DISCARD

ZAPATA

and the Mexican Revolution

ZAPATA

and the Mexican Revolution

JOHN WOMACK, Jr.

New York / Alfred·A·Knopf

1 9 7 0

THIS IS A BORZOI BOOK
PUBLISHED BY ALFRED A. KNOPF, INC.
PUBLISHED JANUARY 15, 1969
REPRINTED THREE TIMES
FIFTH PRINTING, APRIL 1970
Copyright © 1968 by John Womack, Jr.
Library of Congress Catalog Card Number: 68-23947
Manufactured in the United States of America

To my Father & Mother

"YOU CAN ACTIVELY FLEE, THEN,

AND YOU CAN ACTIVELY STAY PUT;

YOU EVEN CAN . . . ACTIVELY HIDE."

Erik H. Erikson

~§[P R E F A C E]§~

T HIS IS A BOOK ABOUT COUNTRY PEOPLE who did not want to move and
therefore got into a revolution. They did not figure on so odd a fate.
Come hell, high water, agitators from the outside, or report of greener
pastures elsewhere, they insisted only on staying in the villages and little
towns where they had grown up, and where before them their ancestors
for hundreds of years had lived and died—in the small state of Morelos,
in south-central Mexico.

Toward the turn of the present century other people, powerful entrepreneurs living in the cities, needed to make the villagers move in order
to progress themselves. And between the entrepreneurs and the villagers
a vivid conflict took shape. Not only in Morelos but in similar districts in
other states this conflict emerged, less dramatic but no less bitter. Everywhere in Mexico, entrepreneurs reasoned that without basic changes in
the country they could not maintain their level of profits or keep the
Republic in business. But wherever bases were changing, villagers protested
—not knowing how to make money out of their fatherland.

In 1910, after thirty-four years of regular government, the high politicians of the regime let a revolt break over presidential succession. Almost
alone among Mexico's villagers, those of Morelos deliberately joined. In a
few months national directors of the revolt gained office. But they proved
as reckless of local traditions as the men they replaced, and the progress
of free enterprise continued. Threatened and bewildered, the villagers of
Morelos revolted again. There ensued nearly nine years of warfare, during
which ordinary farmers and field hands became guerrilleros and terrorists,
endured sieges, and carried on sabotage and passive resistance to pacification. They had several leaders, chief among them one Emiliano Zapata.

Partly because of their insurgency but mainly because of stronger movements of different kinds in other regions, Mexico underwent radical reforms

in the decade after 1910. And in 1920, Zapata dead, the Morelos revolutionaries won official recognition as a legitimate body in Mexico. Implicitly they had forced on its regime a policy of concern for the nation's rural poor. Even today agrarian welfare remains an official commitment in Mexico.

What follows is a story, not an analysis, of how the experience of the Morelos villagers came to pass—how their longing to lead a settled life in a familiar place developed into a violent struggle; how they managed their operations; how they behaved in control of territory and in subjection; how they finally returned to peace; and how they then fared. Zapata is most prominent in these pages not because he himself begged attention but because the villagers of Morelos put him in charge and persistently looked to him for guidance, and because other villagers around the Republic took him for their champion. Through him the country people worked their way into the Mexican Revolution. If theirs was not the only kind of revolutionary experience, it was still, I think, the most significant.

The word "peasant" does not normally appear here. I have preferred other words on purpose, maybe out of crankiness, to make a point. It seems to me that "peasant" generally sounds exotic, suggests a creature that properly fits in an exotic society; and if I were writing the history of a society essentially foreign and out of our time, in the past or the present, anyway strange to us, I would use the word to indicate a particular kind of country person. But I doubt that since the 1860's Mexico has developed in a dimension different from ours. I do not deny that there were and still are peasants in Mexico, but only affirm that by 1910 most families outside the cities there probably were not peasant; certainly most families in Morelos were not. What they were is clear in Spanish: *campesinos,* people from the fields.

Besides, to refer to "peasants" is to verge on raising abstract questions of class. And this is a study not in historical sociology but in social history. It is not an analysis but a story because the truth of the revolution in Morelos is in the feeling of it, which I could not convey through defining its factors but only through telling of it. The analysis that I could do and that I thought pertinent I have tried to weave into the narrative, so that it would issue at the moment right for understanding it.

To produce this book I have knowingly depended on many people, and unknowingly no doubt on many others. First I thank Donald Fleming, who headed me into Latin American history. To the Faculty Committee on Latin American Studies at Harvard University I owe a generous fellowship from the Robert Woods Bliss Fund for 1961–5, and a generous grant from the same fund for the summer of 1966. For their courtesy and efficiency I thank the staffs of Widener Library, the New York Public Library, the Library of Congress, the National Archives, the University of Texas Library, and the University of California at Berkeley Library in the United States; and in Mexico those of the Archivo General de la Nación, the Hemeroteca Nacional, the Biblioteca Nacional, the Biblioteca de la Secretaría de Hacienda, the Museo Nacional de Antropología e Historia, the Instituto de Investigaciones Históricas and the Archivo Histórico at the Universidad Nacional Autónoma de México, the Instituto de Estudios Históricos de la Revolución Mexicana, the Centro de Estudios de Historia Mexicana at Condumex, S.A., the Colegio de México, and the Biblioteca Central Miguel Salinas at the Universidad de Morelos. For their care and cheer in typing the manuscript at various stages I am grateful to Claire Murray, Joslyn Allen, and Carol Thorne. For interesting interviews I state my thanks to Daniel de la O, Diego Zapata, Daniel Gutiérrez Santos, Cristóbal Rojas Romero, and the late Antonio Díaz Soto y Gama. For interviews and permission to use private papers I am deeply indebted to Marte R. Gómez, Porfirio Palacios, José García Pimentel, José Ignacio Conde, Elena Garro de Paz, and Juan Pérez Salazar. For archival directions and tips on facts and interpretations I owe much to Luis González y González, Fernando Sandoval, Manuel González Ramírez, Valentín López González, Antonio Pompa y Pompa, Stanley R. Ross, Juan Luis Mutiozábal, Salvador Azuela, Luis Muro, Lothar and Josefina Knauth, Catalina Sierra Casasús, J. Ignacio Rubio Mañé, Beatriz Arteaga, and Daniel Cosío Villegas. For good recommendations on style I thank my editors, Ashbel Green and Edward Johnson.

Five men in particular were of great importance to me as I worked through this study: José María Luján, for teaching me about the Mexican Revolution; Jesús Sotelo Inclán, for teaching me about Mexico, Morelos, and agrarian struggles; Juan Marichal, for teaching me about Latin America; and Ernest R. May and Oscar Handlin, for teaching me about history. To them I am profoundly grateful. On no account are they responsible for what is wrong or stupid or ugly in the following pages. But little that is good would be there if they had not helped me.

The special sacrifices my friends, my family, and my daughter made for me while I did this work rubbed sores too deep to cure now. I can only ask them to forgive me.

John Womack, Jr.

Cambridge, Mass.
November 22, 1967

⊰[C O N T E N T S]⊱

⊸§[*Illustrations*]§⊸

(*following page 206*)

ZAPATA

and the Mexican Revolution

A People Chooses a Leader

"Like a wound, the country's history
opens in Anenecuilco."
—*Gastón García Cantú*

T HE OLD MAN WAS ABOUT TO SPEAK NOW, and the crowd of farmers
waiting under the arcades behind the village church quieted down
to hear him. They knew the meeting must be important. To make sure
everyone could come, the elders had called it for this evening, on a Sunday.
And to hide it from the hacienda foremen, they had passed the word
around in private instead of ringing the church bell.[1]

Almost all the family men in the village were there, and most of the
other grown but single men. Some seventy-five or eighty had come, kinfolk, in-laws, cronies, and feudists. And now, waiting together in the
shadows of the September evening, they listened carefully for what the
wrinkled old man would say. They knew José Merino was never a man
to ignore. Uncle or cousin to many of them, respected for miles around,
he was chief elder in the village that late summer of 1909 and president
of the village council. The crowd could see he was too tired not to go

---

[1] For an account of this meeting, see Jesús Sotelo Inclán: *Raíz y razón de Zapata.*
Anenecuilco. Investigación histórica (México, 1943), pp. 175–6.

· 3 ·

straight to the point, and as he spoke they listened, quietly and intently.

He was telling them he was too old, over seventy, and too worn-out, that all the elders were too old and worn-out. In the last year, he said, the job had just gotten to be too much for them. To defend the village's land titles and water rights in the fields as well as in the courts required energy they could no longer muster. Traveling back and forth to the state capital in Cuernavaca, journeying even to Mexico City, arranging for lawyers, facing the jefe político (the district prefect) in Cuautla, dealing with the hacienda managers and foremen and field guards—it was too much for old men. And with the new real-estate law passed in Cuernavaca three months before, reforming taxes and titles, the job was getting worse.[2] The elders had served the village as best they could for years, and they served it best now by resigning. The times were changing so fast the village needed more than the wisdom of age. The people of Anenecuilco would have to elect new men—younger men—to stand up for them. That was all, he said, and then he asked for nominations for his own office, the council presidency.

The four old men who composed the council began to take names and prepare for the vote. They needed to offer no advice or admonition: their presence alone guaranteed that the choice would be free, serious, and respected. For seven hundred years Anenecuilco had lived by the strength of will of men like them, and it had no better strength to trust in now. One of the elders, Carmen Quintero, had taken an active and independent part in local politics for twenty-five years, having started his career before some of the men at the meeting were born. Another, Eugenio Pérez, had loaded his rifle to defend village lands as early as 1887. As for the other two, Merino and Andrés Montes, they had been firm and faithful leaders for well over a decade.[3] Nearly four hundred souls made up Anenecuilco, and probably every one of them could look on at least one of the four elders as uncle, great-uncle, cousin, brother, father, or grandfather.[4] Before those four solemn, independent old men, no one would dare try to steam-

[2] Ibid., 173–4. For the text of the law, see *Semanario Oficial del Gobierno de Morelos,* XVIII, 26, 2.

[3] Quintero had been elected to a district electoral college for federal elections as early as 1884. *Periódico Oficial del Gobierno del Estado de Morelos,* XVI, 23, 5. He was also elected to an electoral college for federal elections in 1900. *Semanario Oficial,* VI, 28, 7. For Pérez, Merino, and Montes, see Sotelo Inclán: op. cit., pp. 155, 159.

[4] Elizabeth Holt Büttner: "Evolución de las localidades en el estado de Morelos según los censos de población, 1900–1950" (Maestría de Geografía thesis, U.N.A.M., 1962), pp. 94–7.

roll a vote, or to walk out if defeated. In Anenecuilco village business was too important for muscles or tempers to interfere with.

The nominations were in. Modesto González's had been first. Then Bartolo Parral had proposed Emiliano Zapata, and Zapata had in turn proposed Parral. A vote was called, and Zapata won easily.

It could not have been a surprise. Zapata was young, having just turned thirty a month before, but the men voting knew him and they knew his family; and they judged that if they wanted a young man to lead them, they would find no one else with a truer sense of what it meant to be responsible for the village.[5] He had had his troubles with the district authorities, the first time when he was only seventeen, a year or two after both his parents died. He had had to leave the state for several months then, hiding out on a family friend's ranch in southern Puebla.[6] But no one held that against him: in the countryside troubles with the police were almost a puberty rite. Anyway for the last three years he had been one of the leaders in the group of young men active in village defense, signing protests, taking a junior part in delegations to the jefe político, generally helping to keep up village morale.[7] Recently he had helped to organize the local campaign of an opposition candidate for governor; and though his party had suffered a disastrous defeat—voters intimidated, votes not counted, leaders arrested and deported to labor camps in Yucatán—he had met opposition politicians from all over the state and established connections with them.[8] After the enactment of the new real-estate law, he had begun working regularly with the council.[9]

[5] Dates for Zapata's birth vary. For 1873, see Alfonso Taracena: *Mi vida en el vértigo de la revolución. Anales sintéticos, 1900–1930* (México, 1936), p. 86. For "around 1877," see Gildardo Magaña: *Emiliano Zapata y el agrarismo en México,* 3 vols. (México, 1934–41), I, 104, and the second, posthumous edition of his work, 5 vols. (México, 1951–2), I, 94. For the same guess, see Baltasar Dromundo: *Vida de Emiliano Zapata* (México, 1961), p. 27. For "around 1879," see Baltasar Dromundo: *Emiliano Zapata. Biografía* (México, 1934), p. 21. For 1883, see Octavio Paz: "Emiliano Zapata," in José T. Meléndez, ed.: *Historia de la revolución mexicana,* 2 vols. (México, 1936–40), I, 319. The two most conscientious historians of matters Zapatista, Sotelo Inclán and Porfirio Palacios, both agree on August 8, 1879, for which see respectively: op. cit., p. 169, and *Emiliano Zapata. Datos biográficos-históricos* (México, 1960), pp. 16–17. Following them are Alfonso Reyes H.: *Emiliano Zapata. Su Vida y su Obra* (México, 1963), and Mario Mena: *Zapata* (México, 1959), p. 169.

[6] Palacios: op. cit., p. 20.

[7] Sotelo Inclán: op. cit., pp. 162–6, 172–3.

[8] See Chapter I for an account of this election.

[9] Sotelo Inclán: op. cit., pp. 174–5.

In country terms, the villagers knew, he was not a poor man: the Zapatas lived in a solid adobe-and-stone house, not a hut. Neither he nor his older brother, Eufemio, had ever worked as day laborers on the haciendas, and both had inherited a little land and some livestock when their parents died. Eufemio had liquidated his for capital to start business in Veracruz State—peddling, hawking, marketing, no one knew quite what. But Emiliano had stayed around Anenecuilco. He worked his land, sharecropped a few acres more from a local hacienda, and in slack seasons ran a string of mules through the settlements south along the Cuautla River.[1] He also bought and sold horses in a small way. For lack of land the Zapata family had years before started dealing in livestock, and Emiliano had learned the trade young. He had also learned the pride horses stir in men, and so as he made money he used it on them— buying a new one, outfitting a favorite with a fancy saddle, outfitting himself to sit, worthily booted and spurred, on the shining back of the horse he most admired.

The reputation he earned with horses paid, for hacienda owners throughout central and eastern Morelos and western Puebla, and even in Mexico City, spoke of him as the best trainer around and competed for his services.[2] But their flattering attention never won him over; people always sensed a painful independence about him. Anenecuilcans recalled a story of his childhood—that once as a child he had seen his father break down and cry in frustration at a local hacienda's enclosure of a village orchard, and that he had promised his father he would get the land back.[3] If the incident occurred, he was nine years old at the time, the ninth of ten children, only four of whom lived to adulthood.[4] If the story was apocryphal, still the determination that it chronicled did burn in his glance; and sometimes, though he was as tough as nails and no one fooled with him, he did look near tears. A quiet man, he drank less than most of the other men in the village and got quieter when he did. Once for several weeks he managed the ornate Mexico City stables of a Morelos sugar planter. It was a good chance to start climbing socially and eco-

[1] Serafín M. Robles: "El General Zapata. Agricultor y Arriero," *El Campesino,* October 1951.

[2] Sotelo Inclán: op. cit., pp. 170, 172. Antonio Díaz Soto y Gama: *La revolución agraria del Sur y EMILIANO ZAPATA, su Caudillo* (México, 1960), pp. 245–6.

[3] Dromundo: *Vida,* p. 29.

[4] Surviving besides Emiliano were Eufemio and two sisters, María de Jesús and María de Luz. Sotelo Inclán: op. cit., pp. 169–70. Mario Gill: *Episodios mexicanos. México en la hoguera* (3rd edn., México, 1960), p. 50–1.

nomically—to feather his nest and wind up with his own stables and maybe even a little ranch. But toadying, wheedling petty obligations, maneuvering, operating, pulling deals—it sickened him, literally. Uneasy and depressed, he was soon back in Anenecuilco, remarking bitterly how in the capital horses lived in stalls that would put to shame the house of any workingman in the whole state of Morelos.[5] If he dandied up on holidays and trotted around the village and into the nearby town of Villa de Ayala on a silver-saddled horse, the people never questioned that he was still one of them. Despite his fine horses and suits, Anenecuilcans never referred to him as Don Emiliano, which would have removed him from the guts and flies and manure and mud of local life, sterilizing the real respect they felt for him into a squire's vague respectability. He was one of their own, they felt in Anenecuilco, and it never made them uncomfortable to treat him so. 'Miliano, they called him, and when he died, *pobrecito*—poor little thing. To them he was a neighbor, a younger cousin who could lead the clan, a beloved nephew as rough and true as seasoned timber.

This was the man the villagers elected president of their council. But when they elected him, they were also laying bets that he would stay as they knew him. What convinced them that once in power he would not change and abuse their trust—what kept the question from rising in anyone's mind—was the reputation of his family. Zapata was an important name in Anenecuilco. It had first appeared in local affairs as a rebel name during the War of Independence in the 1810's.[6] Emiliano's father, Gabriel, a quiet, popular, hard-working man with a slight stutter, and his mother, Cleofas, were by all accounts plain folk, but they passed on to their son the rare, plain qualities of unambitious courage and dogged, abiding integrity that glint through the family history. The Zapatas and the Salazars (his mother's people) had it bred into their bones what Mexican history was about. When a Spanish army besieged the rebels in Cuautla during the War of Independence, boys from the neighboring villages sneaked back and forth across the lines for weeks, smuggling tortillas, salt, liquor, and gunpowder to the insurgents: one of the boys from Anenecuilco was José Salazar, Emiliano's maternal grandfather. Two of his father's brothers, Cristino and José, had fought in the War of Reform and against the French Intervention in the 1860's,

[5] Silvano Barba González: *La lucha por la tierra. Emiliano Zapata* (México, 1960), pp. 35–45. Sotelo Inclán: op. cit., p. 173.

[6] Ibid., pp. 138–42.

and years later Emiliano remembered the stories they used to tell him of their campaigns against the Reactionaries and the Imperialists.[7]

Besides, there was another José Zapata, whose career definitely fixed the Zapata family high in village esteem. In 1866–7 during the War of Intervention, the young Republican general Porfirio Díaz organized companies of men all over south-central Mexico to take part in the final push against the French. In every neighborhood he needed a reliable agent to mobilize and lead the local forces. His man in the country around Villa de Ayala was this other José Zapata.[8] Zapata was already an old man, but he knew the region and its people like the back of his hand, and he commanded respect wherever he passed. His home was in Anenecuilco, and after the war ended in 1867 in the restoration of the Republic, the people there and in Villa de Ayala naturally counted on him to lead them in reestablishing a popular peace and order. During the troubled times of the late 1860's and early 1870's he was chief elder in Anenecuilco and held elected posts in the Villa de Ayala municipal government as well.[9] Through these years José Zapata kept faithful connections with Díaz, now an ambitious but ill-advised and confused opposition politician. He organized a secret Porfirista club in Anenecuilco and carried on a clandestine correspondence with his old chief about defending the villagers' lands against the sugar plantations, which he described as a "malign infirmity."[1] Anenecuilcans revered him: when his comrades reported his death to Díaz in 1876, it was "the death of our beloved president, whom we considered almost as a father."[2] And for years afterward they continued along the political course he had marked for them, trusting, even after Díaz came to power and betrayed his earlier promises, that in the end he would remember to help them protect their fields. Still in 1892, in a bitter presidential election, young Anenecuilcans like Eufemio Zapata, Octaviano Gutiérrez, and Teodoro Placencia

[7] Ibid., p. 192.

[8] Victoriano Gómez to the auxiliary mayor of Anenecuilco, July 9, 1867, Archivo de Jesús Sotelo Inclán (henceforth ASI). José Zapata to Narcizo Medina, February 9, 1867, ASI.

[9] José Zapata to the municipal aide of Anenecuilco, October 10, 12, and 19, 1870, ASI.

[1] J. Zapata, A. Solares, and Teodosio Franco to Porfirio Díaz, June 14, 1874, cited in Alberto María Carreño, ed.: *Archivo del General Porfiro Díaz. Memorias y documentos,* 24 vols. (México, 1947–58), XI, 142–3.

[2] Teodosio Franco, Alfredo Solares, and Justino Arriaga to Porfirio Díaz, January 23, 1876, ibid., XI, 300–1. I owe this reference and the preceding one to the generosity of Jesús Sotelo Inclán.

considered it their civic duty to enroll in local Porfirista clubs and vote for the leader old José had given the villagers faith in.[3] Exactly how Emiliano was related to this patriarch, who died three years before he was born, is still unclear, but José Zapata was probably a brother of his grandfather, a great-uncle. In any case his part in village history served to establish Zapata as an honored name there.

Finally, the security of kinship was in the present meeting's very air: Emiliano was also a nephew of the incumbent chief, José Merino.[4] The villagers knew they were in for trouble for the next few years. They had no better bet than Zapata to see them through.

Other offices were then opened to nominations and filled by young men, the unofficial leaders for the last five years of the new generation in the village. Francisco Franco, a close friend of Emiliano's, was elected secretary; Eduwiges Sánchez and Rafael Merino, José's son, were named treasurers; and José Robles became *vocal*, a sort of member without portfolio. It was a short and simple ceremony—the assembly, election, and transfer of authority. Really it was not unusual, since in hard times the traditional procedure was for the elder "judges" to give way to the younger "warriors," and on that Sunday evening, September 12, 1909, the times in store for Anenecuilco looked grievously hard.

Zapata spoke briefly. He said that he accepted the difficult responsibility conferred upon him, but that he expected everyone to back him. "We'll back you," Francisco Franco thirty years later remembered someone in the crowd calling out to Zapata: "We just want a man with pants on, to defend us."[5]

[3] *La Idea Patriótica*, March 10, 1892.
[4] Dromundo: *Vida*, p. 36.
[5] Sotelo Inclán: op. cit., pp. 175–6.

President Díaz Elects a Governor

"Where the captain commands . . ."

THE MEXICAN REVOLUTION HAPPENED because the high politicians of the country openly failed to agree on who should rule when President Porfirio Díaz died. These politicians, nicknamed the científicos, believed it a natural law that the nation could progress only through their control and for their benefit. From the early 1890's on they lectured Mexico about the authority their special science entitled them to, and they eventually convinced great sections of the public of their infallibility. But by 1904 they were floundering in the test of arranging succession to Díaz, who had been president then for twenty consecutive years. In 1908, two years before the next presidential election, the test became a notorious affair of state. And with their maneuvers exposed, the powerful proved naïve, treacherous, and incompetent. In a short time their fashionable order collapsed.

What made the test a crisis was its publicity, and what made it public was Díaz's pride. In February 1908 Díaz had granted an interview to a well-known American "special correspondent," James Creelman, on assignment in Mexico for the popular American monthly *Pearson's Magazine*. Díaz told Creelman he was definitely retiring when his term ended in 1910 and would not, even if his "friends" begged him, "serve again." He "welcomed

... as a blessing" the formation of an opposition party, he said. "And if it can develop power, not to exploit, but to govern," he promised, "I will stand by it, support it, advise it and forget myself in the successful inauguration of complete democratic government in the country."[1]

Then seventy-eight years old, and pathetically obsessed with fixing his place in Mexican history, Díaz intended by these words only to strike the statesmanlike pose he believed worthy of the high rank he held in world esteem. He was sincere but not serious. Resigning, retiring, and promising free elections had long been his favorite gestures, always harmlessly performed for the same audience—for journalists, who could only report, never for Congress, which might accept. And no one had ever taken his words to heart. But there was a difference this time that charged what he said with unexpected significance: Díaz was getting old and could not hide it. Before, talk about retiring was only breath wasted and forgotten. Now, in 1908, it was a morbid reminder that whether he retired or not, he would soon die, and then times would change.

No important politicking had gone on in Mexico for over thirty years without Díaz involving himself in it. By this means he had become the only politician able to maneuver through the intricate maze of alliances and armistices. To ensure his control he kept all deals precarious: in 1908 practically everything central depended on him. The very idea of his departure unsettled people and sent shivers through officeholders high and low. For his own good Díaz should have avoided alarming the public, and he could have done so by turning Creelman away or by having the Mexican press suitably distort his words for Mexican readers. But now toward the end of his life he longed for the genuine gratitude of his compatriots even more than the respect of an Edwardian world, and out of a tardy and indiscreet hope that he might win it by liberal words, he allowed the most influential pro-government newspaper in the country, *El Imparcial,* to publish a full translation of the interview in early March. Like the sudden muffled tolling of a royal funeral bell, the report signaled the ending of one age in Mexico—Don Porfirio's—and the beginning of another (God knew whose), when those left in charge would have to act on their own and without precedents.

But in fact the ceremony was a fake: Díaz was still around. Staging scenes and watching people play them fascinated him. And in the Creelman interview he indulged himself again—asking people and politicians

[1] James Creelman: "President Díaz. Hero of the Americas," *Pearson's Magazine,* XIX, 3 (March 1908), 242.

to carry on as if he had left when he had not and was not about to, and anyway, as everyone knew, would not quit politicking until he lay stiff in his grave. The effect was worse than if he really had died. No politician in the country quite knew how to start acting. Científicos were at a loss whether to pretend the interview had never occurred, or to take it seriously and begin organizing independently for the 1910 elections, bargaining with Díaz for what support they might get. Reformers also worried over a strategy: was the interview a trick to get them to stick their necks out, or a legitimate invitation to bring their informal and amateurish activities into the open and coordinate them in professional parties? By talking about leaving and then not clearing out, Díaz made it hard for Mexican politicians to count on anything. Thus he confused the regular workings of the whole system.

Although in the interview Díaz referred exclusively to national politics and the presidential election of 1910, the confusion he aroused first took effect on the state level. This happened because of the especially complex nature of state political deals, involving deep local interests and clannish loyalties. Normally these deals were like iron. But whenever one cracked and it became necessary to renegotiate who should rule a state, the wrangling was fierce among entrenched local politicians and Don Porfirio's arbitrating agents. Once the exhausted contenders arrived at an agreement, they tried to make it last as long as possible. Through officially selected candidates and rigged elections, the state proceeded in political order. An agreement's durability, however, depended on meticulous attention to all its terms, which in turn depended on their clear definition. The Creelman interview blurred previously clear lines and led to independent movements in 1909 gubernatorial elections in Morelos, Sinaloa, Yucatán, and Coahuila. Officials let politicking get so out of hand that the federal government eventually had to drop its new pretense of neutrality and revert to the imposition of candidates.

The election in Morelos in February 1909 was the first after the Creelman interview in which a serious opposition organized. Ordinarily only the death of a governor in office moved the partners in a state deal to the nerve-racking strain of renegotiation, and that is what happened in Morelos. Governor Manuel Alarcón, having just been reelected for the fourth straight time in August 1908, died on December 15, 1908.[2] He had stayed in office so long partly because the people of his state respected him. As his replacement, they naturally wanted a man like him. And when,

[2] *Semanario Oficial*, XVII, 32, 1; 51, 1. *El País*, December 16, 1908.

through a preposterous miscalculation, they were presented with a very different sort, they resisted. Two years later Mexico began laboring through the first of those enormous, heaving spasms that ruptured central authority and let the revolution loose. What happened in Morelos during that national crisis was mainly determined by what had happened there during the 1909 election.

The affair began without a hint of becoming awkward. The December morning when Alarcón died was ten months after Díaz had intoned to Creelman and the ages that fantastic liturgy of self-sacrifice, liberalism, and democracy. There had already been six gubernatorial elections as well as federal and state congressional elections.[3] And although there were heated private debates and numerous pamphlets urging the formation of independent parties, no group had publicly appeared to take Díaz at his new, tolerant word. When, therefore, on the afternoon of December 21, the Monday following Alarcón's funeral, a clique of sugar planters, lawyers, and state politicians conferred with Díaz in his presidential office, they assumed their new governor would be elected, like those of the year before, according to the regular procedure: on election day the state government would see that the proper candidate won by whatever margin was considered suitable. Who the candidate was, the conference between Díaz and the state leaders would determine.[4]

Picking a worthy successor to Alarcón should have offered no problem. He was himself a perfect model, a native son whose career knitted firmly and vitally into the region's recent history.[5] Alarcón had been born in 1851 on Buenavista hacienda, near the village of Santa María, a few miles north of Cuernavaca, and had passed a childhood as poor and hard as Mexico then had to give. Seven years old when the War of Reform broke out, twelve when the French arrived to install Maximilian, he never had the chance to learn more than farming and fighting. At fifteen he joined the local Republican colonel to resist the occupying Imperialist army. His mother found him and brought him home, but he ran off again—this time farther, to Tepoztlán—and joined the Republicans there. After the war,

[3] In Hidalgo, Guerrero, Tlaxcala, Puebla, Mexico State, and Morelos, where Alarcón had just won. *México Nuevo*, April 2, 1909.

[4] For accounts of the conference, see *El Imparcial*, December 22, 1908; *Diario del Hogar*, January 3, 1909; *Mexican Herald*, December 22, 1908; *México Nuevo*, January 2, 1909; *Actualidades*, January 1, 1909.

[5] In her *Tempest over Mexico* (Boston, 1935), p. 35, Rosa E. King says the people of Morelos wanted "another Indian" for governor, "a popular man." What they meant was a native son.

in 1869, the old Third Military District of Mexico State became the independent state of Morelos. State jobs naturally went to local veterans of the war, and Alarcón, who had taken part in the sieges of Cuernavaca and Mexico City, got an appointment as head of the rurales, mounted federal police, in Yautepec and Tetecala districts.[6] The highwaymen and bandits who swarmed over Morelos at that time soon found it easier to do business elsewhere than in his zone.[7] A military Republican when civilian Republicans were looked on as jaded schemers, Alarcón disapproved of Juárez's successor, Sebastián Lerdo de Tejada, "a Mexican version of Lord Chesterfield."[8] When Díaz, his former army boss, revolted in 1876 against President Lerdo, Alarcón, still a district police chief, bolted to his side and was commissioned to operate in Morelos, Guerrero, and Mexico State. Díaz's revolt triumphed, and a year later the new Porfirista governor in Morelos rewarded Alarcón with a promotion to state chief of rurales. This governor afterward enjoyed the reputation of having wiped out brigandage in the state; actually he only presided while Alarcón and his local officers did the work of running down the outlaws, shooting them on the spot, and slowly, season by season, returning the districts to order.

Porfirian Mexico prized tough policemen, and Alarcón's talents soon won him other posts. By 1883 he was a jefe político.[9] By 1884 he was elected to the state legislature, serving at the same time as lieutenant governor.[1] And he kept his job as state police chief. Despite his poor health, he visited all of Morelos's twenty-six municipalities, acquainted himself with the local notables, and cultivated their support.[2] During the late 1880's and early 1890's he emerged as the strongest politician in the state, and when the current governor died halfway through his term in 1894, Alarcón took over for the interim without hesitation or trouble, had himself elected in his own right two years later, and began a stern but benevolent rule that ended only with his death.[3]

[6] Ireneo Paz: *México actual. Galería de contemporáneos* (México, 1898), p. 43.

[7] J. Figueroa Doménech: *Guía general descriptiva de la República mexicana. Historia, geografía, estadística, etc., etc.,* 2 vols. (México, 1899), II, 370.

[8] The phrase comes from Frank A. Knapp, Jr.: *The Life of Sebastián Lerdo de Tejada, 1823–1889. A Study of Influence and Obscurity* (Austin, 1951), p. 154.

[9] Cuautla district was his. Paz: op. cit., p. 43.

[1] *Periódico Oficial*, XVI, 61, 1; 57, 3.

[2] See Cecilio A. Robelo: *Revistas Descriptivas del Estado de Morelos* (Cuernavaca, 1885), *passim*.

[3] *El Orden. Periódico Oficial del Estado de Morelos*, X, 49, 2–3; 50, 2. *Semanario Oficial*, II, 33, 1.

Before and after he became governor, Alarcón's life was one of public success. The secret was a profound shrewdness about the basic social problem of the state. This was the conflict between the few, powerful sugar planters (or, when as usual they were absent, their managers) and the scores of village leaders and small farmers. Both sides had always been zealous, but the struggle became desperate in the 1880's. Completion of the Veracruz–Mexico City railroad in 1873 had lowered freight rates in central Mexico, and with the extension of a branch line to Cuautla in 1881 and Yautepec in 1883 planters began importing heavy machinery and setting up big sugar mills to supply the large new markets now opened. To grow much more sugar than before, they considered it easier to farm more extensively rather than more efficiently. The race was on to grab land, water, and labor.[4] Through the 1890's and into the new century, the planters had immensely the better of it. But Alarcón gained popularity by at least listening to the villagers' petitions, and sometimes even granting one.[5] By then a plantation owner himself, he had the talent of the triumphant poor boy for inspiring in plain people a sense that he understood them.[6] This talent he needed, because he could not really help them. In Morelos in those years no governor could not have favored the planters, who increasingly resented even verbal tokens of respect for villagers and small farmers. In practice the only thing a politician could do was go through the motions of a compromise, pose, juggle, fake, do magic; at that Alarcón was a home-grown genius; hence his success. Had he lived—had that Mexican country diet not corroded his insides and killed him of gastroenteritis at fifty-seven—he might well have changed the course of rebellion in his state two years later, perhaps by some judicious deal prevented it altogether.

A popular policeman, born of the people and reader of their hearts—who could come after such a man? Four candidates were mentioned in the conference with Díaz on December 21. One was Luis Flores, Alarcón's regular stand-in, the lieutenant governor in Morelos off and on for the last thirty years. Two others were personal associates of Díaz's and leaders in the National Porfirista Party: Demetrio Salazar, a Mexico City lawyer

[4] Domingo Diez: *Bibliografía del estado de Morelos* (México, 1933), pp. clxix–clxxi. See Chapter ii for a detailed discussion of this process.

[5] Ibid., pp. clxxviii–clxxxi.

[6] His hacienda was Temilpa. See Domingo Diez: *Dos conferencias sobre el Estado de Morelos* (México, 1919), p. 56. For an interesting sketch of Governor Alarcón in action, see Mrs. Alec Tweedie: *Mexico As I Saw It* (New York, 1901), pp. 291–353.

who was the son-in-law of a former Morelos governor and especially influential in Cuautla, and Antonio Tovar, a colonel in the army and an old-time politician still popular in the state's villages and small towns. Another possibility was Agustín Aragón, a Jonacatepec native who had become one of Mexico's most distinguished intellectuals.[7] Any of these would have been a sound candidate, a man supported in his own right and commanding statewide respect so that imposing him would not cause serious discontent. But during the talks another figure cropped up—one so unlikely that political gossips the next day confused him with his cousin, then governor of the Federal District.[8] This was Díaz's chief of staff, Pablo Escandón.

Alarcón must have turned over in his grave. A man less like him could not have been found in the whole Republic. Escandóns had graced Maximilian's Imperial court, helped finance the Veracruz–Mexico City railroad, made haciendas famous, and recently, an Escandón having been appointed the Federal District governor, taken over metropolitan society. Among Mexico's fanciest showpieces, veritable luxury-rate tourist attractions, they had shown off so long that by 1900 they had almost lost their capacity for anything else. In the early years of the new century the name Escandón still appeared prominently in newspapers—but in the society columns. Of this mighty, dying tree, Pablo was the last frail twig.

He was only flimsily connected with Morelos politics, and the idea that he could govern in the agile but firm manner of Alarcón was absurd. A delicate soul, educated like many other youths of his class at the Jesuit College at Stonyhurst, England, Pablo had returned to Mexico and entered the family sugar business in Morelos around 1900.[9] He soon secured the Escandón reputation as "progressive." Planters all over the country considered Atlihuayán, the Escandón hacienda near Yautepec, "a model property."[1] Doing business and paying taxes in Morelos soon earned him

[7] México Nuevo, January 2, 1909. For Tovar and Salazar, see Ricardo García Granados: Historia de México, desde la restauración de la República en 1867, hasta la caída de Huerta, 2 vols. (2nd edn., México, 1956), II, 48. Aragón was an editor of the Revista Positiva, a Mexico City "philosophical, literary, social, and political" monthly bearing the motto "Order and Progress" and the date according to the Comteian calendar. See Eduardo Blanquel: "La Revista Positiva de D. Augustín Aragón y la Historia de la Ciencia en México," Memorias del Primer Coloquio Mexicano de Historia de la Ciencia, Vol. I (1964).

[8] El Imparcial, December 22, 1908.

[9] King: op. cit., p. 33. Semanario Oficial, VII, 28, 2–3.

[1] Mexican Herald, December 22, 1908.

minor political rewards. In 1902 he was elected the state's alternate senator and in 1906 was reelected.[2] He also served off and on as the federal deputy from Morelos. But he had not a political bone in his body. President Díaz recognized his real talents: from the time Pablo joined the army (as a captain), Díaz kept him on his staff.[3] A fine ornament, Pablo was to make sure the regime's style was right. He did well and over the years received regular promotions. By 1908 he was a lieutenant colonel.

There he was, one of Mexico's fanciest dukelings, prissy and fawning, looking forward to a long, rich life of fashionable and stately paradings.[4] Then—an apparently trivial assignment—Díaz sent him to Cuernavaca as his official representative to preside over Alarcón's funeral, and life went sour. While he was there tending to the ceremony, a group of planters and their agents, led by Antonio Barrios, Ramón Corona, and Fernando Noriega, visited him. They suggested he get interested in being Morelos's new governor.[5] He did not refuse, and, encouraged, they arranged the conference with Díaz the following Monday. When in Monday's talks it came time to agree on a man, they passed over the others and chose Pablo.

No one knew better than Pablo himself that the choice was politically ridiculous. Being a governor was the last thing he wanted, as he later lamented over tea with a friend in Cuernavaca, the English lady hotelier Rosa King. Mixing in what he called "those beastly local politics" would sicken the heart of any gentleman, he complained to her.[6] Friends generously observed that he was "too aristocratic" for hard work like governing. Others less generously remarked that his career had been limited to the "presidential reception room," and that if he ever saw what went on in Mexico, it was "only through palatial windows or through the crystal panes of his limousine."[7] Nervous civilian politicians worried that his candidacy might signify the predominance of the military party among Díaz's close advisers. But this was silly—imagine Pablo Escandón involved in such gross

[2] *Semanario Oficial*, VIII, 29, 1; XV, 28, 1.

[3] *México Nuevo*, January 2, 1909.

[4] Manuel Márquez Sterling, the Cuban writer and diplomat, penned acid lines on Escandón after meeting him in the National Palace in 1904. See his *Psicología profana* (Havana, 1905), pp. 79–80. See also his *Los últimos días del Presidente Madero (Mi gestión diplomática en México)* (2nd edn., México, 1958), pp. 15–16, 332–3.

[5] *El Imparcial*, December 22, 1908. *Diario del Hogar*, January 3, 1909.

[6] King: op. cit., p. 33. A widow, Mrs. King ran one of the two best hotels in Cuernavaca at that time, the Bella Vista.

[7] *Actualidades*, January 1, 1909.

maneuvers!—and they were quickly reassured. The new independent journal *México Nuevo* described exactly the meaning of his army life. "Colonel Escandón's prestige among the military," it said, "is only the prestige accorded a perfect sportsman."[8]

Why pick a "perfect sportsman" to run a state, especially when he had to follow a native-son governor who had been popular and down-to-earth? It made no obvious sense. But to the planters who conferred with Díaz that December afternoon, the question was not why but why not. Manuel Araoz, the leader of the commission (and vice president of the científico Reelectionist Party), was among the biggest planters in Morelos.[9] His three plantations already included over 31,000 of the state's most fertile acres; local government could have survived on the taxes he alone could have paid. But he wanted even more land under cultivation, to bring an even higher rate of return on his investment. The problem was not paying the price: although land in Morelos cost more than anywhere else in the country except the Federal District, the planters could afford it. What bothered Araoz and his fellow hacendados was getting the land put up for sale. Almost no public land remained available.[1] Even offering attractive terms, the planters could not induce villagers to traffic in the titles to their fields. To acquire the land, they had to resort to political and judicial maneuvers —condemnations, court orders, foreclosures, and defective-title rulings. Manuel Araoz wanted a governor he could use. He preferred to avoid someone like Tovar, a man with grass-roots appeal of his own, who might, even in trivial ways, stand against him. To Araoz and most other planters the Creelman interview meant they could drop the hypocrisy of being "responsible state fathers," organize along clear class lines, and still enjoy official backing. With Alarcón providentially removed, they were free to be as shortsighted as they pleased. So no Tovars for them: a "perfect sportsman," a planter like themselves, a good fellow at the Jockey Club, a tenderhearted socialite who would stay away and let them alone—that was what they were out for.

Díaz himself would probably have preferred someone with more local popularity. In the conference he told the planters he also approved of the

---

[8] *México Nuevo*, January 2, 1909.

[9] For Araoz's politics, see García Granados: op. cit., II, 48. For his landholdings, see the table of haciendas in Appendix A. He also owned two of the twenty-four sugar mills in Morelos.

[1] Manuel Mazari: "Bosquejo histórico del Estado de Morelos" (MS, 1930), p. 109. I consulted this work thanks to the generosity of Valentín López González.

other men mentioned. But Araoz and his friends were important men, and they wanted Pablo; Díaz knew that at least he would be harmless, and he gave way. Pablo protested feebly to Don Porfirio that he did not want the "appointment," but, told it was his duty, he accepted.[2] The next day the other men who had been proposed began denying their availability. And as of December 22 Pablo Escandón was the figure the people of Morelos believed they would have to get used to for at least the next three and a half years.

The Porfirista machine slipped quickly into gear. Barrios, Corona, and Noriega called a meeting of the state's principal businessmen and professionals for December 30 at the Hotel Moctezuma in Cuernavaca. There Corona, the commission secretary, informed them that Díaz had approved their request for Escandón's candidacy and that Escandón had accepted. The meeting at once reinstituted the familiar Central Porfirio Díaz Club, which formally nominated Pablo. The next day a less imposing bunch, local political and social notables from all six districts of the state, convened in Cuernavaca to learn about the club's formation and their candidate's nomination.[3] Escandón himself encouraged these faithful town and village bosses by a brief appearance.[4] And after discussing common local problems, exchanging gossip, and entertaining themselves as politicians away from home will, they returned home to start arranging his election.

At this point everything looked routine. Invitations were going out for the congratulatory banquets for Escandón in Mexico City.[5] True, disgruntled reminders appeared in the independent press that Escandón's candidacy did not necessarily exclude others, that Díaz had also spoken well of more popular men, that if Morelos were left to itself, it would pick Flores (or Tovar, or Salazar).[6] As early as December 23 *Diario del Hogar* had called for a formal opposition campaign. "The moment is precious," it pleaded. But these helpless protests quickly petered out. And even after the Escandonista convention on December 31 in Cuernavaca, there was no public sign of political objection. If the Creelman interview had disrupted the state's politics, the chief beneficiaries seemed to be the planters, who felt entitled to name a toady as governor.

But without fanfare or banquets something exceptional had already

[2] King: op. cit., p. 33.
[3] *Diario del Hogar*, January 3, 1909. *El Diario*, January 25, 1909.
[4] *Diario del Hogar*, January 1, 1909.
[5] *El Imparcial*, January 5 and 7, 1909.
[6] *México Nuevo*, January 2 and 4, 1909.

happened. At the news of the planters' offensive, a native resistance had quietly formed behind the scenes in Morelos.[7] If such ventures were rare, that was only because Díaz usually stymied them, not because there was lack of raw material. In every district of the state—as in every state in the Republic—there were families with grievances against local authorities. For some the grievance was simply poverty; for others, the long exclusion from serious politics because they or their fathers or uncles had joined the wrong side when Díaz first rose to power years before; for still others, a specific gripe against a specific official. These disaffected families formed a vague community of opposition. The oldest and most important knew each other, or at least knew of each other, and certain men were recognized from district to district as opposition leaders. The articulate and prominent among them were townfolk of course, with white collars, shoes, underwear, and important if shaky connections with the establishment. But mostly, and most firmly, the opposition was composed of rural families, dissident clans scattered around the countryside. They usually kept quiet and let the clerks and shopowners and editors and lawyers do the talking, but when they did act they meant business. They were no people to trifle or to trifle with—these villagers and small farmers, the common country people of Morelos. Their ancestors had taken part in some of the most dramatic and difficult episodes of Mexican history. They knew from experience what dignity and independence were, and how long patience and courtesy could legitimately suspend them. And they would not be intimidated. Díaz himself, who had fought and intrigued all through the region, often remarked that "those tramps in the South are tough."[8] When he took over the government in 1876 and began organizing his regime, the rural democrats gradually went underground and the city liberals reconciled themselves to being left out. But they and their sons held on to the liberal hopes of the Restored Republic of 1867. The opposition now springing up against Escandón—the town and country united, the town speaking for the country—was at once a renaissance, a reorganization, and a homecoming for them.

Mexico still belonged to Don Porfirio, however. And whether shopowners or farmers, the Morelos opposition knew better than to waste time on plans for a regular campaign. In the Porfiriato direct electoral con-

[7] Antonio Sedano: "Andanzas militares del Coronel Republicano Antonio Sedano y Algunos Relatos Históricos del Estado de Morelos" (MS, 1919), p. 18, ASI. The opposition was not fully reported in the press until January 7, 1909, by México Nuevo.

[8] Sotelo Inclán: op. cit., p. 186.

frontations rarely took place: practical politics was a matter of making deals. And to force the planters into new negotiations from which a more representative official candidate might emerge, the Morelos opposition had to show Díaz it deserved attention. Strategy required not a full-length campaign but simply one that started with a great burst of energy. If it looked strong enough early enough, Díaz might consider the trouble of suppressing it more costly than the embarrassment of coming to terms with it. The real question for the opposition leaders was whether they would have the time and freedom to impress Díaz. Having calculated their chances in the light of the Creelman interview, they were optimistic. If the planters felt the interview licensed them to act irresponsibly, the opposition leaders felt it guaranteed a longer and more extensive (though never absolute) protection for independent politicking.

The purpose of their work being a deal, there was one man they knew they could not do without. This was General Francisco Leyva, local hero of the War of Intervention and the state's first governor. Now seventy-three years old and residing in Mexico City, he had officially been on the outside looking in for the last thirty-odd years, but that did not mean he did not count. To the insiders in the capital, he represented the outsiders in Morelos, a kind of sergeant-at-arms in the pay of both the seated and the unseated. This post he held by virtue of being party to one of those informal armistices essential to Mexican politics. The armistice—it was with Díaz—had institutionalized and turned to good account a hostility that began in the late 1860's. After the War of Intervention Díaz was angling for a political base from which to challenge President Juárez. One of his most foolish ideas was to try for the governorship of Morelos in 1869.[9] Leyva had earned the office: during the war he had been military commander in the area, and afterward as the district's deputy to Congress he had managed its achievement of statehood.[1] But Díaz horned in, and lost in a free election by

[9] He also ran for president in these years, as well as for chief justice of the Supreme Court (the effective vice president) and for federal deputy of several districts. See Daniel Cosío Villegas: *Historia Moderna de México. La República Restaurada. La Vida Política* (México, 1955), pp. 86–9.

[1] See the Papeles de Francisco Leyva, Folder 8, in the Archivo General de la Nación (henceforth AGN); also Diez: *Bibliografía,* pp. cxlvii–cliii, and Manuel Rivera Cambas: *Historia de la intervención y del Imperio de Maximiliano,* 5 vols. (2nd edn., México, 1961), I, B, 736–7. Leyva had to betray the state he formally served in Congress, Mexico State, to split off its Morelos districts. See Pantaleón Tovar: *Historia parlamentaria del cuarto congreso constitucional,* 4 vols. (México, 1872–4), III, 284–5, 422, 452.

57 to 174.[2] Bad feelings between Leyva and Díaz worsened when Leyva's brother was killed two years later putting down a local rebellion in support of Díaz's revolt of La Noria.[3] After Díaz in 1876 overthrew President Lerdo, on whom Leyva depended, he abruptly dumped Leyva out of power in Morelos and never let him back in state politics. But that did not stop people from informally following Leyva's lead; to scores of Morelos families, Leyva remained the true chief. And this was why he mattered to Díaz. For Díaz ruled two republics—his own official Mexico of Victorian gentlemen in frock coats, and an estranged and frayed Mexico of pariahs. When there had to be words between Díaz and that other, frayed republic, the old chiefs outcast since the 1870's were the only ones who could mediate. If the opposition community scattered around Morelos in 1909 wanted to renegotiate the question of who would be governor, Leyva alone could talk for them.

Around Christmastime, opposition emissaries met the general at his home in Mexico City to discuss their plans. They knew the appeal of his name in Morelos, and they tried to get him to run. He refused, "because he was too old," but he proposed his two sons, Alfredo, a deputy inspector in the Federal District Police Department, and Patricio, an agronomist and official in the Water Division of the Ministry of Public Works.[4] The commission tentatively approved of Patricio.

General Leyva then arranged an appointment with Díaz. On December 28, a week after the planters, he saw the President and inquired how he would look on a rival campaign. That was easy for Díaz to answer: all Leyva could later report to the commission was the President's assurance that "anyone whom the citizens of Morelos freely elect would be welcome to him."[5] Díaz's tongue-in-cheek pieties about popular will and the electoral law were not very encouraging. The oppositionists hesitated to start work. They did not know whether they would be let alone long enough. Not until a week later, January 4, did the Cuernavaca group issue a call for a Leyvista convention on January 7.[6]

There was some last-minute guessing about an alternative to Patricio,

[2] For the most detailed reports on the campaign, see *La Opinión Nacional*, April 22 to July 15, 1869.

[3] Alberto Leduc, Luis Lara y Pardo, and Carlos Roumagnac: *Diccionario de geografía, historia y biografía mexicanas* (Paris, 1910), p. 558.

[4] *México Nuevo*, February 14, 1909. Diez: *Bibliografía*, p. clxxxiii.

[5] *México Nuevo*, January 7, 1909.

[6] Ibid., January 9, 1909.

but the magic of the old general's name settled the question for the convention.[7] The day before it met, dates for the election were officially announced: February 7 for the primary, when the electoral colleges were filled; February 21 for the secondary, when the colleges voted.[8] That meant only a couple of weeks to organize a fast-starting campaign strong enough to make Díaz reconsider. Names had appeal, and the opposition needed all the free appeal it could get: the junior Leyva was formally nominated.[9]

So by January 8, a little over three weeks after Alarcón's death, politics in Morelos had a new look. To resist the planters' open maneuvers for complete domination, an opposition had materialized. Whatever its strategy, it had convened and agreed on a candidate, and the national press was seriously reporting the affair. Merely by involving General Leyva, even through his son, the opposition looked likely to force a new deal. By January 10, just two days after the Leyvista convention, rumors were abroad. Escandón, it was reported, had dropped out of the race at his family's request, and Leyva would probably win Díaz's personal approval.[1] Politicians relaxed. True, the next day Escandón denied the report; and, with Leyvista charges of Escandón's ineligibility on grounds of nonresidence, it became clear that neither side would quit without heavier or sweeter pressures.[2] But this was only the initial test of nerves, and no one doubted that the contestants would soon find a politic way of settling their problem. It was incredible that any candidate would have the stamina to compete six weeks in a state election. Besides, there would be no reason to try—if the traditional opposition strategy worked.

But for the first time in thirty-odd years it did not work. Politics throughout the country had been operating out of kilter for several months. And here in Morelos the regular procedures finally broke down. The contest went on to the end, and when the electoral colleges voted six weeks later, the opposition had not only not traded itself into oblivion but had even won votes. As the campaigning went along, the whole character of the election changed. Political clubs formed outside the safe confines of Cuernavaca, and the original opposition came apart: the country people of Morelos slipped out of the sedate control of their town spokesmen and learned how—and more dangerously, why—to struggle independently.

[7] Ibid., January 6 and 7, 1909. *El Imparcial*, January 8, 1909.
[8] *Semanario Oficial*, XVIII, 2, 3.
[9] *México Nuevo*, January 11, 1909.
[1] *Diario del Hogar*, January 10, 1909.
[2] *México Nuevo*, January 11, 1909.

That the contest lasted at all was unsettling: recording any opposition vote, much less a sizable one, bothered the jefes políticos. But that the opposition worked free was downright alarming. The state's established powers had no fear of Morelos's town liberals. If these little traders, shopkeepers, lawyers, editors, and schoolteachers from the various district seats had plucked up their courage and resisted an offensive disposition of public affairs, they would remain orderly souls. The procedures they would try to keep to would be regular, and there were regular forms for accommodating their opposition. But for country people to speak up was shocking and fearful. When the common people of the state—the villagers, plantation workers, muleskinners, sharecroppers, and small farmers and ranchers —came out in the course of the campaign in open politicking of their own, they tore loose all the settled lines of state politics. The commotion they caused reopened ancient feuds and formed new grudges so intense that even in a calm era it would have taken years for them to die down.

All this happened in Morelos because of the almost accidental simultaneity of more important political developments in Mexico City. No state opposition could last, even if it wanted to, without a powerful sponsor in the capital. Before 1908, the problem rarely arose: no independent groups of national importance existed. After the Creelman interview, efforts to form such groups multiplied, but not until December 1908 did one succeed in bringing together the proper combination of earnestness, respectability, and ambition. This group called itself the Organizing Club of the Democratic Party. The Democrats wanted to prevent the incumbent Vice President, Ramón Corral, from being reelected in 1910 and becoming president if Díaz died before his term ended in 1916. They hoped to convince Díaz of Corral's unworthiness by campaigning as a party to provoke and articulate an anti-Corral public opinion. The 1908 state and congressional elections had taken place too early for local opposition to benefit from their interference. But the scattered gubernatorial elections in 1909, they saw, would offer them both practice for 1910 and preliminary opportunities for educating the public and Díaz. The Morelos election coincided exactly with the moves of the Organizing Club's officers to form their new Democratic Party.[3] Had they organized it sooner, its role in Morelos would have been somewhat different. As it was, the party in early 1909 still had only a loosely defined organization and strategy, and its members were still free to act on their own. According to what Democrats thought their party was for, they joined either side in Morelos.

[3] García Granados: op. cit., II, 45–6.

The two most important Democrats to take part in the campaign were both eminent journalists and both secretaries of the Organizing Club's executive board. But they moved in opposite directions. One was Juan Sánchez Azcona, editor of the recently founded *México Nuevo,* who threw his support to Patricio Leyva on January 13 after an interview with him that day. He had held off until then because the Leyvistas, counting on the traditional pre-election deal, insisted on organizing as personal friends of the old general and refused to form an authentic party with a platform.[4] Sánchez Azcona had helped organize the Democrats precisely because he wanted to stop that kind of politics and introduce a new, impersonal system.[5] But he soon realized there was no time for such serious work in Morelos.[6] Politically independent and personally democratic, he must have been moved by Leyva's populist rhetoric. ("To guarantee the interests of the people is to guarantee the interests of the fatherland," Patricio affirmed.[7]) And Patricio had declared himself opposed to "reelectionism," not so much Díaz's and Corral's reinstallation in 1910 as the general habit of arranging deals instead of permitting and encouraging full-scale rival campaigns. That was probably the crux of the matter for Sánchez Azcona. Considering the origin of Pablo Escandón's candidacy and the hope dimly involved in Patricio Leyva's, he decided to give Patricio the influential support at his command. Also joining the Leyvistas then were Democrats Gabriel and Alfredo Robles Domínguez and Francisco Cosío Robelo.[8]

Other Democrats wanted to use the party to educate the public more specifically—to back the aging but powerful and enlightened governor of Nuevo León, General Bernardo Reyes, for the vice presidency.[9] General Reyes had long seemed a likely heir to Díaz; and under the new cover of a party, the Reyista Democrats now looked forward to a personal deal in the old style. For that, they might use Escandón's military and social connections. Chief among this group was the Organizing Club's other executive secretary, Heriberto Barrón, a notorious Reyes hatchetman. Working closely with him for Escandón was another Democrat and well-known

[4] *México Nuevo,* January 11, 1909.

[5] Juan Sánchez Azcona: *La etapa maderista de la revolución* (México, 1960), pp. 28–30.

[6] *México Nuevo,* January 13, 1909.

[7] Ibid., January 15, 1909.

[8] Alfredo Robles Domínguez: "Mis memorias políticas," serialized in *El Hombre Libre,* September 22, 1930.

[9] Sánchez Azcona: op. cit., p. 30.

Reyista, Diódoro Batalla. Barrón took his public stand on January 21, when he printed a long interview with Escandón in his Mexico City newspaper, *La República*. He was trying to recast Escandón's image to win back some of the independent sympathies Sánchez Azcona had already gained for Leyva. Escandón's cause had suffered especially since he had confessed in a recent interview with a popular magazine that he was totally ignorant about Morelos.[1] In *México Nuevo* Sánchez Azcona never tired of reminding readers of this blunder, nor of reporting jokes about Escandón's Morelos support, which he referred to as the "Cuernavaca Jockey and Sugar Club."[2] Most of all Sánchez Azcona played up Escandón's failure to present even a vague idea of what action he planned for the state should he be elected. Barrón then deftly turned the tables on *México Nuevo* with the January 21 interview in his own paper. Here he provided Escandón with an unimpeachable program—almost word for word the very program the Democratic Party had adopted the day before in its convention in Mexico City.[3]

Freedom for the municipalities from the control of the jefes políticos, increased attention to primary education, guarantees for free speech and press, civic improvements, abolition of a state poll tax—all this, which the *Mexican Herald* compared to Teddy Roosevelt's Square Deal, formed Escandón's program.[4] Few took him seriously, but still the interview was a fine coup for Barrón. The next day *México Nuevo* gallantly ate its words and praised Escandón's "democratic" courage in publishing such a worthy plan.

The interview aroused great interest in independent circles in Mexico City: Barrón had recast not only Escandón's image but also, irrevocably, the terms of the election. It had begun as a local contest tending toward a local deal. It had now become, as well, a war for prestige between the two main factions of Mexico's principal independent political group. And for them there could be no deal. Escandón was bound to win of course, but Democrats on both sides understood that having joined the fight, they had to keep it open and fair to the end. Freely getting out the vote was indeed the whole test. For them the fight was pointless without that final proof

[1] *Actualidades,* January 8, 1909.

[2] *México Nuevo,* January 5 and 14, 1909.

[3] See the "Programa político del partido Democrático," January 20, 1909, cited in [Luis Cabrera:] *Obras políticas del Lic. Blas Urrea* (México, 1921), pp. 391-4.

[4] *Mexican Herald,* February 10, 1909.

on election day, when Escandón would either win or, more or less embarrassingly, have to be imposed. (What they would do if the embarrassment—in plain words, the brutality—was extensive, they apparently did not consider.) The first step in getting out the vote was to publicize the need for it—that is, to forsake the regular procedures of opposition and go directly to the people. The operation was unprecedented, but both the Escandón and the Leyva Democrats went to work.

This complicated immeasurably the business of Morelos's native politicians. Both local teams already had the affair organized in their own terms in Cuernavaca, and publicity was the last thing they were handy at or cared about. But as the Democrats began arriving in the state about mid-January, the local leaders gradually resigned themselves to acting as their agents. The help from Mexico City was disruptive to their organizations, but too tempting to refuse.

The disruption meant less to the Escandonistas. As the official party, they had depended on Mexico City connections—President Díaz, above all—from the first. The jefes políticos, plantation managers, and city fathers arranging Escandón's election were already acting as agents for alien directors before the Democrats came. They simply kept their assigned parts. And the Reyista Democrats did not personally take over or move anyone out: they only made the drive for publicity more professional. With money, ideas, and speakers, they elaborated, refined, and extended the Escandonista campaign, but they did not change its center of control, which remained in Mexico City.

The Leyvistas in contrast, starting as free agents, went through a complete reformation. Their original base was in Cuernavaca, hardly a rebellious city. By ancient custom the weary powerful of the national capital always resorted there to enjoy the deference of the natives. The original leaders, Antonio Sedano and his sons, Ignacio and Enrique, were natives of Cuernavaca and fit products of its climate. Years before, during the War of Intervention, Antonio Sedano had served with General Leyva, and in the 1870's he had remained among his partisans. When Leyva fell in 1876, Sedano fell too—but not into misery or oblivion. Having resigned his commission in the army, he entered business in Cuernavaca and in time became a respected merchant there. For several years he served as a lower-court judge, without salary because he had no law degree, and in 1894 he was elected an alternate on the city council. His relatives also enjoyed a moderate prosperity, holding minor posts in the state bureaucracy, voting in electoral colleges, and educating their children in the Cuernavaca secondary school alongside the children of the foremost families in Morelos.[5] The Sedanos knew the Porfirian modes, political as well as social, and they abided by them. Antonio Sedano and his sons never intended to parade around as "demagogues" or really compete with Escandón. Carefully restricting the whole procedure of negotiation to established channels, they worked only for an official invitation to put forth their terms. In the outlying districts poorer versions of the Sedanos followed the word from Cuernavaca. And dealings had gone as planned, until the Mexico City independents offered their help. The Cuernavaca Leyvistas could hardly turn it down, and as the Democrats infiltrated their organization, their monopoly on the local opposition broke up.

This happened not simply because the Democrats took part, but because they changed the essential point and direction of the Leyvista movement. Although traces of the original effort to get a deal never disappeared, after mid-January they were submerged in the activity of a full-fledged popular campaign. There was no other way for an opposition party to win a big vote without much money or the advantages of official connections. Certainly the Sedanos' methods, designed for very different purposes, would not work; nor, as it soon appeared, would the Mexico City method of informed debate. In practice the problem had an easy answer. What it took to get ordinary people so interested and excited that they might vote for the opposition was a direct promise to them to do something about what made their life hard. If followers could not be dragooned or bought, they could at least be talked into line. Once the movement's aim and strategy were redefined, the Democrats had to reform its organization as well. Generally the reform amounted to expansion—recruiting more members and setting up more clubs around the state. In the two weeks after the Democrats joined the campaign, Leyvistas organized about twenty-five regular clubs in almost as many towns and villages, and published claims to more than 1,500 members.[6] But in the process there also occurred a more significant shift of control, which eventually reorganized the structure of

[5] Sedano: op. cit., pp. 1–18. International Bureau of the American Republics: *Commercial Directory of the American Republics, Supplement, Containing Corrections of Errors in Volume Two of the Commercial Directory* (Washington, 1899), p. 268. *Periódico Oficial*, II, 7, 2; IX, 51, 3. *Semanario Oficial*, III, 51, 6; IV, 2, 2; 29, 2–3.

[6] *México Nuevo*, January 18, 20–23, 25–29, and 31, February 2 and 5, 1909.

opposition in the state and endured after the Democrats had returned to their Mexico City offices.

The shift was that the Cuernavaca Leyvistas moved over to admit the Cuautla Leyvistas to power. And it was significant because it could not remain just a shift, with the two bases then balancing each other. For even in opposition Cuernavaca was conformist, a colony of Don Porfirio's Mexico City. But Cuautla was the heart of Morelos, the real center of state pride and patriotism, with vital country traditions of populist democracy going back far beyond Don Porfirio's time to the earliest, bitter days of the struggle for national independence.[7] Sugar planters considered the peons around Cuautla the touchiest in Mexico.[8] And this defiant spirit even the local businessmen shared. A balance between Cuernavaca and Cuautla could not last, because Cuernavaca stood for a manipulated opposition and Cuautla for a vigorous and true resistance. There was not room enough in Morelos's politics for the two forces; and when the Democrats helped organize Cuautla, they doomed Cuernavaca—and the spirit of moderation.

In effect they had let loose Morelos's common people. On January 22, a Friday and a workday, in the first big demonstration in the campaign, some 1,500 persons attended a rally in Cuautla to celebrate the formation of the Leyvista Liberal Political Club there.[9] The crowd jammed the city's streets and squares cheering General Leyva and his son. It was a signal. All over the eastern and central part of the state—its traditionally independent part—men who had long suffered their own neighborhood's officially imposed boss watched Cuautla, took heart, and followed its lead.

What happened two days later and fifteen miles away in the little town of Villa de Ayala was typical. Refugio Yáñez was a former municipal president of the town, still popular and respected. Pablo Torres Burgos was a schoolteacher—when the town's school had money to stay open—who often helped local farmers on simple legal matters: they knew him to be a goodhearted man and they trusted him. Luciano Cabrera was another bookish Ayalan who had often served as advocate for villagers in land

---

[7] For some of the historical reasons for local pride, see Luis Chávez Orozco: *El Sitio de Cuautla. La epopeya de la guerra de independencia* (México, 1931), and Walter S. Logan: *The Siege of Cuautla, The Bunker Hill of Mexico* (New York, 1893).

[8] *Mexican Herald*, February 7, 1909.

[9] *México Nuevo*, January 25, 1909.

disputes.[1] Together these three formed a Leyvista group, which they named (for a nineteenth-century liberal hero) the Melchor Ocampo Club, and invited villagers in the area to join. Malcontented neighbors and kinfolk from the surrounding settlements flocked in to sign up, nearly eighty in all. Among them were the Anenecuilcans Francisco Franco, who became the club's secretary, Eduwiges Sánchez, Rafael Merino, Emiliano Zapata, and the now aging but once trusting Porfirista Teodoro Placencia.[2] That same day in Jojutla, sixty-five miles southwest, the local Free Vote Club held the campaign's second large Leyvista rally, drawing more than a thousand villagers and peons into the town.[3]

Only a little more than two weeks after it began as a carefully staged maneuver, the Escandón-Leyva dispute had thus become an agitated, public struggle for crowds. By all accounts the Escandonistas proved more professional: holding economic and political power, they could pay or force their employees to attend their demonstrations.[4] But the Leyvistas were more popular. It was an obvious tactic for them to play on rural discontent: posters with the militant village demand for "Land and Water" went up around the state, and "unauthorized" speakers began implying that Patricio would see to a general redistribution of land, even private property.[5] In response, village leaders like Santa María's Genovevo de la O declared for Leyva and began pressing their old claims against neighboring haciendas.[6] The Escandonistas grew jealous, indignant, and then nervous and bellicose; and the Leyvistas, in counterreaction, more provocative and fearless. In a little village northeast of Cuernavaca, for instance, a Leyvista leader, Fermín Bello, was called on by a Cuernavaca policeman and brought back to the city to see the jefe político. The jefe asked Bello how his campaign was going, and Bello told him—well. The jefe then

---

[1] For Yáñez, see *Semanario Oficial*, II, 15, 3, and XVII, 6, 3–4. For Torres Burgos, see Octavio Paz: "Estalla la bomba," *El Universal*, June 30, 1929, and Mazari: op. cit., p. 116. For the help all three gave to Anenecuilcans, see Sotelo Inclán: op. cit., pp. 159–61.

[2] *México Nuevo*, February 4, 1909.

[3] Ibid., January 28, 1909.

[4] Ibid., January 28 and 31, February 2 and 6, 1909.

[5] Diez: *Bibliografía*, p. clxxxiii. The Escandonista press reported these offers through late January and early February; the Leyvista press kept denying that they were authorized, and asking that the Escandonistas identify who made them. See, e.g., *El Diario*, January 30, 1909, and *México Nuevo*, January 31, 1909.

[6] Genovevo de la O: "Memorias," serialized in *Impacto*, December 31, 1949. Personal interview with Daniel de la O.

informed him that since Escandón had to win—"Don Porfirio has disposed it"—his village could not go for Leyva, and that unless Bello dissolved his club immediately, he and his fellows would be shipped off to labor camps in Yucatán as soon as Escandón took office. "Where the captain commands," the jefe concluded in fine Porfirian style, "no sailor gives orders." In any previous election Bello would have gone home and dissolved the club. Now, he refused and went directly to see the Sedanos. That same evening the executive board of the Cuernavaca Leyvista club called a protest meeting and sent a complaint to the minister of the interior.[7]

The drive for crowds strained tempers so severely that politicians, both Escandonista and Leyvista, both local and national, were hard put to confine the struggle to rallies and speeches. What increasingly struck observers as dangerous was not the planters' arrogance, which they took for granted, but the revival of bitterness and open sarcasm among the common people.[8] Impulses of state pride, national patriotism, and a vague but powerful class consciousness were brewing into an almost violent sentiment for Leyva. An old hotel maid in Cuernavaca told Alfredo Robles Domínguez how she felt about the campaign. "Figure it out!" she said. "How could we help liking that kid Patricio, him coming from right around here? Besides, Don Pancho"— she meant Patricio's father—"was a friend of the poor man. He even had a fellow shot when he was governor—a *gachupín* landlord who'd had a peon thrashed almost to death. You don't have any idea," she went on, "how the landlords and especially their *gachupín* managers abuse people around here."[9]

From the fusion of militant pride, heated tempers, raging arrogance, and plain, edgy resentment, there finally exploded on February 1 a riot in Cuautla. When it happened, people were stunned as if they had been half expecting it for a long time: they could not be surprised, but neither could they really believe it. This crucial episode set finally the essential meaning people saw in the campaign, and fixed irrevocably the mood in which they would remember it.

Events in Cuautla the week before the riot had primed the elements

[7] *Diario del Hogar*, February 12, 1909. Among those signing the letter were a few out-of-town Leyvistas in Cuernavaca on business. One was Emiliano Zapata, from Anenecuilco.

[8] *Mexican Herald*, February 3, 1909.

[9] Robles Domínguez in *El Hombre Libre*, September 24, 1930. *Gachupín* is a derogatory term for a Spaniard, or by extension for an arrogant (and white) person speaking Spanish.

of the explosion perfectly. The town's new Leyvista club had tried to stage a rally on a Sunday, January 24, when merchants and laboring people could come in full strength. But the jefe político, Enrique Dabbadie, had refused permission. Nervous because of the big opening-day celebration two days earlier when he had given the Leyvistas full liberty, he feared that if he allowed any more freedom Cuautla district might go for Leyva. The least he might then lose would be his job. Unless he got contrary orders, he was taking no chances: after the first crowd, he had practically put the city under martial law, with federal troops and police and municipal gendarmes everywhere.[1] But Democratic connections and the general pressure of public opinion moved the government in the Leyvistas' favor, and after the Cuautla club filed a complaint, Dabbadie gave way. The Leyvistas received permission to hold a rally the following Sunday, January 31. Through the week they elaborated their preparations, sending out notices and organizing a ladies' auxiliary.[2] Then, almost as a challenge, the pro-Escandón newspaper in Mexico City, El Diario, announced in midweek that Escandón's champions would shortly begin a whistle-stop tour through Morelos.[3] Nationally known orators like Barrón, Diódoro Batalla, and Hipólito Olea would speak from the back of the campaign train at the little stations and haciendas on the railroad line.[4] At larger towns the celebrities would parade into the main square and deliver formal speeches. Their first stop, El Diario noted, would be Cuautla, on Monday, February 1, the day after the Leyvista rally.[5] This was the riskiest place they could have chosen, and the timing was even stupider.

Despite jitteriness the Leyvista rally took place without trouble on Sunday. At the last minute Dabbadie threatened to withdraw his permission for the show, then at four p.m. finally confirmed it, but only till six p.m., when, he said, the federal police would clear the streets. He also refused to let the Leyvistas' band play to welcome the speakers when they arrived at the train station. And he posted rurales around the main square once the rally started. Nevertheless Leyvista clubs from that part of the state—including Villa de Ayala's Melchor Ocampo Club—poured into Cuautla; and considering the provocations they were subjected to, they

[1] México Nuevo, January 31, 1909.
[2] Ibid., February 2, 1909.
[3] El Diario, January 28, 1909.
[4] Ibid., January 30, 1909.
[5] Ibid., January 28, 1909.

behaved remarkably well. They welcomed their speakers without a band, cheered for Díaz and Leyva senior and junior, stayed relatively sober, and got off the streets by six p.m.[6]

But Dabbadie had seen the elation of the crowd and, like a good policeman, sensed what might happen the next day when the Escandonistas came to town. That evening the Ministry of War sent a detachment from the 23rd Infantry Battalion to Cuautla under the command of Colonel Juvencio Robles.[7]

The Escandonista train arrived at Cuautla shortly before noon the next morning. Inauspiciously, cheers for Leyva went up as the distinguished party paraded along the route toward the plaza. Monday being a workday, many in the audience had come not on their own account but because of pressure from Dabbadie. The crowd was not very sympathetic to their elegant guest standing up on the platform with his well-paid rhetoricians. Sporadic shouts of *"Mueran los gachupines"*—death to the *gachupines*—unnerved the speakers. The crowd's enthusiasm lagged, and finally one speaker, Hipólito Olea, asked for a cheer for Escandón. To his outrage and embarrassment, several persons shouted back: "Viva Leyvaaaaa!" Olea flew into a tantrum and began cursing the crowd, calling them "imbeciles" and "ungrateful bums." Rocks sailed up toward him and the crowd quickly turned into a nasty, yelling mob. The rurales got ready to fire, and people scattered in wild disorder.[8]

That evening, the plaza occupied by troops and federal police, Dabbadie posted an official notice—to announce his revenge for the afternoon's spectacle. "It is strictly forbidden," he declared, "to utter insulting cries or to commit any act involving a breach of peace. Offenders," he wound up in an unashamed ex post facto menace, "will be sternly dealt with."[9] Arrests commenced immediately. Local merchants, workers, clerks, peons were marched off to jail—some without charges being filed, many without even having attended the rally, most simply because of their reputations. Local courts refused protection: the few like Pablo Torres Burgos from Villa de Ayala who asked for a restraining order were hustled off just as quickly and jailed for just as long. The arrests continued in following days, until

[6] *Diario del Hogar*, January 31 and February 2, 1909. *El Sufragio Libre*, February 3, 1909.

[7] *Mexican Herald*, February 3, 1909.

[8] *México Nuevo*, February 4, 1909. *La República*, February 4, 1909.

[9] *Mexican Herald*, February 7, 1909.

Cuautla had more Leyvistas behind bars than any other district in the state.[1] And repercussions extended far beyond Dabbadie's bailiwick. The day after the riot, Patricio Leyva lost his job in the Ministry of Public Works for not denying that his agents had promised land to villagers.[2]

In fact not much had happened—a few rocks thrown, some yelling, a lot of arrests and threats, but no bloodshed. But the incident seemed portentous: in the riot everyone thought he saw what he had feared the whole election would amount to. And that made the rest of the campaign an anticlimax. For "decent people," a científico editor in Mexico City lamented, the affair had begun as "a serene, educated, high-toned, and progressive struggle" and had degenerated into "a real war of the sandal against the shoe, of work pants against trousers," of the "saloon element" against "decent people."[3] Suitably reworded, this was how the "saloon element" felt as well. "A real war," a civil war, a class war—that was what haunted minds in Morelos, and in Cuautla the prospect was always most vivid. To such nervous souls the February 1 commotion seemed to put them right on the verge of the cataclysm.

For the election, what followed was irrelevant. To secure its control over the polls, the federal government stationed an unusually large detachment of thirty-five rurales in Morelos during February.[4] Yet local leaders, who knew that after all they would have to go on working and doing business in the state when the election was over, knew also that they could salvage something practical. At least they could reorder parts of the old, broken balance. Even the visiting Leyvista Democrats recognized what had happened and toned down their appeals. Although they defied the Cuernavaca jefe político's prohibition and went ahead with a big rally in the state capital on February 5, they worked to calm the crowd rather than excite it. And the more responsible government agents reciprocated.[5] General Luis C. Curiel, now the commander of the 23rd Infantry Battalion, sheltered two Leyvista speakers at the Cuernavaca rally when the jefe político threatened to hang them on the spot.[6] In the few days before the election the Escandón touring train moved on to Yautepec and Jojutla,

[1] Diario del Hogar, April 17, 1909.

[2] El Diario, February 5, 1909.

[3] Ibid., February 13, 1909.

[4] Reports on Morelos, 1909, AGN, Ramo de Gobernación (henceforth G): bundle 883.

[5] Diario del Hogar, February 9, 1909. Sedano: op. cit., p. 19.

[6] Robles Domínguez in El Hombre Libre, September 24, 1930.

at each stop playing to smaller, more sullen, but at least more restrained audiences.[7] And the Leyvista leaders changed their tune to harp on the virtues of regularity and order. In indignant letters Antonio Sedano explained how Patricio was no revolutionary or subversive, how irresponsible were "anarchistic" ideas of "giving away" the land and water of the rich planters, how "sacred and inviolable" the Leyvistas considered "the right of property."[8]

The obvious efforts at mutual accommodation revived speculation about a deal. When Colonel Tovar arrived in Cuernavaca on February 3, rumors immediately circulated that as someone personally close to Díaz and an old hand in state politics, he had been sent as an officially sanctioned compromise, and Escandón and Leyva would both quit.[9] Faint hopes for a deal still flickered among the most naïve (or desperate) even as late as mid-March, until Escandón had actually been sworn in.[1]

But no deal developed. The Cuautla riot scared opponents into accommodation everywhere except at the polls on February 7, where it scared the government into a firm and general brutality. The jefes políticos especially were determined to take no chances. They speedily and unabashedly resorted to extralegal or illegal measures to assure absolutely Escandón's election in their districts. On their orders federal police jailed many Leyvista leaders in the villages on election day; if, like Genovevo de la O in Santa María, the prey escaped, the police arrested his family as hostages.[2] In some places the jefes políticos arranged with municipal presidents not to post voting lists at all, much less at the proper time. They also rigged the distribution of ballots and packed local polling commissions. Troops and police refused entry to the polls to suspected Leyvistas. Against these abuses Leyvista leaders filed formal protests with the Ministry of the Interior, but to no avail.[3] As a final precaution General Curiel in Cuernavaca remained

[7] *El Diario*, February 3, 1909. *La República*, February 11, 1909. *Actualidades*, February 5, 1909.

[8] *Diario del Hogar*, February 9 and 11, 1909.

[9] Ibid., February 6, 1909.

[1] Later hopes still fastened on Colonel Tovar, though there was hope also for General Curiel. Both were considered "men who knew the problems of the state." *México Nuevo*, February 13, 1909.

[2] De la O in *Impacto*, December 31, 1949. Personal interview with Daniel de la O.

[3] *México Nuevo*, February 7, 1909. *Mexican Herald*, February 8, 1909. *Diario del Hogar*, February 18, 1909. See also Robles Domínguez in *El Hombre Libre*, September 29, 1930.

in hourly communication with Colonel Robles in Cuautla on election day, and federal troops stood on the alert in every district seat.[4]

The general result—Escandón's victory—was a matter of course, but so many interests hinged on its margin and distribution that reliable returns were hard to come by. The official state gazette opted out completely, simply announcing that Escandonista electors had won an "absolute majority" and leaving it at that.[5] Of all the reports of ballots counted, probably the most accurate was the *Mexican Herald*'s, which gave 201 for Escandón and 92 for Leyva.[6] To the planters and the state bureaucrats and policemen, an opposition vote of this size was a scandal tantamount to sedition, and they mounted a new attempt to restore control. Popular agitators responsible—at least those still free and at hand—were jailed; as their fellows signed protests on their behalf, they provided black lists for their own arrests. Peons who had voted for Leyva, or more likely who had not showed up to vote for Escandón, were turned away when they came to work on Monday and had to go further into debt for loans to bribe the foremen to give them back their jobs.[7] Two weeks later the electoral colleges voted, and the returns—again according to the *Mexican Herald,* there being no official count—were 235 to 20.[8] Threats, pressure, and jailings had pared Leyvista votes to less than one quarter of their original, already pared number. Again it was Cuautla that provided the most striking case. Here, even the wildly pro-Escandón *El Diario* had reported 13 Leyvista votes in the primary election. Now, in the secondary, these 13 had vanished completely.

On March 15, 1909, Pablo Escandón was officially sworn in as Morelos's new governor. He would end his term, the official gazette announced, on November 30, 1912.[9] Nobody doubted he would, or that he might win new terms, but however long he lasted, he would never be respected. His election was an insult imprinted in the annals of the state's history—and branded in the minds of its people.

[4] *Mexican Herald,* February 7, 1909.

[5] *Semanario Oficial,* XVIII, 11, 1.

[6] For other returns and their various breakdowns, see John Womack, Jr.: "Emiliano Zapata and the Revolution in Morelos, 1910–1920" (Ph.D. dissertation, Harvard University, 1965), pp. 60–1.

[7] For complaints, see *México Nuevo,* February 9–24, 1909.

[8] For a detailed breakdown, see Womack: op. cit., p. 62.

[9] *Semanario Oficial,* XVIII, 11, 1.

I I

The Planters Progress

"...let them farm in a flowerpot..."

E SCANDÓN THOUGHT HE GOVERNED MORELOS WELL, but in the two years
he held office, he snapped the few remaining threads of civic for-
bearance. Already by mid-1910 the result of his unjust and inept policies
was clear: bitterness had not run so deep in Morelos since the War of
Intervention, more than forty years before. He had practically wrecked
the state's political system, and in one district had even provoked an
agrarian uprising. When Escandón fled in terror in March 1911, the
particular crisis he escaped was months old and largely of his own making.

And largely he made it as he ended it—with escapes, from Morelos and
politics. After less than two weeks in office he asked the state legislature
for permission to go to Mexico City "for affairs of public interest."[1] On
April 23 he asked for a ten-day permit, on May 24 for three days, on June
3 for eight, on June 26 for ten, and so on through the rest of the year.[2]
As for 1910, he spent fully half of it out of state, on three two-month permits.[3]

[1] *Semanario Oficial,* XVIII, 17, 1.

[2] Ibid., XVIII, 20, 1; 24, 1; 26, 1; 29, 1; 33, 1; 38, 4; 41, 2; 42, 1.

[3] Ibid., XIX, 14, 1; 29, 1; 38, 2.

Politically these absences were ruinous. Without even a timid and indulgent supervisor like Escandón, district jefes did exactly as they pleased —which resulted in anarchy and petty despotisms. In Cuautla district, where special conciliatory care should have been taken, Dabbadie seemed intent on revenge. The main bridge in Cuautla caved in, and junk littered the city's streets and main square and park, all because Dabbadie refused to provide the regular public services.[4] He also permitted the sale of pulque and rum on market days, in direct violation of Escandón's orders; and drunk as well as exasperated, the local peons and common people of the town began rioting.[5] What aroused most indignation was that Dabbadie collected contributions to receive Governor Escandón on an official visit, and then never rendered any accounting of expenses. People in the district were certain he had embezzled their donations.[6]

In Cuernavaca, Cuautla, and Jojutla districts, the jefes continued to persecute former Leyvistas. The central Leyvista club in Cuernavaca had filed a complaint with the state legislature, petitioning that the recent elections be nullified. The deputies' reaction was not only to refuse the complaint out of hand but also to assert that the Leyvistas had lodged it only to resist the law that declared Escandón elected. Thus, they argued, the complaint amounted to a breach of the public order, and all who signed it should be arrested for sedition.[7] When this tactic failed, other pretexts served as well. In April the Cuernavaca jefe político had the state's first Leyvista, Antonio Sedano, arrested "for not having washed down the street" in front of his store.[8] Meanwhile, two months after the election, Dabbadie still held Pablo Torres Burgos and Octaviano Gutiérrez, Leyvista leaders from Villa de Ayala, in jail without charge.[9] In June Sedano still sat in the Cuernavaca jail awaiting trial for his misdemeanor. In June also the two Leyvista leaders in Tepoztlán, Bernabé and Ezequiel Labastida, having disappeared soon after election day, were yet to be heard from. Their families presumed they had been conscripted into the federal army —although both were overage—because they had last been seen in a Mexico City military prison.[1] Bernabé Labastida was in fact to spend two years in

[4] *México Nuevo*, May 15, 1909.
[5] Ibid., April 16 and May 1, 1909. *Diario del Hogar*, October 6, 1909.
[6] *México Nuevo*, May 15, 1909.
[7] Ibid., April 7, 1909.
[8] Ibid., June 23, 1909. Sedano: op. cit., pp. 20-1.
[9] *Diario del Hogar*, April 17, 1909.
[1] *México Nuevo*, June 11 and 14, 1909.

a Quintana Roo labor camp, which he survived only by a miracle.[2] Noting these reprisals, village leaders who had already escaped, like Santa María's Genovevo de la O, remained in hiding.[3]

The retirement of the experienced Lieutenant Governor Flores in June 1909 and his death in February 1910 aggravated the state's corruption.[4] District bosses fastened their grip more firmly on their victims and indulged themselves more extravagantly at the public's expense.[5] By February 1910 four large businesses had to close down in Cuernavaca because of harassment from local officials.[6]

Even when Escandón stayed at home to govern, his vagueness and hesitation cost him respect. Impositions that before had at least been managed with dexterity and rigor were now openly botched. In mid-December 1909 the state inspector of prefectures arrived in Yautepec to fix the municipal elections there for the governor's favorites. The inspector muffed the job, and a slate of unacceptable candidates was elected. Escandón then sent the state police chief to nullify the elections. But the police chief could find no clear evidence and tried to force the councilors-elect to resign. As they had not yet formally taken office, he agreed to have them sworn in if they turned over their resignations immediately afterward. Some did resign; but others, once they were in office, refused. It was a rich scandal, and produced a full harvest of ill will against Escandón and his agents.[7]

Luck and common sense deserted the new governor completely when he organized his bureaucracy. He started by firing many officials appointed by Alarcón and replacing them with officials from out of state. These imported bureaucrats knew nothing about the persons their very personal business had to do with, and their ignorance compounded trouble when it developed.[8] And Escandón's appointments often involved him with men worse than ignorant. He made a serious mistake in appointing as tax commissioner Felipe Robleda, a notorious extortionist from Jalisco whose operations soon enraged taxpayers great and small.[9] The rich complained most loudly, but the changes in personnel in the tax office—and elsewhere

[2] Oscar Lewis: *Life in a Mexican Village: Tepoztlán Restudied* (Urbana, 1963), p. 231.

[3] De la O in *Impacto,* December 31, 1949.

[4] *Semanario Oficial,* XVIII, 25, 1; XIX, 7, 1.

[5] *El Sufragio Libre,* December 15, 1909, and March 30 and May 25, 1910.

[6] Ibid., February 9, 1910.

[7] Ibid., December 29, 1909.

[8] Diez: *Bibliografía,* pp. clxxxiv–v.

[9] *Semanario Oficial,* XVIII, 19, 2. *Diario del Hogar,* July 16, 1909.

—ultimately mattered little to them: after initial squabbles, nice under-standings took shape: for those who could afford them, favors were still for sale. The people to whom the changes mattered greatly, however, were those without much money or many connections. The old bureaucrats had grown familiar with local problems, and although the balance of power was unfair, routines had evolved that still offered common people a vague promise of recourse. But now the familiarity and the routine and the hope disappeared. The rich could eventually buy peace from Felipe Robleda, but ordinary citizens had to suffer.

In appointing jefes políticos, Escandón bungled as badly. Only three weeks after being sworn in, he removed the Alarcón-appointed prefect of Cuernavaca and installed Higinio Aguilar, a brigadier general on active duty in the federal army.[1] It was clear that the recent campaign had slackened respect for official order and that the state government needed to reestablish the fear of authority. Also, since Escandón did not plan to spend much time in Morelos, he wanted someone masterful to run the capital district and act as a kind of auxiliary lieutenant governor.[2] But Aguilar was hardly the right choice. He felt no attachment to the people he ruled and let a sadistic police chief run loose in Cuernavaca and antagonize the whole city.[3] In two and a half months Aguilar himself was suspended for defrauding the feeble-minded heir to a Cuernavaca fortune.[4] Escandón finally replaced him with a reliable former municipal president and prefect of Cuernavaca currently serving in the state legislature.

Two other prefectural appointments that backfired, though in a dif-ferent way, were those of José Vivanco and Eduardo Flores in Cuautla. The veteran chief there, Dabbadie, had made himself extremely unpopular during and after the election. But if Escandón wanted to replace him, he should have picked an official already experienced and locally respected. Instead he named Vivanco and then—after Vivanco left in November 1910—Flores.[5] Neither had ever served as prefect or prefecture secretary anywhere in Morelos, and evidently they knew nothing of the work. Cuautla district was the most troublesome in the state, and in the summer

[1] *Semanario Oficial*, XVIII, 17, 1.

[2] There were even rumors that Escandón was going to name Aguilar lieutenant governor formally and then request a license to leave the state, in effect resigning and having Aguilar succeed him. *México Nuevo*, April 9, 1909.

[3] Ibid., June 23, 1909.

[4] *Semanario Oficial*, XVIII, 30, 1. *México Nuevo*, August 7, 1909.

[5] *Semanario Oficial*, XIX, 49, 3-4.

of 1910 rebel leaders began setting up their own order in its southern reaches, in Ayala municipality. Vivanco and later Flores acquiesced completely, and state authority disappeared in the area.[6]

Escandón's worst mistake was his replacement for Lieutenant Governor Luis Flores. When Flores resigned, Escandón should have made an extra effort to find a substitute at least acquainted with, if not versed in, the major problems of Morelos politics. The month Flores resigned, June, was a difficult time for Escandón—he had been in office just three months, he was enacting an unpopular bill to revalue real estate, the Aguilar scandal was just breaking—and he needed all the local powers he could mobilize. But though suitable native administrators were available at least temporarily, he called in Antonio Hurtado de Mendoza, an out-of-state judge with no effective connections or heft in Morelos.[7]

Harmful as they were, all these blunders remained venial: negligence, misinformation, or stupidity might explain them. But when Escandón moved from the organization of government to the practice of ruling, he carried out a policy that was too systematic and clear to be a mistake—the direct service of the planters' economic and political interests. Disputes between plantations and villages were no longer settled obscurely, as Alarcón had often managed. On the contrary, through executive decrees, new legislation, and reforms of the state constitution, Escandón turned openly against Morelos's villagers.

Escandón's actions were in part only another episode in the oppression traditional in those districts of Mexico. Since the sixteenth century, sugar plantations had dominated life there; in 1910 it was an old story that they crowded villages and independent farms, that hacienda lawyers finagled lands, timber, and water from weaker but rightful users, that hacienda foremen beat and cheated field hands. Still prevailing as the excuse was the lordly racism of viceroyal times. For the young Joaquín García Pimentel, whose ancient and illustrious family owned the largest plantations in the state, it seemed that "the Indian . . . has many defects as a laborer, being as he is, lazy, sottish, and thieving."[8] His pious and learned older brother, Luis, who managed the family's vast estates, felt the same way.

[6] Sotelo Inclán: op. cit., pp. 184–8.

[7] *Semanario Oficial*, XVIII, 25, 1. *México Nuevo*, June 13, 1909.

[8] Joaquín García Pimentel: "Condiciones de la gente de trabajo en el Estado de Morelos antes de la revolución de 1910, durante el período de la lucha de 1911 a 1914, y desde esa época hasta la fecha" (MS, 1916), p. 10, Archivo de Luis García Pimentel, Jr. (henceforth AGP).

The local villagers' "natural inclination toward banditry" impressed him deeply, and he often lamented that "Jacobin governments" had removed the villagers' "only restraint and guide: religion," leaving the planters to impose their own cruder controls.[9] On the plantation of another great Morelos family, the Amors, a visiting English "authoress" found the style resembling "that of England in the time of the Barons, when feudal laws reigned and hotels were unknown." The visitor came to understand that the senior Amor "has to look after the spiritual and bodily needs of his people," or ". . . they would only drink away the extra money" he gave them.[1]

But Escandón's policy was also part of a new kind of oppression that had developed with increasing force since about 1880. Its economic source was the international competition the cane- and beet-sugar industries carried on through the nineteenth century. For cane growers the most valuable returns on the struggle were the technological improvements it produced, especially the new milling machines that extracted a much higher proportion of sugar from the stalk than the old presses. These machines became generally available by the 1870's. About the same time a period of political order and strong economic growth began in Mexico. Serious work started on a regular system of railroads, and the promise of a national market emerged. The Morelos planters saw the opportunity; and however much they cherished their bucolic isolation, they at once moved out of it to meet the new demand.[2] They astutely developed interests in processing and selling to match their interest in production. They brought the railroad into the state, imported the new machinery, and planned how to get more land to grow more cane. And as their production increased, they lobbied to reduce municipal and state taxes, to abolish the remaining interstate taxes, and to maintain or raise the national tariff protecting their industry.[3]

The social difference between the old and the new oppression was as profound as the difference between a manor and a factory. Before, various

[9] Luis García Pimentel, Jr.: "Memorias" (MS, 1914), pp. 2, 64, AGP.

[1] Tweedie: op. cit., pp. 339–41.

[2] For an interesting comparison with Brazilian sugar planters, who did lapse into an easygoing and uneconomic ruralism, see Celso Furtado: *The Economic Growth of Brazil. A Survey from Colonial to Modern Times* (Berkeley, 1963), pp. 125–6. It is the market-minded Brazilian coffee planters, as he describes them, who more closely resemble the Morelos sugar planters.

[3] Daniel Cosío Villegas, ed.: *Historia Moderna de México. El Porfiriato. La Vida Económica,* 2 vols. (México, 1965), I, 79–81.

communities and economic enterprises had coexisted without question in Morelos. Sugar plantations, traditional villages, small-farm settlements, single independent farms, day laborers' hamlets, country towns, provincial cities—not all these different kinds of societies flourished, but they were all grudgingly able to survive. Oppression took place, but the individual cases lacked real momentum or coordination. Thus concentration of property in land was sporadic and irregular, for the usual motive was not so much economic calculation as personal greed. Morelos's sugar plantations still functioned in the main tradition of Mexican haciendas, more as symbols than as businesses.[4] When the planters considered the villagers especially unguarded—when the federal or state government seemed unable or unwilling to protect the villagers—then they might take over fields they had long coveted. Sometimes villagers were actually deprived of independent livelihood and had to migrate, or move permanently onto the *real,* the hacienda grounds. But this crisis was more in the nature of an unintended, half-surprising accident: it was not really policy, and no one considered it irrevocable. Happily or not, social variety seemed eternal.

After 1880 this assumption crumbled rapidly. The planters' new chance for sustained profits forecast a new world and generated new social trends. Plantations in Morelos became company towns, their permanent populations ranging from 250 to almost 3,000. The planters organized their own medical and ecclesiastical services, their own stores, schools, police, and powerhouses, and their own regular corps of bricklayers, carpenters, blacksmiths, electricians, and mechanics. To operate the new machines, they imported foreign technicians. They even set up laboratories for research and hired chemists. And as directing agents, they installed new professional managers; the Spanish planters in the state recruited theirs from among Spanish, Cuban, or Canary Island immigrants in Mexico City, and the Mexican planters usually hired experienced Mexicans or trained their own sons. These were haciendas *"comme il faut,"* as one proud Tepoztlán editor crowed.[5]

[4] Fernando B. Sandoval: *La Industria del Azúcar en Nueva España* (México, 1951), pp. 125–46. For the classic essay on this general subject, see Andrés Molina Enríquez: *Los grandes problemas nacionales* (México, 1909), pp. 85–93. The best and fullest treatment is François Chevalier: *La formation des grands domaines au Mexique. Terre et société aux xvi–xvii siècles* (Paris, 1952).

[5] Holt Büttner: op. cit., pp. 101–2. Tweedie: op. cit., pp. 338–40. J. García Pimentel: op. cit., pp. 5, 9. Luis García Pimentel, Jr.: "Recuerdos y reflexiones" (MS, n.d.), AGP. Personal interview with José García Pimentel. *El Progreso de Morelos,* June 4, 1892.

The plutocratization of the Díaz regime through the 1880's eased the planters' way. The Ministry of Public Works sold them almost all the public land left in the state and granted them favorable rulings on their requests for clear titles to other acquisitions. New federal legislation jeopardized previously recognized titles and water rights of many villages. And when the planters took advantage of this fortuity, subservient local courts approved the expropriations.[6] In the late 1860's the planters, or their fathers, had fought hard to keep Morelos a part of Mexico State: they feared that otherwise Cuernavaca and Cuautla districts might break loose from their control.[7] Twenty years later, under Díaz's patronage, they had more power there than before. Increasingly, only the plantations looked like legitimate, progressive institutions. It seemed that other kinds of communities existed as resources for them, that all human beings in Morelos must surrender their personal destinies, superior or inferior, and become mere factors in the planters' cosmopolitan enterprise. The process which individual greed had motivated now emerged as regular, científico practice.

By 1890 it was clear that in this novel boom several important towns, surrounded by plantations, had almost ceased to grow. Jonacatepec, for instance, once a flourishing mule center, now stood like an enclave in the García Pimentels' territory; its situation reminded one educated native of the depressed country towns of Ireland.[8] In dismay at their low census the Cuautla city fathers debated whether their town would stagnate from "being confined between powerful haciendas whose extensive cane fields border on all sides." Some promoters judged that though the restriction would eventually limit the city, they could meanwhile increase its population by urban renewal: in the northern precincts were several unsightly pastures and orchards, belonging to "ragamuffins . . . at once bosses and peons . . . who lend no service to the society where they live"; these properties the promoters wanted to expropriate and subdivide into lots for "poor families who could pay them out in installments."[9] But this was no solu-

[6] Mazari: op. cit., p. 109. For discussions of this process as a national policy, see Wistano Luis Orozco: *Legislación y jurisprudencia sobre terrenos baldíos,* 2 vols. (México, 1895), I, 337–85, and Molina Enríquez: op. cit., pp. 165–96.

[7] Diez: *Bibliografía,* p. clix. It was the many village petitions from the old Third District that moved the Fourth Congress to set up the state. See Tovar: op. cit., I, 151–2, 310; II, 530, 532; III, 89, 422, 428, 508, 676.

[8] *Diario de los Debates del Congreso Constituyente, 1916–1917,* 2 vols. (México, 1960), II, 1083. See also Fernando González Roa: *El aspecto agrario de la Revolución Mexicana* (México, 1919), p. 30.

[9] *La Idea Patriótica,* August 6, 1891.

tion, as the promoters themselves soon acknowledged. Cuautla's cemetery lay only three blocks from the main square and there was no room for more plots. Since the surrounding plantations went on "daily enclosing the city," one editor bitterly observed, "as in a ring of iron," the city fathers had to turn to a village over a mile away for new burial grounds.[1]

In the countryside outside the towns, especially in Yautepec and Tetecala districts, the small, old-fashioned haciendas failed and then merged into the larger, modern enterprises. Some like Dolores retained a subsidiary identity in a grand, combined estate, but others like Apanquezalco or El Charco vanished from the map of Morelos forever. Ranchos, the little rural settlements that were independent but not incorporated as villages, collapsed too. In 1876 the records had carried fifty-three, in 1887 only thirty-six. In 1891 analysts of the recent state census traced the legal extinction of thirty-four ranchos in the last generation, almost a third of them in Tetecala district.[2]

Even villages began to disappear. Those isolated like Tepoztlán in the mountains in the northern part of the state remained fairly safe, but villages in accessible timber country, near railroads, or in the well-watered bottoms were very vulnerable.[3] Although many were entrenched and thriving settlements that could trace their history back before the Conquest and their land titles back to the earliest viceroyal times, none was secure in the current siege. In 1876, the year Díaz took power, there were 118 pueblos recorded in Morelos. By 1887, despite a small increase in state population, there were only 105.[4]

Of these failures the most awesome was no doubt Tequesquitengo's. The villagers there had offended the owner of nearby San José Vista Hermosa plantation, who retaliated by running his irrigation water into their lake and flooding out the whole pueblo. In time only the village church spire remained above water, a reminder of the risks of independence.[5] Through the 1890's and after the turn of the century villages continued to

---

[1] Ibid., January 7, 1892.

[2] José María Pérez Hernández: *Cartilla de la geografía del estado de Morelos* (México, 1876), p. 23. Gobierno de Morelos: *Memoria sobre el estado de la Administración pública de Morelos, presentada al Hon. X. Congreso por el Gobernador constitucional General Jesús H. Preciado, Abril 12, 1887* (Cuernavaca, n.d., 1887?). *La Idea Patriótica*, April 2, 16, and 23, 1891.

[3] Lewis: op. cit., p. 127. Diez: *Dos conferencias*, p. 59.

[4] Pérez Hernández: op. cit., p. 23. *Memoria* (1887).

[5] *El Eco*, May 19, 1889.

disintegrate. By 1909 only a hundred were registered.[6] Hidden darkly in the fields of high, green cane, the ruins of places like Acatlipa, Cuauchichinola, Sayula, and Ahuehuepan rotted into the earth.[7] The stories of these doomed pueblos were widely known among Morelos's country people: kinfolk were often involved in the fights to save them. And their demise was a fearful lesson, leaving villagers no hope of rest.

In particularly tense areas the villages that survived still lost population. Villa de Ayala, for instance, declined from 2,041 inhabitants in 1900 to 1,745 in 1910; and Anenecuilco, in Ayala municipality, went down from 411 to 371.[8] Bit by bit the villagers lost their land—like the orchard of Olaque in Anenecuilco in 1887—but they fought on year after year to preserve what was left. And when they finally lost too much to get by farming, they tried new kinds of work. The Zapata family began raising livestock, as did many around Cuautla when Hospital and Cuahuixtla haciendas had enclosed all the decent farmland.[9]

Not all, however, could go on independently—which was just what the planters counted on. Dispossessed and destitute, many villagers started sharecropping the scrubbiest of the plantation fields.[1] Then, as their debts mounted, they hired themselves out as field hands, still living in their villages but working in contracted gangs. They found wages very high, by the day up to 65 centavos in the dry winter season and a peso during harvest in the spring, and by the job even more, from 75 centavos to 1.25 or 1.50 pesos daily. But they also found prices very high: since Morelos produced only sugar, rice, and rum in volume and had to import cloth and staples like corn and beans, they paid as much to live as in Mexico City.[2] Living in

[6] *Semanario Oficial*, XVIII, 44, 6. Diez: *Dos conferencias*, p. 61.

[7] Magaña: op. cit. (1951–2 edn., here and subsequently), I, 82–4. Diez: *Dos conferencias*, p. 59. *La Idea Patriótica*, April 16, 1891.

[8] Holt Büttner: op. cit., pp. 94–7.

[9] Sotelo Inclán: op. cit., pp. 155–8, 170. *La Idea Patriótica*, December 17, 1891.

[1] If they were lucky, or had local connections, they might contract for land good enough to truck-farm on. Emiliano Zapata sometimes sharecropped on de la Torre y Mier's Tenextepango hacienda. He and Eufemio experimented with varieties of watermelon from Veracruz. Personal interview with Antonio Díaz Soto y Gama. For Ayala's truck trade, see the prefectural reports in *Semanario Oficial*, XIV, 8, 1–2; XVI, 17, 3–4; XVII, 3, 4; 19, 3; 29, 4; 42, 4–5; XVIII, 17, 1–2.

[2] On wages, see J. García Pimentel: op. cit., pp. 7–8; also George M. McBride: *The Land Systems of Mexico* (New York, 1923), p. 32; Lewis: op. cit., p. 94; and *The Mexican Yearbook, 1909–1910* (New York, 1910), p. 392. Anenecuilcans earned only 37 centavos a day in the slack season at Hospital—see Sotelo Inclán: op. cit.,

terms of money, they fell deeper in debt. Finally they left the village for good and like many ex-rancheros moved their families onto the plantation grounds as gente de casa, permanent resident laborers. There on the *real,* if they behaved well, they could at least count on the necessities of life.

Thus, besides land, the planters acquired a dependent labor force. They encouraged this transfer of residence onto the *real,* as Joaquín García Pimentel noted, with "every effort possible." For the "secure and constant labor" of the gente de casa permitted a more efficient specialization of chores within the plantation and, during the rush seasons, relieved the managers of the dangerous and humiliating reliance on local villagers, who hated them and who might desert them for a higher wage elsewhere. Resident labor was especially important for hacendados like the Amors in Tetecala and the García Pimentels in Jonacatepec district, where villages and the seasonal gangs coming out of them were fewer than in the more densely populated central districts; and on the plantations in those relatively remote areas the largest permanent populations concentrated. But other planters, too, regarded it as "a great advantage" to settle workers on their grounds. The relocation did not proceed as rapidly as the planters liked; the Morelos villager, Joaquín García Pimentel observed, "is very attached to the land he was born on and moves only with much difficulty, even when he sees palpably that he would do better"—which often forced plantation managers to bring in migrant labor from Puebla or Guerrero.[3] But in all boldness these entrepreneurs only raised the tempo of their struggle against the villages.

After the turn of the century economic pressures on the planters increased sharply. Their immediate problem was more intense competition within Mexico for the protected domestic sugar market. Not only were their traditional rivals in Veracruz, Puebla, Michoacán, and Jalisco expanding and modernizing their works, but also new rivals appeared in Sinaloa, Tepic district, and most ominously in tropical Veracruz, where American capitalists were investing heavily in large operations. The northern threat Morelos planters could control: they arranged alliances in Puebla

---

p. 185—but this was still well above the national average, 25 centavos a day. On the high cost of living, see "¿Por qué existe y cómo se desarrolla el zapatismo en el E. de Morelos?" *La Tribuna,* May 29, 1913.

[3] J. García Pimentel: op. cit., pp. 1–6. *La Idea Patriótica,* April 2, 1891. Mazari: op. cit., p. 109.

and Veracruz, dumped produce on the market, and expelled the intruders from their commercial domains. But the Americans in Veracruz were different. The Gulf lowlands yielded ordinarily around 30 per cent more cane per acre than the Morelos uplands, which moreover required expensive irrigation and more frequent replanting. If the American effort became a going concern, it might severely damage Morelos's position as the country's leading producer.[4]

Another pressing problem was that national production of sugar now exceeded the domestic demand. Exporting the surplus was the obvious answer, and in 1902 major exports began.[5] Although Morelos planters did not at first take part, leaving the trade to Veracruz and the north, several began exports at least as early as 1905. Leading them was Ignacio de la Torre y Mier of Tenextepango, the state's then most productive hacienda.[6] But the new business only opened a new arena of competition. The costs of production were still high in Morelos, and the international market, lurching from crisis to crisis, was too erratic to depend on.

Also alarming was the new threat of native beet-sugar production, which cane growers assumed would destroy them. From 1906 on agronomists noted "remarkable possibilities" for the new industry. Sonora ranchers declared their vital interest in its foundation, and the federal government offered generous concessions to an American company to start beet-growing in the Federal District or Mexico State.[7] The projects did not materialize, but the danger that they might heightened the Morelos planters' competitive spirit.

Besides these troubles, there was the ultimate menace of exhausting Morelos's rich soil. Estimates were that it could stand constant cultivation of cane without fertilizer for about thirty years; then it would have to lie fallow.[8] So the boom that began around 1880 would begin deteriorating after 1910. The prospect hardly agitated all Morelos planters, but to some—

[4] Cosío Villegas: *Vida Económica*, I, 81. U.S. Department of Commerce and Labor, Bureau of Manufactures: *Monthly Consular and Trade Reports*, October 1908, p. 155; April 1908, p. 140; July 1905, pp. 193–6. International Bureau of the American Republics: *Mexico. Geographical Sketch, Natural Resources, Laws, Economic Conditions, Actual Development, Prospects of Future Growth* (Washington, 1904), pp. 195–6.

[5] Cosío Villegas: *Vida Económica*, I, 81–2.

[6] *El hacendado mexicano y fabricante de azúcar*, XI, 123 (March 1905), 65.

[7] *Consular Reports*, September 1906, p. 101; March 1907, p. 20.

[8] Ibid., September 1906, p. 102. *Mexico. Geographical Sketch*, p. 194.

especially the Ruiz de Velasco family, which had the best scientific training in agriculture—it had long been disturbing.[9]

The increased pressure drove the planters to greater investments, either to diversify the grades of refined sugar or to produce more rum. The Araoz family, for example, imported new machinery worth $350,000 for their Cuahuixtla hacienda.[1] To keep their expensive machines at work, the planters needed to grow still more cane—which obliged them to enlarge their landholdings further. This accelerated expansion was fast turning Morelos into a network of rural factories. By 1908 the seventeen owners of the thirty-six major haciendas in the state owned over 25 per cent of its total surface, most of its cultivable land, and almost all of its good land.[2] And as the planters took over increasingly scrubbier fields, they required increasing supplies of water to irrigate them. Investment in irrigation works probably went as high as that in milling machinery. For his Tenango hacienda Luis García Pimentel put $166,000 into construction of tunnels, canals, aqueducts, dams, sluices, bridges, and cutoff valves, to bring water from the Cuautla River sixty miles away. And along the same river Ignacio de la Torre y Mier and Vicente Alonso together invested over $210,000 in water works for their plantations.[3] During 1908 domestic sugar prices rose considerably, because the government doubled the import duty on sugar to protect the native growers; and surer, fatter profits encouraged further investment and bigger production.[4]

Morelos haciendas thus became famous as the most modern in Mexico.[5] They deserved their reputation. In 1908 the twenty-four mills in the state accounted for well over a third of the country's total sugar production. After Hawaii and Puerto Rico, Morelos was the most productive cane-

[9] See Ángel Ruiz de Velasco: *Estudios sobre el Cultivo de la Caña de Azúcar* (Cuernavaca, 1894), pp. 3–6, and Felipe Ruiz de Velasco: *Historia y Evoluciones del Cultivo de la Caña y de la Industria Azucarera en México, Hasta el Año de 1910* (México, 1937), pp. 73–4.

[1] "La industria azucarera en Méjico," *Revista Azucarera,* VII, 74 (June 1900), 160–1.

[2] See the map in Diez: *Dos conferencias,* p. 60.

[3] Gobierno de Morelos: *Memoria sobre la Administración Pública de Morelos, en los períodos de 1895 a 1902. Gob. Sr. Col. Don Manuel Alarcón* (Cuernavaca, n.d., 1902?), pp. 59–60.

[4] H. C. Prinsen Geerligs: *The World's Cane Sugar Industry, Past and Present* (Manchester, 1912), pp. 164–5. *Consular Reports,* March 1908, p. 236.

[5] Figueroa Doménech: op. cit., II, 374. F. Ruiz de Velasco: op. cit., pp. 30, 74–5.

sugar region in the world.[6] The planters, having committed themselves deeply, were in no mood to relax: between 1905 and 1908 they raised their production over 50 per cent.[7] And they maneuvered for still more land, more water, and more resident laborers. In this development, this planters' progress, the village as a community had no place. The imminent utopia was a plantation.

Villagers did resist these trends, most famously in a case involving Pablo Escandón himself. In 1903 Escandón had directed the manager of his family's Atlihuayán hacienda to put up a fence which took in about 3,500 acres of Yautepec's communal pasture land. Villagers' cattle used to grazing there knocked down the fence in places and wandered back into the territory now under the hacienda's claim. Hacienda guards corralled them and returned them only on payment of a stiff fine. Some impounded cattle died for lack of feed. Others were sold. Others' owners were jailed for letting them trespass. But the villagers would not quit their cause. After months of protesting in vain, the offended persons chose a local farmer, Jovito Serrano, to represent them before the authorities. Serrano took their complaints first to the Yautepec court, which ruled against him. When the Yautepec jefe político refused to review the decision, Serrano appealed to the Cuernavaca district court, which heard the case but upheld the original decision and imposed a hundred-peso fine on the plaintiffs. Still undaunted, Serrano appealed to the Federal Supreme Court and led a commission of seventy Yautepecans to interview President Díaz in Mexico City.[8] Less formally but no less obstinately, villagers elsewhere—in Santa María, Jantetelco, Coatlán del Río, Tepalcingo, and many other pueblos—defied local bosses and tried to defend their ancient claims.[9]

But all resistance the planters or their managers readily disposed of. In most cases the disposition was local, unofficial, and brutal—a proper beating, maybe murder.[1] If these measures were inconvenient, the prefects

[6] Diez: Dos conferencias, pp. 17–19.

[7] Prinsen Geerligs: op. cit., p. 164.

[8] Records of the Atlihuayán-Yautepec dispute are in the Archivo de Zapata (henceforth AZ), Box 30, File 2. For the court record, see Semanario Judicial de la Federación. Tribunal Pleno. Amparos (February–March 1905), 4th ser., XXII, 428–37. There is a legend, repeated most recently in John P. McNeely: "Origins of the Zapata Revolt in Morelos," Hispanic American Historical Review, XLVI, 2 (May 1966), 155, that Zapata took part in the commission. This is unlikely; his name figures in no record of the case.

[9] Mazari: op. cit., pp. 109, 112. Magaña: op. cit., I, 79–80.

[1] For an example, see ibid., I, 81–2.

·

would usually order a rebellious farmer's conscription into the army, which was also brutal. And in the few cases that became public affairs the planters could always appeal to Don Porfirio for an obliging resolution, again brutal. Thus, though the President told the Yautepecans he supported them, and it looked at last as if they might win, their legal exertions suddenly and mysteriously brought them to grief. While Serrano was in Mexico City tending to final details, he was arrested and the Yautepecan land titles and other documents seized. And on June 21, 1904, the Supreme Court upheld the earlier rulings against the villagers. The last that Serrano's family heard of him was a letter he smuggled out as he passed through Veracruz destined for a labor camp in Quintana Roo. With him were thirty-five other Morelos natives, farmers like himself from Tepoztlán, San Andrés de la Cal, Santa María, and San Juanico who had obstructed the planters' progress. Serrano died in Santa Cruz de Bravo, Quintana Roo, in November 1905.[2]

So this new oppression became the common practice. The first generation of planters engaged in it—the ruthless pioneers of the 1880's—had betrayed a nagging fear about the future: the old owner of Cuahuixtla had kept as a personal guard a pack of mean-looking dogs named after the days of the week, Sunday through Saturday, and then the months, at least through March.[3] But the succeeding generation—the ruthless heirs of the 1890's and 1900's—worked in full confidence. In these years the Amor brothers built up an impressive stable of polo ponies, trotters, and racing thoroughbreds on their San Gabriel hacienda, and they imported greyhounds and fox terriers as well.[4] At Santa Clara and Tenango the García Pimentels furnished their magnificent buildings so sumptuously that to a young Cuernavacan they seemed like "the palaces that lie along the Thames." At Oacalo the owner had a ten-acre garden superbly landscaped, complete with a central kiosk, radiating avenues lined with palms and fountains, a bowling lawn, and a tomb for his dead dog. Miacatlán was often the scene of concerts and lavish parties, and Atlihuyán struck visitors as "a delicious mansion one would never want to leave."[5] These Edwardian luxuries were displays not only of new fortunes but also of a new attitude among younger Morelos planters, a serene conviction that they could maintain and even strengthen the controls benefiting them.

By 1909 they were ready to consolidate their system. Where Alarcón

[2] Ibid., I, 85–6.
[3] Robelo: op. cit., pp. 79, 84–5.
[4] Tweedie: op. cit., pp. 342, 347.
[5] Ibid., pp. 320–2. Robelo: op. cit., pp. 5, 30, 54, 61–2, 116–17.

had equivocated, it was Escandón's responsibility as a good científico planter to establish the practice of oppression as policy. The villagers were already weak, their leaders and advocates jailed or driven into hiding because of their Leyvista sympathies in the recent election. And Escandón proceeded without hesitation. The state government's refusal to do justice became a clear rule. Many villagers around Chinameca hacienda lost cattle to the roundup there in 1909, and their complaints were never heeded. The village of Tetelpa lost much of the water it needed for its orchards when, in a dispute over rights to Apatlaco River, the local court ruled for San Nicolás Obispo hacienda. The hacienda manager soon went even beyond the court and cut the village's water off completely. Local orchards were ruined, the village's fruit business and truck farming were finished, and its residents began migrating. In the northern municipalities the contracts for cutting timber off the mountain slopes, always a rich source of corruption, became even more scandalous. Villagers not only lost their timber but the money paid them for it.[6] The most flagrant injustice occurred in Jojutla in the late summer of 1909. There a rice plantation appropriated extra use of the city's water supply. The city council protested, but against Escandón's favorites not even a district seat got effective recourse. And the dispute went on through the fall—with the rice growers using the water.[7]

Escandón's treatment of the pueblos was not merely to make life difficult for them but to break them as independent institutions. In April 1910, for instance, the leaders of Anenecuilco wrote to him in desperation. "As the rainy season is about to begin," they declared, "we poor workingmen must begin getting the land ready for planting. For this reason . . . we turn to the Superior Government of the state, imploring its protection so that, if it please, it might concede to us its backing so we can plant the fields without fear of being plundered and run off by the proprietors of Hospital hacienda. We are disposed to recognize whoever turns out to be the owner of these fields, be it the village of San Miguel Anenecuilco or someone else. But we want to plant the fields so as not to be ruined, because farming is what gives us life. From it we get our sustenance and that of our families."

The request was urgent, and easy enough to grant and arrange. But the reply, when it finally came, was a bureaucrat's insult. Eight days later, a secretary in the state executive office wrote them: "Informed of your note of the 25th of April last, in which you ask that you be permitted to prepare

[6] Diez: *Dos conferencias,* pp. 59, 63.

[7] *Diario del Hogar,* August 31 and September 1, 1909.

and sow the fields which you have claimed, . . . the governor ruled that you be told that you ought to identify the fields to which you refer."

The Anenecuilco leaders wrote back immediately. Frantic at the approach of the rainy season, they suggested various ways the dispute could be settled. They even agreed to pay the hacienda rent for the fields in question—although they had never done so before, and doing so now was in effect recognizing its title—if only the hacienda would let them go ahead with their work. After a week the same secretary replied again: "The proprietor of Hospital hacienda has already been informed of your notes of the 25th of April last and of the 8th of the current month, so that he might say what he considers proper on the request you make in the said notes."[8] Thus Escandón clarified his regime's policy.

His major task, however, was to press the new policy into legislation. The "new orientation," as he later called it, began with the General Revaluation Law for Real Estate, enacted June 21, 1909. In part this law regulated land titles, but its main intention was to devalue the plantations for tax assessments. Planters were now to pay even less tax on their land than before, while the burden was to increase on the already heavily indebted small farmers and other small or middling property owners. A young civil engineer from Cuernavaca, later the best authority on Morelos history, astutely judged this law Escandón's "greatest error."[9] It could not have cost the governor popularity in the villages, where he had none to lose. But in the towns it definitely antagonized merchants and shopkeepers, who might otherwise have accepted his rule but who now filed protest after protest against the new rates; the Cuautla weekly *La Época* became a regular forum for their complaints.[1] In the short run, however, these little people hardly mattered, and Escandón could easily ignore them. Although their resentment was profound, it remained so diffuse politically that even he could manage its suppression. In arranging the new law, the planters who had installed Escandón, men like Manuel Araoz and Luis García Pimentel, had simply decided to drive the state's agrarian crisis to its breaking point and then, unchallenged, snap it in their own favor. It was their first official step in establishing their utopia.

It went so smoothly that during the fall Escandón's aides prepared other

[8] This correspondence is quoted in Sotelo Inclán: op. cit., pp. 179–82.

[9] Diez: *Bibliografía,* p. clxxxv.

[1] *Semanario Oficial,* XIX, 26, 1. For data about the planters' lower taxes, see ibid., 16, 3; 33, 2; 39, 2–3.

steps even bolder. Escandón himself did not take a serious part in the planning because in October he left to direct the protocol of Díaz's meeting with President Taft in Ciudad Juárez.[2] But in late December he returned to outline the new reforms to the state legislature. They were eight amendments to the state constitution, which he admitted would cause "a complete revision" in Morelos politics but which he declared "of urgent necessity" to preserve the "new orientation." The amendments amounted to five changes. One was fiscal, the collection of taxes in June (after the sugar harvest) instead of December (before it), to adjust public and private finances to the economic rhythm of the plantations. The other four changes were political, distinctly enhancing executive authority at the expense of the legislature's already scant power and prestige. One would relieve the governor from having to report on current business at all four legislative sessions; henceforth he would deliver only one *informe,* to open the first session. Another change would permit the governor to leave the state for ten days without formal legislative permission. Another threatened deputies' income, prohibiting individuals from holding and drawing salaries for more than one elected office. The most important change would abolish the legislature's right to approve gubernatorial appointments to the key posts of state accountant and state tax commissioner. Escandón considered the right "an intervention which . . . might become a means of obstructionism" and asked for absolute control over the fiscal bureaucracy. He suggested that the deputies enact his project in their next session in April.[3]

Going into 1910, the planters thus moved almost at will. In making Morelos into the Perfect Plantation, they advanced as easily against the lately disaffected shopowners and merchants as against the traditionally defiant villagers and rancheros. Had the Porifirian system endured another decade, they might well have realized their dream. But through the spring of the new year they came across the first signs of a strategic complication—local interest in a surprisingly vigorous opposition campaign for the presidency. Based in Mexico City, the campaign was the work of scattered political independents only recently organized as the Anti-Reelectionist Party but passionately dedicated to an official challenge of the Porfirista regime. Like the Progressive reformers in the United States, these good souls saw themselves as "enlightened citizens" who would purge "public affairs" of the self-perpetuating gangs of "corrupt politicians" now in control. Their

[2] Henry F. Pringle: *The Life and Times of William Howard Taft. A Biography,* 2 vols. (New York, 1939), I, 463.

[3] *Semanario Oficial,* XIX, 2, 1–6.

slogan was "a real vote and no boss rule," and the party's leader, Francisco I. Madero, the spiritualist scion of a great landed family in the north, was carrying the cause bravely around the nation.[4] Despite increasingly severe persecution, the movement grew larger and stronger.

The campaign itself did not seem important in Morelos. Madero naturally concentrated on the major population and manufacturing centers in the bigger states. The closest his itinerary brought him to Morelos in 1909 and 1910 was Puebla, and Morelos natives were involved only peripherally in the movement. No prominent Leyvista took part. True, in late February 1909 General Leyva and Patricio had helped Madero form the group that eventually became the Anti-Reelectionist Party. But in the summer, months before the party's actual foundation, they had dropped out; Patricio had joined the Robles Domínguez brothers in their currently more militant National Democratic Party, and then quit them too, while the general, giving up on politics, put his personal papers in order and donated them to the National Archives. The Leyvas' champion in Morelos, Antonio Sedano, had also gone to Mexico City and conferred with Madero about aiding him in April 1909, but after the jail sentence he served when he returned to Cuernavaca, he too had abandoned politics. Despite Madero's stern complaints and urgent pleas, neither the Leyvas nor the Sedanos would ask their followers to back the new effort.[5]

Without direction and at great risk, former Leyvista activists in Cuernavaca reorganized anyway as the Leandro Valle Club and declared for

---

[4] This seems a better than literal translation of *"sufragio efectivo y no re-elección."* The impression American muckraking and Progressive political reforms made on Madero and other educated members of his generation was fairly deep. Madero himself asserted that in organizing a state convention to nominate an opposition candidate for governor in Coahuila in 1905, and in presenting an "electoral platform," he and his friends were following "American customs." See his *La sucesión presidencial en 1910* (San Pedro, 1908), p. 11. In this sense Madero belongs with other idealists then active in Latin American politics, men of varying points of view and effect but all convinced that personal morality was the key political virtue—men like José Batlle y Ordóñez in Uruguay, Hipólito Yrigoyen in Argentina, Arturo Alessandri Palma in Chile, Rui Barbosa in Brazil, and José Martí in Cuba. For a good biography, see Stanley R. Ross: *Francisco I. Madero, Apostle of Mexican Democracy* (New York, 1955).

[5] Agustín Yáñez and Catalina Sierra, eds.: *Archivo de Don Francisco I. Madero. Epistolario (1900–1909)* (México, 1963), pp. 324, 382, 399. Robles Domínguez in *El Hombre Libre,* October 17, 1930. Manuel Mazari: "Correspondencia del General D. Francisco Leyva," *Boletín del Archivo General de la Nación,* V, 3 (May, 1934), 450. Sedano: op. cit., pp. 19–21.

Madero. A young men's literary society there under the influence of another erstwhile Leyvista became practically an Anti-Reelectionist club. Sympathetic persons in Yautepec tried to circulate propaganda. In Cuautla the independent editors of *La Época* came out openly for Madero as a presidential candidate. The spiritualists of the Love and Progress Club in Cuautla probably also supported their coreligionary, privately if not publicly in their monthly journal, *El Obrero Espíritu*.[6] But altogether this work was meager. The jefes políticos, who remained sore after the last Morelos election, had already eliminated the most dangerous dissenters and now exercised a tight vigilance. To avoid nettling the authorities, ordinary discontented people shied away from petitions and formal organizations.

The only serious activity took place around Jojutla, where an ex-Leyvista, Eugenio Morales, united more than forty Madero men. A well-established member of the community and an officer in the army reserve for several years, Morales wrote to Madero on March 1, 1910, six weeks before the Anti-Reelectionist nominating convention, to praise his work and to invite him to Jojutla to inaugurate a club.[7] Madero replied at some length, thanking Morales but explaining why he could not accept the invitation and urging him to proceed on his own. Madero told him it was especially important to organize before March 15, so his club could participate in the national convention's preliminary meetings.[8] An Anti-Reelectionist Patriotic League, and its ladies' auxiliary, soon formed in Jojutla, and Morales attended the Mexico City convention in mid-April as the single delegate from Morelos.[9] The Jojutla Anti-Reelectionists were too serious to survive, however. In early May the disturbed local authorities jailed one of the leaders, Lucio Moreno. Held without charge, he remained in jail as late as June 1 and probably spent election day there.[1]

[6] Diez: *Bibliografía*, p. clxxxiv. Valentín López González: *La Historia del Periodismo en Morelos* (Cuernavaca, 1957), pp. 9–10. *El Constitucional*, March 20, 1910. Madero to *La Época*, July 24, 1910, Archivo de Madero (henceforth AM). Manuel Domínguez: *Cuautla. Sucinta receña de la heróica ciudad, cabecera de distrito en el estado de Morelos* (México, 1907), pp. 17–22. *El Obrero Espíritu*, September–November 1910.

[7] Morales became an officer in the army reserve in Jojutla in January 1903. *Semanario Oficial*, IX, 6, 2.

[8] Madero to Eugenio Morales, March 11, 1910, AM.

[9] *México Nuevo*, April 19, 1910.

[1] *El Constitucional*, June 10, 1910. Moreno's wife was president of the ladies' auxiliary.

Despite these abortions, the Maderista campaign had a real effect in Morelos—not in membership lists but in popular attitudes. The simple but astounding fact that a national opposition had formed and was directly disputing not only Díaz's choice for a successor but his own right to stay in office undermined the prestige of his dictatorial regime, invisibly but crucially. Local idealists persecuted and pining away in insignificant little burgs now recognized that they were not alone, or at least need not be; that there were legions like themselves. In watching Madero stand up to Díaz, as an Ayalan schoolteacher later recalled, they were at once encouraged and shamed into hope, the spring of action.[2]

Precisely for fear of arousing this hope, the wisest of Porfirian politicians had never openly challenged Díaz.[3] General Bernardo Reyes, who knew his country well, knew what contesting Díaz's authority would mean— how it could lead to violence, then civil war, then revolution, and the total upheaval of Mexican society, and then, if the United States intervened, the eclipse of Mexican sovereignty. So he had retired from politics when Díaz told him to the previous summer, leaving the field of opposition open. But Madero, because of his comparative youth, his characteristic innocence, and his northern provincial background, never understood the true nature of the Porfirian regime and therefore never understood that a public contest over the presidency could be fatal to the whole order. Madero himself was never revolutionary, but he was, as his enemies in the establishment charged from the first, subversive. The call to join the "democratic movement," as Madero kept referring to his campaign, the promise of "clean" politics, the touching gentleness, concern, and sincerity that Madero projected—all this worked a powerful charm in Morelos, as elsewhere. To the Ayalan schoolteacher, the "principles" Madero announced were "sacred," worthy of absolute "faith."[4] The Anti-Reelectionist campaign had been a crusade: the result was not in the winning of votes but in the winning of hearts. And when on June 13 on the eve of the election the apostle was imprisoned, the halt was not an end but the beginning of a wait. The frayed, insignificant visionaries like the country schoolteacher

---

[2] See Otilio Montaño's speech before the Revolutionary Convention on January 9, 1915, cited in Florencio Barrera Fuentes, ed.: *Crónicas y debates de las sesiones de la Soberana Convención Revolucionaria*, 3 vols. (México, 1964–65), II, 61.

[3] For an excellent essay on this point, and others concerning the revolution, see Daniel Cosío Villegas: "Del Porfiriato a la Revolución," *Novedades*, November 2, 1952.

[4] See the preamble to the Plan de Ayala in Appendix B.

—neighborhood apostles themselves—were those who cared the most. But the agitation had stirred even plain farmers, sharecroppers, and day laborers. People in Morelos, reported a Maderista agent there, stood "ready for all struggles."[5]

Escandón and his associates recognized that this new spirit might disrupt their plans. They had their own complaints about Don Porfirio, because of tight monetary policies, political disappointments, and such; but these were only quibbles, not in the slightest like the current contention. Many of the Democratic politicians and professionals who had campaigned in Morelos in 1909 were now involved in Madero's Anti-Reelectionist movement. And Madero had actually toured the country speaking to huge crowds before his arrest. Already by then the governors of Tlaxcala, Yucatán, and Sinaloa had been embarrassed by local uprisings. In the last two the governors had had to call on federal troops to restore order. If similar riots and rebellion should take place in Morelos, it was clear who would be the immediate targets—cries of *Mueran los gachupines!* still rang in the air from the year before—and Escandón took steps accordingly. The danger was in the villages; against the villages he pressed the attack.

On June 20, 1910, Escandón addressed his deputies in a request to enact the eight amendments he had proposed the previous December, as well as four new amendments. Madero had been in jail in San Luis Potosí a week; but Escandón still feared the disorder his sympathizers might provoke, and to preclude it he now proposed to elaborate into subprefectures the prefectural system he had condemned in his own campaign speeches eighteen months before. Though Morelos was the next smallest state in the Republic, and though it had an excellent system of roads, railways, and telegraph, he lamented that "lack of communications often prevents the administration of authority" and sometimes rendered official action "barely effective." Such unsatisfactory conditions might, he warned, give rise to "serious disturbances, which the government is obliged to prevent." The solution, as he saw it, was not to extend communications nor to remove possible reasons for disturbance, but instead to establish still more "local political authority"—that is, still more executive agents in the persons of twenty subprefects in Morelos's twenty non-district-seat municipalities. Thus, he concluded, the state could exercise force directly, without having to operate through municipal government "in those cases in which this latter

[5] Mazari: "Bosquejo," pp. 112–13.

government might, through bad faith or ignorance, delay action by the governor." The subjefaturas would of course be temporary, he promised: once local isolation ended and dissension disappeared, they would no longer be needed.[6]

Surprisingly, the deputies did not grant his requests at once but only approved them and left them for the fall when they would resume office "elected" as a new legislature. But if they delayed to see whether the opposition's summer restlessness would last after the final election on July 8, they were to find evidence increasing by the week. September must have provided the best proof. Every year the September *fiestas patrias* celebrated the populist origins of the nation. And this year being the independence centennial, federal, state, and municipal governments staged the grandest celebrations ever. But to common people like Emiliano Zapata, who saw the lavish preparations at the Mexico City stables of Díaz's son-in-law, it all seemed a colossal mockery—which they had to pay for.[7] Every country town would glorify the Republic's first martyred apostles and captains, while the Republic's most recent apostle languished in prison. At any time this inconsistency would have been an embarrassment: the pathetic revolts throughout the Porfiriato, in spite of científico assurance that strains could ease only through "evolution," were eloquent testimony to Mexicans' abiding capacity for even hopeless indignation against official treachery. But to the many poor and powerless of the new generation, yearning again for justice but deaf to the old excuses for doing without it, and having moreover recently tasted its promise in a free campaign, the inconsistency was worse—a contradiction, at once ridiculous and intolerable. To them, blatantly deprived of liberty, the official festival of independence seemed a deliberate outrage. As that obscure Ayala teacher (himself a member of Ayala's centennial commission) later remembered, "The tension of the public spirit had reached *a refus,* that is to say, had filled up to the brim."[8]

Having witnessed the popular reaction during the fiestas, the reconvening deputies followed Escandón's bidding. In early October they enacted the twelve amendments he had requested.[9] As of October 15 the governor

[6] *Semanario Oficial,* XIX, 27, 1.

[7] Commissions to organize and collect money for the municipal celebrations had been set up in Morelos as early as 1907. Ibid., XVI, 35, 2; XVII, 6, 3–4.

[8] Otilio E. Montaño: "El Zapatismo ante la Filosofía y ante la Historia" (MS, 1913), AZ, 27:6.

[9] *Semanario Oficial,* XIX, 49, 3.

was authorized to appoint subprefects to take over all remaining municipal autonomy in the state.

It seemed now that the planters were in the clear again, that having fixed their control in Morelos constitutionally, they had solved the complications of the spring and summer and could resume their dynamic progress. True, not all their worries ended. In early November reports started to circulate that ex-candidate Madero, who had escaped from jail and fled to Texas, was calling for a revolution. And the young literati in Cuernavaca who had backed him in the recent election declared their support of his new movement. Betraying their established fathers, they railed against the planters' rule and in the pages of their little magazine, *La Voz de la Juventud,* urged poor folk to join Madero's adventure.[1] But really these were family matters. What counted in Morelos was the Mexico City experts' prediction that the next sugar harvest would be the greatest in the industry's history. In anticipation Escandón installed a new complex of machinery at the mill on his Atlihuayán hacienda.[2] Relaxing in their fashionable homes in the capital, the planters were content: Morelos, which they proudly believed "the richest and most prosperous state in the Republic," at last seemed theirs. And as confidently as they left their plantations to their managers to administer, so now they left their state to Escandón.

The governor was confident too. In mid-November, after the rainy season, he returned from a two-month vacation and settled down to enjoy a winter in Cuernavaca's sun.[3] So little effort did he imagine his job now required that he neglected to appoint the subprefects he had said he needed so badly. And in the lazily supervised municipal elections in late November ex-Leyvistas won seats on at least eight town councils; in Tepoztlán they even captured the municipal presidency. There and elsewhere seats also fell to relatives of ex-Leyvistas or to equally refractory elements, like a Yautepec survivor of the 1903 suit against the present governor.[4] But this

[1] López González: op. cit., pp. 9–11.

[2] *El hacendado mexicano,* XVI, 193 (December 1910), 441; XVII, 194 (January 1911), 15.

[3] *Semanario Oficial,* XIX, 38, 2; XX, 1, 1.

[4] For lists of councilmen, see ibid., XIX, 50, 6–8. For lists of Leyvista club members, see *México Nuevo,* January 18–27, 29–31, and February 4–5, 1909. The seven other towns were Xochitepec, Yautepec, Ayala, Jojutla, Tlaquiltenango, Tlaltizapán, and Jonacatepec.

seemed only a slip, not an omen. Nowhere in Morelos had there been a response to Madero's call for a national revolt on November 20. And sure of his own domains, Escandón drifted into another, dreamy world—reminiscing about England with his friend Mrs. King.

Through the end of the year, however, the complications in the state would not dwindle away. Indeed they multiplied. Far off in Chihuahua the Maderista revolution remained alive, and a crisis developed in Mexico City as the government too slowly mobilized the repression; encouraged, political and criminal fugitives in Morelos began to form bands and emerge from hiding, to test for the first time in nearly two decades the strength and morale of local officials. The bands were small and poorly armed: the group Genovevo de la O collected in the mountains north of Cuernavaca had only twenty-five men, and only de la O had a gun, a .70-caliber musket.[5] But the rebels always appeared in random, difficult places, and Escandón found that his officials could not catch and crush them. Even more disturbing than these renegades, however, was that out in the countryside villagers also began violent resistance to the utopia Escandón had believed secure.

Of the hundred pueblos in the state in 1910, there was probably not one that was not involved in a freshly embittered legal dispute with a neighboring hacienda. And in the current confusion many desperate villagers calculated whether they might serve the cause better by taking direct action. That they would calculate in favor of revolt was most likely around traditional centers of independence and agrarian discontent, like Tepoztlán, Santa María, Tlaquiltenango, and Cuautla. Petty acts of protest, in effect minor rural strikes, did occur in various communities.[6] Almost all these little revolts, however, either disintegrated or plantation managers suppressed or compromised them locally; there is no record of Escandón using federal police or troops to keep order in these weeks.

But one case of village defiance that Escandón and the managers let mature proved fatal. This was the revolt in the troublesome Cuautla district, in its southern Ayala municipality. The four farming communities in this county-sized municipality had struggled for years against the encroachments of Hospital and Cuahuixtla haciendas, and together they were able to carry on a small but direct truck trade with Cuautla and Mexico City. This commercial independence, sustained against great

[5] De la O in *Impacto*, December 31, 1949. See also Mazari: "Bosquejo," p. 115.
[6] Lewis: op. cit., p. 94.

pressure, was coupled with a deep local pride in the role the region had played in the War of Independence.[7] Common people here were probably readier to defend themselves than anywhere else in the state. Farmers in Ayala municipality had never surrendered and paid blackmail to the marauding bandits of the 1860's. They had armed themselves, organized as vigilantes, and fought back. Into the 1890's Ayala remained probably the most militant and most heavily armed rural municipality in Morelos.[8] And this insubordinate tradition endured. In the summer of 1910, when Escandón's war against the state's villages reached its critical stage, it was no surprise that Ayala should be the region where armed resistance developed. Nor was it surprising that of the four settlements in the municipality the little village of Anenecuilco should produce the leader. It had happened before, in the 1860's, and with the same Zapata family.

The new councilmen Anenecuilco elected in September 1909 had first followed the familiar procedure of restudying the village's land titles and trying to find a reliable lawyer to represent it in court.[9] The first lawyer for whose services they contracted (at a stiff fee) proved of little help, and they let him go.[1] They then sought advice from several other sources in Mexico City—among them Paulino Martínez and possibly Jesús Flores Magón, both well-known opponents of the Díaz regime.[2] But all this was of no avail. Even worse, probably for dealing with these controversial figures, the council president, Emiliano Zapata, was drafted into the army

[7] The municipality and its seat, Villa de Ayala, were named for the local hero of the war, Francisco Ayala. See Sotelo Inclán: op. cit., pp. 141–6.

[8] Gobierno de Morelos: *Memoria sobre el estado de la Administración Pública de Morelos. Presentada al H. XI. Congreso por el Gobernador Constitucional General Jesús H. Preciado. Abril 25 de 1890* (Cuernavaca, n.d., 1890?).

[9] Sotelo Inclán: op. cit., pp. 176–7.

[1] They paid the first lawyer, Luis Ramírez de Alba, one hundred pesos. The receipt he gave Zapata, as president of the village council, is dated October 16, 1909, in ASI.

[2] There is a version that Zapata dealt with the notorious anarcho-syndicalist Ricardo Flores Magón. See Sotelo Inclán: op. cit., p. 217. But this is impossible. Ricardo was in American jails from 1907 to August 1910, and then went to Los Angeles to direct the invasion of Baja California. See Lowell L. Blaisdell: *The Desert Revolution. Baja California, 1911* (Madison, 1962), pp. 9, 15 ff. Both Jesús Flores Magón, a brother of Ricardo's, and Martínez had been active Anti-Reelectionists, and Martínez had spoken at the Leyvista rally in Cuautla on January 31, 1909. See the *Diario del Hogar*, February 2, 1909.

in February 1910.[3] It took the efforts of the owner of "the best hacienda in the state and perhaps in the Republic," Ignacio de la Torre y Mier, Díaz's own son-in-law, to get him discharged. In return Zapata had gone to work for him as chief groom in his Mexico City stables.[4]

While Zapata was out of Morelos in the spring of 1910, his fellow villagers ran into serious trouble. Anenecuilcans had complied with the new real-estate law and properly claimed their fields, but these happened to include lands Hospital wanted to keep them out of. In revenge, just at the time for preparing the fields for planting, the Hospital manager warned the Anenecuilcans they would be driven out if they dared to cultivate the disputed area. Then followed the pitiful correspondence with Escandón's office, when their increasingly desperate appeals met with blander replies. When their request was forwarded to the Hospital owner for him to "say what he considers proper," he said it: "If that bunch from Anenecuilco wants to farm, let them farm in a flowerpot, because they're not getting any land, even up the side of the hills."[5]

The villagers kept trying, however. On May 24 they won an interview with Lieutenant Governor Hurtado de Mendoza, who asked them for a list of the persons who had previously cultivated the lands in question. Two days later the list was handed in, along with a new plea for a quick ruling—no longer on the title or possession of the land but just on whether it could be farmed at all, on loan, rented, however possible. Hurtado de Mendoza's other business distracted him, and the village got no answer. Delay followed delay. The rains had already begun.

In the words of Anenecuilco's historian, "Anenecuilco was in fact breaking up and going under." Without these lands the villagers could not support themselves. They would have to split up and move away, which

[3] On February 11, 1910, Zapata was inducted into the Ninth Cavalry Regiment, stationed at Cuernavaca under the command of Colonel Ángel Bouquet. He was released on March 29, 1910, with the same rank he received at first—*soldado*, private. See the documents reprinted in Hector F. López: "¿Cuándo fue consignado Emiliano Zapata?" *El Hombre Libre,* April 5, 1937. The legend persists that Zapata served in the army in 1908, although the best-informed Zapatista chronicler confirmed López's dates. See Serafín M. Robles: "Emiliano Zapata sienta plaza como soldado el año 1910," *El Campesino,* December 1951.

[4] Sotelo Inclán: op. cit., p. 173. De la Torre y Mier was also a federal deputy for Morelos at this time. For the description of his Tenextepango hacienda, see *El hacendado mexicano,* XIII, 148 (April 1907), 484.

[5] For this and following episodes, see Sotelo Inclán: op. cit., pp. 182–8.

would mean the end of a human community some seven centuries old. Adding insult to injury, the Hospital manager rented the lands to farmers from Villa de Ayala, the municipal seat, and the villanos, as they were called, began to plant in the rows already hoed by Anenecuilcans.

This was the decisive point, and it was lucky for Anenecuilco that Zapata had just returned, cranky and resentful, from his gilt-edged centennial opportunity with de la Torre y Mier's stables. Something extraordinary had to be ventured to resolve the local crisis. As president of the village council, Zapata took the decision. Regular procedures having failed, Anenecuilco would act for itself. Zapata gathered together some eighty men in the village, had them arm themselves, and went out to the fields where the villanos were working. He told them he had no interest in fighting with them, that there were Placencias, Merinos, and Salazars in both villages, but that the land was Anenecuilco's and Anenecuilcans would farm it. The villanos retired, along with the hacienda field guard, and Zapata proceeded to assign lots to the farmers from his village. The news went quickly around the state. Even in her Cuernavaca hotel Governor Escandón's friend Mrs. King heard about Zapata during the summer of 1910—about "a fellow over near Cuautla . . . who's been stirring up the people."[6]

Hospital left the Anenecuilcans alone for the next few months, but eventually claimed rent for the use of the land. When they refused to pay, the hacienda appealed to the district prefect and a hearing was called in Villa de Ayala—before the prefect, Vivanco, and the Ayala municipal president, Refugio Yáñez, who had helped Anenecuilco before in land disputes and had served in 1909 as head of Villa de Ayala's Levyista club. Speaking for Anenecuilco, Zapata explained that bad weather had caused a bad harvest and there was no produce or money to pay with. Hospital insisted that the Anenecuilcans sell their cows or work the sum out in day labor in the fields, but the jefe finally decided in favor of the villagers. They would pay no rent at all for 1910, and only what they could in 1911.

It was an astounding victory, but Anenecuilco could not rest on it. Zapata sent a delegation to President Díaz to get the disputed land definitely returned to the village. A ruling favorable to Anenecuilco arrived, and the jefe político passed it on to the hacienda manager and Zapata. The manager disliked the decision, but there was little he could do at the moment. By late 1910 Zapata and the local authorities—Vivanco and Yáñez

[6] King: op. cit., p. 59.

—were practically in alliance. The situation in the countryside was a precarious, armed truce between the local farmers, captained by Zapata, and the hacienda field guards. And until Hospital could arrange for a more reliable prefect, who would protect the hacienda's valuable machinery, irrigation works, and cane, the hacienda preferred to avoid open violence.

In mid-November Vivanco resigned and, after a farewell festival arranged by Zapata, left the state.[7] But his replacement, Eduardo Flores, served the haciendas in the district no better. Officials throughout the country were very nervous during those weeks because of the revolution in Chihuahua, and they were anxious to hedge against reforms by winning local popularity. Thus accommodated, Zapata widened the sphere of his activity. Villanos from the municipal seat joined him now, as well as farmers from the little settlement of Moyotepec farther to the south. Many contributed to the Anenecuilco defense fund and respected Zapata's rulings on village titles and individual allotments.[8] In each disputed area Zapata had the hacienda fences taken down, conferred with the local farmers, and assigned lots. And as the pride of those farmers grew in their defiance, so grew Zapata's reputation.

With reports circulating everywhere about revolts and insurrection, the new jefe finally felt he had to take stock of his district's trouble. He went out with an escort and located Zapata seeing to the distribution of some hacienda-claimed land. What mattered was what always matters in such confrontations—firepower. Zapata had over a hundred armed men with him; Flores's escort numbered ten. Put on the defensive, Flores had to explain his interference. He told Zapata the word was out that he and his men were revolting as Maderistas. Zapata denied the report and said they were only dividing up fields that belonged to them. On that score Flores made no complaint; he asked only if he could count on Zapata and his people if Maderistas did turn up in the area. Zapata assured him he could, Flores left, and the farmers went back to their business.

By the winter of 1910–11 Zapata was the effective authority in that part of the state. The size of the area he controlled was not large, but it was of major economic value and so of strategic importance. Moreover the defiance he and his followers had shown provided a dangerous example for hard-pressed villagers elsewhere. The armed truce throughout the countryside could easily break down in several places. True, the danger the Ayala revolt constituted for the planters' long-range plans to reorganize Morelos

[7] *Semanario Oficial*, XIX, 49, 3–4.
[8] Sotelo Inclán: op. cit., pp. 217–18.

was not ultimate, or even serious—even if it led to defiance elsewhere. In the last resort the federal government could send in troops, crush the insurrection, and jail or shoot the leaders. Even the great Indian rebels of nineteenth-century Mexico were not able to hold out permanently. And as in Yucatán and Sinaloa the past June, the government would have certainly suppressed this much smaller disturbance in Morelos, and Zapata would have been lucky to escape alive—if the Maderista revolution had not succeeded. But over the winter of 1910–11 the movement in the north held together, almost miraculously, and the high politicians of the country floundered in their attempts to have it crushed or bought off. In the confusion that mounted in those months, the Ayala uprising—at first very local and limited in its origins and intentions—took on national significance.

III

The Villagers Join Madero

". . . and after a while we meet . . ."

AS OF MARRIAGES, SO OF REVOLUTIONS: the best take years to turn out well. Madero accomplished the overthrow of Díaz in ten months of planning and action. It was a victory won too soon.

The coalition he managed over the winter of 1910–11 was no tight revolutionary organization, no tested band of comrades like-minded and like-willed and obedient to an undisputed leader. It was a loose congregation of independent rebels, acquainted with each other barely if at all, and only recently united by a common hope. The Maderistas needed at least two or three years of conspiring, hiding, and fighting together before they even tried to take power. Otherwise they could hardly coordinate their affiliated but distinct revolts into a regime. Of these revolts the most distinct was that in Morelos.

From the first the state did not matter much to Madero. In initial revolutionary plans he assigned it a minor part. Mainly because of reports he had heard about the Escandón-Leyva election, he expected support there; but for him the crucial places were elsewhere.[1]

[1] Roque Estrada: *La revolución y Francisco I. Madero. Primera, segunda y tercera etapas* (Guadalajara, 1912), pp. 263–6.

Madero knew he could not afford a general insurrection, financially or politically: it would cost too much, and possibly get out of hand. So his final revolutionary plan featured neat centers of action. Madero proposed three *golpes,* three quick strikes—in Puebla City, Pachuca, and Mexico City—while he reentered the country in the north. Revolutionaries and their civilian and military sympathizers would rise "as a single man," take over the streets and garrisons in those cities, and force the government to deal with Madero as he moved triumphantly through Chihuahua.[2]

Any regional support a revolutionary agent could muster in the countryside around his target would reinforce the movement's general bargaining power. This would be a useful operation of la guerrilla, the little war. But the cities were the keys.

The rebellion in Morelos was then to depend on action in Mexico City. But as preparations began, the plan changed. Madero's Mexico City agent, Alfredo Robles Domínguez, realized that chances for a successful coup there were poor. As he later noted, what happened in the south counted most. And although he never explicitly challenged Madero's strategy, in practice he reversed its emphasis. Under his direction a regional rural insurrection would encircle and press down on the national capital until it surrendered to Madero in the north.[3]

Morelos's part remained minor, nevertheless. Concentrating on Guerrero, Robles Domínguez hoped to take Iguala, isolate the state before federal reinforcements could arrive, and destroy the few garrisons already there. If the rebels failed, they could hide in the mountains, wait for the revolt in the north to draw off the troops pursuing them, and then operate along the Costa Chica in alliance with the revolt in Oaxaca. As for Morelos, the rebels there would serve as auxiliaries to the movements in Guerrero or Puebla, depending on whether they located their bases in the western or eastern districts of the state. Morelos's subordinate role was definitely fixed when the only two likely leaders there—Eugenio Morales and Patricio Leyva—excused themselves from action. Leyva pleaded "ill health," and Morales lamented that he had "grave family matters" to attend to.[4] With no one to count on in the state, Robles Domínguez naturally directed his funds and arms elsewhere.

[2] Ibid., pp. 319–22.

[3] Robles Domínguez in *El Hombre Libre,* November 12 and 14, 1930.

[4] Diez: *Bibliografía,* p. clxxxviii. Leyva's *"ataxia locomotriz muy avanzada"* had not prevented him from conducting a strenuous campaign for governor two years before. Nor did it prevent him from active politicking in 1912–13. For Morales's

This was the scheme as of mid-November. Had its design prevailed, the movement in Morelos would have remained more firmly under central control, would probably have received more respectful treatment as an integrated force, and would therefore not have developed so originally. In a revolution so organized Zapata would hardly have emerged as a state leader.

But the whole revolutionary plan for the south suddenly broke down a week before it was to take effect. On November 13 Robles Domínguez was arrested and jailed in the capital. Jailed with him were his two closest associates in the center of the country, Francisco Cosío Robelo and Ramón Rosales.[5] Their imprisonment removed the Mexico City leadership of the southern wing of the revolution. And on November 18 the Puebla City leadership was removed as well. The chief there, Aquiles Serdán, was attacked in his home by city and federal police and killed along with his brother and several other partisans.

After this debacle revolutionary agents continued to circulate back and forth among Mexico City, Puebla City, and Iguala, but without real authority or resources. Local groups were now free to thrash out their internal differences and develop or decline on their own.

It is remarkable that in these circumstances any movement organized in Morelos. News from revolutionary headquarters in the north could not have come often or been encouraging; and if there was no action in the north, risings anywhere else would be suicide. After a grotesque disappointment on November 20, when he found almost no one to meet him at the Rio Grande, Madero gloomily retreated to San Antonio. Most of December he spent in New Orleans, apparently deserting his cause. During these weeks local malcontents in Morelos were without professional leaders, reliable contacts with official revolutionary agents, or special funds. Yet here and there they began to come together and consider joining Madero's struggle.

In late November, in the nationwide revolutionary depression following the massacre in Puebla City and the embarrassing retreat at the Rio Grande, one group began to meet at Pablo Torres Burgos's house on the outskirts of Villa de Ayala.[6] Probably most of the politically minded farm-

excuse, concocted when Guerreran Maderistas communicated with him in October 1910, see Arturo Figueroa Uriza: *Ciudadanos en armas. Antecedencia y datos para la historia de la revolución mexicana,* 2 vols. (México, 1960), I, 57.

[5] Taracena: op. cit., p. 100.

[6] Magaña: op. cit., I, 97.

ers in Ayala municipality attended one or another of the meetings, but the regulars were Torres Burgos, Emiliano Zapata, and Rafael Merino. Also attending often were three non-Ayalans: Catarino Perdomo, from San Pablo Hidalgo; Gabriel Tepepa, from Tlaquiltenango; and Margarito Martínez, from southern Puebla.

The nominal leader was Torres Burgos. In the country phrase, he "knew how to talk"—how to present a case to the jefe político. But the real chief was Zapata, the president of the joint Anenecuilco–Villa de Ayala–Moyotepec defense committee and currently the effective authority in the southern part of Cuautla district. It was on him that the group depended for its decisions.

Several meetings left the conspirators convinced they should try to establish contact with the Maderista headquarters in San Antonio. Above all they wanted to verify the offer the Maderistas were reportedly making to "proprietors of small holdings" who had lost their lands through abuses of the federal land laws. Already Zapata had seen a copy of Madero's Plan of San Luis Potosí and was studying a clause in its third article.[7]

This clause was a simple agrarian plank in Madero's revolutionary platform, a bid for the support of rural families who had suffered from Díaz's land policy. "Through unfair advantage taken of the Law of Untitled Lands," Madero stated, "numerous proprietors of small holdings, in their majority Indians, have been dispossessed of their lands—either by a ruling of the Ministry of Public Works or by decisions of the courts of the Republic. It being full justice to restore to the former owners the lands of which they were dispossessed so arbitrarily, such dispositions and decisions are declared subject to review. And those who acquired them [the lands] in such an immoral way, or their heirs, will be required to return them to the original owners, to whom they will also pay an indemnity for the damages suffered. Only in case the lands have passed to a third person before the promulgation of this plan, the former owners will receive the indemnity from those to whose profit the dispossession accrued."[8]

At the time this position seemed correct and sufficient to the Ayalan conspirators. True, they knew of few "Indians" in Morelos, but that, they

---

[7] Sotelo Inclán: op. cit., p. 189. For the document, see Manuel González Ramírez, ed.: *Planes políticos y otros documentos* (México, 1954), pp. 33–49.

[8] The law Madero referred to was the *ley de terrenos baldíos,* for a study of which see Orozco: op. cit., I, 587–617; II, 1022–9.

understood, was only how city people called country people.[9] True also, Madero's proposal was not so radical as the promise some knew that an-archo-syndicalist agitators had made, to restore the villages' old ejidos, or communal lands; taking for granted the system of individual private prop-erty established constitutionally since 1857, Madero demanded only that public servants act "morally" in enforcing the law as it stood.[1] But that, as the Ayalans also understood, was all that most villagers and rancheros wanted too. Country families in Morelos revered the 1857 Constitution. To them it was only obscurely an invalidation of communal titles, but vividly and vitally a declaration of nationhood—a cause for which many elder kinfolk and neighbors had risked their lives against the French ar-mies. Despite years of chicanery from constituted authorities, they had never lost respect for the law; Madero interested them now precisely be-cause of his offer of formal justice in the courts. Around Ayala these atti-tudes had become motives. If Zapata could only determine that Madero was sincere, he was willing to join his evidently moribund revolution and try to help revive it.

The conspirators also wondered whom the revolutionary chiefs wanted to run operations in Morelos. No other local group had claimed commis-sions from San Antonio, and for the peculiar circumstances arising in Morelos the San Luis plan had no answer. Article 10 stipulated that in states where in the last two years "democratic campaigns" had taken place, the provisional governor would be that earlier "candidate of the people," assuming he had joined the revolution. (This clause clearly applied to Morelos, Yucatán, Sinaloa, and Coahuila, where after the Creelman inter-view Madero had observed opposition activity with keen interest.) And

[9] Speakers of Nahuatl, the regional Indian language, numbered only 9.29 per cent of Morelos's population in 1910. Holt Büttner: op. cit., p. 48. These concentrated in six villages: Xoxocotla, Chalcotzingo, Tepalcingo, Amilcingo, Tetelcingo, and Tepoztlán. See Othón Flores Vilchis: "El problema agrario en el estado de Morelos" (Facultad Nacional de Jurisprudencia thesis, U.N.A.M., 1950), p. 66, and Robert Redfield: *Tepoztlán, A Mexican Village. A Study of Folk Life* (Chicago, 1930), p. 30. Nahuatl readers were of course even fewer. In his study of Anenecuilco's ancient titles in September 1909, Zapata needed translations from Nahuatl, which he knew nothing of, and he sent his secretary to Tetelcingo, north of Cuautla. There only the village priest, who had studied the language at school in his native Tepoztlán, could decipher the words. Sotelo Inclán: op. cit., p. 177.

[1] For the 1906 program of the anarcho-syndicalists' Liberal Party, see González Ramírez: op. cit., pp. 3–29.

presumably the "provisional governor" would give the revolutionary orders in his state. But in Morelos the former "candidate of the people," Patricio Leyva, was vacillating. If he finally abdicated the leadership, who then would assume authority? Careful and conscientious folk, the Ayalans feared accusations of banditry, and, to avoid them, wanted formal appointments and a definite program. So in those tense weeks they collected money through Zapata's joint defense committee and sent their "speaker," Torres Burgos, north to see Madero.

Torres Burgos probably left for San Antonio in mid-December. It has been questioned that he actually went there, or saw Madero. Probably he did. He was not a man to lie about such a mission, nor was Emiliano Zapata a man to lie to; and Zapata always believed that Torres Burgos had received his orders directly from Madero.[2] If the Ayala emissary did see Madero in San Antonio, it must have been at the end of December or early January. For Madero had not come back from New Orleans until then, and soon afterward he left for Dallas. Fortunately for the Ayalans, his hopes for the revolution had rekindled precisely about this time because of recent successes in Chihuahua.

Meanwhile in Mexico City the planters had sensed the mounting anxiety among their political friends. And although they still trusted Don Porfirio, not bothering to return to Morelos to organize the defense of their properties themselves, they at least took long-distance precautions. For their plantation personnel they ordered arms, and in January they began subsidizing Escandón to reinforce the state's federal police.[3]

The Ayala conspirators then had to decide whether they would let the planters continue their stockpiling and mobilization, or, although without official revolutionary connections, revolt while they had a chance. Zapata's

[2] Those who deny or doubt his trip include Dromundo: *Biografía,* p. 46; Douglas M. Crawford: "The Suriano Rebellion in Mexico, 1910–1919" (M.A. thesis, University of California at Berkeley, 1940), p. 18; and Francisco Cosío Robelo: "Dígale a Zapata que acabe el circo," *Mujeres y Deportes,* February 6, 1937. But in the revised biography, Dromundo says Torres Burgos did interview Madero: *Vida,* p. 47. Cosío Robelo was in jail over the winter of 1910–11 and could not know firsthand. And Crawford, who worked from scanty sources, simply said there was no evidence. None of the San Antonio exiles ever mentioned Torres Burgos's visit, but neither did they ever later deny that he had seen Madero.

[3] Memorandum on the political situation in the state of Morelos, December 29, 1911, Archivo de Alfredo Robles Domínguez (henceforth ARD), Box 7: File 37: Document 5.

decision was to wait for Torres Burgos.[4] Quietly organizing his own forces around Ayala, he tried to restrain the nervous and hot-headed local chiefs he knew. But until Torres Burgos returned, his authority remained only personal. In remote municipalities in the state's northwest and southwest corners, where renegades were already on the loose, he had almost no influence. Even in the region where his reputation gave him power—from Cuautla west to Yautepec, south to Jojutla, and east into Puebla—he still could not dominate neighborhood leaders, many of whom, out of ambition, revenge, idealism, or fear, became increasingly impatient.

The most notable of these leaders was Gabriel Tepepa. A foreman on the Alarcón family's Temilpa hacienda just north of Tlaltizapán, Tepepa enjoyed great respect among the common people around that town and Tlaquiltenango. By then seventy-four years old, a veteran of the War of Intervention and of the revolt for Díaz in 1876, he must have known personally the fathers, grandfathers, uncles, and great-uncles of most of the men he met between Jojutla, Yautepec, and Cuautla.[5] He was a tough old man, the chief of a tough company of local rancheros and villagers, and it had been important for the Ayalans to count him as theirs. But for Tepepa the punctilios of formal affiliation with the Plan of San Luis Potosí mattered little: he was spoiling for a fight.

Tepepa's independence around Jojutla must have encouraged the many former Anti-Reelectionists there. Although these professional democrats were not in contact with Madero, they had received urgings from Maderista conspirators based directly to the south, in Huitzuco, Guerrero.[6] And now, either ignorant of Torres Burgos's mission or, more likely, hoping to monopolize revolutionary authority in Morelos by taking action first, they started operations in rivalry with Zapata's.

In Eugenio Morales's default, the town's other prominent Anti-Reelectionist, Lucio Moreno, seems to have taken the lead. Just released from jail, Moreno was well suited to run the Maderista revolt in the state. Orig-

[4] Joaquín Páez: "Cuatro meses de vacaciones con Zapata," serialized in *El Sol de Puebla,* March 26, 1951.

[5] Jesús Romero Flores: "Mil biografías en la historia de México: Gabriel Tepepa," *El Nacional,* December 15, 1946. Magaña: op. cit., I, 136-7. Serafín M. Robles: "Emboscada del Gobernador Teniente Cnel. Escandón," *El Campesino,* November 1952.

[6] Sergio Valverde: *Apuntes para la historia de la revolución y de la política en el estado de Morelos, desde la muerte del gobernador Alarcón* (México, 1933), p. 38.

inally from Tepoztlán municipality, with connections in Yautepec, he had married and established himself in Jojutla.[7] There his role in the recent election had enhanced his prestige among the malcontents. With this background he could base himself in Jojutla, use Tepepa and his following to control the strategic area north along the Yautepec River, then take Tepoztlán, then Yautepec, and then move against Cuernavaca. He could thus pre-empt a move by Zapata in that direction and hold the state capital when the revolution triumphed.

Torres Burgos had not yet returned when, on February 7, Tepepa revolted in Tlaquiltenango. Rallying quickly to him were his younger partisans in the area—Francisco Alarcón, Timoteo Sánchez, Jesús Capistrán, Lorenzo Vázquez, Emigdio Marmolejo, Pioquinto Galis, and others, each with his own band of fighters.[8] Tepepa then headed north, and a few days later he and Moreno took Tepoztlán. They stayed long enough to burn the municipal archives and ransack the local political bosses' houses; then they passed on into the hills to set up their headquarters and wait for a chance at Yautepec or Cuernavaca.[9] They kept away from the well-armed haciendas, and the state government evidently did nothing to suppress them.[1] Restless without action, Tepepa drifted back south.

Still the Ayalans waited, although more activity took place around Tepoztlán after Tepepa and Morena left. Bernabé Labastida, the former Leyvista leader there, returned from Quintana Roo, bent on vengeance against the local bosses who had deported him. When he found that they had fled, he killed two of their relatives and then set up his own headquarters on the outskirts of the town.[2] Moreno meanwhile stayed in the hills nearby, his eyes fixed on Yautepec and the rich haciendas around it. Another rival had also recently appeared in the area—Amador Salazar, a young Yautepec cowboy and hacienda worker who had helped local villagers in their 1903–5 contention with Escandón, had later been conscripted into the army, and now had returned to settle old scores. But for the moment no one made important moves. Labastida and Moreno had nowhere

[7] Diez: *Bibliografía,* p. clxxxviii. Lewis: op. cit., p. 232.

[8] Magaña: op. cit., I, 98. Serafín M. Robles: "Primeros brotes a causa de la Burda Imposición," *El Campesino,* May 1954. Eduardo Adame Medina: "De Villa de Ayala a Chinameca, 1909–1919," ibid., May 1958.

[9] Lewis: op. cit., p. 233.

[1] The *Semanario Oficial* gives no official notice of *trastornos* (disturbances) during these weeks. See XX, 6–9.

[2] Lewis: op. cit., p. 233.

to go. And Salazar, in contact with Zapata (his cousin) through Otilio Montaño, a former Ayala schoolteacher just promoted to Yautepec, waited like the Ayalans for Torres Burgos to report from San Antonio.[3]

On February 14 Madero reentered Mexico, and revolutionary spirits all over the country began to recover. About the same time word went around central Morelos that Torres Burgos was back. To Zapata he had confirmed Madero's sincerity on the agrarian issue, and he had produced documents naming Patricio Leyva chief of the state's revolution. If Leyva defaulted—by then the obvious case—Torres Burgos himself was to head the movement. He also bore blank commissions for other leaders, to be distributed on the day they took action.[4] The Ayalans' credentials were now in order.

For the next three weeks they only recruited more allies and refined their plans, waiting for the right moment. But in early March the revolution picked up momentum in the north, and several revolts broke out next door in Guerrero. In Morelos the government finally started to mobilize counterrevolutionary forces. It being the peak of the harvest and milling on the haciendas, the planters wanted extra protection for their expensive machines and ripe cane fields. And on March 8 Governor Escandón ordered the reorganization and expansion of the federal police in the state.[5] The Ayalans saw they had to act.

On Friday, March 10, Zapata, Torres Burgos, and Rafael Merino met at the annual Lenten fair in Cuautla. There they agreed on the final details, and the next night, back in Villa de Ayala, they put their plot into operation. Suddenly mutinying, they disarmed the village police and called a general assembly in the square. There the "speaker," Torres Burgos, mounted the little kiosk and read publicly—for the first time in Morelos —the Plan of San Luis Potosí. He went on to report the uprisings in the north, and concluded in *vivas* for the revolution and *mueras* for the government. Otilio Montaño, there from Yautepec for the event, shifted the terms of the appeal with another cry—"Down with the haciendas! Long live the pueblos!" But no one made an issue of the discrepancy; in the ex-

---

[3] Páez in *El Sol de Puebla*, March 26, 1951. Romero Flores: "Mil biografías . . . : Amador Salazar," *El Nacional*, December 15, 1946. Personal interview with Juan Salazar Pérez. On Montaño, see Magaña: op. cit., II, 80, note 1; *Semanario Oficial*, XVII, 44, 3–4; and Páez in *El Sol de Puebla*, April 2 and 11, 1951.

[4] Diez: *Bibliografía*, p. clxxxviii. Rafael Sánchez Escobar: *Episodios de la Revolución Mexicana en el Sur* (México, 1934), p. 167.

[5] *Semanario Oficial*, XX, 10, 1.

citement the political and social struggle seemed identical. And amidst the cheers the younger villagers enlisted. Now formally in rebellion according to the San Luis plan, the Ayalans organized a band of some seventy men from various settlements in the municipality, distributed commissions, and rode south into the countryside. The Maderista revolution had started in Morelos.

The next day the rebels moved down along the Cuautla River, where earlier Zapata had run his strings of mules, to the rancho of San Rafael Zaragoza. There Catarino Perdomo had people already prepared, and almost all the adolescent and adult males joined the revolt, including the local peace officers. So did many dissidents from other ranchos and pueblos who had concentrated there. The rebels then rode on south to a camp in the hills. And then, picking up men and mounts in all the villages and ranchos they passed through, but avoiding towns and haciendas, they moved across the state line into Puebla to organize their campaign.[6]

The military operations that developed in the following weeks betray good evidence of clear and intelligent planning. And although Torres Burgos gave the orders—at least at first—and Zapata remained only one of several revolutionary colonels, the strategy was most likely Zapata's. The objective was Cuautla—geopolitically Morelos's very base, reason, and cause. From there the Ayalans could veto anyone else's control of the state, negotiate for Cuernavaca or attack it directly, and maintain independent access to Mexico City as well as escape routes to the southern hills. But Zapata and the other chiefs knew that their ill-armed and untried men could not fight pitched battles yet, at Cuautla or any other place, as guerreros (warriors) or guerrilleros (bushwhackers). To capture arms and train his volunteers at the same time, Zapata acted first to control the area behind and below a line from Jojutla to Yecapixtla. In this zone the rebels could raid as they pleased, and wait. Then, as federal army and police detachments in the state were drastically reduced or pulled out altogether for reinforcements in the more urgent theaters in the north, they could take villages and towns without much resistance. Gradually they could control the key points along the Interoceanic Railway from Puebla City to Cuautla, and thus secure themselves from an attack in the rear once they took Cuautla. Finally, as the last federal forces were called up and retreated through the route left open beyond Cuautla, the city was bound to fall.

The execution of this strategy was not free and easy, however. Painful,

[6] Magaña: op. cit., I, 98. Serafín M. Robles: "Se Levantaron al Grito de ¡Viva Madero! ¡Muera Díaz!" El Campesino, March and April 1952.

unexpected crises worried the Ayalan Maderistas all through their rebellion. The first was a crisis of leadership that almost splintered the fledgling movement. For over a week Torres Burgos's band stayed in the Puebla
hills, waiting quietly while new recruits came in. One welcome but troublesome addition was Gabriel Tepepa, who had left the inactive Lucio
Moreno to return to his original Ayalan allies. Along with him came all
his younger chiefs. These reinforcements were especially welcome to Zapata
because Tepepa could lend rudimentary but precious military experience
in the task of coaching the rebels and planning attacks; besides, among
the old man's cohorts was Lorenzo Vázquez, whom Zapata had known
as a fellow conscript in Cuernavaca and who could also help on military
problems.[7] Thus strengthened, Torres Burgos decided to bring his guerrilleros out of hiding and into combat. Zapata, still doutful that he had prepared the men sufficiently to fight regular police, much less troops, objected; but Torres Burgos overruled him and disposed his forces for an
assault on Jojutla.

Militarily the choice of target was sound. Since the town had been the
Anti-Reelectionist center in the state, it seemed likely that local support
would produce a cheap victory. Moreover a victory there would yield
extra benefits. It promised loans, forced or voluntary, from the town's
exceptionally rich merchants, and it would establish the Ayalans as the
revolutionary authority in the zone where independent rebels, like Moreno,
had had their base. Politically, however, the choice was dangerously im-
provident. For although Torres Burgos, as the appointed chief in charge,
would have to lead the first major rebel effort, he would have to depend
largely on Tepepa as the chief in fact, since Jojutla was the old man's
stamping ground; and once home, Tepepa's men were his and not Torres
Burgos's. The dissolution of command would not have mattered much
had Tepepa's followers been like the Ayalan chiefs, veterans of the political struggle of 1909 and concerned now about the formalities of political
allegiance and discipline. But none of Tepepa's chiefs had been an active
Leyvista, and now they cared less about organizing and imposing a new
progress than demolishing what they could of the old. Nevertheless, blind
to the jeopardy he placed his cause in, Torres Burgos elaborated his plan.
Assigning Rafael Merino to carry on diversionary movements around
Jonacatepec and Zapata to patrol the Puebla-Morelos line, he took charge of
Tepepa's forces and headed toward Jojutla.[8]

[7] Ibid., December 1951.
[8] Magaña: op. cit., I, 99. *El Campesino,* June 1958.

Unwittingly Escandón helped reveal these strains among the rebels. Under new, sterner urgings from Mexico City after the declarations of revolt in his state, he attempted, with his usual confidence, a show of force. With a picket of cavalry from the Cuernavaca garrison and a few rurales he appeared in Jojutla on March 22 to defend the place against the rebels reported in the area. Two days later, however, Torres Burgos's warriors rode unhindered into Tlaquiltenango, about six miles north. And at the news, and rumors that the rebels wanted to kidnap him, Escandón raced in a headlong flight back to the state capital. In tow were the soldiers and police and all the local officials.[9]

Their desertion ended any chance for an orderly transfer of power from regular to revolutionary authority. When the rebels moved into Jojutla, they refused to obey Torres Burgos's rules against looting and ransacked several places of business, among them stores owned by unpopular Spaniards. This was hardly the reform the earnest Ayalan had anticipated. Shocked at the violence and also, probably, at his own inability to control Tepepa and his men, Torres Burgos made an issue of his command. And in a junta that Zapata and Merino traveled to Jojutla to attend, Torres Burgos decided to resign. With his two young sons, he left and started back to Villa de Ayala on foot. The next day they were surprised and captured along the way by a federal police patrol. As rebels, all three were shot on the spot.[1]

The rebels might now have degenerated into mere renegades or have abandoned Morelos to join the struggle elsewhere.[2] For Torres Burgos had resigned without naming a successor, and his death left the question of revolutionary authority in Morelos as completely in the air as before he had claimed Madero's nomination. Some fifteen chiefs held commissions as colonels in the revolutionary forces. But none could legitimately give orders to the others. Retreating back into Puebla, one party of rebels (including Tepepa) solved the problem in form by electing Zapata "Supreme Chief of the Revolutionary Movement of the South."[3] But in fact the

[9] Sánchez Escobar: op. cit., I, pp. 167–8. Diez: *Bibliografía*, p. clxxxix. José Rincón Gallardo Hope: "Episodios de la revolución del Sur," *Revista de Revistas*, January 29, 1933. The last author was an aide of Escandón's, with him in Jojutla.

[1] Magaña: op. cit., I, 99–100. Diez: *Bibliografía*, pp. clxxxix–cxc.

[2] These were real, not hypothetical, possibilities. See Figueroa Uriza: op. cit., I, 117–18.

[3] *El Campesino*, July 1958.

problem remained. Other chiefs in other parties wanted the post, which looked increasingly important. When the revolution triumphed—and as March went by its triumph seemed ever more likely—the revolutionary boss in the state might then take over as provisional governor or state military or police commander. Now, with the official Maderista affiliation broken, whoever emerged as chief in charge would have to do so the hard way—by convincing his peers he deserved their backing.

This was a feat neither political ambition nor military ferocity could accomplish. The machinery to dragoon local followers did not exist. If a village resented a self-appointed chief, it simply kept its men home. The contest for revolutionary command in Morelos was therefore not a fight. It was a process of recognition by various neighborhood chiefs that there was only one man in the state they all respected enough to cooperate with, and that they had a duty to bring their followers under his authority. The one man turned out to be Zapata, who was a singularly qualified candidate—both a sharecropping dirt farmer whom villagers would trust and a mule-driving horsedealer whom cowboys, peons, and bandits would look up to; both a responsible citizen and a determined warrior. But his elevation to leadership was not automatic, and never definitive. As he himself later wrote to Alfredo Robles Domínguez, he had to be very careful with his men: for they followed him, he said, not because they were ordered to but because they felt *cariño* for him[4]—that is, they liked him, admired him, held him in high but tender regard, were devoted to him. It was because he was the kind of man who could arouse other eminently pragmatic men in this way that neither Tepepa, nor Merino, nor anyone else who cared about the movement ever tried to rival him. If he never bossed them, they never crossed him. But the process of taking command was nevertheless slow and erratic.

In late March around Tepoztlán, where he was probably to arrange a deal with Moreno and other local rebels, Zapata accidentally met an agent from a metropolitan underground group, the Tacubaya Conspiracy, ready to revolt for Madero but with its own, independent program. Zapata asked the agent, Octavio Magaña, to notify the Maderistas in Mexico City that Torres Burgos was dead and that he was provisionally carrying on in the area until Madero named a new chief.

While he awaited Madero's orders (which never came), his posi-

[4] Zapata to Robles Domínguez, June 4, 1911, ARD, 4: 17: 106.

tion in the local movement was crucially strengthened when another agent from the Tacubayans—Octavio's brother Rodolfo—arrived in Morelos a few days after Octavio left. The government had discovered and broken up the conspiracy, and arrested many of those implicated. Rodolfo had escaped and fled south. With him he brought some ten thousand pesos from his father's contribution to the Tacubayans. In view of their ruin Rodolfo delivered the money to Zapata, which provided Zapata with the strongest financial base of all the rebels in the state. And he got it without compromising himself. For although Rodolfo showed him a copy of the conspirators' Political-Social plan, which was substantially more radical than Madero's San Luis plan, and although he expressed approval of its agrarian provisions, there was evidently no pressure for him to switch his allegiance.[5]

Zapata's official connection with the Maderista organization was re-established soon afterward. On April 4 Juan Andrew Almazán—former Puebla medical student, former follower of Aquiles Serdán, former San Antonio exile, and currently self-styled Maderista plenipotentiary in the south—met Zapata at Tepexco, a little village just over the state line in Puebla. There he declared Zapata the Maderista chief in Morelos.[6] The real meaning of his declaration is subject to dispute. Young Almazán had an impressive talent for hoax and skullduggery, and his credentials in this case seem to have been suspiciously vague. In the south he spoke highly of himself, and displayed documents and official papers. But he had quarreled with Madero just before he left San Antonio, and Madero knew enough of him to consider him unruly and unreliable—*díscolo* was his word.[7] The

---

[5] Octavio Magaña Cerda: "Historia documental de la revolución," *El Universal*, July 7, 1950. He garbles the date of this episode. Magaña: op. cit., I, 109–10. For the Plan Político-Social, see González Ramírez: op. cit., pp. 68–70. Article 9 declared: "All properties which have been usurped to be given to the favorites of the present regime will be given back to their former owners." Article 10 promised higher salaries for farm workers. Article 11 obliged "all proprietors who have more land than they can or want to cultivate" to rent fallow fields to those who applied for them, at 6 per cent of the land's taxed value. Article 15 abolished monopolies in agriculture and industry.

[6] Dromundo: *Biografía*, pp. 47–8. Juan Andrew Almazán: *En defensa legítima* (México, n.d., 1958?), p. 19.

[7] José C. Valadés: *Imaginación y realidad de Francisco I. Madero*, 2 vols. (México, 1960), II, 202. On Almazán's early contact with Zapata, see also the interesting comments in Leopoldo Ancona: "El General Almazán y el Agrarismo de Zapata," *Novedades*, October 3, 1939.

true nature of his mission in Puebla and Morelos remains cloudy, but what counts is that he was eventually accepted there as he presented himself—as Madero's "ambassador," the local agent from the central revolutionary directorate. His apparently official dealings with Zapata further legitimized Zapata's leadership.

Unintentionally the científicos themselves now reinforced Zapata's leading position among the Morelos rebels. First they removed the only other figures in the state around whom Maderistas might seriously have collected, the Leyvas. In a desperate effort to quell the national revolt with piecemeal concessions, the científicos had started to replace various authorities, from cabinet ministers to municipal presidents, with less objectionable worthies. In Morelos they could not persuade Patricio Leyva to accept the governorship, but they did entice old General Leyva out of retirement and into accepting a commission as state military commander—which discredited the whole family among local rebels and reformers. Then, compounding the error in an attempt to negotiate with the rebels for a new governor, General Leyva chose to deal with precisely the group that had already acknowledged Zapata as its chief. Meeting in Jonacatepec with Emiliano and Eufemio Zapata (just back from Veracruz), Gabriel Tepepa, and Manuel Asúnsulo (a representative of the Guerrero rebels), the general in effect recognized Zapata as the Maderista chief in Morelos; and he won no concessions.[8]

As the Ayala party gained distinction, especially in the state's southern and eastern districts, new chiefs came into the camp daily. They were men of every breed—Felipe Neri, a twenty-six-year-old kiln operator from Chinameca hacienda; José Trinidad Ruiz, a Protestant preacher from Tlaltizapán; Fortino Ayaquica, a twenty-eight-year-old textile worker from Atlixco, Puebla; Francisco Mendoza, a forty-year-old rancher-rustler from around Chietla, right across the Puebla line; Jesús "One-Eye" Morales, a paunchy, blustery saloonkeeper from Ayutla, just north of Chietla, and a friend of the Zapata brothers since the late 1890's, when they were in hiding there from the Morelos police.[9] With each came a gang of fifty to two hundred new recruits.

[8] Diez: *Bibliografía,* pp. cxc–cxci.

[9] For these biographical tidbits, see Carlos Reyes Avilés: *Cartones Zapatistas* (México, 1928), p. 14; Serafín M. Robles: "Se Incorpora J. Morales, Toma de Chietla, Puebla," *El Campesino,* June 1952; ibid., February 1956; Miguel Ángel Peral: *Diccionario biográfico mexicano* (México, n.d.); *El País,* August 22, 1911; and the private papers of Porfirio Palacios.

By mid-April Zapata clearly ranked as the supreme revolutionary chief in his strategic zone. Exercising his increased authority, he was able not only to order Tepepa and Almazán farther south, to operate along the Puebla-Guerrero border, but also to retain command of Tepepa's chiefs and to integrate them and the new Puebla allies into his own basically Ayalan force. Then, calling up more volunteers from local pueblos and ranchos, he mounted a major offensive against Chietla and Izúcar de Matamoros, Puebla, the latter a key railroad and market town. Rather than defend these places, the new federal police and troops there evacuated them both. And on April 7 Zapata's Maderistas occupied them. The next day federal reinforcements hurried down from Atlixco with artillery and machine guns and drove the rebels out of Izúcar. But in Chietla and in the countryside around, the rebels regrouped and remained in control.[1] The relative success of the operation confirmed Zapata's high standing in the region.

Among revolutionaries in other districts of the state, however, Zapata's authority was more tenuous. In the central zone the bands of Amador Salazar, Felipe Neri, and Otilio Montaño were loyal to the Ayala party, and successful; from Tepoztlán to Yecapixtla and down to Tlaltizapán they carried Zapata's orders and roused recruits in his name. But through the western zone, from Huitzilac in the north to Amacuzac in the south, there roamed rebels and renegades who did not defer to Zapata in the slightest. Genovevo de la O's band west and south of Cuernavaca was at least in friendly contact with the Ayalans, through Salazar, but even so the messages went from "don Ginovevo" to "siñor Emiliano."[2] And other rebel leaders in the same area—like the Miranda brothers and their father, who were also fugitives from the Tacubaya Conspiracy—ignored Zapata completely, turning instead to the powerful chiefs then pressing up from Guerrero.

These chiefs, the four Figueroa brothers from Huitzuco, were formidable rivals of the Ayalans. Strategically, Guerrero was the key state in southern Mexico. And the Figueroas understood well the politics of revolting there. Several years before in Huitzuco the two most ambitious brothers, Ambrosio and Francisco, had been involved in subversion against the Porfirista governor, and Ambrosio had had to take refuge across the

[1] Magaña: op. cit., I, 101. Manuel de Velasco: "La revolución maderista en el estado de Puebla" (MS, 1914), pp. 67–9. I consulted this manuscript thanks to the generosity of José Ignacio Conde.

[2] Páez in El Sol de Puebla, April 2, 3, 6, 11, 17, 18, 20, and 23, 1951.

state line in Jojutla.[3] As he and Francisco knew, it was impossible for revolutionaries to control their large and mountainous state without sundry deals, many with the federal government they opposed; the most direct way to drive such bargains was to push into Morelos and deliver the revolt to the capital's gates. Geography favored this approach, Morelos lying open to the southeast. So, in the Figueroas' case, did local politics. In Jojutla Ambrosio had been a notably successful farmer and rice-mill manager for the influential Ruiz de Velasco family. He had met and impressed most of the merchants and plantation managers in the area, and had served as an officer in the local army reserve from 1903 until he returned home in 1908. Among his old friends he still enjoyed considerable esteem.[4] Moreover, another old friend, Lieutenant Colonel Fausto Beltrán, had recently assumed military command in Jojutla district. And Beltrán, who also now served as General Leyva's chief of staff in Morelos, was trying to persuade the general, the local law-abiding Leyvistas, and the local planters to deal with the Figueroas and buy an armistice.[5] By mid-April the deal was on. Morelos planters, now alert to the danger in their domains, promised to pay Ambrosio a healthy fee for guaranteeing the security of their property.[6] While in the public eye Zapata remained only "one of the ringleaders" in Morelos, the Figueroas had emerged as the strong men of the whole south.[7] In the absence of central revolutionary directions from Mexico City, the conflicts between the Guerrero and Morelos rebels developed without check.

The line along which Zapata had to counteract to forestall the Figueroas was clear. He could guarantee Morelos's political independence after the revolution triumphed only by solidly establishing it beforehand. To this end two successful operations were necessary, though not sufficient. One was political: winning from the Figueroas or the northern revolutionary directorate a formal recognition of the Morelos rebellion's independence. The other, which would enforce the first, was military: holding the strategic places in the state when Díaz began to negotiate with Madero.

Political recognition came first and easier. On April 22 Zapata and Am-

---

[3] Figueroa Uriza: op. cit., I, 31–5.

[4] Ibid., I, 41. *Semanario Oficial,* IX, 6, 2. *El País,* January 12, 1912.

[5] Figueroa Uriza: op. cit., I, 111–12. Diez: *Bibliografía,* pp. cxc–cxci. Figueroa to Robles Domínguez, July 12, 1911, ARD, 2: 8: 36.

[6] Hector F. López: "El maderismo en Guerrero," *El Hombre Libre,* September 3, 1937, and "Datos para la historia de la Revolución," ibid., September 10, 1937.

[7] *El País,* April 18, 1911.

brosio Figueroa met at Jolalpan, a little town in suitably neutral Puebla.[8]
The meeting had been arranged by a Maderista agent, Guillermo García
Aragón. Recently arrived in the area, he had just helped the Figueroas
organize their scattered followers in northeastern Guerrero as a section in
the "Liberating Army of the South."[9] García Aragón had now turned to
formally integrating the Morelos rebels into the Liberating Army. What he
really wanted was to work out at this late stage in the revolution an orderly
cooperation between the would-be hegemonic movement in Guerrero and
the would-be autonomous movement in Morelos. He had nothing of
Robles Domínguez's personal authority with the southern rebels, but any
coordination was better than none.

Among the various resolutions of the Jolalpan conference, the principal was that which formally distributed revolutionary authority. Zapata
and Figueroa agreed—Zapata was commissioned a revolutionary general,
equal to Figueroa—that separately their "columns" would operate freely
in any part of the Republic, headed by their respective chiefs. But, the
agreement specified, "when [joint] operations take place in the state of
Morelos, the supreme chief of the allied column will be Señor Zapata;
when the column is to operate in the state of Guerrero, the supreme chief
will be Señor Figueroa; and when the [allied] column is to operate in
other states, it will be previously agreed who between the said chiefs will
assume the supreme command."[1]

This agreement, sanctioned by an agent from the central headquarters,
was a great victory for Zapata. Not only was he thereby recognized as
Maderista chief in Morelos, but the Morelos movement now had a formally
independent organization. But the victory was so great and easy that it was
suspicious, even ominous: it seems doubtful that the Figueroas meant to
keep their promises.

Subsequent events deepen the doubt. Included as a corollary in the
Jolalpan pact was a plan to attack Jojutla on April 28, which was not what
Figueroa drew his subsidy from the planters for. Curiously, although
Zapata's chieftainship in Morelos had just been specified, Figueroa's col-
umn in the attack was to remain under his own command. And then, as
Zapata began preparing for the operation, disquieting reports reached him.
Much of the information was already common knowledge, like Figueroa's
local connections with the planters and the military commander. But the

[8] Figueroa Uriza: op. cit., I, 120–3.
[9] Ibid., I, 113–14.
[1] Article 5, Jolalpan pact. The document is reproduced ibid., I, 121–2.

latest news was more troublesome. It was about the payoffs, and a deal between Figueroa and Beltrán that at the last minute before the attack Figueroa would withdraw support from Zapata and let him be ruined fighting alone against a heavy federal garrison. There were even stories that Figueroa was scheming to have Zapata assassinated. And on the final intelligence that Beltrán had his artillery pointed northeast, where the Morelos rebels were to attack, Zapata withdrew.[2] But when he so informed Figueroa and requested a new conference, Figueroa refused, went on to occupy the western outskirts of Jojutla without resistance from Beltrán's two hundred troops, and then entered into an unauthorized armistice, negotiated at a nearby hacienda.[3]

On the verge of this pitfall, Zapata reacted cautiously. Despite the complaints of his chiefs and their eager guerrilleros, he retreated to a base in Ayala municipality. Jojutla was rich but not vital: he could afford to lose it if attacking it might get him killed and his movement broken up. Strategically, Cuautla was the state's heart. And having gained all he needed from the Figueroas—formal recognition—he left them to dally with the federals and turned to act where success would benefit him alone.

As he sensed, time was running out. Already the national revolutionary leaders were dickering with Díaz's envoys in El Paso. And Francisco Figueroa was preparing a trip to Mexico City to arrange his regional deal with Don Porfirio.[4] To guarantee the Ayalan position in Morelos, Zapata had now to take towns, not just raid them. Above all he had to establish a clear and undisputed hold over Cuautla. After that, if there was time, he could try for more to enhance the movement's prestige; but Cuautla was indispensable.

He acted quickly and deliberately. Calling a junta in Jantetelco of his twenty-five or thirty main chiefs, he worked out the details of strategy and disposed his forces. In early May allied rebels seized Yautepec and held it for four days, and Zapata defeated a federal garrison at Jonacatepec and occupied the place permanently. Now in the metropolitan press he was "*the ringleader of the state's insurrection.*" In the following days he moved north —always behind Cuautla—raiding the rich but lightly garrisoned factory towns of Metepec and Atlixco in western Puebla, levying forced loans, collecting provisions, and outfitting his men with captured arms and am-

[2] Magaña: op. cit., I, 111–12. Carlos Pérez Guerrero: "Por qué el general Zapata no atacó Jojutla en 1911," *El Hombre Libre,* September 8, 1937.

[3] Figueroa Uriza: op. cit., I, 125–7.

[4] Ibid., I, 129–35.

munition. And then, after news came of the revolutionaries' capture of Ciudad Juárez, while Madero moved closer to a treaty in the north and the Figueroas politicked in Mexico City, Zapata camped at the village of Yeca-pixtla, some twenty-five miles northwest of Cuautla, and organized his attack.[5]

Victory here was long and bloody in coming. The planters had at last extracted a prime protective force from the government—the crack "Golden Fifth" Regiment—and had it stationed in Cuautla. This was precisely the kind of military test that Zapata had earlier tried to avoid. But now he could not wait. It seemed that the Figueroas had actually worked out a private truce in Guerrero that would only aggravate conditions for him in Morelos.[6] Calling on all his chiefs to supply men for a colossal 4,000 to 400 superiority in numbers, Zapata did what he could to carry out a siege with largely untrained, undisciplined, impatient gangs. Though 600 fed-eral troops under an excellent commander, Victoriano Huerta, reached Cuernavaca, they made no attempt to aid their comrades in Cuautla.[7] And finally, after six of the most terrible days of battle in the whole revolution, the federals evacuated and the revolutionaries occupied the gutted city.[8] It was May 19, ten weeks short a day since the Ayalans had rebelled with Torres Burgos. At least Zapata now had one solid base—not enough alone to give him control of the state, but enough to give him the best claim to it.

There was no chance for more. Two days later, on Sunday, May 21, the Treaty of Ciudad Juárez was signed, ending the civil war. On May 25, as agreed, Díaz turned over the presidency to the former ambassador to the United States and current foreign minister, the swank lawyer-diplomat Francisco León de la Barra. Thus began an interim regime to end in free elections in October, which all assumed Madero would win. And on the last day of the month the grizzled old dictator sailed from Veracruz in the German steamer *Ypiranga*—an ordinary Mexican citizen again, bound for exile in the Paris beloved of Edward VII.

But though the fighting ended, the revolution would continue, only

[5] Magaña: op. cit., I, 112. Páez in *El Sol de Puebla,* April 24 and 27, May 4 and 5, 1951. *El País,* May 5, 7, 9, and 12, 1911. Italics mine in the quote.

[6] See Zapata's letter to the editor, *El País,* May 10, 1911.

[7] George J. Rausch, Jr.: "The Early Career of Victoriano Huerta," *The Americas,* XXI, 2 (October 1964), 144.

[8] Magaña: op. cit., I, 113–14. Páez in *El Sol de Puebla,* May 8 and 9, 1951. Figueroa Uriza: op. cit., I, 165–7.

now as official policy—or so Zapata and his chiefs believed. And the policy they planned on most was agrarian reform. This was not to confiscate the plantations. Toward these hated enterprises the rebels had actually been remarkably respectful. They had sometimes raided haciendas, mainly large ones like San Gabriel or Tenango, for the mounts, arms, and ammunition kept there. Rebels had even burned a cane field and sacked the mansion at Tenango in a reprisal against the manager, and at Atencingo, Puebla, they had murdered seven employees.[9] But generally chiefs had provided guarantees to the plantations to finish the harvest and milling. In April Amador Salazar had even put a rebel garrison at Chinameca to protect the harvest then in full swing there.[1] Often chiefs paid for the stock and material they took, or at least signed receipts. Only rarely did they recruit rebels among the gente de casa, who anyway preferred their bonded security, and nowhere evidently did they excite these dependent peons to rise up and seize the plantations they worked on.[2] Like their fathers and grandfathers, the villagers and rancheros who composed the Maderista bands remained traditionally tolerant about the pattern of life in Morelos: they would grant the hacienda its place. But they would also insist on their own place: this was the justice of their revolutionary policy, as they saw it —simply to endorse the village and rancho, to enforce respect for their titles to exist too. So, on occupying Cuautla, Zapata had sent orders to all the pueblos in the district that they should reclaim their lands from the plantations. And when the city's interim municipal president tried to countermand the orders, Zapata had stood by them unflinchingly. In the days that followed, armed parties of sharecroppers and poor farmers began invading fields in the central and eastern districts of the state. The defenseless plantation managers and peons resident on land the squatters claimed had no alternative but to meet the revolutionary demands.[3]

On its face the reform seemed warranted by the San Luis plan. By Article 9 Zapata was the legitimate authority in Cuautla, at least provisionally entitled to carry out Article 3 there—to "subject arbitrary dispossessions" to his "review" and "require the return" of "immorally acquired" land to the "original owners." And few doubted that as revolutionary chief in the

[9] *El País,* April 8 and 17, 1911. Velasco: op. cit., pp. 68–9.

[1] Páez in *El Sol de Puebla,* April 18, 1951.

[2] J. García Pimentel: op. cit., p. 11.

[3] Teofanes Jiménez to de la Barra, August 18, 1911, AZ, 6: J-3: 6. Antonio Carriles to Juan Pagaza, May 23 and 24, 1911, ARD, 6: 28: 10.

state he would carry out this agrarian policy in every district. If other revolutionary generals in other states would not do likewise, that apparently did not disturb him. They must have had different reasons for joining the revolution. As for him, the president of the joint Anenecuilco–Villa de Ayala–Moyotepec defense committee, he had revolted on specific grounds and had contracted a serious responsibility with the men who, on the same specific grounds, had revolted with him. Now that the revolution had triumphed, he was keeping his contract.

But questions remained whether the state really was Zapata's, and whether the Ayala party would count for much in Morelos. For the planters remained powerful and active. Already before the rebels had captured Cuautla, these entrepreneurs were angling to repair their control. It had dawned on them, as the initial problem of policing their property became the scary problem of avoiding financial disaster, that they could not afford otherwise. If they had to go to court to appeal expropriations, then over the summer, just when the crop for next season had to be prepared, the small farmers on the disputed fields would plant corn and beans instead of tending the cane. There would follow another gloomy spring in 1912—low production, idle mills, and lost profits—no happy prospect for businessmen with fortunes invested. Nervously they sought Maderistas who would guarantee tenure as it was, and make the villagers appeal. And these they found in the Leyva-Figueroa coalition they had earlier helped form around Jojutla. General Leyva himself, although he had guessed wrong and accepted his Porfirista commission, was now ready to explain the act as an effort on behalf of reform and to declare himself a revolutionary.[4] Many of his old partisans in Jojutla and Cuernavaca had been sincere Maderistas, though as shopkeepers or lawyers they had not cared to fight, and they considered their sympathies better qualifications than the rebels' for office in a new regime. And the Figueroas, maneuvering toward Mexico City, appreciated friendly understandings to ease their way. It was not that these aspirants would sell out; their intentions were always honorable. It was only that their view of the revolution as a political change and their interest in assuring the change in their favor rendered them candidates for a temporary alliance with the planters. Satisfactions blended, and the new party took shape.

On May 17, two days before Cuautla fell, a delegation of "respectable citizens and merchants" from Morelos had conferred with Ambrosio Fig-

---

[4] Diez, a Leyvista, accepts this version: *Bibliografía*, pp. cxc, cxcii.

ueroa in Iguala and asked him to occupy their state to save them from Zapata. Regretfully, Figueroa refused: he feared an attack from the rear by federals he had not yet compromised with. But a subordinate rebel officer, Manuel Asúnsulo, intervened. He impressed upon Figueroa how the Guerrero revolutionaries might by omission indirectly implicate themselves in Zapata's excesses. He recalled moreover that there were abundant advantages—proximity to Mexico City, for instance—in holding Cuernavaca. Think of the Guerrero rebels marching into the national capital before Madero! Whereupon Figueroa relented and gave Asúnsulo eight hundred troops to move north toward the Morelos capital. Another, smaller force he sent to occupy Jojutla.[5]

The decision had proved wise. That same day, as the negotiations at Ciudad Juárez continued, the secretary of war had ordered General Leyva to arrange armistices in Morelos. The next day the Figueroista chief Federico Morales marched peacefully into Jojutla and assumed command there, notifying Leyva he accepted the truce. Accepting the same offer, Asúnsulo marched his column on toward Cuernavaca, to Xochitepec.[6] From Cuautla, still busy at his siege, Zapata could not resist these advances and furiously refused to talk his way around them. "You are no channel of authority for me," he answered General Leyva on the offer of a truce, "for I take orders only from the Provisional President of the Republic Francisco I. Madero . . . I only tell you that if you do not turn over Cuernavaca to me, and if I take you prisoner, I will have you shot."[7] He also refused even to talk with a peace commission of Cuernavaca city fathers who came to discuss surrendering to him after he took Cuautla. So on May 21 the commissioners rebounded to Xochitepec, where Asúnsulo obligingly offered them "guarantees." That afternoon, General Leyva having resigned in a tremendous, panicky huff, the Guerrerans peacefully occupied the Morelos capital.[8] The next day Asúnsulo received Robles Domínguez's telegram to cease hostilities because of the Juárez treaty.[9]

Thus the planters had regained the local initiative. But even more surprising for Zapata and his Ayalans was the odd reaction from their revolutionary superiors. On May 23, for instance, Robles Domínguez, now out of jail and again Madero's agent in Mexico City, recommended to Zapata

[5] Figueroa Uriza: op. cit., I, 173–5.

[6] Morales to F. Leyva and Castrejón to F. Leyva, May 19, 1911, AZ, 12: 1.

[7] F. Leyva to the secretary of war, June 3, 1911, ibid., 12.

[8] Diez: *Bibliografía,* p. cxciii. Sánchez Escobar: op. cit., pp. 29–31.

[9] Robles Domínguez to Asúnsulo, May 22, 1911, ARD, 4: 17: 2.

that he "suspend attacks" on Calderón, Hospital, and Chinameca haciendas.[1] In fact there were no attacks going on at these places, nor even
threats to attack them—only Zapata's insistence on his local authority
bluntly conveyed to the Chinameca manager.[2] But for the Ayalans it must
have been disturbing that Robles Domínguez had become so tender about
the plantations. On May 24 his specific recommendation became a general
order: an "act of hostility against . . . haciendas" was "an act of war," which
rebels were to "suspend absolutely."[3] And on May 26 in the first revolutionary manifesto since the armistice, Madero himself noted that the
"aspirations contained in the third clause of the Plan of San Luis Potosí
cannot be satisfied in all their amplitude."[4] If this reservation of agrarian
aims proved real, it would be difficult to tell in Morelos whether the revolution had triumphed or not. The Ayalans' military position was precarious
anyway. After months of honest and effective work for the cause, they
faced the possibility that their own trusted leader might set aside their
claim to revolutionary authority in the state—and their projected policies.

It soon became clear that the fate of the revolution in Morelos depended
on the very unrevolutionary compromise that the national leaders had
agreed to in Ciudad Juárez. There Madero and his associates had been
called upon to decide two great issues: Was an epoch ending in Mexico?
And if so, if with Díaz's departure change somewhere and of some kind
was inevitable, what parts and how much of Don Porfirio's epoch should
end? But no one centrally involved in the decisions was sure about them,
perhaps because no one wanted to be sure. Few revolutions have been
planned, carried out, and won by men so uniformly obsessed with the
continuity of legal order as the high Maderistas of 1910–11. There seems
to have been nothing they cared about more than preserving regular forms
and routines. Díaz's regime, like his character, fascinated them: they had
grown up in it, and they never really shook off their ambivalent respect for
the "peace" which, in common with other Mexicans, they could not help
but believe he had established. So, pretending to conciliation, they left open
the question of the epoch's end.

The bargain they struck with the government recorded their evasion

---

[1] Robles Domínguez to Zapata, May 23, 1911, ibid., 5.

[2] Carriles to Pagaza, May 23 and 24, 1911, ARD.

[3] Robles Domínguez to the revolutionary chiefs in his zone, May 24, 1911, ARD,
1: 6: 34.

[4] For the document, see Manuel González Ramírez, ed.: *Manifiestos políticos,
1892–1912* (México, 1957), pp. 210–13.

perfectly. Logically the Juárez treaty should have been a blueprint for transition to a revolutionary government, stipulating the desired changes and formally and dictatorially suppressing opposition to them. But the revolutionary leaders instead exerted only the softest pressure—accepting de la Barra and four other Porfirians in the new cabinet—and returned the issue of change to the voluntary dimension of politics.[5] There, conscientious themselves, they expected their own benevolent democracy to guarantee conscientious negotiations for reform, and of course happy conclusions to them.

Their optimistic evasion proved a fatal mistake. De la Barra was temperamentally not up to being fair. As the American ambassador noted, he was "an absolutely honorable and honest man, cultured, and trained in diplomacy and the gentler arts, but . . . also a sentimentalist and lacking in the firmness and grasp of affairs so essential to one in his position in these critical times."[6] But the Maderistas in the government were not men to take charge. They could not agree, for instance, on the reforms to propose. Since none of the national leaders whose responsibility it was to initiate change had been genuinely alienated from the old regime, none of them had any clear idea of what he hated old or craved new. In forsaking the San Luis plan, they had lost even a crude agenda of priorities. And the profound and urgent longings they had aroused all over the country gave them no time, even if they had the talent, to logroll a revolution with charm and cheer and good intentions. Without regular or revolutionary order centrally imposed, the very foundations of national politics started to slip.

In Morelos the immediate formal setbacks alone were staggering to the Ayala movement. The treaty completely repealed the "political radicalism" of the San Luis plan, reinstating as legitimate the governor, the state legislators, the congressmen, the jefes políticos, and the municipal presidents.[7] Not only were they no longer subject to arrest and trial for having resisted the revolution; the revolutionaries even had to respect their authority again until interim officials might be appointed. Moreover those revolutionaries interested in keeping their Maderista military commissions now found it much less likely that their rank would be confirmed in the army.

[5] For a copy of the treaty, see Cabrera: op. cit., pp. 453–4.

[6] Wilson to the secretary of state, May 23, 1911, National Archives (henceforth NA), Record Group 59: 812.00/1981.

[7] On this point, see the interesting comments by González Ramírez: *Manifiestos,* pp. 219–20.

Even more disastrous than these particular reverses was the reconcentration of national concerns in Mexico City. During the months of civil war, attention had been distracted to Chihuahua, and Morelos had usually enjoyed the freedom of the periphery. The result was a vigorous, village-based populism, with specific demands and a responsible and resolute leader. But when in late May and early June the capital again became the main theater of politics—and a self-consciously conciliatory politics—neither Porfirian regulars nor Maderista neophytes could ignore what took place in the rich valleys eighty miles south. So Morelos underwent the misery of having the central political contests of the new national crisis superimposed upon its own local struggle. The mortal engagement between the conservatives and the reformers that went on beneath the conciliatory façade, the blatant intramural rivalry within each camp, the far-fetched outpourings of anyone who now considered he ought to have a say—all this reverberated into Morelos. The pattern of the contest that resulted was extremely intricate. But as the various coalitions formed and dissolved, the local upshot of the Juárez treaty came clear. With peace, the Ayala party would not get to run the state.

Thus confirmed in their initiative, the planters grew bolder. Shortly after the armistice Gabriel Tepepa returned from the Cuautla campaign to Tlaquiltenango. He and Federico Morales had been personal enemies for years, and their present political differences made a duel inevitable. From Tlaquiltenango Tepepa challenged Morales's authority and manliness by levying a forced loan on several of the most prosperous and unpopular Jojutla merchants—one of them a Ruiz de Velasco in-law. Tepepa was invited into the district seat to collect the loan. When he appeared in the town on May 25 with only a small escort, Morales had him captured and immediately shot.[8] The next day Tomás Ruiz de Velasco, who was to become the Morelos planters' spokesman in the coming months, explained the local political importance of the affair to Robles Domínguez.[9]

The planters pressed on. Naming the interim governor was their next success. Escandón had long since fled the state to return to the England he loved, to represent Mexico at the coronation of King George V; although

[8] Figueroa Uriza: op. cit., I, 198–9. Carriles to Pagaza, May 23 and 24, 1911, ARD. Pedro Lamadrid, Jr., on whom the brunt of the loan fell, was a brother-in-law of Felipe Ruiz de Velasco. With Escandón's complicity, the Ruiz de Velascos had recently helped the senior Lamadrid defraud the state government of 18,000 pesos in taxes. See the Memorandum, ARD.

[9] Ruiz de Velasco to Robles Domínguez, May 26, 1911, ARD, 1: 6: 44.

he had not resigned, he had received a formal six-month leave of absence, and it was understood he would not be back.[1] So in effect the revolutionaries enjoyed the privilege the San Luis plan had originally granted them of installing the new governor. The question was, which revolutionaries? The Ayalans thought the privilege was theirs. On May 26 Zapata entered Cuernavaca and arranged with Asúnsulo to establish a single revolutionary staff, with Zapata picking his own secretary (Abrahám Martínez) as its chief.[2] By May 29 he and Martínez had wired Robles Domínguez three different times asking if he could proceed to name a governor.[3] But there is no sign he got any answer. Meanwhile Asúnsulo was negotiating independently. He first offered the governorship to Manuel Dávila Madrid, a Cuernavaca hotel proprietor who had served on the city's peace commission. The hotelier refused, but recommended Juan Carreón, the manager of the Bank of Morelos. Carreón, like Asúnsulo, was a native of Chihuahua, but he had managed the Cuernavaca bank since 1905 and was an intimate of the planters.[4] On May 31 the banker wrote to Robles Domínguez that he would accept Asúnsulo's offer "with pleasure, as much because I have sympathized with the revolutionary cause, as out of patriotic duty." To prove his patriotism, he went on to emphasize that Zapata seemed incapable of disciplining his men, and that the "principal inhabitants" of Cuernavaca were alarmed at the rumor Asúnsulo would leave the city and turn it over to the native rebel chiefs. He begged Robles Domínguez to have Asúnsulo stay.[5] On June 2 Carreón took office as provisional governor, and Asúnsulo stayed.[6]

The speed and the extent of the planters' recovery of influence was astounding. In a month they had parlayed a neighborhood deal around Jojutla into a narrow and tentative but nonetheless leading control over the state's official fortunes. The coalition they directed held the state capital, the richest town in the south, three district seats—and power over all state civil offices.

Zapata's public response to the planters' operations was strangely passive. Though at Jojutla he could have managed no resistance, at Cuernavaca he

[1] *Semanario Oficial*, XX, 19, 3. *El País*, May 9, 1911.

[2] Martínez to Robles Domínguez, May 26, 1911, AZ, 27: 2.

[3] Martínez to Robles Domínguez, May 28, 1911, ARD, 4: 17: 40. Zapata to Robles Domínguez, May 28, 1911, ibid., 45. Martínez to Robles Domínguez, May 29, 1911, ARD, 1: 6: 92.

[4] Sánchez Escobar: op. cit., p. 32. *Semanario Oficial*, XIII, 9, 6; 13, 8.

[5] Carreón to Robles Domínguez, May 31, 1911, ARD, 4: 17: 63.

[6] Carreón to de la Barra, June 2, 1911, AZ, 17: 8: 5.

could have challenged Asúnsulo. After Cuautla fell, he had been warned
of Asúnsulo's advance and urged to drive on the state capital himself. But
he disparaged the danger. He said that he was not "so anxious," that he
would let "la gente decente"—the proper people—fight it out, and then move
in himself.[7] He must have known, however, that with the Figueroas involved, there was little chance of a fight. In refusing to politick or to attack,
he forfeited the city.

On Tepepa's liquidation he was equally tolerant. Zapata never held
anyone but Morales responsible and never even took special pains to punish him.[8] On May 26, the day after the shooting, Zapata conferred harmoni-
ously with Morales's cohort, Asúnsulo.[9] And on May 29 Zapata, Asúnsulo,
and another rebel who had cooperated with the Figueroas, Alfonso Miranda, declared that differences between the two revolutionary movements
had been settled satisfactorily.[1]

Moreover, despite his disapproval of Carreón, Zapata made no attempt
to dislodge him. True, he did befriend other Morelos chiefs, like Genovevo
de la O, who also resented Carreón. When Zapata entered Cuernavaca on
May 26 he intentionally came in not where Asúnsulo had gone to receive
him but where he knew de la O was waiting. And there he found him, a
gruff, stumpy fellow, dressed in a farmer's white work clothes, lost among
his men; Zapata was deeply impressed. But he let lapse the chance for
organizing a local opposition to the planters' choice. He did not even circulate a protest at Carreón's appointment.[2] In early June he tried feebly to
move his troops into Puebla, out of Carreón's jurisdiction. But he soon
gave up the effort.[3]

Reasons for this passivity were various. At least Zapata still dominated
Cuautla, where he could consolidate his power. And in Cuernavaca Asúnsulo was a cordial person, a young, American-educated mining engineer
who went for ragtime, and was not closely committed to the Figueroas; he
had served in their forces only because he happened to be working in

[7] Páez in El Sol de Puebla, May 10, 1951.
[8] Zapata to Robles Domínguez, June 9, 1911, ARD, 4: 17: 132.
[9] Asúnsulo to Robles Domínguez, May 27, 1911, ARD, 4: 17: 33. Zapata and
Asúnsulo to Robles Domínguez, May 27, 1911, ibid., 35.
[1] Magaña: op. cit., I, 116.
[2] Páez in El Sol de Puebla, May 29, 1951. De la O in Impacto, December 31, 1949.
[3] Robles Domínguez to Zapata, June 2, 1911, ARD, 4: 17: 99. Zapata to Robles
Domínguez, June 10, 1911, ibid., 135.

Guerrero when the revolution started.[4] His comradely treatment of the Ayala party in the state capital, quite in contrast with Federico Morales's belligerence in Jojutla, was a sign he might accept its claim to rule. Besides, Zapata was receiving regular funds to pay his rebel troops and the revolutionary bills: between May 29 and June 2 the Bank of Morelos and the Cuernavaca branch of the National Bank issued him 20,000 pesos for his army's expenses.[5]

Most important, it now looked as if Madero's favor was what counted in Mexico. Though many called the little man a dreamer, he had after all just managed the first successful revolt in thirty-five years. Even his vagueness seemed to reveal hidden powers. He reminded the American ambassador of the Biblical Joseph, "who was called a dreamer but became the practical ruler of a great kingdom and made his brothers princes."[6] And Zapata still believed that despite recent warnings Madero would honor the "holy principles" and "liberating promises" of the revolution. In Morelos the benefits from this presumed shift in the weight of national power would swamp the local reaction. So, relying heavily on his revolutionary affiliations, Zapata took care not to offend his superiors by lack of discipline or respect—even when, like Robles Domínguez, they established a rival faction in his domain. Against every provocation Zapata bided his time, waiting until Madero, once fully informed about Morelos's agrarian predicament, would do the villagers justice. Why dispute with envoys when the chief commands? What Zapata did not yet know was that this chief did not command.

On June 7 Madero arrived in Mexico City to a tumultuous welcome, probably the greatest the national capital had seen since that accorded to the Army of Independence ninety years before.[7] Among the first to greet him at the train station was the country rebel leader from Morelos. The next day after dinner the two conferred at the Madero family's Mexico City house on Berlin Street. Present also were Emilio Vázquez, Benito Juárez Maza, and Venustiano Carranza, all among the high ruling circles of the revolutionary coalition.[8]

[4] Figueroa Uriza: op. cit., I, 174. King: op. cit., pp. 66–8.

[5] For the receipts, see ARD, 4: 17: 81–5.

[6] Wilson to the secretary of state, May 23, 1911, NA.

[7] So reckoned a member of Madero's official party, the historian Ricardo García Granados: op. cit., II, 181.

[8] For this conference, see Magaña: op. cit., I, 130–4.

To Madero's initial plea that he get along with the Figueroas, Zapata acceded. Then, plainly and frankly, he stated his own case. "What interests us," he said, speaking of himself and his followers, "is that, right away, lands be returned to the pueblos, and the promises which the revolution made be carried out."

Madero demurred: the land problem was a delicate and complicated issue, and proper procedures must be respected. What counted more, he said, was that Zapata prepare to disband his rebel troops.

Zapata, careful to affirm his confidence in Madero personally, questioned the federal army's loyalty to an unarmed revolutionary government, national or local. He cited Morelos, where, he said, Carreón was operating completely in favor of the planters. If that happened when the revolutionaries were armed, he asked, what would happen "when we turn ourselves over to the enemy's will?" Obviously Zapata had not caught the new spirit of conciliation. Madero reproved him: this was a new epoch; politics was to be an orderly business; violence would not do.

There then followed a remarkable exchange, when for a moment the vulgar suspense of the Morelos countryside must have charged the atmosphere of that comfortable metropolitan room. Zapata stood up and, carrying his carbine, walked over to where Madero sat. He pointed at the gold watch chain Madero sported on his vest. "Look, Señor Madero," he said, "if I take advantage of the fact that I'm armed and take away your watch and keep it, and after a while we meet, both of us armed the same, would you have a right to demand that I give it back?" Certainly, Madero told him; he would even ask for an indemnity. "Well," Zapata concluded, "that's exactly what has happened to us in Morelos, where a few planters have taken over by force the villages' lands. My soldiers—the armed farmers and all the people in the villages—demand that I tell you, with full respect, that they want the restitution of their lands to be got underway right now."

Madero repeated his promises on the subject. But the interview had disturbed him. Interrupting a busy schedule, he accepted Zapata's invitation to visit Morelos on June 12, the following Monday, to inspect conditions there for himself. Apparently Zapata had outflanked the planters. With Madero as a personal ally, he might beat them. At least it could still seem so.

IV

The Army Campaigns

"...sowing trust, if the word fits..."

INTENTIONAL OR NOT, Díaz's last official act had been a stroke of strategic genius. In resigning he gave Madero the battle but deprived him of the experience necessary to win the war. The strain of an incomplete victory soon pulled the revolutionary coalition apart.

In Morelos the planters nicely sensed this tension—which encouraged them not to despair at the alliance between Madero and Zapata. Efficient and astute as ever, they simply went to work on Madero. Antonio Barrios, the president of the Association of Sugar and Alcohol Producers and Escandón's campaign manager two years before, filed an urgent protest with Madero charging that the Morelos rebels would not voluntarily lay down their arms.[1] Tomás Ruiz de Velasco arranged for himself and a party of Morelos merchants to accompany Madero on his trip to Cuernavaca.[2] And once Madero arrived, Carreón organized a banquet for him in

[1] Association of Sugar and Alcohol Producers to Carreón, June 12, 1911, ARD, 4: 17: 144. Antonio Barrios was also the attorney for Ramón Corona, the proprietor of San Vicente and Chiconcuac haciendas. See Sánchez Escobar: op. cit., p. 167, and the Memorandum, ARD.

[2] *El Imparcial,* June 12, 1911.

the Borda Gardens so aggressively élite that Zapata, formally the state's leading Maderista, refused to attend.[3] So Zapata's invitation backfired. The next day Madero passed on to Iguala, and the day after to Chilpancingo, conferring at length with the Figueroas.[4]

By the time Madero returned to Morelos on June 15 to finish his tour, he was convinced that Zapata was incapable of controlling his reputedly barbaric troops. The ruined buildings in Cuautla, evidence of the terrible six-day battle fought there a month before, Madero saw as evidence of riots and pillaging Zapata had sanctioned.[5] He returned to Mexico City ready to believe the worst about the Morelos rebels.

Important political fissures developed from this personal estrangement. In Cuernavaca Zapata had again requested deliberate action on the agrarian dispute, and again Madero had put him off with promises. Also, both the planters and Zapata were unhappy with Carreón as interim governor, for opposite reasons; but Madero was obviously more sympathetic to the planters' candidates. On the critical question of the moment—the compulsory disarmament and discharge of his 2,500 revolutionary troops—Zapata lost more ground. All he got from Madero was another private promise of an appointment as commander of the Morelos federal police, into which he could incorporate 400 of his men; the rest he had to muster out, and take on an obligation to crush if they rebelled again.[6] The terms amounted to a surrender, possibly the beginning of the end of the revolution the Ayalans had launched three months before. For besides his connection with Madero, which hardly served him well now, Zapata retained no power except that derived from his influence among the state's villagers and rancheros—who themselves looked effective only in the primitive army they had formed during their revolt. To disband his army and to require him to police his own veterans was to dissolve his last political resource. Zapata shrank from the deal, but, isolated as he was, he could not deny Madero's call for trust, and he agreed to demobilize.

The operation began on June 13 at La Carolina, a factory on the northwestern outskirts of Cuernavaca.[7] The supervisor while Madero went south was Gabriel Robles Domínguez, Alfredo's brother, acting as a special

---

[3] Magaña: op. cit., I, 136. *El Imparcial,* June 13, 1911.

[4] Figueroa Uriza: op. cit., I, 201–7.

[5] *El Imparcial,* June 19, 1911.

[6] *El País,* June 14, 1911.

[7] Madero to E. Vázquez, June 13, 1911, cited in Charles C. Cumberland: *Mexican Revolution. Genesis Under Madero* (Austin, 1952), p. 173. Magaña: op. cit., I, 168–9.

commissioner from the Ministry of the Interior. He arranged for rebel soldiers to turn in their arms to state officials at one table; to pass on to a second where he himself, Zapata, and Zapata's chief of staff, Abrahám Martínez, identified them and gave them their discharge papers; and then to collect their discharge pay at a third table—ten pesos to each man from around Cuernavaca, fifteen pesos to a man from farther away, and a bonus of five for turning in a pistol as well as a rifle. State tax officials dispensed these funds, neither Robles Domínguez nor Zapata nor any of Zapata's subordinates having access to them. When the last rebel soldier left, officials had taken in some 3,500 arms and paid out 47,500 pesos. The operation seemed a success, which was persuasive evidence of Zapata's good faith in the bargain.

But as the planters continued to work on Madero, they stopped Zapata from taking even the limited position he had reluctantly settled for. From the first, for the sake of "the true revolution," they had opposed Madero's promise to make the rebel chief commander of the federal police in the state. To protest, Tomás Ruiz de Velasco had followed Madero to Iguala, and though he could not win a retraction there, he did not relax the pressure. Returning to Mexico City, he discovered that Zapata's appointment was not yet formal, that the Maderista minister of the interior, Emilio Vázquez, who was the responsible official, had not yet actually executed Madero's promise. Quickly he made the issue public. Rallying his fellow planters and their sympathizers in the metropolis, he announced a meeting of the "José María Morelos Republican Club" at ten a.m. on June 18.[8] That was a Sunday morning, which required those pious entrepreneurs to go to an early mass; but many came, and the meeting was reported in detail in the press. "This business of supplication ... is over," Ruiz de Velasco proclaimed to his excited audience. Another, elderly speaker declared that "if everyone evades his duties, we can only appeal to armed procedures. We old folk," he perorated, "will carry the arms so the young ones can shoot." A committee to demand an official explanation was formed. Representing the hacendados were Fernando Noriega, a former state deputy and Cuernavaca councilman, and Luis García Pimentel, the richest and the most cultured planter in the Republic. Representing the merchants and small farmers were Damaso Barajas, whose store in Cuautla had burned in the siege, and Emilio Mazari, a recent victim of Tepepa's forced loans in Jojutla. "The advice I give," Ruiz de Velasco concluded, "is that you hitch up your pants. Since

[8] *El Imparcial*, June 18, 1911.

Madero won't attend to anything, since nobody listens to us . . . the road we must follow is that of defiance."[9]

In Cuernavaca Zapata took the planters at their word. The next day, believing himself commander of the state's police, he requested five hundred rifles and ammunition from Governor Carreón, and when Carreón refused, he took them anyway.[1] A telegram from Gabriel Robles Domínguez informing him that "I fixed appointment for chief state police in the form in which we had agreed," and promising to confer with him the next day on this and "other affairs of great interest," seemed to confirm his authority at least provisionally.[2]

The planters had now maneuvered Zapata where they wanted him. The metropolitan *Imparcial*, hardly impartial but certainly still influential, ran the story of Zapata's encounter with Carreón as a yellow-press special, headlined "Zapata Is the Modern Attila." Among other barbarities the rebel chief was accused of causing all the señoritas in Cuernavaca to flee the city, along with the governor.[3] In fact the rebels had kept comparatively good order. Mrs. King, the plucky English lady who catered to Cuernavaca's most notable residents and guests in her Bella Vista Hotel, had no serious complaints.[4] Neither evidently did the various Americans in the city. In other districts recorded grievances were usually about a horse not returned or random abuses by local "last-minute revolutionaries."[5] But the climate was ripe for the planters' propaganda. The revolutionary seizures of land seemed to be outbursts of atavistic communism. Besides, the scattered physical atrocities committed in Morelos loomed especially vivid and ominous: they were perpetrated close to Mexico City, and by men who wore white pajamas and sandals to work, carried machetes, and presented swarthy complexions, in this last betraying themselves unmistakably as members of an "inferior race." This was the clincher. Revolutionary executions were

---

[9] Ibid., June 19, 1911.

[1] *El País*, June 20, 1911.

[2] G. Robles Domínguez to Zapata, June 19, 1911, ARD, 4: 17: 160.

[3] *El Imparcial*, June 20, 1911. Thus began the legend of Zapata as Savage, the badman who careered through the South raping, boozing, and ransacking for eight straight years. This tale reached a climax in H. H. Dunn's *The Crimson Jester, Zapata of Mexico* (New York, 1934).

[4] King: op. cit., pp. 62–70, 76.

[5] Complaints to Alfredo Robles Domínguez involved surprisingly few of Zapata's forces. See ARD, 2: 8 and 4: 17, which contain the correspondence concerning Morelos that summer. Compare them with 4: 16 (Michoacán), 4: 18 (Oaxaca), 4: 19 (Puebla), 4: 20 (Querétaro), 6: 27 (Guerrero and Oaxaca).

always distressing, but if the executioners were recognizably "white" and dressed like civilized beings in pants, boots, and shirts, their deeds remained human. That the "plebes" should execute victims was "Indian," subhuman, monstrous.

Immediately Madero called Zapata to Mexico City to answer the planters' charges that a new revolt had started in Morelos. On June 20 the interview took place in Madero's home. Afterward Madero assured reporters that the planters had exaggerated the trouble, but that he had settled it. Indeed he had: Zapata had promised to retire altogether, giving up his claim to the police command and agreeing to discharge all his men, none of whom would become police. The only force he saved was a personal escort of some fifty men. As for the local agrarian contest, Zapata accepted Madero's forecast that a freely elected and popular state government would resolve it "within the law."[6] As suddenly as they had appeared, the reports of anarchy and revolt in Morelos now disappeared.

So by early July the planters had removed the Ayala party from a contending role in state politics, driving its chiefs out of Cuernavaca and back to their villages. To the planters' dismay, however, this successful veto did not bring back the old order. Since the rebel army had disbanded and federal troops had not yet returned, it was difficult to keep any order at all. Bandits began operations in some areas, blackmailing villages and haciendas. On Madero's advice Carreón asked the minister of the interior for revolutionary troops from other states to serve temporarily in Morelos.[7] But Vázquez—his department in full financial and administrative confusion—ignored the governor's repeated requests.

The police problem was a trifle, however. What worried the planters most was the continued agrarian unrest throughout the state as the planting season began. They had imagined that breaking up the rebel army would dissipate the rebelliousness in the countryside, that to discharge a revolutionary villager was also to discharge his new sense of prowess. But clearly, demobilizing the rebels had not demoralized them. On the contrary, proud veterans now and still full of fight, their revolutionary consciousness ironically enhanced by the official discharge papers they carried, they went back home as missionaries of the new unruliness.[8] Around Cuautla villagers

---

[6] *El País,* June 21, 1911. *El Imparcial,* June 21, 1911. Magaña: op. cit., I, 164–5. The date is wrong in Magaña's account.

[7] Madero to de la Barra, August 15, 1911, cited in Figueroa Uriza: op. cit., I, 225.

[8] For a moving fictional account of this continuing agitation, see Gregorio López y Fuentes: *Tierra* (México, 1933), pp. 80–91.

still refused to surrender the fields they had reclaimed from the plantations.[9] Equally intransigent were the villagers of Cuauchichinola, who had occupied lands enclosed in San Gabriel and Cuauchichinola haciendas. The leaders there were so bold as to publish in the metropolitan press their attack on "tyrannical bosses who have made of Morelos one vast sugar factory." Noting that "our pueblo is one of the most ancient founded by the Mexica and later recognized by the viceroyal government," they asked Madero to honor "the just promises of the San Luis plan" and to protect "the revindication of our rights."[1] Also publicizing their insurgency were the villagers of Jiutepec, who had moved onto lands the Corona family had taken into its San Vicente and San Gaspar plantations. If the Coronas had ever bought the lands, the Jiutepec leaders declared in a public letter to the family attorney, Antonio Barrios, the sale "was a farce to seize the patrimony of the whole pueblo."[2]

Besides, in various towns and villages boomlets developed for Zapata for governor. Although Zapata evidently did not encourage them, many chiefs who had served with him organized clubs promoting his candidacy, "fooling the Indians with false promises," as one reporter lamented. A visitor in Mexico City from Tepalcingo described the commotion in his home town as a "lucha de castas"—a race war.[3] State elections were to take place in mid-August. If the rebel veterans, in spite of their demobilization and dispersal, could influence them, they would reestablish an agrarian party as a legitimate force in state politics.

Thus the planters remained in a bind. Predominant power only was not enough. They could restore the progress they wanted only through restoring their monopoly of political control. In the traditional compromise the villagers could accept, the planters saw the makings of their own financial and social ruin. The slightest breach might be fatal—the feeblest revolutionary success, the mere recognition of the villages' right to exist. This was the first serious crisis the current generation of Morelos planters had had to suffer, and their actions in the following weeks betray confusion and mounting alarm, if not panic. ". . . we are victims of abuses," Emmanuel

[9] Jiménez to de la Barra, August 18, 1911, AZ.

[1] El País, July 3, 1911. "Mexica" is the correct name for the Aztecs.

[2] Ibid., July 5, 1911.

[3] Diario del Hogar, July 24, 1911. El País, July 5, 10, 15, and 18, 1911. See also King: op. cit., pp. 69–70, 74, and Clemente G. Oñate: "Continúo mi aportación de datos para la verdad histórica del zapatismo y demás 'ismos' que cooperaron de la ruina del estado de Morelos," El Hombre Libre, September 15, 1937.

Amor wrote to Madero, half indignant, half bewildered at the Cuauchi-chinolans squatting on disputed fields. "I haven't believed, not for a single moment," he went on ruefully, "that you could consider the socialist pretensions of those persons."[4]

In politics the planters could not agree which course to take, only that Carreón was incompetent. For the Ruiz de Velascos, Ambrosio Figueroa was "the only man who merits the name of revolutionary."[5] Incredibly, a commission including Luis García Pimentel, Manuel Araoz, and Antonio Barrios journeyed to Cuautla and conferred with Zapata, offering to back him for governor and to cooperate with villagers who would take their claims to court. Zapata refused to consider the proposition. Barrios then approached Patricio Leyva, who thanked him but asked that if the planters did back him in the coming elections, they not do so publicly: it would hurt his campaign.[6] Rebuffed by their rivals, the planters looked again into their own camp and turned up an old toady—Ramon Oliveros, who had served them off and on in congress and the state legislature since 1902. The son of a manager of the Amors' San Gabriel hacienda, an ex-timber magnate, and now the manager of a bankrupt Cuernavaca hotel, he sympathized, so his planter friends asserted, "the same with the hacendado as with the peon and the merchant."[7] He had also promised the Amors to cancel the back taxes they owed the state if he became governor.[8] But Oliveros was a lame hope. Proposing him was an open confession of political paralysis.

Events in national politics deepened the planters' local quandary. On July 9 Madero dissolved the Anti-Reelectionist Party and announced the formation of a new Progressive Constitutional Party. His intent was to tighten his control over the revolutionary movement by reorganizing it—without his two most prominent lieutenants of 1910, the brothers Francisco and Emilio Vázquez Gómez, at the moment ministers of education and the interior. Francisco was still the Anti-Reelectionist candidate for vice president, but now Madero wanted a new running mate, a more dependent partner. The rupture was of signal importance in the movement, because Emilio and Francisco would not accept the dissolution of

[4] *El País,* July 7, 1911.

[5] *El Imparcial,* June 19, 1911.

[6] Memorandum, ARD.

[7] Representatives of the Merchants, Professionals, and Agriculturalists of Morelos to de la Barra (n.d., July 1911?), AZ, 12: 7: 1.

[8] On Oliveros, see *Semanario Oficial,* VIII, 32, 1; XV, 28, 1; XVII, 32, 1; Valentín López González: *El Ferrocarril de Cuernavaca* (Cuernavaca, 1957), p. 10; Memorandum, ARD.

the party they remained strong in. Accelerating independent ventures already under way, they worked to keep the old Anti-Reelectionist clubs intact and loyal to the Madero–Vázquez Gómez ticket. So in Morelos, as elsewhere, Maderistas fell to quarreling with each other. Should they follow Madero wherever he led, or should they hold him to his original contract? General Leyva, for instance, cooperated with the Progressive Constitutionalists. But to Antonio Sedano, again active politically, the new party and the attempt to impose a new vice-presidential candidate were "porquerías" —filthy insults—and he refused the general's appeal "not to pose difficulties for Madero." For the campaign Sedano alone distributed nearly two thousand Anti-Reelectionist posters through the state.[9] This dissension among the revolutionaries might please the planters when they considered it in the long run, but here and now they found it a pain: it further obscured which politicians they should deal with.

Even worse, Minister of the Interior Emilio Vázquez began agitating rebel veterans to reinforce his and his brother's position. He had never approved of Madero's conciliatory policy of discharge and had tried to foil it before. Spurned by Madero, he had much less reason to execute it faithfully now. He could not muster the rebels back into federal service, but he could quietly and informally arrange for government arms and ammunition to come into their possession. And so he did, especially in Morelos. Through early July, without organization or definite plans, rebel veterans rearmed there—this time with better weapons than before. The planters' situation, as they themselves complained to President de la Barra, had became "precarious."[1]

Then in mid-month another national imbroglio developed that undid completely the demobilization the planters had earlier brought about, and put the local contest for power back where it had been at the summer's beginning. On the night of July 12 a fracas between revolutionary troops quartered in Puebla City and the federal garrison there ended in a massacre of the revolutionaries.[2] The scandal mattered in Morelos not only because it took place so near but also because Abrahám Martínez, Zapata's chief

[9] Sedano: op. cit., pp. 21–2.

[1] Representatives of the Merchants, Professionals, and Agriculturalists of Morelos to de la Barra, AZ.

[2] For the events in Puebla, see Magaña: op. cit., I, 170–7, and Francisco Vázquez Gómez: *Memorias Políticas (1909–1913)* (México, 1933), pp. 314–34. See also Eduardo Reyes to Agustín del Pozo, July 15, 1911, AZ, 28: 15: 1, a very antifederal report on the massacre, which went also to Zapata.

of staff, had been in charge of the revolutionary troops as a special agent from the Ministry of the Interior. The dispute had started when Martínez arrested several persons in Puebla City, among them two state legislators and a federal deputy, on suspicion of plotting to kill Madero when he visited the city on July 13. Martínez was then himself arrested for disregarding their parliamentary immunity. And in the uproar over recovering the original prisoners, the federal commander finally had his troops storm the revolutionary quarters in the Puebla bull ring. More than fifty people were killed, many of them women and children.

At the news of Martínez's arrest, its reasons and results, Zapata sent word to allied chiefs around the state to reassemble their troops and muster at Cuautla to march to Puebla. The action was unauthorized, but the emergency seemed to warrant it. If Martínez had been arrested for breaking up a plot to kill Madero, and Madero was in Puebla, then maybe the plot would go on. Not knowing that in Puebla Madero had blamed the revolutionaries for the bloodshed and praised the "loyalty and courage" of the federals, nor that Francisco Vázquez Gómez had prepared "trustworthy" federals to defend the city, Zapata wired both Emilio Vázquez and Madero that he stood ready to march.[3] Orders immediately came back for him to stay where he was, which he did; and on his promise to hold Cuernavaca against a revolt, other orders recalled a federal force already dispatched there.[4] And the crisis passed. But in its wake there emerged in Morelos a remobilized and suspicious revolutionary army.

Disbanding this force the second time would not be so easy as the first. In one camp the planters recognized better now the danger of conditional agreements. In another, hopeful politicians had discovered the value of maintaining a controversial simmer in the state. And in a third camp, having learned their lessons from the previous demobilization, rebel chiefs had started to reconsider their loyalties. And as their leader, Zapata had to represent their objections. On July 22 he signed a bold and well-publicized protest which the Vázquez Gómez brothers had encouraged a group of discontented revolutionary officers to initiate against the de la Barra regime.[5]

[3] Vázquez Gómez: op. cit., pp. 335–8. F. Vázquez Gómez to E. Vázquez, n.d. (July 13, 1911?), AZ, 27: 11.

[4] Zapata to Sánchez Azcona, July 13, 1911, AM. Madero to F. Vázquez Gómez, July 13, 1911, Archivo de Genaro Amezcua (henceforth AA). Carreón to G. Robles Domínguez, July 14, 1911, ARD, 2: 8: 53.

[5] For a copy of the protest, see González Ramírez: *Planes,* pp. 52–3. Zapata had not joined in an earlier protest made on July 11, before the Puebla massacre. See ibid., p. 54.

For Zapata, the burden of proof of trustworthiness had now shifted to the government. In practice, he would not become militant, since he still depended on Madero; nor would he cheat about discharging the men he had just called up. He simply would not disband them as credulously and unconditionally as before.

Caught in the middle were Madero and the "White President," as de la Barra liked to be described. Campaigning for the presidency, Madero could not let a rebel chief ruin his efforts at conciliation, but neither could he let the government direct humiliating ultimatums to one of the most prominent sections of his movement. As for de la Barra, having become the vice-presidential candidate of the recently founded National Catholic Party, he could advance his partisan interest only through an immaculately nonpartisan pretense, but after all he had not ordered Zapata to mobilize his men, who remained illegally in arms, like bandits. And he longed to restore official controls.

Until early August, a few days before the state elections, the impossible balance lasted. Then, on August 2, Emilio Vázquez resigned as minister of the interior. The next day Alberto García Granados, promoted from the governorship of the Federal District, replaced him. The change was crucial. Though to Madero the new minister seemed "a most estimable person, whom . . . I recommend . . . in every sense," García Granados was in fact a conceited and ambitious schemer intent on sabotaging the policy of conciliation.[6] Toward Madero he entertained a fine contempt. A seasoned strategist of the old anti-Díaz opposition, he had come to power through the revolution; but as the owner of a sizable plantation in a turbulent district in Puebla, he despised the rebels who had done the fighting.[7] Already he had publicly committed himself to the immediate and unconditional discharge of revolutionary troops, and to the use of the federal army, if necessary, to accomplish it. Regarding Morelos, he was especially eager to exterminate what he considered Zapata's outrageous and pernicious in-

[6] Madero to A. Figueroa, August 9, 1911, AA.

[7] His hacienda, Chagua, was in the lush Huejotzingo district. Though all the names are garbled, the property is listed in John R. Southworth: *The Official Directory of Mines and Estates of Mexico* (México, 1910), p. 224. García Granados was quite concerned with his property during these months. See comments on his involvement in local politics by Archbishop of Oaxaca E. G. Gillow to Minister of the Interior Aureliano Urrutia, July 11, 1913, cited in I. C. Enríquez: *The Religious Question in Mexico* (New York, 1915), pp. 12–13. For postrevolutionary violence in the area, see del Pozo to A. Robles Domínguez, June 5, 1911, ARD, 4: 19: 102.

fluence on the state's economy. "The government does not deal with bandits," was his policy. Unless Zapata submitted to the Ministry of the Interior's order to discharge his forces at once, they would be attacked as outlaws by the federal army.

Resting at the Tehuacán spa in southeastern Puebla, Madero still dreamed of a compromise. Several times he invited Zapata there to confer with him. But Zapata kept begging off. He avowed he feared an assassination attempt if several revolutionary leaders congregated and formed an easy, compact target.[8] The showdown with the government, coming so soon after the Puebla massacre, obviously disturbed him. He reaffirmed his subordination and loyalty to Madero in a public letter.[9] But he would not renounce his duty toward the pueblos to satisfy metropolitan politicians' ideas about order—a stand unreasonable in Mexico City but natural in Morelos. Yet whether he obeyed or defied the new minister's instructions, he seemed to invite the ruin of his cause. Finally he relented, sending his brother, Eufemio, and the chief who was then his first lieutenant, Jesús Morales, to discuss terms with Madero. There was even talk of Zapata coming to Mexico City for negotiations. It appeared then, briefly, that despite official clamors an agreement might somehow be arranged: the questionably mobilized troops would be mustered out, there would be peace in Morelos, and elections would take place the next Sunday, August 13.

Zapata himself evidently intended to retire. During these days, close to his thirty-second birthday, he married a young woman he had been courting since before the revolution. She was Josefa Espejo, one of several daughters a modestly prosperous Ayala livestock dealer had left modestly dowered when he died in early 1909.[1] In rural Mexico marriage was not simply for siring offspring, or for love. Zapata already had at least one child (by another woman) and no doubt assumed—it was a common male assumption—he would have many more by many women he cared about. Marriage was a more solemn proceeding: a contract, a *contrato de matrimonio*, as people called it, entry into which gave a man a place in his com-

[8] Zapata to Madero, July 28, 1911, AM.

[9] *El País*, August 6, 1911.

[1] Serafín M. Robles: "El Caudillo se Casa en la Villa de Ayala, Morelos," *El Campesino*, November 1954. The Ayalan municipal president had performed the civil ceremony earlier, on June 26. See Luis Gutiérrez y Gutiérrez: "*Hoy* visita a la viuda de Zapata," *Hoy*, March 28, 1953.

munity. Marriage was for the grave business of establishing a legitimate family, for creating recognized heirs and securing incontestably one more generation in the clan's name—which was what a man did to institute a private life among his neighbors. On several occasions during the summer Zapata had voiced his "decision" to get out of politics, revealing how he longed for his old country life of horses, market days, cock fights, farm seasons, village elections, local fairs. And his marriage seems an almost deliberate retreat into the local community, a kind of rededication to the community. Had events worked out as Zapata apparently then believed they would, his career would probably have returned to the arena of Ayala muncipality, where, like José Zapata before him, he would have lived out a locally honored life, died a locally grieved death, and been forgotten a generation later.

But what ensued was far from this dream of rest. Neither the planters nor the leading Leyvistas nor the Figueroas nor the conservative politicians rallying in Mexico City had reason to let it come true. And awkwardly but effectively they moved to eliminate the troublesome agrarian party in the state, once and for all. De la Barra, now more confident of his power, took the lead. On August 7, to forestall the chance of a conditional surrender which he could not publicly refuse, he recommended to Governor Carreón that Zapata not come to Mexico City for talks.[2] On August 8 the War Department ordered federal troops to Cuernavaca and Jonacatepec and Ambrosio Figueroa's federal police to Jojutla, surrounding Zapata.[3] The next day de la Barra denied rumors that these forces were to put down a revolt: they were only to provide security, he said, when Zapata's veterans had mustered out again. The White President told a white lie, for the orders he had given the federal commanders were "to suffocate any uprising which might start from the opposition Zapata's men show to their discharge."[4] The same day, almost as a personal insult to Zapata, de la Barra appointed Ambrosio Figueroa governor and military commander in Morelos.[5] To all these measures Madero lent his full support, advising

[2] De la Barra to Carreón, August 7, 1911, AZ, 16: 2: 14. See also the account de la Barra himself later gave of his decision, related in Dearing to the secretary of state, August 26, 1911, NA, 59: 812.00/ 2318.

[3] Report by Victoriano Huerta to the secretary of war and navy on the campaign in the state of Morelos, October 31, 1911, AZ, 27: 8.

[4] *El País,* August 10 and 11, 1911.

[5] García Granados to A. Figueroa, August 9, 1911, cited in Figueroa Uriza: op. cit., I, 229–30.

Figueroa that he should "follow [García Granados's] directions as if they were mine," and asking him to "put Zapata in his place for us, since we can no longer stand him."[6]

Zapata was still at the wedding celebration with his wife and neighbors and chiefs when he received the news on August 9 that more than a thousand troops under the tough and talented Brigadier General Victoriano Huerta had entered Morelos.[7] His renewed commitment to local life—getting married, in Villa de Ayala, almost on his birthday—served now only to drive him back into politics, in defense of that local life. Immediately he wired protests to García Granados and to Madero. To the latter he reaffirmed his esteem and loyalty, asking bluntly, "Do you have any complaints against me?" If Madero could not arrange a halt, he said, he would expect "a frank and sincere statement" from him.[8] He got neither a halt nor a statement. The next day Governor Carreón called off the state elections, due three days later; the reason he gave was "disturbances," which Huerta's arrival had just caused.[9] That afternoon Huerta quartered his 32nd Infantry Battalion in Cuernavaca.

A regular military campaign had begun, to end three weeks later with Madero gravely embarrassed and repentant and Zapata nearly killed. In their political innocence both men believed to the last that they could stall, compromise, or suspend the threat. Neither saw that de la Barra and García Granados would use the strictly limited task of compelling and supervising demobilization as a grand opportunity to invade and occupy the state. This invasion and occupation were not informal extensions of power, but literal military acts. As Huerta reported to the War Department: "The Morelos campaign . . . is what technically is called a campaign of occupation."[1] In the short run the operation was a tremendous conservative success, for it separated the local agrarians from the national revolutionaries precisely when union was what they both needed most.

But after the campaign ended, the parties rival to the agrarians in the state—the planters and the leading Leyvistas—found that they had suffered losses too, not so grievous but still disconcerting. Their trouble was Huerta. At first they welcomed him as "the force to meet force" they had long

[6] Madero to A. Figueroa, August 9, 1911, AA.
[7] Report on G. Robles Domínguez's tour of inspection, August 1911, ARD, 7: 37: 22.
[8] Zapata to Madero, August 9, 1911, AM.
[9] Decree by Carreón, August 10, 1911, AZ, 6: V-2: 52.
[1] Huerta's Report, AZ.

begged for. As Antonio Sedano remarked in a note of thanks to de la Barra, Zapata's men in Cuernavaca had been "a constant menace to the interests of cultivated Society," and Huerta would restore discipline.[2] One of the best combat officers in the Porfirian army, Huerta had special experience in the south, having earned his promotion to brigadier general by crushing revolts in Guerrero in the 1890's, and having observed the rebel action of the past spring in Guerrero and Morelos.[3] But the man was devious and inexhaustibly vicious, and he still ached for the blue sash of a divisional general. Moreover he had a political as well as a professional and personal concern in the Morelos campaign. His hero, General Bernardo Reyes, had just decided to become a presidential candidate in the October election; and accompanying Huerta in Morelos as his private secretary was one of Reyes's most active agents.[4] So any order Huerta imposed in the state would serve purposes not necessarily the planters' or the Leyvistas'. The Figueroas, who knew Huerta from his earlier action in Guerrero, saw the danger from the beginning, and Francisco would not let Ambrosio take up the appointment as governor in Morelos. The consequences of collaborating with Huerta, Francisco warned Madero, might well be "fatal."[5] In time Huerta's champions would also see the evils they had released for themselves in releasing him, that in the long run, instead of crushing the local rebels, he had only propelled them into a new revolution more radical and more determined than before.

Huerta had barely set up his headquarters in Cuernavaca when he began returning very nonsoldierly assessments. "The political situation of the state," he wrote to de la Barra on August 11, "is bad, bad, very bad. . . . I am in accord with the governor of the state, but I respectfully permit myself to declare to you, without failing in respect for the deserving governor, that he is *un hombre de agua tibia*"—a lukewarm-water man.[6]

Huerta and de la Barra had to tolerate this lukewarm governor as long as Ambrosio Figueroa would not accept his appointment. But they quickly deprived him of power to obstruct them by blunders. On August 11, on

[2] A. and E. Sedano to de la Barra, August 12, 1911, AZ, 6: V-2: 40. Two other leading Cuernavaca Leyvistas also thanked de la Barra for sending the federals: see de la Barra to Castañeda and Patiño, August 19, 1911, AZ, 12: 3: Copybook 7.

[3] Vicente Fuentes Díaz: *La revolución de 1910 en el estado de Guerrero* (México, 1960), pp. 31–3, 37–47. Rausch: op. cit., pp. 140–4.

[4] This was Flavio Maldonado: *El País,* August 23, 1911.

[5] F. Figueroa to Madero, August 13, 1911, AA.

[6] Huerta to de la Barra, August 11, 1911, AZ, 12: 1: 17.

orders de la Barra gave him at his prompting, Huerta took over the state's arms and ammunition, which Carreón had controlled but could not, according to Huerta, "keep with due security."[7] The next day de la Barra suspended the state's sovereignty. The pretext was that rebels north of Cuernavaca had ambushed part of Huerta's column when he marched through their neighborhood. Such affrays were common that summer around the whole country. Besides, Zapata had nothing to do with the incident. It was the work of Genovevo de la O's independent veterans, and Zapata did not learn of the action until after it happened.[8] But however limp, the pretext still served. To Carreón's question about the state's autonomy, de la Barra replied that Huerta's instructions were "to continue operations of war to which" he had been "provoked by the attack which the federal forces were victims of . . . said operations will be continued with the energy and speed which circumstances demand unless Zapata's forces surrender unconditionally . . . and disarm . . ."[9]

The obstacle of civil law having been removed, Huerta could pass on freely to occupy and pacify the hostile territory. "To assure the tranquillity of the state's six districts," Huerta calculated he would need 600 cavalry troops—100 garrisoned in each district seat—plus an independent column of 1,500 men. He could then, he wrote to de la Barra, "proceed with the annihilation of the rebels." With fewer men, he warned, he could not "guarantee peace." Morelos would suffer the fate of Chihuahua, wrote this federal general to his conservative president three months after the revolution had supposedly triumphed, "where our troops always came out victorious in battle but never achieved anything practical."[1] Greedily he looked forward to "putting an end to these elements which cause the state so much harm."

He could not proceed immediately, however, because Madero had returned to Zapata's defense. Having received yet another reaffirmation of loyalty from the Morelos chief, as well as an appeal to have the federals withdrawn, and having also received Francisco Figueroa's refusal to cooperate, Madero had decided he would negotiate the conflict.[2] This sur-

[7] Huerta to de la Barra, and de la Barra's noted reply, August 11, 1911, AZ, 16: 1: 25.

[8] De la O in *Impacto,* December 31, 1949. Report, ARD.

[9] Huerta to de la Barra, and reply, August 12, 1911, AZ, 16: 1: 34.

[1] Huerta to de la Barra, August 11, 1911, AZ.

[2] Zapata to Madero, August 12, 1911, AM. F. Figueroa to Madero, August 13, 1911, AA. For a sympathetic account of Madero's efforts, see Ross: op. cit., pp. 188–202.

prised and embarrassed de la Barra. Although he did not formally authorize Madero to negotiate, he was so anxious to protect his image as the immaculate umpire that he acquiesced in private peacemaking.[3] On August 13 Madero arrived in Cuernavaca and the next day on the telephone began talks with Zapata in Cuautla. Their agreement, as Madero wired it to de la Barra that evening, was not so promising as Madero believed. Zapata had learned about the Reyista agents in Huerta's column and had therefore posed unusually stiff conditions.[4] He again declared himself ready to retire and to demobilize his army, but he wanted to keep a select force "to take custody of the state's public security while a legislature is elected, which, in accord with the executive, and under the law, will settle or solve the matter which occupies us—the agrarian matter . . ." He also wanted the federal troops recalled in respect for the state's sovereignty, a new governor who would guarantee revolutionary policies on land, and the removal of unpopular local authorities left over from the old regime.[5] De la Barra could not even consider these proposals. Bombarded with scare stories by Huerta, Carreón, and the Ruiz de Velascos, and now facing international problems as well because of rebel raids on an American ranch north of Cuernavaca, he insisted to Madero on the need to "save the principle of authority."[6] The only real issue, he insisted impatiently, was who would be governor. Figueroa was still reluctant. Why not Ramón Oliveros? he wanted to know—although Zapata had exclusively vetoed him in the previous day's conference.[7] In fact de la Barra hated negotiating with Zapata. "It is truly objectionable," he complained to Madero, "that an in-

[3] See de la Barra's public statement of his position, cited in Magaña: op. cit., II, 40–1.

[4] *El País,* August 6, 1911. Advising Zapata now was Alfredo Quesnel, an out-of-state revolutionary with anarcho-syndicalist connections. Quesnel had clashed with federal commanders in Tlaxcala the previous July. Ibid., July 6, 1911.

[5] Magaña: op. cit., I, 205–11, 215–16. Madero to de la Barra, August 14, 1911, AZ (two messages), 17: 8: 8 and 10. *El País,* August, 16, 1911.

[6] De la Barra to Madero, August 15, 1911, AZ, 17: 8: 11. For the scare stories, see Huerta to de la Barra, August 14, 1911, AZ, 12: 1: 18, and August 15, 1911, AZ, 14: 3: 4; Jojutla residents to de la Barra, August 15, 1911, ibid., 27; Carreón to de la Barra, August 15, 1911, ibid., 10; F. Ruiz de Velasco to de la Barra, August 15, 1911, ibid., 19. For the American trouble, see Dearing to Mrs. H. L. Hall, August 14 and 15, 1911, NA, 84: Mexico, C8, 15. The military attaché of the U.S. Embassy, Captain Girard Sturtevant, accompanied Huerta at least as far as Yautepec. *El País,* August 17, 1911.

[7] De la Barra to Madero, August 15, 1911, AZ, 17: 18: 17.

dividual of his antecedents, whose actions make us fear new outrages, be allowed to maintain [that] attitude you are familiar with."[8] Dickering with Madero, he prepared to let Huerta loose.

On August 15 the head of the War Department, General José González Salas, wired Huerta in code that other federal forces were already advancing from Puebla to Jonacatepec and that he should tell Madero that if Zapata did not agree to disarm that very day, operations would commence from Cuernavaca toward Yautepec.[9] Late that afternoon Huerta impatiently wired de la Barra. If Madero had resolved nothing favorable by the next morning, he asked de la Barra—also in code—to send him five hundred shells for his 75mm. cannon.[1] He planned a "general movement" on Yautepec as soon as he received the munitions.[2] Immediately de la Barra replied, pledging him the proper War Department instructions if Madero gained no "sure promise of immediate and effective disarmament."[3] At nine o'clock the next morning Madero confidently left Cuernavaca. Having just heard from Huerta that no action was under way toward Yautepec, and imagining that "General Huerta thinks as I in everything," he was off for Mexico City to arrange de la Barra's approval of his deal with Zapata.[4] At ten o'clock the vanguard of Huerta's column commenced its operations on the Yautepec road.[5]

But from Mexico City de la Barra reined his forces in again. As a care-taker president, he could not tell Madero to his face that he would not accept Zapata's offer to discharge. Already Maderista politicians were making public charges that the White President had now taken a partisan line favoring Reyes. In a "very urgent" wire de la Barra asked Huerta to stop the advance until after an executive conference with Madero.[6] In reply Huerta played ridiculously helpless. His troops, he said, "after cheer-ing the government of the Republic," had just left to take up battle posi-tions.[7] De la Barra repeated his order to Huerta, with slight ambiguity,

---

[8] De la Barra to Madero, August 15, 1911, AZ, 17: 8: 12.

[9] Huerta's Report, AZ.

[1] Huerta to de la Barra, August 15, 1911, AZ, 16: 1: 24.

[2] Huerta to de la Barra, August 15, 1911, AZ, 17: 11: 7.

[3] De la Barra to Huerta, August 15, 1911, AZ, 14: 3: 20.

[4] Madero to de la Barra, August 15, 1911, AZ, 17: 8: 13. Madero to Huerta, October 31, 1911, cited in Magaña: op. cit., II, 44–6.

[5] Huerta to de la Barra, August 16, 1911, AZ, 14: 3: 28. The wire was in code.

[6] De la Barra to Huerta, August 16, 1911, ibid., 54.

[7] Huerta to de la Barra, August 16, 1911, AZ, 17: 11: 10.

to suspend "every military operation which can be considered as offensive."[8]

The ambiguity was a hint. And Huerta resorted to jargon to grasp the opportunity. His troops' movements toward Yautepec were no longer an "operation" but a "maneuver."[9] He explained their import carefully to the civilian de la Barra. They were to press Zapata "to surrender unconditionally to the just requests of the Supreme Government." The "aggressive stand" of his troops was, he pointed out, "the most eloquent reason for Zapata to submit unconditionally . . ." The lecture went on: ". . . without a demonstration of the incontestable power of the government, its negotiations will give no result; this is why I have mobilized my troops." If Madero's peace talks succeeded "in good time"—which he was doing all he could to prevent—then he would return. If they failed, as he said he believed they would, then he could impose on Zapata the "supreme reason of the government."

De la Barra "cordially praised" Huerta's stand.[1] But however gratifying personally, it remained for the moment an untenable political posture. As Madero prepared to return to Cuautla on August 17, hopefully to conclude the deal with Zapata, the cabinet agreed to suspend "offensive military operations" for forty-eight hours.[2] The War Department ordered Huerta to act accordingly.[3]

Reluctantly Huerta halted his advance, although he sent troops out to burn ranches and he kept sappers preparing the Yautepec road for the artillery carriages. He wired de la Barra asking for a confirmation of the War Department's orders, and begging the President's pardon for the "coarseness" of his "character" in doing so.[4] In a coded reply de la Barra promised that if the Cuautla news was not good by that night—although he had promised Madero forty-eight hours to work in—he would have him "pursue the operations initiated."[5]

Already the movement toward Yautepec had provoked numerous local protests. Only the Cuernavaca Leyvistas had thanked de la Barra for sending Huerta into the state in the first place. And now from Tepoztlán, Tlayacapan, Telixtac, Jalostoc, San Andrés de la Cal, Jantetelco, Yecapixtla,

[8] De la Barra to Huerta, August 16, 1911, ibid., 12.
[9] Huerta to de la Barra, August 16, 1911, ibid., 13.
[1] De la Barra to Huerta, August 16, 1911, ibid., 14.
[2] De la Barra to Huerta, August 17, 1911, AZ, 14: 4: 28.
[3] González Salas to Huerta, August 16, 1911, AZ, 14: 3: 26.
[4] Huerta to de la Barra, August 17, 1911, AZ, 14: 4: 29.
[5] De la Barra to Huerta, August 17, 1911, ibid., 28.

Zacualpan de Amilpas, Villa de Ayala, Yautepec, Cuautla, Atotonilco, Huitzililla, Huazulco, Amilcingo—spokesmen from all these little villages and country towns wired de la Barra that the aggressive federal troops constituted a threat to the sovereignty and welfare of Morelos and should be withdrawn.[6] So also did the "employees, artisans, and mechanics" of the Interoceanic Railway in Morelos and the Cuautla Red Cross chapter.[7] These were folk who had staked all their hopes for local reform on the state elections, and now saw the army called in to prevent them. From Cuautla Zapata sent a blistering note to de la Barra. "The people want their rights respected," he declared. "They want to be paid attention to and listened to. Just because they make a protest, nobody can try to shut them up with bayonets."[8]

More important for de la Barra than these popular outcries was an editorial in the leading Maderista newspaper in Mexico City, in support of negotiations and in veiled reproach of the White President's prejudice against the Morelos rebels.[9] So though Madero did not arrive in Cuautla that night, the President kept Huerta where he was. All the next day, August 18, the general had to wait too. He passed the time in taking up "a suitable position"—at Tejalpa, midway to Yautepec.[1]

Under such pressure Madero and Zapata seemed to feel more sympathetic than before. Although Zapata complained to his chief that "if the revolution had not been on half shares and had followed its course to realizing the establishment of its principles, we would not see ourselves involved in this conflict," he nevertheless reaffirmed again his faith in Madero's sincerity and capacity to resolve the trouble. And Madero in turn, now fear-

[6] Residents of Tepoztlán to de la Barra, August 17, 1911, AZ, 14: 4: 1. All the following come from the same box and file, and bear the same date. For convenience only the sender and the number of the document are listed. Anti-Reelectionist Democratic Club of Tlayacapan, 2. Residents of Huazulco and Amilcingo, 3. Hidalgo Club and people of Atotonilco, 4. Residents of San Andrés de la Cal, 64. Residents of Jantetelco, 65. Residents of Yecapixtla, 66. Residents of Zacualpan de Amilpas, 67. Pablo Torres Burgos Political Club representing the Ayalan people, 68. Branches of the Liberal Democratic Club of Yautepec, 69. Municipal president of Cuautla, 72. Businessmen of Cuautla, 76. People of Cuautla, 77. Delegates of various villages, 78. Democratic Principles Club of Jalostoc, 79. All were marked "don't answer" by de la Barra.

[7] Ibid., 70 and 71. These also were marked "don't answer."

[8] Zapata to de la Barra, August 17, 1911, cited in Magaña: op. cit., I, 217–18.

[9] *Nueva Era,* August 17, 1911.

[1] Huerta's Report, AZ. Huerta to de la Barra, August 18, 1911, AZ, 14: 4: 63.

ful also of a Reyista revival, assured Zapata that he understood "the feelings which inspire you."[2] Madero did not go on into Cuautla on the evening of the 17th, because of the excitement the federal advance on Yautepec had caused there.[3] But the encounter between him and Zapata was warm when he arrived the next morning. At the Cuautla train station Madero gave Zapata the embrace he had given the federal commander at Puebla, and called Zapata his "integérrimo general"—his truest general. Speaking later to crowds in the Cuautla gardens, he pointedly praised the local movement and upheld its "valiant General Zapata" against the "slanders of our enemies." Calling for a new revolutionary union against Reyista intrigues, he said he knew that although the local rebels were discharged, they would always be ready to answer "our first call" and "take up arms to defend our liberties."

The talks that afternoon were genial, too, and their conclusions happy. Not only Zapata and his closest allied chiefs took part, but also, on his invitation, civilian delegates from the surrounding villages. Their agreement, which Madero promptly wired to de la Barra, was more generous and came easier than before. For governor, Zapata and the village delegates preferred Miguel Salinas, the current state director of public education, because he was a native son. But they also approved of Madero's nominee, Eduardo Hay, a loyal revolutionary veteran and Madero's former chief of staff, and they would accept him. For state police commander they would accept Madero's brother Raúl, who would bring in 250 federalized revolutionary troops from the state of Hidalgo. Demobilization they would begin again at an assembly of rebels the next morning, within the cabinet's forty-eight-hour deadline. They made no issue of "the agrarian matter." On their behalf, Madero requested only that de la Barra "get . . . the federal forces regrouped in Cuernavaca and returned to the capital as soon as possible." He planned to stay in Cuautla, he said, until the federals were back in Mexico City "because otherwise it is very difficult to conquer the distrust which people have for them and which is newly justified by the stand assumed by General Huerta . . ."

The next morning in Cuautla, August 19, the agreement started to take effect. Zapata's various chiefs, having assembled from around the state, proceeded finally to discharge what was left of their forces. When the federals did not begin to retire, as de la Barra had not promised they

[2] Zapata to Madero, and Madero to Zapata, August 17, 1911, AA.
[3] Madero to de la Barra, August 17, 1911, AZ, 17: 8: 18. *El País,* August 18, 1911.

would, Madero complained. But at least as long as they stayed in their camp, the discharge would go on.[4]

In those hours all seemed finally to be going well for the villagers. Not so much the terms of the compromise but the fact itself of compromise was monumentally significant. For it augured the government's willingness to tolerate local participation in state politics, which would secure legal recourse against rural injustices. In a few days, it seemed, Morelos would be at peace—with maybe a state agrarian commission, a sympathetic state police, and an interim governor styling himself so fair as to turn over the office even to Zapata if the people elected him.

It was not to be. That very day, while the discharge was calmly in process, de la Barra decided "the decorum of the government" was in jeopardy.[5] Apparently Madero's insinuation that the Morelos campaign was a Reyista plot had shaken the President. Certainly it had aroused rumors that Madero and Zapata had agreed to fake demobilization, so that Zapata could support Madero militarily if Reyes and his adherents in the federal army revolted during the coming presidential election.[6] There was no evidence of a secret deal. But in the immediate context, suspicion counted as proof, at least as pretext. Besides, the cabinet's deadline of forty-eight hours was up, and de la Barra was still receiving "alarming messages" from Carreón and Felipe Ruiz de Velasco about bandit outrages.[7] These "grave disturbances" had not taken place in Zapata's zone around Cuautla but around Tetecala and Jojutla, where Zapata had never had much authority; but for de la Barra's purposes they were still Zapata's responsibility. It was now necessary, he proclaimed, "to proceed to reestablish order—let it cost what it costs." Ambrosio Figueroa he ordered to occupy towns through the state's south and west; federal forces in Puebla he

[4] For these negotiations and communications, see Magaña: op. cit., I, 219–24.

[5] De la Barra to Madero, August 19, 1911, AZ, 17: 8: 28.

[6] *El País,* August 21, 1911. These rumors are recorded as an actual conversation in Antonio D. Melgarejo: *Los crímenes del zapatismo (apuntes de un guerrillero)* (México, 1913), pp. 125–7.

[7] Carreón to de la Barra, August 18, 1911, AZ, 14: 4: 46. F. Ruiz de Velasco to de la Barra, August 19, 1911, ibid., 88. For the doubtful accuracy of these reports, see Madero to de la Barra, August 19, 1911, AZ, 17: 8: 22 and 29. See also Huerta's interesting letter to de la Barra, August 28, 1911, AZ, 12: 1: 20, where he writes: ". . . although I have no complete intelligence service, I have become convinced in the few days I've been in the state of the exaggerated character of all the reports about disturbances of order. That is to say, every time some group of bandits moves in such and such direction, the rumor runs that they are hundreds or even thousands."

directed to move to Jonacatepec, and Huerta he instructed "to impose order in accord with the instructions previously given . . ." These were the original instructions of August 12 and 15 for "operations of war." On specific orders from the War Department Huerta broke camp at Tejalpa and advanced against Yautepec.[8] As his troops approached the town, the municipal president came out under a white flag—and was fired upon. Huerta had taken the President at his word. "It can't be said that a column like that marches in peace," Madero noted with innocent precision; "it is at war." By evening the wide federal column was encamped in the hills at the edge of the town, and the discharge in Cuautla had been suspended.[9]

Madero was at a loss—then and later—to explain this brazen subversion of his efforts. Confused and distraught, he sent Gabriel Robles Domínguez to Yautepec, and after appealing to de la Barra to restrain Huerta, he went there himself the next afternoon, Sunday, August 20.[1] His personal presence in the town, as well as a huge Maderista student demonstration that day in Mexico City, swayed de la Barra again. Husbanding the reputation for impartiality which was his best political asset, the President called a cabinet meeting and arranged a new forty-eight-hour truce. All federal forces were to suspend their advances while Zapata's troops reconcentrated in Cuautla. And there revolutionary police from Hidalgo and Veracruz, not the federal army, would supervise the demobilization and then form the garrison.[2] Outside Yautepec Huerta had already agreed to hold off occupying the town for forty-eight hours; as he wired the War Department, he would need that long to prepare the road for his artillery carriages.[3]

It again appeared that the concessions Madero had carefully secured from both sides would prevent open conflict. Zapata came personally to Yautepec and discussed the new terms with Madero. They amounted to practically the same deal he had agreed to before, and he accepted them. Ordering the immediate evacuation of Yautepec, he then returned to Villa de Ayala to arrange the final discharge, which began the next day in Cuautla after Madero arrived to review the troops. As Madero later admitted, the operation was not faultless, but at least he and Zapata had persuaded the

[8] Huerta's Report, AZ. De la Barra to Madero, August 19, 1911, AZ, 17: 8: 28.
[9] Madero to de la Barra, August 19 and 20, 1911, cited in Magaña: op. cit., I, 225-7.
[1] Madero to de la Barra, August 20, 1911, AZ, 16: 1: 3.
[2] De la Barra to Madero, two letters both dated August 20, 1911, cited in Magaña: op. cit., I, 238-9.
[3] Huerta's Report, AZ. The wire was in code.

leading chiefs of the state to lay down their arms and agree to keep the peace. In gratitude to the Morelos rebels he wrote out vouchers of loyalty for Zapata and twenty-two of his officers, in effect promising them posts in his government.[4] Equally trusting, many local families who had fled the town in fear of a battle now drifted back in.[5]

But as the forty-eight hours passed, the new hopes for peace dwindled. De la Barra kept postponing the appointment of Eduardo Hay as governor. On the evening of the first day of discharge he reinforced the Cuernavaca garrison with 330 federals with machine guns.[6] And when Huerta's troops started occupying Yautepec the same evening, Zapata's chiefs almost rebelled against him.[7]

August 22 was the crucial day. It was increasingly difficult now to persuade the rebels to turn in their arms; they had heard reports that Minister of the Interior García Granados had threatened to prosecute them anyway, and they did not believe the federal troops would not attack them once they had disarmed.[8] And in Mexico City, swamped with more wildly exaggerated "alarming messages" from Carreón and more bombastic political analyses from General Huerta, de la Barra decided to stop trifling with demobilization.[9] The second deadline was up, and the revolutionaries in Morelos were still in arms. There would be no more truces. Huerta sniffed this change in the breeze and leaped to the offensive. The "remedy" he proposed to de la Barra, "with the greatest respect and my best good faith," was "to reduce Zapata to the last extremity, even hang him or throw him out of the country."[1]

On August 23 troop movements began again. The most ominous was Huerta's through Yautepec and toward Cuautla. It was evidently unauthorized and clearly unnecessary, federalized revolutionaries from Veracruz

[4] For these dealings and communications, see Magaña: op. cit., I, 240–5, 249–53.

[5] *El País,* August 22, 1911.

[6] Carreón to de la Barra, and de la Barra's noted reply, August, 21, 1911, AZ, 18: 7: 20.

[7] Madero to de la Barra, August 21, 1911, AZ, 17: 8: 41.

[8] *El País,* August 23, 1911.

[9] Carreón to de la Barra, August 20, 1911, AZ, 16: 1: 28. (Here Carreón complained that Eufemio was about to attack Cuernavaca. Madero replied that he was in fact "sumiso y obediente" in Cuautla. See Madero to de la Barra, August 21, 1911, AZ, 17: 8: 40.) For other complaints, see Carreón to de la Barra, August 21, 1911, AZ, 18: 7: 1, 5, 6, 13, 14, and 20; also Huerta to de la Barra, August 21, 1911, AZ, 17: 11: 16 and 18.

[1] Huerta to de la Barra, August 22, 1911, AZ, 17: 11: 18.

having already garrisoned Cuautla to keep order. And since the discharge of their men was still going on, Zapata and his officers were furious. One group, including Eufemio, wanted to shoot Madero, the "little squirt," as a traitor. Zapata knew what a disaster that would be, and he and Hay, who was there at the time, managed to calm the mutiny. In great distress Madero left for Mexico City, convinced there had been a misunderstanding but that he could again solve the problem in personal talks with de la Barra. But de la Barra never gave him the opportunity. When Madero arrived for an interview, the President excused himself for a cabinet meeting. Quitting finally his efforts to conciliate, Madero wrote de la Barra a long and bitter letter and then left to electioneer in Yucatán.[2] So disappeared the Morelos rebels' last pedigreed champion.

Still fearing bloodshed he could not avoid responsibility for, de la Barra tried in the following days to prevent a direct confrontation between the rebels and the federals, especially Huerta. So Zapata won a few days of grace. But the end was near. Ambrosio Figueroa moved his forces into Jojutla. Federal troops under General Arnoldo Casso López marched up from Jonacatepec toward Cuautla. The editors of the metropolitan daily closest to de la Barra asked whether the rebels in Morelos were "eligible for discharge or for indictments." Tomás Ruiz de Velasco actually filed criminal charges against Zapata; and the federal attorney general ordered his arrest. In reply Zapata published his first manifesto on August 27, To the People of Morelos, defending himself and blaming the government for the trouble in the state. By then Figueroa had executed some sixty local rebels, and was court-martialing more. From Mexico City Madero tried to arrange one last truce through his brother Raúl. But after a cabinet meeting on the 29th, García Granados ruled for the "active pursuit and arrest of Zapata."[3] The revolutionary chief was now an outlaw.

Two days later, as the federals surrounded Cuautla, Zapata made a final protest to de la Barra that he had not declared a rebellion, that he maintained only a small personal escort which Madero had assigned him, and that the government would be responsible for any bloodshed.[4] On the back of the message de la Barra noted his answer: "I lament that the dis-

---

[2] Magaña: op. cit., I, 245–54. There is no record of Huerta having specific orders to take Cuautla, although his general instructions were to proceed with operations of war.

[3] Ibid., I, 255–8. *El País,* August 26, 1911. Dearing to the secretary of state, NA, 59: 812.00/2316.

[4] Zapata to de la Barra, August 31, 1911, AZ, 16: 5: 4.

armament of your forces has not been effective and that parties of bandits have appeared." The cabinet having just decided on the "complete extirpation of banditry" in Morelos, the President then informed Huerta of Zapata's whereabouts and weakness.[5] That same day Casso López and Huerta occupied Cuautla jointly; and the next day, September 1, Huerta headed south toward Chinameca hacienda, where Zapata had escaped.[6]

Impatient to get at his prey, he was ruthless with opposition. "The facts show me," he wrote to de la Barra after crushing resistance around Villa de Ayala, "the necessity to work resolutely and without consideration. These people are all bandits." De la Barra wired his approval: Huerta could proceed "at liberty."[7]

He arrived at Chinameca, however, too late to capture Zapata. The commander there, Figueroa's hatchetman Federico Morales, had already bungled the job and let him get away. Trying to trap Zapata inside the hacienda walls, he had stupidly ordered a charge past the guard at the front gate. Zapata had heard the gunfire, and knowing the plantation grounds, had ducked out of the main building and run into the cane fields that lay to the rear. Three days later he was a bone-tired refugee whom Juan Andrew Almazán accidentally met riding a donkey through a little Puebla mountain town eighty miles to the south.[8]

To many observers the case of the Morelos revolution seemed closed. Madero had shelved the problem and was nervously calculating how he might do in a new violent contest for national power. Zapata himself was in hiding, and his local followers around the state were fleeing for their lives too. By the end of the month, the dirty work finished, Ambrosio Figueroa was persuaded to take over civil and military authority.[9] And Huerta, having now occupied all six district seats, had turned to mopping-up operations. As he reported to de la Barra in his inimitable style, a wheedling rhetoric of cynicism and pomp, he moved through the state garrisoning towns, "sowing trust, if the word fits," and, "with the rifles and with the cannon of the Government of the Republic, preaching harmony, peace, and brotherhood among all the sons of Morelos." By

[5] *El País,* August 31, 1911. Huerta's Report, AZ.

[6] Magaña: op. cit., I, 258–9.

[7] Huerta's Report, AZ.

[8] Almazán: op. cit., p. 22.

[9] Figueroa to de la Barra, October 4, 1911, AZ, 21: 3: 28. *Semanario Oficial,* XX, 37, 3.

September 26 he considered the state "pacified" and his mission there "concluded."[1]

But the planters, who would have rejoiced at "pacification," remained glum. They saw that their troubles were not over, that as Huerta had destroyed the immediate threat to their interests, he had forced into being a new and more dangerous threat. "At liberty" to treat every village he marched into as a nest of "bandits," he thus created "bandits"—men who hated the system he represented as they could not have hated it before. Abusing rural Maderistas, he turned them into Zapatistas; the denomination appeared only in mid-August, after he arrived in Morelos.[2] Worse, in dispersing and terrorizing local rebels, he had driven them for the first time seriously to recruit support or at least to seek protection from the resident peons on hacienda grounds. At Cocoyoc, for instance, the rebels had armed six hundred of the plantation's eight hundred laborers.[3] Worst of all, Huerta had not yet caught Zapata, who had become over the summer a popular idol throughout the state. So despite the official conclusion of the Morelos campaign, the planters did not relax their concern about keeping order. The most enterprising and intelligent, Luis García Pimentel, Jr., began organizing a corps of private police for his father's estates. Fifty guards he mounted, equipped, and armed at the family's expense, hiring as their commander the most experienced peace officer in the state.[4]

The García Pimentels' judgment proved sounder than Huerta's. For Zapata had retreated only to rally. In the mountains along the Puebla-Guerrero border he and Almazán encouraged restless chiefs even in Oaxaca to "revolt as fast as you can."[5] Already Zapata was forming in his own mind the program of this new "counterrevolution," as he then confusedly called it. Daily his old allies, persecuted at home by Figueroa's police, rejoined him and suggested revisions and additions. On September 26 Zapata stated his demands formally in a petition "from the Counterrevolutionaries to the President of the Republic Francisco L. de la Barra." Recognizing de la Barra as President, Zapata and his chiefs declared illegitimate the governors of Morelos, Puebla, Guerrero, and Oaxaca, and demanded popular authorities and military commanders, a postponement of the presidential election, "what in justice the pueblos deserve as to lands, timber, and water,"

[1] Huerta to de la Barra, September 13, 1911, AZ, 12: 1: 24 and 25.

[2] El País, August 17, 1911.

[3] Huerta to de la Barra, August 26, 1911, AA.

[4] L. García Pimentel, Jr., to de la Vega, March 15, 1912, AGN, G: 846.

[5] Zapata and Almazán to Menchaca, September 20, 1911, AZ, 30: 15.

the abolition of prefectures, and amnesty for political prisoners.[6] Almazán, Jesús Jáuregui, and José Trinidad Ruiz delivered the message to de la Barra in person.

The White President agreed to amnesty for political fugitives but ruled out leniency for rebels charged criminally, which included the chief rebel, Zapata. So informed, Huerta plunged on into southeastern Puebla in pursuit of the "ridiculously pretentious bandits."[7] But as he advanced, Zapata drew him on. Then, in early October, faking another retreat deeper into southern Puebla, Zapata reversed and raced two hundred to three hundred men around Huerta's flank. Riding hard through little-known mountain trails, the guerrilleros reappeared suddenly in eastern Morelos, ready to raid again. After Huerta's martial "preaching," recruits swarmed out of the villages and now off the plantations also to swell the rebel army to 1,500. The revived movement was so popular that the available troops and police—now under Casso López—could not contain it. On October 10 the rebels threatened Cuautla. During the next week they moved north into Mexico State, around Ozumba. Picking up more fighters every day, on October 22 and 23 the Zapatistas occupied villages in the Federal District, barely fifteen miles from downtown Mexico City.[8]

Zapata's return to Morelos, coinciding nicely with the presidential election, had provided a kind of local referendum on government policy. The official vote there, which took place despite disturbances much worse than those that had halted the August election for governor, gave victory to Madero's Progressive Constitutionalist ticket in Cuernavaca and Cuautla districts and to the Vázquez Gómez's Anti-Reelectionist ticket in Jojutla.[9] But the popular verdict had obviously been quite different. Against the policy of "complete extirpation," many men had voted with their feet— for the cause of the villages.

The overwhelming local reaction against Huerta's apparent success provoked its own reaction in Congress. As José María Lozano, the most brilliant orator among the deputies, recognized, "Emiliano Zapata is no longer a man, he is a symbol. He could turn himself in tomorrow . . . but the rabble [following him] . . . would not surrender."[1] Finally the up-

[6] For this document, see Appendix B.
[7] Huerta's Report, AZ. Huerta to I. de la Barra, September 27, 1911, AZ, 12: 1: 26.
[8] *Diario del Hogar,* October 10 and 19–26, 1911.
[9] *Semanario Oficial,* XX, 41, 1.
[1] Salvador Sánchez Septién, ed.: *José María Lozano en la Tribuna Parlamentaria, 1910–1913* (2nd edn., México, 1956), pp. 34–5.

rising brought on a cabinet crisis, in which García Granados, González Salas, and Francisco Vázquez Gómez lost their posts. It forced Huerta's replacement as well, apparently ending his career.

Madero was duly impressed, which probably was what Zapata had wanted most. From Parras, Coahuila, where he was waiting for inauguration day, he issued a long—and in part erroneous—public letter explaining why Zapata refused to accept the government's orders. The climax of his message was the assurance that as soon as he took office, Zapata would lay down his arms: ". . . he knows," Madero said, without doubt here addressing himself to Zapata almost personally, "that I will carry out the earlier aims of the government"—those agreed on August 18—"which I believed were the only means of pacifying the state of Morelos, and which Zapata already knows because I communicated them to him in Cuautla."[2]

Another Madero was impressed besides the apostle Francisco. This was his brother the politician, Gustavo. Throughout October reactionary plots to prevent Madero's inauguration developed almost in the open; Reyes had already retired to ominous exile in San Antonio. Against these threats Gustavo sought to reorganize the original revolutionary coalition. In late October he conferred several times in Mexico City with one of Zapata's young aides, Gildardo Magaña, who passed the encouraging news on south.[3] On November 1 Governor Figueroa posted notices in Cuautla pardoning all rebels who surrendered in two weeks.[4] A new kind of pacification was underway. There was fresh hope that finally differences would be settled, and the revolutionary union restored.

When Madero took office on November 6, Zapata had already assembled his troops around Villa de Ayala and was waiting peaceably to begin negotiations. Disturbing news reached the Morelos rebels that Figueroa had accompanied Madero in the inauguration ceremony as the representative of the southern wing of the national revolution. But reassuringly Gabriel Robles Domínguez arrived in Cuautla on November 8, enthusiastic about reconciliation. Observers in Mexico City watched the proceedings closely. According to El Imparcial, "Attila" had expedited a "ukase" to his "hordes" to surrender.[5]

---

[2] The letter is cited in Magaña: op. cit., II, 38–9.

[3] Ibid., II, 63.

[4] El Imparcial, November 2, 1911.

[5] Magaña: op. cit., II, 63–4. El Imparcial, November 8, 10, and 11, 1911. Also at this time Zapata had issued orders to all his officers to permit repairs on railroads and telegraph and telephone lines. Railroad station chiefs and trainmen received copies of the orders.

After three days Robles Domínguez and Zapata and his chiefs had worked out a deal. In effect the agreement would remove the Guerrerans and reestablish the Ayala party as the dominant power in the state, gradually evacuate federal troops and leave local revolutionaries as federal police, guarantee the agrarian aims of the Morelos revolution, and sanction as legitimate protests the rebels' past insubordination.[6]

Robles Domínguez prepared his return to offer the agreement for Madero's approval. But it then became clear that during the negotiations the federal troops in the state had completed foreboding maneuvers. By November 11, taking advantage of the rebels' concentration around Villa de Ayala, General Casso López had surrounded them at close range. Worse, Casso López would not let Robles Domínguez leave for Mexico City. From Cuautla the envoy managed to send an urgent wire in code to Madero, begging him under no circumstances to let Zapata be attacked. "I got excellent conditions," he reported. "Federals want to attack only to break conferences. They refuse to say [what they are up to]." The next day he evaded his guard and went to the capital.[7]

It was Sunday, and Madero saw him without delay at the Chapultepec presidential residence. Exactly how he received the new proposals it is difficult to tell. The promises he had made in August and recently confirmed hardly differed from the conditions Robles Domínguez now presented him. Moreover, as the agreement indicated, Zapata's defiance was simply a state and not a national action. But as president, his fledgling authority challenged almost daily, Madero could not afford to deal on equal terms with a local outlaw, however worthy. So, having heard Robles Domínguez out, he gave him a letter of instructions, an official record of his response:

" . . . let Zapata know that the only thing I can accept is that he immediately surrender unconditionally and that all his soldiers immediately lay down their arms. In this case I will pardon his soldiers for the crime of rebellion and he will be given passports so he can go settle temporarily outside the state.

"Inform him that his rebellious attitude is damaging my government greatly and that I cannot tolerate that it continue under any circumstances, that if he truly wants to serve me, [obeying me] is the only way he can do it.

"Let him know that he need fear nothing for his life if he lays down his arms immediately."

[6] For the agreement, see Magaña: op. cit., II, 65–6.
[7] For this and following communications, see ibid., II, 66–78.

It may well be that off the record Madero made more generous responses, which Robles Domínguez was to pass on privately to Zapata.[8] But if so, the plan miscarried. Because Zapata had not yet disbanded his men, General Casso López decided the conferences between Robles Domínguez and the rebel chief had failed.[9] And when Robles Domínguez returned to Cuautla to renew the talks, the general would not let him go on to rebel head-quarters in Villa de Ayala. All Zapata learned about his offer to make peace was from a courier who delivered him Madero's official demand for a sur-render and a desperate but only half-explanatory letter from Robles Domínguez.

When the courier arrived in the rebel camp, Zapata was already or-ganizing his forces to meet the imminent federal attack. On horseback he read both messages as if—Gildardo Magaña said—he was watching events develop as he had expected. Robles Domínguez's eloquent plea mattered little when Casso López was already drawing up his artillery less than a mile away, on instructions, as it appeared from the other letter, from President Madero himself. In a fury he dismissed the courier. Soon the artillery began firing, and Zapata ordered a retreat. He and his escort held out till evening, then slipped through the federal lines. As before, he headed south into the Puebla mountains, recruiting refugees and partisans along the way.

This was the last hopeful effort at reconciliation. A few days later Robles Domínguez tried to communicate with Zapata about a new agreement, but got no answer.[1] And through eastern Morelos the little war of the guer-rilla started again. In late November Zapata convened a junta of his closest partisans at Ayoxustla, a little mountain town in southeastern Puebla, and there, signing a Plan de Ayala which Montaño had composed, the assembled chiefs finally declared themselves formally in rebellion against the federal government. Madero was inept, treacherous, and tyrannical, they pro-claimed. Only through violence could they gain justice for the pueblos. To lead the Ayala revolution they called on a national hero, the chief who had emerged as the most famous Maderista commander in the earlier San Luis revolution and who was now the loyal but restless head of Chihuahua's

[8] For a consideration of the evidence, see Womack: op. cit., pp. 216–17.

[9] Casso López's Report to the secretary of war, November 30, 1911, Archivo His-tórico de Defensa Nacional (henceforth AHDN), XI/481.5/177, 290–302. For secur-ity reasons I was not permitted to consult the original documents in this archive. I owe consultation of notes on them to the generosity of Luis Muro.

[1] G. Robles Domínguez to Zapata, November 15, 1911, ARD, 7: 37: 42.

federal police, Pascual Orozco. "I am resolved," Zapata wrote to Magaña in Mexico City, "to struggle against everything and everybody . . ."[2]

In early December, probably on his brother Gustavo's advice, Madero sent another commission to see Zapata at a camp on the Puebla-Morelos border. But the commissioners bore no new offer. To the chief whom Madero had embraced in the August crisis in Cuautla, in the worst days of a time of lies and broken promises, to the chief whom Madero had then classified among all his many revolutionary generals as his "truest general," to this chief the commissioners could now not even assure amnesty and a pardon if he laid down his arms. The only guarantee they could assure him was a safe trip into exile. And Zapata, recalling the long months of strain he and Madero had labored through together, exploded in resentment. "I've been Señor Madero's most faithful partisan," he told the commissioners. "I've given infinite proofs of it. But I'm not any more. Madero has betrayed me as well as my army, the people of Morelos, and the whole nation. Most of his [original] supporters are in jail or persecuted," Zapata continued, incensed at the purges he knew were going on in his own state and thinking they must be underway elsewhere too, "and nobody trusts him any longer because he's violated all his promises. He's the most fickle, vacillating man I've ever known." What should they tell the president? the commissioners asked. "Tell him this for me," Zapata concluded, "—to take off for Havana, because if not he can count the days as they go by, and in a month I'll be in Mexico City with twenty thousand men, and have the pleasure of going up to Chapultepec castle and dragging him out of there and hanging him from one of the highest trees in the park."[3]

So in a bitter and defensive divorce from the national movement ended the first phase of the Morelos revolution. Henceforth it developed on its own. The aching hopes for union were useless, because both Madero and Zapata had committed themselves in dead earnest to an endeavor—a revolution—which they did not know they saw very differently. At the beginning no one in the revolutionary coalition distinguished between a "social" and a "political" revolution. In June, shortly after the fatal troubles had begun, Zapata had given a wistful interview to a reporter as he waited in a Mexico City train station, ready to return home. "It can't be said of me," he told the reporter, "that I went off to the battlefields under the pressure of poverty.

[2] Zapata to Magaña, December 6, 1911, cited in Magaña: op. cit., II, 95–6. For the full text of the Plan de Ayala, and comments on its origins and significance, see Appendix B.

[3] *Diario del Hogar,* December 18, 1911.

I've got some land and a stable . . . which I earned through long years of honest work and not through political campaigns, and which produce enough for me and my family to live on comfortably. . . . Now I'm going to work at discharging the men who helped me," he continued, "so I can retire to private life and go back to farming my fields. For the only thing I wanted when I went into the revolution was to defeat the dictatorial regime, and this has been accomplished."[4]

That was all Madero and the other revolutionaries said they wanted too—"to defeat the dictatorial regime." But the difficulty was that different men had different criteria for judging when the dictatorial regime had been defeated, or even precisely what the dictatorial regime was.

When had the revolution triumphed? For Zapata, the southern provincial, the exasperated chief of his village, the answer was straightforward: when the agrarian dispute in his state was equitably settled, or at least when deliberate moves had been taken in that direction. For Madero, the northern provincial, a landlord's gentlest son, floating in reveries of goodness, the answer was both more and less: when Mexicans prospered and loved one another, or at least when he took office. The difference between the very nature of their expectations was profound. And when they finally realized it, they could turn to no organized party or committee for adjustment and discipline. Under terrific pressures they had to mediate their conflict themselves. But as they indicated by their almost desperate desire to trust and be trusted, they had nothing of the true politicians' ruthless knack for disagreeing in peace—at other people's expense but for their security. Their original commitment had been too hopeful: Zapata suspected betrayal in every disagreement, and Madero could see the selfishness in any view but his own. Of all the revolutionaries, they were the least suited to live with their differences.

[4] *El País,* June 22, 1911.

The Official Revolutionaries Perform

"Not only the so-called científicos . . ."

IN MEXICO CITY REVOLUTIONARIES TOOK OFFICE, and Prince Albert coats replaced khaki jackets. But in Morelos the war continued. Through the whole Madero term two local revolutionary parties would fight to determine what the revolution there would be. From the start the aim of the law-abiding revolutionaries was clear: trusting in support from their metropolitan patrons, they wanted to legislate popular reforms and decree them officially. After December 15, when the *Diario del Hogar* published the Plan de Ayala, the aim of the rebellious revolutionaries in Morelos was clear too. They wanted popular reforms carried out in the field, whether a clerk in an office authorized them or not. As before against Díaz, Zapata and his chiefs were waging war against Madero; but now they specified as well that the struggle was to benefit the nation's country people, that dispossessed farming families would recover their lands or receive new grants from expropriated haciendas, and that not advocates but actual veterans of the struggle would dominate the resulting regime. In the conflict both parties worked for popular change, but in different worlds. In the conflict they also changed themselves.

Until mid-1912, when the federal government restored home rule in

Morelos, both revolutions going on there were movements of opposition—
one loyal, the other insurrectionary. For the rebels the proper tactics seemed
simple to devise and execute. Zapata and his chiefs evidently believed, as
did many other observers, that Madero would soon fall. Even before the
apostle's inauguration, dangerous challenges to his authority had developed.
In October Emilio Vázquez had retired to San Antonio, where he met
General Reyes and obviously began to plot a revolt in alliance with him.
On October 31 Vazquista agents in Mexico City signed their own Plan de
Tacubaya, denouncing Madero and proclaiming Vázquez president. In
early November the metropolitan police exposed a Vazquista-Reyista conspiracy to assassinate the new President. A month later they uncovered
another such plan among high-ranking military officers with Reyista connections.[1] And though General Reyes failed to start an uprising when he
reentered Mexico in mid-December, and instead ended up in jail, still the
Vázquez Gómez brothers, who had tricked him into the failure, remained
critical threats to the government.[2] In the north there were many discontented revolutionaries, like the ambitious Pascual Orozco, whom they
might persuade to rebel. In these promising circumstances all Zapata and
his chiefs evidently thought they had to do was fight—to maintain their
rebel standing for the little while until Madero fell, when they could press
a new government to meet their demands or fall itself.

So they hardly bothered about organization. The junta issuing the
Ayala plan comprised most of the rebel chiefs who had been and would
later be prominent in Morelos, including besides the Zapata brothers and
the plan's author, Montaño, veterans like Francisco Mendoza, Jesús Morales,
José Trinidad Ruiz, Amador Salazar, Lorenzo Vázquez, Emigdio Marmolejo, and Pioquinto Galis. But the junta had no fixed camp, much less
a regular headquarters. Nor did a full-time secretary manage its business:
Abrahám Martínez, who had earlier served as Zapata's chief of staff, was
still in jail in Puebla City; Montaño, the intellectual of the movement, was
trying now to become a warrior; and other minor aides drifted in and out
of the various rebel camps too erratically to coordinate operations. Moreover several important local chiefs did not yet belong to the Ayala junta.

[1] For the Plan de Tacubaya, which is not the Plan Político-Social of the Tacubaya
Conspiracy, see González Ramírez: *Planes,* pp. 55–60. For the plots, see *Diario del
Hogar,* November 9 and December 18, 1911.

[2] Special Report of Private Detectives in San Antonio, January 2, 1912, Archivo
General de la Secretaría de Relaciones Exteriores (henceforth AGRE), L-E-857R:
File 9 (sic, in fact, 3).

Missing among others were veterans like Felipe Neri, Genovevo de la O, Francisco Pacheco, Jesús Jáuregui, Ignacio Maya, and Pedro Saavedra—all currently in rebellion but not formally under Zapata's orders. And not all those having sworn allegiance to the Ayala plan were firm in their loyalties. In early January Jesús Morales tried to arrange a private deal with the federal government. Not long afterward Mendoza disarmed and banished José Trinidad Ruiz, incorporating Ruiz's men into his own force.[3] In these weeks the action the Zapatistas carried on in Morelos was less a revolt than a rural riot.

Almost immediately bandits started operating too. This development was especially ominous, because harvests would soon begin on the plantations and trigger the yearly boom in the markets throughout the region. The rebels did not want competition from other outlaws in selling protection to the planters, and they did not want highwaymen preying on the country folk who needed to trade to build up their fund of cash. On December 20 Zapata issued general orders to his Liberating Army of the South to provide "every class of guarantees in the villages and fields and on the roads, . . . to respect and aid civil authorities who have been legally and freely elected," and not to let revolutionary forces or pacificos "destroy or burn the property of the haciendas, because these will be the patrimony and source of work for the villages." He also instructed officers to permit troops to return home to harvest crops or care for their families. There was no word on agrarian reform. Concluding, Zapata admonished his officers "to bring to the consciousness of our troops that the better we behave, the more adherents and help we will have among the people and the faster will be our triumph."[4] To the "beloved pueblos" themselves he published a manifesto on December 31. There he professed the legitimacy of the Ayalan revolutionaries' goals and disclaimed responsibility for "those individuals who, protecting themselves with my banner, commit outrages and abuses and carry on feuds. . . . These persons," he declared, "I ask all my partisans and the pueblos in general to throw back with energy, for these I consider enemies of mine who try to discredit our blessed cause and prevent its triumph."[5]

But despite the liabilities of disorganization, the rebel junta remained

[3] Morales to Madero, January 7, 1912, AZ, 28: 12: 1. Encarnación Muñoz: "Breves apuntes históricos" (MS, 1913), p. 62, AZ, 31: 1.

[4] Gonzalo Vázquez Ortiz to O. Magaña, December 25, 1911, cited by Magaña Cerda in *El Universal*, December 10, 1950.

[5] For the manifesto, see González Ramírez: *Manifiestos*, pp. 505–6.

amorphous. For finances it still depended on local contributions, a few forced loans, and the sporadic philanthropy of interested metropolitan politicians. For arms and ammunition it had only those captured from federal army and police patrols and those randomly supplied by gunrunners coming down from Mexico City.[6] In early January an aspiring Zapatista agent in Cuautla pleaded for the junta to send him a letter of introduction and instructions so he could "ORGANIZE, SYSTEMATIZE, and GENERALIZE" the revolution. It was "indispensable," he urged, "to establish a *Center* in Mexico City . . . to direct, give character to, and assume political responsibility for the movement." This arrangement, he argued, would give the movement "IMPULSE and SOLIDITY."[7] Already he had appealed twice for instructions and received no reply; no record indicates he fared more happily this time. The Ayalan chiefs evidently had no hankering for an elaborate structure, of national or local inspiration.

Loosely associated as they were, they still moved on the verge of seizing military control of the state. More than a thousand federal troops under General Casso López and around five thousand rurales under various commands remained in Morelos. But the only places they effectively held were the towns they were stationed in, the district and major municipal seats. In some cases, especially among the rurales, the commanders were excellent; and on paper they had crafty tactics for their mounted police—constant pursuit, night marches, mobile provisioning.[8] But almost all officers and troopers came from other states, Jalisco and Guanajuato mainly, and they were as ignorant of the twisting trails and ravines they now had to maneuver through as they were unfamiliar with the local villagers, whom they inevitably harassed and who then informed on them to the rebels.[9] The planters too resented the expense and disruption the soldiers and policemen caused.[1] The result was that the federal forces rarely budged from their quarters. When they did venture onto the roads, their commanders normally took them out in awkward battalion strength. So in the southeast Zapata, Mendoza, and Morales led guerrilleros practically where

---

[6] Antonio Díaz Soto y Gama: "Un noble amigo de Zapata," *El Universal*, December 13, 1950. *El País*, February 19 and 25, and June 15, 21, and 26, 1912.

[7] Unsigned letter to Zapata, January 4, 1912, AZ, 28: 12. His emphasis.

[8] General Instructions to Commanders and Officers of Rural Police, 1912, AGN, G: 647.

[9] Induction contracts of rural police in Morelos, January, 1912, AGN, G: 846, 925.

[1] *El Imparcial*, December 20, 1911, and January 21, 1912. L. García Pimentel, Jr., to de la Vega, March 15, 1912, AGN.

they pleased in the countryside. In the northeast, up into Mexico State as far as Ozumba, José Trinidad Ruiz was the dominant power. Having preached in various little towns in that zone, he knew the people and the terrain well; the police commander charged with suppressing the rebellion there all but admitted the impossibility of his task.[2] Only after Mendoza disarmed Ruiz did the federals recover a feeble control in the area. In the center of the state Salazar and Neri ruled as thoroughly as ever, attacking garrison towns and moving at will through the villages. And in the northwest—in the strategic country north of Cuernavaca, around Santa María and Huitzilac—de la O had scared the rurales into complete passivity. Few battles occurred in his zone because not even the federal regulars dared to contest his authority.

The rebels had become so powerful in Morelos that by mid-January their example had infected malcontents elsewhere. In Tlaxcala, Puebla, Mexico State, Michoacán, Guerrero, and Oaxaca, revolts sympathetic to the Ayalan movement had broken out. An embarrassing southern crisis thus formed for the federal government, already deeply disturbed over the widening estrangement of Pascual Orozco in the north. On January 17 Madero agreed to accept Ambrosio Figueroa's resignation from the governorship of Morelos, as much to regain the loyalty of local moderates as to let Figueroa put down the uprisings in his own state. And two days later, to resolve the crisis directly, the minister of the interior declared martial law for four months in Morelos, Guerrero, and Tlaxcala, and thirteen districts in Mexico and Puebla. But still the rebellion flourished. In late January the rebels almost took Cuernavaca. Some three thousand had gathered in the countryside around the state capital, from Tepoztlán to Temixco to Huitzilac; and after a federal spoiling action failed at Santa María on January 26, the rebels commenced vigorous, evidently coordinated attacks through the whole area. Under de la O's command they fought three- and four-hour battles every day for more than a week. From rooftops in Cuernavaca fascinated observers could see the explosions of federal artillery shells in Santa María and watch the black smoke rise up the mountainside as the village burned. But the rebels sustained the offensive, and every day they seemed closer to ruining the federals and occupying the capital.[3]

For the other, law-abiding revolutionaries in Morelos, to whom poli-

[2] Francisco J. Enciso to Reynaldo Díaz, December 23, 1911, AGN, G: 645.

[3] *El País,* January 19, 20, 27–29, and 31, February 2 and 4, 1912. *El Imparcial,* January 19, 1912. De la O in *Impacto,* January 21, 1950.

tics mattered more than tactics, this crisis in part simplified their work and in part complicated it. The blessing it brought them was Figueroa's resignation, which greatly improved their chances of recovering local control of the state government and enacting reforms. As governor, Figueroa had tried to establish a Guerrero clique in Cuernavaca. Depending on his lieutenant governor, Aurelio Velázquez, and the Cuernavaca district judge, Ruperto Zuleta, both of whom were imported Guerreran politicos, he hoped to secure Morelos in favor of his own family's national ambitions. Since local revolutionaries wanted to manage the state themselves, Velázquez and Zuleta could arrange a political base for their boss only among old Escandonistas and hangers-on who had just lately gained office and were now reluctant to retire. Thus in the December municipal elections the Guerrerans had found no better candidate for municipal president of Cuernavaca than the hack Ramón Oliveros, who lost. For the gubernatorial elections due January 14 Velázquez and Zuleta had not been able to find any plausible candidate among the local notables and finally proposed yet another Guerreran, whom even their native collaborators would not accept. To repair Figueroa's authority and to prevent a native victory in the race for governor, Velázquez had started a sweeping purge. He dismissed from the state bureaucracy many new appointees whom he considered unreliable and recommissioned those who had served Alarcón and Escandón. He abolished salaries for municipal presidents, which required them to assume compromising debts or resign. Although he did not actually eject any municipal presidents, as General Casso López did in three Puebla border towns, he did remove town councilmen in several places. Also under his auspices police commanders abused local governments and even executed suspicious officials without trial. And when these measures proved in vain and it seemed that the club of toadies Judge Zuleta had organized to elect the governor would flop, then Figueroa had called off the elections—on January 12, two days beforehand. So Figueroa's resignation and retreat from Morelos a few days later amounted to a reprieve for the local champions of legal change. Rallying, they proceeded to fortify their position.[4]

Already they had strong bases. Not only in Cuernavaca but in Yautepec, Cuautla, Jonacatepec, and many smaller towns they had won power in the recent municipal elections. Their representatives were not ex-Porfiristas, ex-Escandonists, or ex-Leyvistas: neither Felipe Escarza, the new municipal

[4] *Diario del Hogar,* January 5, 6, and 16, 1912.

president of Cuernavaca, nor Julio Cárdenas in Yautepec, nor Everardo Espinosa in Cuautla, nor José María Alcázar in Jonacatepec had a record of active participation in any party or movement. Evidently they were political neophytes. They were also not wealthy men: Alcázar, who ran a dry-goods and grocery store, was the only citizen of credit among them.[5] Nor had they been agents or attorneys for the planters in the state. And they were all really natives of the towns they now governed, not merely residents in passing. Without connections in Mexico City or even in Cuernavaca, they most likely came into their offices only through the local, literally familiar operations of respect, duty, consent, and fealty. As Figueroa departed, it seemed they might lead their neighbors to success in their peaceful campaign for reform.

The new interim governor, Francisco Naranjo, Jr., was also an encouraging factor. He was not a native son, as local revolutionaries would have preferred, but he was at least a northerner, from Nuevo León, and not another Guerreran. And he was a reputedly sincere and honest veteran of the popular cause in the north. The son of a Porfirista military hero, he had still in the time of Don Porfirio risked a comfortable engineering career to help found the radical Liberal Party. For agitating he had once gone to jail, and his father had had to appeal to Díaz personally for his release. An Anti-Reelectionist in 1910, he had joined the Maderista revolution in its earliest weeks.[6] Afterward he was one of the few irregular colonels trusted to retain his commission and the command of the corps of riflemen he had organized. Now he came to Morelos, unlike Figueroa, publicly intent on doing good for the local people. He had tried to enlist as his lieutenant governor an old friend and a cofounder of the Liberal Party, the militant anarchist Antonio Díaz Soto y Gama. Soto y Gama refused the appointment: the government had committed "an extremely grave error," he explained, in mistaking the "deep social problem" in the south as banditry, "to be resolved with artillery barrages . . . in the Russian manner": although he did not aspire to "agrarian communism," he noted, nor to "the impossible utopia of absolute equality," he would not be an accomplice in "the war to the death against the victims of Capital."[7] But

[5] Ibid., December 11, 1911, and February 28, 1912. *El País*, July 3, 1912. *Commercial Directory*, pp. 168, 199, 224.

[6] Rubén García: *El Antiporfirismo* (México, 1935), pp. 32–3. Francisco Naranjo: *Diccionario biográfico revolucionario* (México, 1935), p. 143.

[7] *Diario del Hogar*, January 25, 1912.

Naranjo alone was still a welcome ally for the local revolutionaries. He came obviously disposed to help them in calming the rebellion and improving the popular welfare.

On arrival in Cuernavaca he began a careful study of the reasons for the unrest and violence. "I found," he later recalled, "that Morelos lacked three things—first plows, second books, and third equity. And it had more than enough latifundios, taverns, and bosses." The information that Yautepec had no room to expand its cemetery, or that Cuautla had no place to dump its garbage, was a shock to this earnest engineer from the vast, open steppes of the north. Like Soto y Gama, also a northerner, he referred to the frustration and constriction of local communities as a "problem," less a deliberate oppression than a special kind of riddle.[8] With the reformers already in municipal offices around the state, he might "solve" it.

Help was also forthcoming through more obscure channels. President Madero's brother Gustavo had quietly arranged the release of Zapata's former chief of staff, Abrahám Martínez, from jail in Puebla City, and on January 25 brought him and two other former aides of Zapata's, Gildardo and Rodolfo Magaña, to a private meeting in Mexico City. Granting the justice in Zapata's resentment, Gustavo still insisted on "our duty to try again for a reconciliation." In fact it was not so much patriotic generosity as political anxiety that moved Gustavo, since Pascual Orozco had privately broken with the Maderos a week before and was now about to break publicly with them in Chihuahua. But the deal agreed on in this caucus would serve Naranjo's benign purposes in Morelos. On January 26 Martínez and Rodolfo Magaña left in secret for Zapata's camp to relay Gustavo's plea for renewed negotiations and a truce.[9]

The crisis that had produced these boons for the law-abiding revolutionaries soon proved a curse for them as well. Naranjo could not attend to their interests, because the rebels permitted him no space or time to maneuver in. To the revolutionaries fighting in the field the new governor's sympathies made no difference. What mattered to them was the force he directed into their territory. Indeed it was his attempt to flush them out of Santa María that provoked the tremendous attack on Cuernavaca in late January. Although the rebels briefly relaxed the offensive in early February, de la O and other chiefs like Vázquez and Salazar, who had just reinforced him, published a notice that on February 6 they would start blowing

[8] *El País,* August 5, 1912.

[9] Michael C. Meyer: *Mexican Rebel. Pascual Orozco and the Mexican Revolution, 1910–1915* (Lincoln, 1967), pp. 47–52. Magaña: op. cit., II, 108–9.

up every train coming into the state.[1] Meanwhile Martínez, having conferred with Zapata, wrote back to President Madero that he would rejoin his old chief to help him however he could.[2] And on February 6, as they had warned, de la O and his allies resumed their drive against the state capital even more ferociously than before. In desperation the federal commander in the city ordered the immediate burning of Santa María and its surrounding woods, where the rebels had their base. Naranjo could not stop him. And on February 9 federal troops stormed into the village, soaked the houses and buildings with kerosene, fired them, and retreated. Artillery shells exploding into the woods touched off flames there. By evening the village was in ashes, the charred timber in the hills around still aglow and smoking.

Thus federal forces had again treated the nearby Cuernavacans to an awe-inspiring spectacle. To a reporter for *El País,* a metropolitan Catholic daily, the action seemed a worthy effort "to destroy Zapatismo, which is threatening to destroy what we hold highest, our nationality."[3] But to the rebels—especially to de la O, whose young daughter died in the fire— it was an abjuration of all the rules of war.[4] After the federals left, the rebels moved back into the area and recommenced their campaign, which was to go on for over a month.

In this emergency the hopes of Naranjo and his prospective protégés in the town councils were impossible. Avoiding a fiasco, the new governor would not reorder state elections. For the sake of continuity and because he had no other official on the spot to turn to, he kept Aurelio Velázquez as lieutenant governor. Abuses and expulsions of local councilmen therefore continued.[5] And revolutionaries ready to propose reforms had to shelve their plans.

Still worse for them was that in a panic President Madero had appointed a new military commander for Morelos who aggravated the rebellion and so prolonged the period of legal suspensions. The new commander was Brigadier General Juvencio Robles. Years before in Indian wars on the northern frontier he had learned the army's procedure for crushing rebellions, and coming now into the south, he intended to fight villagers and rancheros as he had fought tribesmen. Already he had experience of Morelos

---

[1] *Diario del Hogar,* February 14, 1912.

[2] *El País,* February 9, 1912.

[3] Ibid., February 10, 1912.

[4] De la O in *Impacto,* January 14, 1950.

[5] *El País,* February 1, 1912.

and its commotions: in 1909, as a colonel, he had commanded the Cuautla garrison on the day Escandonista voters "outnumbered" the Leyvistas. On February 3, after a long conference with the secretary of war, he told reporters how he saw the state: "All Morelos, as I understand it, is Zapatista, and there's not a single inhabitant who doesn't believe in the false doctrines of the bandit Emiliano Zapata." Having thus lumped the planters, their attorneys and managers and employees in the mills and in the fields, the peaceable reformers, the passive admirers of the rebels, the rebels operating independently, the rebels operating in alliance with Zapata, the rebels operating under Zapata's authority, and the bandits themselves all together as one enemy, Robles remained confident. In "a relatively short lapse of time," he predicted, he would "reduce that falange of gangsters who presently scourge the state . . . with their crimes and thefts worthy of the savage."[6]

Once in Morelos he went straight to business. On February 10, on his instructions, federals arrested Zapata's mother-in-law, his sister, and two sisters-in-law in Villa de Ayala and took them as hostages to Cuernavaca.[7] The same day the federal commander in Yautepec had the house of Municipal President Julio Cárdenas searched. The evidence the troops found was hardly incriminating—an old, broken pistol, six moldy cartridges, and some political credentials seventeen years old—but the commander ordered Cárdenas to resign, and Cárdenas had to flee for his life. Three days later the commander had fourteen local suspects shot: four Yautepecan farmers and ten workers from the Cocoyoc plantation, where rebels had armed many peons the previous summer. Cárdenas issued public protests, as did his fellow municipal president, Everardo Espinosa of Cuautla, who also had to flee.[8] But they had no effect.

Robles shortly put into regular practice a favorite policy, "resettlement." Modeled on Spanish proceedings in the recent Cuban War of Independence, and on similar British action in the Boer War and American action in the Philippines, "resettlement" was a deliberate definition of an indefinite war. By 1910 it had become the standard method in the Mexican army for suppressing popular guerrillas. It required first forcing the rural pacificos out of their villages and ranchos and into concentration camps on the outskirts of larger towns, where federal supervision was easier. Then flying columns could move freely into the country-

6 Ibid., February 4, 1912.
7 Robles to the secretary of war, February 11, 1912, AHDN, XI/481.5/178, 90.
8 *Diario del Hogar*, February 18, 27, and 28, 1912.

side and treat whomever they met as "hostiles." In the end demoralized and exhausted rebels would surrender, and the federals would scour the area clean of those who still resisted. The peculiar feature of Robles's use of this method was that he burned places he wanted the population to evacuate. "If," as he later noted in his defense, "the Zapatistas returned to occupy those pueblos and make barricades out of their houses so as to battle the federals, besides obtaining the necessities of life from the inhabitants, there was nothing more rational and logical than to destroy those Zapatista redoubts and prevent the residents from giving arms, ammunition, and food to the gangsters."[9] So the burning that had been a stroke of desperation a few days earlier at Santa María now became a system.

On February 15 Robles sent out a strong force south of Jojutla to initiate his policy. Along the Chinameca River near the Guerrero border the troops reached the little village of Nexpa. They found only 136 people still there, 131 of them women and children. After driving them out of their houses, they set fire to the ramshackle buildings. "The residents cried and pleaded that the pueblo which had seen them born not be destroyed," reported the *El País* correspondent. "... in the midst of the greatest terror and consternation the flames did their work, and a dense, black column of smoke rolling laboriously up the sides of the mountain announced to the Zapatistas hidden there that they no longer had a home ..." All the Nexpans went back to Jojutla as federal prisoners, and stayed under guard in an army corral. Robles eventually released them but would not permit them to return to their ruins; they had to check in daily with Jojutla police.

Other federal forces "resettled" other populations. San Rafael and Ticumán were burned. So was Los Hornos, where Zapata had had a headquarters and where the federals captured Lorenzo Vázquez's family and sent them, like Zapata's, back to Cuernavaca as hostages. Elotes also, a little rancho in the same region, the federals put to flame. And in Villa de Ayala they burned down many houses. Robles and his superiors might well grant, as the Catholic editors of *El País* did, that these actions were "liberal in cruelty." But, as the editors themselves insisted, "heroic remedies" were necessary. Otherwise, they argued, "we fear that the state of revolt might become chronic." The truth about Morelos was "horrible," the editors observed. "Zapatismo has adepts who amount to legion; its coreligionaries can be counted in many thousands . . . therefore [rebel] espionage is magnificent." Unless Robles pursued his plan of "the total

[9] *El País*, August 31, 1912.

destruction of the shanty towns which serve as refuge for Zapatistas," Morelos would become "the tomb of our heroic army."[1]

Thus justified, "resettlement" continued. On February 20, after learning that the still-active rebels north of Cuernavaca received supplies from muleteers who passed through Coajomulco and Ocotepec, Robles had those two villages burned as well. He did not dare burn the huts in which the resident peons of the plantations lived, but with the peons themselves he was as ruthless as with villagers and rancheros. His commander in Yautepec had eighteen more workers from Cocoyoc hacienda executed. Even high-ranking plantation personnel did not escape Robles's scrutiny. In late February he had the San Vicente and Chiconcuac managers and some of their assistants arrested for giving ammunition to the rebels in return for protection. Tried and found guilty in court-martial, the defendants were sentenced to six months in prison.[2]

Although this curse had nearly swamped them, the law-abiding revolutionaries persisted in private attempts to restore peace and constitutional rule. On February 20 old General Leyva arrived in Cuernavaca and began conferring with delegations from neighboring pueblos. It was public knowledge that he had no influence with Zapata and the chiefs under his orders; the general himself declared "categorically that no negotiations would start with Zapata, Abrahám Martínez, and other ringleaders and thieves." But it still seemed possible that he might arrange a truce with de la O and the rebels based in Santa María. "The Indians in their majority went into the revolution," the general explained to the press, "because they had been despoiled of their lands." His mission, he went on, was "to examine with the governor of the state the titles to the properties the Indians claim, and then to proceed in justice." To rebels guilty of no crime but rebellion, he could offer amnesty.[3]

Meanwhile pillars of Cuernavaca society began publishing formal requests that Robles not burn certain pueblos. Vouching for the loyalty of the families there, they embarrassed him into at least temporary and scattered restraints. Encouraged, local notables elsewhere published formal defenses of their towns too, and won similar provisional guarantees. Although burnings and plunderings continued, influential citizens thus gained exemption for a few, favored places.[4]

---

[1] Ibid., February 17–20, 1912. *Diario del Hogar,* February 18 and 23, 1912.
[2] Ibid., February 24, 1912. *El País,* February 21, 25, and 26, March 2 and 7, 1912.
[3] Ibid., February 21, 22, 24, and 26, 1912.
[4] Ibid., February 25 and 28, March 3 and 4, 1912.

Concurrently the deposed municipal presidents' drive to remove Aurelio Velázquez was about to succeed. The turning point came when Julio Cárdenas publicly accused Velázquez of trying secretly to organize support in Morelos for the subversive Vázquez Gómez brothers. Velázquez and politicians like him "are dishonoring the administration of Señor Madero," Cárdenas charged, "because these men are everything but Maderistas."[5] Velázquez shortly resigned, and on March 2 a close friend of Naranjo's, Jacobo Ramos Martínez, took over as lieutenant governor. Almost immediately he began trying to arrange contact with Zapata, to deal with him as General Leyva had hoped to deal with de la O.[6]

But the rebels would not quit. By now they had lost more than their lands. Having seen their homes burned and their kinfolk shot or imprisoned, they felt little obligation to consider the government's offer to accept their surrender. Besides, from the reinforcements Robles had scared out of villages and plantations into their camps, they were even more numerous than before. And they had even less reason for compromise when in early March the news arrived that Pascual Orozco had finally revolted in the north: the government, it seemed, would soon collapse, and they would ride into the state capital as conquerors. Neither Leyva nor Ramos Martínez could persuade them to negotiate. And as federal troops and police withdrew to the Federal District for reassignment in Chihuahua, the rebel chiefs extended their zones of active operations and accelerated the pace of their attacks. Through March de la O engaged the best federal regulars in the state almost daily around Huitzilac. For the whole month Neri and Salazar besieged the weak garrison at Tepoztlán. Eluding the rurales, Lorenzo Vázquez carried out frequent successful raids on haciendas in central Morelos. Mendoza campaigned powerfully from Axochiapan to Zacualpan. And the two Zapatas mounted alarming assaults in southern and western Puebla, in a threat to that state's capital.[7]

Robles tried to seize the offensive, but although he could sometimes capture a rebel base or locate rebel bands and disperse them, he could not bring the rebellion under control or even slow it down. After March 23, when Orozco won a crucial battle in southern Chihuahua, the rebels in

---

[5] *Diario del Hogar,* February 28, 1912.

[6] *El País,* March 2, 1912. *El Diario,* September 29, 1912.

[7] De la O in *Impacto,* January 21, 1950. Robles to the secretary of war, April 10, 1912, AHDN, XI/481.5/178, 198–212, 229–33, 274–5. G. Sánchez to the inspector general, March 18, 1912, AGN, G: 846. Muñoz: op. cit., pp. 63–8. *El País,* March 29, 1912.

Morelos became even bolder. The state seemed almost theirs. From Mexico City Pablo Escandón wrote in despair to his political tutor, still in exile in Paris, that "if things go on as they are going, surely we will retrogress to our former position as A NATION OF THE LAST ORDER, A TRUE NIGGERDOM."[8]

For the rebels April was the critical month. The other two parties committed in the struggle remained on the defensive, practically on the run. The continuing emergency in the north further depleted federal forces and supplies in Morelos, so that Robles abandoned the countryside completely and tried to hold only the major towns. And the rebels' rivals in revolution, the reformers intent on legal change, could extract no more concessions from the beleaguered federal government. In his April 1 report to Congress Madero had specifically stated that not until he was in military control of Morelos would he authorize "studies and operations" on "our age-old agrarian question." Regarding the southern troubles, he was obviously in a sore mood. "Fortunately," he noted, "this amorphous agrarian socialism, which for the rude intelligence of the farmers of Morelos can only take the form of sinister vandalism, has found no echo in other regions of the country."[9] The poor prospects for restoring order were especially vivid to the hacendados, who had lost whoppingly in the current harvests. When a federal agency started inquiries about purchasing lands for resale to poor farmers, several Morelos planters offered their estates for sale.[1]

Still pressing as hard as they could, the rebels were not able to carry their local advantage into a decisive triumph and institute their own government in the state. They did disrupt rail service, and they did occupy important towns. On April 1 Neri and Salazar finally captured Tepoztlán. On April 2 Zapata attacked and took Jonacatepec. On April 6 Zapata, Mendoza, Vázquez, and other chiefs began a combined assault on Tlaquiltenango, Tlaltizapán, and Jojutla, actually entering the last city several times. But the rebels could not secure their victories. In every case the federals returned

[8] Escandón to P. Macedo, March 29, 1912, "El Archivo de la Reacción," *El Universal*, October 12, 1917. His emphasis.

[9] "Informe leído por el C. Presidente de la República Mexicana al abrirse el cuarto período de sesiones del 25 Congreso de la Unión, el 1 de abril de 1912," *Diario Oficial*, CXIX, 27, 405–13.

[1] *El hacendado mexicano*, XVIII, 208 (March 1912), 81; 209 (April 1912), 121; 210 (May 1912), 161. Secretaría de Fomento: *Trabajos e iniciativas de la Comisión Agraria Ejecutiva* (México, 1912), included in Jesús Silva Herzog, ed.: *La cuestión de la tierra, 1910–1917*, 4 vols. (México, 1960–2), II, 168.

to the contest and reoccupied the towns. In Jojutla they took revenge by executing some fifty captives.[2] Evidently the rebels did not have the ammunition for serious campaigns. Stealing from careless federals and police and buying from the black market in Mexico City, they could raise constant uproar in guerrillas; but they could not steal, buy, or transport enough to fight regular battles. Sooner or later the federals always had more bullets to shoot.

So the fighting went on week after week. Often it was very bloody, especially around Huitzilac, which the federals shelled and burned. In late April de la O and Salazar again mobilized some four thousand men around Cuernavaca and even set up cannon to bombard the place; the city fathers wanted to surrender.[3] But the attack never happened. And no attack elsewhere settled any issue definitively in the rebels' favor. They remained masters only in the countryside, which was a social but not a political base.

Through early May the rebel chiefs' failure became clear: they had not lost the struggle, but they had not won it when their chances were best. To rebuild their caches of ammunition, Neri and Salazar suspended major campaigns and raided very seldom. De la O drifted northwest into Mexico State, also to repair his forces. And after a depressing junta the Zapatas, Montaño, Mendoza, Capistrán, and other chiefs retreated into eastern Guerrero, attacking Tlapa to capture supplies, but losing.[4] Zapata hoped that Orozco might send him arms and ammunition from the north by sea to a little port on Guerrero's Costa Chica.[5] But Orozco himself had no materiél to spare, because of the recent U.S. embargo on the shipment of war goods into Mexico, and he evidently never acknowledged Zapata's requests.[6] In late May some chiefs, though not Zapata, resumed active operations through northern and eastern Morelos. And Zapata directed letters to the Chamber of Deputies, the cabinet, and the diplomatic corps, giving notice of an attack on Mexico City "from one moment to the next."[7] But

[2] Robles to the secretary of war, April 10, 1912, AHDN. J. Refugio Velasco to the secretary of war, May 26, 1912, ibid., XI/481.5/178, 221–4. Robles to the secretary of war, April 4, 1912, ibid., 234–8; May 7, 1912, ibid., 492; May 19, 1912, ibid., 249–53, 258–63. Magaña: op. cit., II, 133–4.

[3] *El País,* April 25, 1912.

[4] Muñoz, op. cit., pp. 79–90.

[5] Zapata to Orozco, May 6, 1912, ARD, 8: 43: 17.

[6] Meyer: op. cit., pp. 70–1, 73–5, 81–2.

[7] Robles to the secretary of war, May 25, 1912, AHDN, XI/481.5/178, 513–31. Villar to the secretary of war, May 22, 1912, ibid., 533–4, 539–40. *El País,* May 25, 1912. Wilson to Madero, May 25, 1912, NA, 84: Mexico, C8, 15.

this was an idle threat. The army captain who had been selling the Morelos rebels thousands of Winchester cartridges from federal arsenals was in jail.[8] And though rebels could here and there ride into metropolitan suburbs, they could not hold their ground when rurales appeared. Besides, it was now the rainy season and time to plant, and many rebel soldiers went home to work in their fields. Trains to Cuernavaca started running roughly on schedule again.

As the violence slackened, the law-abiding party awkwardly but effectively gained the initiative in the state. Already in early May Governor Naranjo had felt sure enough of his support to send Madero a long, stern letter, asking him to restrain the rampaging General Robles. He received the testy reply that a governor should not complain when the federal executive had dictated "measures . . . opportune in a time of war"; but he did not relax the pressure.[9] In mid-May, as Orozco faltered in the north, Naranjo announced that the government would soon recover control in the south as well, which was less a military judgment than a political pretext for restoring constitutional authority. Looking forward to May 19, when the four months of martial law would end, the governor, his lieutenant, and their local allies began preparing for state elections. They maneuvered with startling speed and coordination, revealing the close connections they must have fixed among themselves by then. And on May 19, as constitutional guarantees went back in force, voting for the electoral colleges took place in all but a few municipalities. A week later the colleges elected a fairly uniform crew of reformers to the state legislature and Congress. For General Leyva, dying now in Cuernavaca, it was a final, sweet vindication.[1]

An unexpected delay passed before the state deputies actually took office, partly because authorities in Yautepec could not hold elections and probably also because Robles objected to the resumption of civilian rule. Moreover scattered rebel raids still went on, now and then disturbing rail traffic into Cuernavaca and Cuautla.[2] Nevertheless the chances for compromise seemed weekly to improve. Having assured a credulous Madero that the war would soon end, Robles was reassigned to Puebla.[3] Through the June and early July rains the rebels remained in the doldrums. Travelers coming

[8] *El País,* May 25, 1912. See also Alfonso Taracena: *La Tragedia Zapatista. Historia de la Revolución del Sur* (México, 1931), pp. 27–8.

[9] Testimony of Ramos Martínez, April 2, 1913, AZ, 27: 6.

[1] *Semanario Oficial,* XXI, 20, 1; 21, 1. Diez: *Bibliografía,* pp. cc–cci.

[2] *El País,* May 15, 17, and 19, June 28, July 5, 1912. *El Diario,* July 6, 1912.

[3] Madero to Robles, June 15, 1912, AM.

into Mexico City from Cuautla reported that the guerrilleros around there had run low on all supplies and could not keep their bands intact. At the U.S. Embassy, too, information was that the "Zapatistas [were] badly disorganized on account of many internal dissensions."[4] The new minister of the interior, Jesús Flores Magón, believed conditions were ripe for new talks with Zapata and sent a secret envoy to his camp.[5] Grave losses also for the rebels were the arrests in Mexico City of their leading agents, Gonzalo Vázquez Ortiz, Abrahám Martínez, Gildardo Magaña, and Luis Méndez. Their documents and confessions betrayed which planters were paying forced loans, where black-market arms and ammunition came from, and who were the metropolitan channels of subversion.[6] Meanwhile in Morelos Naranjo and his associates strengthened their organization and refined the program of reforms they would legislate. Finally on July 12, nearly six weeks late, and still without Yautepec represented, the deputies were sworn in. The peaceful revolutionaries were now no longer the opposition but the government.

On July 17 the new deputies convened in the state capitol, Cortés's marquisal palace, to serve out the last session of Morelos's twenty-second legislature.[7] Like the municipal presidents elected at the end of the previous year, they were almost all men of only local standing. City folk, they owned no farms, managed no plantations. Characteristically they ran the general store in their home towns; one, Eugenio Morales, was the proprietor of a little factory in Jojutla. None was notably prosperous or prominent in the state. None had taken an active part in the Maderista revolution in 1910–11. And few had official experience in politics. Morales was the savviest politician among them—a veteran of the Leyvista and the Anti-Reelectionist campaigns, and a Jojutla town councilor in 1911. Two others had had bits of training: Pedro Guzmán, the alternate deputy for Jonacatepec, had been a clerk for the jefe político there in 1904; and José D. Rojas, the deputy for Tepoztlán, had belonged to a Leyvista club.[8] The rest were thoroughly green in the intricate business of wheeling and dealing in power. Respected grocers or druggists or harness dealers at home, the new deputies were ob-

---

[4] *El País*, June 12, 1912. Schuyler to the secretary of state, June 17, 1912, NA, 59: 812.00/4232.

[5] For the envoy's interview with Zapata, see *El País*, August 7, 1912.

[6] *El País*, June 14, 15, 21, 22, 26, and 27, July 7, 16, and 17, 1912.

[7] *Semanario Oficial*, XXI, 29, 1–2.

[8] *Commercial Directory*, pp. 224–5, 268. *Semanario Oficial*, XII, 12 (Supplement), 13. *México Nuevo*, January 18, 1909. *El Imparcial*, August 22, 1913.

scurities in Cuernavaca. But they assumed authority in earnest, eager to improve the welfare of the common people they knew.

The circumstances they labored in remained tense. Cramping them from the first was the brevity of their term, which was to end on September 15. In the two months left to them when they took up their seats, they could hardly hope to pass all the new laws they wanted. Another worry was another series of elections starting on August 4, for the twenty-third legislature, the governorship, and thirteen district judgeships. For the incumbents, who had thrilled to Madero's cry against boss rule, it was an especially pointed question whether they should try for reelection. If so, they tarnished themselves as men of principle. If not, they risked the dissipation of their revolutionary spirit and the ruin of their revolutionary program. Anyway, whom should they back for governor? Should they let Naranjo stay in office during the elections and so help decide who the new governor would be? Thus immediate political concerns tightened the already close strain of legislating reform. And, most threatening, the rebels remained in arms. As Zapata told the government's secret envoy: "... the revolution in Morelos is not a local revolution ... not until Madero's downfall will we enter into peace agreements." After a lapse in operations to accumulate supplies, the rebels resumed almost daily attacks on federal outposts and troop and passenger trains. Three days after the legislature convened, de la O's rebels attacked and burned a train at Parres station, just over the state line in the mountain parks of the Federal District. There were nearly a hundred casualties, many of them civilian passengers; only thirteen of fifty-three soldiers in the escort survived. Precisely on account of this massacre, Madero called an extraordinary cabinet meeting, where Minister of the Interior Flores Magón proposed a reimposition of martial law in Morelos and various other states and a reinforcement of Robles's southern army. The rebels battled on, however. In late July Zapata and Jesús Morales seemed about to capture both Jojutla and Yautepec; the latter the federal commander almost lost from the inside when the townspeople themselves revolted against his garrison.[9]

The new deputies nevertheless gamely began preparing for their task. To secure their base they formally requested on July 23 that the federal government send more troops to the state; these they got two days later,

[9] *El Diario*, July 12, 22, and 23, 1912. *El País*, July 19, 21, 27, and 29, 1912. *Nueva Era*, July 26 and 28, 1912. Magaña, op. cit.: II, 139-41.

four hundred strong, with two sections of artillery.[1] They then resolved to dump Naranjo for an interim governor who was a native son. This was a troublesome and convoluted maneuver. Naranjo did not want to retire until he had tried out on Morelos his own program of reform: the suppression of political prefectures, the expropriation of land necessary for urban growth and roads, the repeal of the constitutional provision permitting reelection, and the organization of a regular police for the main towns.[2] Besides, to dump him was to open the contest for his post between supporters of the two rival candidates for governor in the imminent elections. The candidates, a freshly spirited Patricio Leyva and Agustín Aragón, the intellectual whom the científicos had considered in 1909 before choosing Escandón, were already campaigning hard, and both appreciated how important it would be to control the state executive office on election day. In the legislature Eugenio Morales even argued, long and energetically, for keeping Naranjo through the interim, evidently because he feared that a Tepoztlán faction that favored Aragón might win the struggle for the office if it came open. But despite their differences and the high stakes involved, the deputies arranged a felicitous deal. Taking leave of Naranjo, they named as interim governor Aniceto Villamar, a respected Tepoztlán lawyer and an associate of Aragón, and then named as his lieutenant governor Francisco Sánchez, a loyal Leyvista since 1909.[3]

Finally, in a key move, they gained for this deal and their subsequent projects the approval of the federal government. Madero in effect apologized to Patricio Leyva for the behavior of the army in Morelos and urged him henceforth to have justice done in cases of abuse. When the elections were over in a few days, he averred, "political agitators will have no pretext for continuing their anti-patriotic labor, and the pacification of the state will be carried out with relative facility."[4] Not every federal disposition was in the new legislature's behalf. On August 6, for instance, the government again decreed martial law in several states, including Morelos, to take effect on August 25 and last six months.[5] Although the decree did not suspend the new legislature, it did restore to military commanders certain

[1] *Semanario Oficial*, XXI, 31, 2. *El Diario*, July 27, 1912.

[2] *El País*, August 5, 1912.

[3] *Semanario Oficial*, XXI, 30, 5–6; 31, 1–3; 32, 3–5, 7. On Villamar and Aragón, see *El País*, March 4, 1912; on Leyva and Sánchez, see *México Nuevo*, January 18, 1909.

[4] Madero to Leyva, August 7, 1912, AM.

[5] *Nueva Era*, August 7, 1912.

liberties that could obstruct civilian authorities' attempts at reform. But generally the government was a source of help for the new deputies. Through Villamar's personal and Leyva's written representations to Madero, they gained several beneficial concessions.

Of these the most important was the recall of General Robles and the assignment of General Felipe Ángeles to command southern operations. No veteran of Indian wars, Ángeles was rather a military intellectual—a brilliant, French-trained artillery officer who had recently been appointed director of the National Military College. In Mexico City he enjoyed a glowing reputation as an officer of honor and civilization. He was also deeply ambitious, but had the political sense to advance his career subtly and always in seeming modesty. Not only would he not burn villages, he even came to Cuernavaca publicly committed to proceed "in accord with the new governor . . . in arranging pacts with the Zapatistas." Consequently, despite Zapata's rebuffs, Minister of the Interior Flores Magón created yet another channel for limiting hostilities and perhaps working out a truce. The government, he noted, was "forever most ready . . . to enter into dealings with Zapata." He discouraged private negotiations, like those the Ruiz de Velascos were trying to start with the rebels around Jojutla, but he himself sponsored Naranjo and Ramos Martínez, who were still trying as his agents to meet rebel chiefs.[6]

A further service the federal government provided was a keener surveillance of the planters who persisted in paying the rebels for protection. On August 1 federal officers even arrested three managers, at Cocoyoc, Atlihuayán, and Oacalco haciendas, for furnishing ammunition to local rebels.[7] Thus through early August the peaceable advocates of change in Morelos settled the preliminaries of their performance. And during the month, in a remarkable burst of words and gestures, they enacted their revolution.

On August 5, at the ceremony for swearing Villamar into office, the president of the new legislature introduced the drama. "Not only the so-called científicos . . . should occupy themselves with the problems of social improvement," he proclaimed, "but also the humble representatives of the people, who know them well and have felt with them all the bitterness of life." To achieve "true democracy" did not require "many years or new generations," he declared, ". . . only the good will to serve the Fatherland and to tolerate no more defaults." Praising on the one hand the "heroism" of the state's Maderista revolutionaries of 1910–11, like Zapata, he directly

[6] *El Diario,* August 4 and 7–12, 1912. *El País,* August 10 and 11, 1912.
[7] Ibid., August 2 and 3, 1912.

upheld on the other the legitimacy of the present federal government and suggested formally that Villamar appeal through the families of the rebels that they stop fighting against it. In conclusion he asked the new governor to put "all his enlightenment and talent into ruling wisely over [the state's] destinies and achieving its pacification."[8] So commenced the most radical phase in Morelos's forty-three years of legislative history.

Leading this drive was Eugenio Morales. Already he had had more political practice than the other deputies. Besides, the summer before he had been in contact with a feminist-anarchist group in Mexico City—which evidently had given him a taste for ideological forays.[9] On August 7 he proposed the first series of constitutional amendments that he and his comrades in office believed would solve the essential problem they saw in the state. Twelve articles Morales wanted to change, all to ensure local controls over the state government. In particular he wanted to reduce the powers of the executive, which Escandón had greatly expanded. Articles 16 and 60 he would reform to qualify for the governorship only citizens who really were native sons, who had not lived two consecutive years outside the state (except on official business), and who had resided in the state for the two years immediately previous to the election in which they were candidates. Articles 34 and 39 he would restore as they were before Escandón had had them changed, which would reaffirm the legislature's right to a formal report from the governor at each of its four sessions and its right to appoint state treasury and tax officials. Morales wanted to suppress altogether Articles 81, 82, and 83, and part of Article 70, to abolish prefectures and subprefectures. And Articles 23, 61, 89, and 95 he would reform to abolish the electoral colleges and institute direct elections in the state.[1]

Morales's proposals went on to the proper legislative committee, and the deputies turned their attention to new reforms. Especially agitating in these days was "our age-old agrarian question," as Madero had wearily called it. Both current candidates for governor had professed their interest in the issue. Patricio Leyva had revived his slogans of 1909 about reconstituting the villages' ejidos and water rights. And Aragón, who nurtured an increasingly populist spirit, had expounded sentiments that were almost subversive. "In Morelos," he had publicly declared, "those who follow Emiliano Zapata in good faith and without more designs than the improvement of their social condition . . . represent those who know civilization only by

[8] *Semanario Oficial,* XXI, 33, 1–6.
[9] *Diario del Hogar,* July 17, 1911.
[1] *Semanario Oficial,* XXI, 35, 1–3.

name. And it is only honest to recognize it frankly, *their longings are legitimate.* . . . if the hacendados of Morelos illegally enjoy lands and water," Aragón had vowed, ". . . I will be on the side of the Indians, with the laborers . . ."[2] In the voting of the electoral colleges on August 12 Leyva won easily in ten of eleven districts, but it remained obscure exactly what his agrarian program would be.[3] And in private the new deputies continued to debate how they could answer the questions they detected in the countryside. Not all agreed on the questions, much less the answers, but most did believe that there were real rural grievances in the state—which was, in Mexico in 1912, a revolutionary position.

The federal government kept on supporting these efforts at reform even after another railroad massacre. On August 12 at Ticumán, between Yautepec and Jojutla, a rebel band under Amador Salazar attacked a train and killed thirty-six federals and thirty civilian passengers, among them two metropolitan reporters. The wildest demands for vengeance were instantly current in Mexico City.[4] But General Ángeles refused to expand the war. And the response from the National Palace was to let officials in Cuernavaca react magnanimously, rather than compel them to start new "resettlements." Villamar issued a manifesto recognizing that the rebels were not bandits and urging them, "not as your governor but as your brother," to make peace. Then, he promised, "calm and impartial tribunals . . . and consultative juntas" would resolve "the agrarian question . . . through equitable arrangements with the landlords, who without doubt also hope for the establishment of peace." A still more vivid and deliberate sign of federal trust in the local regime was the permission it gave for the release of Zapata's family from the Cuernavaca jail. And in the cabinet Flores Magón upheld the local reformers' hopes for restoring the ejidos.[5]

The performance of the law-abiding revolutionaries in Morelos reached its climax in late August. After accepting provisionally the constitutional amendments Eugenio Morales had proposed, and passing tax laws in favor of small enterprises, urban and rural, the deputies took up the "agrarian question" directly. In their labor they brought forth three mice. On August 31, resuming his role as the chief of the revolutionary legislators, Morales

---

[2] Mateo Rojas Zúñiga: *La gobernación de Morelos de 1912 a 1916 y la opinión pública. Dos cartas acerca de la candidatura del Ingeniero Agustín Aragón* (México, 1912), pp. 14–15. His italics.

[3] *Semanario Oficial*, XXI, 36, 1. For partial returns, see *El Diario*, August 13, 1912.

[4] *El País*, August 13, 1912. *El Diario*, August 17, 1912.

[5] *El Diario*, August 18, 25, and 28, 1912. *El País*, August 28, 1912.

recommended a 10 per cent increase in taxes on the haciendas. His motive, as he explained it, was not to press planters into selling marginal lands to needy farmers but simply to raise revenue for municipal governments. Another proposed solution to the agrarian problem came from the deputy representing the district around Tetecala, Antonio Sámano. His idea was that, "by the measures which are due legal procedure," the state acquire as public domain the market places on various haciendas. This proposal earned a eulogy from Morales, who stressed that it would "redound to the good of the pueblos and the benefit of free trade." Finally, another emboldened deputy moved for the foundation of a state college of agriculture and mechanics. All three proposals were formally approved, and filed for consideration by the next legislature. Evidently exhausted, the deputies adjourned.[6] So ended the session that had been the most radical in Morelos's legislative history.

Meanwhile a clear calm had matured in the field, less because of the speeches in the Cortés's palace than because of the political maneuvers of Villamar, Ángeles, Naranjo, and Ramos Martínez. To rebel chief and rebel trooper alike they appealed, publicly and privately. And though no chief amnestied himself, many guerrilleros did quietly return to their villages and ranchos. And as they suffered no federal harassment, many of their companions followed their example. After the fiery terror of Robles's campaign, country families now became loyal out of sheer gratitude—like Zapata's mother-in-law, who wrote to thank Ramos Martínez that "my girls don't cry any more."[7] Ángeles waxed intensely proud of this diplomatic success. To reporters he decried the "inexpressible lack of tact" which had earlier led to the burning of "innumerable pueblos" and given villagers "more than enough reason . . . to consider the federal forces and police as their greatest enemies." In contrast he boasted that through his application of "reason and justice . . . there was no revolution here in the South," that he had transformed a campaign "for a military commander" into a campaign "for a chief of police." And in fact, although Generals Huerta, Robles, and Casso López tried to have him court-martialed for these broadcast remarks, Ángeles had described conditions in Morelos with fair accuracy.[8]

Not only had villagers now stopped joining the rebellion, they had even

[6] *Semanario Oficial,* XXI, 36, 2–7.

[7] Felicitas and Guadalupe Sánchez V. de Espejo to Ramos Martínez, September 22, 1912, AZ, 28: 12.

[8] *Nueva Era,* August 24 and 25, 1912. *El Diario,* August 24 and 29, 1912. *El País,* September 1, 2, 7, and 8, 1912.

started asking rebel chiefs not to camp in their vicinity. And the chiefs, to avoid antagonizing their base but remain in revolt, had to move into other states, de la O shifting his operations into Mexico State in late August and the Zapatas and Mendoza shifting theirs into Puebla. In early September Zapata tried to organize a coordinated movement against Mexico City, to disrupt the official celebration of the national holidays in mid-month, but despite hard attacks around Tetecala and Jonacatepec, the plan fell through.[9] Only small bands of outlaws were left in Morelos, and it seems that many of these actually were bandits, as Ángeles claimed, not rebels. No large battles developed anywhere in the state. The skirmishes that went on normally involved federals and rurales only as companies.

Thus, when the twenty-third legislature convened on September 16, the peaceable revolutionaries exercised extraordinary authority in the state, socially as well as politically. Had they elaborated and amplified the reforms already presented, they might have established themselves as the legitimate rulers in Morelos, and the rebel chiefs would have had to quit the fight there, to surrender or to hunt a following elsewhere. Two years later both Zapata and de la O would recall this as the time when they had been most uncertain about ultimately winning.[1]

What ensued in this legislature, however, was less reform than argument that reform was impossible. From the previous legislature only two deputies returned to their seats, two eminently inconspicuous souls.[2] And the other deputies now coming into office were revolutionaries distinctly more conservative than their predecessors. Only one, Octaviano Gutiérrez, had been a prominent Leyvista in 1909. The rest were more sober figures, sympathetic to protests against injustice but too aware of the attendant risks to venture into action. Among them were politicos already accomplished in Cuernavaca dealings, like Leopoldo Fandiño, an attorney for the Alonso family, who had served in the Cortés palace from 1904 to 1908, or Juan Alarcón, who had been there from 1906 to 1910. Others like young Domingo Diez came from the state's "best families." Still others like Benito Tajonar and Lauro Arellano had had long experience in municipal government.[3]

---

[9] Ibid., September 2, 1912. *El Diario,* September 3, 1912. Muñoz: op. cit., pp. 112–16. Ángeles to the secretary of war, September 7, 1912, AHDN, XI/481.5/178, 950–1. Ocaranza to the Cuautla chief of line, September 17, 1912, ibid., 980–93, 995–1000.

[1] Díaz Soto y Gama: *La revolución,* p. 119.

[2] For the roster, see *Semanario Oficial,* XXI, 36, 1.

[3] Ibid., XII, 33, 1; XV, 32, 1; XVII, 32, 1; 6, 3–4; XIX, 50, 7. *Memoria* (1890).

Besides, several like Arellano were regular men of means, not hick-town general-store proprietors but upstanding merchants from busy market towns. And at least two were thriving commercial farmers—León Castresana, who owned an eight-hundred-acre rice plantation near Jojutla, and his alternate, Isaac Flores, who had a rice plantation of nine hundred acres.[4] In Cuernavaca these swells felt in their element. As the previous deputies had yearned to become the champions of popular change, these new deputies yearned to become the guardians of civil order. With a full two years in which to make their reputations, and the prospect then of promotion to federal deputy or even senator, they quickly assumed the role of challenged statesmen.

The issue that excited them most was the suppression of the rebellion, which was already decomposing. To aid in the effort they acquiesced in various military suspensions of civil rights. And in mid-October they made their concern official policy. Querying the lieutenant governor on whether he had used state funds to bribe rebel chiefs to surrender, they suddenly blasted the federal government's version that violence had almost ended in Morelos. Tajonar especially harped on "the alarm which exists among the inhabitants of Cuernavaca because of the . . . reduced garrison" there. At his insistence the legislature appealed to Congress for "due protection against the daily more notable advance of the revolt." Diez too joined in this public profession of responsibility, urging a study of "the way to prepare for the defense of society." Evidently, after an embarrassing exposure in the metropolitan press, Governor Villamar stopped sending pleas to rebel chiefs to accept amnesty. And other secret emissaries slacked off in their probings. In early November the legislature appealed again for "help" in restoring "security" in Morelos.[5] Eventually the constant pressure had its effect. In late November a new, conservative minister of the interior revoked Ramos Martínez's commission to deal with the rebels and ordered him "to render accounts immediately and to come inform this capital."[6] And Governor Villamar began notifying the new minister every few days of rebel movements, or the lack of them. Governor Leyva maintained this service, after taking office on December 1, at an almost daily rate into 1913.[7]

[4] Southworth: op. cit., p. 218.
[5] *El País*, October 29, November 9 and 24, 1912. *Semanario Oficial*, XXI, 42, 3–6; 43, 4.
[6] R. L. Hernández to Ramos Martínez, November 30, 1912, AGN, G: 889.
[7] For this exchange, including twenty-nine communications between November 29, 1912, and January 7, 1913, see ibid. See also *El País*, November 23 and 26, 1912.

The pending proposals for reform had gained no such devotion. The new deputies first consigned them to special committees "for study and opinion." Like the new minister of the interior, they believed that "impatience" reflected lack of civic virtue, that "every evolution, every project, needs scrupulous study, in order that we not make a mistake and have to regret it."[8] But when they finally started receiving the committee's reports, they remained quite indifferent to the "problems of social improvement" that their predecessors had wanted to solve. On October 17 in a secret vote they unanimously voted down the bill authorizing the state to acquire hacienda market places. When the bill for the agricultural and mechanical college came up, they voted it down too. And on October 22 they postponed indefinitely the vote on Morales's bill to raise plantation taxes. Not until November 8, six weeks after convening, did they consider Morales's proposed amendments to the constitution. Of the twelve they voted down the five that were the most democratic in promise, the one on citizenship and the four on direct elections. The others they approved, with minor additions and clarifications, to strengthen their own legislative control over state politics.[9]

From these gentlemen came only two proposals for reform.[1] One was in defense of certain villages, a bill that Diez introduced on December 10. His idea was to prohibit "the exploitation of woodlands on a grand scale" in Morelos and to assure that "those same woodlands will be exploited individually by the residents of the pueblos which own them." The main beneficiaries were obviously to be Santa María and surrounding villages, where many families depended on local stands of timber to make the charcoal they peddled.

Various deputies supported Diez's project. And the times did seem propitious for its enactment. In Mexico City a presidential commission had published its report advising restoration of village lands, a reformist had been appointed minister of public works to consider agrarian problems, and six different bills had come up in the new Congress for popular changes in rural life. The most impressive bill, which the brilliant Luis Cabrera had introduced on December 3, was for "the reconstitution of the ejidos."[2] Discussions unthinkable before were raging in the federal government—radi-

[8] Ibid., October 8, 1912.

[9] *Semanario Oficial*, XXI, 38, 1; 49, 2; 43, 3, 5.

[1] Ibid., XXI, 51, 2–4; 52, 2–3.

[2] For the commission's report and the bills, see Silva Herzog: op. cit., II, 163–310. For the new minister, see González Roa: op. cit., pp. 223–5.

cal discussions not of whether but of how to defend the nation's country poor against capitalist entrepreneurs. In states like Aguascalientes and Guanajuato agrarian reforms were already underway. And in Cuernavaca Governor Leyva had stated his own sympathies for the movement at his inaugural speech on December 1: "The reconstruction of the ejidos contains the whole problem which presently agitates this rich region. It is not true ... that the Zapatistas seek a redistribution of lands [sic]. Their desire—and I believe," he noted, "that they have a right to demand it—is the reconstitution of the ejidos, that the small holdings which were confiscated from them be returned." This act of justice, he concluded, ". . . will bring back to agriculture many who today have the character of revolutionaries."[3] Since the woodlands bill Diez now advocated was not even a restitution but only a limited protection of resources in the future, and moreover did not affect the sugar plantations, its passage should have been easy.

But it failed, largely because Governor Leyva opposed it. The bill was unconstitutional, Leyva argued, for the deputies had no power to legislate on communal property. Diez was shocked. "We have before us one of the causes of the present revolution . . . ," he declared. "If we don't go to the aid of the inhabitants of the pueblos and [instead] leave them exposed to the abuses of contractors, we'll never see our desires for the reestablishment of peace realized. . . . We have two paths, to protect the contractor . . . or to protect the inhabitant of a village possessing its woodland." Other deputies had their excuses ready, however. As one explained, he wanted to promote the welfare of the pueblos too, but it was necessary "to attend to the reasons of the executive." By six to five the legislature voted to postpone consideration of the bill until the next session. Diez made no further protest. He had already excused himself in concluding the defense of his bill: "If the project is thrown out, my conscience will be clear. I will have done what I humanly can do."

The other reform proposed in this legislature was in a bill that Fandiño introduced on December 13, to reduce taxes for those who had suffered losses in the 1910–11 revolution. Here the obvious beneficiaries would be the planters who had paid forced loans and not been repaid, and the merchants in Jojutla and Cuautla whose stores had been sacked. The next day by a vote of nine to two the legislature approved the project, expanding its coverage to those who had suffered losses from 1910 to the present date.

Thus in their own eyes Leyva and his lawful revolutionaries proved what a worthy government they were. To them, as Diez later indicated, it

[3] Cited in Magaña: op. cit., II, 200–1.

seemed a titanic victory simply to have "normalized" constitutional procedures.[4] Now, they believed, they had years to work out the answer to other, social questions. Not politics but logic was the source of the solutions they wanted, and as rational men in pursuit of the truth they could not, they reasoned, go finally wrong. Although Madero did not share their view on ejidos, for instance, his new public works minister did; and when the legislature closed, Leyva sent Tajonar to the minister, not to arrange a deal to press indulgence from Madero but to consult the maps and deeds registered in the minister's files and over time to frame a case to persuade the President.[5] In Cuernavaca the sense of hope was pervasive. The city's Christmas festival took place that year in the old Porfirio Díaz Theater, the biggest building in town. "That happy night," Mrs. King later remembered, "when all thought of war was pushed outside the circle of light, and soldiers and townspeople yielded to joy!"[6]

In the countryside, however, feelings were less jubilant. There the denial and postponements of reforms did not seem proof of political talent or wisdom but signs of another betrayal. The excuse that introducing and defending a bill in the legislature was "what I humanly can do" rang hollow to village leaders who had risked their lives in persuading rebel chiefs to operate elsewhere. To farmers who had laid down their arms in hopes of recovering their land in peace, it was incredible that only a study of their misery was now possible. In Cuernavaca the law-abiding revolutionaries might well have consolidated the political authority they had assumed there in September, but in the villages they had wasted the popular, social authority that they had also inherited.

This was a dangerous forfeiture, because the rebel chiefs could now reclaim local loyalties. Through the whole parliamentary performance, they had remained in action. It was not automatic that they should all have carried on the fight, and it is still not clear why they all did. In early October Zapata himself had been ready to confer with Ramos Martínez in Jolalpan.[7] It may be, as contemporary analysts reported, that he would have entered a provisional truce but that de la O and Salazar, who had massacres on their records, refused to go along.[8] Anyway, no truce came about—which

[4] Diez: *Bibliografía,* pp. ccii–cciii.

[5] Manuel Bonilla, Jr.: *El régimen maderista* (2nd edn., México, 1962), pp. 113, 215–16.

[6] King: op. cit., p. 105.

[7] Eufemio Zapata to Ramos Martínez, n.d. (October 1–3, 1912?), AZ, 27:16.

[8] *El País,* September 29 and 30, October 1, 3, 5, 6, and 13, 1912.

was what counted. In mid-October a short-lived military uprising in support of Don Porfirio's nephew Félix Díaz took place in Veracruz, reducing garrisons and dividing officers in Morelos; and rebel chiefs started shifting operations back into the state. As hope in the official revolution soured in the villages, Zapata and his allies again became popular figures there, manifest in their stubborn revolt as the tried and true champions of the people.

They soon flourished militarily too. They were shrewder generals now, and they devised a new strategy neatly fitting their movement in Morelos. The central plan was to charge the main cost of their campaigns not to the pueblos but to the plantations. At a junta in San Pablo Hidalgo on November 1 the Zapatas, Mendoza, Montaño, Salazar, and Neri agreed on the fiscal details. Levying a weekly tax on each hacienda in Morelos and southwestern Puebla, they allotted the various zones of collection among themselves and sent circulars to the planters about the ruling. If a planter would not pay, the responsible chief was to burn his cane fields. Various planters did not pay. And by early January the rebels had burned fields at Atlihuayán, Chinameca, Tenango, Treinta, Santa Inés, San José, and San Gabriel, inflicting losses on the planters alone of over two million pesos. But off and on some planters did pay the tax, providing the rebels irregular but still large and welcome income.[9] Thus the rebels not only saved their reputation in the villages but also earned more revenue.

Tactical opportunities also derived from the new strategy, because rebel chiefs no longer had to depend on the villages even for their manpower. In destroying cane fields, they destroyed the jobs many resident and occasional plantation workers would have had during the harvest, and so opened up for themselves new pools of potential recruits. Chiefs like de la O and Mendoza, whose regulars had declined to one hundred or one hundred fifty in September, mobilized marching forces through January of five hundred to one thousand.[1] They could now plan more ambitious operations than a

[9] Muñoz: op. cit., pp. 126–7. *El País,* October 30, November 12–15, 1912, and January 4, 1913. Mendoza to the Tenango manager, January 16, 1913, and to the Tenango representative, January 19, 1913, AGP.

[1] Muñoz: op. cit., pp. 120, 143. *El País,* January 21, 1913. There is no documentary or circumstantial evidence that the Zapatistas pledged their support to Francisco Vázquez Gómez in these weeks, as the Vazquistas claimed. On a Manifesto of San Blas, dated December 15, 1912, and proposing Vázquez Gómez for provisional president, there is the signature of "Major General of the Southern Army Emiliano Zapata." See United States Senate: *Revolutions in Mexico. Hearing before a subcommittee of the Committee on Foreign Relations,* 62 Cong., 2 sess. (Washington, 1913), pp. 871–6. But this subscription seems a forgery, at least a proxy's commitment without warrant.

raid or an ambush; major coordinated attacks were again possible. And although he discriminated more carefully than Huerta or Robles, Ángeles too resorted to bombarding and burning suspect villages and executing captives en masse. The forces he sent out were no longer patrols but expeditionary columns of eight hundred to twelve hundred troops.[2]

Embarrassing political uproars resulted from this rebel recovery in the countryside. Each new field on fire was a disgrace for the federal government. The minister of the interior would not let the planters pay off the rebels, and even jailed Escandón and his manager briefly for buying protection; but neither he nor the minister of war could muster forces to prevent the burnings. The planters were in a desperate fury, "between the sword and the wall," as their friends on El País put it. In mid-November they offered to pay the federal government a special tax for the organization of a special rural police, in vain. The burning of fields continued into the new year. By late January over half the state's already picayune production had gone up in flames.[3] "I'm making it plain to you," Felipe Ruiz de Velasco wrote to the minister of the interior, "that the situation is intolerable . . ."[4]

Even so the government in Cuernavaca was in no grave danger. Internally the party of lawful revolution was sound, its members confident and its leaders secure. Despite the rebels' rural success, neither Cuernavaca nor any other important town was about to fall. True, without the favor of their powerful patrons in Mexico City the local revolutionaries in office would have no ground to stand on. But in early February, despite continued wrangling in the federal capital, it seemed unlikely that the favor would cease. It seemed less likely still that the patrons themselves would disappear.

[2] El País, January 19 and 26, 1913. Nueva Era, January 23, 1913. Ángeles to the secretary of war, December 6, 1912, AHDN, XI/481.5/178, 1398–1407, 1417, 1568–9.

[3] El País, November 12 and 15, 1912, January 14, 24, and 26, 1913. Nueva Era, January 10, 1913.

[4] Hernández to the Jojutla commander, January 6, 1913, AGN, G: 889.

Refugees Win a War

"*. . . everything that signifies law,*
justice, rights, and morals . . ."

B EFORE DAWN ON FEBRUARY 9, 1913, a barracks revolt broke out in Mexico
City. Led by General Manuel Mondragón, the rebel troops released
General Reyes and Félix Díaz from prisons where they had been consigned
for their earlier rebellions, and tried to install them in power in the National
Palace. By noon loyal troops had practically put down the mutiny. General
Reyes had been shot to death in the fighting at the Zócalo; Mondragón and
Díaz had holed up in an old armory-fortress a few blocks southwest of the
Alameda, apparently doomed. But in the morning's battle the regular commander of the capital's garrison had suffered a wound, and President Madero had appointed a new commander––General Victoriano Huerta. And
in the following days, with the connivance of the American ambassador,
Huerta secretly arranged with Díaz and Mondragón for their revolt to
succeed. While the negotiations went on, a sham artillery duel devastated
much of the city's downtown and killed hundreds of innocent civilians.
This was the mournful Decena Trágica, the Ten Tragic Days. When the
cannons finally quieted on February 19, Madero and his Vice President
had resigned, and Huerta, his hero Reyes now dead, emerged as a caretaker

president; and there was a new, Felicista cabinet. Three days later Madero and the former Vice President were assassinated.

It briefly appeared that Huerta, Félix Díaz, and the Reyistas would achieve a stable coalition by which they could restore the old lines of progress—or better still, without the canny and sometimes refractory Don Porfirio, institute an even more efficient rule. But they were disastrously mistaken about their own capacities and their common compatriots' longings. The awful public drama of Huerta's betrayal and Madero's murder shook the country to the very roots, giving rise to passions and impulses and organizations more radical than any since the crusade for Independence a hundred years before. Huerta never even established as much order as Madero had maintained. Instead he aggravated turmoil into a terrible crisis, and Mexico moved into a profound social revolution.

In Morelos, as elsewhere, the process began in confusion. Among the revolutionaries in office it worked in especially tortuous ways. Telegraph reports of the revolt reached Cuernavaca almost immediately, as did Madero himself, who came to confer with Governor Leyva and General Ángeles.[1] And at first the local authorities backed the President. Madero felt so sure of the state that after he returned to Mexico City the next day he ordered Ángeles to follow him, bringing two thousand troops along. But as the violence in the national capital continued and seditious agents came down to suborn the remaining garrisons, local suspense mounted. And when the coup succeeded, Leyva and his fellows were on tenterhooks. In the dreadful assassinations they could read the end of their own careers and hopes for political and social reform. On Leyva's advice the legislature voted not to congratulate Huerta and Félix Díaz. But Huerta was supposed to be only a temporary figure, and according to most informed opinions, enlightened civilians were soon to take over the government again. In the end it seemed wiser for the revolutionaries in office to keep their peace and their place; later they could help reorganize a national movement for reform. Soon Leyva and most other Morelos politicans resignedly declared themselves Felicistas. On March 5 the legislature voted its "adhesion to the new government."[2]

Other official elements in the state vitiated this resolution, however. Several federal police corps of northern Maderista origins would not accept the

[1] Bonilla: op. cit., pp. 173-4. King: op. cit., pp. 107-11. Mrs. King says that Madero stayed in her hotel while in Cuernavaca, and that she was asked to fly the British flag for his protection—which she did.

[2] *El País*, March 7 and 13, 1913.

new regime. And several others also now in opposition in the Federal District fled into Morelos to join their dissident comrades. Besides, municipal authorities began treating with local rebels.[3]

Among the revolutionaries in the field, confusion was also current. Most remained in action during the Decena Trágica and gained much ground. But it was unclear in whose name the gains were. The local rebels' defiance was not in defense of the falling government. Although rumors circulated that Zapata and de la O had decreed a provisional armistice to aid the loyalists, and although some observers even believed that Zapata was offering sanctuary to Madero, there was evidently no such deal, not even an attempt at one.[4] For in those tense days the chiefs met in no junta to make the decision. Probably the rebels refrained from attacks only to let the thousands of federal forces in the state withdraw to Puebla and Mexico City, whereupon they moved into the evacuated towns and haciendas. So when Huerta took office, many rebels wondered whether they should recognize the new government.

Most leading chiefs were in no doubt about the stand they should take. They remained as belligerent as before, because they considered Huerta and the Felicistas as illegitimately in power as Madero had been, and even more treacherous and cruel than him. The Zapatas and de la O knew Huerta well, they knew his minister of foreign relations and acting vice president, de la Barra, and they knew his minister of the interior, Alberto García Granados. From these familiar antagonists they expected no understanding. To de la O, who had received invitations from Mexico City to "confer," Zapata sent instructions on February 27 to "take your precautions . . . and attack the enemy as often as he presents himself." On March 2 he, Mendoza, Vázquez, and several others formally notified Huerta that their rebellion would go on. On March 4 they similarly protested to Félix Díaz "against the imposition of the illegal government of General Huerta."[5]

But there were serious defections. In Izúcar de Matamoros, which they had occupied, Jesús Morales and Otilio Montaño gleefully celebrated the victorious coup. Montaño soon repented, but Morales, then the third- or fourth-ranking rebel general, even came to terms with Huerta's agents and went on to Mexico City announcing to all in range that Zapata and the other

[3] Jesús Romero Flores: *Historia de la Revolución en Michoacán* (México, 1964), pp. 83–4. Magaña: op. cit., II, 267–72.

[4] For these legends, see for example Bonilla: op. cit., pp. 215–16.

[5] Muñoz: op. cit., pp. 146–57. De la O in *Impacto*, January 21, 1950. Magaña: op. cit., III, 25, 90–2.

chiefs would soon lay down their arms too.[6] Various lesser chiefs, like Simón Beltrán, Joaquín Miranda, and his sons Alfonso and Joaquín, Jr., likewise came to terms.[7] So did the ex-Zapatista José Trinidad Ruiz, who had been carrying on an independent rebellion. Others leaned in the same direction. They leaned harder when they learned that in Chihuahua Pascual Orozco had accepted a remarkably generous deal and recognized Huerta; since Orozco still figured as the national chief in the Plan de Ayala, they had good reason to follow suit.[8] It seemed significant that the Morelos rebels started no grand offensive. Having occupied Jonacatepec, Tlaltizapán, Yautepec, Tepoztlán, Tetecala, and many other towns, they were now an entrenched power in the state. But their strength was in their union, which no one could take for granted.

Adding to the uncertainties of Morelos were agents working at cross purposes to end the local rebellion. In pursuit of peace, for instance, Felicista representatives swarmed around the state angling to deal with individual chiefs. The minister of war asked the bishop of Cuernavaca to help in the "speedy pacification of the country" and commissioned a priest to treat with de la O. Pascual Orozco, Sr., representing his famous son, came directly to Zapata's headquarters. But when Leyva or local politicans tried similar negotiations, the Felicistas accused them of "official Zapatismo," of plotting an allied resistance with the rebels. And President Huerta meanwhile remained contemptuous of any compromise. He reappointed Juvencio Robles military commander in Cuernavaca, which recalled how "with an iron hand and disdaining womanish contemplations" Robles had fought the rebels before. And when, as if in reprisal, rebels attacked a military train on the way to Cuernavaca and killed seventy-five federals, Huerta declared martial law again through the south.[9] In contingency he planned to deport fifteen thousand to twenty thousand laborers from Morelos to Quintana Roo and bring in replacements from other states. As he confided to the U.S. ambassador, the new laborers "may not be as efficient at first to perform the work required by landowners in Morelos, but they will at least be ignorant of the roads and trails of the state . . . and less apt to be tempted by promises from Zapata." The "best means to handle" the rebel chiefs,

[6] *El País,* February 27, March 5 and 6, 1913.

[7] Ibid., February 24, 1913. Magaña: op. cit., III, 87–8.

[8] Meyer: op. cit., pp. 97–8.

[9] Magaña: op. cit., III, 92–3, 100–1, 106–7, 144, 158–9. *El País,* March 2–5, 8, 9, 13, 20, 23, 26, and 27, 1913.

he later told the ambassador, "is an 18 cents rope wherefrom to hang them."[1] Still, in restraint, he did not yet have Robles take up his assignment.

In this discord and contradiction not even the planters, now in official favor again, could agree on the theme of their advice to the government. Some, like Corona, Araoz, and Escandón, who had not set foot in the state since 1911, advocated the harsh vigor of Robles as the firmest guarantee of security. And they lobbied constantly to ensure that his appointment would be effective, that he would bring abundant forces, and that once in Morelos, he would stay. Others, like the Amors and the García Pimentels, deplored the policy of terror and urged diplomatic arrangements. Among the state's planters, only the two young García Pimentels, Luis, Jr., and Joaquín, had personally witnessed the grief and destruction Robles had earlier caused, and only they discerned that in attacking villagers as rebels he had created rebels. Robles's "procedures," young Luis decided, were "not only stupid but completely counterproductive and odious." But he and Joaquín could not prevail upon their colleagues in the industry. As a class in crisis, the planters could not rally. Although they had been school chums abroad and had become Jockey Club cronies, polo teammates, business partners, even in-laws, they now could summon no spirit of solidarity. In doubt, each maneuvered for himself. The result was that they contributed to the disorder of their state and to their own ruin.[2]

Through March and into April a crude and uneasy coexistence persisted in Morelos. Politically no contests broke out: Leyva, who was suspected of disloyalty to the new regime, left the governorship to take a safer, less conspicuous seat in Congress; and his local partisans duly formed their Felicista clubs. No federal reinforcements arrived to reclaim the towns the rebels held, for at the moment Huerta had turned his attention instead to the north—to the powerful states of Coahuila, Chihuahua, and Sonora—where popular leaders and dissident governors were organizing a much more formidable resistance to his regime. And the rebels themselves halted serious violence to let the few plantations still in business finish harvesting and milling, so they could later tax the product. Hostile gestures continued of course, like Zapata's public letters to Orozco and Huerta condemning their "mercantile transaction . . . to assassinate the Revolution." The most spectacular gesture was Zapata's arrest of various peace commissioners, including the

[1] Wilson to the secretary of state, March 14 and April 1, 1913, NA, 59: 812.00/6849 and 7101.

[2] L. García Pimentel: op. cit., pp. 2, 5–7. *El País,* March 15, 1913.

Orozco party, and his subjection of them to show trials. Well into April the trials of these hostages lasted, to emphasize to Mexico City and to wavering rebel chiefs the principles of the Ayalan opposition. Here and there rebel patrols actually skirmished with small army and police detachments. But no regular military operations developed. As Minister of the Interior García Granados complained, Zapata and his chiefs were buying time, watching how the northern resistance went.[3]

By mid-April, however, crucial decisions were at issue in Mexico City. In the north Governor Carranza of Coahuila had published his Plan de Guadalupe, formally founding a national "Constitutionalist" movement to oust Huerta and arrange legitimate succession to Madero. And in the United States the newly elected President Woodrow Wilson gave no sign that he would recognize de jure a government that was not even de facto. Huerta decided to crack down everywhere he could. To Morelos, finally, he sent his trusty General Robles. He thus plunged the state into a chaos from which it would emerge in fundamental and irrevocable change.

The governor in Cuernavaca when Robles arrived on April 14 was Leyva's right-hand man, Benito Tajonar. The next day, the day before the legislature was to convene in its second session, Robles informed Tajonar that he had "final orders" from Huerta to have himself named governor. Tajonar refused: the legislature had to consent. And the deputies agreed that Robles was constitutionally ineligible because he was not a native of the state. Precisely to prevent such impositions they had amended the constitution in their previous session.

The next day Tajonar addressed the legislature as it convened. ". . . only God with his power," he declared in a veiled reference to Robles's demand, "will make me turn over the command which the people have conferred on me."[4] The legislature's president, Leopoldo Fandiño, answered the address and expressed the deputies' endorsement of Tajonar, "who never," he said, "would consent to the violation of the state's sovereignty . . ."[5] The only persons in the hall not applauding were several military officers.

[3] Ibid., March 7, April 4, 10, and 11, 1913. Zapata's letters are cited in Magaña: op. cit., III, 130–7. For the show trial records, see Palafox's charges against Ramos Martínez, March 21, his charges against the Orozco commission, March 27, and Minutes of Conferences, March 30, April 1, 2, 4, and 10, 1913, all in AZ, 27: 6.

[4] Diez: *Bibliografía,* p. ccv.

[5] Cited in [Jan Leander DeBekker:] *De cómo vino Huerta y cómo se fue* (México, 1914), pp. 280–1. *El País,* April 17, 1913.

The deputies then adjourned. That evening, with Tajonar and other Leyvista leaders in Cuernavaca, they prepared to move the government the next day into the mountains northwest of the city—where they must have believed de la O would give them refuge.[6] But Robles had already reported the legislature's proceedings to Huerta; and in the middle of the night, before the conspirators could escape, he had them all arrested on Huerta's orders. Under military guard they were immediately packed off to the Mexico City penitentiary. Other Leyvistas still free, like Antonio Sedano, fled into hiding in the metropolis. Thus the party of lawful reform in Morelos disappeared.

Robles then took over the state capital. Later in the morning he assembled Cuernavaca's Escandonista dregs and declared he had suppressed the legislature's rebellion. On the excuse that Leyva's being sworn in as a federal deputy had left the state no government, he would hold civil authority as well as military, he informed them, until the Senate named a new governor.[7] No official challenged him, and a month later, despite individual protests, the Senate voted overwhelmingly to ratify President Huerta's choice for interim governor—General Robles.[8]

For the desperate planters the institution of this dictatorship was an ugly but nevertheless hopeful move. Like the editors of *El País,* they believed that Morelos now needed "a strong government, of military character, capable of reestablishing order." And on April 21 they treated Huerta to a grand banquet at the Jockey Club. The speech they heard was frank, and shocking. A federal campaign would start the next day in Morelos, Huerta announced, and he asked the planters, "the favored of fortune," to support him "without reserve, making a sacrifice of the properties you own in the state . . . because the lives of our brothers and our own interests are at stake." To assure success, he warned, he would have "recourse . . . to extreme measures, for the government is going, so to speak, to depopulate the state, and will send to your haciendas other workers . . ." The reason, he explained, was that country people in Morelos were "all Zapatistas. . . . It is necessary to clean out all such [types], and you must not be surprised," he concluded, "if perchance something abnormal happens, for the state of things demands procedures that are not sanctioned by law but which are

[6] Diez: *Bibliografía,* p. ccvi.

[7] DeBekker: op. cit., pp. 282–3. Sedano: op. cit., p. 22. *El País,* April 18, 1913.

[8] *El Imparcial,* May 11 and 15, 1913. Among the protesters was Morelos's own senator, José Diego Fernández.

indispensable for the national welfare." But it was also a promising speech: within a month, Huerta affirmed, he would "establish complete peace."[9] Accordingly they responded with warm offers to organize "volunteer corps" at their own expense, to garrison the haciendas and free the federal troops to pursue "the bandits."[1]

The planters' new hopes were in vain, however. The announced campaign did not start. Worse, what Huerta had done in declaring war on the state's rural population was simply to swell the rebels' ranks, to bind together a previously fragmented opposition, and to drive the whole force of resistance under the command of Zapata. Partly because the metropolitan press had consistently portrayed Zapata as the peerless master of revolt everywhere in the south, and partly because in fact he was the first chief of a definite, uncompromising movement in Morelos, Zapata was the natural resort of locals in distress. As other, baffled chiefs now looked to him for a lead, so too refugee villagers and rancheros and frightened peons turned to him for orders.

And these they received, in organized form. Zapata's headquarters was no longer the casual collection of temporary secretaries and passing aides that it had been a year before. Now in professional control of rebel business was a new director, Manuel Palafox. While other secretaries, arrested on missions, languished in the Mexico City penitentiary, and while Montaño neglected administration to become a hero of arms as well as letters, Palafox had quietly and gradually emerged as the rebels' major domo. Earlier experiences had trained him nicely for the post. A onetime engineering student in Puebla City, his home town, he had worked as a salesman and accountant for companies in various parts of the Republic, from Oaxaca to Sinaloa. There he had learned the finer points of hustling, precision, thoroughness, and scheming. Palafox had first met Zapata in October 1911, when as an employee on Tenango plantation he had delivered the offer of a bribe to the rebel camp; Zapata had almost had him shot then. But later Zapata had released him on a mission to Emilio Vázquez in San Antonio, and after he returned Zapata had grown increasingly dependent on his managerial talents—perhaps on his political counsels too.[2] In prosecuting

[9] *Mexican Herald,* April 23, 1913.

[1] *El Independiente,* April 26, 1913.

[2] E. Marmolejo to Palafox, December 3, 1918, AZ, 30: 19, and December 25, 1918, AZ, 27: 13. Marte R. Gómez: "Notas sobre el Gral. Manuel Palafox" (MS, 1966). I was able to consult this manuscript thanks to the generosity of its author, who intends to incorporate it into a forthcoming study, "Galería de Secretarios de Agricultura de México."

the case against the peace commissions in the recent show trials, Palafox had consolidated his position in the headquarters. Short, spindly, pock-marked, he was now only twenty-six, but in him throbbed an ambitious energy so intense that he could impose a regular system even in the hectic affairs of his chief's office. As he coordinated plans and dispatched instructions, rebel operations went on in clearer patterns.

Early in the morning of the day after Robles seized power in Cuernavaca, Zapata began a major attack on Jonacatepec. Garrisoned by nearly five hundred troops under the command of General Higinio Aguilar, the town held out for thirty-six hours before falling. It was just the kind of victory the rebels wanted. The booty was immense: 330 Maussers, 310 horses and saddles, two machine guns with ammunition—as well as General Aguilar himself, 47 other officers, and the surviving troops. Aguilar and all his men were brought to rebel headquarters in Tepalcingo. For propaganda purposes Zapata pardoned them on the condition that they not fight again against the revolution.[3] Aguilar was astounded. An experienced old crook, he saw he could play both sides. Out of gratitude and greed he joined Zapata and lent the rebels his valuable professional military training. More importantly, he provided a go-between for Zapatista purchases of arms and ammunition from corrupt federal officers.

The rebel offensive continued. On April 23 Zapata laid siege to Cuautla. On May 1 rebels blew up a military train in a station on the Mexico-Morelos border: almost one hundred soldiers died. After May 5 constant attacks took place around Cuernavaca.[4]

Against this challenge Huerta could hardly delay action any longer. But with a distinct threat building in the north in the Constitutionalist movement, he could also hardly tolerate a protracted diversion of five thousand to eight thousand troops in the south. The conscripts he had been drafting in Morelos for service elsewhere were too few to make up for a massive military commitment in the state. The escape Huerta devised from this dilemma was ingenious and characteristically bold and brutal. On the one hand he took the risk of temporarily increasing Robles's forces to about five thousand. And on May 9 Robles officially resumed his favorite procedure, "resettlement." Within a week, he decreed, all inhabitants of pueblos, ranchos, and smaller hamlets had to "reconcentrate" in the closest district seat, or in one of a few other major towns. Pueblos suspected as "nests of bandits" would be burned and razed; and anyone caught in the

[3] Magaña: op. cit., III, 160–1. Muñoz: op. cit., pp. 165–9.
[4] *El País*, April 24, 1913. *El Imparcial*, May 3, 1913. Magaña: op. cit., III, 178–9.

countryside without a license would be summarily tried and executed. On the other hand, to compensate in the north for the troops thus occupied in Morelos, Huerta authorized a huge increase in the local draft. The increase was possible because Robles was to take his conscripts from among the reconcentrated population.[5]

Robles initiated the plan with great success, dragooning hundreds of farmers and field hands into service each week and shipping them off in cattle cars to Mexico City. From there the "recruits" passed on as cannon fodder to the north or as military laborers to other short-handed states. This draft had few precedents in Mexican history, and those of a special kind. It was not like the common judicial sentence of rowdy individuals or the impromptu conscription used in the country's political wars of the nineteenth century; it resembled rather the calculated genocide that the government had practiced in racial wars against rebellious Indians in Sonora and Yucatán. There Robles had learned his trade, and now in Morelos he applied it again. "Why, I am trying to clean up your beautiful Morelos for you," he told an indignant Mrs. King. "What a nice place it will be once we get rid of the Morelenses! If they resist me, I shall hang them like earrings to the trees." By June 1 he had deported nearly one thousand captives.[6]

The draft caused such a shock that it became the subject of a local song, "The Crimes of the Tyrant Huerta:"

> The draft, the hateful draft,
> That sowed desolation
> On the whole beloved soil
> Of our noble Nation.
>
> The worker, the artisan,
> The merchant and the peon,
> They carried them off to the ranks,
> Without any compassion.
>
> He sent them to the North,
> That lowdown badman Huerta,
> To die unjustly
> On the fields of battle.

[5] *El Imparcial*, May 5, 9, 10, 11, and 14, 1913.

[6] King: op. cit., p. 93. *Mexican Herald*, May 31 and June 1, 1913. Magaña: op. cit., III, 180.

> Thousands of orphans
> Stayed forever alone,
> For their fathers were dead
> On campaign without a reason.

The balladeers also sang about Robles, in commemorating "The Extermination of Morelos:"

> God forgive you, Juvencio Robles,
> For so much barbarity and so much badness,
> So much shame, so many horrors
> As you've committed in our little province.[7]

This was "something abnormal" indeed. And despite Huerta's warning of what to expect, the planters were surprised. For as Robles carried on, they saw that he established not even an incomplete peace. He was strong enough only to lay waste, not to secure control. The policy of concentration, as Luis García Pimentel, Jr., noted, was "a farce." The federals could not finally depopulate the villages: when villagers saw a column coming to evict them, they fled into the ravines and hills; after the column had sacked their houses and left, they filtered back. Ironically, García Pimentel remarked, the only real concentration was the work of the rebels, who often got fugitives to form permanent camps in hiding.[8] So the planters were losing many of their workers to the draft and more to the rebels, without a sign of when or whence the government would send new workers. And since they had not yet organized their "volunteer corps" for self-defense, and the army would still not station garrisons on their grounds, their haciendas remained subject to rebel raids and forced loans. If the planters could not restrain Robles, he would destroy them in destroying the state.

Through various appeals the Morelos planters tried to exercise the responsibility they now perceived. Some evidently maneuvered to have Robles reassigned to another zone and to have a less incendiary commander appointed in Cuernavaca. Others insisted that he stay, and be reinforced. Evidently they believed that they could also take part in the war, at least in the defense of their property, which would prevent Robles from doing

[7] Both songs cited in Merle E. Simmons: *The Mexican CORRIDO as a Source for Interpretive Study of Modern Mexico (1870–1950)* (Bloomington, 1957), pp. 121, 293.

[8] L. García Pimentel: op. cit., p. 2.

irreparable damage and thus preserve a basic stability in the state. From Huerta the planters won an agreement in late June permitting them to retain 30 per cent of their employees, whom they were to register, post bond for, and arm. In a National Agricultural Congress in early July they helped arrange a formal deal with the Ministry of the Interior to arm and munition plantation guards.[9] But these projects remained on paper. No private guards were organized or armed, and Robles careened on, wrecking plantations and villages alike. The new officers who reinforced him, like General Alberto T. Rasgado and Colonel Luis G. Cartón, were even more destructive.

The disruption of local life grew ever more fierce. In June Robles shipped out over two thousand conscripts, leaving their families to fend for themselves in his concentration camps. He also seized control of markets in Cuernavaca, Cuautla, and Jojutla, to cut off the supplies to outlying villages and force their inhabitants to come into his camps.[1] More often country folk fled to rebel camps in the hills, but misery prevailed there too. Waiting hours in hiding for a drink of water; going for days without tortillas or salt; constantly prey to malaria and pneumonia; rarely eating meat, and then barely cooked; almost never getting cigarettes, liquor, or medicine; sleeping at night in the rain, rolled up in a blanket on the wet ground—this was the lot of those who escaped Robles. In the chaos, reported a metropolitan correspondent on the scene, "a regular battalion" of ten- to twelve-year-olds followed rebel bands around, scavenging and looting worse than their elders. In Puente de Ixtla the widows, wives, daughters, and sisters of rebels formed their own battalion and revolted "to avenge the dead." Under the command of a husky ex-tortilla maker called La China, they raided wildly through Tetecala district. Some in rags, some in plundered finery, wearing silk stockings and dresses, sandals, straw hats, and gun belts, these women became the terrors of the region. Even de la O treated La China with respect.[2] Everywhere in Morelos communities disintegrated. Desolating village after village, federal commanders drove people into new associations: neighborhoods and families disappeared, their refugee parts to be swallowed up in roving rebel armies. Thus in months Robles and his henchmen shredded the tough fabric of provincial society that would have required decades of peaceful development to unravel.

[9] *El Imparcial*, June 5, 10, 13–15, 25, and July 2–4, 1913.
[1] Ibid., June 22 and 28, 1912. *Mexican Herald*, June 30, 1913.
[2] *La Tribuna*, May 29, June 3 and 4, 1913.

Throughout the Republic similar convulsions were going on. It was clear that a profound civil war was underway, a war more engaging and more violent than any experienced in Mexico since the War against the French Intervention. And in the south it was Zapata, the champion of the pueblos, who took the lead in defining the popular cause. As the ballad-eers crooned,

> Goodbye, Cartón and Juvencio Robles,
> Adios, Rasgado, you wild hot thing.
> Take your battalions back to Huerta,
> And your strategy so mean.
> Tell him there are no more villages,
> Nor bandits to chase,
> Only Zapata and his squadrons,
> Always ready for you to face.[3]

In and immediately around Morelos Zapata took special pains actually to organize the popular forces. This was now a vital task. The struggle had become so ferocious that some local chiefs, on the verge of moral collapse, were as ready to fight each other as the federals. Worse, they abused villagers in their rivals' or even in their own bailiwicks, which eroded the rebel base. Zapata reproached bullies individually, but only in an army of clarified purpose and coordinated commands could he expect his orders to have a serious effect. And beyond Morelos new strains were at work. As the Ayala plan gained currency through the central and southern states, local leaders learned of its agrarian provisions, and many, whose people had suffered dispossessions of land like those in Morelos, declared themselves partisans of Zapata. Eutimio Figueroa and Miguel de la Trinidad Regalado in Michoacán; Jesús Salgado, Julio Astudillo Gómez, Encarnación Díaz, and Heliodoro Castillo in Guerrero, where the Figueroas lost influence entirely; Everardo González, Julián Gallegos, and Valentín Reyes in Mexico State; Honorato Teutle and Domingo Arenas in Tlaxcala; and scores more in Puebla, the Federal District, Oaxaca, Hidalgo, Veracruz, even San Luis Potosí, Durango, and Chihuahua—they were all Zapatistas, adherents to the Plan de Ayala.[4] But these allies remained scattered, out of touch with each other and with the headquarters in Morelos, not even confederates. At long distances Zapata obviously could not direct their military operations, but unless he gave them general polit-

[3] Cited in Simmons: op. cit., p. 293.
[4] Palacios: op. cit., pp. 117–18.

ical guidance, they might easily fall to fighting among themselves, making separate deals with the government, or offending local populations to the discredit of the cause.

To clarify his political position, Zapata amended the Ayala plan. Since late April he had considered how to reform it, and finally on May 30 he published a manifesto by Montaño specifying the changes.[5] Huerta was declared a "usurper . . . whose presence in the presidency of the Republic accentuates more and more each day his incompatibility with everything that signifies law, justice, rights, and morals, up to the point that he is reputed worse than Madero." And Orozco, for his compromise with Huerta's "pseudo-government," was judged "unworthy" of the honor the Morelos Revolutionary Junta had originally bestowed upon him in naming him national chief. In Montaño's solemn phrase Orozco had become "a social zero, that is, without any acceptable significance." Zapata himself now assumed officially the chieftainship of the Ayala movement.

To outline military relations and revolutionary goals, he also formally reorganized the rebel high command as the Revolutionary Junta of the Center and South of the Republic. He himself, as chief of the rebel army, was ex officio president of the junta. Other members included Eufemio Zapata, Montaño, de la O, Pacheco, Salazar, Neri, and Mendoza. The secretary was Palafox.[6] A few weeks later there issued from the Zapatista headquarters a new set of instructions for revolutionary officers, probably composed by Palafox. Like the earlier instructions of December 1911, these rules carefully specified the officers' two major responsibilities, to their troops and to the villages they occupied. But unlike the earlier code, and indicating how much larger and more professional the movement had become, the new rules provided that officers should "pay the soldiers wages, or better said, help out the troops where it is possible," levy forced loans on prosperous merchants and landlords, replace local officials "in accord with the will of the people," and report operations every two weeks to their zone chiefs or to the central headquarters. Most remarkable was the decentralization of the authority to carry out the agrarian reform prescribed in Article 6 of the Ayala plan. Before, it seems that only the Morelos junta could review villagers' titles and restore their lands; and in only one case, in Ixcamilpa, Puebla, had the junta formally done so.[7] But now officers in

---

[5] Zapata to Montaño, April 25, 1913, AZ, 30: 1. For the text of the manifesto, see González Ramírez: *Planes,* pp. 84–5.

[6] Magaña: op. cit., III, 183.

[7] Palacios: op. cit., pp. 81–2.

the field were to lend their "moral and material support" to villages presenting titles and filing reclamations. Although the new rules contained no mention of the radical Articles 7 and 8 on outright expropriation, even this grant of limited jurisdiction in agrarian disputes signified a clear assumption of sovereignty and a deliberate attempt to put a stated policy into practice.[8]

The effectiveness of the new regulations varied greatly from one district to the next. The character of revolutionary authority in a specific area depended on a multitude of factors, among them the temperaments of the local federal commander and rebel chief, the strategic value of the territory, the interest the government and the rebel headquarters had in it, and the particular nature of its political and social circumstances. Nowhere in Morelos, for instance, were the rebels long enough in control to institute agrarian reforms. And here and there little hamlets were wiped out by rebels—the houses sacked, the women raped, the horses and mules confiscated, the cattle driven away for black-market sale to a corrupt federal colonel, the pigs butchered on the spot, the chickens carried off for a later meal. But although outrages occurred, it seems quite unlikely that common people through Zapata's zone of immediate influence suffered much at rebel hands. Local chiefs had a stake in following the rules simply to prove themselves of value to the headquarters that might one day be a government. If they hanged municipal officials or merchants who would not pay their quotas, they still did not alienate working farmers and their families.[9] In the deep and abiding respect plain people felt for Zapata, they revealed that at least they understood the suffering they did endure. In folksongs balladeers sang that "all through the South, they love him loyally / for he gives them Justice, Peace, Progress, and Liberty."[1]

As it reorganized and became genuinely Zapatista, the whole southern revolution flourished. Zapatista guerrilleros even raided Mexico City's suburbs. In reaction Robles accelerated the terror in Morelos, "to cut out the evil at its roots," the press explained, "exterminating the Zapatista seed so that it will not germinate again . . . " On policy he ordered more burnings, and having already burnt out most minor targets, his officers Rasgado and Cartón now put to flame even municipal seats like Yecapixtla, Xochitepec, Villa de Ayala, and Tepalcingo. As in 1912 they also had women and children arrested as hostages, among them Zapata's mother-in-law and four

[8] For these instructions, see Magaña: op. cit., III, 267–8.
[9] *La Tribuna,* May 31, June 4 and 7, 1913.
[1] Cited in Simmons: op. cit., pp. 286–7.

of her daughters, who were consigned to military prison in Mexico City on charges of espionage. And "the hateful draft" continued: nearly thirteen hundred conscripts departed from Morelos in July. The destruction was appalling. As an agent for the White Cross reported, the state was "only a rough sketch of what it was two years ago. . . . those ample plantings of cane, rice, and so many other food products have disappeared, now converted into a sad heap of ashes, the monotony of the burned fields interrupted only by one or another deserted hamlet also half-ruined by fire."[2] Again responsible planters tried to intervene, despite the government's public offer to import thirty thousand Japanese to replace their lost peons. Joaquín García Pimentel privately communicated a plea for peace to Eufemio Zapata.[3] And he and other planters extorted a promise from the new minister of the interior that Robles would permit fugitive workers to return to the haciendas; they also won new approval of the "volunteer corps." But again their efforts were abortive.[4] As Robles, Rasgado, and Cartón persisted in their rampage, the refugees multiplied and the revolutionaries grew stronger in numbers and determination.

The climax of Robles's blundering campaign to crush the rebels was the capture of Huautla, a mining settlement in the rough hills southeast of Jojutla. There Zapata had located a temporary headquarters, and there had gathered many runaway villagers and peons from elsewhere in the state. The taking of Huautla would not break up the Zapatistas, as Robles, who had fought guerrillas for years, must have known. In that difficult terrain all the federals then in Morelos could not hope to fix the rebels in place and annihilate them. The rebels would simply disperse, escape through the federal lines, and relocate their headquarters in another camp; at most they would lose some stores. But Robles also knew that victory in a staged battle was the surest warrant for promotion. And through July, with great fanfare, he prepared his attack. To reporters he related how from Cuernavaca he would direct in enveloping maneuvers three columns under Generals Rasgado and Antonio Olea and Colonel Cartón, and how, after the federals had surrounded and blasted the rebels, the Zapatista movement would dissolve. The battle "will certainly be bloody," the reporters learned, "since in Huautla no stone will be left on stone." But afterward, Robles declared, "the pacification of . . . Morelos will be a fact."[5]

[2] El Imparcial, July 7, 8, 12, 14, 15, 19, and 26, 1913.

[3] Eufemio Zapata to J. García Pimentel, June 28, 1913, AGP.

[4] El Imparcial, July 30, 1913. L. García Pimentel: op. cit., p. 4.

[5] El Imparcial, August 2 and 3, 1913.

In early August the celebrated drive began. There followed days of grandiose reports of attacks and "secret" preparations for more attacks. Meanwhile Zapata was quietly evacuating the refugees and the bulk of his local forces south into Guerrero and Puebla. But the show went on. Once, Cartón missed his cue and charged his column right into the settlement, which he found already abandoned; but he quickly retreated and rejoined his fellow commanders in their phony action. Waiting for the word from Robles, who was busy burning towns in the Federal District, Rasgado, Olea, and Cartón occupied themselves in burning the villages and ranchos in their area. Finally on August 19 they moved into the empty settlement together. There they found the bodies of Pascual Orozco, Sr., and two other peace commissioners whom Zapata had had executed in revenge. Among their other discoveries, they said, were the Zapatista archives and a cache of forty thousand rifles with ammunition, which they never produced. "Zapata's hordes have today been completely destroyed," Robles wired Huerta, "and properly speaking, the Morelos campaign has concluded."[6]

In the metropolitan press this was a tremendous triumph. Flowing from it came a deluge of promotions for the officers and troops involved in the affair. Colonel Cartón became a general. And Robles attained the army's highest rank, divisional general. Even the planters believed their prayers had been answered, that Robles had suppressed the rebellion and the revolution. And down to Cuernavaca the most august hastened in a party—Ramón Corona, Antonio Escandón, and Luis García Pimentel, Sr., with their ever-ready chamberlain, Ramón Oliveros. For the first time in months the city was host to "an elegant 'soirée.'" Actually Robles had managed a successful holding operation in Morelos. With reinforcements he now commanded seven thousand men there, which had enabled him to recover military control of the six former district seats. And he had given the control a political veneer in reestablishing the prefectures and appointing jefes.[7] For that "the favored of fortune" could be grateful.

But in the field, where the federals were still like shingles in the sea, the revolution did not subside. Zapata and the other chiefs displaced at Huautla simply carried on their operations elsewhere. The most remote Zapatista action in these days was a mutiny in Mérida, Yucatán, by Morelos

---

[6] Ibid., August 5, 7, 12, and 17–20, 1913. L. García Pimentel: op. cit., pp. 5–6.

[7] *El Imparcial,* August 21, 22, and 26, 1913. Among Robles's appointees was Eugenio Morales, municipal president of Jojutla with the authority of prefect.

conscripts, but closer to home—throughout Morelos and into the Federal District, Mexico State, Tlaxcala, Puebla, Guerrero, and Michoacán—the regular Zapatista bands went on tearing up railroad tracks, wiping out federal outposts, and raiding towns. Thus, despite Robles's entrenchment in Morelos, the general revolution of the center and south remained in full effect. And by late August the failure of the federal mission was obvious. Robles had only proved again what he had already proved a year before—that with enough force and firepower he could defend urban enclaves in the countryside, but he could not scare the surrounding population into order. The most he had accomplished was a vicious stalemate that served no interest but his own. And Huerta was not the kind of superior to accept as an excuse the lament that the natives were stubborn. From his own brutal perspective he might well have asked Robles, as Morelos balladeers asked him in song, "What fault is it of the people who live here/ that you can't win in the end?"[8]

Moreover Robles's failure came at an especially trying time for the government. Huerta had recently consolidated his own power in the administration, removing the Felicistas from the cabinet and sending Félix Díaz as an envoy to Japan, but he nevertheless badly needed recognition from the United States; without it European bankers refused him loans. And President Wilson still believed that the interim Mexican President did not merit his blessing morally or politically. He had just recalled his ambassador, who had argued in favor of Huerta, and sent a "personal representative," John Lind, to investigate conditions in Mexico. And, as Huerta knew from his foreign minister, this "confidential agent" had decided soon after arriving in the country that the government was neither legitimate nor effective. The evidence the agent found was the well-organized Constitutionalist movement in the north and the active resistance through the center and south. The terms he therefore offered for recognition were hard—the declaration of a national armistice and the promise of early, free elections in which Huerta would not be a candidate—and Huerta would not consider them, whatever the alternatives. He had already scheduled elections for October 26, and although he had publicly insisted he would not run for (and retain) the presidency, he did not want to commit himself to the U.S. government. This recalcitrance President Wilson resented. On August 27 he addressed his Congress on the Mexican question,

[8] Ibid., August 23 and 25, 1913. Magaña: op. cit., III, 230–2. Song cited in Simmons: op. cit., p. 293.

noting Huerta's inability to establish order and urging Americans in Mexico to leave at once.[9]

Under increasing American pressure Huerta could no longer afford such costly and useless diversions as Robles's. He would now invest all his prime offensive forces in the north, where the political and military threat was most portentous, and in the south he would leave only reduced, defensive garrisons. On September 4 the minister of war called Robles to Mexico City for a long conference, after which Robles announced he would take a two-week rest. More conferences followed, which must have given him little time to relax; but on September 13 his vacation was lengthened indefinitely when he was removed as Morelos's governor and military commander. Replacing him was Brigadier General Adolfo Jiménez Castro, who had served in Morelos the year before under Ángeles.[1] He was to preserve the stalemate, but less violently and less expensively.

And so he did, to the relief of merchants, planters, and refugees.[2] Under Jiménez Castro the federal commanders of the three thousand to four thousand troops left in the state became in practice city police chiefs. Not fit to make regular war, they barely sustained the little war of the guerrilla. Occasionally they directed battalions into the countryside for a burning, but usually they kept their forces holed up in the district seats. There the officers sweetened their tour by embezzling state and municipal funds and selling government property, while the troops passed their days boozing on pulque or warm beer, shooting pool, and pining away for the northern villages from which they had been drafted.[3] And within its limits the strategy worked. The garrisons were just strong enough and near enough to each other to make the cost of a rebel attack prohibitive in lives and ammunition. Through the ruined villages and fields and hills and ravines the revolutionaries moved almost at will, collecting rents from a plantation here, robbing a train there; but against the main towns all they dared try was a raid.

For Zapata this little war soon became a dangerous bind. Like revolutionary leaders elsewhere around the Republic, he evidently understood

[9] For an account of the agent's activity in Mexico, see George M. Stephenson: *John Lind of Minnesota* (Minneapolis, 1935), pp. 208–329.

[1] *El Imparcial,* September 5, 13, and 23, 1913.

[2] Ibid., September 25, 1913. L. García Pimentel: op. cit., pp. 1, 3, 6. J. García Pimentel: op. cit., p. 13.

[3] Diez: *Bibliografía,* p. ccviii.

that Huerta's October 26 elections might be crucial. If Huerta lasted until then, and if he kept his repeated promise not to be a candidate, the científicos and religious conservatives who would probably win office might gain American recognition. But to bring Huerta down before then, or at least to cause such a national disturbance as to invalidate the elections, the revolutionaries would have to do more than merely remain in action. And when finally Huerta did fall, the southern revolutionaries would need firmer control over their region than raids would give them; they would need to hold cities, to threaten or even to enter the federal capital itself. So Morelos, where no tactic more complicated than raiding was feasible, could no longer serve as the Zapatistas' central zone of operations. The proper strategic base for the new war of place and position in the south was northern Guerrero, and there Zapata moved his headquarters in late September. Because the Ayala revolution had developed so extensively through the south, he could organize the campaign from there as well as from Morelos.

The pressing question was whether he would have time to mature a major offensive before the elections. To launch the drive he would need to knit the various bands under his orders into at least the skeleton of a regular army—in less than a month. Even without a deadline the task was awesome, since each chief cherished as his own the "company" he had recruited. But once in Guerrero, depending on his secretary Palafox, Zapata went to work.

On October 4 new instructions for the Liberating Army of the Center and South issued from headquarters, again probably composed by Palafox. Designed to break down the clannish loyalties among the revolutionary forces and to consolidate direction and authority in a regular military hierarchy, these rules greatly elaborated the formal structure of the army. Chiefs were to name corporals and sergeants, for instance, "so that they . . . may mobilize their troops with more exactitude and rapidity." Any subordinate was to obey any superior, whether he belonged to his outfit or not. Soldiers in combat or on march were to stay in their assigned units and not mingle into others, "because they will be the cause of disorders and confusion." Any soldier who left his post in battle or in retreat was a deserter, and on missions requiring them to abandon their units soldiers had to carry written orders. Besides, the procedures for entering villages, collecting loans, and distributing wages were made more explicit. And the prohibitions against pillaging and otherwise abusing the population were made stricter. As for reforms, they figured even more dimly here than they had in the previous set of instructions: a chief could authorize the suspension of guarantees—that is, replace a local official or confiscate property—only in the case of "enemies of the Revolution who it can be proved help the bad illegal government," which gave the "enemies" the benefit of the doubt.[4] For the moment, as Zapata and Palafox had apparently decided, the strategic need was not to disjoint the region but to broaden and diversify the revolutionary appeal, or at least to narrow the range of resistance against it.

Within a week unexpected events in Mexico City relaxed the urgency of Zapata's situation. On October 9, encouraged by the Constitutionalist General Francisco Villa's recent capture of Torreón, a key rail junction in southern Coahuila, the Maderista militants still in the Chamber of Deputies brought on a crisis in the government. Protesting the disappearance and suspected murder of a Maderista senator the day before, they warned President Huerta that if he allowed any more outrages against Congress it would "hold its sessions where it might have guarantees."[5] Their veiled threat to move to a city behind the Constitutionalist lines forced Huerta's hand. The next day he dissolved Congress, ordered the arrest of 110 deputies, and assumed dictatorial powers until the elections returned a new government. It was clear that he had thus doomed himself, for he had destroyed all chances that the United States would recognize the elections' outcome. And revolutionary factions around the country could now organize their coalitions and campaign with some deliberation.

In the south Zapata shortly caught the critical import of what had happened. Meeting in southern Morelos on October 19 with Palafox and other counselors, he agreed to send envoys to arrange a "unification" with the main revolutionary chiefs in the north and to deal with the United States for recognition of the allied movement as belligerent.[6] The next day he published a Manifesto to the Nation, proclaiming that "Victory approaches, the struggle comes to its end."[7] And on October 24 he wrote to Francisco Vázquez Gómez in Washington, D.C., authorizing him to represent the southern revolution at the White House and to ask for a loan to buy ammunition.[8] The enthusiasm and the maneuvers were premature: Huerta

[4] Zapata to the forces under his command, October 4, 1913, AZ, 12: 8: 1.

[5] DeBekker: op. cit., p. 367.

[6] Service record of Luis Íñiguez, May 2, 1913, to September 16, 1915, AZ, 27: 17. Zapata's appointment of ambassadors, October 29, 1913, AZ, 28: 17: 1.

[7] Cited in Magaña: op. cit., III, 252–7.

[8] Zapata to F. Vázquez Gómez, October 24, 1913, AZ, 27: 6.

did not resign for another nine months, the envoys never got out of Guerrero, and Vázquez Gómez accomplished nothing. But Zapata did right to count October's crisis as the turning point.

Slowly, as the northern revolutionaries absorbed the government's attention, Zapata's campaign took shape in the south. His strategy was sound, an insightful play on Guerrero's political geography and system of communications. Iguala was where the railroad from Mexico City ended, and it was a hard two- or three-day march past the malarial Balsas River and then through mountains to Chilpancingo, the state capital. On Zapata's orders major Morelos chiefs like de la O, Salazar, Neri, and Mendoza would continue to busy federal troops in their home districts. Zapata himself, who would keep his headquarters in southern Morelos, would direct distractive efforts there and in southern Puebla, as well as coordinate the forces in Guerrero on the sly. Then, holding the federals in Iguala by threats in Morelos and along the Morelos-Guerrero-Puebla border, he could isolate and capture Chilpancingo. The prestige of such a victory— no other southern state capital was near falling to the revolution—and the arms and ammunition captured there would fuel simultaneous attacks on Acapulco, whence he could communicate by sea with the north, and on Iguala, the key city of the whole region. And from Iguala he could pull together revolutionary forces all across the center and south of the country for a final, massive drive through Morelos and against Mexico City.

In building his army Zapata encountered remarkably few political difficulties. Already the main chiefs in central and northern Guerrero—Salgado, Díaz, Gómez, and Castillo—had formally recognized the authority of the Zapatista headquarters. And now, whether from true sympathy with the Ayalan cause or from band-wagon calculations, they accepted Zapata's leadership in fact. Another important Guerrero chief, Julián Blanco, based along the southern Costa Chica, soon joined them. Blanco had earlier fought against Zapatistas in Guerrero for the Maderista state government and had become a local Constitutionalist when Huerta seized power, but on November 23 he too signed the Ayala plan. In the following weeks he and the other allies and Zapata worked out the terms of their cooperation.[9] On January 18, 1914, Blanco and Montaño, acting for Zapata, signed a treaty at Blanco's own headquarters confirming his allegiance.[1] Only in Morelos did chiefs kick their traces. Mendoza, for instance, evidently resented spending his men and ammunition in diversionary raids.

[9] Zapata to Blanco and Montaño, December 26, 1913, AZ, 30: 1.
[1] Cited in Magaña: op. cit., III, 294–5.

To push the campaign in his zone Zapata even had to send in another, more respectful chief, Ignacio Maya.[2] And in a dander Mendoza started negotiating with Joaquín García Pimentel to surrender.[3] But the deal never came to pass. In all cases Zapata maintained the loyalty of his forces as he organized them. So impressive was the revolutionary confederation he was building that federals defected to enlist in it.

Cramping Zapata's plans most tightly was the lack of military supplies. To hold the loyalties of scattered chiefs, to equip an army of their impatient followers, and then to conduct daily coordinated operations over a broad front, Zapata needed more arms and ammunition than raids, pilferage, or petty black-market purchases could provide. But no shipments ever came from the northern revolutionaries, or from Vázquez Gómez in the United States. In the Zapatista headquarters the search for arms and ammunition became obsessive. The smallest caches were subject to the revolutionary claim. Just as old José Zapata had demanded arms from malingering neighbors for use against the French, now Emiliano Zapata demanded them for use against Huerta. "I have information that you have hidden away certain war supplies," he wrote to one chief not under his command. ". . . I recommend to you that you send me immediately six rifles of those that you have . . . if you do not . . . it will be ordered that of the cattle which belong to you 50 be confiscated, which will be brought to this headquarters."[4]

Careful preparations for the move on Chilpancingo continued through January and February. While Zapata negotiated for alliances with other Guerrero chiefs, he also specified the operations the committed chiefs would undertake and the contingencies they might act on.[5] The Morelos chiefs learned to synchronize their attacks, so that in a single day federal commanders would have to repel raids on three or four district seats, not knowing whether any or all of them were in earnest. And strategic towns in northern Guerrero were taken and permanently occupied.[6] At these moves alarm coursed through the War Department, but there were no reinforcements to send.[7] By late February the revolutionaries were ready. Jesús

[2] Palafox to Mendoza, November 11, 1913, AZ, 27: 17.

[3] Mendoza to J. García Pimentel, December 19, 1913, AGP.

[4] J. Zapata to Narcizo Medina, February 9, 1867, ASI. Zapata to Andrés Figueroa, January 25, 1914, cited in Figueroa Uriza: op. cit., II, 566–7.

[5] Zapata to Montaño, February 3, 1914, AA.

[6] Magaña: op. cit., III, 291–2, 298–9, 304–5. Figueroa Uriza: op. cit., II, 569–79.

[7] *El Independiente,* March 3 and 12, 1914.

Salgado, whom Zapata had made responsible for the attack, called a junta of chiefs at Cuetzala, a mountain town northwest of their objective.[8] There they worked out the final details of the parts each would play.

On March 9 Blanco's troops took up their positions south of the state capital. To the west stood Salgado's division. And to the north stood Castillo's. On March 12 Zapata arrived with nearly two thousand reinforcements from Puebla and Morelos and set up a temporary headquarters at Tixtla, a few miles to the northeast. Revolutionary forces now totaled nearly five thousand, against some fourteen hundred federals under the infamous General Cartón. And two days later on Zapata's orders a siege closed up the city. Even in this emergency the War Department could dispatch no relief column; units of the Jojutla garrison had mutinied on March 12, paralyzing the defense of the whole southern zone.[9] The final assault Zapata had scheduled for March 26; but on March 23 the Guerrero chief Díaz arrived with his troops, eager for action. Disregarding orders, he led a charge which the other forces followed and which broke the federal lines. Early the next morning the revolutionaries took control of the city's center.[1] As the American consul in Acapulco wired to Washington: "The fall of Chilpancingo was the result of the most decisive action yet fought in this region."[2]

With his officers, over six hundred troops, and many supplies, Cartón escaped along the road to Acapulco, but chiefs Blanco and Ignacio Maya alertly pursued him; and he finally surrendered forty miles south at a village called El Rincón. The federal troops, most of them conscripts, were simply disarmed and set free, and many joined the revolutionary forces. But the officers—General Cartón and forty-three others—were returned to the Zapatista headquarters at Tixtla, and Zapata ruled that they be court-martialed. Some were released, but those identified as incendiaries were sentenced to death and executed. Among them was General Cartón, shot in Chilpancingo's public square on the morning of April 6.[3]

Simultaneous with these trials the Zapatista headquarters had called a junta in Tixtla of the main revolutionary chiefs in Guerrero. According to

[8] Magaña: op. cit., III, 309–10.

[9] *Mexican Herald,* March 14–18, 1914.

[1] For varying descriptions of the battle, see Magaña: op. cit., III, 310–15; Figueroa Uriza: op. cit., II, 583–6; Custodio Valverde: *Julián Blanco y la revolución en el estado de Guerrero* (México, 1916), pp. 48–9; and Daniel R. Trujillo: "Memorias Revolucionarias de un suriano Zapatista," *El Legionario,* March 15, 1958.

[2] Edwards to the secretary of state, March 30, 1914, NA, 59: 812.00/11356.

[3] The trial proceedings and results are in Magaña: op. cit., IV, 11–18.

Article 13 of the Ayala plan, they were to name a provisional governor. Between General Blanco and General Salgado they chose Salgado. And as a self-styled "Director of the Provisional Government" he took office on March 28 and immediately began purging and reorganizing the state bureaucracy.

Politics, however, was generally left to trusted subordinates, as Salgado and Blanco resumed the military offensive. Blanco headed south, frightening the American consul in Acapulco so badly that he called for (and got) a U.S. warship to stand offshore.[4] And Salgado moved north. By April 8 his forces had taken Iguala. And in the following days, reinforced by Jojutla mutineers, they took Taxco and Buenavista de Cuéllar as well, and Salgado even sent reinforcements to revolutionaries in Michoacán and Mexico State.[5]

By then Zapata had returned to Morelos to direct operations. His resources for attack had increased greatly. All the cannons, machine guns, rifles, ammunition, and government funds captured at Chilpancingo and El Rincón had been dutifully turned over to his headquarters.[6] Although Zapata had to resupply the Guerrero chiefs in order to preserve harmony, he still kept a sizable store for Morelos and Puebla. And thus equipped and encouraged, he eagerly pressed the campaign. The day the revolutionary government took office in Guerrero he had published a manifesto to the Morelos chiefs, urging them to continue attacks and reminding them of the reports they would soon have to submit to headquarters. In early April de la O raided into southern Mexico State, and Mendoza and Eufemio Zapata attacked and occupied plantations and villages in southeastern Morelos and southern Puebla. To chiefs as far away as Michoacán Zapata sent instructions about the drive he intended to mount against Mexico City.[7] By mid-April revolutionary forces controlled practically all Morelos's villages, ranchos, and small towns, and were daily attacking the district seats.[8] The only haciendas they had not yet taken were the García Pimentels' Tenango and Santa Clara. There, alone among the state's planters, Luis, Jr., and Joaquín had actually organized a private guard (ten Japanese soldiers under a French officer) and had remained personally to help defend their

[4] Edwards to the secretary of state, April 2, 1914, NA, 59: 812.00/11395.

[5] Magaña: op. cit., IV, 18–22.

[6] Figueroa Uriza: op. cit., II, 586–7.

[7] Concha de Villarreal: "El indio tarasco decapitado por agrarista," *Todo,* November 4, 1937.

[8] Magaña: op. cit., IV, 168–71. L. García Pimentel: op. cit., pp. 11 ff., 51–8.

father's holdings. But before the revolutionary onslaught even these valiant young men were about to despair. Waiting dejectedly for new attacks, Luis gained no consolation even in confessing and receiving communion in the local parish church. So deeply depressed was he that only when he fell further into a trivial, vulgar amusement, when "we started to listen to some raucous phonograph records," did his spirits revive. The "patriotic speeches, historical scenes, songs and pieces of music—all the infernal repertory of the wicked machine, which before I detested, now seemed," in his hysterical misery, ". . . a magnificent distraction."[9] Fatalistically he prepared to abandon his heritage in the state.

Again, however, the Zapatistas were running short of ammunition. Even the Chilpancingo booty was insufficient to power more than a few major battles. It required upward of two hundred thousand rounds for a force of three thousand to four thousand revolutionaries to besiege a town for five days, and materiél in this volume was hard to find in the south. The revolutionary armies in the north, operating in regions with more marketable wealth—cattle or cotton—and with easy access to American munitions dealers, had early established a reliable trade across the international frontier and could plan and sustain long campaigns. But Zapata had nothing valuable to sell, nor a safe market to sell it in. From Guerrero mines Salgado minted silver pesos, but these barely served to keep the state government and local economy functioning. And the planters, who had earlier paid dues for protection, now had no cane to protect and so paid no dues.

To meet the extraordinary needs of a regular campaign, Zapata had first tried in October to negotiate an American loan, but he had received no sign of help from Vázquez Gómez. Then, busy as he was during the Guerrero offensive, he had sent agents to the American representatives in Mexico City, one to the American consul-general and another to Confidential Agent John Lind himself—to finagle funds for the purchase of ammunition. These efforts continued even after Lind returned to Washington in early April. Once Zapata tried to maneuver Lind into arranging a loan by promising not to advance on Mexico City, which he could not have done anyway. But Lind only advised Zapata to see the Red Cross for charity.[1] Even if Zapata could have contracted a loan and bought bullets in the United States, it would have been practically impossible to transport tons of lead overland for fifteen hundred miles from the border, the last five

[9] Ibid., p. 64.
[1] Stephenson: op. cit., pp. 265–6.

hundred miles by mule. So, without steady supplies, Zapata could not maintain the proper rhythm in his campaign. The drive against Mexico City slackened. The only strategy now feasible was to keep up the pressure of the guerrilla in Morelos and Puebla and wait for a break.

But then the break came—for the revolutionaries in the south and north a stroke of luck as sudden and as crucial as the dissolution of Congress six months before. On April 21, in an awkward attempt to bring Huerta down, President Wilson directed United States military forces to occupy the port of Veracruz. In the next week, as during the Decena Trágica, federal troops were called in from all the central and southern states to the Federal District as emergency reinforcements. Those in Morelos evacuated four of the state's six district seats—Jonacatepec, Cuautla, Yautepec, and Tetecala, all of which immediately fell to the Zapatistas besieging them.[2] And at last the García Pimentels too retreated. On hearing the news from Veracruz, young Luis felt "a deep sensation of impotent rage against so many elements that seemed to unite and plot against me." Seeing that he would have to leave now, he went straight to the plantation chapel "to hide what little of value had remained in it," and there, he later remembered, "I could not help getting down on my knees and weeping like the man who has taken a supreme resolution . . ." In "a great anguish" he gathered together the few people still on his grounds and on April 24 joined a federal column headed north out of the state.[3] Everywhere in Morelos the last remnants of the old order and the old progress were dwindling away, and the revolutionaries were rushing in. Cuernavaca itself was so weakened that the commander there urged all foreigners, and ordered all Americans, to leave the city: he declared he could no longer be responsible for their safety.[4]

Although neither the Mexican nor the American government wanted war, and both knew it to be unlikely, Huerta served his own purpose in portraying the American intervention to the public as the first step in a full-scale invasion. In his support the metropolitan press exploded into the patriotic fury characteristic of turn-of-the-century journalism. "While Mexicans Cut Gringo Pigs' Throats," trumpeted one headline, "In the Churches the Gloria Rings Out."[5] For many, the shock of American sailors and marines landing at Veracruz recalled General Winfield Scott's landing of

[2] Magaña: op. cit., IV, 171–4.

[3] L. García Pimentel: op. cit., pp. 66–79.

[4] King: op. cit., p. 135.

[5] *El Independiente,* April 23, 1914.

1847—which ended in Mexican disgrace. To the still uninformed revolutionary leaders, Huerta explicitly conceded amnesties and proposed alliances in a national struggle to repel the "pigs of Yanquilandia."

In Morelos Huertista emissaries quickly made their way to the camps of most leading chiefs. On April 24 federal officers invited de la O to surrender to the government and help fight the Americans. Two days later de la O received the same invitation from Joaquín Miranda and his son Joaquín, Jr., the ex-revolutionaries turned Huertista. To Mendoza's camp came a similar proposal from a similar agent, Jesús Morales. But no Zapatista chief accepted the envoys' offers. In each case the chiefs informed the headquarters, now in Tlaltizapán, of what they had discovered and asked for instructions. On his own de la O even arrested the Mirandas as traitors and sent them to headquarters for trial. Mendoza did the same with Morales. And at Tlaltizapán the resistance to collaboration was adamant. There the Huertista commissioners were not even able to submit the offers they bore; Palafox sent his own courier to the new military governor in Cuernavaca to learn the official terms. The Veracruz affair made his "blood boil," Zapata declared, but he would not consider union with Huerta. If the Americans did invade, he said, he would defend the Republic—but independently, as chief of the Ayala revolution, and in no connection with the federal forces. As various friends in Mexico City, like Antonio Díaz Soto y Gama, reported to the southern headquarters on the limited nature of the American action, they confirmed the Zapatistas in their decision. In a court-martial Palafox judged the Mirandas and Morales guilty of treason and had them shot. And calling up chiefs from Guerrero and Puebla, Zapata ordered the resumption of the southern campaign.[6]

Again his plan was to push into the Federal District, into Mexico City itself if possible. The strategy reflected the clear sense Zapata had acquired of the real constitution of Mexican politics. During three years of revolt he had learned well not to trust other parties to carry out reforms that only he and his chiefs had fought for. The very name of his fighting force revealed how he conceived of the civil war: whereas the Constitutionalist Divisions of the North, Northeast, and Northwest were subordinate parts of a pretended national army, Zapata's Liberating Army of the Center and South was the independent agency of his region. The security of Morelos's villagers, as Zapata now saw, derived not from the good will of the federal

[6] Magaña: op. cit., IV, 183-4, 188-96.

executive but from the national influence of the state's leader, and for him the surest way to national influence was through the disciplined participation of his army in the capture of the national capital.

Only two concentrations of federals remained in Morelos, the garrisons at Jojutla and Cuernavaca. The revolutionaries eliminated the first in overwhelming attacks in early May. Of the twelve hundred federals engaged there, most finally defected to the revolution with their arms and ammunition; less than ninety staggered back to Cuernavaca. The state capital was a harder place to take. A natural fortress standing in broken hills with deep barrancas cutting around it, the city defied all tactics but those of the siege. In late May Zapata had it surrounded and in early June he closed it up. There he left the last federals in the state, occasionally reinforced, relieved, or provisioned, but hopeless and harmless.[7]

Meanwhile he had already directed other revolutionary forces into action in the Federal District. In the mountain villages scattered through the bottom half of the district Zapatistas appeared almost daily, to wipe out little army detachments or to claim the allegiance of the people and recruit warriors.[8] On June 10 Zapata ordered southern chiefs to concentrate all their forces except rear guards "to continue our advance toward the capital of the Republic."[9] By late June a Zapatista occupation of the city seemed imminent to a special American agent there.[1]

On the verge of victory the Zapatista chiefs ran into a new temptation, to take the capital on conditions. This chance Huertista agents began posing in the south after a crucial Constitutionalist triumph in the north, at Zacatecas, and during an ominous Constitutionalist advance in the west, on Guadalajara. The high politicians of Huerta's party harbored a terrific hatred for this northern movement—partly from fear that since it was so rich, organized, and cohesive that if it came into power they could not manipulate it, and partly from resentment toward its leader, Governor Carranza, an old Porfirista who had betrayed his origins and yet emerged in command anyway. But the Zapatistas they still held in contempt, as shorter, darker-complexioned, and more countrified people, "Indians." And having recognized that they could no longer win, the Huertistas therefore started trying to trick the southern rubes into a deal, to bring

[7] Ibid., IV, 217–29. See also King: op. cit., pp. 152–202.

[8] Magaña: op. cit., IV, 206–8.

[9] Headquarters circular, June 10, 1914, AA.

[1] Canada to the secretary of state, June 23, 1914, NA, 59: 812.00/12323.

them into power, to divide the national revolution, and so to preserve a central role for themselves. But Zapata resisted such maneuvers. Probably on Palafox's counsel he issued instructions to his chiefs on July 1 to publish no declarations without clearing them through headquarters—"to avoid bad interpretations, fatal deviations, and twisted intentions whose realization would redound to the harm of the cause of the People."[2] At the Zapatista as at the Constitutionalist headquarters the demand was for unconditional surrender.

Finally in defeat and disgrace, Huerta resigned on July 15 and fled into exile on the same boat that had borne Don Porfirio away, the *Ypiranga*. But his government remained; the army would not quit fighting. Ascending to the presidency in an obvious last-ditch ploy was Francisco Carbajal. Interim President Carbajal was the former Porfirian Supreme Court justice who had, to his eternal discredit with the nation's revolutionaries, negotiated and cosigned the infamous Juárez treaty on behalf of Díaz's government. The bait was another compromise.

No revolutionary bit. Although Zapata lost most in bargaining advantages as the Constitutionalists moved in closer from the west, he opposed negotiations as intransigently as ever. When on July 17 nervous revolutionary agents from Mexico City reported to him the news of Huerta's resignation, as well as the "terrible" fear in the metropolis that he would storm and sack the capital, without hesitation he brushed aside hints that he promise guarantees. He planned, he told the envoys, to mobilize immediately twenty thousand men and advance them on the capital. Within three days at most, he declared, they would occupy the city. His officers were under strict orders to allow no sacking, but politically he would grant no concessions.[3] "It is good to repeat," he told his chiefs, "that we will carry out no transactions with any government if it does not turn over the Supreme National Powers to the Revolution, without qualifications of any kind."[4] As proof, he launched an attack the next day against Milpa Alta, an important town in Mexico City's southern suburbs; it fell two days later.

On July 19 Zapata and his leading chiefs carefully defined their official position in an Act of Ratification of the Plan de Ayala. Noting that they sought "before anything else the economic improvement of the great major-

---

[2] Headquarters circular, July 1, 1914, AZ, 27: 21.

[3] Zapata to the chiefs, officers, and soldiers under his command, July 14, 1914, ARD, 12: 34A: 1.

[4] Santiago Orozco to the chiefs, officers, and soldiers of the Liberating Army of the Center and South, July 17, 1914, AZ, 27: 21.

ity of Mexicans" and that they would "always oppose the infamous pre-
tension of reducing everything to a simple change in the personnel of
government," they formally refused to recognize any authority not constituted by the leaders of the nation's great popular armies. Three specific
obligations they undertook to defend "even at the cost of their blood and
their lives." First, they would not "cease their efforts" until the Ayala plan's
agrarian provisions were "elevated to the rank of constitutional precepts."
Second, they confirmed the ousting of Pascual Orozco and the election of
Zapata as national chief of their revolution. And third, the southern chiefs
would not consider "their work concluded" until "the servants of Huer-
tismo and other personalities of the old regime" were purged from all
offices and a new government was established "composed of men devoted
to the Plan de Ayala, men who forthwith carry agrarian reforms into
practice."[5] For Palafox this document was fundamental. He recommended
that Zapata have it widely distributed among the revolutionaries.[6]

Although the end was near, Carbajal and his cohorts still hoped for a
deal. One veteran politico, for instance, wrote to Zapata on behalf of a
Citizens Committee for National Defense. He assured Zapata that Carbajal
favored the Ayalan plan's proposals, especially those on the land question!
For this and other generous concessions he requested only that Zapata suspend hostilities and send delegates to sign a treaty.[7] Carbajal himself
tendered equally bogus offers to Zapatista agents in Mexico City. To two
young students who interviewed him while he shaved one morning he
made the amazing promise that he would turn over to Zapata the capital,
its arsenals, and its garrison. In exchange he asked only for Zapata's word
that he would respect "the lives and properties" of the metropolitans. He assured the boys that the southern chiefs could achieve no understanding
with Carranza, whom he peevishly described as "glutting himself with his
triumphs."[8]

These fleeting overtures excited no audience, however, at the Zapatista
headquarters. Zapata still counted on getting his forces into the city on
their own steam, possibly through the coordination of an uprising downtown with an assault through the suburbs.[9] And Palafox followed the

[5] Act of Ratification of the Plan de Ayala, July 19, 1914, ibid.

[6] Palafox to Zapata, July 24, 1914, AA.

[7] Samuel Espinosa de los Monteros to Zapata, July 25, 1914, ARD, 12: 34A: 2.
For the other concessions, see Womack: op. cit., pp. 312–13.

[8] Magaña: op. cit., IV, 208, 210-13.

[9] Zapata to Heliodoro Arroyo, July 26, 1914, AA.

activities of Zapatista agents with a keen eye, so that "the Revolution might not be prejudiced in any way."[1] Although the Constitutionalists had now pushed through Guanajuato and into Querétaro and daily strengthened their bargaining position, Zapata remained bitterly opposed to talks. The only dealings he approved of were with army officers, whom he evidently trusted more than politicians. He sent one envoy directly to them, a reliable revolutionary who had attended the National Military College. And on August 10 he published a decree offering amnesty to officers not guilty of civil crimes and to the troops in general.[2]

By now the Constitutionalist armies were so close to the city that the most Zapata could have gained would have been a joint occupation. Surprisingly, he gained no role at all. In the end the metropolitan politicos decided to treat exclusively with Carranza's representatives, and Zapata could not stop them. On August 13 at Teoloyucan, a little town in north-central Mexico State, authorities from the War Department surrendered the federal army to the leading Constitutionalist general, Álvaro Obregón; not even a Zapatista observer was present. In a flash the Teoloyucan treaties revealed a grim truth about the revolution. The crucial victory the Mexican people had just won, in a hard eighteen months and largely by their own devices—this victory they had accomplished as in-laws, not as blood kin, in cooperation but not in union. The question that now charged their relations was whether the various leaders they had created almost in their own image could combine to organize and save their victory.

Although the treaties might deny the Zapatistas, they could not make them disappear. True, Zapata had missed a good political chance; but at least, in avoiding disreputable compromises, he had failed in full revolutionary honor. Clearly the Zapatistas had helped to overthrow Huerta and to drive the revolution, its discoveries and its hopes, into the course of the nation's history. Indeed, as anyone in the capital could see, there the Zapatistas undeniably were, the lights from their campfires on the mountains to the south flickering in the August night.

[1] Palafox to Ángel Barrios, August 7, 1914, AA.
[2] Cited in Magaña: op. cit., IV, 209–10.

VII

The Countrymen Disavow
the Constitutionalists

"They're all a bunch of bastards."

AFTER EIGHTEEN MONTHS OF CIVIL WAR Mexico City had again fallen to the revolutionaries. And tentatively, then jubilantly, people from Sonora to Chiapas celebrated the return of peace. Peace was news, like an earthquake or a miracle. On street corners the balladeers sang about it.[1]

Of all the states Morelos had probably most reason for relief. Its rich countryside lay devastated. Only a few sugar plantations had marketed anything of a harvest, and that under Zapatista auspices; the others had seen their business "almost paralyzed."[2] The state's district seats, even its capital, were ghost towns—the houses and shops empty, roofless, gutted by fires that left the cracked and broken walls black with smoke. In the villages summer weeds were thriving in the quiet ruins. In the last year alone Morelos had lost over one fifth of its total population.[3]

But although there was peace, there was no rest—in Morelos or any other state. Again Mexico's revolutionary leaders proved unable to join

---

[1] See the songs cited in Simmons: op. cit., pp. 132-3, 521.

[2] *El hacendado mexicano*, XX, 231 (February 1914), 41; 232 (March), 81; and 233 (April), 121.

[3] Holt Büttner: op. cit., p. 23.

forces for the sake of their common popular cause. Before, with Madero, they had quarreled over what the revolution was; now, after Huerta, they quarreled only over how to manage and guarantee it. But the divisions were nonetheless bitter.

Two major parties grappled for control. Both were factions within the Constitutionalist movement. One was the group supporting Governor Venustiano Carranza, the founding father of the movement and now its First Chief. The other was the opposition that had collected around Francisco Villa, the onetime bandit who had become the most powerful revolutionary general in the country, "the Centaur of the North." Superficially the Villistas and the Carrancistas resembled each other. Both had military organizations, Villa's being his famous Division of the North and Carranza's the Divisions of the Northeast and the Northwest. And both still seemed incoherent conglomerations of rival elements, with former Maderistas on both sides, as well as many parvenu revolutionaries and even some old científicos and Reyistas. A visiting American muckraker could tell them apart only by finding out which enjoyed the support of Wall Street.[4]

But as the American sensed, there was more at stake than power. In deciding which party to join, a young Mexican journalist perceived the difference. His words on Villismo, which he finally joined, reveal a nice insight into its character. *"Descontentadiza,"* he called it, and *"libérrima, inconsciente, arrolladora"*—restless and hard to please, utterly free, unconscious, overwhelming.[5] More a force of nature than of politics, the Villista party was commotion rampant. These northern drifters could give their populism no real point. Cowboys, muleskinners, bandits, railroad laborers, peddlers, refugee peons, the Villistas had no definite class interests or local attachments. And to certain ambitious operators, like General Felipe Ángeles, this disorder was an opportunity. Repudiating Huerta, Ángeles had joined the revolution in hopes of becoming its military boss and later, perhaps, president. The headquarters he found easiest to mastermind, because no one else could or would, was Villa's; and there he based his intrigues.[6] But even he could not give a clear direction to Villismo.

[4] Lincoln Steffens: *Autobiography* (New York, 1931), p. 715. According to him, Villa carried the taint.

[5] Martín Luis Guzmán: *El Águila y la Serpiente* (9th edn., México, 1962), pp. 213–14.

[6] Luis Fernando Amaya C.: *La Soberana Convención Revolucionaria, 1914–1916* (México, 1966), pp. 17–18, 24–5. Basilio Rojas: *La Soberana Convención de Aguascalientes* (México, 1961), p. 61.

Villa was the very incarnation of irregularity, and his men took him as a model.

Carranza's party, on the other hand, rested on its claims to formal legitimacy. The new, nationalist entrepreneurs who composed its high command and local cadres were intensely more deliberate than the Villistas. If they plundered, it was not for fun but on business. The fortunes the Carrancista generals sought were huge beyond the drifters' dreams, guaranteed, and (the utmost requisite!) officially certified and socially acceptable. And to achieve them they had a positive, unequivocal policy. First they would purge the government completely, which was why they feared Ángeles, who they suspected would compromise with his old army colleagues to win power. And then they would organize their own regime, a sound system of reform in which they could succeed—to the presidency.

At the edge of this contest stood the Zapatistas. Like Villismo, their movement was populist, unofficial. But their party, born of the independent Ayala revolution, enjoyed extraordinary political solidarity. In isolation and poverty the Zapatistas had early secured a solid base in Morelos's villages and defined their purpose as the defense of the pueblos. And recent recruits had tightened their cohesion with a stringent and militant ideology. The newcomers were metropolitan intellectuals, refugees from the anarcho-syndicalist House of the World Worker, which Huerta had closed in May 1914. On being outlawed, the World Workers split. Many went underground in the capital, later to join the Carrancistas and help organize workers into Red Battalions. Others escaped south into Morelos or kept close contact with those who did—like Antonio Díaz Soto y Gama, Rafael Pérez Taylor, Luis Méndez, Miguel Mendoza López Schwerdtfeger, and Octavio Jahn. The men going south, citified radicals all, followed no special anarcho-syndicalist line. Pérez Taylor, Méndez, and Mendoza L. Schwerdtfeger concerned themselves mainly with the urban working class and seemed vaguely Marxist. Jahn was a French syndicalist, reputedly a veteran of the 1871 Paris Commune. And Soto y Gama, a young lawyer who had helped found both the Liberal movement in 1899 and the Socialist Party in 1912, was a passionate disciple of Tolstoy's and Kropotkin's creed of the good peasant.[7] But together these professional revolutionaries provided a theory, in the latest jargon, of "Land and Liberty." And at the Zapatista headquarters Palafox took them in and gave them various sec-

[7] Rosendo Salazar: *La Casa del Obrero Mundial* (México, 1962), pp. 145–9, 187, 212–15. Miguel Mendoza L. Schwerdtfeger: *¡Tierra Libre!* (México, 1915). Personal interview with Soto y Gama.

retarial assignments. Soto y Gama took the lead in elaborating and refining ideas; the doctrine of agrarismo and the cult of the agraristas that emerged were chiefly his work. Thus through the summer and fall of 1914 the Zapatistas seemed increasingly to propose agrarianism not merely as a necessary element of national policy but as the paramount or even exclusive policy. Zapata himself and his native chiefs were not actually so ambitious: they never changed the modest slogan of the Ayala plan, "Reform, Liberty, Justice, and Law." But their local intransigence apparently confirmed their new agents' rigid proclamations.

Already by the time of their victory over Huerta, the nation's leading chiefs had started preparing for the new round politically as well as militarily. In Chihuahua Villa and Ángeles had retired to build their strength. And in the center and south the informal cooperation between Constitutionalists and Zapatistas in the field—the comradely deals that had developed especially in Michoacán, Mexico State, and the Federal District— soon stopped.[8]

The Carrancistas laid out their claims unmistakably. On the evening of the day the federal army surrendered to Obregón, August 13, Zapatista reconnaissance patrols noted that the federals were not evacuating the little towns they still garrisoned in the southern part of the Federal District until Constitutionalists replaced them at their posts.[9] Unknown to the Zapatistas, this transaction followed to the letter the surrender Obregón had negotiated earlier that day at Teoloyucan.[1] Thus the Carrancistas blocked Zapata's way into the capital.

The Zapatista chiefs should not have been surprised by this hostility. They had already heard that in the north the Constitutionalists had wiped out the few chiefs there who adhered to the Ayala plan.[2] And Zapata himself had never made any secret of his independence from the lordly Carranza. As early as May 1913 he had publicly referred not to Carranza

[8] Magaña: op. cit., IV, 275–92. Romero Flores: op. cit., pp. 124–5. I. Thord-Gray: *Gringo Rebel (Mexico, 1913–1914)* (3rd edn., Coral Gables, 1961), pp. 380–7.
[9] Magaña: op. cit., IV, 240. Thord-Gray: op. cit., p. 388.
[1] See Articles 3 and 4 of the Evacuation and Dissolution Conditions, in Juan Barragán: *Historia del Ejército y de la Revolución Constitucionalista,* 2 vols. (México, 1946), I, 600–2. See also Obregón's general orders to Lucio Blanco, whose troops relieved the federals in the villages south of Mexico City, in Armando de María y Campos: *La Vida del General Lucio Blanco* (México, 1963), p. 104.
[2] Manuel Palafox: "La paz que Carranza propuso a Zapata," *El Universal,* June 28, 1934.

alone but to several chiefs as the leaders of the "armed movement of the North."[3] By October 1913 he had noticed the unusual claims of the "Carrancista movement."[4] Still, when he appointed "ambassadors" to arrange a union with the northerners, he sent them not to Carranza's headquarters only but to six other chiefs as well. In February 1914 a Constitutionalist agent conferred several times with Zapata, urging him "to put himself in accord with General [sic] Carranza, or better said, recognize him without qualifications and unconditionally. By taking this step," he assured Zapata that "he would soon see himself and his party satisfied in their political and agrarian aspirations." But this and other Constitutionalist efforts proved fruitless. "My arguments were heard," the agent later lamented, "but not heeded, and finally were rejected." "You see," Zapata had told him "how no one, not even Villa, recognizes Sr. Carranza."[5] Toward the end of the war, having received ugly reports about Carranza from anarcho-syndicalists and from desperate conservatives, Zapata advanced his position. Not only would he not recognize Carranza as First Chief, he told a Carrancista envoy—Gerardo Murillo, a World Worker intellectual better known as the painter Dr. Atl—but he now insisted also that "all the revolutionaries of the Republic recognize the Plan de Ayala," which named him, Zapata, Supreme Chief while a national junta designated an interim president.[6] Soon afterward, Zapata's secretaries, Palafox, Soto y Gama, and Reynaldo Lecona, censured Carranza to other Carrancista envoys as an "unhealthy element" and "a bourgeois . . . who therefore could not recognize the Plan de Ayala."[7] And under their influence Zapata even impugned Carranza's personal sincerity. The day after Carranza arrived in Mexico City, Zapata wrote freely to Lucio Blanco, one of the three or four highest-ranking Constitutionalist generals: "I will tell you in all frankness that this Carranza does not inspire much confidence in me. I see in him much ambition, and a disposition to fool the people . . ."[8]

And if the Carrancistas had refused the Zapatistas entry into the capital, the Zapatistas had also permitted no trespassing on their domains. During

[3] *El Imparcial,* May 1, 1913.

[4] Zapata to F. Vázquez Gómez, October 24, 1913, AZ.

[5] G. García Aragón to A. Robles Domínguez, August 5, 1914, ARD, 9: C: 24.

[6] Minutes of the conference between Zapata and Dr. Atl, July 28, 1914, AZ, 27: 21.

[7] Unsigned report to A. Robles Domínguez, n.d. (early August 1914?), ARD 11: 31: 32.

[8] Zapata to Blanco, August 21, 1914, AZ, 27: 21.

these days some three hundred Constitutionalists in search of pasture for the northern armies' horses and mules moved a large herd into the upland plains around Chalco. The Zapatista commander there surrounded and disarmed them, and sent them as prisoners to the southern headquarters at Yautepec. There the troops were set free, but the officers remained in custody.[9]

Moreover it was no secret that Zapatistas had had dealings with Villa, Carranza's most dangerous rival. As soon as Villa became prominent in the Constitutionalist campaigns, Zapata had recognized him as a chief of the same rank as Carranza. Villa was the first of the seven chiefs to whom he had directed his "ambassadors." And in November 1913 a personal liaison actually commenced. For lack of funds the Zapatista "ambassadors" were not able to go north, but Gildardo Magaña did go at his own expense. The year before, during Madero's regime, young Magaña had spent some months in the Mexico City penitentiary with Villa. There, having helped him with the rudiments of reading and writing, he had earned Villa's friendship. He had also explained the Plan de Ayala to him.[1] So when Magaña reached Matamoros, by the roundabout way of Veracruz, Havana, and New Orleans, he naturally considered Villa his most likely northern prospect.[2] And no obstacles hindered him. Carranza was then on the other side of the country in Sonora; and the revolutionary general running the states of Tamaulipas and Nuevo León, which he had to cross to get to Villa in Chihuahua, was Lucio Blanco, who had himself recently earned a reputation for agrarian sympathies by expropriating a local hacienda and dividing it among its peons. Chief of Blanco's staff was a close childhood friend of Magaña's, Francisco Múgica. In this climate Magaña's hopes flourished, and shortly after Villa's dramatic victory at Ciudad Juárez on November 16, he headed there for a conference. It was impossible to tell how firm Villa's "social" devotion was, but at least to his wellwisher Magaña he sounded sincere. He had turned down Carranza's proposals to repeal the few agrarian reforms initiated earlier in Chihuahua under a Maderista regime. He was even planning to set up a state agrarian commission to continue them. He also praised other northern chiefs with agrarian sympathies, like Calixto Contreras and Orestes Pereyra in his native Durango. And although he had never met his compañerito Zapata, he agreed warmly with his desire for the union of "revolutionaries of

[9] Magaña: op. cit., IV, 242.
[1] Ibid., II, 146–64.
[2] For his account of the trip, see ibid., III, 271–4.

principle." To prove his interest, he started a correspondence with Zapata.[3]

By March 1914 Villista agents had an attentive audience in Zapata: the news they brought could excite a general junta of leading southern chiefs.[4] By mid-August, reports were current in Mexico City of how Villista envoys were respected figures at the Zapatista headquarters. One Villista, with whom Magaña had earlier conferred, came specifically to ask Zapata to "show himself energetically against Carranza."[5]

In the Carrancista camp, however, many chiefs also valued an understanding with Zapata. Radicals themselves, they appreciated his struggle for agrarian reform. Besides, they feared the ultimate consequences of losing him to Villa. A Villa-Zapata axis would obstruct the Constitutionalist seizure of power, which might permit an astute conservative clique to take charge. Especially they feared Felipe Ángeles, with his federal loyalties and connections. Even to forestall his rise, they dared not broach the subject of Zapata to their First Chief. To Carranza, Zapata's "rabble" was the same as Emilio Vázquez's 1912 "mob," and neither much better than Orozco's traitors, with whom both had allied against Madero; and he absolutely refused any union with the Morelos movement.[6] But independently, while Villa and Zapata slowly cultivated their mutual relations, Carrancista spokesmen in the center and south had done what they could to sway Zapata to their side, or at least to keep him away from Villa. On July 27 Carranza's private secretary wrote to Zapata, offering him military supplies in return for support of the First Chief.[7] Then came Dr. Atl's interview in Yautepec.

These Carrancistas saw their main hope in the fact that Zapata had not formally committed himself to Villa. The southern connection with the Chihuahua movement remained casual and cautious. Nor had Zapata turned absolutely against the Carrancistas, for in Michoacán, Guerrero, Mexico, and Puebla he remained at peace with them. But this was no sign of sympathies. It was simply that Zapata trusted no other national leader; and until he did, he would stay independent. "Revolutions will come and revolutions will go," he had told the Carrancista agent in February, "but I

---

[3] For the conference, see ibid., III, 284–8.

[4] García Aragón to A. Robles Domínguez, August 5, 1914. ARD.

[5] Marte R. Gómez: "La Reforma Agraria en las filas villistas" (MS, 1965), pp. 33–4. I consulted this manuscript thanks to the generosity of its author.

[6] Alfredo Breceda: *México Revolucionario, 1913–1917,* 2 vols. (Madrid, 1920; México, 1941), I, 435.

[7] Zapata to Alfredo Breceda, August 21, 1914, AZ, 27: 17.

will continue with mine." Such a stand Villa could tolerate, even encourage. But Carranza could never tolerate it, much less recognize it: independent revolution jeopardized his claim to the chieftainship of all legitimate resistance to Huerta. As Zapata's southern operations succeeded, Carranza grew more annoyed and more intransigent. It became increasingly difficult for his subordinates to prepare for any compromise.

Still, when the war ended, nothing formal took place—even after the Carrancistas closed up the Zapatistas' way into the capital and thus openly posed for the first time the possibility of an alliance between Villa and Zapata. Despite resentment on both sides, the passage to an understanding remained clear for the time being. No revolutionary chief so dominated his camp that he could proceed crudely over the feelings of his lieutenants. And before public commitments occurred, many Carrancista leaders felt regular negotiations were necessary—whether to satisfy their reformist fellow officers that Zapata was impossible to deal with, to weaken the resolve of enemy officers, or actually to see if any chance remained for a political settlement. And the Zapatista leaders responded for similar reasons—to unify themselves, to divide the other camp, and to try out their own hopes for peace. Besides, the people were groaning for a rest. And so talks began.

After Obregón occupied Mexico City, Carrancistas and Zapatistas conferred almost daily. While Carranza waited at Tlalnepantla to enter the capital, a self-styled Zapatista agent, Alfredo Serratos, interviewed him and other leaders and agreed to take their offers to Zapata. There also two members of de la O's staff saw the First Chief on their own account.[8] And their visit impressed Carranza sufficiently for him to write to Zapata, suggesting a "personal interview" wherever Zapata might choose.[9] Among the Carrancista officers in Mexico City angling for a deal with Zapata, Lucio Blanco took the lead. Realizing the danger of revolutionary divisions, he met in strict secrecy with four other Carrancista generals on August 17 and decided to send a confidential agent south. The agent was to deliver Blanco's personal gift to Zapata, a .44 Colt revolver with gold inlay, and to assure Zapata that there were Constitutionalist chiefs who would force Carranza to enact agrarian reforms.[1] Then on August 18 Dr. Atl intervened again by writing Zapata on Blanco's behalf about a conference.

[8] Magaña: op. cit., IV, 247–51.
[9] Carranza to Zapata, August 17, 1914, AZ, 27: 17.
[1] Thord-Gray: op. cit., pp. 395–8.

But though the exchanges continued, they did not establish grounds for mutual accommodation or even slacken the tension. On his claim to executive authority through the Plan de Guadalupe Carranza was adamant. He wanted peace, but he would not compromise. Fearing for Mexico's very existence as a nation if Villa's party took power, he saw in Zapata only an accomplice to Villa's subversive work of disorder. Anything Zapata did was bad, even if Carranza had proposed similar action. "This business of dividing up the land is ridiculous," he told envoys from de la O, when he himself had already declared that land reform was inevitable. What counted for Carranza was that reform have an official source, that it literally issue from a metropolitan office. And to him the Zapatistas were only country renegades, upstart field hands who knew nothing of government. If they had fought Huerta, so also they had backed Orozco against Madero. He warned one Zapatista commission that unless the southerners laid down their arms he would order attacks against them "as bandits."[2]

Zapata was no less stubborn. For him also the sore point was the constitution of an interim government, which would control the elections of the new federal and state regimes. If Carranza became president, Zapata believed with good reason, he would stifle the southern movement and disable the agrarian cause. In Zapata's eyes only a regime constituted according to his Ayala plan could guarantee the eventual enactment and enforcement of agrarian reform. This was not because of the plan's reformed Article 3, which declared him the revolution's Jefe Supremo, but because of Article 12, which provided the machinery to replace him—a grand junta of the chiefs of the nation's great popular armies, which itself would name an interim president. And like Carranza, Zapata would admit no compromise before recognition of his plan. The information his secretaries continually gave him about Carranza confirmed him in his notions: the northern First Chief, so went reports, was a thieving, ambitious old *cabrón*, surrounded by conniving lawyers indifferent to the miseries of common people.[3]

In careful disrespect he refused to dignify his agents to Carranza as formal delegates. To Carranza himself he wrote that "the persons who have approached you as representatives of mine are not, and I have no representative at all in Mexico City." Noting that "the triumph of the cause of the people, which you say has arrived," would not in fact be secure

[2] Magaña: op. cit., IV, 261–70.
[3] A. R. Serratos to Magaña, October 1, 1914, AZ, 27: 7.

"until the revolution of the Plan de Ayala enters" the capital, he stated how "very necessary" it was for Carranza and the other northern chiefs to sign the southern plan. As for the personal interview Carranza had suggested, Zapata declared his readiness for it: "for which," he concluded, "I recommend that you come to this city of Yautepec, where we will talk in full freedom . . ."[4]

From Zapatista headquarters regular propaganda issued against the would-be First Chief. To Villa Zapata wrote that Carranza's presidential aspirations were "very dangerous." The old man's greediness would cause another war, he said, "for in no way will we revolutionaries who sustain the [Ayala] plan permit it to be mocked in the slightest."[5] In Mexico City a Zapatista agent told the Brazilian minister that his chief "would never recognize Carranza."[6] And over Amador Salazar's signature there appeared a curious, confused manifesto, probably composed by Montaño, wherein he declared his misgivings that "Señor Carranza, already in possession of the Provisional Government of the Republic [,] has not yet made any frank unreserved statement as to his attitude toward our General in Chief Emiliano Zapata . . ."[7] On August 23 Zapata made his first bid for United States attention in a long open letter to President Wilson, in which he condemned "Mr. V. Carranza and his clique of ambitious politicians."[8] Two days later he wrote to Villa again that "the time has come for a provisional government to be set up" by the revolutionary chiefs. If Carranza proceeded otherwise, Zapata boasted of "70,000 men with Mausers" who would fight the war to the end.[9] Privately he did not underestimate the Carrancista forces. About this time Soto y Gama predicted sanguinely to him the Carranza would fade away in at least a year or two. Zapata disagreed: it would take much longer, he foresaw, until Carranza's generals grew exasperated and deserted him. But as long as it took he would hold out.[1]

The pressures for peace remained strong, however. The metropolitan press reinforced them by publishing rumors of Carrancistas and Zapatistas

---

[4] Zapata to Carranza, August 17, 1914, AA.

[5] Zapata to Villa, August 21, 1914, AZ, 27: 17.

[6] Canova to the secretary of state, August 21, 1914, NA, 59: 812.00/12959.

[7] To the Liberating Army of the Republic of Mexico, August 23, 1914, ibid., 13006 1/2.

[8] Zapata to Wilson, August 23, 1914, AZ, 27: 17, and NA, 59: 812.00/12998 1/2.

[9] Zapata to Villa, August 25, 1914, AZ, 27: 17.

[1] Personal interview with Soto y Gama.

exchanging views.[2] Most important, the American consular agents in the capital tried to sponsor negotiations. Indirectly their efforts did bring about the only formal talks that took place between the two parties.

For months the Americans had hoped to bring Zapatistas and Constitutionalists together "to insure cooperation in the establishment and maintenance of peace" after Huerta fell.[3] And on August 23 Carranza "intimated" to one agent, John Silliman, "that possibly the good offices of the United States might be effective in arranging a conference with Zapata and himself."[4] Almost certainly he intended that the Americans should invite Zapata to Mexico City, which would require Zapata to humble himself politically or discredit himself diplomatically. The next day Carranza told Silliman outright that he would accept an offer from him "to arrange a conference" with Zapata.[5] This was "a delicate matter," as the agent knew, but he resolved it discreetly by having a representative of the American Red Cross convey the desire for talks to Zapata. The Red Cross agent, Charles Jenkinson, had "a lengthy and confidential conference with Zapata" on August 25. But his report was discouraging. Zapata's attitude toward Carranza was "decidedly unfriendly," Jenkinson observed. Although the southern chief insisted "that a conference between Carranza and himself is imperatively necessary," he repeated that "it must be at his own military camp." Jenkinson also found "Villa emissaries with Zapata" and remarked that "they were treated with the highest consideration." Nevertheless—and no doubt to Carranza's dismay—he judged it "quite probable that Zapata would compromise on some nearer place for conference at American suggestion but not otherwise." These views Silliman and Jenkinson recounted to Carranza on August 26, although "it was not considered expedient to go into particulars."

Carranza was now in a difficult bind. Having asked for the American intervention, he could hardly condemn its fruits. However, excruciatingly sensitive as he was to foreign meddling in Mexican affairs, he did not want agents of the United States government really involved in negotiations between him and his domestic rivals. Therefore, bending to keep from breaking, he gambled. On the one hand, he did not dismiss the possibility of American mediation. Although he rejected again the proposal that he meet Zapata at Yautepec, and although, as Silliman noted, he "still continues to

[2] *El Liberal,* August 18–20, 1914.
[3] Lind to the secretary of state, April 3, 1914, NA, 59: 812.00/11396.
[4] Silliman to the secretary of state, August 23, 1914, ibid., 12967.
[5] Silliman to the secretary of state, August 24, 1914, ibid., 12986.

belittle Zapata," he did indicate that if all other contacts failed he would let the United States President furnish intermediaries for the bargaining. On the other hand, he reserved the right to play out his own dealings with Zapata first.[6] Thus he restored Mexican control over negotiations, on the condition that he engage in them.

Luckily for him the latest Carrancista delegate to Zapata now filed a promising report. This was the work of Juan Sarabia, a former Liberal, former editor of the *Diario del Hogar*, which had first published the Ayala plan, and an old friend of Antonio Díaz Soto y Gama. Authorized by the Federal District chief of police, he and an aide, Ramón Barrenechea, had gone to Cuernavaca "to confer with General Zapata about achieving the unification of the armies of the North and South in order to consummate the peace which the Fatherland needs so much."[7] Once in Morelos, Sarabia had taken the opportunity to size up Zapata, his headquarters, and his forces. None impressed him. The southern army was well supplied from the materiél captured in Cuernavaca, but, despite Zapata's boasts, Sarabia learned that it comprised active units of only fifteen thousand men—and those still poorly trained and organized. At headquarters Palafox held the staff "completely in check," but to Sarabia he seemed "a mediocrity de pueblo (in all senses)." Zapata himself was "like a Messiah" to his partisans, but "of education or politics," Sarabia concluded, "he has not even a notion. . . . He is puffed up with pride . . ." Still Sarabia found reasons for hope. The other secretaries around the headquarters—Soto y Gama, Luis T. Navarro, Genaro Amezcua, and Montaño—he regarded as intelligent and amenable souls, "good friends of mine [who] . . . in a given case would do something for peace."

Even Zapata, he believed, might respond to the right appeal. When Amezcua explained to his chief that Sarabia bore a letter from Antonio Villarreal, Zapata had shown immediate interest. He knew Villarreal as another comrade of Soto y Gama's in the Liberal Party, and had heard from Magaña of the agrarian reforms Villarreal had recently carried out as revolutionary governor of Nuevo León. Just four days before he had

---

[6] Silliman to the secretary of state, August 26, 1914, ibid., 13015.

[7] For this conference, see Sarabia's report of the arrangements between Ramón R. Barrenechea and Emiliano Zapata, August 25, 1914, ARD, 11: 31: 64, and Sarabia to John Kenneth Turner, January 26, 1915, cited in Carlos Basave del Castillo Negrete: *Notas para la historia de la Convención Revolucionaria (1914–1915)* (México, 1947), pp. 76–93.

written to Villarreal, praising him as "a patriot and an honorable man . . . who will know how to defend the cause of the people."[8] And now to Sarabia he spoke "very highly" of him again, and of Luis Cabrera and Lucio Blanco as well. On Amezcua's suggestion, without consulting Palafox, he gave Sarabia written authority to invite Villarreal, Cabrera, and Blanco to confer in Cuernavaca. In the note he expressed his "best wishes to arrive at a cordial arrangement with all revolutionaries who sustained the same principles."

On balance, then, Sarabia reported to Carranza that it would not be "difficult, much less impossible, to have [Zapata] enter into a satisfactory deal." He advised that one last commission go to Morelos, and that Lucio Blanco and Villarreal compose it. He further advised that the Carrancistas even grant Zapata his demand for a national revolutionary junta to name the interim president, since the Carrancistas were so numerous that they could control it. And if this last effort at peace failed, he said, it would not take a long campaign to starve the Zapatistas out.

Carranza remained as skeptical as ever, but to keep the Americans out of his business he had to negotiate. Indeed the circumstances of these talks would be as favorable as he could get: because of the Zapatista invitation, he would not have to attend the conference in person but could send the envoys Zapata had asked to see. So he appointed the commission. He suspiciously did not let Blanco go, and he did not authorize the delegates to grant any concessions. But in the general excitement these reservations went unnoticed. And on August 27 the commission left for the south—Luis Cabrera, then Carranza's closest civilian adviser, and Villarreal, accompanied by the go-between Sarabia. To the revolutionary editors of *El Liberal* it seemed "almost a certainty that a favorable result will be reached." In their pages Dr. Atl rhapsodized about his own "long conference" with Zapata a month before and referred to "the national esteem" owed to the "tenacious and invincible" southern warriors. "I have the firm conviction," he declared, ". . . that General Antonio I. Villarreal and Attorney Luis Cabrera will be able tomorrow to bring to the inhabitants of the capital and to . . . the whole nation the word that is necessary, not only for our peace but also to do justice."[9]

This was a fantasy. When the Carrancistas arrived in Cuernavaca to

[8] Zapata to Villarreal, August 21, 1914, cited in Magaña: op. cit., V, 16–17.
[9] *El Liberal*, August 28 and 29, 1914.

talk, their surprise at what they saw immediately betrayed how slight were the chances for an understanding. For as they came down into that ruined, provincial capital they entered a world completely different from Mexico City. Cuernavaca had become a town that Morelos's common country people had taken over, camped in, and turned into their own. And all the strengths and weaknesses of common country people pervaded the town's atmosphere. To their discomfort, the Constitutionalists could not tell who was a chief and who was not: except for stray *charros*, Zapatista leaders dressed like their followers in the sandals and white work clothes all Morelos farmers wore. Many could not read or write. And when they voiced their opinions in meetings, it was in the manner of simple folk distinguished less for eloquence than for dumb courage—with a meandering and ungrammatical and then suddenly straightforward honesty.

Worst for the Carrancista envoys was the provincial suspicion they encountered. As wordly men accustomed to variety of scene and company, and to the sociable courtesies of politicians, they found themselves offended by the plain, bitter pride the Ayala revolutionaries took in their local cause. "The only form by which the Zapatistas understand the triumph of the Revolution," Cabrera and Villarreal later reported, "is for the Plan de Ayala to triumph in all its parts. . . . The very name of the Plan de Ayala is so important that it is believed indispensable to mention it as accepted in order to convince the [southern] revolutionaries that [their] plan has triumphed."[1]

The enmity the invited envoys sensed was in part a deliberate creation, emanating from the Zapatista headquarters. There Palafox, whose authority his aides had breached in suggesting the talks, had recovered control and reinstated his policy of no compromise. For him, to concede powers to Zapata's rival Carranza was to favor the careers of his own rivals in the Carrancista headquarters; and this generosity he was no longer capable of. During the last months he had developed a consuming itch for command. His signature, once modest and clear, was now grand and full, tumescent. Little Manuel Palafox had become a figure of national prominence, a potential minister at least. If he could help engineer the disgrace of Carranza and the disintegration of the Carrancista party, he would certainly take a seat in the revolutionary cabinet.

Backing him in his plan to embarrass the Carrancista agent was a recent arrival in the southern camp, Alfredo Serratos. The evident aim of this Zapatista-come-lately was also self-promotion. Already he had intervened in

[1] For this report to Carranza, see Magaña: op. cit., V, 82–90.

relations between Carranza and Zapata, falsely claiming before each chief that he represented the other. An old Maderista and a friend of Soto y Gama, Serratos disliked Palafox personally—"a perverse and sanguinary man," he later dubbed him—but for the moment he swallowed his disgust and encouraged Palafox. It may be that Serratos was secretly a Villista agent: he had been a man of political and military mark in Hidalgo, which was Felipe Ángeles's native state, he later cooperated closely with Ángeles, and he finally returned north to join the Villista army.[2] In any case the role he now assumed was to intensify the antagonism between Carranza and Zapata. But the xenophobia in Morelos did not originate with Palafox and Serratos, outlanders themselves.

The real source of the current suspicion was the fear prevailing in the state, a fear born of the abuses and treachery strangers had perpetrated there in the past. Again perfectly representative of his people's feelings—even in their weakness—was Zapata, the chief of Morelos. Zapata knew the importance of the meeting with Villarreal and Cabrera. It offered hopes for the integration of the local reforms he and his men had already won into a national system. But it was precisely the meeting's importance that made it dreadful to him. In some uncanny way the common people of Morelos had picked a leader they could not have been surer of: that is, Zapata could not have felt more responsible toward them. A man obsessed with staying true, he could not betray a promise for the life of him. But courage of one kind can hint at cowardice of another; and Zapata was afraid—not for himself, but of himself, of unwittingly betraying the trust his peers and their people had invested in him. This was why he hated Mexico City: why in 1910, after his release from the army, he quit a promising job in Díaz's son-in-law's metropolitan stables and came home instead to Anenecuilco, why in 1914 Zapatista agents told Carranza their chief would not come to the capital to confer. To Zapata, as the agents said, Mexico City was "a nest of politicians and a focus for intrigues."[3] Zapata himself minced no words about politicians. "Those *cabrones*!" he called them in a later conversation with Villa. "As soon as they see a little chance, right away they want to get in on it, and they take off to brown-nose the next big shot on the rise! That's why I've busted all those *cabrones*. I can't stand them. . . . They're all a

[2] Jesús Hernández Bravo: "El General Serratos Combatió a Zapata y Hoy lo Defiende," *El Hombre Libre,* May 28, 1937. Alfredo Serratos: "El General Serratos Refuta Unas Apreciaciones," ibid., June 2, 1937, and "Bocetos para la historia: el abrazo Villa-Zapata," *El Universal Gráfico,* November 24 and 25, 1952.

[3] Magaña: op. cit., IV, 251.

bunch of bastards."[4] He would go to Mexico City, his agents had told Carranza, "only when circumstances permitted nothing else and always to stay only as long as necessary." But now Mexico City had come to him. Could he trust his plain horsedealer's sense to tell a trick from a deal? As Palafox reminded him, the northerners had never shown any "social preoccupation" like that in the Ayala plan. With rage he must have remembered another series of August compromises three years before. The Carrancista envoys might be friendly, but they were strangers and they had come to talk high politics; and Zapata left town.

Thus, when Cabrera, Villarreal, and Sarabia arrived in Cuernavaca on Thursday afternoon, August 27, they learned that their host had gone—to Tlaltizapán, a quiet little tree-shaded town sixty-five miles to the south, a cool oasis among the steaming rice paddies around Jojutla. No explanation excused his departure. He would be back, the envoys were told, mañana.

Such was the vacuum the Carrancista negotiators entered as they prepared to learn how they could win the Zapatistas away from Villa and prevent a new civil war. In their favor they felt there operated only one factor—the state's exhaustion. A Carrancista agent had already reported that "several Zapatista chiefs of some significance . . . [were] resolved to abandon their chief Zapata in case he does not arrange something with Señor Carranza, for they are tired of such a long and cruel struggle . . ." Among the Zapatista troops, also, the agent reported a "marked desire for peace, for they feel their energies worn out and poverty giving the orders in their households."[5] In his report Sarabia had also mentioned the ordinary soldiers' "fatigue and desire to go home to work in peace." Various Zapatistas had asked him, he said, what the Carrancistas were up to "because they wanted to rest. Naturally they do not renounce their beliefs, but one does notice in them the desire even to desert because of the misery they find themselves in; and if they do not do so, it is for the fear they have of being shot by a firing squad, which their chief Zapata would irremissibly do."[6] This exhaustion, the demoralized fatigue that dirt farmers and field hands collapsed into when they believed that they had fought enough and that there was no good cause to waste yet another planting season—this was the undertow of the tide of suspicion swelling over Cuernavaca. Ordinary people feared betrayal, but they also feared more war.

[4] See the stenographic record of the Villa-Zapata interview, printed in González Ramírez: *Planes,* pp. 113–21.

[5] García Aragón to Robles Domínguez, August 5, 1914, ARD.

[6] Sarabia's Report, ARD.

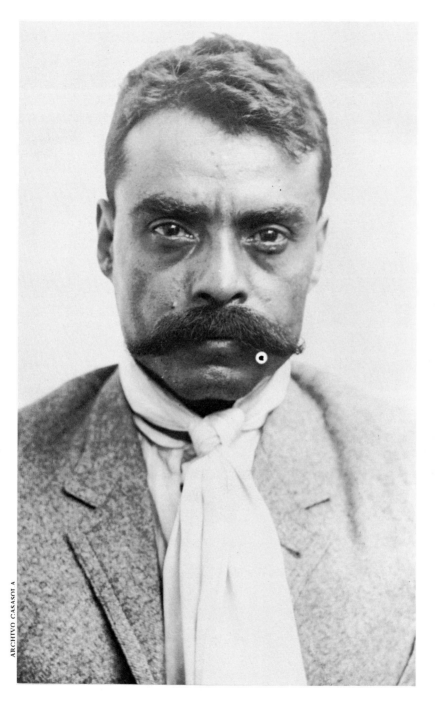

Emiliano Zapata, 1914

ARCHIVO CASASOLA

Emiliano Zapata in the early days of the Maderista revolt, 1911

Eufemio (left) and Emiliano Zapata (right), 1911

Manuel Palafox   *Francisco Pacheco*

Zapatista commissioners to the Convention of Aguascalientes: front, second from left, Paulino Martínez; third from left, Antonio Díaz Soto y Gama

Female prisoners from Morelos villages, federal hostages in 1913

Young Zapatista troops, around 1914

Hostages in Mexico City, 1913, among them Zapata's mother-in-law and four of her daughters

Zapatista troops breakfasting at Sanborn's restaurant, after occupying Mexico City for the first time.

General Felipe Ángeles

*In dark glasses, General
Victoriano Huerta*

Genovevo de la O

December 6, 1914. Emiliano Zapata, center, with big sombrero; on his left, with bandaged head, Otilio E. Montaño; on Zapata's right, on eagle chair, Francisco Villa

Amador Salazar

Fortino Ayaquica, around 1915

Fortino Ayaquica (right) in the 1930's

Otilio E. Montaño   *Gildardo Magaña in 1912*

Right to left: Francisco J. Múgica, Minister of Communications; Gildardo Magaña; President Lázaro Cárdenas; and Manuel Ávila Camacho, Minister of War, 1938

A young Zapatista

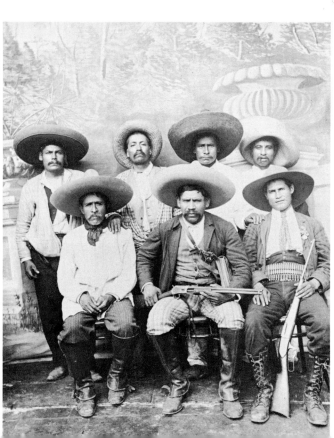

General Juvencio Robles

Front, center, a typical Zapatista chief, Refugio Sánchez, from Tepoztlán

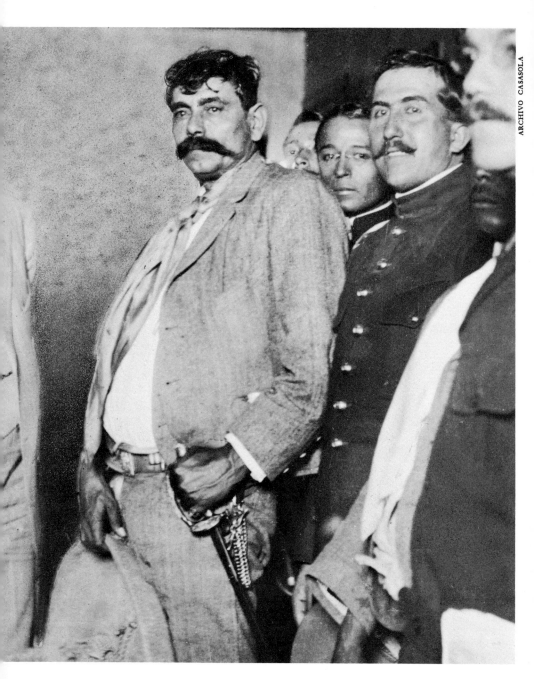

Hand on saber, Eufemio Zapata

Pablo González

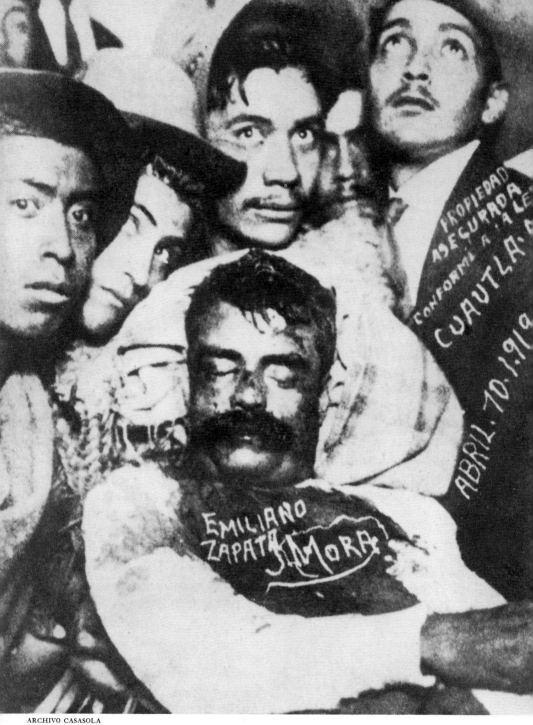

Emiliano Zapata, dead, in the Cuautla police station, April 10, 1919

While they waited for Zapata to return, Cabrera and Villarreal agreed to unofficial discussions. The first took place the evening of their arrival. Ominously, no local Zapatista chiefs attended—only Palafox, Serratos, Soto y Gama, Amezcua, and a few other recently enlisted secretaries, at least one (Dr. Alfredo Cuarón) from Felipe Ángeles's staff.[7] Recognizing their difficult situation, the Carrancistas maneuvered with appropriate caution. But in Zapata's absence Palafox lorded it over the meeting. From his first words Sarabia noticed his "despotic, dominant, and presumptuous character." Every slip by Cabrera and Villarreal—and even some failures to slip—Palafox turned into evidence of deceit. With obvious relish he dictated the course of the proceedings, intoxicated by his first starring role before a national audience.

Cabrera and Villarreal could not get a word in edgewise. Carranza and the Constitutionalist generals had to "submit unconditionally" to the Ayala plan, Palafox insisted. Until their "submission" occurred—"Palafox used this word," Sarabia said, not adherence—Zapata would refuse to consider formal negotiations. Cabrera and Villarreal replied gingerly that they could accept the plan's "principles," especially those about land reform, but suggested that other national problems existed which the Ayala plan did not treat. Why not call a convention to compose a general revolutionary program, incorporating the Zapatista demands on land reform with other legitimate plans? A proposition very similar to this Palafox himself advanced a week later, admitting to an agrarista writer in Mexico City that the Ayala plan by no means offered solutions to all the nation's problems, and that it would therefore form only part of national revolutionary policy.[8] But now, with Cabrera and Villarreal, he refused to compromise. On the contrary he demanded "with idiotic stubbornness" that the Plan de Ayala be accepted "without changing a word, a comma"—his very words, Sarabia recalled. Otherwise, he warned, the Zapatistas would go to war against Carranza. Reminded of how disastrous another civil war would be for their country, Palafox minimized the evil. He waved a paper which he said was "the letter from General Villa in which he submits to the Plan de Ayala." In another war only Carranza would suffer, he retorted in what would later prove a very painful misjudgment.

Friday came and still Zapata did not return, and Palafox called another meeting. This time he wanted the discussions official. As Villarreal and

[7] Federico Cervantes: *Felipe Ángeles en la Revolución. Biografía (1869–1919)* (3rd edn., México, 1964), p. 173.

[8] Palafox to Antenor Sala, September 3, 1914, cited in Magaña: op. cit., IV, 313–15.

Cabrera represented Carranza, he would represent Zapata: he asked formally for the envoy's credentials. They explained how they had happened to come—on Zapata's indirect invitation at Sarabia's prompting—and declared honestly that they were only Carranza's "unofficial representatives" and carried no formal credentials or instructions. They did, however, have Carranza's verbal authorization to treat certain matters in private with Zapata himself. This information, Cabrera and Villarreal later reported, "appeared to cause a certain surprise and not a little disappointment." But Palafox went on with his vehement harangues: "The only basis of peace which the revolutionaries of the South admit," the envoys heard again, "is . . . the absolute submission of the Constitutionalists to the Plan de Ayala in all its parts . . ."

About noon on Saturday Zapata finally arrived. But the chances for serious negotiations still looked bad. At the dinner that Zapata, his chiefs and staff, and the envoys ate together, the southern attitude toward the Carrancistas was openly belligerent. Zapata himself, Sarabia remembered, was "reserved and shy"; but an allied chief, a great, burly burr-head from Sinaloa, Juan Banderas, accused the Carrancistas of having attacked his forces around Chalco, and Palafox, recalling "the rigor" with which he had prosecuted the Huertista commissioners a year before, led Sarabia to believe he might have the present envoys shot too. Sarabia could see Zapata growing angrier.

Then came the formal discussions. They did not constitute a general junta of the southern chiefs, and they did not amount to real bargaining. Gathered that afternoon in the temporary headquarters in the Bank of Morelos were Zapata, Palafox, Serratos, and Banderas, and Cabrera, Villarreal, and Sarabia. For three hours the Carrancistas waited while Zapata talked in private with Palafox and Serratos, and Banderas tried to bait Villarreal into a fight. At last Zapata returned to the envoys "with an unmistakable expression of concentrated fury." To Cabrera's diplomatic statement of Carranza's desire for a personal interview, so that the two chiefs could work out an understanding, Zapata replied that he got along with everyone—"if not agreeably then screwing-fighting it out"—and that if Carranza wanted to see him, let him come to Cuernavaca.

After this outburst Zapata hardly spoke. Palafox took over to reiterate his familiar demands that Carranza sign the Ayala plan and agree to all its provisions. When Zapata did speak, it was to ratify Palafox's position. As the conference went on, Zapata grew increasingly furious—as if enraged by the very idea of discussing the petty rights and wrongs of what he had fought three and a half years for. The only active part he took in the talks occurred when all the conferees had agreed that to ease tension in the Federal District the Carrancistas would formally surrender to the Zapatistas the villages they already held south of Mexico City, and would also turn over to them the town of Xochimilco, a strategic prize, the location of the capital's waterworks. This offer, Cabrera and Villarreal reported, Zapata rejected "with energy" as "a favor." But Palafox and Serratos persuaded him to accept it.

The talks ended about eight thirty that evening, and left the Carrancistas thoroughly bewildered. More confusion followed. The Zapatistas had promised the envoys passes so they could return through the lines to Mexico City that night, but then at two a.m. on Sunday they were told they would have to wait for another conference. Sarabia complained to his friends Soto y Gama and Amezcua the next morning and finally obtained the passes, and the exasperated envoys returned to compose their report.

They now understood that a "conflict" was "imminent between the Revolution of the North and that of the South." They could only note that Zapata had finally specified four conditions to "avoid the war." Carranza and his generals had to sign the Ayala plan. Xochimilco would go to the southerners. Carranza would have to retire as the Executive Power, or else accept a representative from Zapata, probably Palafox, "with whose accord transcendental decisions will be dictated and appointments to public posts will be made." And when these three demands were met, new formal conferences would take place in the Zapatista headquarters to carry out the electoral and agrarian provisions of the Ayala plan. The terms were patently unacceptable; Cabrera thought Carranza might consent only to the implicit demand for a decree on agrarian reform. But at least the envoys had obtained a clear and authoritative statement of the southern position.

But they remained at a loss to explain why this position was so "unjustified and ferocious." Cabrera, Villarreal, and Sarabia were steady champions of agrarian reform. In their own party they had defended the Ayala movement as an authentic popular revolution and Zapata as its legitimate chief. Yet in Morelos they had found only insults. Villarreal decided that the fault was not Zapata's. As he wrote to the southern chief, it seemed to him that "all the difficulties, all the intransigencies, all the threats of war came principally from Sr. Palafox."[9] Cabrera gave a similar opinion to an American agent, "that Zapata is weary of fighting but . . . private secretary

[9] Villarreal to Zapata, September 5, 1914, AZ, 27: 21.

[Palafox] ... imposes these conditions."[1] To a Socialist friend in the United States Sarabia was less charitable in his judgment. "Zapata is an imbecile," he wrote. ". . . although it appears that in good faith he wants to improve the humble people [sic], in practice he winds up a blind instrument of skillful rascals like Palafox and Serratos . . ." But these were reactions, not analyses. What counted was that Zapata had let Palafox's tirades serve as his declaration of independence and that he stood by the demands of the conference. Unwittingly Sarabia confessed his inability to fathom what had happened: "I expected from [Zapata] and his people," he wrote his American friend, "something completely different from what I saw when I had the misfortune of knowing them up close."

In fact the conference carried special meanings for every individual Zapatista involved. For Palafox and Serratos the talks probably were an occasion to advance a Villista connection, in order to further their own careers. For other Zapatistas like Soto y Gama and Amezcua, they were an opportunity to reunite the "revolutionaries of principle" and their anarcho-syndicalist aides in all three major camps—Villa's, Carranza's, and Zapata's. For many local rebel chiefs, they were proof that isolation remained the best policy. But for Zapata and probably to most Morelos country folk, they were only the critical phase in the months-old process of frustration with Carranza.

In this last sense their outcome was foredoomed. First Chief Carranza sparked not the faintest sympathy among Morelos farmers and field hands. A senator in Porfirian congresses, a corpulent, imperious old man with a ruddy face, blue-tinted spectacles, and Boulanger whiskers, sitting in his saddle as if in a chair, Carranza was politically obsolete. Rebel and revolutionary he might now be, but in another world—an established and civilized world of clean linen, breakfast trays, high politics, and ice buckets for wine. If Zapata, whose natural arena was the country town of Cuautla, had become a Carrancista, it would have been an astoundingly shrewd maneuver; but it would have been a fluke. In this second August crisis, as in the first, Morelos country folk acted through Zapata; and as they drew back from Carranza in disgust, distrust, and disappointment, so, as one of them and as their chief, Zapata drew back too. True, for him to go definitely against Carranza at this point was to encourage Villa to start another war, infinitely more grievous than the war just won. But in Morelos now alle-

[1] Belt to the secretary of state, September 3, 1914, NA, 59: 812.00/13095.

giance to a man like Carranza was impossible. For the Zapatistas, which included everyone in the state, the Cuernavaca talks had never been negotiations, only pretexts for the final confirmation of their hopes and fears.

The failure of these talks—Carranza publicly refused Zapata's conditions on September 5—still produced no alliance of the Morelos revolution with Villa's. And individual Carrancistas kept trying to apologize or argue the Zapatistas out of their hostility: both Cabrera and Villarreal wrote to Zapata trying to explain how they had been misunderstood, and why, and to assure him that they meant no harm.[2] The American consular agents in Mexico City also resumed their efforts at arranging peace. To avoid irritating Carranza, who complained that earlier American intervention had inflated Zapata's ego, they asked for and received instructions from the State Department to "say to Zapata that this Government earnestly desires that he shall confer with the Constitutionalists and cooperate with them in securing the needed reforms."[3] But these overtures failed. Zapata was determined to operate on his own, and if the significance of the Cuernavaca episode escaped any Mexico City leaders, Zapata lost no time in raising another signal of his independence. On September 8 there issued from his Cuernavaca headquarters a decree to execute Article 8 of the Ayala plan.[4]

This article provided for the nationalization of the goods of persons who opposed, directly or indirectly, the Ayala revolution. And it applied to urban as well as rural property. Liberating Army generals or colonels were to initiate the proceedings, and municipal authorities were to report inventories and their disposition to the southern headquarters. Rural property would pass to pueblos who needed lands, or go to support orphans and widows of the revolutionary dead. The income from urban property was to be used to form credit institutions for small farmers and to pay pensions to revolutionary orphans and widows. As for the "fields, timberlands, and waters" that the revolutionary authorities would nationalize and redistribute, these could not be sold or "alienated" in any way: legitimate possession of them passed only through heirs.

Within Morelos parts of the Ayala plan had already taken effect. Where

[2] Zapata to Cabrera, September 19, 1914, AZ, 27: 12. Cabrera to Zapata, September 23, 1914, ibid. Zapata to Cabrera, October 4, 1914, AZ, 27: 7. Villarreal to Zapata, September 5, 1914, AZ.

[3] Silliman to the secretary of state, September 5, 1914, NA, 59: 812.00/13116, and Bryan to the Brazilian minister, September 7, 1914, ibid., 13117.

[4] Cited in Magaña: op. cit., V, 102–3.

it was feasible, villagers had reoccupied disputed fields as local Zapatista chiefs had reoccupied the towns and district seats.[5] Evidently, since the original promulgation of the plan, recovery was all that Zapata had formally let his officers enforce. Of course Zapatista chiefs had also in fact freely confiscated property where they had to or where they could, but Zapata had never authorized the practice. But now with the Constitution suspended, and with a radical headquarters staff, he was ready to proceed further. As at Cuautla, where Eufemio Zapata now ruled, agrarian commissions of locally respected farmers were shortly appointed and began their revolutionary work.[6] The results would remain provisional until a new Zapatista government took office in the state, but they nevertheless indicated what the chiefs who would install that government expected from it. And the section on urban property sounded a warning to Mexico City on what might happen if the Zapatistas occupied the capital.

This general defiance—the impossible conditions demanded at Cuernavaca, as well as the nationalization decree—publicized well Zapata's unbending resistance to Carranza. Zapata now seemed so committed against Carranza that desperate ex-federal and Orozquista-Huertista commanders started petitioning to join or cooperate with the southern army. The most conspicuous of these were Benjamín Argumedo, Higinio Aguilar, and José Trinidad Ruiz. Congratulating Zapata for his "noble opposition" to Constitutionalism, "a macabre operation of the White House to draw out of our beloved soil the riches . . . of this blood-stained Fatherland," they asked him how he would regard them if they rose in rebellion in Veracruz. They had their own plan and program, they admitted, and wanted to take the port from the Americans still occupying it.[7] Juan Andrew Almazán entered his plea too, alleging a long service on behalf of the southern cause and begging forgiveness for having joined Huerta.[8] By September 12 the American consular agents recognized that further dealings between Zapata and Carranza were out of the question.[9] During the previous week Zapatistas and Carrancistas had actually exchanged fire around Tenango, Mexico, and Atlixco, Puebla.[1]

In this crisis, however, Zapata hesitated to press his claim militarily. In

[5] Trinidad Paniagua to Zapata, August 2, 1914, AZ, 27: 17.
[6] Eufemio to Emiliano Zapata, September 19, 1914, AZ, 27: 12.
[7] Argumedo, Aguilar, and Ruiz to Zapata, September 10, 1914, ibid.
[8] Almazán to Zapata, September 19, 1914, AZ, 28: 7: 1.
[9] Silliman to the secretary of state, September 12, 1914, NA, 59: 812.00/13166.
[1] El Liberal, September 12, 1914.

the first place he alone could not conceivably win a war. His stores of captured arms and ammunition were abundant—two million cartridges and twenty or thirty effective artillery pieces, with their own shells—but his field forces of fifteen thousand were too few and tactically still too disjointed for regular battles; and in guerrillas he could not now advance.[2] Also, internal dissensions had developed in his army. In Cuernavaca de la O fiercely resented Palafox's exercise of jurisdiction in his zone and threatened to apply his own justice in cases he considered important.[3] Moreover, if Zapata could gain a chance for his reforms only through alliances with other revolutionary factions, it was still unclear with whom he should treat in national revolutionary politics. He remained tentatively in favor of Villa. But he could not tell for sure whether the leading Carrancista generals would stay loyal to their First Chief or desert him to join Villa in a new coalition. And hoping for the latter decision, he might provoke the former if he mounted attacks now. So, although Zapata had broken openly with Carranza, he did not launch a direct, violent challenge against him. In preparation for the day when he might do so, he granted the ex-federals' and Huertista's pleas for enrollment on the condition that they sign the Plan de Ayala and take orders from his headquarters; these veteran mercenaries he would use in Puebla and finally against Mexico City.[4] But for the time being he only held the line and looked for a trustworthy deal. In mid-September he sent Gildardo Magaña north to confer with Villa, and he kept another agent, Manuel Robles, in discussions with the Carrancista chiefs in the capital.[5]

Of increasing interest to Zapata was a revolutionary junta Carranza had promised to call soon in Mexico City. Carranza had intended that the junta simply confirm his Constitutionalist claim to authority; but as Manuel Robles reported to Zapata, several important Carrancista chiefs like Obregón and Blanco were at work for the sake of peace to expand the meeting into a general revolutionary junta, including the Villistas and the Zapatistas.[6] Through September it remained at issue who would dominate the junta. And Zapata refused to consider accepting an invitation.[7] Nevertheless he stayed in contact with those chiefs trying to organize an open con-

[2] Sarabia's Report, ARD.

[3] De la O to Palafox, September 26, 1914, AZ, 27: 12.

[4] Zapata to Argumedo, Aguilar, and Ruiz, September 21, 1914, AZ, 27: 12.

[5] Railroad pass for Magaña to Torreón, September 12, 1914, ibid.

[6] Robles to Zapata, September 13, 1914, ibid.

[7] Zapata to Paulina Maraver, October 3, 1914, AZ, 27: 7.

vention—through Magaña, who not only saw Villa but wrote back to Carrancista friends in Mexico City, and through another agent, Leobardo Galván, who attended the caucuses of the peacemaking Carrancistas.[8] And when the junta, which met first in Mexico City on October 1, reconvened in Aguascalientes on October 10 as the Sovereign Revolutionary Convention, Magaña was there to report on its new character.[9]

It was a reformed assembly, not under Carranza's control, not even in sympathy with him. Of the more than one hundred delegates in Aguascalientes, only a few were still loyal to the First Chief. Most were Constitutionalists like Obregón who had come to believe that they could save their revolution and their nation only by dumping their leader. And sitting now among them were thirty-seven Villistas. The Conventionists devoted much attention to the matter of Morelos. On October 12 the chief Villista, Felipe Ángeles, proposed that they formally invite the Zapatistas to join. The next day Ángeles arranged for an observer whom he styled a Zapatista general and delegate to sit in a place in the meeting hall.[1] On October 14 the Conventionists declared themselves the sovereign authority in the country. And the day after, they commissioned Ángeles to go to Cuernavaca to invite the southerners personally. Although Zapata cautiously made no response, the secretaries at his headquarters were eagerly preparing themselves for a trip north.

On October 17 the Ángeles commission arrived in Mexico City—Ángeles himself, Rafael Buelna, Calixto Contreras, and Guillermo Castillo Tapia. There they conferred at length with Lucio Blanco. Two days later they left for Cuernavaca in the charge of Alfredo Serratos, and arrived the same evening. The first person Ángeles sought in the town was Dr. Cuarón, who presented him to Palafox. Immediately they arranged an interview with Zapata for the next day at noon.[2]

It was the first time Zapata and Ángeles had met. Remembering Án-

---

[8] Magaña to Columba C. de Magaña, October 5, 1914, ibid. Amaya C.: op. cit., pp. 67–8.

[9] Magaña to C. C. de Magaña, October 10, 1914, AZ, 27: 7.

[1] For the first days of the Aguascalientes Convention, see Barrera Fuentes: op. cit., I, 84–277. For evidence that the honored observer, Guillermo Santaella y Santibáñez, was a Zapatista of Ángeles's own manufacture, and in fact a Villista agent, see Santaella y Santibáñez to Hipólito Villa, October 23, 24, and 26, 1914, AZ, 27: 7.

[2] For this mission and minutes of the interview between Ángeles and Zapata, see Magaña: op. cit., V, 198–204.

geles's restrained conduct as Madero's last military commander in Morelos, Zapata was especially cordial to him. As for the invitation, he explained, he would have to ask the opinions of his various chiefs. Sending delegates to the Convention clearly amounted to a decisive act of policy for the local revolutionaries, and on this question he could not rule alone. While they waited for the chiefs to reply, Zapata conferred with Villa's "gray lieutenant." He did not want to send accredited delegates to a meeting dominated by Carrancistas, he told Ángeles, even if they were independent Carrancistas. The acting president of the Convention was Villarreal, against whom the Zapatistas held a bitter grudge for his role in the August conference in Cuernavaca. Until the Convention accepted the Plan de Ayala, Zapata said, he could not recognize it as legitimate. But how, he wondered, could he present his case to the assembly and get it to vote the plan without having his spokesman admitted? And how could he have them admitted, with "voice and vote," without recognizing it? Perhaps he could send a "commission" first and, if it succeeded, then a "delegation."

On October 22 the conference began formally in the Cuernavaca headquarters. It was a curious setting in which to decide the fate of a revolution so rooted in local pride and grief. Again, except for Zapata himself, no important Morelos chief took part. Again, almost all the Zapatista "colonels" representing the movement were secretaries, men of the pen, the number, and the word. And only one was a native of the state. The reason the Morelos chiefs thus abdicated their authority is still obscure. It was as if their very concern for the local cause inhibited them from involving it seriously in national affairs. Plain villagers themselves, they must have sensed that they had no business committing the Ayalan revolution to an uncertain alliance like the Convention. Having become national figures, they had incurred the obligation of acting nationally but not, they feared, the capacity for it. The only responsible course, they apparently believed, was to let those who proclaimed themselves experts in grand dealings do the grand dealing; meanwhile they would try to defend the little places that were their own. Afraid, like Zapata, of betraying their people, they turned over the chances for doing so to the intellectuals they had always at heart despised.

This time Palafox kept quiet: he was seeing his plans realized. Ángeles did most of the talking. He began by summarizing what he and Zapata had agreed to be Zapata's position, that the southern headquarters could not recognize the Convention's sovereignty until it obtained Carranza's resignation and granted representation—as Ángeles carefully put it—to "the faction which we might call exclusively agrarian, symbolized by the revolution of the South." This latter point the Zapatistas took to mean formal adherence to the Ayala plan. And one of them wanted to know why they should even send a commission if the Convention might not vote the plan's approval. Here Ángeles responded with embarrassed vagueness, since he hardly wanted to promise direct and full recognition of the plan. Swamping the query in pomposity, he emphasized Mexico's need for peace "at any price." Otherwise, he warned, the U.S. Republican Party, if it triumphed in the 1916 elections, would "work for Intervention"—a remote bogeyman, to say the least, a year and a half away in coming even if he materialized.

The secretaries compromised, and Zapata let them. In the final draft of the conference minutes, the typed words still stood—"it is necessary that . . . the Convention recognize the Plan de Ayala." The last four words were marked out, however, with the same pen the conferees used to sign the document; and in their place, between the lines, was written "the principles of the Plan de Ayala."[3] The Convention could easily approve the southerners' principles, and decide later what they counted for in practice. And on this basis the Zapatistas appointed their "commissioners" in the form Zapata had earlier contemplated.

In all there were twenty-six, including Paulino Martínez as the chief, Juan Banderas, Soto y Gama, Gildardo and Rodolfo Magaña, Leobardo Galván, Amezcua, Dr. Cuarón, Manuel Robles, and eleven other persons at the present conference. Otilio Montaño was also named, but he was ill and did not now take up his appointment.[4] Again, remarkably few Morelos natives were to represent the revolution born in the state. Of those leaving for the north, the only commissioner of true local extraction was Galván, a lawyer from Tepoztlán.

In Aguascalientes the Conventionists waited hopefully, but they were soon to be disappointed. For what Zapata had decided was not calculated to ease their peacemaking tasks. The southern commission left Cuernavaca on October 23, packed into the same automobiles Ángeles and his men had arrived in. And the next day the train they traveled on from Mexico City passed through Aguascalientes without stopping. Zapata's commission went on one hundred miles north directly to Villa's headquarters at Guadalupe, just beyond Zacatecas. There Martínez clinched the deal with Villa's ad-

[3] Minutes of the meeting in Cuernavaca, October 22, 1914, AZ, 27: 7.

[4] Zapata to the secretary of the Convention, October 22, 1914, cited in Magaña: op. cit., V, 230–1.

visers; the other Zapatistas reassured themselves of Villa's concern for the southern cause, and picked up their expense money.[5] If Zapata was to authorize "foreign entanglements," he would have none of the pretense of parliamentary coalitions within an assembly. As the leader of a popular military movement, he would go whole hog and publicly ally with Villa's popular military movement.

On October 26 the Zapatista commissioners finally appeared in Aguascalientes, and the next morning the Conventionists gave them a thrilling official welcome into the theater where they met. As the commission's leader, Paulino Martínez then took the rostrum. After praising Zapata and Villa as "the genuine representatives ... of this homeric struggle ... Indians both of them," he stated the southern position. In effect he declared that he and his fellows intended to make the Convention give up its pretense to revolutionary impartiality and become the political vehicle of a Villa-Zapata military axis against Carranza.[6] Behind the scenes Ángeles maneuvered —to grant the Zapatistas their claims on paper, and to ride the Villistas into the presidency.

Henceforth the deliberate Zapatista drive for control never stopped. Immediately after Martínez spoke, and on the delegates' demand, Soto y Gama went up to the rostrum. The radical young lawyer had languished too many months in Palafox's shade at the southern headquarters not to grab this chance to shine for his cause. In a long, extemporaneous discourse, he established himself as the Zapatista tribune. Explaining Mexican history, denouncing Carranza, insulting the national flag, and eulogizing the Mexican people as eloquently as ever Kropotkin had the Russian, he set loose a terrific uproar. But after nearly homicidal interruptions, the cries that followed his speech and shook the building were vivas for Villa and Zapata.[7]

The task of winning the Convention's acceptance of the Ayala plan proved more difficult than causing commotion. For the Constitutionalists still formed a majority; and if they were willing to see Carranza be removed from power, they did not want either Villa or Zapata to replace him. But through adroit compromises and Soto y Gama's oratory Martínez wangled a deal he could boast of to Zapata.[8] In the October 28 session, after con-

[5] Martínez to Zapata, October 28, 1914, AZ, 27: 7, the first of two letters of this date.

[6] For his speech, see Barrera Fuentes: op. cit., I, 505–9.

[7] For his speech, see ibid., I, 509–14.

[8] Martínez to Zapata, October 28, 1914, AZ, 27: 7, the second of two letters of this date.

fused debates that lasted all day, he got the Convention to approve "in principle" the plan's Articles 4, 6, 7, 8, 9, and 12.

In itself Martínez's achievement was hardly an overwhelming triumph,
Articles 6 through 9 being the land reform articles that Cabrera and Villarreal had already agreed to "in principle" two months before. But the context
of the favorable vote lent it momentous significance. The Aguascalientes
Convention was then the effective government of Mexico, and its adoption
of the Ayala articles, even in principle, was the first official commitment to
a policy of rural welfare in the nation's history. That four years earlier
the científicos had controlled high policy almost completely in favor of the
great landlords, that during Madero's administration agraristas still seemed
eccentric social engineers, and that now a government should announce the
country poor's special right to its services—this alone marked where and
how far the revolution had advanced the public's sense of justice. And the
driving force of the change had been the Morelos revolutionaries.

Even so Zapata understood how little he had actually won in practice.
Most dangerous for him was that he had now half-recognized the Convention's sovereignty, although the Convention had not yet done away with
Carranza. When Martínez asked him for full delegated authority, Zapata
replied that he could not send it. Not until the Convention definitely removed Carranza, he said, could he recognize its sovereignty fully by ac-
crediting his commission as a delegation.[9]

On October 30 the Conventionists took the steps he requested. Leading
delegates like Obregón and Ángeles proposed to dismiss Carranza from his
position as First Chief and Executive Power, and to proceed to name an
interim president. After more long and uproarious argument, the resolution
carried in a closed session by 112 to 21. The assembly had now committed
itself to an ostensibly independent line that was in fact pro-Villa. And in
the next few days the break with Carranza was completed. On November
4, celebrating the withdrawal of Carranza from Mexico City, Martínez and
his fellow delegates reported happily to Zapata that the "Division of the
North behaved admirably and showed itself a true ally. To their constant
and invariable agreement is owed our victory."[1]

The repercussions of this "victory" in Morelos, however, were not so
cheering. It was soon clear there that the Villistas looked forward to "a
few more shootings," as Villa put it to Soto y Gama; that Villa and Ángeles

[9] Zapata to Martínez, November 2, 1914, two letters of this date, both cited in
Magaña: op. cit., V, 240–3.

[1] Martínez et al. to Zapata, November 4, 1914, AZ, 30: 8.

wanted to dominate the independent Carrancistas like Obregón rather than share power with them, which only rallied them again around Carranza; and that coming out in the wash was a war—in which the Zapatistas would have to take part.[2] As early as November 10 Villa wrote to Zapata that "the time for hostilities has come . . ."[3] And the Conventionist minister of war sent orders to the southern headquarters "to initiate an active campaign against the city and state of Puebla."[4] In letting their secretaries involve them with Villa, the Morelos chiefs had thus committed their people to a fight that was not theirs.

In this new alliance the Zapatistas were obviously uncomfortable. Late in the evening of November 24, after the last Carrancistas had evacuated Mexico City, the first southern contingents filtered quietly, almost embarrassedly, into the capital. Uncertain of their role there, they did not sack or plunder but like lost children wandered through the streets knocking on doors and asking for food. One night they heard a great clanging and clattering in the street—a fire engine and its crew. To them the strange apparatus looked like enemy artillery, and they shot at it, killing twelve firemen. Zapata himself was no calmer. Late on November 26 he arrived in the capital. The Carrancista chiefs before him had moved into fine private houses downtown—the residences of the científicos now in exile—but Zapata holed up in a grimy, gloomy little hotel a block away from the railroad station where trains left for Cuautla. He was invited to ceremonies in his honor at the National Palace, but would not attend. Reporters interviewed him, but he hardly muttered sentences. And when the Villistas moved into the northern suburbs to join forces with him on November 28, he took off back to Morelos.[5]

So leery was Zapata that he worried his new allies. A Villista agent in Cuernavaca even reported that Zapata had resumed his independence. The American consular agents were disturbed too: they hoped for a strong Villa-Zapata coalition to restore order in Mexico. And on December 2 a trusted Villista chief (Roque González Garza), the special American agent assigned to Villa's headquarters (George Carothers), Juan Banderas, and Serratos arrived in Cuernavaca to cajole Zapata into a more genial attitude.

---

[2] Antonio Díaz Soto y Gama: "Francisco Villa," *El Universal,* August 24, 1938.
[3] Villa to Zapata, November 10, 1914, AZ, 30: 8.
[4] José I. Robles to Zapata, November 10, 1914, ibid.
[5] Cardoso to the secretary of state, November 29, 1914, and Silliman to the secretary of state, November 30, 1914, NA, 59: 812.00/13940 and 13939. *El Sol,* November 28, 1914. *El Nacional,* November 30, 1914.

They delivered Villa's personal letter to him. They assured him of Villa's sincerity. They promised him he would be safe in Mexico City. They impressed upon him the need for a serious "understanding" with Villa. And in the end Zapata agreed to return for a conference on December 4, not in the capital but at a halfway place in his territory, Xochimilco.[6]

The carefully staged meeting occurred as planned. It was the first between Zapata and Villa, and supposed to herald a glorious revolutionary union. With Zapata came his main secretaries, his brother Eufemio, his cousin Amador Salazar, even his sister María de Jesús and his little son Nicolás. In flowers and colored streamers Xochimilco was decorated as for a fair. The schoolchildren sang songs. There was a town band for serenades. At high noon Villa arrived with a small escort. Montaño made "a hearty speech of welcome," reported an American agent at the scene, and gave Villa an abrazo. He then introduced the Centaur of the North to the Attila of the South. After a few greetings, the two chiefs passed to the town schoolhouse where they sat down in a crowded upstairs room to confer.

As the American agent observed, the two men made "a decided contrast." Villa was "tall, robust, weighing about 180 pounds, with a complexion almost as florid as a German, wearing an English [pith] helmet, a heavy brown sweater, khaki trousers, leggings and heavy riding shoes." Next to him Zapata seemed a native of another country. Much shorter than Villa, the American noted, "weighing probably about 130 pounds," he was a dark and "thin-faced" man, "his immense sombrero sometimes shading his eyes so that they could not be seen. . . . He wore a short black coat, a large light blue silk neckerchief, pronounced lavender shirt and used alternately a white handkerchief with a green border and another with all the colors of the flowers. He had on a pair of black, tight-fitting Mexican trousers with silver buttons down the outside seam of each leg." Villa, the American could see, "did not have any sign of jewelry on," but "Zapata wore two small old-fashioned gold band flat rings on his left hand." Nearby sat Zapata's sister, whom the American mistook for his wife. "Everything she had on her person could probably have been purchased for about $5.00 American money. Her fingers were covered with the flat band old-fashioned rings, that looked more like brass than gold, of which she had more than a dozen." And next to her was Zapata's son,

[6] Cobb to the secretary of state, December 6, 1914, NA, 59: 812.00/13966. Serratos in *El Universal Gráfico,* November 25, 1952. Villa to Zapata, December 1, 1914, AZ, 27: 2.

asleep through the whole conference and "clothed in a pair of loose-fitting white cotton trousers and shirt of the same material, home-made and badly made."

For half an hour the two chiefs sat "in an embarrassed silence, occasionally broken by some insignificant remark, like two country sweethearts." Zapata "seemed to be studying Villa all the time." Not until Villa mentioned how "high and mighty" Carranza was did they warm up to each other. "I always said so," Zapata exploded, "I always told them, that Carranza is a son of a bitch." Ranting and joking about the old First Chief, they talked freely for nearly an hour. Now and then Palafox or Serratos or González Garza would pipe up to say yes. Zapata ordered some cognac, and though Villa, a teetotaler, asked for water, he bravely gulped the drink Zapata handed him in a toast "to their fraternal union." Villa "nearly strangled. His face contorted and tears sprang to his eyes, while he huskily called for water." Having chased his fire down, he offered Zapata a swallow. "No," Zapata replied courteously, "go ahead and drink it." A decided contrast, indeed.

The informal conference then broke up as Villa, Zapata, and Palafox retired to another room. For an hour and a half they discussed how to crush the Carrancistas left in Puebla and Veracruz. Villa boasted of his military stores and generously offered to furnish Zapata whatever he needed to carry on his campaigns. Afterward there was a dinner and speeches. The American agent was relieved. He saw evidence of a "good understanding" between the two chiefs, "which holds great promise for the early establishment of peace in Mexico."[7] Two days later the Division of the North and the Liberating Army of the Center and South formally and festively paraded into Mexico City to occupy it together. For posterity the photographers at the National Palace framed an ebullient Villa chuckling on the presidential throne, a dour Zapata on his left.

This mirage of union soon vanished. For Zapata the truth came out during the campaign in Puebla, which he left Mexico City to direct on December 9. Along the way he learned from an astute agent in the capital of the continuing efforts of old Porfiristas, Felicistas, Huertistas, and ex-federals to insinuate themselves into the revolutionary ranks. "Today we still have to temporize with these types," the agent reported three different intriguers saying, "but soon it'll be another thing. Ángeles, who is

[7] Canova to the secretary of state, December 8, 1914, NA, 59: 812.00/14048. González Ramírez: *Planes*, pp. 113–21.

ours, has Villa in his hand. As for Zapata, who is a savage, it'll be necessary to eliminate him . . ."[8] Villa's behavior lent credence to the report.
The artillery he had grandly promised at Xochimilco was not sent until
very late, and then only on Zapata's repeated request; and then the Zapatistas had to haul it by man- and mule-power through the pass between
the great volcanoes, Popocatépetl and Ixtaccíhuatl, because Villa provided
no locomotives for transport.[9] And while Zapata waited for the guns outside Puebla City, he heard of much graver and more portentous perfidy:
on December 13 Villista officers in Mexico City murdered his chief
delegate to the Convention, Paulino Martínez.

On December 15 Zapata peacefully occupied Puebla City, the Carrancistas having evacuated it as soon as the artillery arrived. But even in the
euphoria of this easy victory, Zapata did not hide his misgivings. To Villa
he wrote almost chidingly of the frequent reports "that our enemies are
working very actively to divide the North and the South, . . . for which
reason I see myself compelled to recommend that you take the greatest
care possible on this particular."[1] Although Zapata knew the strategic
importance of holding Puebla, he returned to Morelos in evident confusion
and disgust.

By the end of the month the vaunted Villa-Zapata coalition was a
public failure. Although the Convention went on as a political body, Zapata
practically abandoned his military duties to it and settled down in retirement in Tlaltizapán. The troops from Morelos that he had taken on campaign followed him home, uninterested in the glory of conquest. The main
force left in Puebla was a corps of former Orozquistas under Juan Andrew
Almazán, who with his cronies Argumedo and Aguilar made deals with
local Felicistas and let Huertista officials out of jail. And although
Villista chiefs protested indignantly to Zapatista headquarters, and although Palafox himself urged Zapata to exercise more surveillance over
the mercenaries, Zapata made no move, verbal or physical, outside Morelos.[2]
In Mexico City Palafox bore the brunt of Villista resentment. The same
American agent who had seen a "good understanding" on December 4
now saw that "the break between [Villa] and Zapata is not remote, and

---

[8] Dolores Jiménez y Muro to Zapata, December 9, 1914, AZ, 27: 19.
[9] Cronista de la Revolución: "Sobre Veracruz," *Excélsior*, July 21, 1929. *La
Opinión,* December 19, 1914.
[1] Zapata to Villa, December 16, 1914, AZ, 27: 19.
[2] Palafox to Zapata, December 21, 22, and 23, 1914, ibid.

when it comes Señor Palafox will be one of the first Villa will attend to."[3]

Carefully, methodically, the Carrancista generals assessed this discord among their rivals and assumed the offensive. By January 4 of the new year Obregón had troops in Puebla's suburbs and the next day after hard fighting he took the city. He thus began in earnest his campaign to crush Villa, whom the Carrancistas, discounting Zapata, saw as the primary danger. Not until Obregón and his comrades destroyed the Villistas could they hope to establish a new regime; then the southern trouble would shrink to an irritating local core that they could treat at their leisure. In the following months, while this terrible war raged in the north, Morelos remained at peace—the state's first peace since the fighting had begun four years before and the last until it ended five years later. And the people there were able to have their own revolution.

[3] Canova to the secretary of state, December 30, 1914, NA, 59: 812.00/14131.

VIII

The Pueblos Carry Out
a Revolution

*". . . hanging on tight to the tail of
our jefe Zapata's horse."*

W HILE MORELOS'S SECLUSION LASTED, the state was almost a frontier.
Dispossessed and destitute families had indeed inhabited the place
for centuries; now, psychologically, they arrived. What they conquered,
cleared, leveled, and settled was not a territory, which they only recovered,
but a society, which they thus recreated. Like other immigrants and pioneers,
they proceeded fitfully—sometimes by the compulsion of immediate needs,
sometimes by dreams they would not surrender. But in this social wilderness
they moved in a remarkably constant direction toward the establishment of
democratic municipalities, country neighborhoods where every family had
influence in the disposition of local resources.

In central and southern Mexico the utopia of a free association of rural
clans was very ancient. In various forms it had moved villagers long before
the Spaniards came. Its latest vehicle was the Zapatista army: ironically,
Morelos's country families had clarified their civilian notions in military
service. The Liberating Army of the Center and South was a "people's
army." And to the men who fought in its ranks, and to the women who

accompanied them as private quartermistresses, being "people" counted more than being an "army." For leadership they still looked more readily to their village chiefs than to their revolutionary army officers. At first, during the early years of the guerrillas, they had suffered no tension in their allegiance, because village chiefs and revolutionary officers were commonly the same persons, or close relatives, or old friends. But in the big campaigns against Huerta, as the skeleton of a regular army formed, amateur warriors had started to become professionals, and commanders had had fewer personal connections with local civilian leaders. Although village councils normally cooperated with the army, ordinary soldiers had more and more divided, or at least different, loyalties. The war did not go on long enough, however, for the Liberating Army's militarist tendencies to harden. Rather the army and the village leaders worked out in practice a federal chain of command. The army chief passed his orders down to the village chiefs, or their deputies who campaigned with him, and they in turn passed the orders on to their respective followings. This mediation usually contained the tension between rival authorities.[1]

As for the tension among villages, or among village contingents on duty, the civil war itself had relaxed it. Already before the war village leaders had been acquainted with at least the reputation of each others' families; and their common struggle generated a cohesion among them. People from traditionally rival places like Santa María and Huitzilac had died defending each other, which bound the survivors in a close sympathy.

Far from an autonomous military corporation, like Villa's or Orozco's drifters, the revolutionary army that took shape in Morelos in 1913–14 was simply an armed league of the state's municipalities. And when peace returned in the late summer of 1914, the villagers refounded local society in civil terms. As soon as they could, they elected provisional municipal and judicial authorities and claimed surrounding assets. They even refused to let railroad crews cut down timber for crossties and fuel or draw water for locomotives.[2] To harried Conventionist officials in Mexico City, this

---

[1] On the traditional character of the Zapatista movement, see François Chevalier: "Un factor decisivo de la revolución agraria de México: 'el levantamiento de Zapata' (1911–1919)," *Cuadernos Americanos,* CXIII, 6 (November 1960), 165–87. On the Zapatista army, see Gómez: op. cit., pp. 114, 133, and Carlos Pérez Guerrero: "Cómo vivían los bandidos zapatistas," *Mujeres y Deportes,* February 6, 1937.

[2] Robert E. Quirk: *The Mexican Revolution, 1914–1915. The Convention of Aguascalientes* (Bloomington, 1960), p. 206. Palafox to Zapata, December 21, 1914, AZ, 28: 19: 1.

was the work of perverse and superstitious peasants. But the villagers themselves saw the case otherwise: old railroad-hacienda contracts were no
longer valid; the timber and water were theirs now. Having supported
and composed the revolutionary army, these country folk reasoned that they
should be the beneficiaries of its success. More important, they had also
learned in the war that military leaders ought to respect them, and that if
they did not, others should appear who would. Village authorities all over
the state espoused this new toughness, and it constituted the firmest in-
hibition against neighborhood dictators.

Zapata and most of his chiefs shared these popular expectations about
civilian rule. They also had not lost their sense of who they were—the sons
of the pueblo, field hands, sharecroppers, and rancheros. Their original
authority had been in local councils. And the pretensions they developed
were honest, country pretensions. No native Morelos revolutionary dressed
in khaki, the current national fashion for aspiring politicos. When a Morelos
chief wanted to look elegant, as Zapata did at Xochimilco, he dressed as
for a fair at the district market, in rings and gaudy colors and flashy silver
buttons. The only uniforms in Morelos's revolutionary army were those
sported by Amador Salazar's personal escort: they were green *charro* out-
fits.[3] The esteem the local chiefs always appreciated most was the esteem
of fellow villagers. Like villagers, and as the Ayala plan proscribed, they instituted a civil state as soon as they could, electing de la O provisional
governor. When de la O's military duties occupied him otherwise, the
chiefs in a secret ballot elected a new governor, Lorenzo Vázquez. And
Vázquez prepared to call regular elections for the governorship, the state
legislature, the higher state courts, and the municipalities.[4]

Corps of conquest seldom disband smoothly on the frontier, and knots
of military power remained in Morelos. Recurrent complaints reached Governor Vázquez that local chiefs abused municipal presidents, mocked
civil officials, and refused to give up nationalized territory. In mid-March
Vázquez had to appeal to Zapata for "moral support" against "some badly
intentioned persons who have the mistaken belief that the [state's] authori-

---

[3] Marte R. Gómez: *Las comisiones agrarias del sur* (México, 1961), p. 87.

[4] José Urbán Aguirre: *Geografía e Historia del Estado de Morelos* (2nd edn.,
Cuernavaca, 1963), p. 252. Amado Cháverri Matamoros: "El Archivo de Zapata," serialized in *La Prensa,* September 27, 1935. Zapata told Soto y Gama that he wanted a
secret vote to replace de la O because he wanted no politicking—no argument or sway-
ing of opinion because of his or some other chief's stand. Zapata himself voted for
Francisco Pacheco, he told Soto y Gama. Personal interview with Soto y Gama.

ties must be under the soles of any revolutionary at all who has himself no more authority than the power of his arms."[5]

But this bullying was casual and personal, and not a sign of an intention to rule. The Morelos chiefs rarely if ever met in junta to make regular decisions. Peers of their rural realm, they still communicated only through the first peer, Zapata, at his court, the Tlaltizapán headquarters. In a grave emergency many might have repaired together to the court for consultation, advice, or orders. But happily for them, grave emergencies did not occur in Morelos in 1915. Few even left their neighborhood to campaign. Despite abuses, their sense of obligation, like Zapata's, was directed not to the army but to the villages. To protect the new government Vázquez asked Zapata to subordinate revolutionary commanders to municipal authorities, to make them turn over confiscated property to the state, and to help organize a "public security force"—either the traditional village vigilantes or state police. And Zapata approved Vázquez's requests, to guarantee "the good functioning of all administrative affairs and to maintain order and tranquillity in all the pueblos of this state."

Zapata had already rebuked military chiefs who interfered in village affairs. When he himself took part in settling local troubles, as he did more than once, he limited his involvement to enforcing decisions the villagers reached on their own. When, for instance, during the agrarian reform it came time to mark the boundaries between Yautepec and Anenecuilco fields, he accompanied the district agrarian commission into the countryside to a tecorral, a stone fence, where the representatives of both communities had gathered. The oldest men around had come along as experts. For years these elders had struggled in their neighbors' defense, and Zapata listened to their judgments "with particular deference," recalled a young member of the commission. As Anenecuilco's president and as the Liberating Army's commander-in-chief, he then instructed the agronomists who would do the surveying. "The pueblos say that this tecorral is their boundary," he told them, "and that's where you are going to trace me your marks. You engineers sometimes get stuck on straight lines, but the boundary is going to be the stone fence, even if you have to work six months measuring all its ins and outs . . ."[6] Significantly, Zapata never organized a state police: law enforcement, such as it was, remained the province of village councils.

[5] Vázquez to Zapata, March 14, 1915, AZ, 28: 18: 1.
[6] Gómez: *Las comisiones,* pp. 76–7.

The local people themselves recognized how responsible the army chiefs generally were. Zapata especially they trusted, as the champion who would right all wrongs. High in the mountains near the Puebla border Soto y Gama's brother Conrado, serving on the State Agrarian Commission, met an old woman in a little isolated village. Not knowing even whether she understood Spanish, he asked her what she thought of General Zapata. "What do you want us to say?" she answered, "—us poor mountain Indians who go along hanging on tight to the tail of our jefe Zapata's horse."[7]

The result was the real possibility of local democracies. Although the chiefs retained extraordinary power, passing it down to a trustee when they left on campaign, their control was never institutional nor so restrictive as the Porfirian bosses'. And although Zapata's personal provision of guarantees was irregular, because access to him was irregular, he was a nevertheless respected chief justice. The revolutionary society that actually developed in Morelos never outgrew contention between the new civil and military authorities, but at least the contest was genuine, and the location of legitimacy clear. From the beginning the movement had been a deliberate enterprise by country chiefs to restore the integrity of the state's villages, to gain local rights of participation in national progress. When Madero initiated the revolution in November 1910, Morelos rural leaders did not flock to his cause without weeks of hard reckoning and calculation. And when they did join him, it was for conscious, practical reasons—to recover village lands and establish village security. When later they reacted against Madero's refusal to keep his promises, they defined their opposition with a public plan. And despite Madero's great popularity, many villagers supported them, actively or passively. If, in the war against Huerta and afterward, their local concerns seemed a liability, the state chiefs remained uncomfortable with grander, vaguer projects: in the villages they were at home, and the rest they left to their secretaries. In this insistent provincialism was the movement's strength and its weakness.

The authority reconstituted in the villages provided the ground for the state's agrarian reform. And the reform in turn reinforced the villages by concentrating in them control over agricultural property. As Palafox declared in September 1914, the "repartition of lands will be carried out in conformity with the customs and usages of each pueblo. . . . that is, if a certain pueblo wants the communal system, so it will be executed, and if

[7] Díaz Soto y Gama: *La revolución,* pp. 262–3.

another pueblo wants the division of land in order to admit small [individual] property, so it will be done."[8] Thus emerging as the sources of power and livelihood were the most traditional agencies of local society.

This resort to the past was different from the Carrancista agrarian reform. On January 6, 1915, Carranza signed a decree according to which state authorities would control the provisional allotment of lands to claimants. And because of the war, state authorities might be military as well as civil, natives of their zone of command or not, ignorant of its local "custom and usages" or not. Carranza expressly noted that the reform was not "to revive the old communities nor to create others like them but only to give . . . land to the miserable rural population which today lacks it. . . ." He further specified that "the property of the lands will not belong to the pueblo in common but is to be divided in pleno dominio—fee simple . . ." In practice those who took charge of expropriations and redistributions were enterprising generals contemptuous of old ways and intent on success in the new. And the graft was wondrous. So firm a grip did these Carrancista chiefs fasten on the benefits of the reform that a year later in another decree Carranza had to proclaim that the military were to intervene "only when the action of the political authorities might be difficult," and even then only on special instructions from the chief executive, for a limited purpose and a temporary period. But in the Carrancista areas the entrepreneurs remained in charge. As they managed it, agrarian reform was to help create a new, national economy in which they could flourish.[9] For the Zapatistas, it was the discharge of a national duty to uphold the dignity of local life. The regime that would form in Morelos would come about not through the orders of bureaucrats or generals but through the cooperation of village leaders.

The revolution in land tenure in Morelos in 1915 was an orderly process, largely because of Manuel Palafox. His ambition brought himself and other agraristas into the Conventionist government, and his peremptory conduct there assured official ratification of local reforms. This seemed only the beginning of a historic career. When the Zapatistas had occupied Mexico City, Palafox had entered the precincts of glory and stateliness, the classic forum of the heroes of his country. He was then a mere twenty-nine years

[8] Cited in Magaña: op. cit., IV, 314.

[9] For these decrees, see Manuel Fabila, ed.: *Cinco siglos de legislación agraria en México, 1493–1940* (México, 1941), pp. 270–4, 280–1. For a short commentary on the 1915 decree, see Eyler N. Simpson: *The Ejido: Mexico's Way Out* (Chapel Hill, 1937), pp. 56–62.

old. What this meticulous, cunning, intense little man conceived his destiny to be is still unknown, his private archives supposedly having burned, his associates mostly having died or learned to vilify him, his few surviving confidants secretive or in doubt about him; but it seems likely that he imagined himself another great reforming figure in the line that went back through the immortals of the mid-nineteenth century, Benito Juárez and Melchor Ocampo, back to the enlightened founding fathers of the Republic. During his stay in the capital he behaved as if by design to lay claim to historians' attention. Bold and ingenious in his program, determined, arrogant, incredibly busy, Palafox sprang into action at the first opportunity. Leaving a reliable aide, Santiago Orozco, to run the southern headquarters, he set up another Zapatista headquarters in Mexico City after the Xochimilco conference. And from his office in the Hotel Cosmos— "The Leading International Hotel in Mexico City, San Juan de Letrán 12, with two telephones"—he maneuvered strenuously to advance the agrarista cause.

Within days Palafox became secretary of agriculture in the Conventionist cabinet, the ranking Zapatista in the government. And to the reporter who asked him on the day of his appointment if he meant now, like officials before him, "to study the agrarian question," he replied, "No, señor, I'll not dedicate myself to that. The agrarian question I've got amply studied. I'll dedicate myself to carrying [reform] into the field of practice . . ."[1]

Immediately the American agents singled him out as a troublemaker. When one agent asked him for safe-conduct passes to visit an American-owned hacienda in a Zapatista zone, "he told me," the agent reported, "that he could not give them, as all of these estates were to be divided up, and the land distributed to the poor." The agent explained that this property was American. Palafox's answer was scandalous: "he replied, that it did not make any difference whether it was American or any other foreign property; that these estates were to be divided up . . ." The agent promised his superiors further reports on Palafox. "I can foresee," he wrote, "that he will be an element destined to give the Minister of Foreign Affairs a great deal of avoidable work." By late December, identifying Palafox as the one who would divide properties "whether they belonged to Americans or Chinamen," the agent filed a conclusive judgment on him. "He is impossible," the agent had decided, "and his rabid socialistic ideas could never be of any help in solving the problems in a beneficial manner for his country."

[1] "Hace 50 años," *Excélsior,* December 14, 1964.

Gloatingly the agent then anticipated how Villa would "attend to" Palafox when Villa and Zapata split.[2]

In early January Palafox organized his department. Besides founding a National Bank of Rural Loans and directing the establishment of Regional Schools of Agriculture and a National Factory of Agricultural Implements, he began reviewing village petitions for lands. On January 14 he set up within the department a special bureau of land division. To villagers even in Hidalgo and Guanajuato he sent word to reclaim their fields.[3]

The administration of agrarian reform began in Morelos as soon as Palafox found technicians to carry it out. These came voluntarily, from the graduating class of 1914 of the National School of Agriculture. The 1913 class had gone to Chihuahua to serve in Villista headquarters, but various personal bonds drew the 1914 class to the south. Another of the Soto y Gama brothers, Ignacio, taught in the school. The students liked and respected him, and his attachment to the Morelos revolution influenced them deeply. Also it happened that the oldest student in the class, Alfonso Cruz, had known Palafox in Sinaloa before the revolution, and now as an aide of the secretary he recruited his mates into service with the Zapatistas.

In mid-January the Convention formally appointed ninety-five of these young agronomists to agrarian commissions "charged with the survey and division of lands" in Morelos, Guerrero, Puebla, Mexico, and the Federal District. Twenty-three were to go to Morelos—in six parties, one for each of the state's former political districts. In the end five of the Morelos-bound commissioners did not take up their appointments. But Morelos was the closest, safest, and most exciting place, and many assigned to other states went there. So on January 30, bearing their tripods, levels, and chains, forty-one youths presented themselves in Cuernavaca. They had arrived early, partly from eagerness for work, partly from a fear of the Carrancistas, who had just reoccupied Mexico City and driven the Convention also to Cuernavaca.

To run the district offices, Palafox then contracted thirty-five civil and military engineers temporarily exiled in Morelos. These included Conrado and Ignacio Díaz Soto y Gama, a highly respected young agronomist, Felipe Santibáñez, and Felipe Carrillo Puerto, later famous as a radical

---

[2] Canova to the secretary of state, December 17 and 20, 1914, NA, 59: 812.00/14122 and 14131

[3] Silliman to the secretary of state, January 13, 1915, ibid., 14195. *La Convención*, January 5, 6, 14, and 15, 1915.

governor of Yucatán. Four other agronomists from earlier classes of the
agricultural school appeared, and Palafox contracted them too. He quickly
organized them and the most recent graduates into district commissions
and distributed their various assignments.[4] To supervise their work, he
named Alfonso Cruz head of agrarian operations in the state.

The size of the individual commissions varied slightly, depending on
how many young assistants accompanied the district chief and subchief.
The Tetecala commission numbered nine persons; Jonacatepec and Yautepec had eight; Cuernavaca, seven; Cuautla, six; and Jojutla, five. The staffs
remained fairly stable: by the end of the year every commission had under-
gone at least one change in chiefs, but only the Jonacatepec group had
replaced assistants.[5]

The commissions shortly took up their assignments, the non-Cuerna-
vacans moving their equipment by wagon to the several former district
seats. There the local Zapatista commanders allocated them buildings near
the center of town for their offices and quarters. These were mostly old
mansions, deserted by their wealthy inhabitants and now nationalized
property. Some houses had furniture, some did not; but the assistants'
morale stayed high—even with the drastic shortage of girls—and Zapata
and Palafox arranged for the local commanders to protect the commissions
in their duties.[6]

Once a commission was installed in its quarters, the assistants put their
instruments in order and the chief had notices posted that they were ready
for business. Many villages had already taken over the fields they had
fought the plantations for, and often much more land besides; but they
quickly accepted the offer for legalizing their claims. The first representatives came in and requested surveys, and in groups of two or three the
young men went out to see the pueblo chiefs. There they would inspect
what the local farmers called "la mapa," the village's land title which often
dated from viceroyal times. And then, provided with a work crew to carry
the equipment and hack out the brush, they would move "in almost a

---

[4] Gómez: *Las comisiones*, pp. 18–21, 44, 50.

[5] Ibid., pp. 190–5. Santibáñez served as agrarian agent on the Yautepec commis-
sion, which included Marte Gómez as an assistant. Carrillo Puerto was agent for the
Cuautla commission, which included as an assistant Fidel Velázquez, presently sec-
retary general of the Mexican Workers' Confederation. As for the Soto y Gamas,
Conrado went to Guerrero as the Iguala district agent, and Ignacio directed the
Rural Loan Bank.

[6] Ibid., pp. 51–7.

military operation" into the countryside to determine where the boundary lines ran. This was no easy chore. As points of reference, "la mapa" often showed "a big rock," "a leafy fig tree," "a rounded-off hill," or "a deep canyon." For directions the assistants would have to consult local elders, and even then get nothing precise. In some cases the vagueness was intentional: it covered up a village's greediness. Pueblo chiefs knew that the plantations now lay open to invasion and that the most aggressive villages would take over the most and the best land. It would have been surprising if in these circumstances some villages did not try to pre-empt good fields. But in general village leaders seem to have acted with restraint. Ordinarily their confusion was in good faith. At least they recognized the commission's formal authority in land matters and presented such maps as they had.

Still, serious conflicts arose. For although the commission respected local custom in its surveys, there were insoluble village rivalries that only compromise could ease. A plantation might have arrogated one village's lands decades before, then subsequently rented them for years to farmers from another village. How to dispose of the fields now? In such cases the assistants would call the parties involved into a junta and hope for conciliatory attitudes. The villages were extremely suspicious, however, and with their representatives to the juntas they often sent along their military leaders and gangs of local toughs. If a village representative felt the junta was about to wrong his pueblo, he would refuse to accept its rulings. "We're not sucking hind tit," he would inform the commission, and to the cheers of his hometown following he would withdraw from the talks.[7]

The commissioners might then either turn to a more prestigious authority, the district revolutionary chief, or even General Zapata himself, or they might proceed with their contested survey. The second course was likely to involve them in a violent feud between the rival villages. And the higher appeal they preferred to invoke as a last resort. So all they could do was to try new negotiations. And in time the youths' hard work and their obvious sincerity won them the villagers' trust. "These ingenieritos are no dandies," the local farmers reported. "They can take walking all day as much as we do, and then in the evening they go on with their papers."[8]

The Temixco-Santa María case especially helped the commissions gain acceptance in the countryside. Rural families all over the state knew about the struggle between the hacienda and the village north of Cuernavaca.

[7] Ibid., pp. 62–9.
[8] Ibid., pp. 71–8.

In the last years of the Porfiriato the hacienda had gained what then seemed a definitive victory. And in the civil wars the village was practically razed. But the first act of the Cuernavaca commission was to go out to restore Santa María's traditional lands. The villagers greeted the ingenieritos warmly, with bouquets and speeches. And on February 19 the formal ceremony of restitution took place.[9] Former inhabitants returned, and Santa María came back to life. The case was renowned as a sign to other villagers that they could count on the commissions to honor their titles.[1]

When finally a village had its boundaries surveyed, and received its allotted section of a neighboring hacienda, the district commission left it autonomous. According to Article 6 of the decree of September 8, 1914, the village could keep its land under a common title and distribute cultivation rights, or it could distribute the titles themselves to individual smallholders—however it elected. Neither the state nor the federal government had any jurisdiction in such affairs. As Zapata wished and as Palafox had declared, "custom and the usages of each pueblo" would determine the local property system.[2] The federal government retained only the power to prevent title-holders, whether communal or individual, from selling or renting their lands—which would protect them against collusion between crooked village politicians and speculators. In the impossibility of enforcing a general prohibition against greed, restricting the right to fall victim to it was the best the government could do. Evidently no local farmer protested against the restriction.

Thus the villages of Morelos were born anew. In the months the six commissions functioned in the state they surveyed and defined the boundaries of almost all the one hundred-odd pueblos there, incorporating into them most of the local farm land, stands of timber, and irrigation facilities.[3] The regime—or series of regimes—that they chartered became a regular entrenched system. By early March Zapata notified the current Conventionist president, Roque González Garza, that "The matter relating to the agrarian question is resolved in a definitive manner, for the different pueblos of the state, in accord with the titles which protect their properties,

[9] "Informe que rinde el Jefe de la Comisión Agraria en el Distrito de Cuernavaca . . . February 19, 1915," *El Nacional*, November 20, 1932.

[1] Gómez: *Las comisiones,* pp. 64-5.

[2] For other comments on Zapata's refusal to consider ideologically derived patterns of land reform, see Díaz Soto y Gama: *La revolución,* pp. 272-4.

[3] For an account of the various commissions' work, see Gómez: *Las comisiones,* pp. 64-78.

have entered into the possession of said lands . . ." Subsequent disputes among villagers or villages, he declared, would go to the secretary of agriculture for rulings, either directly or through a special commission or a civil court.[4]

The land not included in the village dominions remained at the disposition of Secretary Palafox, who could leave it as private property, or after indemnization expropriate one third of it in the public interest, or confiscate it outright as the holding of an enemy of the revolution. Some planters had assumed that by sweet talk and the offer of capital and expertise they might recover their haciendas, at least in part. "If I'm not badly informed," Joachim Amor wrote to Zapata from Mexico City in October 1914, "you wouldn't look with displeasure on the reestablishment of work on the plantations, in view of the great poverty which reigns there." For his investment he only asked "the very natural condition that you give your consent and impart your protection and aid so we can work." He wondered incidentally if Zapata might not arrange to free his fellow planters, Ignacio de la Torre y Mier, Manuel Araoz, Romualdo Pasquel, and José Pagaza, from the Mexico City penitentiary, so they too could contribute to the state's recovery.[5] But Palafox, with his "rabid socialistic ideas," had astounded metropolitan observers by retaining control of all lands the villages did not take. Apparently he did not even pay indemnities but simply confiscated the surplus territory. Still there were planters and plantation attorneys who did not believe that the local revolutionary chiefs shared this presumed lunacy. But they quickly learned their mistake. As an American consul wrote to Washington in distress, "A few days since [my conversations with Palafox,] Ramón Olivares [sic], a fine type of Mexican, educated in the United States and in England, a member of the American club, is reported to have been brutally murdered near Cuernavaca by the Zapatista Governor of Morelos, the notorious Genoveva [sic] de la O . . ."[6]

The sugar mills and distilleries Palafox also confiscated. These were "in a complete ruin," as Zapata himself admitted: what the federals had not destroyed or stolen from them in the 1913–14 war, the villagers and refugees had later made off with. But both Zapata and Palafox wanted to put the mills back in operation, not as private enterprises but as public services. There the villagers who continued to produce cane could bring their harvests. There refugee peons could resettle to earn a wage. And there

[4] Cháverri Matamoros in *La Prensa,* September 27, 1935.
[5] Amor to Zapata, October 21, 1914, AZ, 27: 7.
[6] Silliman to the secretary of state, January 13, 1915, NA, 59: 812.00/14195.

the government could collect the profits for revenue. Repairs and the mobilization of laborers and draft animals began as soon as Palafox took office. And by early March four mills were again in business in Morelos— Temixco, Hospital, Atlihuayán, and Zacatepec. In charge of them were native generals, de la O, Emigdio Marmolejo, Amador Salazar, and Lorenzo Vázquez, respectively. The meager proceeds they took in they returned to headquarters to defray the "very many extraordinary expenses," as Zapata called them, ". . . of military hospitals, barracks, help to ambulance columns, and aid to the widows of revolutionaries killed on campaign . . ." In time, Zapata was sure, the wealth of the state would surpass even its former abundance, and then "we will see what is the best way to use it."[7]

Other than revolutionary observers also entertained these speculations, which seemed increasingly germane after Conventionist armies reoccupied Mexico City in mid-March and the Convention returned there as the central government. Attracted now to Morelos were various sharpers, carpetbaggers, pitchmen, and hucksters. Precisely in eliminating the planters and promoting an economic revival in the state, Palafox had put them onto the scent. They could well understand, ace fleecers themselves, that the secretary had dispossessed the old owners; but they could not believe that he would keep the property as a public domain. By all the laws they took for gospel it was inevitable that for a fee or a cut Palafox would transfer land to new private owners. To them, nationalization seemed only a quaint procedure for replacing one crew of capitalists with another.

Among these characters, the jauntiest and most persistent was a New Englander who had spent the last twenty years in Mexico, Hubert L. Hall. A businessman, a Mormon, and an inside-dopester on his adopted country, Hall impressed Americans who met him quite favorably. As one agent reported, " . . . he is entirely trustworthy and a man of high character. . . . Senator Smoot knows him very well . . ."[8] Morelos was of special interest to Hall. For a while he had run a hotel in Cuernavaca, and by 1910 he had acquired land in the timber country around Santa María; the first complaint to the United States embassy about damage to American property in Morelos had come from Mrs. Hall, in August 1911.[9] During the rebellion that followed Hall had to write off his investment in the state. In March 1913, when it seemed the Zapatistas might make peace, he had tried to

[7] Cháverri Matamoros in *La Prensa*, September 27, 1935.
[8] Lind to the secretary of state, March 23, 1914, NA, 59: 812.00/20609 1/2.
[9] Dearing to Mrs. H. L. Hall, August 14, 1911, NA.

recoup his losses by organizing a company for "the division of lands" in which he offered fifty thousand pesos in shares to Zapata and ten thousand pesos in shares to each of the other main chiefs.[1] The plan fell a cropper, however, and in the ensuing war Hall had seen his Mexican prospects gravely jeopardized. But as the revolutionaries emerged triumphant in mid-1914 he had recognized that in the chaos of reconstruction he might parlay his connections and bluff into a real fortune. Back in the United States, he persuaded the State Department that he was a "personal friend of Zapata," almost wheedled diplomatic credentials to present to the southern head-quarters, and did get an official allowance for his trip home. Only Zapata's warning that "it would not be safe for that gentleman to come to his camp" had stymied Hall then.[2] But now the go-getter returned to Morelos, pretending anyway to diplomatic status, as buoyant as ever and with a new scheme.

The racket he proposed was the Liberating Army Cooperative Colony. This was to be a private company capitalized at 180,000 pesos, which two hundred founding members were to subscribe in thirty monthly install-ments. The founders were to be the leading revolutionary chiefs and sec-retaries "who struggled so dauntlessly for the liberty of the people in the past" and whom Hall would now enlist in "the great labor of education and redemption of the same people, by means of colonizing land, establish-ing cooperatively and with the aid of the government works of irrigation, industry, and manufacture where very many laborers will be employed." Specifically the founders were to direct the operations of a massive agricultural combine holding over 64,000 acres in the rich Cuerna-vaca valley. The combine would include lands formerly attached to Temixco, Ocuila, San Vicente, and Atlacomulco haciendas, lands which Hall expected Secretary Palafox to grant to the company as a "concession." There the newest methods in farming and ranching would be standard. Also to be established were agricultural schools and experiment stations, cooperative markets, shops, warehouses, stables, and a weekly news-paper. One share in the company's stock would go to the head of each family laboring on the colony, one to each married couple, one to each grown child living in a family, and one to each widow. If other groups of two hundred revolutionaries wanted to found affiliated colonies, they could

[1] Magaña: op. cit., III, 97.
[2] Bryan to the Brazilian minister, August 28, 1914, NA, 59: 812.00/13015. Silli-man to the secretary of state, August 29, 1914, ibid., 13040.

freely do so; and if the land around them was insufficient, they could take fields away from contiguous haciendas or pueblos, "naturally without prejudicing their rights." But Hall preferred to start the first colony around Cuernavaca, "craddle [sic] of the great revolution of the South, whose spirit and high ideals we wish to commemorate and perpetuate in this altruistic and beneficent manner."

The chiefs and secretaries Hall actually conned into this enterprise were evidently not many or important. In his first (and only) flyer in March he claimed seventy founders already subscribed, among them Palafox, Montaño, Lorenzo Vázquez, Leobardo Galván, Santiago Orozco, Genaro Amezcua, and Antonio and Ignacio Díaz Soto y Gama. But of these only Ignacio Díaz Soto y Gama had a seat on the colony's organizing committee or the provisional board of directors over which Hall presided. As secretary of both groups, this dashing agronomist composed the company's advertising literature. Probably only he took a serious part in the project. In the English translation that Hall rendered of the prospectus he modified some of Soto y Gama's wildest boasts: where for example the original read that "all the other prominent chiefs of the Conventionist army" had enrolled as founders, Hall wrote that "invitations have been extended to General Emiliano Zapata and all the other principal officials of the Ejército Libertador" to enroll. No record yet discovered indicates that these chiefs or the others named even conferred with Hall, much less signed pledges of subscription.

In early April Hall approached Palafox himself in Mexico City. "Desiring to assist," the good Mormon declared, "in the great humanitarism labor which the Mexican government is now undertaking in its efforts for the economic, moral and educational benefit and progress of its citizens, especially in the agrarian question which for years I have studied and have been deeply interested in both theoretically and practically, I have invited a number of leading citizens to unite with me to organize a Cooperative Colonization Association to labor and operate in connection with the government, in such parts of the republic as it may be seen to be of advantage to do, beginning its labors in the State of Morelos, the cradle of the revolutionary movement of the South, and which was of so pronounced and Agrarian Character, having met with a willing and hearty response from over one hundred of the foremost men of the military government, officials, agricultural, artesian and commercial classes who have manifested an ardent desire to commence the work as soon as possible, and to that end, we have organized a provisional organization to take the necessary first steps to secure our desire." Then he asked for the land grant. The request, he believed, was "most reasonable and moderate as compared with concessions and attractions for Colonists offered by the governments of Canada, Australia, the Argentine, Brazil and the United States." As an old hand in such matters, he reminded Palafox that "The concensus of opinion of the experienced men who have studied the colonist and emigrant problem of Mexico *is that it can only be accomplished successfully here, when operated on a large scale, and largely aided and fostered by the Government . . ."*[3]

Palafox's response, however, was not "willing and hearty." Although he evidently made no formal refusal, he did not grant the land Hall wanted. And he started inquiries to check if Hall was in fact an American agent. By mid-April he knew from Washington that "Hall has not been nor is now employed in the Department of State nor represents it in any form."[4] No further trace of Hall appeared in the affairs of Morelos. And the villagers' version of agrarian reform proceeded apace. From his headquarters in Tlaltizapán Zapata guaranteed it. As another American agent reported after meeting him there on April 16: "He believes it is right that the property of the rich should be taken and given to the poor."[5]

So solid and vigorous was the local revolution that it continued independently of the shifting fate of the Zapatista politicians in Mexico City. After returning to the capital in mid-March Palafox and Soto y Gama carried on a ferocious struggle with the Villista president of the Convention, Roque González Garza. The Villistas resented not only the Zapatistas' pretensions to power and their drive for social reforms but also, most rankling, the weakness of the southern military effort against the Carrancistas. The Zapatistas in turn protested that they could not make, buy, or collect from Villa enough ammunition to mount regular campaigns, and that anyway they deserved an equal role in forming policy; most disgusting to them was how the Villistas shrank from social reforms, in agrarian or other matters. Above all they feared that the Villistas might retreat north and leave them in the lurch. And to hold their allies in place they practically put them under guard, appointing Gildardo Magaña governor of the Federal District and Amador Salazar commander of the Mexico City garrison. When in early April Palafox demanded that González Garza allot funds to pay for uniforms for the southern army, the President refused and on the is-

---

[3] For all the documents relating to the Hall episode, see Lind to the secretary of state, March 23, 1914, NA. The spelling, syntax, and emphasis are Hall's own.

[4] Bryan to Duval West, April 12, 1915, AZ, 28: 6.

[5] Duval West, Report to the President, May 11, 1915, NA, 59: 812.00/19181.

sue tried to eject Palafox from the cabinet. Soto y Gama arranged a truce, but Palafox remained so offensive to the President that on May 1 González Garza did force his resignation. The news enraged Zapata, who came up to Mexico City—in what proved to be his last trip to the capital—and demanded Palafox's reinstatement, in vain. Then a month later Soto y Gama engineered González Garza's defeat in the Convention, a new, frailer executive took office, and Palafox returned to his post.[6] But these metropolitan intrigues did not really interest Zapata, which was why they went on and on. And they did not carry into Morelos. There people were moving on their own course, in no need of outside sponsors or patrons. And there in full force the revolution continued.

In the spring harvests began, the first fruit to mature from this progress of the pueblos. The crops the farmers now brought in were not the planters' cane or rice but the traditional foodstuffs, corn and beans. As the rainy season came on, Governor Vázquez distributed among the municipal governments 500,000 pesos—a loan from the Convention—which were to go to local farmers as credit for seed and tools. By mid-June reporters found all the fields in the state under cultivation, again mainly in corn.[7]

Zapata did not approve of this development, which would leave the sugar mills idle. At least since 1911 he had foreseen that reorganized haciendas might be a bountiful source of public wealth, and recent talks with agronomists had confirmed his idea that the mills should continue to operate as "national factories." Farmers growing cane and selling it to the mills would earn money, he understood, and so be able to save, buy new goods, and use new services. Accordingly he had ordered spare parts to replace those on damaged machines. And three more mills reopened for business. Again native chiefs were in charge—Modesto Rangel at El Puente, Eufemio Zapata at Cuautlixco, and Maurilio Mejía, Zapata's nephew, at Cuahuixtla. Later, Santa Clara reopened under Mendoza. But assisting them technically now were agronomists from the Rural Loan Bank, under the imaginative direction of Ignacio Díaz Soto y Gama. Zapata himself urged villagers to quit growing vegetables and instead produce a cash crop. "If you keep on growing chile peppers, onions, and tomatoes," he told Villa

[6] For an account of these struggles based on González Garza's archive and favoring him, see Quirk: op. cit., pp. 211–23, 232–52. For a Zapatista version, see Palafox to Zapata, March 28, 1914 [sic, 1915], AZ, 27: 10; Palafox to Zapata, April 13, 1915, AZ, 30: 6; A. Díaz Soto y Gama to Zapata, May 17, 1915, AZ, 28: 23: 1; Palafox to Zapata, June 25, 1915, AZ, 27: 1.

[7] *La Convención*, May 20 and June 17, 1915.

de Ayala farmers, "you'll never get out of the state of poverty you've always lived in. That's why, as I advise you, you have to grow cane . . ." Through conditional gifts of money and seed, he did persuade some villagers to resume the cultivation of cane.[8]

But most families went on truck farming. Rather than rehabilitate the hacienda, they obviously preferred to work and trade in foodstuffs that had always seemed the mainstay of the pueblo. And during the summer they restocked Morelos's district markets with the familiar beans, corn, chickpeas, tomatoes, onions, chile peppers, even chickens. While Mexico City was on the verge of starvation at this time, common folk in Morelos evidently had more to eat than in 1910—and at lower real prices. So profuse was the production of food that despite the constant infusion of Conventionist currency into the state's economy, there was little sign of inflation. In the fondas, the crude country inns where revolutionary officers, local officials, and metropolitan refugees ate, the young agrarian commissioners got by easily on four pesos a day.[9]

In such clear relief the character of revolutionary Morelos emerged: in the very crops people liked to grow, they revealed the kind of community they liked to dwell in. They had no taste for the style of individuals on the make, the life of perpetual achievement and acquisition, of chance and change and moving on. Rather, they wanted a life they could control, a modest, familial prosperity in the company of other modestly prosperous families whom they knew, and all in one place. An experiment, for instance, they would try only after they were certain it would work—after, that is, it was no longer experimental. And profits they appreciated only if they had an orthodox use for them.

Even among those in official command the tone of relations in the state in 1915 was intensely, almost intentionally, rural and rustic. In sartorial fashion the standard was white pajamas, the southern farmers' work clothes. Headquarters secretaries wore them not only through affectation but also because they were safer in them. On visits to Cuernavaca allied revolutionaries from the north doffed their khakis; otherwise they courted insults

[8] Serafín M. Robles: "El Zapatismo y la Industria Azucarera en Morelos," *El Campesino,* August 1950. Porfirio Palacios: "Todo es según el color. . . . El problema del azúcar y la visión de Zapata," *La Prensa,* February 19, 1944.

[9] Gómez: *Las comisiones,* pp. 39, 59–60. On the Conventionist currency, which came into Morelos through payments to the southern army, see Francisco Ramírez Plancarte: *La Ciudad de México durante la revolución constitucionalista* (2nd edn., México, 1941), pp. 450–5.

and even assaults if they wandered far from the central plaza. Anyone in trousers, a shirt, and boots was a *catrín,* a dandy. In language the familiar, second-person address was the norm, and country slang and dialect prevailed: a fellow or a buddy was a *vale* (literally, a voucher), to shoot was "to bust" (*quebrar*), "fun" (*el gusto*) was trick riding and roping, the enemy was *los Carranzas, pobre* (poor) came out as *probe, somos* (we are) as *semos, fue* (he was) as *hue.* For entertainment there were no fancy liquors or shows imported but only the same local diversions as before the war—warm beer and raw rum (*resacado*), cock fights, and "fun" on horses.

The heart of the state was now in Tlaltizapán. In this restful little town in the hollows leading down into the Jojutla rice fields, where towering dusky green laurels cast the square and streets in permanent shadow, where the wind suddenly moving in the tops of the trees could hush the talking below, where in the quiet the sound would rise of water rippling through the maze of local creeks and canals—in this resort Zapata had made not only a headquarters but also a home. And here, as the American agent who came to meet him could see, all the farming families in the state looked to him "as a Saviour and a Father."[1] Here, unlike in Mexico City, there was no busy display of confiscated luxury, no gleeful consumption of captured treasure, no swarm of bureaucrats leaping from telephone to limousine, only the regular, measured round of native business. The days Zapata passed in his offices in an old rice mill at the northern edge of town, hearing petitions, forwarding them to Palafox in Mexico City or ruling on them himself, deciding strategy and policy, dispatching orders. In the evenings he and his aides relaxed in the plaza, drinking, arguing about plucky cocks and fast and frisky horses, discussing the rains and prices with farmers who joined them for a beer, Zapata as always smoking slowly on a good cigar. The nights he spent back in his quarters with a woman from the town; he fathered two children at least in Tlaltizapán.[2] For his birthday in August the townspeople held a fiesta, and the local señoritas put on a stir-

---

[1] West, Report, May 11, 1915, NA.

[2] Zapata fathered at least five sons and four daughters. His wife, Josefa, bore him two children, Felipe and María Asunción, both of whom died in infancy. See Herminia Aguilar: "Doña Josefa Espejo, Vda. de Zapata," *El Campesino,* May 1950. Other children were "hijos naturales." Surviving at least to adulthood were Nicolás, born in 1906; Eugenio, probably born in 1913; María Elena, probably born in 1913; Ana María, born in 1914; Diego, born in 1916; María Luisa, probably born in 1918; and Mateo, born in 1918. See Gill: op. cit., pp. 69–74.

ring program—"parade, speech, hymn to labor, waltz, dialogue, speech, parade, poetry, speech, fantasia, dialogue, children's comedy, monologue and speech, national anthem . . ."[3] In this haven Zapata indulged such dreams of glory as he had. Beside the church on a hill at the southern edge of town he wanted a mausoleum built, as a collective tomb for himself and his closest chiefs. In Tlaltizapán he had found the moral capital of his revolution.

The extravaganza of the year was a bullfight in Yautepec. There Salazar had a little plaza de toros built opposite the train station, and Juan Silveti, a celebrated novillero later to become one of Mexico's best toreros, came to perform against two young bulls from Ignacio de la Torre y Mier's prize Toluca herd. Revolutionary chiefs assembled from throughout the state, some in Pullman cars. Zapata of course came up from Tlaltizapán. He and Salazar even took a preliminary part in the fight, riding rings around the bulls, dodging their charges, and wearing them down for the artless peons who were serving Silveti as banderilleros.[4]

No social event more elegant than this occurred in Morelos in 1915, because no sophisticates were there to stage or attend it. The devotees of refined culture had long since left for the metropolis, some in terror, others in exultation, like Montaño, who became Conventionist secretary of education. The only old nabob still in the state was de la Torre y Mier, released from the Mexico City penitentiary but kept out of pocket and under house arrest in Cuautla. The nearest that gay blades in Homburgs and ladies with boas were spotted was in Amecameca, a rail junction across the line in Mexico State; there a mob lynched one smart couple.[5] Reforming out of its own origins and on a frontier, revolutionary Morelos was a very suspicious society, not easily hospitable, much less generous, to those who seemed not to belong. Local families had fought hard and long to recover their rural heritage. And in their agrarian state they wanted only other country families like themselves. There was a method in this intolerance, this deliberate coarseness, this willful ignorance of urbane ways. For city folk were the born bearers of ill tidings. Even the dogs knew to bark at them.

Thus, when the first omens of the state's inevitable doom appeared in the north, no native and few other Zapatistas recognized them. The omens

[3] Felicitación Que los Vecinos de Tlaltizapán ofrecen al Sr. Gral. Emiliano Zapata . . . August, 1915, AZ, 28: 5.

[4] Gómez: *Las comisiones,* pp. 121–3.

[5] Ibid., p. 102.

were the reports of three successive, tremendous defeats that the Carrancista General Obregón had inflicted upon Villa—two in early April at
Celaya, the third in early June at León, all in Guanajuato, in the strategic
great basin northwest of Mexico City. Obregón, who had lost an arm at
León, now emerged as a master of war. Despite the news Zapata did not
open a second front. In the capital Palafox and Soto y Gama worried not
about the collapse of the army the Convention depended on but about the
land reform bill they expected to introduce soon.[6]

But the crisis came on anyway. On July 11 a Carrancista army under
Pablo González occupied Mexico City. The Convention retreated in disorder to Toluca, where it maintained the pretense of a national government. And Salazar's Morelos troops in the metropolis and Federal District
withdrew south. Six days later González evacuated the capital again, to
protect Obregón's lines of communication with Veracruz against a Villista
attack in Hidalgo; and when he left, Zapatista forces sneaked back. But it
seemed certain that he could return when he chose: although Villa maintained his battered army in the field, the nation's military balance had
shifted decisively in the Carrancistas' favor.

At last southerners began to read the signs. As outlanders, the young
agrarian commissioners stranded in Morelos lost their illusions first. Sadly
they planned no more vacation trips to the capital.[7] Zapata himself finally
went into action. To hold off González's return, he personally commanded
on July 30 a powerful attack of 6,000 men against 1,700 Carrancistas northeast of Mexico City. Other attacks took place simultaneously throughout
the area. But none could contain the Carrancista advance. On August 2
González reentered the capital, this time to stay.[8] In Morelos merchants
began trying to refuse Convention currency.[9]

Still, no alarm charged the state. Zapata returned to rest in Tlaltizapán,
honored at his birthday party and evidently more preoccupied with the
doings in the Toluca Convention than with his crumbling military position.[1] On the advice of Palafox and Soto y Gama he believed that an inter-
American conference then organizing in Washington to treat the Mexican
problem would result in Carranza's downfall, and that the Carrancista

---

[6] Palafox to Zapata, June 25, 1915, AZ.

[7] Gómez: *Las comisiones,* pp. 119–20.

[8] See Pablo González's official report on his operations from July 17 to August
2, 1915, cited in Barragán: op. cit., II, 611–17.

[9] Pacheco to Zapata, August 5, 1915, AZ, 28: 5: 1.

[1] Zapata to Palafox, August 26, 1915, ibid.

chiefs would soon rejoin the Convention.[2] If so, he had no need to waste ammunition and men.

But weekly the decay of his position became more obvious. As Villa lost one key town after another in the north and as the inter-American conference failed, Zapata returned to action. To harry the Carrancistas in the rear, he launched strong attacks into the Federal District and Mexico State. In late September he even captured the power plant at Necaxa, the source of metropolitan electricity. But he could not hold it nor any of the other towns and villages he had taken. Everywhere the Carrancistas pushed him back, more firmly in control of the Valley of Mexico than any commanders since 1910. In Puebla and Mexico State local Zapatista chiefs began accepting amnesties from the Carrancista government, which gravely disturbed the chiefs in Morelos.[3] The state's seclusion had ended. Its revolutionaries were now on the defensive.

On October 10 the refugee Convention in Toluca divided for the last time, the Villistas and the President fleeing north. The Zapatistas escaped again to Cuernavaca, where, under Palafox's guidance, they reconvened the rump as the official and exclusive embodiment of the national revolution. These pretensions soon suffered irreparable deflation. On October 19 President Wilson extended the United States's de facto recognition to Carranza's government. He also prohibited all arms shipments to Mexico except to Carranza's authorities. The American decision thus fixed politically the new balance of power which the Carrancista armies had already won militarily. And it marked the beginning, after five years of civil war, of Mexico's reconsolidation. Carranza had finally realized his claim to sovereign legitimacy. Although the Carrancistas could not yet dominate the whole nation, they could prevent any other faction from displacing them. Henceforth they would rule.

In Morelos, however, the native attitude remained skeptical. The local chiefs had no clue to how solid the northern movement had also become. They still considered Carranza a mere leftover from the old regime, another haughty landlord who aspired to restore the Porfirian order. And not withstanding "Mister Wilson's" recognition, they doubted that he could retain the loyalty of the genuine revolutionary generals around him. Having

[2] Soto y Gama to Zapata, August 17, 1915, AZ, 28: 6: 1.

[3] "Para la historia," *La Prensa,* September 22, October 31, November 3 and 19, 1931. (Henceforth citations of this series will refer only to the date of *La Prensa.*) Silliman to the secretary of state, September 27 and 30, 1915, NA, 59: 812.00/16135 and 16333.

witnessed desertions and treacheries galore during the past five years, they reckoned Carranza would not last long. By now they had already resisted and helped bring down three federal governments, each apparently stronger than his. So the strategy they pursued was the same as before: vigorous raids in the south, to discredit the government and tempt ambitious loyalists to revolt.

With less excuse the Zapatista secretaries also disparaged Carranza's sudden ascendancy. Voicing the official Morelos response through the Convention now in Cuernavaca, they encouraged the stubborn native hopes. Secretary of Agriculture Palafox dominated the Convention absolutely and tolerated no gesture of compromise. As he and Soto y Gama lost power, they became more intransigent in policy. In 1915–16, in an exaggerated but less dramatic way, the same complex of tensions developed as in 1914— Zapata's retreat from serious politics, and Palafox's rigid opposition.

On October 26 Palafox published a Manifesto to the Nation, probably composed by Soto y Gama. It was the first official southern response to Carranza's new government, an introduction to an extensive Program of Political and Social Reforms which the Toluca Convention had voted a month earlier and which the Cuernavaca rump now issued, slightly amended, as its own. The program itself was an interesting draft of the basic changes the Conventionists believed necessary to save the nation. It was a more detailed catalogue of improvements than a similar Carrancista project published the previous December, and it contained promises of legislation both more stringent and more moderate, depending on the subject, than the various decrees Carranza had promulgated on land, labor, municipalities, divorce, education, taxes, and mineral concessions.[4] That same day Palafox delivered on one promise, publishing a radical agrarian law that gave the secretary of agriculture immense authority over urban and rural property and natural resources. By this remarkable law the Department of Agriculture would be the central agency of a stupendous nationalizing reformation of Mexico.[5] But the introductory manifesto was a gross mistake, betraying a fantastic misconception of the national context in which the proposed reforms might have an appeal. Lambasting Carranza's "ill-

---

[4] Manifesto to the Nation, October 26, 1915, AZ, 28: 5: 3. The text of the program of reforms is also in González Ramírez: *Planes*, pp. 123–8. For Carranza's promises, see ibid., pp. 158–64. For a study of his decrees, see Nettie Lee Benson: "The Preconstitutional Regime of Venustiano Carranza, 1913–1917" (M.A. thesis, University of Texas, 1936), pp. 96–128.

[5] See Appendix C for the text of this law.

fated faction" for "an infamous and incredible pact with the great land-holders," the southern secretaries specifically accepted "with pleasure the manufacturer, the merchant, the mineowner, the businessman, all the active and enterprising elements which open new paths for industry and provide work to great groups of workers . . ." But "the hacendado," they intoned, "the monopolist of all the lands, the usurper of nature's wealth, the creator of national misery, the infamous slave-trader who treats men like beasts of burden, the hacendado being unproductive and idle—him the [Zapatista] Revolution does not tolerate." The southern program was "quite simple," as they summarized it: "War to the death against the hacendados, ample guarantees for all the other classes of society."

This was the rhetoric of 1911 or 1913, not late 1915, and no revolutionary not already a committed Zapatista could thrill to it. For the old landlords, the supposed villains, no longer had power in Mexico. Most languished in jail or exile. As a class they hardly even existed. True, outside Morelos the nation's villages had not emerged dominant. But the state and district chiefs who led them were not likely to champion an agrarian revolt now, since thanks to Carranza precisely they had become the new landlords. As for the careerists in business and labor, they already had a government to depend on and lobby in. And so far it served them well. That thus a new regime had actually formed, cohesive and durable, that Carranza was a front not for the Amors, the Escandóns, and the García Pimentels, but for the clever and ruthless young operators from the north who commanded the revolutionary armies, that the danger for Morelos villagers was not in familiar reaction but in alien progress—this crisis the southern secretaries had no notion of. In their blindness they reinforced the local chiefs' tenacity.

The ruin of the native revolution in Morelos was therefore no caving in but a ragged, bitter, and confused giving way. Through the fall Zapata arranged raids from Oaxaca to Hidalgo. Indeed his forces were more active now than when Villa had needed them. But the raids gained nothing in territory or prestige. They did not even demoralize the government, whose generals took over more and more towns in the states surrounding Morelos.[6] The raids, moreover, cost dearly in ammunition, which because of the American embargo was daily more scarce. At Atlihuayán hacienda Zapata kept a primitive munitions factory working, recharging old Mauser and .30-.30 shells and for slugs plugging them with little pieces of copper cable stolen from Mexico City suburban trolleys and power works; but

[6] *La Prensa*, November 17, 21, and 24, 1931.

the supply was irregular and inadequate.[7] Meanwhile the Villista army collapsed completely in the north, and attention refocused on the south. In late November the government announced plans for a "definitive" campaign against the Zapatistas, "right in their hideouts in . . . Morelos."[8] Isolated as never before in the revolution, the state would soon be under siege. The young agrarian commissioners began applying for permits to get out. Scared and desperate, one became alcoholic; others sneaked off to the capital without waiting for passes.[9]

Zapata tried to tighten security over local resources for defense. The management of the munitions factory he removed from Secretary of War Pacheco's control and brought into the headquarters.[1] He also ordered his army to prohibit trade between Zapatista and Carrancista zones "in every article," primary necessities or not—"to take away from the enemy all those elements which could serve for his sustenance."[2] And he began to reclaim the sugar mills from the chiefs, to assign them to the Rural Loan Bank to operate directly.[3] But even at the first small harvest in these "national factories," and the prospect of a little revenue, he was gloomy. He wanted to give the proceeds to the peons working in the mills: "Who knows," he told his secretary, "what they will have to suffer later on?" Guiltily he insisted that the imminent woe was not his fault "but that of events which have to come."[4]

The government's offer of amnesty, publicized since August, greatly increased the strain on the local chiefs. Suspecting a defection, one would try to disarm another's forces. But this jumpy vigilance only tended, as Zapata warned in reprimand, "to deepen the personal enmities which exist between chiefs . . . which we must avoid at all cost."[5] Fearful that subversive telegrafists might sabotage his military operations, de la O tried to control the wire offices in his zone.[6] In a squabble over an artillery piece, his men killed one of the most daring and proficient Zapatista field commanders, Antonio

---

[7] Ibid., October 10, 1931.

[8] Ibid., November 28, 1931.

[9] Gómez: *Las comisiones,* pp. 138–59.

[1] Zapata to Pacheco, November 7, 1915, AZ, 31: Copybook 2.

[2] Headquarters circular, February 9, 1916, AA.

[3] Gabriel Encinas to Mendoza, January 25, 1916, AA.

[4] Palacios in *La Prensa,* February 19, 1944.

[5] Zapata to L. Vázquez, November 15, 1915, AZ, 31: Copybook 2.

[6] Zapata to de la O, December 11–12, 1915, ibid.

Barona.[7] In the southeastern zone Mendoza was so offended by intruding rival chiefs and by innuendos about his loyalty that he challenged Zapata to name a new chief there.[8] And along the front allied chiefs actually took amnesties. Most disturbing, these defectors came mainly from Pacheco's division in Mexico State and the Federal District, which guarded the northern entrances to Morelos. They were Zapatistas of recent conversion whom Pacheco, as Conventionist secretary of war, had commissioned in droves; and they deserted now as speedily as they had joined. One, however, was a grave loss: Vicente Navarro, a tough and canny chief who had defended the pass at Contreras. When he took an amnesty, the Carrancistas moved right down to La Cima on the threshhold of Morelos.[9]

Still, the high native chiefs did not flag in their defiance. Mustering forces of two thousand to three thousand men at three or four different rendezvous, they struck in coordinated attacks into the Federal District, southern and central Puebla, and southern Mexico State. If a chief had ex-federal officers on his staff, he got fifth-column help from ex-federals serving on the other side. Especially along the Puebla border these friendly enemy officers would sell supplies, pass on intelligence, and arrange private truces so fighting could go on elsewhere.[1] To the southwest, after Carrancistas pushing up from Acapulco took Chilpancingo and Iguala and penetrated into Morelos, de la O drove them back in a terrific counteroffensive. Sweeping down into Guerrero, he and Jesús Salgado wiped out garrisons and field forces alike re-covered the country in "fine and prosperous" crops. By late December de la O had carried the war into the Carrancista home territory around Acapulco. Outside the city, the American consul there reported, the Carrancistas showed an "absolute lack of any positive control."[2] Throughout the end of 1915 and the first weeks of 1916 the Morelos revolutionaries put up such a fierce resistance around their state that the vaunted government campaign against their "hideouts" could

[7] *La Prensa*, December 5, 1931. Gómez: *Las comisiones*, p. 91.

[8] Mendoza to Zapata, January 4, 1916, AZ, 27: 5.

[9] *La Prensa*, November 3, 10, and 19, and December 8 and 29, 1931. Meléndez: op. cit., I, 369–70.

[1] Confidential memorandum, n.d. (late 1915–early 1916?), AGRE, L-E-794: 31 [sic, 19] : 20. Confidential report, n.d. (late 1915–early 1916?), ibid., 32. J. G. Nava to César López de Lara, October 29, 1915, ibid., 34.

[2] Edwards to the secretary of state, November 3, 1915, and January 25, 1916, NA, 59: 812.00/16834 and 17256.

not start. "Only the lowest class Indians can pass the lines with safety," noted the new American chargé d'affaires; "anyone else would undoubtedly risk his life."[3]

But the government merely raised the pressure. In late January it amplified its own agrarista propaganda: the National Agrarian Commission, it promised, would "initiate works for the restitution and grants of ejidos to the pueblos."[4] On February 1 the undersecretary of war announced that twenty thousand new troops would join the ten thousand already assigned to the south. He also threatened to use the government's recently acquired flotilla of airplanes to give "a mortal blow" to the Zapatistas.[5] And his department finally took steps to remove ex-federals from posts where they could obstruct operations.[6]

Again the public Zapatista response was a fire-breathing Manifesto to the Nation. The only reasons for "the fratricidal struggle staining the . . . Fatherland with blood," the headquarters secretaries ranted, were the "boundless ambition of one man of unhealthy passions and no conscience," Venustiano Carranza, and the sycophancy of the group that surrounded him.[7] Even in private they exuded cheer. To Zapata Palafox confided his hope "that in the near future when we dominate Mexico City and other regions of the country, . . . then as I've always hoped, a great number of agrarian commissions will form, so that they will go into all the states of the Republic."[8]

But the chiefs were not so certain. Among them the government's continuing vigor and resolve had prompted darker judgments—doubts whether to go on in principled violence, which would invite the Carrancistas to repeat the work of Huerta and Robles in the state, or to bargain for peace and local autonomy by recognizing Carranza. This was a dilemma especially painful to the chiefs in the northwestern zone, where the brunt of a Carrancista invasion would fall. There the ranking figure was Pacheco, based in Huitzilac. Already he had lost much outlying support and many key points of defense. And as powerful Carrancista legions massed at La Cima, they obliged him to decide whether he should make a deal or pre-

---

[3] Parker to the secretary of state, November 18, 1915, ibid., 16896.

[4] *El Demócrata,* January 23, 1916.

[5] Ibid., February 1, 1916.

[6] Estado Mayor del General Vicente Segura: *Historia de la Brigada Mixta "Hidalgo," 1915–1916* (México, 1917), p. 23.

[7] Manifesto to the Nation, February 7, 1916, AZ, 27: 2.

[8] Palafox to Zapata, February 7, 1916, ibid.

pare for battle. On his decision the Carrancistas would walk into Morelos or have to fight for every hill and ravine. Pacheco was a mystic: in all affairs he did, he said, as God bid him.[9] Now he listened for the divine word.

On February 20 Zapata authorized Pacheco to communicate secretly with General Pablo González, who commanded the Constitutionalist forces at La Cima.[1] What Zapata intended—to initiate peace talks, arrange a local truce, or suborn González—remains unclear, though it was probably the last.[2] It also remains unclear whether Pacheco followed Zapata's instructions, or from the first undertook an independent course. At heart neither chief probably knew exactly what he was up to: depending on González's response, different proposals might arise.

Then de la O and his lieutenant, Valentín Reyes, discovered the correspondence between Pacheco and González. De la O and Pacheco were old rivals, because of a feud between their native villages of Santa María and Huitzilac; and recently the contest had become more heated.[3] With good reason de la O was suspicious as well as jealous. And Reyes apparently expected that he could displace Pacheco and succeed to his command. They both warned Pacheco against treason.

Pacheco immediately complained to Zapata that de la O and Reyes were bothering him. And Zapata in turn informed the two chiefs that it was with headquarters' authority that Pacheco had entered "into dealings and communication with the enemy . . ." The object of the talks, he assured them, was "to learn the aims of the Carrancista General Pablo González and other chiefs who second him with respect to the cause which we defend." The headquarters had received Pacheco's reports on what had happened so far, Zapata said, and it would support Pacheco "as long as the conferences which he had with [the Carrancista generals] were for the benefit of the Revolution, and something advantageous was gained without damage to the principles of the Plan de Ayala."[4]

Pacheco soon hinted, however, that the Good Lord had disposed as de la O had guessed. With hostilities suspended and supposedly in the midst of delicate talks, he complained gruffly to Zapata about his troops' poor pay.

[9] Personal interview with Soto y Gama. Octavio Paz: "Trágico fin del General Pacheco," *El Universal*, December 3, 1933.

[1] *La Prensa*, July 7, 1932. Zapata to Pacheco, March 4, 1916, AZ, 31: Copybook 3.

[2] For a contrary view, see Rafael Alvarado: "Zapata intentó asesinar al General Pablo González," *Todo*, November 5, 1942.

[3] Zapata to de la O, January 8, 1916, AZ, 31: Copybook 2.

[4] Zapata to Reyes and to de la O, March 4, 1916, AZ, 31: Copybook 3.

"I would appreciate it," he wrote, "if you would order the paymaster-general to attend to the paymasters of my division . . . so [my soldiers] who find themselves daily attacking the enemy and away from home . . . can buy corn and not run into difficulties."[5] And suddenly on March 13, under no fire, he evacuated Huitzilac and retreated south to Cuentepec. The Carrancistas moved immediately and without resistance down past Huitzilac as far as La Cruz. Seven miles away, Cuernavaca prepared for a bombardment. Through binoculars the Carrancista officers could see white surrender flags hung out of windows there. On March 18 González himself arrived in La Cruz to inspect the positions his forces held on the heights above the Morelos capital.[6] By then the weary Conventionists had fled on down to Jojutla. De la O obstructed González's advance and saved the front for the moment. But strategically the defense of the state was now impossible.

Incredibly, Pacheco remained free. Even after the Cuentepec municipal president corroborated de la O's constant charges of treason, Zapata stayed loyal. On March 23 he assured Pacheco that "up to today" he had given no credit to rumors of his treachery; and he warned de la O against shooting Pacheco until he had thoroughly investigated the case and proved Pacheco's guilt beyond a doubt.[7] Boldly inspired now, Pacheco complained that de la O had mistreated his troops and sacked Cuernavaca.[8] But as he maneuvered on south, evidently angling to flank Jojutla and capture the Convention, his luck ran out. At Miacatlán one of de la O's patrols caught and shot him. Zapata kept his troops in arms, redistributing them among other chiefs.[9]

Hardly had this loss sunk in when a worse blow struck. On April 16, on his way back to Yautepec after reconnaissance west of the town, Amador Salazar was killed by a stray enemy bullet that hit him in the neck. In the shock of death he stayed upright in the saddle. Finally, as his big sombrero slipped, his aides saw what had happened.[1] So on the eve of attack by the most formidable army they had yet faced, the Zapatistas were without two of their highest chiefs and best commanders.

Meanwhile González had moved his forces in a ring around the state. He, like the other high politicians and generals of the new regime, was im-

[5] Pacheco to Zapata, March 11, 1916, AZ, 27: 3.
[6] El Demócrata, March 21, 1916, Meléndez: op. cit., I, 370.
[7] Zapata to Pacheco and to de la O, March 23, 1916, AZ, 31: Copybook 3.
[8] Pacheco to Zapata, March 27 and 28, 1916, AZ, 27: 3.
[9] Zapata to I. P. Zabala, April 13, 1916, AZ, 27: 4.
[1] Meléndez: op. cit., I, 371–2. Gómez: Las comisiones, pp. 123–4.

patient to end the southern problem. A Constitutional Convention was on their agenda, to legitimize Carranza's reformist decrees, but preparations for it could not begin in earnest until the nation was more or less at peace. Besides, Villa had just provoked an international crisis, raiding murderously into Columbus, New Mexico, and bringing back in pursuit of him a U.S. Army punitive expedition; and on the eve of constitutional reform the Carrancistas could not afford the reappearance of even the possibility of the old Villa-Zapata axis.[2] González now commanded thirty thousand troops, well-supplied and in high spirits, and for his own reputation he was bent on achieving an impressive success. From Jojutla, as if to rally the local forces, the die-hard Conventionists reissued their October 26 manifesto and program of reform.[3] But the surviving Morelos chiefs no longer deluded themselves. They knew the state would shortly be a battleground again, and they were already organizing the procedure, military and civilian, for evacuating the state's villages.[4]

On April 27 González set up his headquarters at Tres Marías and resumed operations. By April 29 government troops held positions surrounding Cuernavaca. At six a.m. on May 2 González directed the final action; and after a short, sharp attack, the state capital fell.[5] Zapata had come up from Tlaltizapán to direct its defense, but withdrew just in time to escape. In the next two or three days almost all the state's other main towns fell to the government commanders. The War Department even had a plane bombing Zapatista lines. By May 6 González reported to Secretary of War Obregón that the campaign was practically finished.[6] The Liberating Army barely held Jojutla, its Tlaltizapán headquarters, and a few scattered villages. And late efforts to suborn Carrancista commanders were to no avail.[7]

As it entered Morelos, the Carrancista army seemed the old federal army reincarnate. Its troops came not as liberators but as conquerors of the local population, which was itself the enemy and enjoyed at most only the rights of prisoners of war. When the Carrancistas took Cuautla, they hanged the

---

[2] On the crisis, see Clarence C. Clendenen: *The United States and Pancho Villa. A Study in Unconventional Diplomacy* (Ithaca, 1961), pp. 234–69.

[3] Manifesto to the Nation, April 18, 1916, AZ, 27: 4.

[4] Zapata to municipal presidents, March 30, 1916, AZ, 27: 3.

[5] *El Demócrata,* May 10, 1916.

[6] Ibid., May 5 and 8, 1916. Oscar Lewis: *Pedro Martínez. A Mexican Peasant and His Family* (New York, 1964), p. 101.

[7] Letters from Almazán, Eufemio Zapata, and Maurilio Mejía to one commander, General Vicente Segura, in Puebla, and his replies, are in Estado Mayor: op. cit., pp. 104–19.

parish priest as a Zapatista spy.[8] On May 5 González ordered every person in the state to turn in his arms: continued possession of them would be grounds for the "severest penalties." At Jiutepec on May 8 the Carrancista General Rafael Cepeda assembled 225 prisoners and after a summary trial had them all shot.[9]

In terror pacíficos swarmed out of pueblos in the line of the Carrancista advance. Fleeing south into Guerrero or east into the high, volcano country, they littered the roadsides with material thrown away to lighten their loads. They jammed little villages still for the moment safe, like Tehuiztla, south-west of Jojutla. This hamlet "presented the look of a fair," reported an observer there in early May, "but a fair of pain and rage. People's faces were furious. They would barely mumble out a few words, but everyone had a violent remark for the Constitutionalists on the tip of his tongue. In conversations, comments on the news alternated with reports which emigrants asked of each other about roads, villages, little settlements stuck up in the steepest part of the mountains, inaccessible, unheard of places—so they could go there to leave their families . . ."[1]

By mid-May the Carrancistas had shipped nearly thirteen hundred prisoners to Mexico City. Some were combatants, some were not. All of them, declared the military commander in the capital, General Benjamín Hill, were bound for Yucatán: and not only them, but all future prisoners. There, General Hill indicated, they would have the "opportunity to work . . . under the vigilance of civil and military authorities"—which would make them "men useful for society and for their families."[2]

From Tlaltizapán Zapata tried desperately to organize municipal police to keep local order as one army replaced another in the state.[3] But police who assumed such responsibility only invited the first fire against their families. For the invading Carrancistas, who considered the villagers themselves outlaws, the transfer of power had to be violent. In mid-June, after another crushing attack, González's forces took Tlaltizapán itself, and a tremendous booty. They also executed 286 persons—132 men, 112 women, and 42 minors of both sexes, as the local register of burials recorded them.[4]

[8] Porfirio Palacios: "Zapatismo vs. Gonzalismo," *Todo,* December 24, 1942.

[9] *La Prensa,* May 5, 1932. *El Demócrata,* May 10, 1916.

[1] Anonymous memorandum on events around Jojutla, May 4, 1916, AZ, 27: 5.

[2] *El Demócrata,* May 16, 1916.

[3] Circular to municipal presidents and assistants, May 31, 1916, AZ, 30: 12.

[4] Palacios: *Zapata,* p. 230. *El Demócrata,* June 15, 1916. *La Prensa,* June 25, 1932.

Helpless in regular battles, Zapata, his surviving chiefs, and the men who stayed with them retreated back into the rough hills.

As the Carrancistas drove into the Zapatista capital, it seemed that the local revolution had failed completely, that the villagers' efforts to carry out their own changes had been a profound mistake and that only on dictation from Mexico City could reform occur and last in Morelos. If so, the idea of a popular revolution was a delusion. If so, the Plan de Ayala was mere rural fustian, and Zapata not an insightful leader but simply a brave and angry clod.

IX

The Guerrilleros Survive

". . . to dispute with the enemy . . ."

POOR MRS. KING! A harassed refugee now in crowded Veracruz, her young daughter prey to every passing revolutionary officer, and she herself victim of a recurring nightmare, she felt at times that her nerves would snap. During the day she was usually calm. But at night in the dream the good widow saw her Cuernavaca property ruined. While she "stood impotently by, screaming," Zapatistas knocked down her dear Hotel Bella Vista and "methodically piled up the stones to form a pyramid."[1]

She had "invested everything" in the Cuernavaca hotel after her husband's death. Its fortunes, so she had remarked with Victorian innocence, were her fortunes; and now in the summer of 1916 she could not stand "these horrible fancies" of total loss. She knew the Constitutionalist army had recently occupied Morelos, and it occurred to her that in repairing her things there she might repair her life. She went back, but Cuernavaca presented an awful scene: "Black, battered, bullet-pierced walls where had been comfortable, happy homes, bridges destroyed, approaches to the town cut

---

[1] For her account, see King: op. cit., pp. 5–6, 263–99. The phrases in quotes are hers.

off, everywhere signs of the dreadful conflict that had taken place. . . . My head had known it would be like this," she said, "but my heart was not prepared. We drove down the silent streets past abandoned, deserted houses; not a soul in sight. A dog, nosing in a heap of rubbish, slunk away at our approach, and the clatter of the wheels awoke strange echoes in the emptiness. . . . I was sobbing, 'But there is no one here! Where are the people? Where are the people?'" Her hotel, as she had feared, was demolished. "The great dining room that had been my pride was bare," she later recalled, "—nothing left in it, only pigs and chickens living there together quite happily."

For three days she escaped into a compulsive euphoria about rebuilding that verged on hysterics. Then in a desperate test of her hopes she asked General González's permission to begin work. The general, as she however learned, "had his own obsessions." As Zapatistas went on fighting, González ached to crush "his elusive foe in any way he could compass it." Mrs. King's petty laments wearied him. "This is no time to talk of reconstruction, Señora King," he barked. "The work of destruction is not yet çompleted." "But our homes! Our property!" cried Mrs. King. "'Oh, Señora,' he said, almost angrily, 'That is of the past. That is all over.'"

In a daze she walked back to the quiet square where her ruined hotel was, feeling that "I had died along with my valley-nestled home." "This," she decided, "is the end of Rosa King." At the edge of town, on the hill beside the state government building, looking down the cobbled streets, out over the ravines below and across the valley to the mountains north and east, she began to remember her childhood and to wonder how all her strivings could have failed. A final and nearly lunatic despair seized her. She called out loud toward the mountains, "Are you dead, too?" Echoes came drifting back, like cries to her.

At this instant it struck her that there were people in the mountains— the plain people she had missed in town. At once she thought of how ancient their struggle was "to hold their freedom and their country." The idea that they had fought and would go on fighting, as "strong, steadfast, eternal" as the mountains, inspired her. A vision ran through her mind of men hiding out there in the hills, "with their rifles and their leader, finding cover and nourishing herbs among the stony ledges." "And then," as she later remembered, "I knew I had not died." There was a bond between her and those country folk, between her and the world, which the loss of her property could not undo. She returned to Mexico City, and in the following months, despite even more calamities, she felt herself grow stronger.

As she recovered, so did the local revolutionaries. The impassioned experience of the last five years, culminating in an eighteen-month effort to establish local, popular welfare, had created a consuming sense of union among Morelos's rural families. Together they had enjoyed the high hopes of their own reform, and together again they had suffered the awful disaster of González's invasion. "It seemed," recalled the observer of the refugee crowd at Tehuiztla, ". . . that a single family had reunited there. Everybody talked to everybody else with complete confidence. People lent each other help, and men and women who had never seen each other talked as intimately as old friends." A few stayed in Guerrero, like one Tepoztecan sure that "the situation [in Morelos] was hopeless and that I would be killed and that [my wife and children] would perish."[2] But most, having deposited their families in "inaccessible, unheard of places," came back "to dispute with the enemy," said the Tehuiztla observer, "the land he was trampling over." In revolution these people had learned to think of Morelos as theirs, and only theirs. To them the occupying Carrancistas seemed as foreign as the American troops still in the north, who they believed, as Zapata had by now publicly charged, were there on Carranza's invitation to defeat Villa.[3] Patriotism required, as Mrs. King had guessed, not that they respect so strange and disreputable an authority as Carranza's but rather that they oppose it heart and soul. And when in early July Zapata and the other chiefs returned to organize resistance, the villagers rallied around them—this time even grimmer, even more deeply determined. By now they knew better how to die than to abandon their homes.

The risk of resistance in Morelos in mid-1916 was dreadful. For Pablo González stood to fix a claim on an important post in Mexico City if he established Constitutionalist rule in the state: this official dignity he craved, and he had thirty thousand troops to win it. From his early years in Nuevo León and Coahuila before the revolution he had wanted success and approval. An orphan at six, a peddler at fourteen, once even an emigrant into the United States, then a petty merchant and politician in a little Coahuila farm town, and a revolutionary for Madero in 1911, he had strained all his life, alternately careful and reckless, for the opportunity he had now.[4] His only handicap was a fear of failure that had numbed his brain and left him as stupid as he was ambitious. By 1916 a solemn, ceremonious palooka,

[2] Lewis: *Pedro Martínez,* p. 102.

[3] Manifesto to the Mexican People, May 29, 1916, AZ, 27: 5.

[4] José Morales Hesse: *El General Pablo González. Datos para la historia, 1910–1916* (México, 1916), pp. 9–18.

sporting smoked glasses and a floppy Stetson, González suffered a reputation as the only Carrancista general of division never to have won a battle. His high rank he owed to Carranza, who had arranged his promotions because he needed a general he could control to balance Obregón, whom he could not. But González's torpidity of wit was so thorough that over the short run it was a potential strength; on the make, he was at random capable of any tactic, ingenious as well as inane. Although his luck had not been good so far, in Morelos it might go right.

Already he had carried out the preliminaries of his mission with impressive dispatch, eradicating Conventionist authority in the state. Municipal governments, the state government, the Conventionist national agencies —this loyal Carrancista regarded them all as illegitimate and reactionary. And all he had deposed. All the Conventionist laws and rulings he had also nullified. Included of course among the abrogated acts were the redistributions Palafox had made in titles to land.

Now González turned to fulfill his "supreme duty and decided goal, to reestablish order and work in the whole state." In this enterprise he behaved oddly for a revolutionary called Constitutionalist. He did not restore the civil constitution of Morelos that Juvencio Robles had suspended in 1913. Instead, like Robles, he governed formally as a military dictator. His headquarters in Cuernavaca was the governor's office. Likewise, in the other main towns his subordinate commanders assumed civil authority. And in the villages where no garrisons or detachments were, the district commanders appointed agents responsible to them alone. In mid-August González had another governor replace him, General Dionisio Carreón, but Carreón too governed as a military dictator.[5] No municipal or legislative elections therefore took place, as they did elsewhere in the Republic, and no civil courts opened. Nor did González carry out social reforms to implant the revolution he represented. The most he accomplished, as he boasted, was that "lives and interests have been respected, there have been established municipal services, schools, provisioning stations for the people, facilities for commerce, etc., etc."[6] In mid-July he did decree the formation of a State Agrarian Commission in Cuernavaca, to operate as Carranza had directed in his decree of January 6, 1915. And he indicated that local commissions would soon be set up in the former district seats.[7] But thus he only staked out his own authority over the disposition of all farm

[5] *El Demócrata*, August 21, 1916.
[6] Manifesto to the Natives of Morelos, July 9, 1916, AZ, 28: 4: 1.
[7] *El Demócrata*, July 25, 1916.

property in the state. And he evidently did not use the authority, as he could have, to order provisional restitutions or grants of land to petitioning villages. Only around Axochiapan did a subordinate, Vicente Segura, honor village claims for restitution.[8]

What González supervised as Constitutionalism in practice was the plunder of Morelos. The pickings were fine. On the mountains through the northern parts of the state there was abundant timber. As reporters hinted, the valleys were thick and green with newly planted food crops.[9] And as González himself noted, large herds of cattle were grazing in rich pasture land—over one thousand head around Tlaltizapán alone. Besides, stores of the sugar and alcohol produced in the recent cane harvest remained in the mills the Zapatistas had rehabilitated. The milling machines themselves were still in the haciendas. And finally there was the materiél the Zapatistas had had to leave. The locomotives, boxcars, cannon, and ammunition might go back to the War Department, but other items were in high demand among private buyers. At Tlaltizapán, for instance, the booty comprised six boxcars of paper, three boxcars of coal and other minerals, five thousand kegs of blasting powder, loads of dynamite, nitroglycerine, fuses, caps, nitric acid, and tanning bark, a car of sulphur, fifty tons of copper, five boxcars of machinery for manufacturing cartridges, several printing presses, and one hundred hides.[1] All this was the spoils of war, and as González managed it in the next few months, it all disappeared—to reappear in markets in Mexico City. Along the way González and most of his staff and subordinates came into the money. For them the Morelos campaign was a great chance for patriotic boodle, the most irresistible kind. In cashing in their power, they deprived the Zapatista "bandits" of precious resources. Such was the revolution González installed in the state, a "work," as he termed it, "of reconstruction and progress."

To villagers who contemplated defending themselves against this version of social change, González quickly made clear the reprisals they could expect. The occasion was a warning he delivered in early July, after Zapatista raiders had almost wiped out Constitutionalist garrisons in Santa Catarina and Tepoztlán. Evidently the local folk had served the raiders at least as spies. If they or other villagers again obstructed his "beneficent and healthy labor," he declared, they would oblige him "to proceed with extraordinary severity against all the pueblos of the state." He could not permit the

[8] Estado Mayor: op. cit., pp. 34, 41, 45–6, 95–101.
[9] El Demócrata, June 15, 1916.
[1] La Prensa, June 25, 1932.

enemy beaten in the field to find refuge in the villages, among people "who hypocritically call themselves peaceable." Henceforth, he proclaimed, villagers had to cooperate with the Constitutionalist commanders and turn in Zapatistas. Otherwise the whole population would "incur the most terrific responsibilities" and suffer "summary punishment without appeal of any kind."[2]

Still, the Zapatistas mobilized defiance. Strategically they disbanded the old twenty thousand-man semi-regular army. Even twenty thousand regulars were not enough to hold back González's legions, and after the losses of the recent campaign the Zapatistas did not have enough ammunition to equip a third that many for more than small actions. Anyway, without control over the produce in the valleys, the local revolutionaries could not support a large, positional force. Instead they reverted to guerrillas. Breaking into small, wide-ranging units of one hundred and two hundred men each, based in temporary camps in the hills and intimately familiar with the terrain and people of their respective zones, they were easier to feed and harder to find. And from early July on guerrilleros staged raids and ambushes painfully embarrassing to González. After the Santa Catarina and Tepoztlán massacres, an unusually large force of one thousand men struck into the Federal District through Ajusco and up to Milpa Alta, where it captured valuable military stores and then withdrew. At Tlayacapan Zapatistas battled a Constitutionalist detachment for seven hours on July 16. A day later two hundred Zapatistas attacked the garrison at Tlaltizapán. A week after that another force of two hundred attacked the garrison again.[3]

Not all the surviving veteran chiefs would actually fight. Some remained nominally in the resistance but in practice delayed at their bases, pretexting a lack of ammunition for their uncertain inertia. Worse, they still taxed the villagers around them for supplies, or even let bandits move into their zones. Justified or not, their delinquency disgusted Zapata. And he tried to shame laggard chiefs into combat—as much to mollify the villagers they had riled as to disrupt Constitutionalist control. In mid-August he publicly condemned "the cowards or egoists . . . who have retired to live in towns or camps, extorting from the pueblos or enjoying wealth they have taken over in the shadow of the revolution," and giving "promotions or appointments to persons who do not deserve them." They were as bad

[2] Manifesto to the Natives of Morelos, July 9, 1916, AZ.
[3] *El Demócrata,* August 8 and 20, 1916. *La Prensa,* July 9, 14, and 21, 1932.

as the old federal officers, he declared, "[who] weighed on the Nation and caused it great expenses without lending any positive service." And he proclaimed them unworthy to lead "an armed movement which battles for the good of the people and not for the formation of a new class of idle and useless men . . ." Dishonorable discharges from the Liberating Army were in order, he decreed, for commanders who without authorization had retreated in the face of the enemy since May 1—since, that is, the major campaign in which the Constitutionalists had occupied the state. Also discharged were "chiefs, officers, and soldiers who instead of fighting the enemy use their arms to abuse the citizens of the pueblos and to take away from them their scarce means of subsistence," as well as chiefs who refused to obey current orders to resume operations. They all had to turn over to headquarters their arms, ammunition, staffs, escorts, and troops. The promotions and appointments they had made were to go before headquarters secretaries for review.[4]

The first chief to suffer this disgrace was Lorenzo Vázquez. Since 1911 Vázquez had been among the chiefs Zapata trusted most, in council and in the field. But during the critical weeks of the Constitutionalist invasion, he had roused grave suspicions against himself. He, Montaño, and the since executed Pacheco had complained that the defeat the state was going down in was the fault of the Conventionists, Palafox and Soto y Gama especially, who had prevented an understanding with the Constitutionalists. Then, after Pacheco's execution, Vázquez had taken into his camp two officers from Pacheco's staff, reportedly two of those who had persuaded their former chief to retreat before González.[5] And the line of defense around Jojutla, which was his to hold during the June battles there, Vázquez had not held long enough for Zapata to get supplies or civilians out of Tlaltizapán. Subsequently he had reorganized no forces and carried out no raids. And on August 15 Zapata ordered his dishonorable discharge for "notorious cowardice." Later, chiefs who failed to come back from Guerrero were also discharged. Among them was Leobardo Galván, a general and a former delegate to the Convention.[6]

Still, going into the fall of 1916, the Zapatistas probably had around five thousand men in the field. Probably two thousand to three thousand more

[4] Decree of August 10, 1916, AZ, 28: 4: 1.

[5] Declaration of Inocencio P. Zabala, April 14, 1916, AZ, 28: 5. Meléndez: op. cit., I, 375.

[6] General Order of August 15, 1916, AZ, 28: 4: 1. General Order of January 13, 1917, AZ, 30: 13.

were on active reserve, to replace casualties or to spell the fatigued. And despite Constitutionalist amnesties and pay-offs, most of the chiefs fighting on were those who had been with Zapata from the first. In the southwest around Tetecala and Puente de Ixtla Pedro and Francisco Saavedra were constant threats to Constitutionalist garrisons and patrols. In the south around Jojutla the readiest bushwackers were Eutimio Rodríguez, Gabriel Mancera, and Modesto Rangel. At Huautla Zapata had his own headquarters. In the southeast around Jonacatepec, as always, Mendoza was in frequent skirmishes with the enemy. Moving around the northeast from his base in Tochimilco, Puebla, Fortino Ayaquica carried on regular operations. Along the Mexico State–Morelos border around Ozumba and Amecameca, the forces of Vicente Rojas and Everardo and Bardomiano González often fought their way into key towns. Around Cuautla Sidronio Camacho kept the Constitutionalist garrison practically paralyzed. And from there over to Yautepec and down to Tlaltizapán Eufemio Zapata, Emigdio Marmolejo, Jesús Capistrán and Juan Salazar staged one raid after another. North of Yautepec and around Tepoztlán the most energetic chiefs were Timoteo and Mariano Sánchez and Gabriel Mariaca. And in the northwest and west, reaching into the Federal District, Mexico State, and down into Guerrero, were the forces of de la O, which Valentín Reyes, Rafael Castillo, and Julián Gallegos took out on repeated assaults.[7] The Constitutionalists never caught or disabled any of these bands.

Moreover the Zapatista challenge remained strictly Zapatista. Tempting appeals had reached Zapata to join a Felicista rebellion, which Félix Díaz had returned in the past February to start in Veracruz and Oaxaca.[8] Because of the financial resources of the exiles who backed him, among them several ex-planters from Morelos, Díaz had quickly won the affiliation of numerous other anti-Carranza leaders around the Republic. By mid-1916 his movement had become the most serious opposition in Mexico.[9] And the Felicistas, the Constitutionalists, and the American diplomats in Mexico City all believed that Zapata would affiliate too.[1] But as quickly as others had joined Díaz, Zapata refused any connection—and this just when he needed help most. In Puebla he cooperated militarily with mercenaries

[7] Meléndez: op. cit., I, 372–3.

[8] Zapata to Mendoza, April 6, 1916, AZ, 31: Copybook 4.

[9] For a Felicista account of Díaz's 1916–17 adventures, see Luis Liceaga: *Félix Díaz* (México, 1958), pp. 362–462.

[1] James L. Rodgers to the secretary of state, June 23, 1916, NA, 43: American-Mexican Joint Commission: Rodgers dispatches (henceforth AMR): Box 9: 408.

now Felicista, like Higinio Aguilar and Juan Andrew Almazán, but he gave them no entry into Morelos nor ever coordinated his forces with theirs. And to clarify his political position he sent out circulars to his chiefs informing them of Díaz's return and forbidding them to recognize him "in any way."[2] Ideologically the Morelos revolution remained the movement of the Ayala plan.

González's reaction to the resurgent Zapatistas was unerringly obtuse. It was, as he had warned, "to proceed with extraordinary severity" against the pueblos, where active resistants no longer were. And in the particular procedure he employed he confirmed himself as the immediate spiritual heir of the most infamous figure in Morelos history, Juvencio Robles. For beginning on September 15, the eve of the national independence holiday, he ordered the concentration of the state's rural families in the main towns for subsequent deportation.[3] The order amounted to another declaration of war against the village as an institution. In stark contrast, on the same day in almost all other states, municipal elections were to take place to found local autonomy. Meanwhile, the plunder of Morelos continued. Among their victims, *los Constitucionalistas* had by now become known as *los consusuñaslistas*—"the ones with their fingernails ready" to scratch out loot.

Zapata took nice advantage of this bungling to discredit González and his revolution in the state. On September 15 he decreed a General Law on Municipal Liberties. Composed by headquarters secretary Conrado Díaz Soto y Gama and aides, the law was a formal fulfillment of various promises in the Conventionist program of reforms. In its five initial articles it paralleled the brief decree Carranza had issued on municipalities. Declaring that "municipal liberty is the first and most important of democratic institutions, since nothing is more natural or worthy of respect than the right which the citizens of any settlement have of arranging by themselves the affairs of their common life and of resolving as best suits them the interests and needs of their locality," Zapata abolished all federal and state control over town councils in administration and finance. In effect he thus abolished the system of political prefectures. And he ruled that elections be direct. But in thirteen other articles the law was markedly more communalist than the Carrancista decree. In this section of distinctly southern inspiration Zapata recognized a danger Carranza had ignored completely. Unless citizens took direct part in the "principal affairs" of their town, he warned,

[2] Circular, June 7, 1916, AZ, 28: 4: 1.
[3] *El Demócrata*, September 25, 1916.

local bosses would manage the election of their cronies to the council and "there will be achieved only the establishment of a new despotism . . . to replace the old jefes políticos." To prevent the ensuing "abuses and scandalous businesses or immoral traffic, to submit to the approval of all the citizens the most important business of communal existence, such as the alienation or acquisition of lands, the approval of salaries and expenses, the celebration of contracts on lighting, paving, collection or conduction of water, and other public services," he prescribed several means for civic control of town councils. Only local residents were eligible to vote or hold office. Officials could serve only one year and had to wait two more before they could run for re-election. Questions involving the municipal budget, the purchase or sale of municipal property, municipal contracts, loans, and indebtment had to go before a publicly announced general junta, with its own freely elected executive committee, for full discussion and a majority vote. And a certain minority of citizens could at any time call for detailed accounts, or even impeachment hearings, by a petition to the revolutionary headquarters for a general junta.[4]

To discredit the Constitutionalists further, Zapata offered the local pueblos fiscal guarantees in a decree on state and municipal revenues. Where Carranza had not even referred to income for town councils, the Zapatista secretaries here stated on principle that "to prepare and make effective municipal liberty," pueblos had to have "enough funds and resources to pay amply for their needs." And they did not, as the Carrancista secretaries later would, leave the state government to take in all taxes and then decide how much to return to the towns. They noted precisely which tax sources belonged to the state and which to the municipal governments. Among the fourteen sources reserved to the latter were pawnshops, cantinas, and the new-fangled gas stations. Considered most important was the municipal right to levy a monthly sales tax on local grocers, butchers, bakers, and other purveyors of "primary necessities." In the enabling clause the Zapatista secretaries also shrewdly ruled that so long as the war went on, and no state government existed, the town councils could collect the state's taxes as well as their own.[5]

A change Zapata made in his tactics about this time helped to preserve his own support in the pueblos. Although he continued to operate in guer-

[4] General Law on Municipal Liberties, September 15, 1916, AZ, 28: 2: 1.
[5] Law on State and Municipal Incomes for the State of Morelos, September 18, 1916, ibid.

rillas, he now selected targets more on political than on military grounds—which intensified the fighting where it shocked Mexico City but curtailed it around ordinary villages. The change was a sign that Zapata had finally taken heed of Villa's example in the north. There, commanding only two hundred or three hundred men but staging scandalous raids, like those into the United States, Villa had posed a serious danger for Carranza's new government: in late September the American troops were still in Mexico, and negotiations were still dragging on to get them out.[6] At least since May Carranza had feared that Zapata might launch similar attacks in the south, dramatic assaults to prove that the government was a sham.[7] Struggling through the summer to regain his balance in Morelos, Zapata was not up to terrorist theatrics; but in a long report from an agent in Puebla City on September 27 he read a persuasive case for trying them. The agent, Octavio Paz, admitted that Carranza's military control was generally sound but insisted that his political situation was extremely precarious. The elections for the Constitutional Convention Carranza had recently called were bound to divide the ambitious chiefs around him. And if the United States had decisive evidence of the regime's internal weakness, it might well rescind recognition. If the Republican candidate "Hugges" won the imminent presidential elections, as Paz reported bets of five to one he would, then the rescission was even more likely. Paz recommended attacks on trains and on Puebla City, which, he said, would create as much international furor as Villa's rampages in the north.[8]

On October 1 Zapata first indicated publicly that he had a new field of action in mind. In an Exposition to the Mexican People and to the Diplomatic Corps, after complaints about Carranza's political and economic policies and a condemnation of the coming Constitutional Convention as a vicious fake, he declared suggestively that "there is not a single line of communication which it can be said is controlled by Carrancismo."[9] Almost immediately he mounted an operation vividly impressive to foreign agents in the capital. On October 4, in a battle the American chargé d'affaires described as "one of the heaviest . . . between Constitutionalists and Zapatistas . . . in months," Zapatistas captured the pumping station at Xochimilco which supplied the capital its water. A week later another band

[6] Clendenen: op. cit., pp. 270–95.

[7] Cándido Aguilar to J. L. Rodgers, May 22, 1916, NA, 43: AMR: 9: 369.

[8] O. Paz, Report, September 27, 1916, AZ, 28: 2: 1.

[9] Exposition to the Mexican People and to the Diplomatic Corps, October 1, 1916, ibid.

attacked the suburb of San Ángel, only eight miles from downtown Mexico City.[1]

Through the fall this was the pattern of Zapatista operations—to suspend combat in Morelos and to press it harder at sore spots elsewhere in the center and south. In Puebla, Tlaxcala, southern Hidalgo, Mexico State, Michoacán, Guerrero, and Oaxaca, local gangs more or less Zapatista put on numerous raids. And rarely was the place of attack a village out in the country, or the motive to challenge a garrison. More and more often the action was along a railroad or around a mill, factory, or mining town, to attract the attention of foreign consuls.[2]

Despite a new interest in movements outside Morelos, Zapata kept sharp watch over the guerrilleros still in the state. He allowed them no excuse for resting in their camps but egged them on to follow the example of chiefs like Everardo González and Valentín Reyes, who raided two or three times a week into Mexico State and the Federal District. More important, Zapata urged them to maintain good relations with the pueblos. Although at times he reprimanded municipal officials for ignoring legitimate guerrillero claims, his overriding concern was that the men fighting in the field retain the sympathy of the people in the villages.[3] He circulated orders among his chiefs to respect persons and property in contested areas, to see to the establishment of municipal and judicial authorities in all towns, and to let local officials work "in full liberty."[4] In particular he tried to avoid feuds between chiefs, which might involve innocent villagers who would later refuse pasture, food, and quarters to needy warriors back from battle.[5]

Zapata's pressure for discipline was so strong that other chiefs issued instructions for their own zones. From his camp at Tochimilco Fortino Ayaquica ordered chiefs of detachments in surrounding pueblos to shoot on the spot any person caught in the act of banditry or abuse of local rights. Suspicious persons they were to send to his headquarters.[6] Ayaquica's initiative won him the Morelos headquarters' praise.[7]

[1] Parker to the secretary of state, October 5 and 12, 1916, NA, 59: 812.00/19449 and 19530.

[2] Meléndez: op. cit., I, 373.

[3] Zapata to Ignacio Sagredo, October 23, 1916, AZ, 28: 2: 2. Zapata to Mendoza, August 5, 1916, AA.

[4] Circular to Chiefs of the Liberating Army, October 9, 1916, AZ, 30: 12.

[5] Zapata to Mendoza, November 13, 1916, AZ, 28: 2: 3.

[6] Instructions to Chiefs of Detachments, October 10, 1916, ibid., 1.

[7] Revolutionary Information Service, October 26, 1916, ibid., 2.

Meanwhile González had become lethally impatient. His dream of an impressive professional military administration had faded. As the clearing campaign stalled, even saving face was a problem. Every week he had to report more hamlets seized from resistants—and a hundred or so more Constitutionalist casualties.[8] In frustration his subordinate commanders vented their rage on whomever they found. On September 30 Colonel Jesús Guajardo executed 180 residents of Tlaltizapán—men, women, and children. The families were Zapatista, he asserted: they would not pay a forced loan he had levied on them.[9]

And the sacking continued, as frantic as ever. Anything portable, it seemed, wound up on the Mexico City market. One day Mrs. King received a visit in the capital from three army officers who asked her to identify some bathtubs they had just bought from a Cuernavaca shipment. She accompanied them to a warehouse near the central train station—and yes, she told them, the tubs were from the Bella Vista. Great was the officers' relief: their purchases were good quality! Mrs. King protested that the tubs were hers, that she wanted them back. The officers refused. They had, they explained, only "confiscated" what she had "abandoned."[1]

A few months later, writing to a colleague in another zone, a secretary at the Morelos headquarters recalled the Constitutionalists' ferocity with bitterness still fresh. "Never did anyone believe," he wrote, "that there would be ruffians who surpassed Huerta's . . . come and see," he asked, "—pueblos completely burned down, timber leveled, cattle stolen, crops that were cultivated with labor's sweat harvested by the enemy . . . to fill the boxcars of their long trains and be sold in the capital." As for the concentration, his comment was brief but pungent: "Robles, damned a thousand times, is little in comparison." To clear out the countryside, he said, the Constitutionalists drove people like "a herd of pigs" to loading platforms and then shipped them in boxcars and cattlecars to Mexico City. There they scattered them into the slums around the railroad yards, absolutely destitute. Families left in the state fared hardly better. "This business of seeing three or four men pulling a plow, taking the place of the beasts they owned but which the Carrancistas stole from them—this," the secretary testified, "is a revolting thing."[2] Years later Morelos villagers remem-

[8] *La Prensa,* September 27 and October 4, 1932.

[9] Palacios in *Todo,* December 24, 1942.

[1] King: op. cit., p. 302.

[2] Juan Espinosa Barreda to Alberto Paniagua, March 30, 1917, AZ, 28: 1: 3. For Mrs. King's comments on refugees in Mexico City, among whom she found her former servants, see op. cit., pp. 301–2.

bered the invaders of 1916 with so much hate that they even confused them with the federals of 1912–13, referring to all their woes since 1911 as the work of the Carrancistas.[3]

The balladeers could plumb the true depths of local despair only by laughing—

> For God's sake, Venustiano, change your plans.
> Tell your soldiers not to ax
> The poor hogs, cows, and chickens
> And the turkeys in their attacks.
> Tell them the jugs aren't Zapatista,
> Nor the pots nor pans nor skillets,
> The old butter-moulds, the meal, and dough,
> Nor the seed we've stored, the shawls, and dishes.[4]

But the Zapatistas only grew bolder in their raids, and in November they forced González to the breaking point. Their tactics were two spectacular acts of terror on the Mexico City-Cuernavaca railroad. On November 7 near Joco station in the Federal District they blasted a train headed south up Mount Ajusco. In Mexico City busy metropolitans heard the explosion and the rifle fire that followed, and looking at the southern slopes, they could see the smoke from the burning wreckage. Some four hundred military and civilian passengers died in the massacre.[5] González was then in the capital, engaged in the most delicate politicking with Obregón and Carranza. Excruciatingly embarrassed, he opened a formal investigation of the attack and returned to Cuernavaca to make his own inquiries. There on November 11 he expedited a Draconian order. "Anyone," he declared, "who directly or indirectly lends service to Zapatismo, or to any other faction opposing Constitutionalism, will be shot by a firing squad with no more requirements than identification." Also suffering a summary death penalty would be anyone caught on roads or paths without certified safe-conducts from the Constitutionalist headquarters in Cuernavaca; anyone near railroad right-of-ways "without satisfactory explanation"; anyone not resettled in the specified towns; anyone who had given his personal safe-conduct pass to another; and anyone who had vouched for someone dishonestly requesting a safe-conduct pass.[6] González threatened in vain.

---

[3] See, e.g., Lewis: *Pedro Martínez*, pp. 84–6.
[4] Cited in Simmons: op. cit., pp. 147–8.
[5] *El Demócrata*, November 8 and 9, 1916. Taracena: *Mi vida*, p. 395.
[6] *El Universal*, November 14, 1916.

A few days later, a little higher up the same mountain, Zapatistas blasted another train. Again the casualties were appalling. And again metropolitans were witness to González's incapacity even to police the capital zone. The American chargé d'affaires took due note of the Constitutionalist failure in the south.[7]

González was in a fury, but he was helpless. Even with thirty thousand men he had miscarried his assignment. And he could extract no new reinforcements from Secretary of War Obregón, who needed all the troops and supplies he could muster in more critical operations—chasing Villa in Chihuahua and Félix Díaz in Oaxaca, and keeping close guard on the American expedition still on Mexican soil. González's only recourse was private rant, that Obregón had deliberately shortchanged him in men and funds and had probably subverted him too, and that the Zapatistas were "barbarians, . . . loathsome satyrs [of] bestial instincts, . . . felons and cowards by nature" who would not fight fair.[8]

In Cuernavaca González resigned himself to defeat. He dutifully let the political burlesque continue in which members of his staff won local "elections" to represent Morelos in the Constitutional Convention opening December 1. Acting as branches of the recently founded official party, the Liberal Constitutionalist, the garrisons at Cuernavaca, Cuautla, and Jojutla chose three headquarters officers as regular delegates and three more as alternates. Only one, Colonel Alvaro Alcázar, representing Jojutla, was a native of the state: the politician in an old merchant family from Jonacatepec, he had served on the town council there in 1911. The others were northerners, from Sonora, Nuevo León, Coahuila. The Liberal Constitutionalist commanders also nominated Carranza for president, and after considering one of their own number, General Gustavo Elizondo, for governor, they nominated Carranza for that post as well.[9] But González had no illusions now about his real power in the state. After convening his generals to discuss the campaign, he announced on November 22 a plan

---

[7] Parker to the secretary of state, January 10, 1917, NA, 59: 812.00/18161.

[8] Pablo González: "Verdades para la historia," in Partido Reconstrucción Nacional: *Recopilación de Documentos y Algunas Publicaciones de Importancia* (Monterrey, 1923), pp. 239–43.

[9] *El Universal*, November 9 and 18, and December 5, 1916. See also S. Valverde: op. cit., pp. 183–4, and Gabriel Ferrer Mendiolea: *Historia del Congreso Constituyente de 1916–1917* (México, 1957), p. 168. On the origins of the Liberal Constitutionalist Party, see Eugene M. Braderman: "A Study of Political Parties and Politics in Mexico since 1890" (Ph.D. dissertation, University of Illinois, 1938), pp. 156–9.

supposed to intensify operations but in fact to retreat. The instructions
he issued were to clear five hundred meters on both sides of the railroad
track from Contreras in the Federal District down to Cuernavaca, and to
move headquarters back to Mexico City.[1]

Left practically to fend for himself, Military Governor Carreón could
only wait for the end. His commanders were like those elsewhere who,
observed the American chargé d'affaires, "seem to have abandoned the
field almost entirely and to be devoting their time to politics and grafting."[2]
They were especially eager to appropriate the corn harvest now coming in.
Meanwhile Constitutionalist troops grew weaker every day. Already they
had been decimated by malaria. Another scourge was dysentery, contracted
from living on fruits like the mango in a nearly tropical climate. And as
winter came on, a typhoid epidemic developed in the Federal District and
spread into the state. The few shipments of morphine and quinine that
reached Cuernavaca went on the black market, for private resale back in
the capital. By now military hospitals in González's zone held seven thousand sick, exhausted, ill-fed, demoralized soldiers. Others even more
miserable sought shelter in side-tracked boxcars or makeshift huts. Some
died in the street.[3]

After the harvest Zapata suddenly resumed the offensive in Morelos. On
December 1, from headquarters re-established in Tlaltizapán, he launched
coordinated surprise attacks against garrisons in Cuernavaca, Yautepec,
Jojutla, Treinta hacienda, Jonacatepec, Axochiapan, Paso del Muerto, and
Izúcar de Matamoros, Chietla, and Atlixco, Puebla. The decrepit Constitutionalist defenses caved in. Jojutla and Treinta fell the first day, the
Zapatistas knocking five hundred hapless soldiers out of action. The other
places remained under siege, and rail traffic between Cuernavaca and
Iguala ceased. From Mexico City González released reports in the following days that his forces had dislodged Zapatistas from various villages, but
each dislodgement occurred closer to the Federal District.[4]

In late December the Constitutionalists began to pull out of Morelos,
taking whatever they could with them. And coming in after them and
sometimes around them in gory ambushes, the Zapatistas reoccupied the
main towns. On January 7 they rode into Jonacatepec, and the next day

---

[1] *La Prensa,* November 22 and December 1, 1932.

[2] Parker to the secretary of state, November 8, 1916, NA, 59: 812.00/19793.

[3] Partido Reconstrucción Nacional: op. cit., pp. 243–4. *La Prensa,* October 11,
November 19, and December 6, 1932.

[4] Ibid., December 29, 1932, and January 7, 1933. Meléndez: op. cit., I, 373–4.

fought their way into Yautepec. By January 10 they again held Cuautla. During the next week they moved into Tetecala, then Miacatlán, and then Cuernavaca.[5] They had retrieved no supplies, but they had recovered their state.

For a few weeks delirium prevailed in Tlaltizapán. From there it seemed that Constitutionalism was about to collapse, that González was withdrawing his forces as the federal generals had withdrawn theirs when Huerta fell. Soto y Gama dashed off a program of economic and financial measures the Liberating Army would carry out when it again occupied Mexico City.[6] Octavio Paz, now in San Antonio, also misjudged the federal retreat. He reported back to headquarters the intelligence that "our triumph appears a fact" and urged an immediate push north from Cuernavaca, to beat Pancho Villa to the capital![7] After the United States lifted its embargo on shipments of war materiél in mid-January, Zapata signed another Manifesto to the Mexican People, declaring that "the nightmare of Carrancismo, running over with horror and blood, is at its end," and assuring the nation again of southern "generosity" to all classes except the landlord.[8] From headquarters there also issued a new nationalization decree.[9] And on paper the Liberating Army underwent drastic regularization —into an active and a first- and second-reserve militia, from the squad to the division level, complete with an engineering and a medical corps and military tribunals.[1]

It was soon clear how far off this judgment was. That González should fold was no sign that the government would too. At the Constitutional Convention in those very days the Carrancistas were proving the basic strength and solidity of their party. And in debating and writing into the new Constitution reforms for social welfare, they revealed an acute sense of national responsibility. They even horned in on the Zapatistas' agrarianism. Among those who advocated a radical defense of the pueblos was a delegate from Puebla, Luis T. Navarro, who as a Maderista deputy in 1913 had found refuge from Huerta among the Zapatistas, had served eighteen months with them in Morelos and Puebla, and now in 1917 de-

[5] Revolutionary Information Service, January 10, 1917, AZ, 30: 13.
[6] Measures of Economic and Financial Order, January 10, 1917, AZ, 27: 18.
[7] Paz to Soto y Gama, January 15, 1917, AZ, 29: 13.
[8] Manifesto to the Mexican People, January 20, 1917, AZ, 30: 13.
[9] Decree on Nationalized Goods, January (n.d.), 1917, AZ, 28: 10: 3.
[1] Decree to the Liberating Army, January 31, 1917, AZ, 30: 13.

fended their honor and their cause in a Carrancista Convention.[2] And in Article 27 the radicals prevailed, guaranteeing that villages had the right to hold property as corporations, that the pueblo was a legitimate institution in the new order. Militarily, outside Morelos, the Carrancistas had actually improved their position in the south. In Guerrero and Puebla they had organized local contacts into skeleton governments. In Tlaxcala, where dispossessed villagers like those in Morelos had organized into a similar agrarian movement and then in 1915 declared for Zapata, the Constitutionalists had arranged a deal with the local chief, Domingo Arenas. Near Huejotzingo, Puebla, on December 1, 1916, Arenas had accepted "a humanitarian and patriotic invitation" to "unify" his forces with the Constitutionalists. In return he became a general of brigade, all his officers held their ranks and commands, the Arenas division began duty as the garrison at San Martín Texmelucan and began receiving its pay and supplies from the War Department, and Tlaxcalan villagers won provisional approval of the land seizures they had carried out. Zapata shortly declared Arenas a traitor to the Ayala plan, but he could not shake the Tlaxcalan chief's position.[3] Through this deal and others the Constitutionalists consolidated their control in the country. And in early February the last American troops in Mexico returned to the United States. Having retaken Morelos, the Zapatistas had not triumphed; they had only survived.

During February Zapata and his chiefs corrected their sights. They did not concentrate their forces to drive into the Federal District or against Puebla City. Rather, they planted them in bunches at the key passes into Morelos, to hold a line around the state. And the defense looked so tough that González did not even try to breach it. In early February he went down as far at Tres Marías to inspect the few Constitutionalist outposts in the vicinity. Three weeks he spent in those cold and foggy heights, peering down through the clouds into the Cuernavaca valley, brooding. Although he announced that he would soon "activate the campaign," he acknowledged that he could not run trains on south. And when he returned to Mexico City in late February, he took with him even the out-

[2] Luis Sierra Horcasitas: *Patria. Obra Histórica-Revolucionaria. Primera Parte* (México, 1916), pp. 65–8. *Diario de los Debates del Congreso Constituyente,* II, 1080–4.

[3] Act of Surrender of General Domingo Arenas to the Government of Venustiano Carranza, December 1, 1916, AA. General Orders of December 15, 1916, AZ, 28: 2: 3.

posts he had left before.[4] Militarily, the Zapatistas had made Morelos into a quagmire. González could have stormed back into the state, but he would only have bogged down deeper. On the defensive, the Zapatistas were at least safe.

The work the chiefs and secretaries now resumed was the work they had been at before the invasion, the refoundation of the state as a commonwealth of villages. This they did in part to secure more tightly the popular base of their movement. In part also they were out to confirm to observers in Mexico and beyond, and to themselves as well, that only they were sincere in their respect for the pueblo, that in comparison the Carrancista agrarian reform was a fraud. In similar straits outlaw revolutionaries elsewhere made deals with the government, lapsed into banditry, became mercenaries, affiliated with the Felicistas, anyway forgot the reason they had originally given for their revolt. But in Morelos the commitment to keep local rural communities intact and in operation remained as strong as it had ever been. After six years of fighting, the revolutionary chiefs there evidently could not conceive of another purpose to their struggle. As for the secretaries, still certain they could not have been wrong, they stayed loyal too.

If the Zapatistas had not changed, local conditions of life had, however —for the worse. Most striking was that the hacienda had disappeared. Its resident laborers long fled, deported, conscripted, or recruited, its fields in corn or weeds, its buildings broken down and burned, its mills dismantled, the plantation was no longer a center of production, not even of habitation. It was visible in Morelos in 1917 only as a ruin, a place for lizards and archaeologists. Less obvious but equally crucial was the change in the villages. There families still congregated, but many were in places they hardly knew, where they had fled for refuge and stayed in fear. And around the villages too the fields lay empty of crops, last year's cornstalks still standing dry and yellow-gray under the winter sun. In the pastures there were no cattle. Nor were there pigs or chickens roaming as before through the bleak, cobbled village streets. Only now and then women or children passed out of doors, to dart from one stove-in building to another on their errands. And old local leaders were gone, killed or deported or hiding out. In this misery and social disarray bandits reappeared, as they always had during such times in Morelos. To refound the state, the Zapatistas could no longer depend on the pueblos to reorganize on their own.

[4] *El Demócrata*, February 8, 15, and 27, 1917. *La Prensa*, February 16, 1933.

Nor could they count on the crippled municipal councils to guide recovery. Without reduced but still active haciendas to work for, without local resources to draw on, without local men to trust and follow, the pueblos required direction they could not generate themselves. This the Zapatistas had to provide.

The agency of organization was an office whose creation Zapata had suggested in late November 1916. Sensing that the traditional authority no longer existed in many villages, and anticipating the disorders the Constitutionalists would leave in their wake as they pulled out, he complained to Soto y Gama that "all those who helped me to set fire to the house now don't want to help me put it out." He urged Soto y Gama and the other secretaries to tour the pueblos to explain "that if I rose up in arms, it was not to protect bandits nor to cover up abuses, but to give full guarantees to the pueblos, protecting them against any chief or armed force that violates their rights."[5] On November 28 Soto y Gama formally set up the office in Tlaltizapán as the Consultation Center for Revolutionary Propaganda and Unification. Initial members numbered fifteen, including Soto y Gama, Palafox, Montaño, the Magaña brothers, Enrique Bonilla, Prudencio Casals R., Ángel Barrios, and Leopoldo Reynoso Díaz.

The consultants' duties were generally as Zapata had outlined them, to give the pueblos their bearings again. They were to deliver lectures in the villages on the mutual obligations of revolutionary troops and pacíficos; to give public readings and explanations of headquarters manifestoes, decrees, and circulars; and to mediate feuds between chiefs, between chiefs and pueblos, and between pueblos. And from this experience they were to advise headquarters in the framing of laws and reforms. Most important, they were to organize subsidiary juntas in all villages under revolutionary control, as Associations for the Defense of Revolutionary Principles.[6]

The first association Soto y Gama, Gildardo Magaña, and Enrique Bonilla set up on December 12 at Tochimilco.[7] In the following weeks many others formed throughout southwestern Puebla and central and eastern Morelos. There they functioned as local branches of the Zapatista party, the first popular organizations both civilian and secular that had ever

[5] Antonio Díaz Soto y Gama: "Cargos infundados contra Zapata," *El Universal,* May 4, 1955.

[6] Basic Rules for the Consultation Center for Revolutionary Propaganda and Unification, November 28, 1916, AZ, 28: 2: 3.

[7] Foundation of the Tochimilco Association for the Defense of Revolutionary Ideals, December 12, 1916, ibid.

existed in many villages. Associates had no official authority, and they were under strict orders not to interfere with municipal government business; but in practice they dominated local society. On paper each association comprised four officers and six voting members, elected every four months by direct vote in the pueblo. Re-election for a year after leaving office was forbidden. Candidates had to be "revolutionary or at least to sympathize with the principles which the revolution defends." Other qualifications were local residence, majority of age, literacy, and no record of having exploited local people either from public office or through "influences . . . with past governments."[8] But since only a few villages still contained ten such men not already in the Liberating Army, and even fewer had the forty whom a year's round of elections would require, the associations remained simple cadres. In almost all of them, the dominant figures were a few brothers or cousins who had retained local respect without having gone off to war. Together they filled maybe half the seats, which they traded around at each term.

The associates' responsibilities were various. Among them was that of taking part in "the elections of all classes of authorities, formulating candidacies which guarantee the interests of the pueblo, exhorting citizens to fulfill their electoral duties, and organizing them for the elections." The upshot was that associates controlled the irregular municipal elections in Morelos in 1917 and 1918 and probably exerted secret but nonetheless real influence in the regular elections in Puebla.[9]

In routine matters the associates served as commissars. Their principal business was to make sure that the military respected the civil authorities. And they managed mediation in scores of disputes between municipal officials and chiefs of garrisons. The conflicts were usually over the control of local resources—crops, pasture, draft animals, vacant plots. Because of all the migrations and resettlements, it was harder now to say who had the best claim to use a certain field or team of oxen. The soundest claim in a pueblo was a reputation for having used the thing in question before. Yet the revolutionary troops, who had put no more than a rifle to use for the last year, also deserved support or the means to support themselves; and

[8] Rules for the Associations for the Defense of Revolutionary Principles, May 23, 1917, AZ, 29: 10.

[9] Many documents on the activities of various associations in 1917 are in AZ, 28: 3, 20, and 22. For the Puebla elections, in which an ex-Zapatista candidate for governor ran strongly around Atlixco and Izúcar de Matamoros, see Porfirio del Castillo: *Puebla y Tlaxcala en los días de la revolución* (México, 1953), p. 260.

their jefes were quick to protect their interests. So rival authorities competed, each for its own constituency and each professedly for the sake of the revolution. To specify the respective rights and obligations of the villagers and the guerrilleros, the Tochimilco associates sponsored negotiations between the town council and Ayaquica's headquarters. Under a special charge to fulfill revolutionary promises on "the agrarian question," they obtained a treaty on December 21 distinctly in the pueblo's interest. The agreement became a model for other villages throughout the Zapatista zone. And associates corresponded frequently to report on its workings. A warm camaraderie caught on among these commissars, who began to fancy the notion that they were the true guardians of the revolution.[1]

Their most consequential work was to make ordinary villagers see transcendent value in the struggle they were engaged in. As associations formed, the members assumed most of the duties of civic education which the Consultation Center had originally performed—reading and explaining headquarters announcements to local general juntas, ironing out neighborhood feuds, contracting revolutionary lecturers. They also took on the responsibility of improving public schools. The motive for the service, as they later stated in their constitution, was frankly the desire "to get propaganda into the bosom of families and to get the heads of these [families] to inculcate good principles in their children and other relatives, to make them take an interest in the Revolution and understand that on its triumph depends the happiness of honest workingmen and the progress of Mexicans in the material order as well as in the field of social and political liberties and rights and in the moral and intellectual order." In harshly limited circumstances the associates accomplished more than González even tried. Over the winter, through tiny private donations and special taxes that they "advised" town councils to collect, they established or reestablished primary schools in probably fifteen or twenty villages. By mid-April the associates in Tochimilco, Zacualpan, and Jantetelco even had night schools for adults in session. And in Tochimilzolco they were about to open a trade school for adults.[2] The academic lessons that students in the Zapatista schools learned were rudimentary but still valuable. Besides, for country folk the experience of hearing a teacher say that the resistance

[1] Tochimilco agreement, December 21, 1916, AZ, 30: 12. President of the Alpanocan association to the president of the Tochimilco association, February 26, 1917, AZ, 28: 3: 1.

[2] Circular No. 12, April 17, 1917, AZ, 28: 21.

still going on was for the fatherland and for poor people, and that the Zapatistas were national heroes—this was unforgettable.

Soon after reoccupying the state, Zapata began organizing a government
to reinforce the pueblos. The first law he decreed was an original plan
Palafox had prepared, to establish a special agrarian authority in each village "to represent and to defend . . . the pueblos in affairs of land, timber,
and water." Palafox recognized that "from time immemorial" some villages had named representatives in their agrarian disputes, but now he
wanted to make the post a regular office "with faculties and obligations well
defined," independent from the municipal council. Every village, he declared, had to elect at least two representatives by a direct vote, to serve for
a year (without salary) concurrent with the town councilors. Nominees
had to be over twenty-five, "notoriously honest," natives of the village in
which they were up for election, and resident there for at least the last
five years. Re-election could occur only after two terms. Removed from the
municipal council and incumbent now on these officials were the immense
responsibilities of managing their pueblo's communal property, the ejido
—of renting vacant fields, of assigning plots to resident families, of granting permits to divert streams or exploit a section of the local woods. Above
all, as Palafox listed it, was the responsibility of guarding "the titles and
maps of the ejido," the veritable proofs of the village's right to exist.[3] In
thus fortifying local control over the local economy, Zapata acted to guarantee forever the traditions he did not believe his people could do without.

These intentions shortly received elaboration and formal revolutionary
approval. On March 1 a major junta of chiefs and secretaries took place in
Tlaltizapán. There in a session of the Consultation Center they discussed
for three days the various problems of their revolution and the strategies
and policies they should try to carry out. According to the only account
still available, the debate was free and lively. On some subjects, particularly
strategic alliances, the junta postponed decision.[4] On others the consensus was clear. Among these, it appears, was how to rule Morelos. For the
time being the revolutionaries would set up no office of national authority

[3] Law relative to Representatives of the Pueblos in Agrarian Affairs, February
3, 1917, AZ, 28: 10: 1. About five weeks later the Constitutionalist secretary of
agriculture ruled similarly that in the agrarian reform he administered local agrarian
committees, not municipal authorities, had the rights to hold title to ejidos and to
manage them. See Fabila: op. cit., pp. 315–16.

[4] Fortino Ayaquica: "Cómo perdió la vida el general Domingo Arenas," serialized
in *El Hombre Libre*, September 8, 1937.

to replace the defunct Convention. Superior orders would come from the Tlaltizapán headquarters, which Palafox now divided into Departments of Agriculture, War, Education and Justice, Treasury, and Interior; but they would be general orders, not administrative but organic. Most attention would go to municipal affairs.

In the following weeks three basic laws issued from Tlaltizapán, all to strengthen the pueblos. The first was Zapata's March 5 decree on the mutual claims of the villages and the revolutionary armed forces. In refinement of the past December's Tochimilco treaty, he granted civil officials remarkable powers for a state under siege. Primary was the right of pueblos to elect their local governments and to maintain their own courts and police. In their jurisdiction municipal authorities could "arrest, disarm, and remit to headquarters" any chief, officer, or soldier who did not furnish credentials of his commission. To the army, villagers owed no more than the classic duties of pacíficos in an area of guerrillas—to serve as messengers and guides, to bring the troops food and supplies during combat, to help the wounded and bury the dead, and to provide garrisons their own farm plots. In contrast the military prerogative was sharply limited. Officers had rights only to contract with municipal governments for food, pasture, and quarters for garrisons and troops in transit, and to court-martial backsliders from the Ayala plan. And to the villagers, revolutionary commanders owed substantial respect. After seeing that pueblos in their zone had elected governments, they had to refrain completely from intervention in civilian disputes. In particular they had to respect the municipal distribution of land, water, and timber, and "subject themselves to the pueblos' rulings and customs." No personal services or labor of any kind could they exact from the villagers. Nor, since the land the villagers farmed was their own, could they charge them rent. The obligation phrased most portentously was surely the obligation village leaders cared most about: on pain of court-martial army personnel could not "take over fields from the pueblos or from those that formed part of the old haciendas, for each member of the army, whether he is a chief or not, will have a right only to the lot of land which comes to him in the distribution [the villagers grant]."[5]

Not two weeks later came the second major law, to constitute the state's political system. Here Zapata and his secretaries defined the autono-

[5] Law on the Rights and Obligations of the Pueblos and the Armed Forces, March 5, 1917, AZ, 28: 3: 2.

mous municipality as the nuclear unit of government. But recognizing that pueblos "isolated from each other as now happens" often fell into "rivalries, hates, and bad understandings," they instituted a new office to serve "as a bond of union between the municipios." This was the district presidency, similar to the elective prefectureships that had existed in Sonora and Zacatecas twenty-five years before: when they voted for their municipal officials, townspeople would also vote for a district president, who would ensure order and responsibility in the town councils in his domain.[6] At the top was a governor, whom the revolutionary chiefs would pick as before for the provisional period and who had to rule in accordance with a three-man governor's council, which the chiefs would also appoint. In the same law the Zapatistas at headquarters also provided for regular popular participation in government through other than official channels. Here the reform was an invention of their own. Through a hierarchy of juntas—villagers meeting in their pueblos on the fifteenth of each month, their elected delegates meeting in the proper municipal seat on the twentieth, and appointed municipal delegates meeting in the district seats on the first—they hoped to keep local people immediately and constantly involved in politics.[7]

Barely a month later Zapata issued the third basic decree, a thirty-two-page organic law for the state's town councils. Noting that "in these moments of general disorder . . . municipal authorities are bound to encounter serious difficulties in their labor, principally [since] . . . the majority of those who now sit on the councils lack practice in administrative affairs," the headquarters secretaries spelled out how the new officials should proceed. In detail they described the territorial composition of a municipality, the strictly impartial character of its government, the creation of municipal assistancies in outlying pueblos, the various powers of the municipal president, councilors, assistants, and employees, and the official duties in administration, finance, health, security, education, justice, entertainment, and so on.[8]

In practice the Zapatista government of Morelos in 1917 was a crude

[6] For the Sonoran and Zacatecan precedents, see Moisés Ochoa Campos: *La Reforma Municipal, Historia Municipal de México* (México, 1955), pp. 315-16, 322-3.

[7] General Administrative Law for the State of Morelos, March 17, 1917, AZ, 28: 1: 2.

[8] Organic Law for Town Councils for the State of Morelos, April 20, 1917, AZ, 28: 21: 2.

and disjointed operation. No record has appeared of the election of a district president, or of the meeting of a village, municipal, or district junta. Also the revolutionary chiefs evidently never named a provisional governor or a governor's council. To make the laws that he issued effective, Zapata had to send out one circular after another—ordering chiefs not to confiscate cattle that farmers brought back into the state, authorizing town councils to license peaceable citizens to carry arms "for their security and defense," drafting local rowdies into the revolutionary army, restraining exasperated officers from abusing refractory pacificos, badgering commanders and municipal authorities to set up schools and courts.[9] But it seems that at least the town councils worked, most of them, most of the time. Certainly there were local officials firm enough in conviction and control to raise complaints to the headquarters, and to get them resolved in the pueblos' favor. If no real polity formed in the state, nevertheless definite patterns of authority re-emerged. And although the Zapatista secretaries cultivated them, they were a native, natural growth. As in 1915, they were civilian and populist.

Meanwhile on the lines around the state the fighting went on. Raids and ambushes continued weekly. And just over the border at all four corners frequent and bloody battles occurred—in the southwest around Iguala, in the southeast around Chietla and Izúcar de Matamoros, in the northeast around Cholula and Ozumba, and in the northwest around La Cima.[1] Zapata tried especially hard to mount an attack on Puebla City, the capture of which would be a grave shock to the government. His spies informed him that the city was full of discontent and short on ammunition, that if he could muster forces to sustain fire for more than five hours, he could take the place.[2] For weeks he negotiated with the Tlaxcalan Domingo Arenas, to win him back to the cause and to engage his division in the

[9] Circular on the rights of the citizenry, February 14, 1917, AZ, 28: 3: 1. Circular to municipal presidents, March 2, 1917, AZ, 23: 3: 2. General Orders of March 5, 1917, AZ, 28: 1: 1. Circular to chiefs, March 17, 1917, ibid. Circular to chiefs, March 18, 1917, ibid., 2. Circular to municipal presidents, March 12, 1917, ibid., 1. Circular on schools, March 28, 1917, ibid., 2. Circular on courts, March 28, 1917, ibid. As usual in rural communities, the local complaint about school was that the children were needed to work. See the municipal president of Atenango del Río to headquarters, June 3, 1917, AZ, 29: 13.

[1] Meléndez: op. cit., I, 374. *La Prensa,* March 25, April 6, May 4 and 16, and June 1, 1933.

[2] Paz to Zapata, October 27, 1916, and January 15, 1917, AZ, 29: 13.

Puebla campaign.[3] A Felicista chief mediating between Zapata and Arenas even advised Zapata to extend the offensive. "With a general push in the states of the South," he wrote, "that is, with a simultaneous attack on several towns, we would soon send Carranza [like Díaz and Huerta] to the Ypiranga."[4] Zapata never accomplished the Puebla attack, much less the broader southern drive, but his forces patently maintained the military initiative in the strategic country west and north of Puebla City. To defend the town of Cholula the Constitutionalists had to make it into a fortress.[5]

The Zapatistas' survival was humiliating to González. On March 11 elections for Congress and the presidency had come off in every state in the Republic, except Morelos, the center of his zone of operations.[6] But still he could squeeze no new supplies or reinforcements from the War Department. On May 1 his rival, Obregón, resigned as secretary there, but what followed was worse. Because of the Department's marked political function, President Carranza took on its powers directly, which, considering his other preoccupations, only confused its direction and impaired its efficiency; and now González could not even cry sabotage from above.[7] The undersecretary of the Department proved unable to discipline clerks or combatants, now formally organized as the National Army. Field commanders, happier in the cantinas than in a fight, faked battles, padded their casualty lists, and for exercise went out to pillage. For months González toiled on like this. Winking at one officer's corruption, censuring another's, and then proclaiming barefaced a string of victories in the south that should have carried him through Morelos and on at least into Guatemala, the unlucky general saw his political fortunes trickle away week by week. Not all the kermesses he attended in the metropolitan suburbs could comfort him. Always the press described the Zapatistas on the run, only to announce in outrage the next day a new raid on a national train or outpost. Government spokesmen reported hundreds of Zapatistas surrendering, yet Carranza pressed Congress for permission to extend execu-

[3] Zapata to D. Arenas, March 7, 1917, AZ, 28: 1: 1. M. Caraveo to Zapata, March 23, 1917, ibid., 2. Zapata to D. Arenas, April 13, 1917, AZ, 28: 21: 1. Ayaquica in *El Hombre Libre,* September 6 and 8, October 4, 6, and 15, 1937.
[4] Caraveo to Zapata, March 26, 1917, AZ, 28: 1: 2.
[5] *La Prensa,* April 25, 1933.
[6] Ibid., March 11, 1933.
[7] Gabriel Ferrer Mendiolea: "Los secretarios del Presidente Carranza," *El Nacional,* June 29, 1954.

tive authority in the disputed zone.[8] At last the Zapatistas' vitality disheartened González. Unable to crack or to crush them, he received on July 7 a two-month leave of absence to go to the United States "on personal business."[9]

But though the Zapatistas recovered, no calm settled over Morelos. By then indeed it had become clear that the Zapatistas too were in a grievous bind. The very fact of survival had brought them into a new crisis, for although they had reorganized the state and were holding out well, they now had to decide why they struggled on. They could no longer easily assume that Carranza would soon fall and his regime disintegrate. After all, Carranza had managed national elections and the installation of a regular government in Mexico City and every state capital but Cuernavaca. He had aggravated discontent, but not critically. In April, after the United States declared war on Germany, he had looked in trouble for his neutralist foreign policy; but instead the war guaranteed his control, as Zapata learned from his agent in San Antonio.[1] Protest as they would against Carranza's assumption of the presidency on May 1, the Zapatistas could not sap the calculated loyalty of those northern generals who dreamed of succeeding to power without rebellion.[2] The secretaries at headquarters might forecast the regime's imminent collapse, but chiefs who had been at war for five or six years read the omens differently. Basic questions surfaced.

Should these veterans finally lay down their arms and recognize the government? They had the example of Domingo Arenas to consider. In accepting the Constitutionalist invitation to "unify," he had secured peace and autonomy for his territory, and through the villages there he was more revered than ever. For the Morelos chiefs, however much they resented Arenas's defection, his achievement was impressive. And the provision for communal property in the new Constitution seemed a plausible guarantee that if they retained power in the state, they could enforce agrarian reform there. Besides, once they had recognized the government and extracted money and supplies from it, they could always revolt again—as many other chiefs had, and as they were urging Arenas to now.

---

[8] *La Prensa,* June 22, 1933.

[9] Ibid., July 8, 1933.

[1] Zapata to Arenas, April 5, 1917, AZ, 28: 1: 1. Magaña to Zapata, April 25, 1917, AZ, 28: 21: 2. Zapata to Magaña, April 27, 1917, ibid. Magaña to Zapata, May 4, 1917, AZ, 29: 10. Paz to Zapata, May 23, 1917, AZ, 29: 13.

[2] Protest Before the Mexican People, May 1, 1917, AZ, 29: 10.

Or should they join Félix Díaz? Since Carranza had announced his plans for a new Constitution the year before, and especially since the new charter had taken effect, Don Félix had paraded as the champion of the Old Liberalism of the 1857 Constitution. His movement had become more popular and more formidable; and wealthy exiles in New York still financed him. If Carranza did fall, the Felicistas looked likeliest to dominate a new government. The Old Liberal cause Díaz now claimed to represent was the cause for which the fathers and grandfathers of many Morelos chiefs had fought. To them as to many chiefs in other states through the center and south, his appeal for recruits and allies was increasingly attractive.

Or should they go on independently? And if so, how should they justify the continued sacrifice to the villagers in whose name they fought? As independents, should they ignore other important dissidents around the country? Or should they establish relations with them? On what terms? Should the terms be uniform for all allies, or vary depending on local conditions? Who would do the negotiation?

As the need to answer these questions grew through 1917, so did the strain on the Zapatista chiefs and secretaries. At the Tlaltizapán headquarters intrigue flourished. Zapata and the other chiefs apparently preferred to let the questions ride, in hopes that they would disappear. But the secretaries, who sensed more keenly the political opportunities an astute decision might lead to, pressed and maneuvered to impose their opinions. Every gesture triggered suspicions. Fears of defection and treachery abated only if Zapata intervened personally to vouch for the suspect.

For all the strain was hard. For some, especially those already on the skids, it was intolerable. After his discharge the previous August, Lorenzo Vázquez had languished for several months at headquarters practically under house arrest. He still venerated Zapata, his old army buddy and his chief since 1911, but Palafox and Soto y Gama scared and repelled him; they had turned his jefe against him, he lamented to other chiefs.[3] In early 1917, just as the local revolutionaries recovered the state, he fled south—to the little town of Buenavista de Cuéllar, on the Guerrero line, where a colony of outcast and self-exiled Zapatistas had gathered. In the following weeks he commiserated with another also-ran, Otilio Montaño. Like Vázquez, the portly, pompadoured schoolteacher had always been loyal to Zapata but had nevertheless lost out at headquarters. Although Zapata liked him, he had never greatly respected him. Montaño talked too much, and

[3] Personal interview with Palacios.

rarely to the point. An anarchist, a positivist, a pastoralist, he often bored Zapata, or made him laugh. Besides, he could not write a simple sentence. His literary style couched philosophical musings best; it did not serve for plain correspondence. Worst, he had early proved politically unreliable. In 1912 he had advised Zapata that they should quit the struggle and flee: as disguise he could wear dark glasses and Zapata could shave his moustache. The Ayala chief did not take kindly to Montaño's panicky counsel. He replied that since he was "no fairy, bullfighter, or friar" he was not about to shave his moustache, much less desert his followers.[4] In 1913, at the time of Huerta's coup, Montaño had almost recognized the government, as the chief he was then advising, Jesús Morales, actually did. In 1915–16 he had associated closely with Pacheco and Vázquez. By early 1917 he had become, as he had earlier described Madero, "a 'Social Zero' and a 'Political Zero.' " To get him out of Tlaltizapán Soto y Gama appointed him the Guerrero agent for the Consultation Center.[5] Thus in disrepute Montaño and Vázquez began to discuss whether they should leave the movement.

In early May a revolt broke out in Buenavista de Cuéllar. It was a confused affair. The rebels demanded recognition of Carranza, although the nearest national garrison was too far away to help; and yet they fought under the slogan, "Respect for the Rights of Others is Peace," which was an old Liberal motto and therefore a Felicista reference. Only two facts were manifest. The rebels rejected the authority of the Tlaltizapán headquarters, and their chief, reluctantly or not, was Lorenzo Vázquez. Zapata moved quickly to put down the mutiny, ordering an attack on Buenavista on May 5. The suppression went easily, and on May 7 headquarters announced that Vázquez had been hanged for treason.[6]

But the sequel was even more painful. Prisoners from Buenavista charged that Montaño had been their brains, that he had proposed the slogan and advised the uprising. It was almost certain that at least twice in the last six weeks he had been through Buenavista, and although he had not been precisely at the scene of the revolt, informants produced letters which they alleged he had written and which linked him with Vázquez.[7] Most

---

[4] Antonio Díaz Soto y Gama: "El Caso de Montaño," *El Universal,* May 18, 1955.

[5] Soto y Gama to Montaño, January 5, 1917, AZ, 30: 13.

[6] Martín Demófilo Moreno: "Con fantásticas inexactitudes no se escribe la historia de un pueblo," *La Prensa,* July 16, 1930. Meléndez: op. cit., I, 375. Zapata to Victoriano Bárcenas, May 5, 1917, AZ, 29: 10. Revolutionary Information Service, May 7, 1917, ibid.

[7] Montaño to Zapata, March 18, 1917, and Zapata to Montaño, April 3, 1917, AZ, 28: 1: 2.

incriminating was that Montaño had not reported in Tlaltizapán during or after the revolt, but had headed toward the rebel town. Quite near there loyal Zapatistas had seized him. Montaño protested that he was innocent. But Palafox and Soto y Gama took up the case, urging an indictment.

Zapata delayed action, obviously not wanting to prosecute his old companion. Most other veteran chiefs could not believe Montaño's guilt either, and anyway they were inclined to forgive him.[8] But after several days Zapata did what he had to do: call a court-martial to try Montaño for complicity in treason. Presiding over the court was Palafox, and appointed to the other seats and offices were more of Montaño's enemies and rivals. Personally Zapata could not take the inevitable verdict. He informed the headquarters secretary of justice that he would pardon Montaño of any crime less than that charged. And then on May 15, the day the trial began, he left Tlaltizapán until it was over.[9] At one a.m. on May 18 the revolutionary tribunal found the little schoolteacher guilty. Later in the morning Montaño delivered his last oration, proclaiming that "the politicians who are now in the headquarters" had framed him in an "infamous intrigue," that never for a moment had he betrayed the Ayala plan, which he himself had written, and that Zapata had weakly let his enemies destroy him but that the people of Morelos would finally do him justice. At the end he asked for a priest. Refused, he flew into a rage of resignation, signed his sentence and a long formal protest, and said goodbye to his family.[1] At noon he was executed by a firing squad. Even the court felt obliged to justify the sentence and express regret.[2]

Other chiefs collapsed in other ways. Of thirty national soldiers captured in a battle in March, Valentín Reyes himself shot every one.[3] Around Cuautla Zapatista officers tore down the remains of the sugar mills at Casasano, Calderón, Hospital, and Cuahuixtla, against superior orders. Worse, they then smuggled the scrap metal into national zones in Puebla and the Federal District, where it sold at high, World-War-I prices. Among the crooked officers was Luciano Cabrera, the Ayalan who had defended Ane-

---

[8] Moisés Bejarano: "Breves Apuntes Sobre la Muerte del Gral. Otilio E. Montaño" (MS, n.d., 1960?), p. 5. I consulted these notes thanks to the generosity of Juan Salazar Pérez. Bejarano was part of the squad guarding Montaño.

[9] Zapata to Gregorio Zúñiga, May 15, 1917, AZ, 29: 10.

[1] Bejarano: op. cit., p. 8. "El testamento político de Otilio E. Montaño," Excélsior, January 21, 1919.

[2] Revolutionary Information Service, May 18, 1917, AZ, 29: 10.

[3] Serafín M. Robles to Zapata, March 13, 1917, AZ, 28: 1.

necuilco before the revolution and had joined Pablo Torres Burgos and Zapata in the first days of the Maderista revolt.[4] Eufemio Zapata tried to suppress this illegal traffic, but he too was on the verge of breaking. He had never been as strong a character as his brother, and the retreats after 1915 had left him completely at loo e ends. Famous already for drowning his miseries in alcohol, loudly an t violently, he began to berate his comrades. In May 1916 he had accused Mendoza of being "crazy, because I know that you run around hiding and in disguise . . ."[5] In January 1917 he wrote to another fellow revolutionary, whom he called "an illiterate in every sense," demanding an apology for some slight and warning that unless he got it, "you'll have to get wise to what my machete knows."[6] In March he even wrote insults to his brother, asking sarcastically if he should permit a local bully to steal as he pleased.[7] In mid-June he threw his last tantrum. He lost his temper with the father of one of his leading subordinates, Sidronio Camacho, and beat the old man. In revenge Camacho shot him down in the street on June 18, and he died that evening. Camacho then took his men northeast into national territory and accepted an amnesty from the government.[8]

Thus by the summer of 1917 the Morelos revolution was back in force, but also in the throes of a critical struggle simply to hold together. The Zapatistas' recovery and reorganization of the state did not change their hostile isolation from the powers in Mexico City. And precisely because they were sincere revolutionaries and not bandits or vandals, they could not derive from the dispute alone a motive to keep themselves going. Although twelve or fifteen important chiefs were still alive and still professed loyalty to the cause, although they still fought indomitably on the lines around their native state, and although they retained profound support in the villages, they were now at odds among themselves as they had never been before. Outlaw revolutionaries in a country where revolutionaries governed, they could no longer agree on the goals or tactics of their movement. Should there even be a movement? It was time for crucial decisions.

[4] Eufemio to Emiliano Zapata, May 29, 1917, ibid.
[5] Eufemio Zapata to Mendoza, May 12, 1916, AZ, 27: 5.
[6] Eufemio Zapata to an unnamed person, January 8, 1917, AZ, 30: 13.
[7] Eufemio to Emiliano Zapata, March 28, 1917, AZ, 28: 1.
[8] Figueroa Uriza: op. cit., II, 741. E. González to Zapata, June 19, 1917, AZ, 29: 13.

The Resistance Reforms

*". . . our unforgettable General Zapata fell
never to rise again."*

AFTER THE DEATHS OF MONTAÑO and his brother, Zapata lost faith in the advice he got in Tlaltizapán. "His normally taciturn character," a young headquarters guard later remembered, "had became dark, crabbed, irascible, somewhat neurasthenic, to the point that even the men of his escort feared him when he called them."[1] But reaching him through his grief were words he soon listened to. They came from Tochimilco, from Gildardo Magaña, the ranking secretary there. Magaña was a peacemaking man.

As a boy he had learned generosity, to resolve the tensions of the misfit life his family led. The place he was born in, Zamora, Michoacán, was a prosperous and modern town when he grew up there in the 1890's and 1900's. Lying in an "astonishingly fertile" valley, surrounded by "rich and productive haciendas" where tobacco, grains, sugar cane, fruits, and live-stock flourished, the town had swelled to a population of over twenty-six thousand in 1910. Special sources of pride were three grand hotels, an elec-tric light system, and the streetcars running out to the train station and suburban villages. But Zamora was also, as a younger Magaña brother later recalled, "the most fanatic city in the most fanatic state in Mexico." The

---

[1] Bejarano: op. cit., p. 4.

people there were not mere Catholics but clericalists, who cherished their cathedral and churches not as sanctuaries but as glorious monuments to their own superior unction. For them religion was less a way of worship than a way of putting on the dog. During the War Against the Intervention, Zamorans had cheered when the French occupied their town to save them from the Liberals, who would have reduced them to plain republican equality. The incubator of these pretensions was the diocesan seminary, the only secondary school in the town. There since the 1830's Zamoran fathers had sent their sons, not so much to make them priests as to steep them in Latin, philosophy, and "the theological sciences," to instill the pride of orthodoxy in them.[2] There many Magañas had studied, and there Gildardo and his brothers went like proper Catholic boys. But their father, Conrado, was a man of spirit rare in Zamora, and what he taught his sons at home and through example set going in them challenges to all they took in at school.

Conrado Magaña had himself attended the Zamora seminary, to become, as his parents hoped, a priest. But repudiating his forebears, scorning his clean-shaven, black-skirted teachers, he had gone into business when he graduated. By the 1890's he ranked among the leading merchants in town, the proprietor of strings of eight hundred mules that his agents worked in trade from Tabasco to Colima. Most shocking to his fellow Zamorans, he was a proudly self-proclaimed Liberal. He warmed to the memory not of Maximilian and the French but of the old anticlerical nationalists like Benito Juárez and Michoacán's own Melchor Ocampo. His first son he named Melchor. Like a good Liberal, he delighted in supporting the persecuted opposition press in Mexico City and the provinces, buying up twenty-five or thirty subscriptions to radical newspapers and distributing them among his associates. On the centennial of Juárez's birthday in 1906, a gloomy day for most Zamorans, Conrado Magaña collected all the local cowboys, rancheros, and mule drivers he knew and staged a parade into the town that climaxed in a protest against the Porfirista regime. Convinced of the power of education, he sent his sons to the seminary not because of but despite its religiosity. For the same reason, to give them the advantage

[2] T. Philip Terry: *Terry's Mexico. Handbook for Travellers* (México, 1909), p. 149. José Bravo Ugarte: *Historia sucinta de Michoacán,* 3 vols. (México, 1964), III, 170–4, 179–81. Eduardo Ruiz: *Historia de la guerra de intervención en Michoacán* (2nd edn., México, 1940), pp. 48–50. José Guadalupe Romero: *Noticias para formar la historia y la estadística del Obispado de Michoacán* (México, 1860), pp. 107–9. Jesús Romero Flores: *La revolución como nosotros la vimos* (México, 1963), pp. 50–1.

of the little enlightenment available in Zamora, he sent other children from families who could not afford the school by themselves.[3]

From these stresses Gildardo Magaña somehow emerged strong and whole. What he had learned was to mediate: not to compromise, to surrender principle and to trade concessions, but to detect reason in all claims in conflict, to recognize the particular legitimacy of each, to sense where the grounds of concord were, and to bring contestants into harmony there. Instinctively he thrived on arguments, which he entered not to win but to conciliate. To his brothers, though he was the third youngest of ten children, he always seemed the oldest—"by nature of the type," an American acquaintance later observed, "we call conservative and prudent." His father also noticed his talents, which he took as managerial, and sent him to Philadelphia to study business.[4]

Gildardo became a Liberal like his father. In 1908 the Magañas moved to Mexico City, and there he and his brothers, abetted by their father, plunged into the opposition then mounting against Díaz. Joining metropolitan clubs tending toward anarcho-syndicalism, they wound up in the abortive Tacubaya Conspiracy of March 1911. In flight from the law, they went south to join the closest uprising, that of Zapata in Morelos. Since then they had remained loyal to the revolution started in Ayala, Gildardo in the lead.

But in revolution Gildardo still yearned for union. From the summer of 1911 on he had dedicated himself to settling differences he considered only misunderstandings. With the Maderos first, then with the Constitutionalist chiefs in the north in 1913–14, and then with Villa and Ángeles and the Conventionists in 1914–15, he had worked to play down mistrust and reform coalitions. Each time he had failed, but the impulse to reconcile never ceased. In 1916 he had not stayed in Tlaltizapán, where the backbiting was so fierce, but had passed on to Tochimilco, where he could operate in cleaner air. Around there he helped to keep local chiefs in line and to protect the villages from excessive revolutionary demands. Tall, husky, baby-faced, too young and mannerly to seem to rival older chiefs, too big for those his own age to scare, he became a regular arbiter in the area. It was he who took charge of the efforts to win Domingo Arenas back to the

[3] Personal interviews with Octavio Magaña Cerda.

[4] Carlos Reyes Avilés: "Gildardo Magaña. Breves Datos Biográficos," in Meléndez: op. cit., II, 470. William Gates: "The Four Governments of Mexico. Zapata—Protector of Morelos," *World's Work*, April 1919, p. 657.

Zapatista fold.[5] And the advice he gave his chief Zapata now, in the fullness of the wisdom of his barely twenty-six years, was utterly typical of him— to seek allies within the government.

The general idea of outside contacts hardly recommended itself to Zapata. On that pretext had occurred every major defection from the Morelos revolution. Besides, for a year now he had had agents in the United States and Cuba, and they had accomplished nothing. In San Antonio, where Zapata had sent him to get money for arms and ammunition, Juan Espinosa Barreda had contracted only promises of aid and influence from a crackpot local lawyer, Henry Ben Cline. And Cline, also a Protestant preacher and a fervent Prohibitionist who wanted Zapata to win so he could make Mexico dry, never delivered on the promises.[6] Following Espinosa Barreda to San Antonio was Octavio Paz, to spy on other Mexican exiles and report on American politics. Paz had returned detailed intelligence, but he had located no serious new champions or sympathizers.[7] And in Cuba Genaro Amezcua was a thorough disappointment so far. In April 1916 Zapata had commissioned him to go to the United States to propagandize and buy arms and ammunition. A month later he turned up in Havana instead, where he remained in mid-1917 practically unheard from.[8] Other agents whom Zapata had recruited for operations in Mexico, like Carlos M. Peralta, who as "Atl" managed Zapatista espionage in Mexico City, or Alfredo Miranda, who as "Delta" had spied in Puebla City, ran out of information whenever they ran out of funds; Miranda had even accepted amnesty from the government.[9] In Tlaltizapán the advice to make new contacts—and among the Constitutionalists—sounded almost subversive.

But coming as it did from Magaña, Zapata soon approved the suggestion. He trusted Magaña, who though neither a villager nor a native of Morelos had never betrayed local interests in earlier negotiations. Besides, Zapata had already recognized that in the end he would have to deal with men like Obregón, and that he could do so with a clear conscience: in July he had authorized the publication of "A Toast to Alvaro Obregón," in honor of the Sonoran chief's recent criticisms of the Carranza administration. Zapata's decision headed the Morelos revolution into a distinctly new

[5] Ayaquica in *El Hombre Libre,* October 15, 1937.

[6] Cháverri Matamoros in *La Prensa,* September 12, 13, and 16, 1935.

[7] Zapata to Paz, April 15, 1916, Archivo de Octavio Paz (henceforth AP). Paz to Diódoro Arredondo, December 21, 1916, AP. Paz to Palafox, January 15, 1917, AP.

[8] Service record of Genaro Amezcua, April 1910 to May 1920, AZ, 12: 5.

[9] Cháverri Matamoros in *La Prensa,* September 16, 1935.

course. While he stayed in Tlaltizapán trying to hold the local movement together, his proxy Magaña would try from Tochimilco to find friends in other camps.[1]

One likely source of aid went untapped. This was the Morelos colony in Mexico City, which no longer comprised the planters but mainly old Leyvistas who had joined Carranza since 1914. Patricio Leyva, Antonio Sedano, Benito Tajonar, Domingo Diez, Miguel Salinas's son León, Manuel Mazari—these exiles wrangled among themselves and disapproved deeply of Zapata, but they still loved their native state and wanted to spare it misery; and they had connections in the government. If Zapata had directed Magaña to ask them for help, they might well have given it.[2] But precisely because they were natives, and therefore his rivals, they were the last persons Zapata would invite to take part in local affairs. Besides, he did not want favors from Carranza, but to force Carranza from the presidency.

For the time being Magaña also shied away from the Felicistas, though financially and strategically they remained the government's most formidable opponents. The revolutionary opposition that Zapata expected Magaña to organize had little in common with the reactionary opposition Félix Díaz and his cronies in New York had launched, and Magaña was careful to avoid any sign of affiliation with them, much less subordination. He continued joint Zapatista-Felicista military operations in western and southern Puebla, but in propaganda he always announced them as purely Zapatista.

In mid-August the overtures began—to Villa and Emilio Vázquez. To the latter, whom Paz had watched in San Antonio and found more reliable than his brother, "especially on the agrarian question," Zapata sent his "greetings." Tentatively resuming the vague collaboration they had carried on in 1912, he only urged Vázquez to continue his work for "our common ideals" and to aid Paz. With Villa Zapata was more specific. Although Villa no longer threatened the government militarily, he remained a potential political danger at large in Chihuahua; and Zapata regarded his participation in the projected coalition as indispensable. To demonstrate revolutionary unity he asked Villa to sign a new Manifesto to the Nation for publication on September 1. He also asked Villa if he would name Emilio Vázquez his representative in Washington.[3]

---

[1] [Genaro Amezcua:] *Méjico Revolucionario a los pueblos de Europa y América, 1910–1918* (Havana, n.d., 1918?), pp. 88–9. Reyes Avilés: *Cartones,* pp. 42, 53.

[2] Mazari: "Bosquejo," p. 123. Sedano: op. cit., pp. 24–5.

[3] Zapata to E. Vázquez and to Villa, August 18, 1917, AZ, 29: 13.

Meanwhile Magaña prepared to communicate with the national commander in Puebla. This was General Cesáreo Castro, a chief Carranza trusted implicitly, a native of Carranza's own hometown in Coahuila, but also a chief of agrarian leanings, "a revolutionary of principles" whom Magaña had met in Monterrey in 1914. The go-between Magaña located was Colonel Eduardo Reyes, a native Pueblan, stationed in Atlixco. Off and on since mid-1911 Reyes had been in contact with his revolutionary neighbors in Morelos, and for what Magaña convinced him was a patriotic cause he now took the grave risk of treating with them again. On August 20 he and Magaña began corresponding on how to initiate dealings with General Castro.[4]

The new venture almost ended in disaster before it got going. For the last six weeks Magaña had been waiting for Domingo Arenas to declare himself a Zapatista again, as he had promised in a secret interview in early June. Persistent complaints from Magaña and Ayaquica about the delay provoked various excuses from Arenas, and finally a note that he wanted another conference with them on the prospects for revolt. He invited them to meet him at noon on August 30 at San Pedro Coaco, a tiny hamlet just north of Tochimilco on the slopes of the Volcano Popocatépetl. Near there they met at the time agreed, with their aides and escorts. Ayaquica was already very suspicious of Arenas, having heard that Arenas planned to take him and Magaña dead or alive to Puebla City. And now he and Magaña heard it outright—a proposal from Arenas that they accept amnesties like his. The discussion broke into furious yelling. The escorts maneuvered around for a good first shot. And then the shooting started. Arenas fired point-blank at Magaña, and missed. Magaña punched Arenas, collapsed into a wrestling match with the spindly Tlaxcalan, who had only one arm, and finally stabbed him in the belly with a hunting knife. Still Arenas got loose. He was running to escape after his aides when the Zapatista escorts shot and killed him. Magaña left immediately for Tlaltizapán to report the episode to Zapata.[5]

But the Manifesto to the Nation duly appeared on September 1. It had three main propositions: Carranza was a bogus revolutionary; the Republic's true revolutionaries still fought for "principles, [notable comma] whose most concrete expression is the Plan de Ayala"; and the new regime would rest on the ruins of latifundistas like Luis Terrazas, Íñigo Noriega,

[4] Statement of services of Eduardo Reyes, April 17, 1919, AZ, 30: 36.
[5] Ayaquica in *El Hombre Libre,* November 3, 5, 8, 12, and 15, 1937.

Enrique Creel, and Ignacio de la Torre y Mier.[6] The last proposition mattered most. For not by accident the latifundistas mentioned, prominent
figures in the old regime, were now prominent in exile in New York for
the sums they contributed to the Felicista movement.[7] The manifesto served
as a kind of plebiscite among revolutionaries. Those who signed it set themselves not only against Carranza's false revolutionary government but also
against Félix Díaz's false opposition.

Through the fall these efforts continued, with no striking success but
with no egregious failure either. Zapata himself devoted unusual attention
to the enterprise. Although Palafox embarked on a crusade against Carrancista spies infiltrating into Morelos, which might eventually have implicated Magaña, Zapata kept him in check and encouraged Magaña to try
new contacts. In particular he recommended appeals to Vicente Segura, the
Carrancista commander who had given land to villages around Axochiapan
the year before, and to Lucio Blanco, in exile in Laredo, Texas.[8] He also
sent young Octavio Magaña on a secret mission to San Antonio to check on
Paz's work. And at last he had southern propaganda sent to Amezcua in
Havana, who had it published in the press there.[9]

Slowly in response the War Department organized a new offensive in
the south. It was difficult for Carranza and his advisers to tell whether the
Zapatista attempts to negotiate in Puebla signified a more sophisticated
strategy or an inclination to surrender.[1] Anyway the reaction was to force
the issue in battle. As in 1916, national battalions were to surround Morelos
and then pinch together, catching the Zapatistas in the middle, leaving

[6] Manifesto to the Nation, September 1, 1917, AZ, 29: 13.

[7] Liceaga: op. cit., pp. 406, 426. The geography of Mexican exile politics was
interesting. The most conservative elements retired to Paris and Biarritz and contributed little money or prestige to a cause they obviously considered lost. It was as
if they too had been liberated, from the responsibility of leading an "Indian" country
they were ashamed of. The merely rich—the científico entrepreneurs—operated
mainly in New York, and were the most effective. Destitute lawyers, politicos, journalists, and hatchetmen hung out mostly around the Caribbean and in the Mexican
communities through the American Southwest. There is a mine of information on
this subject for 1918 and 1919 in AGRE, L-E-837: 12.

[8] Circular to municipal authorities, September 10, 1917, AZ, 28: 10: 1. Decree
against traitors, September 20, 1917, ibid., 2. Palafox to Mendoza, October 16, 1917,
AZ, 29: 1. Zapata to Magaña, November 3, 1917, ibid. Excélsior, September 13, 1917.

[9] Amezcua: op. cit., pp. 100–2, 106–15, 119–28, 138–47, 151–9.

[1] Excélsior, August 11 and 14, 1917.

them no escape, and then crushing them "once and for all."[2] Command of the operations first went to General Castro, but finishing Zapatismo was a juicy bit of patronage, and González soon took over again. After the rains ended, fighting for his political life, he drove his generals into action. Even so, few budged. The advance into Morelos was only into the eastern zone, and there largely the feat of Sidronio Camacho, the ex-Zapatista who had joined the nationals after killing Eufemio Zapata, and Cirilo Arenas, Domingo's avenging brother. The Zapatista chiefs around Cuautla lacked the ammunition to make resistance effective, and firing only to harass the invaders, they pulled out. On November 19, after heavy artillery bombardments, González's regular generals marched into Cuautla. Within two weeks they had also taken Jonacatepec and Zacualpan.[3]

In Mexico City the Carrancistas waxed jubilant. At last, they imagined, González had really mounted the definitive campaign in Morelos and would soon have the state in order. The prospect of the fortunes they still dreamed they could get out of the old haciendas especially excited them. In the new daily *Excélsior* appeared the lively "hope that in a very short time, probably by the next harvest, important sugar productions will be obtained from the different mills . . ." González too believed he was on the verge of a grand success. His plans, he announced, were to rebuild "the plantations of cane." Although he omitted reference to land reform, he sparked no objection from the Department of Agriculture, where for two months the director of the agrarian bureau had been Patricio Leyva.[4]

But no momentum carried the nationals on. As the campaign bogged down, the metropolitan press lamely explained week after week that the definitive phase was not the previous but the next operation. Camacho retained control around Cuautla, but moved no farther toward Yautepec or Tlaltizapán. Arenas headed back to more familiar territory. From Guerrero General Silvestre Mariscal advanced only up to the Morelos line, unable to take Puente de Ixtla and penetrate the state. Neither Castro in Puebla nor Salvador González in Mexico State began a coordinated push.[5]

Coolly Magaña went on with his diplomacy. His most promising negotiations were still with Eduardo Reyes, to arrange contacts with Castro. But

[2] Ibid., October 4, 1917.

[3] Ibid., September 2 and November 24, 1917.

[4] Ibid., December 3, 1917. *Boletín Oficial de la Secretaría de Fomento, Colonización e Industria,* II, 7 (October 1917), i.

[5] *La Prensa,* October 19, 26, and 28, November 23, and December 2 and 16, 1933.

he did not neglect dealings with other likely confederates. In early December he drew Alfredo Robles Domínguez, by then a federal deputy and a major figure in national politics, into an exchange of letters.[6]

In mid-month the rationale of his efforts suddenly came clear. A revolt broke out in Coahuila, because the defeated candidate for governor there would not accept his loss. Joining him in rebellion were other prominent but now disgusted local leaders, among them once trusted national commanders. Implicated also were exiles like Lucio Blanco, a native Coahuilan himself, who took the opportunity to sneak back into Mexico. In sympathy or in connivance national troops also mutinied in Veracruz.[7] News of the uprisings threw the Zapatista headquarters in Tlaltizapán and Tochimilco into a flurry of correspondence. Magaña wrote to rebels in San Luis Potosí, urging them to unite with other "healthy elements . . . in common accord" and assuring them that such was the intention of "the great majority of the revolutionaries of the country, with whom we are already in communication." Zapata himself wrote to encourage a Hidalgo malcontent in league with the Coahuila rebels. Following events closely, he exhorted Magaña to try especially hard for contacts with the fugitive Lucio Blanco and the national commander in Tlaxcala, Pedro Morales.[8] Two impressive manifestoes promptly issued from Zapatista headquarters, To the Revolutionaries and To the People. In both the call was for union. The Coahuila revolt proved, went the argument of the first, that Carranza alone kept the revolution from its final establishment as a popular government. The Ayala plan was now only the banner of "the country people," not the complete code of solutions to the Republic's woes. For provisional president Zapata wisely proposed no one, and antagonized no one. The president would receive his mandate, he promised, from a new junta of the nation's revolutionary chiefs. In the second document the headquarters secretaries played nicely on politicians' impatience with official abuses in the recent congressional elections. They styled Carranza an old Porfirista who would never carry out the reforms he had promised and again emphasized his personal responsibility for the recurring disorder. "Everyone," read the manifesto, "military or civilian, social reformers and simple liberal democrats, socialist men of action and men platonically in love with the revolutionary ideal"—

[6] A. Robles Domínguez to Magaña, December 11, 1917, AZ, 29: 1.

[7] La Prensa, December 14, 1933. María y Campos: op. cit., p. 203. Revolutionary Information Service, Bulletin 5, January 3, 1918, AZ, 29: 8.

[8] Magaña to S. and M. Cedillo, December 25, 1917, AZ, 29: 1. Zapata to Azuara, December 26, 1917, and to Magaña, n.d. (late December 1917?), ibid.

all longed for a revolutionary coalition to bring peace. "The only obstacle" was Carranza.[9]

The hopes inspiring this skillful propaganda were too high. In Coahuila the rebel generals could not make their troops follow them into revolt. In Veracruz the mutiny failed. Loyal officials nipped in the bud a dangerous conspiracy in Toluca to revolt in support of the Coahuilans. By early January 1918 the threat had collapsed. Scattered protests and outbursts of violent resistance to Carranza's rule continued among disgruntled politicians and commanders around the country; in Guerrero General Mariscal almost revolted. But no movement became serious.[1]

Still Magaña and Zapata proceeded in their effort. Thanks to excellent espionage, Magaña found out the details of the bitter competition now raging within the government. The critical disaffection of the Sonoran Generals Obregón and Hill, their retrenchment in the Liberal Constitutionalist Party, and their accord with leading civilians like Robles Domínguez to form an oppositionist majority in Congress, Pablo González's resignation from the Liberal Constitutionalists, his drift into partnership with other important rivals of Obregón, and their "unconditional" commitment to Carranza—this was the wrangling Magaña knew best how to hear the theme and fugues in. And he explained it clearly to Zapata, who understood and asked for more. So while Magaña and Zapata maintained connections with the rebel Coahuilans, to secure their help for future subversion, they hoped eventually to gain stronger allies.[2]

At the same time Magaña was busy at yet another maneuver, the presentation to Carranza himself of Zapatista terms for a truce. By February, working through Castro and the undersecretary of war, he had his proposals before the President. As a "preliminary base for any action toward peace," the Zapatistas wanted a cease-fire along the current front and a promise of civil guarantees to the villages and towns in the surrounding national zone. In return they would pledge not to attack national forces and to protect tradesmen and pacíficos crossing their lines. On this understanding, they would negotiate in good faith to restore regular rule in "the South." Implied

[9] To the Revolutionaries of the Republic, and To the People, December 27, 1917, ibid.

[1] *La Prensa,* January 6, 1934. Zapata to Magaña, January 18, 1918, AZ, 29: 8. *Excélsior,* January 20–30, 1918. Braderman: op. cit., pp. 167–9.

[2] Magaña to Francisco Coss, January 14, 1918, and to Zapata, January 19, 20, and 23, 1918; Zapata to Magaña, January 26, 1918, and to Luis Gutiérrez, Jesús Dávila Sánchez, and Coss, January 28, 1918, AZ, 29: 8.

throughout the memorandum to Carranza was that the Zapatista army would remain intact and in control of Morelos. In short, if Carranza would recognize the legitimacy of the state's native revolutionaries, they would recognize his government.[3] The deal Magaña had proposed was practically what Carranza had earlier agreed to with Domingo Arenas. For the President, however, Arenas had been only a minor chief of local standing, easy to accommodate, whereas Zapata notoriously represented hopes and attitudes about Mexico's development that agitated the country and were, Carranza believed, perverse. For him to recognize Zapata was to grant the chance of reforms that could "compromise the people." "I never was a revolutionary, nor am I, nor will I ever be," Carranza remarked a few weeks later. "I am a fervent Constitutionalist, and I pride myself upon having reestablished the constitutional order. Everything has been done."[4] He did not refuse Magaña's proposals; evidently he did not even deign to answer them.

Through February the Zapatista search for allies took on a new and grim urgency. Troubling Zapata and Magaña now were reports from a curious visitor in their territory, an American tycoon turned theosophist-archaeologist. He was William E. Gates, in Mexico formally to do research but really to hunt material about current Mexican politics. Gates knew Mexico well, in a weird way. After graduating from Johns Hopkins (at the bottom of his class, '86) and ignominiously secluding himself in business in Cleveland, he had discovered Madame Blavatsky's *Secret Doctrine* —which let him in on the mysteries of "ancient America." Privately, while he amassed a fortune and an esoteric library, he delved into Mayan hieroglyphs and history. Toward 1910, in his late forties and still unmarried, he had left Cleveland and moved to a bustling theosophical community outside San Diego, to pursue his studies full-time. There finally he bloomed as a true Hopkins man, becoming professor of American archaeology and linguistics at the theosophists' School of Antiquity, publishing an article on Mayans in the bulletin of Harvard's Peabody Museum, producing a paper on concepts of language for an anthropological congress in Geneva, helping found the San Diego Museum, praying for peace, and voting for Wilson, a fellow Hopkinsian, in 1916. And in 1917 Gates too swam into international affairs. To a new friend up in Santa Monica, like himself an aging pilgrim in southern California and an old Latin hand besides, H. L.

[3] Memorandum for the undersecretary of war and navy, February (n.d.) 1918, AZ, 30: 36.
[4] *Evolución,* March 30, 1918, cited in Braderman: op. cit., p. 166.

Hall, formerly of the Liberating Army Cooperative Colony in Morelos, Gates confessed his itch to decipher the mysteries of modern Mexico. This, he assumed, would not be snooping but serving his country and its neighbor, "not," as he later insisted, "because of interests, for I have none, but because I care for my Indians [and feel it is] my bounden duty" to put the facts about them "at the disposal of the administration." In June 1917 he wrote to Secretary of War Newton D. Baker (Hopkins, '92), whom he had known a decade before as a Progressive city solicitor in Cleveland, and informed him about his trip. A month later, "predisposed to Carranza," he arrived in Yucatán.[5] Seeing how the Carrancista governor ran the state, he saw red. The governor was practically a "Bolshevist," the theosophist concluded, the boss of a "Mexican I.W.W." Gates began to hate Carranza, and to collect evidence against him. In Mexico City, where he became an honorary professor at the National Museum and for the first time in thirty-two years wrote a note on his career to his class secretary, he talked with the British minister, who recommended that he interview Zapata.[6] Thus, proud and presumptuous, Gates came to see Magaña in Tochimilco in early February 1918. There he spoke with authority, in Spanish. And Magaña took him at his inflated word—for a strong Wilsonian, a close friend of the U.S. secretary of war, and a university professor. Mainly Magaña appreciated his offer to speak on the Zapatistas' behalf in Washington. He sent him on to Tlaltizapán.[7] And there Gates delivered to Zapata the painful news that when the Great War ended, as it soon would, and Carranza fell, as he surely then would, the United States would not tolerate more conflicts in Mexico.

Although self-appointed and sincere, Gates was no mean diplomat. In a protocol he composed to state U.S. policy in Mexico, he granted Zapata and other revolutionaries an option: to work out a union by themselves before the war ended. But if they could not manage the union, he declared,

[5] On Gates, see *The Johns Hopkins University Register*, 1885-6 through 1909-10; Emmett A. Greenwalt: *The Point Loma Community in California, 1897-1942. A Theosophical Experiment* (Berkeley, 1955), pp. 119-20; J. McKeen Cattell: *Leaders in Education. A Biographical Directory* (New York, 1932), p. 344; and William Gates: "The Four Governments of Mexico. Creole, Mestizo, or Indian?" *World's Work*, February 1919, p. 385. See also his correspondence with Baker in United States Senate: *Investigation of Mexican Affairs. Report and Hearings before a subcommittee of the Committee on Foreign Relations*, 66 Cong., 1 sess., 2 vols. (Washington, 1920), I, 310-28, and his correspondence with Hall in the New York *Evening Post*, August 5, 1919.
[6] *The Johns Hopkins Alumni Magazine*, VI, 3 (March 1918), 292.
[7] Magaña to Zapata, February 2, 1918, AZ, 29: 2.

then "in the name of humanity Mexico must not be permitted to destroy herself." He grandly promised to help Wilson "forestall the approach" of a military operation. But he cautioned Zapata: "See that Mexico does not make intervention necessary for her own salvation."

Zapata believed Gates's report. And unlike the actual interventions of 1914 and 1916, this mere warning scared him. Earlier, right or wrong, he had considered the gringos' maneuvers so irrelevant (1914) or so directly in support of Carranza (1916) that they required no change in southern strategy. But now, so cutting was the threat the American professor brought that he would not let him spell it out. When Gates tried to finish reading his protocol, repeating that "Mexico must not go on in self-destruction," Zapata shut him up. "I don't even want to hear it," he said.[8] But he had caught the point of the lethal generosity the American expressed: he would have to redouble efforts at unification. Unless he and the other rebels and dissidents in the country organized soon, two gruesome dangers awaited them. Either they would lose their followings to Carranza, who would use the imminent American menace to unite all factions behind him, or, if he fell, they would in their confusion and disarray forfeit the nation's sovereignty to the United States, at least temporarily. To Zapata both alternatives were abhorrent, both in effect treason. Gates passed on south into Oaxaca to interview rebels there; Zapata remained in Morelos, sensitive now to yet another responsibility, "national decorum."

On February 8 a circular issued from Tlaltizapán to Liberating Army chiefs and officers. After the ritual preface that victory was near, it announced that since "the unification of all revolutionary elements is the basis of peace and the necessary condition for the immediate and complete triumph of our ideals," any nationals who defected "to help us from now on like good compañeros" were entitled to full guarantees from the Zapatista forces. Two days later, for the first time in two years, Zapata named a special envoy to deal with outlaws in other states. The envoy was to go to Guanajuato and Zacatecas to unify "the criterion and action" of revolutionaries there. On February 14 he started a regular correspondence with Amezcua in Havana. At the end of the month he gave Magaña "full authority to treat with all chiefs and officers who serve or served in 'Constitutionalist' ranks and who have asked or are asking to unite in the Revolution."[9]

---

[8] Gates in *World's Work*, April 1919, pp. 661–2.

[9] Circular to Chiefs and Officers, February 8, 1918, AZ, 29: 2. Zapata to Albino Guerrero, February 10, and to Magaña, February 25, 1918, ibid. Zapata to Amezcua, February 14, 1918, AZ, 12: 5.

New elaborations shortly appeared in the Zapatista appeal for union. An important manifesto in mid-March, To the Revolutionaries of the Republic, did not even mention the Ayala plan. The cry was simply to get together, no need seeming "more imperious" than union. In "a new invitation, this time formal and definitive," Zapata asked revolutionaries in general "to put aside small differences, to meet, to discuss matters, and to agree." On the same day headquarters issued another manifesto for distribution in factory and mining centers. In this invitation to "brothers of the cities" to join "your brothers of the fields" in the struggle against Carranza, there was a final, passing reference to "the triumph of our principles, of those subscribed to in the Plan de Ayala"—but no demand that workers accept the same principles. As if signing either manifesto was too public an act to ask of leaders who might otherwise sympathize, headquarters also sent out a form letter in which Zapata invited Señor Blank to collaborate privately for the President's overthrow. Triumphant together, they would then institute land reform, emancipate the proletariat, etc. Again no reference to the Ayala plan appeared. On March 24 Zapata signed a decree that the Liberating Army would admit defecting nationals at the ranks they presently held, whether they had joined Carranza recently or served him from the beginning.[1]

The tendency of the new concern for instant allies was to appeal to the Felicistas too, who still carried on the richest and most broadly based rebellion. Actively if variously associated with Don Félix now were chiefs like Manuel Peláez, who controlled the Tampico oil field and extorted fortunes from American and British companies; Joaquín Jiménez Castro and the Cedillo brothers in San Luis Potosí; Juan Andrew Almazán in Nuevo León and Tamaulipas; José Inés Chávez García in Michoacán; Marcelo Caraveo, Pedro Gabay, Roberto Cejudo, Constantino Galán, and Higinio Aguilar in Veracruz and Puebla; José Inés Dávila and Guillermo Meixueiro in Oaxaca; Alberto Pineda in Chiapas.[2] But just because of its strength, Felicismo was hard to deal with. In treating with Felicistas, Zapatistas might seem to win them for the revolutionary opposition, but they might also seem to slide themselves into the reactionary opposition. Magaña, who had to cooperate militarily with Felicistas in

[1] To the Revolutionaries of the Republic, and To the Workers of the Republic, March 15, 1918, AZ, 29: 4. Zapata to ———, March 15, 1918, ibid. Decree to the Inhabitants of the Republic, March 24, 1918, ibid.

[2] Liceaga: op. cit., pp. 420–1, 430–8, 456–7. E. David Cronon, ed.: *The Cabinet Diaries of Josephus Daniels, 1913–1921* (Lincoln, 1963), p. 214.

Puebla, warned Zapata against political agreements with them anywhere. To ally with them was to become their accomplices, and this, he judged, would ruin the southern cause. But here Zapata was not so anxious. Although he wanted no formal affiliation with the Felicistas either, he valued the strategic possibilities that a tighter military connection with them could provide, and he appreciated now the international impact of a revolutionary union including the Felicistas. Let our agents negotiate, he replied to Magaña; only limit their instructions and disavow them if they go too far.[3]

The attractions of an understanding with the Felicistas became even more obvious in April. Four jarring revolts broke out against the government that month. Rebelling were Cirilo Arenas in Puebla and Tlaxcala, Luis Caballero in Tamaulipas, the troops of Pedro Morales in Tlaxcala, and the troops of Silvestre Mariscal in Guerrero. Each revolt derived from its own peculiar origins, but all four became more or less Felicista. Magaña studied them closely, sending his interpretations on to Zapata.[4] How to benefit from these uprisings? In Morales's and Arenas's zone the Zapatistas could exert immediate popular influence, and in the one "Indian" episode of the whole Zapatista revolution secretaries composed manifestoes in Nahuatl for distribution through Tlaxcalan and Pueblan villages, to congratulate local chiefs on their defiance of Carranza and to coax them into a renewed allegiance to Zapata.[5] But to harness the rebellions in Tamaulipas and Guerrero for Zapatista purposes would require treating with the leaders there, who already leaned toward Don Félix.

Despite misgivings, Zapata finally appointed an ambassador to visit the main Felicista camps. His choice was Reynaldo Lecona, a friend of Soto y Gama's and a trusted junior secretary at headquarters since 1914. Bearing the March manifes es and decree, other propaganda, and special invitations to a general junta in Morelos where delegates could work out a plan for union "under one banner," Lecona headed east in late April.

In the same spirt Zapata signed a remarkable document in Tlaltizapán on April 25. It was a new Manifesto to the Mexican People, and a masterpiece of popular-frontsmanship. The author was Conrado Díaz Soto y

[3] Magaña to Zapata, April 11, 1918, and Zapata to Magaña, n.d. (mid-April 1918?), AZ, 29: 3.
[4] Magaña to Zapata, April 27, 1918, and Revolutionary Information Service, Bulletin 1, April 28, 1918, ibid.
[5] Manifesto to the Pueblos in Arenas's zone of operations, and Manifesto to the Chiefs, Officers, and Soldiers of the Arenas Division, April 27, 1918, ibid.

Gama, who here refined all his wiliness into the most sweetly politic phrases. "Where is the Revolution going? What do the sons of the people arisen in arms propose for themselves?" he asked. The answer was a bland reiteration of commonly accepted revolutionary aims—"to redeem the indigenous race, giving it back its lands and by that its liberty; to have the laborer in the fields, the present slave of the haciendas, converted into a man free and in control of his destiny through small property; to improve the economic, intellectual, and moral condition of the worker in the cities, protecting him against the oppression of the capitalist; to abolish dictatorship and win ample and effective political liberties for the Mexican people." The means he suggested were even blander—"to fix points of detail, to obtain the solution adequate to each problem, and not to forget the special conditions of certain regions or the peculiar necessities of specific groups of inhabitants, it is necessary to count on the accord of all the country's revolutionaries and to know the opinion of each of them." To prevent "a new exclusivist faction or new absorbing personages" from dominating the revolutionary movement, the gallant Conrado offered "the following procedure, of easy and simple application: when the revolutionary forces occupy the capital of the Republic, a junta will take place which the revolutionary chiefs from the whole country will attend, without distinction of factions or flags. . . . In that junta the national voice will let itself be heard . . . once the provisional revolutionary government is established, Congress can, as the authentic and genuine organ of the general will, resolve conscientiously the national problems."

Only in hints did Conrado reveal the Zapatistas' new political position. Noting initially "the snares and intrigues of the reaction," but omitting condemnations of the new 1917 Constitution and glorifications of the old 1857 charter, he separated the Zapatistas from the Felicistas but did not divorce them. Lambasting Carranza personally but granting the claims of all "honorable" revolutionaries, even paying tribute to those who now served Carranza although they resented him, he encouraged an affair between the Zapatistas and the loyal oppositionists without a mention of marriage. Again omitting reference to the Plan de Ayala, even to "the South," referring always to "the Revolution" as a single body, yet harping on "the special necessities" of "certain regions" and "specific groups," and every time raising land reform as the prime revolutionary goal, he indicated that for recognition in Morelos Zapata and his chiefs would recognize the government. This was a far cry from the aggressive speeches of the Zapatista delegates in the Convention in 1915, farther still from the demands Palafox had pressed upon the Carrancista emissaries in the summer of 1914. Indeed it amounted in national terms to an abrogation of the Ayala plan itself, in part a reversion to the stand of September 1911, when Zapata had not yet defined his action as a drive for social reform in the whole Republic but still conceived of it as a local movement for justice in the courts. The only trace left now of the plan he had fought nearly seven terrible years for was the slogan at the end of the manifesto—"Reform, Liberty, Justice, and Law." To secure these benefits, and peace, for the people in the place he cared most about, and to help prepare the country against the foreign intervention he feared, Zapata had forsaken his independence and declared himself ready for a "work . . . of concord and fraternity."[6] In no subsequent national pronouncement did he refer to his old Plan de Ayala.

From Tlaltizapán the manifesto was sent on to Tochimilco. There Ayaquica and a visiting Felicista chief, Caraveo, signed it. And from there Magaña dispatched agents with copies into Mexico City and into Felicista territory to the east and northeast. The most serious effort since 1911 to re-incorporate the Morelos revolution into the national movement was now underway. Because the immediate control over its direction and pace was in Tochimilco, Zapata took an extraordinary interest in the organization of the headquarters there. Mildly annoyed, Magaña assured his chief that he would keep his office functioning properly.[7] But Zapata's attention remained in focus on the diplomatic dealings, as intensely as it had been before on restoring the villages their lands.

Local commotions still mattered in Tlaltizapán. Because of the poverty in which González had abandoned Morelos the year before, villagers had reaped very meager harvests in early 1918. The stark misery and destruction Gates had seen in the state reminded him of war-torn Belgium—"Rheims and Ypres and St. Quentin in the small."[8] And now as the rains began, the villagers jealously guarded the seed they were planting for the next harvest. Zapata tried to protect them from military exactions.[9] But thieves and bandits having sprung up in these hard times, villagers fought back on their own. From their experience in the Associations for the Defense of Revolutionary Ideals they had become quite militant about their rights. And organized and armed for self-defense, they repelled intruders without much

[6] Manifesto to the Mexican People, April 25, 1918, ibid.
[7] Zapata to Magaña, May 2, 1918, and Magaña to Zapata, May 4, 1918, AZ, 27: 15.
[8] Gates in *World's Work*, April 1919, p. 657.
[9] Decree on the Rights of the Pueblos, March 5, 1918, AZ, 29: 4.

discrimination. Inevitably mistakes occurred. Although Morelos had its share of them, the worst was in late April in Puebla, south of Tochimilco, where there had recently been association elections.[1] Fed up with blackmail and bother during their planting, the vigilantes of the pueblo Amecac fired on a squad of Caraveo's allied Felicistas. Stories later differed about exactly what happened. For their part the Amecacans charged that when they refused to give the officer in command of the intruding troops the food and pasture he had requested, he had ordered his troops to seize stores from municipal buildings. The local authorities then defended themselves, they reported; shots were exchanged, men fell dead on both sides, and the Felicistas fled with the villagers in hot pursuit. The unlucky officer, on the other hand, alleged that when he and his men arrived peaceably at Amecac, they overheard remarks like—"Now only a few have come, so let's do away with them." While he dined with the municipal assistant, he said, he heard shots and ran outside and saw the villagers massacring his men. He could not tell how many he had lost.[2]

Whoever told the truth, the scandal embarrassed Zapata. Ayaquica, in whose zone Amecac was, wanted its whole population consigned to Tlaltizapán for a tough investigation. The aggrieved troops, he admitted, were not local natives, coming originally like Caraveo from Chihuahua; but if villagers now resisted outlanders, he warned, "they will do the same tomorrow with our forces." Another angry chief wanted to disarm all villagers, "because provided with the permit for carrying arms for the defense of their interests, they commit offenses [against us]."[3] Zapata tried moderation, appointing Caraveo to a mission in Guerrero, summoning to headquarters only "the most respectable citizens" of suspect pueblos, urging Magaña not to aggravate the case around Tochimilco. But it took days of palavering to repair relations with the aggrieved villagers, and over three weeks to induce Caraveo to go to Guerrero without revenge.[4] Two and a half months after the shooting, Zapata still had to rule on the dispute it had opened, confirming the villagers' right to bear arms but only with a license and to defend themselves or the Ayala plan. Six weeks after that, in a "patri-

[1] Dromundo: *Biografía,* p. 168. Reports from Alpanocan and Tepanapa locals to Tochimilco central, April 13 and 29, 1918, AZ, 29: 3.

[2] Magaña to Zapata, May 2, 1918, AZ, 27: 15.

[3] Ayaquica to Zapata, May 2, 1918, and T. Cortés Cabrera to Magaña, May 1, 1918, ibid.

[4] Magaña to Caraveo, May 4, 1918, and to Zapata, May 5, 1918, and Zapata to Magaña, May 7, 16, and 23, 1918, ibid.

otic appeal" to fractious pueblos in his zone, he reconfirmed their right to arm for defense against "bad men and bad revolutionaries."[5]

In the Tlaltizapán headquarters itself there was also grave trouble. Crucially important was the dismissal of Manuel Palafox. As foreign policy had become Zapata's central concern through the past year, Palafox had lost influence with his chief. Worse, he lost his respect. Not only was Palafox of no use in conciliatory efforts, because of his arrogant temper and because he had personally insulted men in other camps with whom Zapata now wanted to deal; he also seemed in retrospect the individual responsible for the Zapatistas' present plight—the man they could blame for their disastrous involvement with Villa in 1914, their alienation of worthy chiefs in the Constitutionalist party, and their abiding reputation as the most intransigent group in the revolutionary movement. In February Gates had noticed Palafox's anomalous role in Tlaltizapán. "When it was politics, and Mexican or international questions," he observed, "Palafox was not there—off with other duties. When it was a matter of practical dispositions about titles, crops, irrigation, he was." On the American's inquiry about Palafox's demotion, Zapata confirmed his guess. Jilted, Palafox had plunged compulsively into administering local reforms. The day Gates arrived at headquarters he barely sat down to eat, he later recalled, "before Palafox was explaining all the operations of irrigation, their agricultural loan bank, making advances to the farmers just as they went on stage by stage in the cultivation, seeing to it that the crop was marketed and the loan repaid; all well devised to educate the farmers to economic independence. The dinner got cold while he talked." Gates politely praised the reform for being "in agreement with our most modern lines." In pathetic delight Palafox then bragged to Soto y Gama, "The señor says this is the best system in the world." By now he could not restrain himself from claiming that he had actually written the Plan de Ayala. Through the spring Palafox broke down. It seems that in doubt of his sex he behaved indiscreetly and became an object of contempt at headquarters. Zapata almost had him shot. Only on Magaña's warning that another execution after Montaño's would be too much, Zapata relented and sent the ruined little man to Magaña in Tochimilco, "to lend his services as you judge convenient."[6]

[5] Circular to municipal authorities, July 16, 1918, AZ, 30: 23. Patriotic Appeal to All Pueblos Deceived by the So-called Government of Carranza, August 22, 1918, AZ, 27: 9.

[6] Gates in World's Work, April 1919, pp. 658, 660. Zapata to Magaña, May 26, 1918, AZ, 27: 15.

Still no local imbroglio distracted Zapata from his concentration on winning new friends and forming a union. Through the Amecac and Palafox crises he continued to consider with Magaña which rebels to invite into their union, which exiles to ask back into the revolutionary movement, which federal deputies to encourage in opposition.[7] Responses to Lecona's mission among the Felicistas began to come in. And a note arrived from a friend of Gates's in Mexico City that the "scholar" had talked with high United States officials, who, he said, would now arrange a change in American policy toward Carranza. This was pure puffery—on his return to the United States in May Gates had had a "few minutes' talk" in Washington with the harried Secretary of War Baker, who had promised no more than courtesies—but, knowing no better, Zapata and Magaña took the note straight.[8]

Through the summer, as congressional elections approached, Zapatista negotiations grew even more elaborate. Letters and appointments and pleas for signatures on manifestoes went out to all manner of Carranza's opponents—to Villa and his agent in the United States, to major and minor Felicistas, to other independent rebels.[9] After Octavio Magaña returned from San Antonio in mid-July to report that Paz had been in sad shape, alcoholic and out of the swim of exile politics, and that contrary to his intelligence the Vázquez Gómez of "agrarian tendencies" and standing with the Americans was not the lawyer Emilio but the doctor Francisco, Zapata became prodigally tolerant about political associates. ". . . what counts now to my way of thinking," he wrote to Gildardo Magaña in early August, "is to put up several persons who'll do as much as possible, and then afterwards we'll see what slant to give the business." Although he granted that the doctor was "bad," he remarked that he was also "very sharp in politics and would do something." Without waiting for an answer, he repeated his opinion to Magaña "that to look for men perfectly wholesome in ideas and clean of [bad] antecedents . . . is almost in vain." As agents and allies he wanted men with connections already established, "for they have the advantage of being practical, of knowing all the angles

[7] Magaña to Zapata, May 16 and 19, 1918, ibid.

[8] Manuel Peláez to Zapata, May 21, 1918, and Zapata to Magaña, May 23, 1918, ibid.

[9] Among these are Zapata to M. Díaz Lombardo, May 28, 1918, ibid.; to J. Cabrera, July 4, 1918, AZ, 30: 23; to S. Salazar, J. J. Baños, G. Olarte, M. Romero, J. Carrera, and L. Salazar, July 12, 1918, ibid.

of politics, and of knowing how to measure circumstances."[1] Within the next week he had signed letters to Felipe Ángeles and to Emilio and Francisco Vázquez Gómez, urging them to cooperate, start a revolt in the north, and arrange for a recognition of belligerency from Washington.[2]

In mid-August, after the elections cost the Liberal Constitutionalists their majority in Congress, Zapata at last addressed himself directly to the most important dissident of them all, Obregón. He sent two letters, probably the creations of Soto y Gama, to encourage Obregón to revolt. In the first he warned that "the reaction threatens the conquests of the Revolution like an avalanche" and asked that Obregón climax "his enterprise as a fighter, helping to liberate the nation." In the second he condemned Carranza as a dictator, insisted on unification as a simple act of patriotism, and asked again for the "valuable cooperation of revolutionaries who up to here have maintained themselves at a distance from us." In the same week he also signed letters to Obregón's chief aide in Mexico City, Aarón Sáenz, and to the Liberal Constitutionalist deputies of the past Congress, congratulating them and inviting them south if the government persecuted them. When Magaña found in refuge in Tochimilco a former national officer who had served under Obregón in the great battles against Villa in 1915, he had him write his old commander too, to assure him the Zapatistas respected him.[3]

Obregón did not revolt. Nor did he, who never received his letters, or his aides, who did receive theirs, reply on paper to the Zapatistas: even if Obregón expected later to treat with Zapata, he could hardly afford to leave a written record of his plan for Carrancista spies to find and publish. But undaunted, Zapata resorted again to Francisco Vázquez Gómez, naming him in late August his confidential agent to the United States. If Gates's tale was true, then Vázquez Gómez could convince the American government to recognize the united revolutionary factions as belligerents.[4]

Most probably Carranza was aware that Zapata communicated with

[1] Report to Zapata, July 10, 1918, ibid. Zapata to G. Magaña, August 4 and 6, 1918, ibid., 20.

[2] Zapata to E. Vázquez, August 11, 1918, and to F. Vázquez Gómez, August 12, 1918, ibid. Zapata to F. Ángeles, August 11, 1918, AZ, 27: 9.

[3] Zapata to Obregón, August 17 and 24, 1918, and to Sáenz and to the Liberal Constitutionalist deputies, August 24, 1918; Leonel Ramírez to Obregón, August 22, 1918, AZ, 30: 20.

[4] Reyes Avilés: *Cartones,* p. 56, *n.* 1. Zapata to F. Vázquez Gómez, August 30, 1918, AZ, 30: 20 and 27: 9.

his opponents and enemies. Certainly Pablo González knew, as the leading general among the Carrancista "unconditionals" and the chief in command in the zone where Magaña still negotiated with Castro and Reyes. González despised Zapata as fiercely as ever. But he was in no position to stop the Zapatistas' dealings. Militarily he could not yet mobilize the forces to capture Tochimilco or Tlaltizapán without weakening garrisons and striking columns in action against the Felicistas. Anyway these months were the rainy season, when artillery and cavalry attacks would have bogged down the afternoon of their initiation. Politically also González was in a bind. If he forbade Castro to receive propositions from Magaña, he forewent the opportunity, which he wanted to retain, of enticing Magaña and Ayaquica into accepting amnesties. In frustration he had sounded out a former aide of Zapata's, retired in Mexico City, about returning to Morelos to lure Zapata into an ambush. But the man refused and tried to send a warning south, and González had to jail him.[5] The upshot was that national troops hardly moved on the lines they held around and in Morelos. True, national officers reported constant combat, "more battles," commented an ex-undersecretary of war acidly, "than the Cid himself fought before and after his death."[6] But even though Zapata, de la O, Mendoza, and Ayaquica carried out operations into Puebla, Guerrero, Mexico State, and the Federal District, national commanders began no counter-offensive.[7] Through the fall they occupied no more territory than that they had taken a year before around Cuautla and Jonacatepec.

And through the fall the Zapatista attempts to negotiate continued. To Felicistas, to Francisco Vázquez Gómez, to national officers right in Morelos, to already allied revolutionaries in other zones, and again to Obregón, couriers carried out letters from Tochimilco and Tlaltizapán.[8]

---

[5] Manuel N. Robles: "Lo que supe de la muerte del General Emiliano Zapata," *La Prensa,* September 19, 1955.

[6] *Excélsior,* June 15, 1918.

[7] Ibid., September 8, 9, and 24, and October 20 and 23, 1918. Zapata to Magaña, August 6, 1918, AZ, 30: 20. Memoranda of the U.S. military attaché, September 14 and November 4, 1918, NA, 59: 812.00/22245 and 22361.

[8] A few among these letters are Zapata to C. Galán, M. Carvanzo, and R. Cejudo, September 1, 1918; to S. Cedillo, F. Vázquez Gómez, L. Caballero, L. Gutiérrez, and Almazán, September 5, 1918; to Obregón, September 17, 1918; Magaña to J. A. Castro, September 7, 1918, AZ, 30: 26; Zapata to E. Figueroa, August 5, 1918, ibid., 20; to Cal y Mayor, October 12, 1918, ibid., 25. L. F. Bustamante: "Dizque Don Pablo no Autorizó la muerte de Emiliano Zapata," *El Universal Gráfico,* November 10, 1937.

Not all the replies in favor of union were attractive. One, for instance, came from an agent whom Manuel Peláez, now independent from the Felicistas, had stationed in Puebla—Federico Córdova. In mid-September Córdova passed on to Marcelo Caraveo, also now loyal to Peláez rather than Don Félix, a report from anonymous metropolitan "señores": the White House was convinced no revolutionary presently in opposition "can control the situation" by himself; these same "señores" could get military supplies and a $50,000,000 American loan if the revolutionary factions would unite under Peláez; as a guarantee for the loan, Peláez would give "the oil wells on his property" around Tampico. In turn Caraveo passed the report on to Magaña, noting that "apparently the Gringos and Peláez have arrived at a deal . . . " Magaña shortly sent back a frosty answer from Zapata. After acknowledging Peláez as "a true and conscious revolutionary" and repeating his wish for a "solid and secure" revolutionary union, Zapata replied that "we must operate with the most necessary prudence and indispensable tact to crown the work duly—that is, without prejudice to the popular interests we defend and without any slight to national decorum, of which the people have always shown themselves so jealous." In sum, he refused Peláez's invitation and reiterated his own.[9] But other replies were encouraging. Reading between the lines of several, in late September Zapata appointed Alfredo Robles Domínguez his "general representative" in Mexico City, and in early October Magaña dispatched the appointment along with the manifestoes of March 15 and April 25, other propaganda, and a brief on Zapatista contacts in the British Legation. Like Vázquez Gómez, only quietly on the home front, Robles Domínguez was to advocate foreign recognition of the outlaws as belligerents.[1]

As winter came on, a new and profoundly anxious tone sounded in Zapata's correspondence. He had local worries galore now. The Spanish influenza, rampant throughout the world in these months, appeared in Mexico City in early October and spread immediately into the south. There were the perfect grounds for an epidemic—prolonged fatigue, starvation diets, bad water, continual moving. In the mountains where the poorest villagers were and where many chiefs had their camps, the biting winter cold broke the health of thousands. In the towns bodies accumulated

[9] Caraveo to Magaña, September 20, 1918, and Magaña to Caraveo, September 24, 1918, AZ, 30: 26.

[1] Zapata to Robles Domínguez, September 25, 1918, and Magaña to Robles Domínguez, October 2, 1918, ibid., 25.

faster than they could be buried. By December Cuautla sheltered only 150 to 200 civilians. Cuernavaca was a refuge of less than five thousand. As for the open countryside, a family might as well have tried to inhabit Gehenna. In makeshift huts men, women, and children lay in shivering chills for days, without food or care, until one by one they all died. Wise survivors deserted their dead and fled into Guerrero, to safer climes south of the Balsas River. National patrols discovered whole villages abandoned literally to "the peace of the graveyard." In Mexico City Carrancistas found a grisly comfort in such news. "Spanish Flu," one headliner proclaimed, "Continues Its Pacification Work in Morelos."[2] Through deaths and emigration the state lost a quarter of its population in 1918, numerically not so large a loss as Huerta had caused in 1914 but proportionally no doubt larger than any since those of the great plagues of the sixteenth century. Among the sick were many Zapatista soldiers and the whole staff at Tochimilco; though no important secretary died, most were invalid for weeks. In addition Zapata had recently lost several agents and gunrunners, arrested in Mexico City and Toluca. Short of able-bodied men, his chiefs were now short of supplies and ammunition too. Moreover, Palafox and a fellow secretary, Enrique Bonilla, had run off from Tochimilco to Cirilo Arenas's camp; it looked likely that they would make their defection final.[3] And González had mounted a new campaign in the south. But pressing on Zapata through all these torments, taking on the force of their pain as it bore down, moving him to the verge of both relief and despair, was his preoccupation with the end of the World War—whether the menace Gates had conjured up the past February would now prove real, whether the United States would intervene again in Mexico.

In late November Zapata wrote to Felipe Ángeles in Texas. Maybe France, where Ángeles had gone to school, could help restrain the Americans. Could not Ángeles use his "intimate friendship" with Field Marshal Foch, Zapata asked obliquely, to win Foch's "powerful moral influence" in support of "the cause of the Mexican people"? Two weeks later he stated his fear directly to Magaña. Modest as usual on topics he felt ignorant about, he asked Magaña and Soto y Gama to consider, "if you think it

---

[2] *Excélsior*, November 26, 1918. See also ibid., October 25, November 1–10, and December 3, 9, and 11, 1918; Manuel Mazari: *Breve estudio sobre la última epidemia de influenza en la ciudad de México* (México, 1919), p. 21. S. Valverde: op. cit., p. 186; Manuel Arvide Rendón: "Labor desarrollada en el Sur en 1918," *El Legionario*, June 1953. Holt Büttner: op. cit., pp. 22–3.

[3] *Excélsior*, October 15, 1918. Magaña to Zapata, November 3, 1918, AZ, 30: 21.

advantageous to our cause," how to "approach the Allied Powers, to propose something favorable to the interests of the Republic and those of the Revolution." This attempt he regarded as critically important, "for it appears to me that once the European-American question is solved, the United States of America will throw itself on our nationality."[4] Then would arise the impossible choice Gates had implied, to join Carranza in national defense or to acquiesce in foreign supervision. Meanwhile he had Magaña resume serious dealings with Castro and Reyes. Increasingly in correspondence with them there appeared attacks on "elements markedly reactionary," in rebellion like the Felicistas or in office like the Carrancista "unconditionals." The theme of Zapatista appeals was now blatantly patriotic. "If peace doesn't come in a very short time," Magaña warned Castro, "if we Mexicans don't deal with each other fraternally, since the end of the European war has left the hands of the American colossus free, we are threatened with the most humiliating of interventions, the result of which would be at least the definitive wiping out of our sovereignty as a nation."[5] This was no trick, to traffic in love of the fatherland, but an honest alarm.

González, to whom Castro remained loyal, plainly saw his and his subordinates' patriotic duties in a different light. For him these duties reduced in Morelos to the re-establishment of Carrancista officials. And in early December, the rains having stopped, the Zapatistas having weakened drastically in numbers, health, and reserves of men and supplies, and the government having consolidated its power in the new Congress, González accelerated his military operations. With eleven thousand troops, moving from Cuautla and Jonacatepec and from lines around the state, he quickly occupied the four other main towns—Yautepec, Jojutla, Cuernavaca, and Tetecala. Scattered Zapatista forces tried to resist, but within days they had everywhere dispersed and retreated into the hills.

This time González ran the Constitutionalist revolution in Morelos more professionally. To secure the occupation, he put garrisons in forty or fifty towns and villages and hastened repairs on the railroads. To satisfy metropolitan curiosity about his statesmanship, he appointed municipal authorities, confirming some he found in office, replacing others with

[4] Zapata to Ángeles, November 21, 1918, ibid. Zapata to Magaña, December 8, 1918, AZ, 30: 19.

[5] Magaña to Castro, December 3, 1918, ibid. See also Magaña to Castro, November 3 and 10, 1918, and to Reyes, November 10, 1918; and Reyes to Magaña, November 9 and December 8, 1918, ibid.

trustier types; speculation began over whom he would name provisional governor and district judges. To fix his generals' interest in preserving local order, he seized various plantations, which he then arranged for them to rent from the government. And to assure prospective investors and entrepreneurs, he commenced a policy of repopulation, offering free fares to Morelos for laborers from anywhere in the Republic. As he indicated, his intention was "to reconstruct that rich state which before was so flourishing."[6] Among the places he took was Tlaltizapán. Now and then Zapata could fight or sneak back into the town. But from mid-December on he was a fugitive. So were de la O, Mendoza, and the others.

In hiding, the Zapatistas had new temptations pulling at them. From Arenista territory Palafox had issued in November a Manifesto to the Southerners, urging them to desert their chief and join a separatist agrarian movement that he had launched. In alliance with Everardo González, whom he claimed to have already won over, they would struggle on for the Ayala plan—whose slogan he had amended to "Land and Liberty." Other allies he mentioned were Arenas and Caraveo, both, he did not mention, now partisans of Peláez.[7] Palafox as a person was still in disgrace among the Zapatistas, but at least through him any chief but Zapata could now gain entrance into a more promising, oil-rich rebellion. From the other side, Castro in mid-December offered amnesty to Magaña "and all those like you who work in good faith." Since Castro was in close touch with the President, the offer came practically from Carranza himself. If the Zapatistas were sincere patriots, Castro suggested, they would rejoin the national revolution to fortify the government against its enemies, and then try to change it from within. In form, he explained, he could not grant the amnesty "except on the basis of unconditionality," but "I remain pledged," he went on, "that if [the grant] is effected, it will be with absolute guarantee for your lives, families, and interests."[8] On these terms, surrendering not in Morelos to González, who might prosecute and shoot them no matter what he said, but in Puebla to Castro, who had always treated them honorably, individual Zapatistas could regain the privileges of service in power.

Yet the Zapatista organization remained intact. No ranking veteran chief of the Morelos revolution disowned Zapata for another leader in re-

---

[6] For the military operations and the reorganization of the state, see *Excélsior*, December 3, 7, 9, 11–14, 16, 21–2, and 26, 1918.

[7] For the manifesto and a cursory Carrancista analysis, see ibid., January 24, 1919.

[8] Castro to Magaña, December 19, 1918, AZ, 30: 19. See also Reyes to Magaña, December 8, 1918, and Magaña to Zapata, December 10, 1918, ibid.

volt. Although Palafox sent personal appeals to some southern chiefs, even in their current straits they replied with irrevocable insults. ". . . a poor devil of mistaken sex like you can't call himself a friend of men like we really are," retorted Maurilio Mejía. Less arrogant but equally abrupt was the refusal from Emigdio Marmolejo: "All the lies you tell me, go tell them to people who don't know you, because here in Morelos, I'll be frank with you, you'll manage to surprise no one, least of all in the stupid form you proceed in . . . Knowing you as I do, as an intriguing and ungrateful man, I find it very natural that now . . . you speak badly of he who showered you with favors and considerations which, we now see more clearly, you did not deserve."[9] Nor did any major native chief surrender to the nationals, or even provisionally move his operations into Puebla. In this disheartening crisis the chiefs who had been together from the start eight years before—Zapata, de la O, Mendoza, Ayaquica, Jesús Capistrán, Francisco Alarcón, Timoteo Sánchez, Gabriel Mariaca, Pedro and Francisco Saavedra, Zeferino Ortega, Magaña, Mejía, and Marmolejo—still stayed true to each other. During the winter they did lose some minor chiefs and many troops who accepted amnesties from González and Castro; their bands became so small that they could not even carry on guerrillas. But they did not lose the basic loyalty of their people. With only one exception (a stray unit under Victoriano Bárcenas, originally from Guerrero, which proved the rule), the amnestied forces did not cooperate with the nationals in betraying their former comrades, much less in helping to suppress them. Instead, officers and men quietly returned home to tend their puny, patchy crops, as they had been doing before the occupation. Like their leaders' retreat, their surrender was strategic. In the fields and the villages they waited for a chance to rise again. Meanwhile they went on serving their old chiefs when and how they could. Food they gave them, and shelter and intelligence. Literally they nourished the local revolution and kept it alive.

Zapata remained nevertheless in regular contact with Magaña, and their negotiations continued without a pause. News from agents in Mexico and Puebla City having heightened his fears of American intervention, Zapata insisted that Magaña harp on the patriotic theme in dealings with Castro.[1] He approved Magaña's statement of support for an Alliance of

[9] Mejía to Palafox, November 27, 1918, AZ, 30: 21. Marmolejo to Palafox, December 3 and 25, 1918, AZ, 30: 19 and 27: 13.

[1] Report from Atl (Carlos Peralta), n.d. (December 1918?), AZ, 30: 19. Zapata to Magaña, December 13, 1918, ibid.

Proletarians in Mexico City and kept up correspondence with neighboring rebels. But his overriding concern now was for connections among Carranza's still loyal opponents, to persuade them to oust Carranza before the United States acted against him. To Amezcua in Havana Zapata had long reports and propaganda sent, to broadcast from there too his latest, residual claim that "to reconstruct the national revolutionary party, it is indispensable to set Carranza aside," and to repeat his promise that the Zapatistas would then collaborate with the Liberal Constitutionalists and other "men of advanced principles."[2]

At once encouraging and foreboding for this tack were the increasingly reproachful diplomatic notes that the United States sent to Carranza about Mexican oil decrees. The notes, copies of which Magaña received and forwarded to Zapata, were welcome evidence that Carranza as President jeopardized the nation and that patriots had to hurry to discharge him; and yet they were also a grotesque, insinuated warning that to increase attacks against him was to bring the American action on.[3] But Zapata did not waver. At his urging Magaña prepared a bold New Year's Day Manifesto to the Mexican People that featured Carranza as the single source of all the Republic's tribulations, foreign and domestic. Lambasting Carranza again for abuses in state and congressional elections, and praising the Liberal Constitutionalists again, Zapata now charged publicly that Carranza's neutrality during the war had been false, that he had protected "the interests of Kaiserism," taken the part of "imperialism against democracy," offended "French and British capital," and worst, "in the matter of oil," had dictated "laws worked out in accord with the German Minister." For resulting conflicts, Zapata declared, "no one but Carranza will be the great culprit." Only if revolutionaries dumped him, he concluded, "will we again be the masters of our destiny."[4]

Through January the Zapatista tack shifted again. Deciding that Castro had never intended to forsake Carranza, only to convince Zapatistas to take amnesties, Magaña broke off negotiations with him and Reyes. Immedi-

---

[2] Zapata to Magaña, December 17, 1918; to H. Aguilar, December 25, 1918; and to Amezcua, December 15, 25, and 30, 1918, ibid.

[3] Magaña to Zapata, December 31, 1918, ibid., and January 5, 1919, AZ, 30: 24. For the American notes, see United States Department of State: *Papers Relating to the Foreign Relations of the United States, 1918* (Washington, 1930), pp. 687–792.

[4] Magaña to Zapata, January 5, 1919, and Manifesto to the Mexican People, January 1, 1919, AZ, 30: 24.

ately his interest in Francisco Vázquez Gómez revived. To Havana he wrote to ask Amezcua to write to Vázquez Gómez in San Antonio, to coordinate their propaganda and declarations.[5] And to Zapata, back in Tlaltizapán in late January, he sent mail and a revolutionary program from Vázquez Gómez—along with a report from San Antonio that many exiles there, including Ángeles, Villa, and Villarreal, backed Vázquez Gómez, and that the prestigious doctor was "in constant communication with President Wilson [then in Versailles!], who gives him complete confidence and support." Magaña's own advice was to unify all the outlaw revolutionaries under the direction of this "man of much talent," to proclaim him Supreme Chief of the revolution. In Vázquez Gómez's program he saw only two flaws. They were glaring—a failure to mention the restitution of lands, timber, and water to the pueblos, and a failure to explain that the revolutionaries would not reimpose the 1857 Constitution where it nullified "the revolutionary principles." But Magaña had amended the program appropriately and believed Vázquez Gómez would agree to the changes "in his own interest" to stay in office. Without waiting for Zapata's reply he sent off to Vázquez Gómez a provisional approval of the amended program.[6]

On February 4 Zapata answered Magaña, obviously relieved. The guilty strain of claiming national authority was over now: in the end he could resume his pride in his local role: he was "happy" to accept Vázquez Gómez's Supreme Chieftainship, he wrote, "especially when as you weil know I have never had more aspirations than those of seeing my people happy and absolute owner of the fruits of their labors." The next day he signed a long letter of accommodation to Vázquez Gómez. It probably came from Magaña's typewriter. Patently for an American audience, containing not a whiff of Palafox's "rabid socialistic ideas" of 1915, it was a remarkable statement on behalf of "the spirit of enterprise" in industry, commerce, mining, the oil business, finance, and agriculture. Implied only once was a demand for an agrarian reform, to satisfy "the need the Mexican people experience for lands for the formation of small property," but explicit was the assurance that "we do not encourage in any way sense-

[5] Magaña to Castro, January 14, 1919, and to Amezcua, January 15, 1919, ibid.
[6] Magaña to Zapata, January 31, 1919, ibid., and to F. Vázquez Gómez, February 1, 1919, AZ, 30: 29.

less radicalisms . . . tending to suppress in agricultural matters the all powerful spring of private initiative." The only restrictions Zapata here declared legitimate were on "monopolies which threaten to destroy the free play of social forces."[7]

To Villa and Peláez he shortly dispatched letters informing them of his decision and urging them to recognize Vázquez Gómez too. The doctor was "an old revolutionary, cultured and upright," he reminded them, "with deep-rooted and firm convictions and amply acquainted in diplomatic circles." On February 10 he signed a manifesto Magaña had composed, To the Mexican People and Revolutionaries. "To carry to a happy end and leave totally consummated the unifying labor whose bases were presented in the manifestoes of March 15 and April 25 of last year," the manifesto announced formally the nomination of Vázquez Gómez as the Zapatista candidate for "the Supreme Chieftainship of the Revolution." Like the current eulogies of presidential candidates for 1920, it ran on and on in praise of "El Doctor," who for a Mexican audience became more reformist and emerged "in a word . . . a link of union for Mexicans." An extra bulletin from headquarters soon followed to the same effect.[8]

Pablo González meanwhile strived to make his rule in Morelos effective. The lessons of his earlier debacle having sunk in, he maneuvered more cautiously than before. Already a dark-horse candidate for the presidency in 1920, he could not afford another fiasco now. Thus, though in steady control of every important town but Tlaltizapán, he steered clear of areas where de la O's terrorism might put him to shame. Cuautla he used as his base: the railroad between there and Mexico City was safer than the Cuernavaca line, and the surrounding farmland was easier to patrol. There González kept his army headquarters and set up the state capital. There he installed a new governor, an aide from his staff, Colonel José G. Aguilar. There he employed prisoners of war in rebuilding the town at fifty-five centavos a day, plus food. And from there he returned to the capital in late February to declare to the press that "most of the state's haciendas

[7] Zapata to Magaña, February 4, 1919, and to F. Vázquez Gómez, February 5, 1919, ibid.

[8] Zapata to Villa and to Peláez, February 9, 1919; Manifesto to the Mexican People and Revolutionaries, February 10, 1919; Extra Bulletin, February 14, 1919; Magaña to C. Aguilar and to L. Ibarra, February 15, 1919, and to Ángeles, February 16, 1919, ibid.

are already in action and give jobs to many people . . ." He had provided well for his generals: "in tracts of some consideration," he boasted, "work goes on at the plantations of Santa Inés, Cuahuixtla, San Carlos, Atlihuayán, Calderón, Tenextepango, Zacatepec, Treinta, San José Vista Hermosa, El Puente, Hospital, and several others. Very good harvests are expected from them all . . ." So far he had not reinstituted an agrarian commission in the state, nor indicated officially or unofficially whether he planned to. In 1919, as in 1911, the farmers who prepared the fields to receive the summer's rain were in law mostly sharecroppers and day laborers. But to González their individual fates were only trivia in the oddly familiar progress he nobly predicted, "an era of prosperity for the state." As his friends on *Excélsior* headlined, in a style reminiscent of científico editors, "Morelos Returns to the Life of Order."[9]

Even in González's absence national control prevailed. Around Cuernavaca General Gustavo Elizondo arranged an informal truce with de la O. Elsewhere Zapatista chiefs lay low. The only skirmishes worthy of record were those in which nationals momentarily pinned down a Zapatista party on the move. Zapatista troop surrenders went on in driblets. And in peace the local economic recovery continued. Along the newly opened railroads and wagon roads trade resumed with the Federal District and Puebla. Market towns bustled again. Booming at the fastest clip was Cuautla, which quickly regained some four thousand inhabitants, not quite two thirds its population in 1910 but plenty in the present circumstances. There in early March, marking the town's renaissance, the national commander promoted the big Second Friday of Lent fair—where eight years before Zapata, Pablo Torres Burgos, and Rafael Merino had laid their final plans for joining the Maderista revolution.[1]

But politically the occupation had stalled again. Three months had passed, and despite vigorous efforts the nationals had not managed the surrender or capture of a single major Zapatista. Even more frustrating was that some chiefs actually lived at times in the towns, and now and then appeared in public. "Do you want to enter your horse in the races at the Cuautla fair?" Mejía wrote to Mendoza in Jonacatepec. "There'll also be cockfights, and we need good cocks. Could you get us any?"[2] And still at

---

[9] *Excélsior*, March 1, 6, and 12, 1919.

[1] Ibid., March 13 and 19, 1919. Meléndez: op. cit., I, 376. Dromundo: *Vida,* pp. 259–60. Memorandum for Chief of Naval Operations, Weekly Report for Week Ending March 10, 1919, NA, 45: Subject File W-E-5: Box 654.

[2] Mejía to Mendoza, January 25, 1919, AZ, 30: 24.

Tochimilco, moving when threatened to the nearby hamlet of Tochimizolco, remained the central Zapatista headquarters.

To González's deepest chagrin Zapata himself stayed notoriously at large. In late February an energetic national force had driven him out of his base southeast of Jojutla and chased him toward Jonacatepec, and then along the state line toward Tochimilco. But he maintained authority over his chiefs, directing their movements in the area and keeping them respectful of the villagers they depended on. "When asking for food," he instructed them in early March, "you will do so with good words, and whatever you want, ask for it in a good manner, and always showing your gratitude. . . . the better we behave," he concluded, "the sooner will we triumph and have all the pueblos on our side." The popular protection he had earned was apparently inviolable. No one would turn him in, despite gossip of gigantic rewards. Instead, from every town his spies informed him about national operations. The bartenders and whores in Cuautla served him especially well because of their contacts with the personnel of the national headquarters there.[3]

From mountain retreats Zapata and Magaña continued their subversive diplomacy. Magaña had an agent warn Peláez not to listen to the apostate Palafox, who had gone to his headquarters near Tampico. In reply he received an offer from Peláez of fifty thousand pesos and ammunition. On March 10 he commissioned his brother Octavio to go to Mexico City, "to hold conferences with the elements who work for the candidacy of General Álvaro Obregón for president." And on March 17 Zapata signed a defiant open letter to "Citizen Carranza." In phrases probably Soto y Gama's, Zapata addressed himself "for the first and last time" not "to the President of the Republic, whom I do not recognize, nor to the politician, whom I distrust," but "to the Mexican, the man of feeling and reason, who I believe must be moved sometime (if only for an instant) by the anguish of mothers, the suffering of orphans, the worries and anxieties of the fatherland." Simple in language, specific in reference, contemptuous yet sober in tone, aggressive yet responsible in advocation, the letter was an impressive indictment of the Carrancista regime. After a late, passing notice that Vázquez Gómez could arrange peace and revolutionary union, it ended in a plea to Carranza "as a patriot and a man" to resign for the sake

[3] Magaña to Zapata, March 2, 1919; Zapata to Magaña, March 3, 1919; and Circular, March 4, 1919, AZ, 30: 32. Elías L. Torres: "No te descuides, Zapata," *Jueves de Excélsior*, April 8, 1937.

of the country. In the next few days Magaña had copies sent to allied outlaws and distributed in the capital and other big cities.[4]

Zapata's perseverence increasingly chafed the Carrancistas. Already
the presidential campaigns for 1920 were on, although Carranza had tried
to squelch them as "premature"; and continued resistance to the President's
authority impaired his political reputation and hampered his efforts to
control the succession. With Peláez and Díaz and their cohorts still in
arms against him, with Villa still on the loose in Chihuahua, with Ángeles now back in the country to help Villa, with another violent dispute over
a governorship exploding in Tabasco, Carranza took particular offense
at Zapata. The others he could plausibly dismiss as reactionaries or mere
rivals for power, dangerous but not essentially relevant to the new order
and progress in Mexico. But symbolically in Zapata, a popular outlaw who
famously stood for the rights of country folk, he faced an undeniable
moral challenge in the coming elections.

Abroad too the Zapatista survival embarrassed the government. Confused with the survival of the other rebels, it seemed proof either that
Carranza was not popular or that he was not strong enough to merit
foreign recognition. That in fact he was neither was a notion already
current in the United States, thanks largely to William Gates. In January
Gates had published in the influential *North American Review* an article
on his recent tour. The lowdown, as Gates gave it, was that Carranza
was not a legitimate president: that "we find at his side the German
Minister and the I.W.W.," that national forces in the country were "as
Germans in Belgium, or Bolsheviki in Russia," that in contrast the only
"happy people" he had seen were in zones that Zapata, Félix Díaz, and
other rebels controlled, and that these chiefs formed "a unified political
revolution to restore constitutional government, wipe out the socialistic
legislation, and come back to a position of respect internationally." To
the Zapatistas Gates paid special tribute. "The Mexican revolution (really
started by Zapata in 1909, before Madero) will never end until the mountain peasants of Morelos come into their own," he declared; "you might
as well fight the Swiss." Though farfetched in its images and misleading
in its account, the article was vividly detailed, freshly informed, and per-

---

[4] C. Aguilar to Magaña, March 4, 1919, AZ, 30: 32. On Obregonista-Zapatista con-
tacts, see Octavio Magaña Cerda: *Yo acuso a los responsables, El pueblo que nos juzgue*
(México, 1961), pp. 26–34, and Hill to Obregón, April 20, 1919, cited in González
Ramírez: *Planes*, pp. 263–4. Zapata to Carranza, March 17, 1919, AZ, 30: 32, reprinted
in Palacios: *Zapata*, pp. 258–66. Statement of Gildardo Magaña, November 20, 1924,
AZ, 25: 3.

suasively argued, and it attracted the attention Gates wanted. In February he began a five-part series in the monthly *World's Work*. There, under the suggestive title "The Four Governments of Mexico," he elaborated his argument that Carranza was both tyrannical and weak and that his opponents represented the true yearnings of the Mexican people. In late February the editors of the *Literary Digest* summarized Gates's initial article, noting that only Zapata had the "honest intention" of returning land to "the Indians." And in delight or alarm Mexican editors gleaned the story from there and publicized it in their own papers. They also gave headlines to the news Palafox sent them that the Zapatistas had nominated Vázquez Gómez as Supreme Chief. For Carranza, Zapata had become a heavy liability. By mid-March the President was in a mood to approve the editorial his journalist friends quoted from *The New York Times*: "Order, the resumption of sugar planting, the sugar industry and agricultural work generally, the revival of communications, education, and peaceful life depend in Morelos upon the utter downfall, the permanent absence, or the extinction of ZAPATA. . . . he is beyond amnesty."[5]

So the Zapatistas had reason for a measured optimism. With Gates's advertisement, they remained even in defeat a significant faction in revolutionary politics. And if they held together and held out, according to their old strategy, they might soon witness Carranza's collapse and then after nearly a decade of struggle bring their local revolution into a triumph the new national leaders would recognize. In a spasm of last-minute precaution Magaña and the other secretaries and aides in Tochimilco wanted to suspend military operations, to avoid capture or death on the eve of success. They would go on dealing in words, as in the letter they wrote for Zapata to send to Gates thanking him for the "justice" done to the "Revolution of the South" and asking him to communicate with Vázquez Gómez for more publicity.[6] But they considered dealing in bullets too risky now. They urged Zapata simply to hide and wait until the crisis broke.

Zapata had other ideas. Having led his men in the field from the beginning, he could not understand why he should retire toward the end. The proposal went against his grain personally, and politically it involved

[5] William Gates: "Mexico To-day," *North American Review*, CCIX (January 1919), 68–83, and in *World's Work*, February–June 1919. "Mexico To-day a Storm-Center of Misery and Danger," *Literary Digest*, LX, 8 (February 22, 1919), 50–4. *The New York Times*, March 18, 1919. *Excélsior*, March 19, 1919.

[6] Zapata to Gates, March 24, 1919, AZ, 30: 32.

its own risks. Would not his disappearance provoke divisions among the other chiefs just when solidarity counted most? How could he keep the respect of Mendoza or Ayaquica or Saavedra, much less that of de la O, if they did not know for sure that he was still alive, if they could not see him or hear of him in combat? Besides, as he learned from his spies in Cuautla, an opportunity had recently come open for a sensational military coup in Morelos. The reports were of bitter discord between Pablo González and the best cavalry officer in the south, Colonel Jesús Guajardo, commander of the Fiftieth Regiment. In mid-March González had ordered Guajardo to operate against the Zapatistas in the mountains around Huautla. Hours later he had caught the handsome young officer carousing in a local cantina; Guajardo tried to duck out the back door, but González had had him tracked and arrested. Although Guajardo was devoutly loyal to González, although as a native Coahuilan he relished crushing the "Zapatista trash" (in his President's phrase), although he was locally famous for his avowed longing to test himself man to man with Zapata, González had had him jailed. The incident became a scandal. And at the news on March 21 Zapata had written a note for a courier to smuggle to Guajardo, inviting him to join "our troops, among which you will be received with due considerations."[7] Guajardo was back in the field now, punished, the spies said, but harboring a hot grudge against his general. The stakes in negotiating further with him were irresistible. If he and his regiment defected, the Zapatistas might again seize control in Morelos's main towns—just when, as in 1911, the national crisis opened. The arguments in Tochimilco for caution did not move Zapata. He would not treat with Guajardo at a distance or from a hiding place. Others at the headquarters could do as they pleased, but in late March he bid goodbye to the diplomats and secretaries there and in high hopes came back home into action in Morelos. "I remember him as if it had been yesterday," a young aide wrote nearly a decade later. "He was going with greater energy into the struggle, with new enthusiasm, like someone who knows he is going to finish a good job."[8]

In early April Zapata was killed. It happened in an ambush, plans for which were in train even as he returned to the state. The note he had sent to Guajardo had not reached him, but wound up instead on González's

[7] Zapata to Guajardo, March 21, 1919, AZ, 27: 14. For Guajardo's troubles, see "Carranza autorizó la muerte de Zapata, dice Pablo González," *Novedades,* October 28, 1942.

[8] Reyes Avilés: *Cartones,* pp. 45–6.

desk, and suggested to González a counter-plan. He would have Guajardo play along with Zapata until he could catch him dead or alive; if the latter, González would arrange a court-martial and public execution. González knew that by now Zapata presented a challenge to the government that death would not liquidate, however cleverly it came. But to let him roam brazenly around the countryside was to invite a worse challenge. The notices about Zapata in the American press, the news of the Zapatista commitment to Vázquez Gómez, the taunts in Zapata's open letter—this had incensed the President, and in recent conferences with him González had gathered how deeply Carranza would appreciate the elimination of his southern foe. Trapping and killing Zapata might discredit a regime already out of popular favor, but Carranza could also claim that the stroke proved his power and the futility of opposition.

In Cuautla in late March, with Zapata's letter to Guajardo, González set his scheme going. First he double-checked with Carranza. Then, officially authorized, he ordered Guajardo released and remanded to the Cuautla headquarters. There in a humiliating scene in the officers' dining room, he primed him for his instructions. After having him wait outside all through supper one evening, he ordered him in as he took coffee, asked the other officers and guests to leave, and then calmly accused his young colleague of being not only a drunken lout but also—a traitor. Zapata's letter he produced as proof! Guajardo, González merrily recalled twenty-odd years later, was stunned. He must have seen his whole career, not to say his life, about to end unjustly. He had taken a fine pride in his military talents: being jailed had genuinely hurt him, and the disgrace and doom he now groaned in was raw grief. González finally drove him to tears before he took pity and explained the plan to him. Helpless, Guajardo agreed and answered Zapata's letter. If Zapata promised him guarantees, he would bring over his men and supplies when the time was right.[9]

Now the feeling out began. On April 1 Zapata wrote again, agreeably surprised at Guajardo's ready compliance. The esteem he voiced for Guajardo's "convictions" and "firm ideas" was more than ritual flattery. There was a dashing, tough-dandy streak in the national officer that Zapata took a liking to. Tentatively he asked Guajardo to stage his mutiny the following Friday, April 4. For his first action he wanted him to arrest and hold for a revolutionary court-martial the only amnestied Zapatistas who had helped the nationals suppress their former comrades, Victoriano Bárcenas

[9] Guajardo to Zapata, n.d. (March 30, 1919?), AZ, 27: 14.

and his band, then in Jonacatepec. Guajardo replied immediately, promising deeds to match his reputation but giving a reasonable excuse for waiting a few days. A shipment of twenty thousand rounds of ammunition was due in Cuautla between April 6 and 10, he said, and he needed it before revolting. But escorting the shipment, as he did not say, would be González, then in conference with Carranza in the capital; most probably Guajardo feared to act without his chief around.[1]

Zapata graciously but insistently wrote back not to wait so long. He sent an aide, Feliciano Palacios, to Guajardo's base camp at Chinameca to report on the deal's progress. Palacios detected nothing suspicious, and assured Zapata that Guajardo was "very spirited and determined." Over five hundred men were at his orders, the aide disclosed, and properly munitioned and supported they ought to take Jonacatepec easily.[2] Zapata remained impatient, but accepted Guajardo's postponements.

By Monday, April 7, all was ready. The ammunition had arrived. González was back. And Zapata had received promises of other national defections and specified his battle orders against Jonacatepec, Tlaltizapán, and Jojutla. To divert attention from Morelos, Zapatistas attacked Cholula, Puebla, that day. That night in Cuautla Guajardo made his last preparations and the next morning finally declared himself in rebellion against the government. As he left Cuautla, a captive Zapatista free on bond there, Eusebio Jáuregui, sent Zapata another recommendation in his favor.[3]

Guajardo marched directly to Jonacatepec, as Zapata had ordered. There other national officers joined his bogus mutiny, and together on the morning of April 9 they occupied the town in Zapata's name. Keeping his agreement with Zapata, Guajardo arrested Bárcenas and his turncoats. But then he had them shot.[4]

Zapata had come with his escort to Pastor Station, a little train stop on the Interoceanic line south of Jonacatepec, to await Guajardo. His spies had picked up rumors of a trick, but Zapata restrained his suspicions. At

[1] Zapata to Guajardo, April 1, 1919, and Guajardo to Zapata, April 1, 1919, ibid. *Excélsior,* April 7, 1919.

[2] Zapata to Guajardo, April 2, 1919, AZ, 27: 14. Palacios to Zapata, April 3, 1919, AZ, 30: 36.

[3] Palacios to Zapata, April 7, 1919, ibid. Zapata to Guajardo, April 6, 1919, cited in Palacios: *Zapata,* pp. 273–5. *Excélsior,* April 9 and 10, 1919. Jáuregui to Zapata, April 8, 1919, AZ, 27: 14.

[4] Report of the events that ended in the death of Emiliano Zapata, March–April 1919, ibid. Salvador Reyes Avilés to Magaña, April 10, 1919, AZ, 30: 36.

the news from Jonacatepec he instructed Guajardo to come on. Their escorts were to be thirty men apiece. About 4:30 that afternoon the two met at Pastor—Zapata with thirty men, Guajardo with a column of six hundred and a machine gun. Zapata was nevertheless cordial, giving Guajardo an abrazo, congratulating him, and accepting the present of his prize horse, a sorrel known as the Golden Ace. Together they went on south a couple miles to Tepalcingo. Privately Zapata still had misgivings, and he tried several times through the evening to get Guajardo to join him at his quarters for supper with other Morelos chiefs—to press him and test him. The invitations were in vain. Guajardo begged off with a stomach ache, and finally asked to return that night to Chinameca, to make sure, he said, that González did not capture his stores of ammunition there. Zapata agreed: they would meet at Chinameca early the next morning and discuss their next move. Guajardo left, and Zapata spent the night at a camp in the hills on the way there. Reinforcements now accompanied him, 150 men in all, too many for Guajardo to try to capture him from.[5]

Shortly after dawn on April 10 Zapata and his escort were up and riding. This was Zapata's home ground. Chinameca hacienda lay along the Cuautla River barely thirty-five miles below Villa de Ayala. It was one of the first places he had seized after joining Madero in 1911. And as he recalled later in the day he had almost been trapped and killed there in that summer's crisis. Many times he had ridden these same country trails—as a young man, headed for markets or stock auctions, then for the last eight years as a rebel, revolutionary, and outlaw, hiding and hunting. He knew every path, creek, and fence. The countryside was cool and fresh in the early April morning. The rains and planting had already begun. In August he would be forty. Of his children he knew only the eldest, Nicolás, now thirteen; and he had hardly reared him. There was no omen about the day, a plain Thursday; dealing with Guajardo heightened the tension, but the basic strain of trust, fear, and hope was old and familiar. At about 8:30 in the morning he and his men came down out of the hills to Chinameca.

Outside the hacienda and backed against its front walls stood various shops, and in one Zapata and Guajardo conferred. Inside the walls Zapata's

[5] Palacios: *Zapata,* pp. 276–8. The base of this account is the notes of Adrián Castrejón, a chief in Zapata's escort. For Guajardo's Official Report to General Pablo González, Chief of the Corps of the Army of Southern Operations, April 14, 1919, see *El Universal,* April 16, 1919.

escort rested. But the talk of ammunition and attacks was soon interrupted by reports that nationals were in the area. Zapata quickly directed Guajardo to guard the hacienda, and then organized patrols from his own men and sent them out on reconnaissance. He himself led one patrol. Although there was no sign of the enemy, Zapata posted sentries and returned to the hacienda environs. It was 1:30 in the afternoon. Only Guajardo's troops were inside the walls now, except for the aide Palacios, who was in conference with Guajardo about collecting twelve thousand rounds from his cache of ammunition. Zapata waited. Invited in to join Guajardo for dinner and close the deal, Zapata chose to keep waiting. But as Guajardo's officers went on repeating the invitation, tacos and beer sounded better. The day had started early, and there had been a lot of rough riding. By two o'clock Zapata was growing impatient; finally at 2:10 he accepted. Mounting the sorrel Guajardo had given him the day before, he ordered ten men to come with him inside the hacienda gate.

"Ten of us followed him just as he ordered," a young aide at the scene reported to Magaña that evening. "The rest of the people stayed [outside the walls] under the trees, confidently resting in the shade with their carbines stacked. Having formed ranks, [Guajardo's] guard looked ready to do him the honors. Three times the bugle sounded the honor call; and as the last note died away, as the General in Chief reached the threshold of the door . . . at point blank, without giving him time even to draw his pistols, the soldiers who were presenting arms fired two volleys, and our unforgettable General Zapata fell never to rise again.

"The surprise was terrible," continued the aide in his report. "The soldiers of the traitor Guajardo, stationed . . . everywhere, nearly a thousand men, were firing on us. Soon resistance was useless. On one side we were a fist-full of men thrown into consternation by the loss of the Chief; and on the other side a thousand of the enemy . . . were taking advantage of our natural confusion to attack us furiously. . . . This was how the tragedy was." Killed also in the trap were Palacios—when the volleys cracked at the gate, his hosts inside shot him—and two others who rode in Zapata's last escort. The survivors fled for their lives down to Sauces, a camp a few miles south.[6]

They had had no chance to retrieve Zapata's body. Hardly had it hit

[6] Palacios: *Zapata*, pp. 279–82. Reyes Avilés to Magaña, April 10, 1919, AZ. Killed in the firing at the gate were two aides, Agustín Cortés and Lucio Bastida. Reported dead at first were Castrejón, Gil Muñoz Zapata, and Zeferino Ortega. They were, however, only wounded, as was Jesús Capistrán.

the ground when Guajardo's troops, on orders, ran out and pulled it inside the hacienda. Two hours later Guajardo had the body loaded on a mule and was nervously leading his column back toward Cuautla. About 7:30, as the evening of the murder began to darken the hills around, the column passed through Villa de Ayala, and someone telephoned the news ahead. At headquarters González found it almost too good to be true. Who could tell if Zapata had not reversed the trick, and was not now bringing in Guajardo's body, about to spring an attack on his would-be assassins? What if Guajardo had actually defected? González prepared his troops. But shortly after nine o'clock Guajardo's column arrived in Cuautla without incident. Out of the night from the south it filed into town, clopping and jingling past the cemetery and the Señor del Pueblo church, the front ranks pulling to a halt on Galeana street before a store facing the main plaza. González and his officers came out to see, and Guajardo had the body dumped onto the pavement. González aimed a flashlight at the face. It really was Zapata. Immediately González returned to his office and "with the highest satisfaction" wired Carranza that Guajardo had carried out "el movimiento preparado." And he recommended that Guajardo be promoted to brigadier general for his service. Amid noisy, shoving crowds, meanwhile, Zapata's body was carried to the local police station. There it was identified conclusively—Eusebio Jáuregui was a witness—and photographs were taken as proof.[7]

The next day giant red headlines broadcast the news in Mexico City. Minding their connections, Carrancista editors rejoiced at the finish of "the Famous Attila." For González, "this prestigious military man" to whom "the triumph frankly corresponds," they advocated "enthusiastic congratulations." Hopefully they saw the Republic "purged of a harmful element." Deliberately they repeated the official argument that the death of "the bloodthirsty ringleader" was the death of Zapatismo and "an important advance . . . toward the effective pacification of an important region of the country . . ." Journalists speaking for Obregón ran stories more spare and restrained, however. And in comments on "The Legend and the Man" the editors of *El Demócrata* were notably subdued in their congratulations to Guajardo, González, and the President. They referred only to "a strategem ably plotted and bravely carried out." Toward Zapata himself they were notably charitable. Although they denied him "great

[7] Report of the events . . . , March–April 1919, AZ. *Excélsior,* April 11, 12, and 14, 1919. Copy of the certificate of the identification of the corpse of Emiliano Zapata, April 11, 1919, AZ, 30: 36.

excellencies of genius and character," they did not condemn him as a bandit or badman. They granted that "he had taken in the consciousness of the natives the proportions of a myth." The pueblos had followed him, they explained, because he had given them "a formula of vindication against old offenses . . . which already existed latently and [which] his cry of insurrection did no more than condense in tempestuous storm-clouds." To destroy the myth of Zapata, they concluded, would require reforms to destroy the injustices that had generated him.[8]

In private the affair irked many established revolutionaries. Army officers especially resented the promotions coming to Guajardo and his partners in the plot. Some even complained to the President, and leaked their gripes to the press.[9] Other more generous revolutionaries plunged into the gloom of divided loyalties. A young aide in the government's General Supply Office, Jesús Romero Flores, later remembered the morning he read the reports. He and his superior, General Francisco Múgica, considered themselves "on the extreme left." As delegates to the 1916–17 Constitutional Convention, both had advocated radical articles on land, labor, and education; in swinging the votes to drive the reforms into the charter, Múgica had been the key figure in the key committee. Although in the early days in 1911 Múgica had once volunteered to fight Zapata, he had come through the years to admire his long and constant struggle. Besides, he could not deny his childhood friendship with the Magaña brothers—whose father had helped him through the Zamora seminary and later as an oppositionist newspaperman. Romero Flores also sympathized with the southern agraristas, and he too, another Michoacano, knew the Magañas. On learning of the assassination, he thought the times were "black." He and Múgica spent that Friday morning at their office "deeply moved, almost without speaking." This new death reminded him of the past winter's terrible flu epidemic, when "a feeling of sadness and fear seemed to envelop everything." When he read the government's boast of treachery, his depression burst into indignation against "the mob of wheeler-dealers" in power.[1]

---

[8] *Excélsior,* April 11 and 12, 1919. *El Universal,* April 11 and 12, 1919. *El Demócrata,* April 13, 1919.

[9] *El Universal,* April 16, 1919.

[1] Summerlin to the secretary of state, April 16, 1919, NA, 59: 812.504/176. Jesús Romero Flores: "Evocación luctuosa de Emiliano Zapata," *El Nacional,* April 10, 1956, and *La revolución,* p. 166. Armando de María y Campos: *Múgica. Crónica Biográfica* (México, 1939), pp. 12–16. Personal interview with O. Magaña. For Múgica's early gesture against Zapata, see Múgica to Madero, June 24, 1911, AM.

In Cuautla González spent Friday and Saturday arranging local publicity for the corpse. He even had movie cameras record the burial at the Cuautla cemetery Saturday evening. The spectacle, he reasoned, would dispel all doubts about whether it had been Zapata who had died—which would sap the surviving Zapatistas' resistance and discourage villagers from protecting them. Thousands, including Zapata's two sisters, came in from the surrounding pueblos to view the body. As these "humble people" filed up to the coffin and then for an instant paused and looked into it, they would, wrote an *Excélsior* reporter, "tremble from head to toe." What shivered them was probably not, as the eager reporter believed, fear of "the ringleader" but the horrifying surprise of their own guilt: years before they had located a man whom they asked to stand up for them, and he had stood up for them, and now they saw him dead. Beyond Cuautla the word spread around the state, and with it the shock of the loss. "It hurt me as much," a Tepoztecan remembered later, "as if my own father had died."[2]

On April 16 González published a manifesto to stop the mourning. "Zapata having disappeared, Zapatismo has died," he insisted. "Zapata was simply a gangster," he proclaimed in answer to the recent Obregonista editorial, and those who now tried to glorify him as "a martyr" were "unscrupulous politicians." Their inference that "the death of the man does not matter because ideas remain immortal"—this González pronounced an "enormous profanation!" And to prove that "no precise and high idea can subsist with [Zapata's] memory," he went on to ridicule the Plan de Ayala. It was hardly more than "a cry which Emiliano's followers were taught to repeat mechanically, to disguise with something their ignorance and naïveté . . . a gibberish of empty phrases and curses against científicos and political bosses which only reveals the vanity of thought of its authors . . ." At the end was a menacing invitation to pueblos that had been Zapatista to return to a peaceful life and no longer support the bandits. "The motto which from today forth will guide the acts of the government, without any vacillation whatever," González concluded, "is—for men of order and work, protection and guarantees; for troublemakers and rebels, inflexible and exemplary punishment."[3]

To González's dismay the shock of the assassination did not break the local spirit. As one anonymous vandal carved into a post in Cuernavaca's

[2] *Excélsior,* April 13, 1919. Lewis: *Pedro Martínez,* p. 108.
[3] *El Universal,* April 17, 1919.

Borda Gardens the day after the murder, "Rebels of the South it is better to die on your feet than to live on your knees."[4] Nor did the spectacular burial and the threats finally depress people. Like Romero Flores, the country folk of Morelos found themselves outraged. Many would not believe Zapata was dead. Odd stories began to circulate. One went that Zapata was too smart for the trap, and had dispatched a subordinate who resembled him to the fatal meeting. Anyway, it went on, the corpse on display was not Zapata's. Zapata had a mole on his right cheek, or a birthmark on his chest, or the end of the little finger on his roping hand missing—or something, anything, that González's exhibit did not have. In a few days the Chief would reappear as always. Then stranger reports were passed on. The horse he rode the day he died, the sorrel Guajardo had given him—it had been seen galloping riderless through the hills. People who saw it said it was white now, white as a star. And someone thought he had even glimpsed Zapata himself on it, alone, heading hard into the Guerrero mountains to the south. The belief that he had not died was a consolation, both for shame at not fighting any more and for anguish at having charged him with an impossible responsibility, having trusted him to death. But it was not a healing consolation. Among the rural families now laboring to hold on in the new order, the ache of sorrow persisted. After all, a doubtful, painful belief in the incredible was a way of staying loyal to the Chief even after he had gone.

Still, might making right, González's plan seemed to have worked well enough. His official control of Morelos remained steady. In the main towns the returning merchants and shopowners were too happy about peace to complain out loud, and the poor people there and in the villages around were under too close a guard to protest publicly, much less to riot. The general assumption was that the Zapatista organization would now go to pieces. As if to seal the episode, Carranza agreed to promote the officers and troops who had trapped Zapata. Guajardo not only ascended to brigadier general but also collected a fifty thousand-peso reward, part of which he honorably distributed among the men who had done the killing. Orders went out to federal authorities in Puebla to arrest Colonel Reyes, the mediator privy to many secrets, and now disposable.[5]

[4] Frank Tannenbaum: *Peace by Revolution. An Interpretation of Mexico* (New York, 1933), p. 139.

[5] Palacios: *Zapata*, pp. 285–7. Testimony of G. Magaña on behalf of E. Reyes, October 20, 1920, AZ, 30: 28.

The Zapatistas Inherit
Morelos

"It's family business."

T HE GREAT REVOLUTION MADERO started in 1910 took a full decade to end. At first a moderate movement, it might have subsided early in parliamentary wheeling and ministerial dealing. But the científicos feared the issue of compromise and let Huerta force the movement out of regular politics. In protest and rebellion the revolutionaries became legion, and militant. And in victory in 1914 only they stood in command, at odds only among themselves. But so tremendous were the popular energies aroused in the struggle that even the radical Constitution of 1917 provided no more than a tentative settlement. True, by then the revolution was over in substance. Except for Carranza the leading public figures were men unheard of or inconsequential seven years before. The army was new, as was almost all the bureaucracy. So were the schools, newspapers, and pride in the fatherland. Agriculture, the country's base, was in new hands. But having lead the movement this far, Carranza could not establish it as a regime. No bewhiskered landlord, no ex-Porfirian senator, no president who seemed at sixty as eightyish as Díaz, could bring the revolution into focus and fasten its spirit in an engaging cause. Throughout Carranza's administration the characteristic mood among the new national leaders was impatience verging on despair, disgust, and cynicism; even those who kept the official peace did so grudgingly. Not until a popular hero became president, not until ordinary men could trace the pattern of their own lives grandly magnified in the life of the chief, could the new leaders revive the people's hope in the revolution and re-enlist their commitment to it. If he did not emerge, the whole revolutionary enterprise might well fail. It was time for him in 1920.

In a quick revolt in the spring of that year Mexico's new leaders consolidated their holdings and overthrew Carranza. And there the popular hero was, tough, cunning, fleshier than in his days at war but still as alert as ever, dapper now in a three-piece suit and watch chain, his retreating forelock slicked down smooth, a right arm missing, and a habitual look on his face of pain and tension, yet always cracking jokes—Álvaro Obregón. Like the crisis of 1910, the 1920 crisis was about succession and therefore involved only the highest politicians. The streets singers described it nicely:

> The People are very calm
> As they watch this fuss and mess.
> They say very calmly,
> "It's family business."[1]

But unlike the earlier crisis, it did not trigger a national collapse. And although the shift of control was slight, it was nevertheless momentous. When Obregón achieved the presidency, the Mexican revolution resumed its true direction.

In Obregón's drive revolutionaries in Morelos played parts decisively important for the state. On the choices they made as officials or fugitives to resist, ignore, tolerate, or join him depended the choice he would make of whom to favor and whom to thwart there afterward. And on this choice depended the kind of party that would then work as the local wing of the national revolutionary movement. Through 1919 and into early 1920 no authority in Morelos was Obregonista, within or outside the law. But as they all maneuvered for positions in the 1920 showdown, they prepared unawares for a crucial rendezvous.

The orders prevailing in Morelos through 1919 remained Constitutionalist, coming ultimately from Carranza or González. Although on June 20 González moved his headquarters from Cuautla to Puebla City, the commanders he left in the state were his firmest partisans, generals like

[1] Cited in Simmons: op. cit., pp. 162–3.

Francisco Cosío Robelo, Estanislao Mendoza, Fortunato Zuazua, and Salvador González, northerners mostly, and devout Pablistas. In a new wrinkle of Constitutionalist reform their direct political agents were no longer northern staff officers but natives of Morelos, natives not seen there since 1913 but at least natives originally. These were the old Leyvistas, returning from oblivion to perform in office again. On June 17 in Cuautla Benito Tajonar had moved provisionally back into the governor's chair he had lost six years before. And moving into humbler posts around the state were his moldier counterparts, some recently returned from Mexico City, Puebla, or Guerrero, and others resurrected from a once healthy but now unnecessary local seclusion.[2] But their native roots were no base of independence. To the federal government, Morelos was legally still in the suspended status it had been in since 1913. The present civil officials all served on appointments—even elective authorities like the municipal presidents, which Carranza himself named in the old district seats and which Tajonar named in the other towns and villages. Supervising their bureaucratic operations was González's aide, the former governor and new lieutenant governor, Colonel Aguilar. No plans were announced for the election of a legislature or a regular governor. The revolution that ensued was thus no local growth but a transplant, another happy collaboration of patrons and protégés.

A week after his inauguration Tajonar proclaimed his intentions in a manifesto "to the inhabitants of Morelos." His mission, he said, was "to try for the resurgence of this our state to the prosperous life, to the greatness it always had, . . . its reconstruction in general." The attempt would be difficult, he admitted, because "bad sons of the state had led it astray . . . , duping its good faith, fooling its longing for liberty, and exploiting that faith of true believers"; but by "the Constitutionalist ideal" he promised "harmonization and . . . reorganization." His particular interest, he emphasized, was "social improvement." And to manage it he offered not "a program" but four "measures." In fiscal affairs he proposed "a policy of conciliation tending to the perfect harmonization between capital and tax." In juridical matters he proposed to end "every prejudice . . . and every personal influence" and "to fulfill to satisfaction this desire of the people, who have been hungry for justice." In politics he took his inspiration from "the proceedings initiated by General Pablo González, [which] will tend to prepare properly the town councils in the state to enter into

2 S. Valverde: op. cit., pp. 233, 236.

the exercise of their autonomous liberty." But "all my attention" he proposed to dedicate to public schools: "the enlightenment of the people" being "my principal desire," he declared, "I will spare no effort or sacrifice whatever to fight . . . illiteracy, the origin of our material and collective backwardness and the single cause of the formation of tyrannical and despotic governments." And he vowed to prevent "astute clericalism" from infiltrating into the schools, though "by this," he assured his subjects, he meant no "red-radical liberalism." Finally he made "a formal call to all Morelenses without any distinction" to help him raise "this our unfortunate state, like the Phoenix bird, from its ashes to be again what it always has been, great, strong, and respected." To "irredentist Morelenses, to those who perdure in the unhealthy labor of irreducibles," he made a special call to stop "their rebel attitude" and cooperate in "the reconstructive work." The reason González had appointed him came out in his concluding cry for allegiance as "a son of the state, a brother of yours."

Garbled, obscure, repetitive, and contradictory, Tajonar's manifesto proved a reliable guide to his administration. He took his first action three days after he took office. To restore the state treasury, "the touchstone and fundamental base" of his government, he decreed a General Fiscal Law—which was, only slightly amended, the General Fiscal Law that Escandón's legislature had passed in May 1910. This, he declared, "fulfills to satisfaction the end which is pursued."[3]

But meanwhile, in contempt of Tajonar, González, and Carranza, the Zapatista chiefs remained in the field. Steeped in the experience of Zapata's chieftainship, in the memory of his down-to-earth constancy through the years, they had borne the shock of his death and commenced a remarkable effort to carry on as before. Five days after the assassination another manifesto had issued from a Zapatista camp in Morelos "to the Mexican people." It was a profession of "a triple task: to consummate the work of the reformer, to avenge the blood of the martyr, to follow the example of the hero." Recalling how the struggle for Independence had gone on after the deaths of Father Hidalgo and General Morelos, it was also a declaration that "the oppressed multitudes" of the Republic had already accepted "the saving principle of the division of lands" and that when they triumphed, which was "only a question of time," they would transform "all Mexicans . . . from slaves into rebels and from pariahs deformed by worldly servitudes into free men, worthy of the respect of History."

[3] *Periódico Oficial del Estado de Morelos,* 3rd Ser., No. 1, pp. 1–4.

And in the concluding dedication it was a renewal "before the Mexican Nation [of] our oaths of fidelity to the cause." The last words came almost in chokes, in which nine years of fatigue, grief, frustration, and despair gushed out in defiance, in a rancid warning that "we will fight to the end against Carranza's outrageous dictatorship, immoral and corrupt, more shameless than that of Porfirio Díaz, more lying and machiavellian than that of Francisco [León] de la Barra, more imbecilic and hypocritical than that of Huerta, the assassin." Signing in an impressive display of solidarity were thirty-four major and minor chiefs and secretaries—Magaña first, then Mendoza, Jesús Capistrán, Pedro Saavedra, Ayaquica, de la O, and other veterans.[4]

The Zapatistas' defiance was more than verbal. Because of the popular disgust and guilt over Zapata's death, they went on receiving protection, supplies, and information from country folk. And in the weeks after the assassination, with local clandestine help, they even mounted terrorist reprisals against civil and military authorities. Army officers especially felt "tracked and hunted" like animals in these "mysterious aggressions." In Jojutla one night Zapatista terrorists shot and almost killed the municipal president, who prudently retired to Mexico City for treatment.[5]

Far from ceasing resistance, the Zapatista chiefs were most interested in who would lead it. During the summer they went through a succession crisis of their own. For them the stakes were immense—the mantle of Zapata himself, the right to determine Zapatista strategy in the coming uproar over the presidency, the command of southern defense in an American intervention, the rewards of final victory. And out of responsibility and ambition the chiefs rubbed each other's feelings raw. But they never broke up, much less fell to fighting among themselves. From start to finish their crisis remained "family business" too—how to bring the brood home right.

The main contenders for the leadership were Magaña and Mendoza, representing deeply different strategies. At forty-eight Mendoza was the oldest of the surviving Zapatista generals. A true warrior, he had served actively at the head of his forces since April 1911. The hardest southern campaigns had been his heydays: peace, for other chiefs a time to return to civil concerns, was for him a time to expand and strengthen his battalions. Although he had acquired aides and secretaries for his correspond-

---

[4] Manifesto to the Mexican People, April 15, 1919, AZ, 30: 36.
[5] *El Demócrata*, April 25, 1919.

ence, and although they gave him political advice, he had no serious political contact with other revolutionary or reactionary camps. What he cared about now as before was combat, and what he always stood ready for was a battle or a getaway. For Mendoza to take charge of the movement was ultimately to preserve its integrity and its isolation. His secretaries might manage negotiations and maybe even a deal, but they could not guarantee that he would long honor it or use it to good advantage; and the movement would continue out of whack. That Zapatista authority should devolve upon the now twenty-eight-year-old Magaña, however, would be a change of powerful consequence. For not only would the diplomatic dealings he and Zapata had started certainly continue, but as a politician of rare talent and many intimate connections in Mexico's new ruling class he was also much more likely than Zapata or any other Zapatista chief to sense the balance of the deals he made, to keep them in effect, and to get maximum benefits from them for his constituents. Of all the Zapatistas, Magaña was the man to bind the native revolution in Morelos into a new national regime.

The contest began in confusion immediately on Zapata's death. That very evening, when the aide who had seen the assassination sent his official report to Magaña in Tochimilco, he had implicitly recognized Magaña's claim. The next day, however, the aide sent an official report to Mendoza as well. Observing that "the [Zapatista] troops of the state of Morelos remain . . . without a chief," he explicitly recommended that Mendoza take provisional command of them at once and call a junta for the election of a new chief. "Given that you are the senior general and of merits well recognized," he wrote to Mendoza, "I expect that all the compañeros will accept this ruling."[6] Another complication was a note from Mejía to Mendoza to assemble the Morelos chiefs in Tochimizolco "so that reunited we might agree on something . . ."

Magaña moved quickly to secure his claim. On April 14 in a meeting at Tochimilco he and Ayaquica and their underlings agreed that "as soon as possible" a general junta should take place for "a definitive accord" on a new commander in chief, and that until then local chiefs should operate in their usual zones and the Tochimilco headquarters would "go on functioning . . . as when Zapata was alive." The next day Magaña dispatched circulars to the various chiefs asking them to join him "as quickly as you can," or to send "a duly authorized subordinate." On April 17 Mejía wrote

[6] S. Reyes Avilés to Mendoza, April 11, 1919, AZ, 30: 36.

again to Mendoza, stressing the "highest urgency" of the junta and begging him and his chiefs to come to Tochimizolco "at the latest on the 21st."[7]

Mendoza would not acquiesce. Although he indicated he would attend the junta, he kept postponing the trip. Entrenched in his camp at San Miguel Ixtlilco, a tiny hamlet on the Morelos-Puebla border south of Tepalcingo, he did not even send apologies. At first he may have dallied from fear of going into the zone of Ayaquica, his oldest and most jealous rival, or from trouble in assembling the Morelos chiefs, or from simple boredom with the formalities of succession.[8] But the delay worked conveniently in his favor to dissipate Magaña's institutional authority. And by early May it was clearly a deliberate balk, practically a mutiny. On May 5 Magaña saw fit to remind Mendoza that until the election of a new chief the Tochimilco headquarters remained "the superior office of the Liberating Army," as before Zapata's death. And on May 7 he issued another circular publicizing that Vázquez Gómez had just accepted the appointment as Jefe Supremo of the Revolutionary Union, asking for new pledges of allegiance to him, and repeating the request for nominations of candidates for Zapatista commander in chief.[9] But Mendoza went on independently. Chiefs close to him corresponded directly with Vázquez Gómez, notifying him of Zapata's death and asking him for orders on succession.[1] Mendoza himself would not answer the May 7 circular, which would have implied recognizing Magaña at least as a mediating agent with Vázquez Gómez. Nor would he nominate a candidate for the chieftainship or name a delegate to the general junta. And joining him now was Mejía, who three weeks before had urged him to stay in line.

Among other Morelos chiefs Magaña still had strong support. On May 17 Jesús Capistrán replied to the circular, recognizing Vázquez Gómez and nominating Magaña for commander in chief. Five other chiefs close to Capistrán shortly did the same. And on May 23 Magaña deftly promoted his own candidacy in yet another circular insisting that "now more than ever we must stay united" and that Zapata had always regarded internal disputes as "treason to the cause." If the Zapatistas could not hold together, he hinted darkly, they would drift into camps where

---

[7] Circular, April 15, 1919, and Mejía to Mendoza, April 17, 1919, ibid.

[8] Magaña to Mendoza, April 15 and 17, 1919, ibid. Soto y Gama to Mendoza, May 4, 1919, AZ, 30: 35.

[9] Magaña to Mendoza, May 5 and 7, 1919, ibid.

[1] Joaquín Camaño and others to F. Vázquez Gómez, May 5, 1919, ibid.

agrarianism counted for little. The appeal again was for a speedy junta.[2]

But as Magaña moved toward taking control, he galvanized the opposition. Mejía was blatantly against him now. Never steady or reticent, dubbed "el mulato" for his passion, Mejía had become even more erratic since his uncle's death. Through mid-May he excited hesitant chiefs to dissent and dissident chiefs to protest. And on May 25 from his camp in Axochiapan they sent a formal declaration to Magaña that "in our humble opinion this call [for a junta] is premature and impracticable . . ." Their reason was feeble: too many fugitive chiefs were busy in military "operations" for a majority to attend Magaña's junta (though not the one they were at), and a vote from less than a majority would be invalid and divisive. But a poor excuse was better than none, enough anyway to introduce a demand that Magaña resign most of his secretarial prerogatives. Although the Tochimilco headquarters would remain as before in organization and personnel, the oppositionists now wanted Magaña to consult with "the principal chiefs of our army" on "all affairs of vital importance." Specifically they wanted "notification of all the correspondence received in those offices, both from the Jefe Supremo . . . and from the compañeros who head other armies in different regions of the country, as well as a copy of the answer which is given to each." The first signatures were Mejía's and Mendoza's. But even Capistrán signed, probably in fear of an open split in the movement if he did not help postpone a decision.[3]

Magaña relented, as few other secretaries would have. Rather than force the issue, he resolved to wait—especially in view of the national conflicts that developed after Obregón announced his presidential candidacy on June 1. In a manifesto proclaimed from Sonora Obregón did not merely deny Carranza's claim to pick his successor, but also radically and ingeniously redefined the terms of the national political struggle. The gist was that only two parties had ever existed in Mexico, the liberal and the conservative, "of tendencies diametrically opposed." At present only one party was active, the liberal: "its tendencies are advanced, but it is divided into an infinity of groups which vary among themselves only in details . . ." But the conservatives were angling to recover power, in the persons of revolutionaries who had betrayed their principles. The current political contest

[2] Capistrán to headquarters, May 17, 1919, and Z. Ortega, B. Abúndez, V. Aranda, F. Alarcón, and F. P. Saavedra to headquarters, May 19, 1919, ibid. Circular, May 23, 1919, ibid.

[3] Mejía and others to Magaña, May 25, 1919, ibid.

was therefore no trivial tilt between rival aspirants for the presidency but a climactic test in which all true revolutionaires had to pull together to save their common triumph and finally secure its establishment. Strongly implied in this argument was an appeal for support from those revolutionaries who among "an infinity of groups" happened still to languish outside the law. The Zapatistas obviously figured in the liberal movement Obregón proposed to rally. For in condemning conservatives who paid off "hatchetmen" and increased "the number of martyrs, . . . always the best fuel for inflaming the bonfire of popular wrath," he pointed straight at Carranza and González and honored the memory of the victim of Guajardo. Magaña took real hope from the manifesto, which he urged Amezcua to publicize in Cuba.[4] If he could avoid an intramural feud in Morelos, convince observers elsewhere that the Zapatistas were still in business, and keep his own political fences mended, he would at least maintain the possibility of a national deal in the difficult months to come.

Without a challenge on his own ground Mendoza now acted as Zapatista commander in chief. Encouraging him in his presumption was his secretary, Arturo Deloy, an obscure young man who evidently came from Puebla City and had once been an aide to Palafox. Through June Deloy started independent correspondence with neighboring chiefs to report the maneuvers of one to another, as if he were now to coordinate Zapatista operations. On June 13 Mendoza took it upon himself to attack a refractory hamlet near his camp, killing all the inhabitants and burning all the houses. On June 30, to strengthen villages loyal to him against incursions from other chiefs, he confirmed their right to arm for self-defense. And when Pablo González published a manifesto to the pueblos in his zone warning them not to hide fugitive Zapatistas, the "counter-manifesto" issued not from Tochimilco but from San Miguel Ixtlilco. In mid-July Mendoza accused Ayaquica of trying to suborn his chiefs and of abusing pueblos in his own zone, and almost attacked him. Only the most amenable responses from Ayaquica and Magaña staved off ruinous hostilities.[5]

In this confusion and suspense national leaders of opposition saw an alluring opportunity. For them the Zapatista movement was now fair game. Although its military value was scant, for its name alone it was a

---

[4] For the manifesto, see Luis N. Ruvalcaba, ed.: *Campaña Política del C. Álvaro Obregón, Candidato a la Presidencia de la República, 1920–1924*, 5 vols. (México, 1923), I, 40–59. Magaña to Amezcua, June 24, 1919, AZ, 30: 34.

[5] Cháverri Matamoros in *La Prensa,* October 1, 4, 8, and 9, 1935. Ayaquica and Magaña to Mendoza, July 22, 1919, AZ, 30: 39.

political prize, the winning of which would enhance the eminence and credit of any presidential hopeful—immediately for those outside the law, in 1920 for those still inside. And over the summer complicated intrigues evolved to subsume the movement, or at least a tractable rump. Few overtures evidently went to Magaña, the shrewdest negotiator. But for the other Zapatistas the temptations to accept alien direction grew.

From early July on de la O received Obregonista notes at his camp at Tepeite in the mountains north of Cuernavaca. The sender, Colonel Aurelio Calvo, was an escapee from the Mexico City penitentiary hiding out on Mount Ajusco. Whether he operated initially on orders or on his own is still the Obregonistas' secret, but it was wise for them to have an understanding with the chief who remained capable of cutting the Mexico City-Cuernavaca railroad. Although Calvo was very tentative in his approach, he patently had not come as a fugitive himself to persuade de la O to recognize Carranza. Although de la O was suspicious, he did not discourage the contact.[6]

The most formidable bid for the movement came from Manuel Peláez, still the rebel boss around Tampico. To compete on a national scale with his main rival in rebellion, Félix Díaz, Peláez needed allies and adherents in the south, and since the previous September he had bargained for Zapatista support. Although Zapata had then refused him, Peláez had not fouled his chances for a deal later: when Palafox had come to his camp around the turn of the year, the greeting Peláez gave "that Iscariot was completely disrespectful."[7] By mid-1919, having reassigned Caraveo to Chihuahua, leaving Higinio Aguilar as his lone partisan in southern Puebla, Peláez needed support in the south even more badly than before, and he looked again to the Zapatistas. As agents to advance his proposition among them he had Aguilar and his agents in Puebla City and Izúcar de Matamoros. And as a sponsor to recommend him he had the notorious, at least erstwhile Zapatista, who now after Zapata's death was useful and welcome in his camp—Manuel Palafox. Since mid-April Palafox had been writing to Zapatistas on the fringe, urging them not to give up or go Felicista.[8] And in June he had sent out a circular to the chiefs in Morelos and Puebla, declaring that he was in the Oaxaca mountains on a mission

[6] De la O in *Impacto*, January 21, 1950.

[7] C. Aguilar to Magaña, March 4, 1919, AZ.

[8] Palafox to Sabás Crispín Galeana, April 15, 1919, AZ, 27: loose documents. Galeana currently operated around Tlapa, Guerrero, where he cooperated with local Felicistas. See Liceaga: op. cit., p. 523.

for the dead Zapata and asking for his old comrades' aid. Magaña had alertly tried to check this subversion. In a long circular of his own he repeated the unsavory story of Palafox's severance from headquarters and blasted his claim to Zapata's confidence.[9] But the squelch was not definitive. As Palafox no doubt explained when he returned to Peláez's camp about this time, the reluctance of the Morelos chiefs to recognize Magaña as commander allowed a strange bedfellowship between Magaña's old and new rivals. And in Palafox Peláez had the best man to play on the chiefs' weaknesses. Through him ran the best odds for Peláez to garner not only individual Zapatistas' declarations of allegiance but also the national Zapatista title of Jefe Supremo still reserved for the exiled Vázquez Gómez.

The Pelaecista intrigue began in late July with a frosty letter from Peláez to Magaña. Politely but firmly Peláez disapproved of the Zapatista commitment to Vázquez Gómez, argued that revolutionaries should not make nominations for Jefe Supremo until they had achieved a "material unification" of operations in the field, and lastly, delaying that union, postponed financial and military aid to the Zapatistas.[1] He might as well have asked Magaña how much Zapatista recognition cost. A thinly veiled ultimatum, the letter paralyzed Magaña diplomatically.

On July 25 Aguilar's agent in Izúcar extended a Pelaecista feeler directly to Mendoza's camp. To Deloy the agent passed on Palafox's regards and a notice that Peláez had ordered Palafox into the south "to see the chiefs and to organize forces and give them supplies for war and also to let [our] people know that he is about to start giving them salaries." From Peláez the agent relayed a promise "to give you everything you need." Deloy was to reply to Palafox arranging a conference where they could settle the details.[2]

From San Miguel Ixtlilco the response was a cautious encouragement. On July 29 the newly promoted General Deloy answered Palafox, asking what he proposed. And on August 4 Mendoza wrote to Peláez's personal agent in the south, Federico Córdova, to learn when and where Peláez would send the promised supplies. Neither Deloy nor Mendoza evidently informed Magaña of their dealings. Nor evidently were other chiefs involved.

The Palaecistas promptly pressed the courtship, each trying his special

[9] Circular, June 30, 1919, AZ, 30: 34.
[1] Peláez to Magaña, July 22, 1919, AZ, 30: 39.
[2] Cháverri Matamoros in *La Prensa*, October 8, 1935.

line. On August 10 Palafox disclosed in a long letter to Deloy that he wanted "to unify the Southern elements" to carry on the agrarian struggle. In a crackling tirade he told why the movement had foundered, revealing as he wrote the still fresh pain of his own jealousies, disappointments, and grudges. Zapata had liked "good horses, fighting cocks, flashy women, card games, and intoxicating liquors" too dearly, he snapped, to lead the movement as he should have. After 1914, he charged, Zapata lapsed into a "lethargy of inactivity . . . The dead leader's energies and aptitudes disappeared because of the excess of vice which he sustained with 22 women, for if he had no time to attend to that many skirts, less time still he had to attend to the revolutionary affairs of the South." And in the following machinations, he ranted, Magaña had seized power at headquarters, caused divisions and disunion, and almost had him assassinated—which was why he had fled. Vázquez Gómez came in for some of Palafox's vitriol too, as a figure whom "no revolutionary of prestige" considered important, a has-been whom Magaña alone supported. Palafox's conclusion was an appeal to shift Zapatista loyalty to his version of the Ayala plan and presumably his choice for Jefe Supremo. In a postscript he urged Deloy to remind Mendoza of "the offenses" Zapata had given him. Less invidiously Federico Córdova suggested only more effort at togetherness and the election of "a good jefe," either Felipe Ángeles or Manuel Peláez. In September, he wrote to Mendoza, Peláez himself would arrive in the south "with elements sufficient for the development of operations in these regions." Meanwhile Aguilar's local agents went on reporting to Deloy.[3]

But through August the intrigue failed. In the end neither Deloy nor Córdova nor Aguilar nor Palafox could entice Mendoza to break with the local movement he had soldiered for so long. If he would not truckle to Magaña, by now one of the clan, much less would he front for Peláez, a perfect outlander. In reply to Palafox on August 20 Deloy demurred at pledging Mendoza to collaborate with him. He granted that the old Ayala plan needed reform and that Palafox's version might satisfy "some revolutionary agraristas," but he insisted on the dangers of dissension in the movement—which, he hinted, Palafox would aggravate. "All my work with General Francisco Mendoza," he wrote, taking his cue from his chief, "is for union." Although Aguilar's spies continued their reports to Deloy, the Pelaecista correspondence stopped.[4]

[3] Ibid., October 4, 7, and 8, 1935. Córdova to Mendoza, August 14, 1919, AZ, 30: 3.
[4] Cháverri Matamoros in *La Prensa,* October 4, 8, and 9, 1935.

Magaña now moved to resolve the crisis, calling in late August for a general junta on September 2. To reassure the Morelos chiefs, he specified the place of meeting as Capistrán's camp at Huautla. And this time agreement came astonishingly easy. At Huautla the junta opened on the day announced. Despite national patrols, over thirty chiefs attended with their escorts and staffs. Among them were de la O's delegation from Tepeite and the contingent from Tochimilco, including Magaña, Ayaquica, and Soto y Gama in person; Mejía and Mendoza did not attend, but their lieutenants did. The debates went quickly. And on September 4, exactly twenty-one trying weeks after Zapata's death, the assembled veterans voted to elect a new commander in chief. Representing the various factions, tendencies, and zones in the movement were five candidates—Timoteo Sánchez, Mejía, de la O, Capistrán, and Magaña. In the balloting the first three collected one vote each, Capistrán got eleven, and Magaña won with a majority of eighteen. So free was the election that four of Ayaquica's group voted for Capistrán and three for Magaña; all of Mejía's and Mendoza's chiefs voted for Magaña. The electors then swore to respect the majority's decision. Formally Magaña was now Zapata's successor.[5]

He arranged immediately for publicity, to convince absent dissenters to accept him and to proclaim the Zapatistas' re-entrance into national politics. The official manifesto was issued on September 5, composed by Soto y Gama and a young aide, Carlos Reyes Avilés. "The Revolution of the South has just taken a great step," they declared, exuding relief. "It has just obtained a beautiful result, more important than a hundred victories on the fields of battle, by coming to agreement on the election of a General in Chief, of a military as well as a political director." This accord, the happy secretaries wrote, was proof that Zapata's death had not left the cause "disorganized, like a body without a head." On the contrary, they raved, "the South goes on as before the death of its leader, an organized movement, which, guided by high ideals, strong through union and conscious of its goals, marches without hesitation toward its noble object: the emancipation of the country folk through the conquest of the land." Of course, they tactfully admitted for the sake of Mendoza and the other old chiefs, Magaña was no Zapata. But by craft of policy, they suggested, he could do what the dead chief had done by force of personality. Anyhow, they insisted, recognition of the Huautla vote would be the best expression of the principles Zapata had taught. "This is the greatest desire of the under-

[5] Magaña to Mejía, September 2, 1919, AZ, 30: 38. Record of the Huautla junta, September 4, 1919, ibid.

signed," Soto y Gama and his aide concluded in memoriam, "that on congratulating their brothers on the triumph achieved, they exhort them to follow in every detail the example, the lessons of honor, seriousness, and firmness, and the glorious road which our already immortal Emiliano Zapata left marked for us."[6]

In particular Magaña addressed conciliatory appeals to Mendoza. Still sore, the old man replied to headquarters on September 10 that "various chiefs" had informed him of their dissastisfaction with the Huautla junta and that he would not endorse its decision until the other dissenters agreed to.[7] Magaña persisted, however, in requesting his support. And he assumed authority over former guerrilleros, mainly from Mendoza's forces, accusing them of abusing pacificos in the pueblos they had retired to, and ordering them to report to headquarters for licenses to bear arms.[8] Capistrán also worked to placate the old man. And on September 24 Mendoza gave in. Convinced, he said, of Magaña's "noble principles and fine qualities," forswearing "ambition and perfidy," and consoling himself in the thought that "history will give to each man the prize which belongs to him," he formally recognized Magaña as "general in chief."[9]

Yet dissension continued, for Mendoza still protected Mejía and Mejía still intrigued. Although no evidence has clarified whether Mejía communicated with Peláez, Palafox, or Córdova, he suspiciously kept maligning Vázquez Gómez as Jefe Supremo and claimed connections with Aguilar and Cirilo Arenas. Decrying the vote of the Huautla junta, he went on stressing the differences among Zapatista chiefs after most were ready for renewed solidarity. He even tried once, on entering Huautla and finding Capistrán and his lieutenant gone, to raise the pueblo in revolt against its chief. Only a delay by the local citizens foiled Mejía: Capistrán returned in time to scare him off and prevent a scandal that would have been gravely embarrassing.[1] So provocative had Mejía become that another veteran, Adrián Castrejón, implied to Magaña that he should have him shot. ". . . it is very opportune to treat this affair seriously," he declared in the only lucid sentence in a barely literate letter, "and once and for all take

[6] Manifesto to the Revolutionaries of the South, September 5, 1919, ibid.

[7] Magaña to Mendoza, September 5 and 7, 1919, and Mendoza to Magaña, September 10, 1919, ibid.

[8] Circular to municipal presidents, September 20, 1919, ibid.

[9] Capistrán to Mendoza, September 20, 1919, and Mendoza to Magaña, September 24, 1919, ibid.

[1] Capistrán to Magaña, September 29, 1919, ibid.

the measures most convenient to avoid greater disturbances in the future."[2] But the trouble was too complex for Magaña to settle violently. The assassination of Mejía would parallel the assassination of his uncle, would corroborate the government's propaganda about Zapatista disintegration, and might drive Mendoza back into open independence.

Finally the squabbling came to a close, in the peaceful and personal way Magaña liked. The key was a letter Capistrán sent to Mendoza in late September, a long, handwritten plea, riddled with misspellings but eloquent in its earnest, deliberate style, for Mendoza to accept for good the Huautla vote. He had heard news, Capistrán declared, that Mendoza had balked again at Magaña's succession—"which if true will carry us to ruin, nullifying us as revolutionaries and making the sacrifice of nine years sterile for our suffering and beloved people." Capistrán comfortingly reported to his "distinguished friend and companion" how the delegates at the junta considered him "one of the old chiefs who are left to us, one whom we love and respect," and how they had taken his views into account in their decision. On the election Capistrán was most persuasive. "As an honorable man and as a sincere coreligionary, I assure you," he said, "that [it] was carried out in absolutely legal form." There were no threats, no carbines aimed to force a signature. "Do you believe it possible that we might admit an imposition of that nature?" The "entire world is watching us," he insisted, "to see if we are worthy to continue the grandiose work begun by the most honorable and greatest patriot which Mexico has produced since the venerable Father Miguel Hidalgo y Costilla launched the cry of liberty for our beloved Fatherland." He wanted an interview to talk out misunderstandings. Frankly he asked Mendoza "to pay no attention to those who for their own ambitions try to fool you to the prejudice of all." Bluntly he blamed Mejía for the current contention. The next day, complaining to Magaña about Mejía's shenanigans in his zone, he suggested the orders he wanted if Mendoza would not rein Mejía in: he had his people mobilized, he said, and ready for an expedition.[3] But on Capistrán's appeal Mendoza came around. A week later, having discussed the local trouble at length, the two chiefs wrote to headquarters expressly condemning Mejía's intrigues. Their note was a clear and definitive recognition of Magaña's leadership, and Mejía shut up. In reply Ayaquica

---

[2] Castrejón to Magaña, September 24, 1919, ibid.

[3] Capistrán to Mendoza, September 28, 1919, and to Magaña, September 29, 1919, ibid.

and Magaña indicated to Mendoza that they would stifle intrigues in their camp against him.[4]

Now in fact the Zapatistas' succession crisis was over, six months after it had begun. And thanks to Magaña, their organization had survived intact. With the authority of experience he called for national "integration and concord" in a triumphant mid-October Manifesto to the Revolutionaries of the Republic. For provisional president he again proposed the Zapatistas' Jefe Supremo, Francisco Vázquez Gómez—"a man calm and unruffled, a civilian and not a belligerent, neutral in the midst of regional or factional differences," a man who would "harmonize discrepancies."[5] As he described Vázquez Gómez's virtues, Magaña described his own. The local reunion he had managed was no betrothal, but neither was it a deal in bad faith and only for the moment. In touching each nervous chief so as to move him, in bringing them all to agree, in coaxing a consensus, he had proved that even without Zapata they could trust each other. And together, since González still could not catch them, they remained a considerable factor in local and national revolutionary politics.[6]

Through the fall this trust became immediately vital to the Zapatistas. For maturing then was the international crisis dreaded in Mexico since the war ended in Europe, a direct challenge from the United States. Precipitating it was the disappearance on October 19 of the U.S. consular agent in Puebla City, William O. Jenkins.[7] Two days later Federico Córdova informed the American embassy that he had kidnapped Jenkins on orders from Peláez, to demonstrate the Carrancistas' inability to police even major cities. On October 26 Jenkins reappeared safe and sound. The case might have closed there: despite raging from Jenkins and his friends in the U.S. Congress, the formal U.S. reaction from Secretary of State Lansing was eminently mild. But Carranza, who had just introduced his candidate into the presidential campaign, chose to represent the case to inflate his prestige. Under his auspices Puebla officials soon charged that the

---

[4] Capistrán, Mendoza, and P. Casals R. to Magaña, October 6, 1919, AZ, 30: 4. Ayaquica to Mendoza, October 10, 1919, and Magaña to Mendoza, October 12, 1919, ibid.

[5] Manifesto to the Revolutionaries of the Republic, October 15, 1919, ibid.

[6] *Excélsior,* October 21 and 29, 1919.

[7] Ibid., October 20, 1919. For a discussion of this incident from a diplomatic perspective, see Charles C. Cumberland: "The Jenkins Case and Mexican-American Relations," *Hispanic American Historical Review,* XXXI, 4 (November 1951), 586–607. Unless otherwise noted, the subsequent quotes from Mexican and American officials come from this article.

American agent has connived in his own abduction to discredit Carranza, which implied that Carranza was so strong he annoyed the United States, that opposition to him was now tantamount to treason, that the Carrancistas were the only firm guarantors of national sovereignty. On November 15 Jenkins was arrested and held briefly for questioning. The United States was "greatly surprised and deeply concerned," said Lansing. Four days later Jenkins was rearrested and imprisoned for trial. And by November 21 the crisis was in full bloom, in big red headlines in the Mexico City newspapers.[8] To Mexicans the thrust of events seemed clear. For the last six months most of the important American journals had expressed bellicose sentiments toward the Mexican government. In July and August witnesses at hearings of the U.S. House Rules Committee, among them William Gates, had lambasted Carranza and urged a benevolent intervention into Mexico. Since September the aggressive Republican Senator Albert B. Fall had conducted hearings on Mexico before his subcommittee on Foreign Relations: the most impressive witnesses advocated force to protect American investments. Several Republican governors had just been re-elected, another symptom of gringo fury.[9] And now Secretary Lansing warned of "a very serious effect" on Mexican-American relations, for which Mexico would be "solely responsible." Rigged or not, the Jenkins case was a perfect pretext for a new American intervention. In the crisis Mexican leaders had various roles to play—official, outlaw, and exile. In Morelos the politicos and generals in command were automatic patriots, merely loyal to the government on which they depended. But for the Zapatista chiefs it was grievous to admit a distinction between national and partisan interests, then to choose, then to face each other. Only in trust could they survive the ordeal.

Magaña took the initiative for the Zapatistas and quietly prepared to offer the government their support. To mediate with Carranza he turned to Lucio Blanco, whom the Zapatistas remembered fondly for his agrarista reputation and his generosity toward the south in 1914–15, and whom Carranza had recently called back to counter Obregón's popularity in the army. Through early November Blanco negotiated for a passport for

[8] E.g., *El Universal*, November 21, 1919: "Jenkins Case About to Provoke International Conflict."

[9] United States House of Representatives: *Appointment of a Committee for Investigation of Mexican Situation. Hearings Before the Committee on Rules*, 66 Cong., 1 sess., 2 parts (Washington, 1919). *Investigation of Mexican Affairs*, I, 3–744. *Excélsior*, November 6, 1919.

Magaña and arranged the channels of communication with Carranza. And once the international conflict became critical, Magaña sent his word to the presidential office. Practically, "in view of the Jenkins case and the generally difficult situation the Republic is in," he offered to surrender. "I wish," he wrote, "to enter into a deal with authorities to arrive at an agreement on the form in which we can end our rebellion and collaborate in quick and complete pacification of the country."[1]

This was an extraordinary maneuver. Despite the impending danger of intervention, most other outlaw chiefs remained in opposition. From Chihuahua Villa evidently made no gesture, conciliatory or defiant. Neither evidently did Peláez, whom a witness in Senator Fall's hearings was soon to declare "a splendid type of Mexican, . . . friendly towards Americans."[2] As for the Felicistas, who knew best what continued subversion might mean, they gave no sign of sympathy for a unified anti-American resistance: they even increased their military operations, especially around Veracruz.[3] The strategy of these intransigent chiefs was familiar, deriving from a political tradition as old as social strife in their part of the world—that the paramount, intolerable enemy was the enemy at home, that help from outside was a godsend. But Magaña's sense of his country was new. It was a conception current in Mexico for no more than the last seventy-five years and prevalent only now in his generation of leaders—that the primary enemy was always foreign, that formal and real cooperation with domestic rivals in a national emergency was the only responsible course, that the unforgivable sin was to taint the sanctity of the native contest. And so Magaña's strategy was new. If he helped Carranza, he might help forestall an American intervention and publicize the legitimacy of his party as well. Had Zapata lived, Zapatista strategy could not have been so flexible. In his head Zapata had finally learned that the defense of the villages of Morelos was not equivalent to the defense of the nation, that in great crises the local cause was subsidiary. But in his heart it seems that the two struggles had been one to the end. Probably he would never have acted on the Jenkins issue, maybe letting Magaña assure the government he would fight the gringos but hardly agreeing to "end our rebellion" besides. It took Magaña

[1] Blanco to whom it may concern, November 11, 1919, AZ, 30: 4. Anonymous (from the text, clearly Magaña) to the chief clerk in charge, n.d. (November 23, 1919?), AZ, 30: 32.

[2] See the testimony of William F. Buckley, December 6, 1919, in *Investigation of Mexican Affairs,* I, 840.

[3] Liceaga: op. cit., pp. 590–2.

to certify that the Zapatistas had come to a conscious recognition of themselves as fundamentally Mexicans.

On November 27 Blanco notified Carranza that Magaña had arrived incognito in Mexico City "in virtue of the rather strained international situation" and that he wanted a personal interview. Carranza agreed to see him the next morning. And at nine a.m. on November 28 Blanco, an aide, and Magaña arrived at Carranza's home. There, while Blanco and the aide waited in the antechamber, Zapata's successor conferred privately with Carranza and his chief of staff, the young brigadier general Juan Barragán. Magaña declared, wrote Barragán in a memo three weeks later, that "in view of the information he had from . . . newspapers reaching his camp about the difficulty of the international situation, and being a Mexican before a rebel, . . . he was disposed to reunite the groups of armed people who were at his orders and to study the most appropriate form of suspending hostilities." For Mexicans to go on fighting among themselves if war broke out—this "he believed antipatriotic."

Carranza then asked him: "And what do you want?" "Only guarantees," Magaña answered, only respect for his and his chiefs' persons, properties, and civil and political rights, only the recognition of their allegiance. Carranza heard a simple selfish cadging and he gladly waxed charitable, promising Magaña "every class of guarantees . . . and," the President went on, "if you get to needing the support of the forces of the Army to terminate your work . . . , count on that too." Magaña declined the offer, noting that his return to Morelos in the company of the national army "would perhaps give results contrary to those which I propose." To clarify his position, he reminded the old man that "before anything else I would need to exchange impressions with the main chiefs of the group and in accord with them to give a solution fitting and worthy of the situation." As he made no insulting proposal to Carranza, which would rightfully, he said, raise doubts about his sincerity, so he expected no insulting proposal from Carranza. The President would not quibble and told his guest to proceed as he thought best. "If anything unforeseen comes up," he suggested, "you can communicate with General Barragán, who's already in on this affair." The interview ended with mutual statements of esteem—for its purpose, a success.[4]

Meanwhile in Puebla City Ayaquica had appeared publicly to turn him-

---

[4] Statement of Juan Barragán, December 15, 1919, AZ, 30: 37. For a contemporary version of the meeting, see *Excélsior,* November 30, 1919.

self in. With another local chief, a Pelaecista he cooperated with, Ayaquica announced to reporters that he had information to cast light on the Jenkins case. Having read about the case and the international crisis it had provoked, and being a Mexican "more than anything," he could not, he said, "keep silence to the prejudice of the national integrity . . ." The information which the Pelaecista chief sent at once to the American embassy, was a denial that Jenkins had conspired in the kidnapping—evidence that the government should release him. Ayaquica and the Pelaecista then returned to the mountains, but left delegates to arrange a surrender; and on November 29 Pablo González himself came to Puebla to confer with them.[5]

By now the conflict with the United States was on the verge of violence. On November 28 Secretary Lansing had read the riot act to the Mexican ambassador in Washington. Because Jenkins was still in jail, Lansing declared that "the patience of this country [the United States] was nearly exhausted and had almost reached the breaking point, that the tide of indignation among the American people might overwhelm and prevent further diplomatic discussion and force a break in our relations and that a break would almost certainly mean war . . . [which] would be carried to an end with all the power of this nation." The next day he dispatched an insolent note to Mexico City, accusing the Mexican government of "willful indifference" to the feelings of the American people and practically demanding Jenkins's immediate release. The American press intensified the crisis in lead stories and on the editorial page. And on December 3 it came to a climax. That day in the Senate Fall offered a resolution that he and a State Department representative had just devised. It was a request that the Senate approve beforehand the State Department's action in "the pending controversy" with Mexico, and that moreover the Senate ask President Wilson to withdraw recognition from Carranza and "to sever all diplomatic relations now existing between this Government and the pretended Government of Carranza."[6] On approval the resolution was referred to the Foreign Relations Committee. Imminent, it seemed, was another American intervention into Mexico, much more determined, free-swinging, and dangerous than those of 1914 and 1916. The headlines in Mexico City blared out the news of American airplanes and ships ready to strike.[7]

[5] El Heraldo de México, November 28, 1919. El Universal, November 30, 1919.

[6] Congressional Record, 66 Con., 2 sess., Vol. LIX, Part I, p. 73. The State Department representative was Henry Fletcher, the U.S. ambassador to Mexico, in Washington for consultation. See Investigation of Mexican Affairs, I, 843C.

[7] El Demócrata, December 3, 1919.

On December 4, the talks with González having gone well, Ayaquica came into Atlixco to surrender. With him were several other Zapatista chiefs and secretaries and 250 armed men. And the next day, after they turned in their arms, González granted them all amnesties, twenty pesos each, and safe-conduct passes. Ayaquica then went back to Tochimilco and became the municipal president. The rumors were that other Zapatista chiefs would soon surrender too, following Magaña's and Ayaquica's example.[8]

Precisely at this time the international conflict began to abate. On December 4 Lansing asked the Foreign Relations Committee not to act on the section of Fall's resolution about severing Mexican-American relations. On December 5 Puebla officials let Jenkins go free on bail. And on December 8, having read a memo from Fall on the need for a tough resolution, the invalid President Wilson declared that he would "be gravely concerned to see any such resolution pass the Congress."[9] But in Mexico, where Jenkins's case remained before the court and where the persistent salvos from American congressmen and editors resounded ominously, the trend toward peace did not become obvious for several weeks. And as the crisis seemed to continue, scattered rebel chiefs continued to accept amnesties in support of the government. In Morelos small Zapatista bands turned themselves in almost every day through early December. And chiefs who remained nervously in hiding sent emissaries to indicate their interest in recognizing the government. By mid-month officials at González's headquarters claimed that more than twenty Zapatista jefes of first rank had surrendered in Morelos and Puebla, among them veterans like de la O, Mendoza, Jesús and Próculo Capistrán, Adrián Castrejón, Timoteo Sánchez, and Gabriel Mariaca. Most, like de la O and Mendoza, had not actually come down out of the hills, but those who did received a cordial welcome; there was even a local effort to name Jesús Capistrán municipal president of Jojutla or Jonacatepec. By December 21 so many chiefs had apparently laid down their arms that González considered the pacification of the south complete and announced the closure of the southern headquarters in Puebla as of January 1.[1] The help Zapatistas had given in securing official order in Morelos and Puebla was dramatic testi-

---

[8] *El Universal*, December 5, 6, and 24, 1919. *Excélsior*, December 6 and 9, 1919.
[9] Cited in James H. Callahan: *American Foreign Policy in Mexican Relations* (New York, 1932), pp. 578–9.
[1] *El Universal*, December 16, 24, and 25, 1919. *Excélsior*, December 17, 1919.

mony that Magaña spoke truly for them, that they cared most about the fatherland.

But as it became clear that the crisis was over, the Zapatistas found their movement in an awkward position. Some chiefs like de la O, Mendoza, and Mariaca remained outside the law, still in arms and still in hiding and now with no reason to accept amnesties. Others like Magaña, Ayaquica, and Capistrán appeared as declared champions of constitutional authority, even as officials, unexpected but nevertheless renowned converts. And in the new, calmer context their patriotic recognition of the government looked like a political recognition of Carranza. Thus González described it in his final report on southern operations. Rebels had surrendered, he implied, not for the sake of their country but simply because in the regular progress of his campaign he had forced or persuaded them to stop fighting. "The incident of the American Consul Jenkins . . . has no importance whatever from the point of view of pacification," he wrote.[2] And now that leading Zapatistas were stuck among the Carrancistas, they could not easily get out. Although Capistrán and Ayaquica were fairly free in their own bailiwicks, Magaña in Mexico City was practically under house arrest.[3]

This Zapatista association with the government, however qualified, carried a heavy meaning. The drift was not that amnestied chiefs might go down when Carranza fell, since in the chaos of the last days they could escape and join the new party coming to power. Nor, since personal bonds restrained them, would they turn against their comrades still in arms and disable their movement forever. Rather, in their theatrical surrenders they had implicated themselves not only in Carrancista politics but also in Carrancista policies—which jeopardized the reputation of their movement in the towns and villages.

For politically, despite the restoration of order, the Carrancistas would permit no autonomy in Morelos. On December 4 Governor Tajonar decreed that in 1920 as in 1919 municipal presidents and councilors would serve on executive appointment. And despite subsequent petitions for elections of municipal and state governments, and reports of official promises of elections, no elections took place.[4] The only vote the Carrancistas prepared for was the presidential election. But to fix the state for the Carrancista candidate, they tightened their administrative control. As lieutenant governor they discharged Colonel Aguilar and installed a more savvy

[2] Ibid., December 18, 1919. Partido Reconstrucción Nacional: op. cit., p. 50.
[3] Soto y Gama to Paz, March 26, 1920, AP.
[4] *Periódico Oficial,* 3rd Ser., No. 9, p. 4. *El Heraldo de México,* December 11, 1919.

and more reliable Coahuilan, José María Rodríguez, who set about welding the municipal presidents into an efficient electoral bureaucracy.

In economics the Carrancistas granted an agrarian reform, but of peculiar impact and only for their peculiar revolutionary purpose. Observing that no public record existed of the transactions in local real estate since 1914, Tajonar decreed a new registration of deeds. For those who had bought, sold, or inherited real property in the state in the last five years, or contracted to pay or collect rent or service on land there, or only wanted a local title confirmed, the governor designated the period from October 15 to December 31 as the time when they could pay taxes and have claims ratified.[5] The result was not the protection of the pueblos but their destitution, and the resurgence of the planters. In early November Luis García Pimentel, the de la Torre y Mier and Araoz heirs, and other former nabobs started pressing the federal government to dispossess the generals to whom it rented plantations in Morelos, as well as third parties who sublet from them, and to repossess the planters who had held the land in 1914. Because they impugned the honor and threatened the fortunes of González's generals, they gained prompt backing from the Obregonistas on *El Demócrata*. There a reproachful editorial appeared on "The Sugar Industry, Militarized." It was wrong, the writer declared, for the government to have seized the haciendas, and wrong again for it then to have rented them to the military, who ran the mills like barracks, treated workers like conscripts, and did not safeguard the machinery. It was better, he urged, to restore the haciendas to the old owners, who for their "interest . . . and special experience" were "those called to operate them with success and to give lucrative employment to the greatest number possible of mechanics and laborers."[6] The Carrancistas also detected the political energy of the demand. And to win the planters' sympathy, or at least to ally their enmity, Carranza acceded to their reinstatement. During December and January the landed exiles returned to Morelos. If, like García Pimentel's son Joaquín, they actually returned from exile abroad, they arranged permits for repatriation through the President's secretary, who gave the order to Section 3 of the Ministry of the Interior.[7]

The practice of Carrancista policy in Morelos became brazen. On January 19, to seal central direction of local politics, Rodríguez replaced

---

[5] *Periódico Oficial,* 3rd Ser., No. 8, p. 3.

[6] *El Demócrata,* November 10 and 12, 1919.

[7] L. García Pimentel, Jr., to his mother, February 25, 1920, AGP.

Tajonar as governor.[8] Meanwhile the planters busily revamped their haciendas. Although few were so bold as Luis García Pimentel, Jr., who returned "to these blessed lands" in person, they all had agents in the field pushing operations eagerly. The problems were knotty. How, without huge funds, which they no longer had, could planters buy seed before the rains began, or repair their demolished buildings, milling machines, and irrigation canals, or hire hands for the current short harvest, the cultivation over the summer, and next year's big harvest—and stay financially independent? How would they even recruit hands in a local population only 55 per cent of 1910's, or tempt experts into a devastated zone? But in Mexico there were no minds more inventive nor souls more enterprising than theirs. Hectically foreclosing on their own debtors and selling cheap the corn from their sharecroppers' rent, they raised quick cash. Going in as partners, they pooled money for the emergency. Buying a lot of bad and a little good seed, they accumulated enough to make a planting. Recouping stolen equipment and repairing only essential machines and canals, they left the rest to repair as they went along. Renting out fields for a year at piddling rates, they got them farmed and their titles recognized; next year they could increase the rents. Driving their managers as hard as Luis, Jr., drove himself and his foreman, twelve hours a day, "like a black," they toiled in a labor of love. After all, they had the land to depend on again, and as young Luis reminded his parents, "The truth is that these lands are very good." And improvising and straining, they made impressive headway as the weeks went by. "The combination of prehistoric methods with the railroad," declared Luis, "is one of the most curious things. But out of it are coming some green stalks of cane." Most important, the planters recovered largely on their own account, not slipping into the trusts that had formed to take over estates in Puebla, not incurring other, foreign obligations. Happily promising to send back melons and fruit to the García Pimentel children in Mexico City, Luis like the other planters assumed "a good future" for sugar haciendas in Morelos.

In the villages the revived planters' progress rankled. It was even more offensive than the progress the Carrancista generals had accomplished. Whereas the generals' control of the plantations, though onerous, had been a military occupation, therefore not definitive, indeed inevitably subject to civil and possibly popular revision, the planters' resumption of titles seemed an official reconsignment of the state to their charge for keeps; and the

[8] Urbán Aguirre: op. cit., p. 252.

planters could feel the popular resentment against them. The people around Jonacatepec, young Luis lamented to his parents, were "really very bad and very ungrateful. Many have come to *beg*, [but] to greet me and to ask me about you" there had come only one woman. He reckoned that a fear of Zapatista reprisals had inhibited locals from showing affection toward him, the generous old landlord's son, but he revealed his own fear of the locals themselves when he requested and took along a military escort just to go out to Tenango and back. Worse, the villagers overwhelmed him with "questions," Luis complained, "some of the old vintage, and others modernist," about their rights to land, timber, and water. Beyond doubt he assured his parents: "Today militant Zapatismo is entirely dead, and the bands that remain are few and without importance." And yet, sensing the tension in the Morelos air, grouching that villagers would soon start to ask for ejidos, he observed: "The Zapatismo that has not died nor will die is pacific Zapatismo, for these people have thievery in their blood and nothing nor nobody will be able to take it out of them."[9]

The longer the Zapatista chiefs remained inactive while the planters recovered, the more moral authority they forfeited in the pueblos. And this rot jeopardized not only their movement but the whole revolution in Morelos. For if they finally lost their popular reputation, then the only local party with roots in the villages would have disappeared—which meant that a new order in the countryside, like the old, could only be imposed. For Morelos the Zapatistas' fate in 1920 was crucial, the last phase of the most significant revolutionary issue opening in 1910 and unresolved since. At stake still was whether there could be a local revolution, or even local influence in the national revolution.

In the confusion oppositionists from outside the state resumed their intrigues. Again the Pelaecista venture was the most serious, this time featuring new agents and a new, more tactful diplomacy. It began in early January when a Pelaecista chief, Rafael Pimienta, arrived at Gabriel Mariaca's hideout near Tetecalita and offered him a steady supply of arms and ammunition from Mexico City. Unlike Palafox the previous summer, he asked no political commitment in return; he only declared that Peláez sought to restore the 1857 Constitution with agrarian reforms, which was now all the Zapatistas proposed too. Mariaca was not sure how to answer. Dutifully he wrote to Magaña for instructions, but received none. Then,

[9] L. García Pimentel, Jr., to his mother, January 22 and February 25, 1920, AGP. His italics.

"finding myself isolated and with the firm interest of fighting for our cause," as he later explained, he accepted the offer. He even provided Pimienta a guide to Everardo González's camp in the mountains of southeastern Mexico State, where Pimienta planned to bring the supplies for distribution.[1] In other Zapatista camps the appeal of Felicismo was more attractive, and during January more than twenty rattled minor chiefs requested and received commissions as Felicista officers from Felicista headquarters in Veracruz. On January 18 four Zapatista generals from Morelos arrived in person at the Veracruz camp and put themselves under Don Félix's orders.[2] From his camp at Tepeite de la O remained in contact with the Obregonista Colonel Calvo.

But Magaña had not abdicated. Already against Palafox and against Mendoza, he had proved that he was no man to quit a fight simply to avoid trouble. Precisely because he knew the feeling of a genuine peace, he was restless in the compromising immobility the Carrancistas confined him in. And when he got news in early January that Carrancista and oppositionist propaganda about him had disconcerted various chiefs, who wanted "instructions . . . to define our situation," he began preparations to escape from the dead peace of Mexico City, to return to the struggle in the field and secure the bases of a true settlement.[3] On January 11, citing recent reports of "reactionaries" trying to suborn "the serious and well-intentioned element" in the south, he notified Lucio Blanco that he was leaving to stop "that work of intrigue which prejudices us so much." Always politic, he did not break contact with Blanco but named an agent, a Puebla lawyer long helpful to the Zapatistas, to continue dealings with him and General Barragán; besides, he promised to correspond with Blanco, and sent him the key to the code they would use.[4] By late January he was back in the Puebla mountains, an outlaw again. As before, he slighted the military to concentrate on the diplomatic effort, cooperating with the amnestied Ayaquica but naming Genaro Amezcua and Vázquez Gómez as Zapatista delegates to an exile junta about to take place in the United States.[5]

Magaña's return heartened the movement in Morelos. The rash of Zapatista defections to the government and the Felicistas now ceased. The

[1] Mariaca to Magaña, January (n.d.) and March 13, 1920, AZ, 30: 15 and 16.
[2] Liceaga: op. cit., pp. 596–7.
[3] J. Ramos to Magaña, January 2, 1920, AZ, 30: 15.
[4] Magaña to Blanco and to Felipe T. Contreras, January 11, 1920, ibid.
[5] Magaña to Amezcua and to F. Vázquez Gómez, January 30, 1920, ibid. A third delegate Magaña named was Augustín Arriola Valadez, a radical Mexico City editor.

Pelaecista chief Pimienta, however, Magaña wisely made no objection to, and through the following weeks Pimienta smuggled the military supplies he had promised into Mariaca's camp. Meanwhile the secretaries strove to recoordinate the Zapatista organization. And in early March, having quietly arranged it with the municipal president, Soto y Gama reinstituted a clandestine central Zapatista office in Tlaltizapán. There he planned monthly meetings for the secretaries and aides from all Zapatista camps, "to unify totally the revolutionary criterion on the various national problems." Accord was urgent, Soto y Gama advised Mendoza in inviting his staff, "now that the triumph of the cause we fight for is so near."[6] Officially the Jefe Supremo of the Zapatista organization was still Vázquez Gómez, whose agent in Mexico City beseeched Magaña to stay loyal to him and not stray into allegiance to Peláez. And on Vázquez Gómez's behalf, more than twenty local chiefs were ready for action by mid-March—including the veterans de la O, Mendoza, Mariaca, Francisco Alarcón, Pedro Saavedra, Valentín Reyes, Zeferino Ortega, Vicente Aranda, Everardo González, and Sabino Burgos. Among them they mustered some 2,500 guerrilleros and another 1,500 reserves. In a military junta Mariaca and de la O supervised the distribution of the supplies Pimienta had brought. As Mariaca reported to Magaña, they awaited only his orders to begin operations.[7] After four months of scission and misgivings, the Zapatistas were again a force in local and national politics, thanks again mainly to Magaña.

It was a most opportune rally. For in mid-March, when the Carrancista candidate for president began his speaking campaign for the June election, the national crisis of succession began to open publicly. Obregón, Pablo González, and the Carrancistas moved into contention that was daily more legalistic and portentous. Lurking nervously in the wings were the exiles, rebels, and outlaws.

Magaña, with decisiveness wondrous for his twenty-eight years, now changed the allegiance of his movement. With insight even more wondrous, he guessed right about where to pledge it—to Obregón, as soon as Obregón's personal agent in the south, Brigadier General Juan C. Zertuche, asked him for it. And after sending word to chiefs in Morelos, Guerrero, Mexico, Puebla, even in Michoacán, he himself went on an

[6] Soto y Gama to Mendoza, March 3, 1920, AA.

[7] Severo Leal to Magaña, February 29, 1920, AZ, 29: 7. Soto y Gama to Amezcua, March 23, 1920, and S. Burgos to Amezcua, March 24, 1920, AA. "Mexico, Estimate of the Military Situation, March 5, 1920," NA, 45: 658. Mariaca to Magaña, March 13, 1920, AZ.

Obregonista mission into the most strategic zone in the south, the Mixtec-del Valle passes, where Puebla, Oaxaca, and Veracruz meet. This was Díaz country, Don Porfirio's base fifty years before and his nephew Don Félix's base now; until late March the only Zapatistas around operated as Feli-cistas. But then Magaña arrived, reclaimed local chiefs, and began organiz-ing them to declare for Obregón and hold the region for him when the crisis broke.[8]

Back in Morelos the new alliance set quickly. On March 27, six days after police had jailed more than seventy prominent Obregonistas in Mexico City, among them five federal deputies, Calvo came in person and on orders to Tepeite and reported to de la O that in the capital it seemed he had sur-rendered. "Tomorrow," de la O replied, "I'll prove to them that I haven't sold out." And the next day at Tres Marías he blew up a passenger train bound for Cuernavaca. Among the survivors was the assistant military attaché at the U.S. embassy, whom de la O held for ransom. A day later he had raiders attack into the Federal District and ransack Milpa Alta for supplies. "General Obregón wants to be your friend," Calvo then assured de la O. "And what proofs do you bring me of what you tell me?" the gruff little chief asked, pressing for materiél. Calvo caught the hint and offered "to stock you with arms and ammunition." In a few days the de-liveries began.[9] Snubbed, the Pelaecista Pimienta shrank to a tag-along in the new deal and settled for service as de la O's chief of staff.

In early April the break in the national crisis began. In a last, clumsy stab at controlling the opposition, Carranza insisted on appointing a devout Carrancista general as commander in chief of Sonora, the home base of the Obregonista party. On April 2 the undersecretary of war ordered Obregón to return from a campaign tour to testify before a court-martial in Mexico City about allegedly subversive connections with a recently amnestied Felicista chief. On April 6 Obregón appeared before the court and found himself no longer a mere witness but a likely defendant. On April 10 the Obregonista governor and legislators of Sonora declared their state practi-cally independent of the federal government. In Mexico City the police

---

[8] Palacios: *Zapata*, p. 294. Liceaga: op. cit., p. 608. Zertuche had taken a central part in Obregón's campaign until March 1, when he dropped out of sight "to fulfill a commission." See Ruvalcaba: op. cit., II, 354. For more on Zertuche, see Ricardo Calderón Serrano: "Un soldado de la Revolución," *El Nacional,* January 22, 1947.

[9] Ferris to the secretary of state, March 29, 1920, NA, 59: 812.00/23531. Summer-lin to the secretary of state, May 12, 1920, NA, 45: 659. De la O in *Impacto,* January 21, 1950.

moved to the brink of arresting Obregón and his closest lieutenant, Benjamín Hill. On April 11 at a private dinner in the modish Chapultepec restaurant Obregón wormed Pablo González into an understanding that amounted to a benevolent Pablista neutrality. And early on April 13, the day he was to hear the charges against him, Obregón fled the capital.[1] The showdown was on.

From the first the Zapatistas figured intimately in Obregón's cause. For both Obregón and Hill escaped south; and though Obregón, disguised as a railroad worker and riding a train through Morelos into Guerrero, could postpone an appeal to the local outlaws, Hill, who reached only the southern suburbs of the capital, needed them at once. On the day of the escape, a Tuesday, he wrote to de la O proposing a time and place for his rescue. The Zapatistas were too far away to meet him when he asked, and he had to hide out in a sand quarry outside Mixcoac. But on Thursday de la O answered, congratulating him and promising to send what he later described as a "suicide expedition" after him the next day. "The chiefs already carry orders to lend every aid and to keep due consideration for comrades," de la O assured Hill, "and I for my part will arrange to have everything ready here." Calvo got Hill to a place where the Zapatistas could find him, and over the weekend Valentín Reyes led five hundred raiders into the Federal District near Contreras and picked the Obregonistas up. Returning on Sunday, the expedition ran into a column of two hundred nationals, whose fire killed Calvo and eight others. But the next day Reyes safely deposited Hill with de la O in a camp at La Cima.[2] And on Tuesday, April 20, a week after Obregón's flight, Magaña published an official welcome to the new rebels. Probably penned by Soto y Gama, it gloomed through a brief dirge about Díaz, Huerta, and Carranza, and then lifted into a regular rhapsody in praise of "the honorable men of Constitutionalism, the Obregóns . . . who go off again today to the field of battle. . . . Welcome be you, brothers! . . . receive the fraternal embrace of your brothers, who on the heroic mountain, among the aeries of eagles who die facing into the sun, have known how to keep burning the fire of liberty, the infinite longing to be free Mexicans. . . . United thus we will have won." In an invigorating warm-up for his debut in the Chamber of Deputies, the author closed to the tune of "the bugles of triumph." One last image he could not stifle:

---

[1] Ruvalcaba: op. cit., III, 7–222.

[2] De la O in *Impacto*, January 21, 1950. *El Liberal*, April 19 and 22, 1920. *El Universal*, April 20, 1920. *El Demócrata*, April 18–21, 1920.

"the white flag of peace" unfurling to show the motto of "France of '93, Liberty, Equality, Fraternity."[3]

Already Magaña had involved amnestied Zapatistas as well. To Ayaquica in Tochimilco he had sent reports which, Ayaquica replied, "have cheered me greatly because now I do believe we'll work out our affairs." Ayaquica assured Magaña he had arranged a deal with a local national commander "to mobilize myself at the right time." And as Magaña's "friend and compañero" he sent back to him a courier to report verbally on "many other things which you should know."[4]

Meanwhile in a single week the Obregonista revolt had developed into a major national rising. From northern Guerrero, where local officials gave him refuge the day he escaped, Obregón had immediately dispatched coded telegrams to his partisans and likely allies around the Republic. Promptly there issued from the Sonora government a formal repudiation of Carranza's authority. On April 15 the national military commanders in Sonora declared themselves exempt from his orders as well. Seconding them in the next few days were civil and military authorities in Sinaloa, Michoacán, and Zacatecas, and lesser officials in other states. In the northeast Manuel Peláez merged his forces into the new movement. And on April 20 the governor, legislators, and commander in chief of Guerrero also formally repudiated federal authority. So the same day did the heads of the Mexican Labor Party, now in refuge with Obregón in Guerrero.[5]

By now officials in Morelos were itching to go Obregonista too. Although Governor Rodríguez remained firmly loyal to Carranza, the municipal presidents had slipped out of his control and had almost all voiced sympathy for the new rebels. And the military commanders in the state, General Francisco Cosío Robelo in Cuernavaca and General Salvador González in Cuautla, both neutral Pablistas, acted as if to encourage a revolt in their zone. After hearing from Obregón on April 14, Cosío Robelo had not budged since. Neither had González. Even when orders had come for Cosío Robelo to pursue de la O and Hill, he had not moved, and the rebels had continued freely through the southern Federal District and northern Morelos, recruiting villagers to fight on the promise of arms, a peso a day, and "free hands" to loot; to attack them, the War Department finally had to call in General Gustavo Elizondo from Mexico State. On April 21 Gon-

[3] *El Demócrata,* May 13, 1920.
[4] Ayaquica to Magaña, April 15, 1920, AZ, 27: 6.
[5] Figueroa Uriza: op. cit., II, 824–36. Ruvalcaba: op. cit., III, 350–3.

zález evacuated Cuautla, leaving the town to its own defenses. The same day the undersecretary of war visited Cuernavaca personally to check on its garrison and discovered that Cosío Robelo had already withdrawn the bulk of his troops down to Puente de Ixtla, where they might as easily join Obregón as resist him. Although the undersecretary returned to Mexico City the next day with Cosío Robelo's profession of loyalty, the nationals in Morelos remained inactive, and security there deteriorated further.[6]

The climax of the Obregonista revolt began on April 23, when the rebel authorities of Sonora published a Plan of Agua Prieta. This was a formal political program for the nation, to throw out the Carrancistas, install Sonora Governor Adolfo de la Huerta as provisional president, and reconstitute the government in new elections. There now being two supreme executives, Carranza in Mexico City and de la Huerta in Sonora, loyalists and rebels had to define who was legitimate. And on the issue the rebels multiplied in swarms, especially in the army. As Luis Cabrera, Carranza's minister of finance, observed, "More than a rebellion, it's . . . a real military strike."[7] Through the following week the uprising developed into a mighty national boom.

The repercussions swept Morelos into the main stream. When the news of the Agua Prieta plan reached Cuernavaca, Governor Rodríguez hurriedly convened a junta of municipal presidents to declare for Carranza. But instead of Carranza the assembled officials declared for Obregón and the Sonorans. And Cosío Robelo, at last on the go, congratulated them, discharged Rodríguez, and ordered the distribution of arms to municipal militia around the state.[8] Villages uncertain about accepting the Obregonista commission, for fear of antagonizing the Zapatistas, sent couriers to Magaña's headquarters in Puebla; but Magaña advised their full commitment to the revolt, and Zapatista veterans now returned to action as partisans of Obregón. As they took up positions in their villages or rejoined their old chiefs in the field, the Liberating Army of the South took shape again.

[6] *El Demócrata,* April 21, 22, and 26, 1920. *El Liberal,* April 24 and 25, 1920. Joaquín D. López: "Rectificación al General Francisco Cosío Robelo," *El Universal,* December 29, 1930.

[7] For a copy of the plan, see González Ramírez: *Planes,* pp. 251–5. For declarations of support, see Clodoveo Valenzuela and Amado Cháverri Matamoros: *Sonora y Carranza* (2nd edn., México, 1921), pp. 299ff. For Cabrera's remark, see *El Demócrata,* May 3, 1920.

[8] S. Valverde: op. cit., p. 237. For an account sympathetic to Rodríguez, see Urbán Aguirre: op. cit., pp. 223–5.

The local rites of rebellion proceeded frenetically. On April 25 the undersecretary of war stripped Cosío Robelo of his rank "for lack of military spirit," but in vain. That same day, a Sunday, Pablo González fled the capital, giving Pablistas everywhere their cue. On Monday Obregón came up briefly from Iguala and Cosío Robelo came down from Cuernavaca, and in a festive reunion in Puente de Ixtla they clinched their deal. In absentia Salvador González announced his affiliation with them. And on Tuesday Cosío Robelo formally declared for the Sonorans, placing his five thousand well-armed and munitioned troops under Obregón's orders. On Wednesday General Elizondo, the Pablista whom the War Department had ordered to Cuernavaca to crush the rebels, joined them. That day also a loyalist general occupied Cuautla, but hopelessly evacuated it and retreated back to the capital. By the end of April every organized group in the state was Obregonista—all the national army corps, all twenty-six municipal governments and militia units, and all the Zapatista bands. And the planters were in flight again.[9] For still uncertain villagers Magaña confirmed his earlier advice in a Circular to the Pueblos of the Southern Region on May 1. "In a special way" he recommended that "all sympathizers of our cause impart their moral and material help to all honorable revolutionaries, including among these the new compañeros who, disillusioned now with the lies of Carrancismo, are returning to the field of struggle, to contribute with their effort to the triumph of the Revolution." His final warning was that of an exhausted man about to gain power: "Today as yesterday we will be friends of pueblos who are with us. But we will know how to punish those who fail in the gratitude they owe to the sacred memory of our immortal Emiliano Zapata."[1]

At 7:15 a.m. on May 2 Obregón and his aides left Iguala on a jubilant train trip back north toward the capital. Passing into Morelos, they stopped at Zacatepec, where Hill, Salvador González, de la O, Pimienta, Reyes, Mariaca, and other chiefs were waiting. To nearby Jojutla they all retired to cool off in a junta in the Mazari family's house and to arrange commands and contingent strategies for the coming drive into Mexico City. Giddy at this late, sweetest success, de la O could hardly contain himself. "I've got half a Republic in my pocket," he told Obregón. That afternoon the party went on to Cuernavaca. There Cosío Robelo and Elizondo had prepared

[9] *El Demócrata*, April 26 and 28 and May 2, 1920. *El Liberal*, April 26–9, 1920. *El Universal*, May 9, 1920. Francisco Cosío Robelo: "Rindiendo Cuentas," ibid., December 27, 1930.

[1] Circular to the Pueblos of the Southern Region, May 1, 1920, AZ, 30: 18.

a welcome, and Obregón spoke to a large attentive crowd from the balcony of Mrs. King's old Bella Vista hotel.[2] With the rebellion thriving elsewhere in the country, no doubt could remain that the Obregonistas would shortly advance into the Federal District—without outlaw Zapatistas high in their ranks.

Threats to the new southern union persisted. From Mexico City the Carrancistas still tried to mount a resistance, sending an airplane or two to bomb rebel positions at La Cima, Tres Marías, and the Cuernavaca train station: but to no avail, as the rebel forces continued to concentrate for their offensive.[3] From distant San Antonio too came a desperate plea from the abandoned Vázquez Gómez to Magaña not to accept Obregón, which was, he groaned, only "to accept Carrancismo without Carranza." But this was an exile's wail into the wind, as wistful and as futile as the songs of the Aztec poet-king whose name Vázquez Gómez had taken for a pseudonym.[4] Like Carranza, only a year his senior, the doctor was already a political corpse. And Magaña did not even answer him. In Obregón Magaña could see a man with all the political talents he admired in Vázquez Gómez, but young, intensely vital, and actually about to become president. And to Obregón he cleaved. So did the other Zapatistas. And fused into one, their ranks swelling as they advanced, the allied rebel armies passed through the evergreen forests and mountain parks of the southern Federal District and came down into the open central valley.

Finally on May 7 Carranza and the last loyalists fled the capital, trying to reach Veracruz. By then Obregón was in Xochimilco, waiting, escorted by the troops of de la O. The next day they all moved up to Tacubaya, still waiting while Obregón's agents prepared the city to receive him. There a reporter asked Obregón: "Do you believe the alliance with the South will be lasting?" The reply was a little jewel of statesmanship, a straight public answer veiling and confirming a private offer. "I believe it is definitive," Obregón said. "And it will have as a consequence a multitude of benefits for that region."[5] On May 9, as Obregón re-entered Mexico City a conquering hero, de la O rode with him in close company. Four days later Magaña

[2] Ruvalcaba: op. cit., IV, 56. Mazari: "Bosquejo," pp. 117, 126. De la O in *Impacto*, January 21, 1950. Gustavo Casasola: *Historia Gráfica de la Revolución Mexicana, 1900–1960*, 4 vols. (México, 1964), II, 1381.

[3] *El Demócrata*, May 4, 1920. *El Liberal*, May 3, 1920. Urbán Aguirre: op. cit., pp. 225–6.

[4] Netzahualcóyotl to Magaña, May 4, 1920, AZ, 30: 18.

[5] *El Universal*, May 9, 1920.

and Soto y Gama arrived in the capital too, in dark suits and hats now like proper dignitaries, to be photographed showered in their friends' confetti, dumbly gripping ceremonial bouquets.[6] For these Zapatistas the ordeal was over.

Swiftly and skillfully Obregón and his Sonoran partners organized their government. They suffered one ugly episode—to escape from rebel pursuers in Puebla, among them local Zapatistas, Carranza deserted his train, retreated into the rough mountains in the state's northern districts, and was there assassinated on May 21 by traitors who had joined his guard.[7] But the Obregonista leaders stayed inculpably steady, evincing a phlegmatic disgust at the treachery, arresting the assassin, and going on with their deals. The day of Carranza's funeral in Mexico City, on May 24, they arranged for Congress to elect Adolfo de la Huerta provisional president, by 224 votes to Pablo González's 28. On May 26 the general who had been the rebel commander in chief in Sonora, Plutarco Elías Calles, took charge of the War Department. Four days later de la Huerta arrived in the capital. And on June 1 he was sworn into office for an interim term of six months.[8] The smoothness of the transition impressed even the street singers, by now skeptical to the bone about politicians. As one observed:

> It's all one single party now,
> There's nobody left to brawl.
> Buddies, there's no more war now,
> So let's get on with the haul.

He even let loose a prediction, an indulgence balladeers had grown extremely chary of, that

> The people will give their vote
> To General Obregón,
> Because he's the only chief
> Who bridles ambition.[9]

---

[6] Ibid., May 10, 1920. *El Demócrata,* May 13, 1920. Casasola: op. cit., II, 1394, 1403–4.

[7] A. Barrios's Report to Magaña, May 16, 1920, AZ, 30: 18. *El Demócrata,* May 17, 22, and 23, 1920. *El Universal,* May 17 and 23, 1920. *Excélsior,* May 19 and 20, 1920. For a sensitive novel about this episode, see Fernando Benítez: *El rey viejo* (México, 1959).

[8] *El Universal,* May 24 and 25, 1920. *El Demócrata,* June 1 and 2, 1920.

[9] Song cited in Simmons: op. cit., p. 168.

Zapatistas were prominent in this rapidly consolidating new regime. On June 2, twenty thousand Agua Prieta partisans marched in review through the Zócalo, among them the forces from Morelos. And watching with the honored new leaders from a balcony of the Palacio Nacional, beside the faintly smiling Pablo González, stood the squat, swarthy de la O, frowning into the sun. From an angle he looked almost like Zapata, dead now for over a year. (If de la O had been killed and Zapata had lived, Zapata would probably have been there in his place, with the same uncomfortable frown, persuaded by Magaña to join the boom for Obregón but probably worrying, as Magaña was not, about when he might have to revolt again.) After the parade official photographs were taken in the Palacio's ornate salons. De la O endured one, with his lieutenant Valentín Reyes on his right and Pablo González and other generals to his left. Everyone else set himself and posed. Only de la O stared with crude suspicion straight into the camera, exactly as Zapata had always done. Morelos's best men did not know what a pose was. But there a native chief sat anyway, a peer of the nation's highest commanders. At gala banquets that summer it was no planter's attorney who represented the people in the little state south over the mountains, but the jefe of a village where most folk peddled charcoal for a living.[1]

The Zapatistas came in for power as well as exhibition. On June 2 Secretary of War Calles formally incorporated the Zapatista Liberating Army, until then an irregular force under Obregón's orders, into the national army as the Division of the South, and de la O and Magaña became divisional generals.[2] In politics Magaña was exceptionally handy because of his long connection with chiefs in many camps, both those now in office and those not yet accommodated. Among his own chiefs still in the field, he clarified the nature of the new regime and convinced the last reluctants, like Mendoza, to accept it for good. For chiefs once Zapatista but now Felicista and still outlaws, he could arrange amnesties. With returning exiles like Antonio Villarreal he and Soto y Gama resumed familiar contact immediately. Most helpful was Magaña's dealing with Villa's agent in San Antonio in support of the President's negotiation for Villa's surrender and retirement. The government was in a "magnificent disposition," Magaña

[1] Casasola: op. cit., II, 1432, 1434, 1464. *El Demócrata,* June 20, 1920. *El Heraldo de México,* June 25, 1920.

[2] Ibid., June 4, 1920. *El Universal,* June 4, 1920. Palacios: *Zapata,* p. 295.

wired to San Antonio, and "with every pleasure General Villarreal and Southern elements will mediate."[3] Swayed by this and other appeals, Villa finally signed a peace treaty on July 28 and secured the Obregonistas' reputation as the only revolutionaries who could unify the country. Second only to Magaña as a Zapatista operator was Soto y Gama, because of his old connections with radical intellectuals and professionals who were now key factors in politics inside and outside the government. Under Obregón's auspices Soto y Gama reunited his cronies from the Convention of 1914–15, talked in new recruits, and on June 13 founded the National Agrarista Party. Local friends organized clubs in Morelos, Guerrero, Puebla, Tlaxcala, Mexico, Hidalgo, San Luis Potosí, Durango, Guanajuato, Jalisco, and Chihuahua. In the congressional elections in August only seven Agraristas won seats as deputies, but through Soto y Gama's contact with Obregón they exercised authority in the chamber ten times what their numbers warranted. During October Soto y Gama served as the chamber's second vice president, and during December two other Agraristas were its first and second vice presidents; Agraristas also sat on prime committees—credentials, constitutional questions, foreign relations, and agrarian affairs.[4]

For Morelos the most precious influence Magaña and Soto y Gama had was in the Department of Agriculture. There the secretary was Villarreal, provisionally during the interim term and then, when Obregón became president on December 1, on a regular appointment. After their early statement of faith in his sense of "revolutionary duty," Magaña and Soto y Gama had kept the pressure hard on him. And in office he obliged them. As director of his department's agrarian bureau he dismissed Patricio Leyva and named Valentín Gama, a relative of Soto y Gama's and five years before a minister of commerce in the Convention. And Gama promptly named Genaro Amezcua, now back from Havana, his official agent in Morelos.[5] Publicly exhorted and supported by Soto y Gama's Agraristas, Villarreal managed through 1920 the first serious efforts at general agrarian reform—the Un-

[3] P. Martínez to Magaña, June 2, 1920, and Mendoza to Magaña, June 6 and 15, 1920, AZ, 30: 22. G. Lozano Sánchez to Magaña, July 2, 1920, ibid., 31. Magaña and Soto y Gama to Villarreal, May 16, 1920, ibid., 18. Magaña, A. Barrios, and O. Paz to M. Díaz Lombardo, June (n.d.) 1920, ibid., 15.

[4] Vicente Fuentes Díaz: Los partidos políticos en México, 2 vols. (México, 1954–6), II, 24. Directorio de la Cámara de Diputados del XXIX Congreso de los Estados Unidos Mexicanos (México, 1921), pp. 12–34, 53–70.

[5] Boletín Oficial de la Secretaría de Agricultura y Fomento, V, 5–8 (May–August 1920), ii, iv.

cultivated Lands Law of June 23, the National Agrarian Commission Circular of October 6, and the Ejido Law of December 28.[6] Thus, for the pueblos of Morelos, Soto y Gama and Magaña were advocates-superior, for cases at the top. Local access to central authority did not remain so direct as in mid-May 1920, when an obscure Zapatista colonel in Jonacatepec wired a complaint to Obregón that the García Pimentels were abusing farmers around the town, and only two days later Obregón wired back his support, "with every pleasure." But however convoluted, the channels of protest and petition still ran open into the executive offices of the government. As Soto y Gama reported to Mendoza, the highest Obregonistas "hear us and pay attention to us."[7] If not exactly "a multitude of benefits," the villagers had gained the chance of defense from powerful men and the prospect of relief—a revolutionary change from 1910.

At home in 1920 the Zapatistas had emerged in almost absolute control. Chief was General de la O, the state military commander, "a patriarch," as one journalist viewed him, "with an attitude reminiscent of the Bishop of Jerusalem."[8] Next was the newly appointed governor sworn in on July 10, Dr. José G. Parrés, a native of Hidalgo but the Zapatistas' leading medical attendant in Morelos at least since 1918. The lieutenant governor was Carlos M. Peralta, formerly "Atl," the head of Zapatista espionage in Mexico City in 1917. Next came the state's three federal deputies, first among them Soto y Gama's local agent, a native of Tlaltizapán and a militant Zapatista since April 1911, Leopoldo Reynoso Díaz, and then his chosen adjuncts, Mariano Montero Villar and Francisco de la Torre, both products of the Zapatista headquarters; only the senator, Benito Tajonar, was a fluke.[9] On about equal rank stood Amezcua, seeing to the business of the Agriculture Department in the state. Then came the chiefs of the local Defensas Sociales, the civilian militia still armed and on call. Through June and July, egged on by Pimienta and other intriguers, de la O acted as if to disarm the defensas and station detachments of his own regular force in the towns.

[6] Personal interview with Soto y Gama. For comments on the importance of these laws, see Simpson: op. cit., pp. 81–8, and Frank Tannenbaum: *The Mexican Agrarian Revolution* (New York, 1929), pp. 185–6, 330.

[7] S. Robles to Obregón, May 19, 1920, and Obregón to Robles, May 21, 1920, AZ, 30: 18. Soto y Gama to Mendoza, July 1, 1920, AA.

[8] Francisco Bulnes: *Los grandes problemas de México* (2nd edn.; México, 1956), p. 58.

[9] S. Valverde: op. cit., pp. 239, 253. *Directorio de la Cámara* (1921), pp. 20, 24, 27. *Directorio Cámara de Senadores XXVIII Leg.* (México, 1920), p. 6.

There were several ominous confrontations between the rival units. In reaction the militia chiefs appealed for help to Magaña, who had originally organized many of the defensas from Zapatista headquarters in 1918–19. One chief even proposed to Magaña that he run for governor, presumably to counter de la O.[1] In early August Magaña forwarded the complaints and his recommendation to the President. Militiamen who wanted to retire should receive six-months discharge pay, he advised, and the rest should remain in arms as a rural police, although they would draw no wage from the federal government. Parrés having asked him to direct the state's Agrarian Commission, Magaña asked further that an escort of a hundred militiamen remain available to him for special duty at the government's expense.[2] The upshot was about as he projected: to avoid offense to de la O he stayed out of Morelos, but the militia retained their arms, and the chiefs went on as the neighborhood lions.

Only at the bottom and in the Zapatistas' shadow were there revolutionaries of another breed in office. These were the district judges and municipal presidents, councilors, and assistants, some newly appointed in the recent revolt, most the characters Tajonar had installed the year before. But they were now subject to local election, and they invented past careers of service from which they came out salty campaigners, intimates of Emiliano. Soon they even believed their inventions.

The Zapatista officials quickly carried their revolution into practice again. On August 18 in his second decree Parrés started pensions for the families of local men killed in the revolution. And on September 4 in Decree Number 5 he initiated a new agrarian reform in the state. "Considering," he said, "that the Southern Revolution led by General Emiliano Zapata was for the vindication of the proletariat of the field, . . . that the Plan de Ayala . . . had as a watchword principles among which . . . the most important is the restitution and grant of ejidos to the pueblos and the emancipation of the eternally exploited field hand, . . . that the historic moments in which Morelos lives are the result of . . . the effort of all those citizens who sustained cruel struggle in the southern mountains, . . . that our brothers' bloodshed, the crying of the orphans, and the pleading of the widows the Revolution has left . . . demand that the survivors . . . fulfill their promises," he formally organized the agency "to crown the offer made in Villa de Ayala by the martyr of Chinameca." This was the State Agrar-

---

[1] Soto y Gama to Mendoza, July 1, 1920, AA. *Excélsior,* August 3 and 5, 1920. Castrejón to Magaña, July 9, 1920, AZ, 30: 31.

[2] Memorandum to de la Huerta, August 6, 1920, ibid., 30.

ian Commission he had wanted Magaña to direct. It was to operate as prescribed in Carranza's decree of January 6, 1915, sanctioned in Article 27 of the new Constitution the Zapatistas had recognized in declaring for the Agua Prieta plan.[3]

By the new law Morelos became a place where villagers could remain villagers, decently and by right endowed, economically enfranchised. Any cluster of farmers in the state who qualified legally as a pueblo, ranchería, congregación, or comunidad could together now apply to the governor to reclaim old or to gain new land around their settlement. Within twenty-four hours after receiving the petition, Parrés declared, he would consult his Agrarian Commission to determine the validity of the case and the extent of the territory due, and issue his decision. If he approved, as he seemed to say he always would, the commissioners would then have local agents transfer provisional title to the village and remit the relevant documents to the National Agrarian Commission, which Villarreal presided over, for study and a recommendation to President Obregón. If the President approved, as he had vowed to, the title became definitive. To include as many farmers as possible in the reform, Parrés emphasized that refugee camps populated in the turmoil of the war and legally still without status as civil corporations had the right to petition him for it; obviously he intended to grant it. Compared with Palafox's reforms, the new law would cramp the villagers it gave ground to. Before, a village's definitive title to land had been complete and in perpetuity. Now it was only in usufruct, to revert to "the Nation" if abused. And by fiat the secretary of agriculture might well meddle deep in village business. Certainly Congress and the President could make strange changes in local relations.[4] For as it took formal custody of rural communities, the federal government also took a formal role in them. But compared with the measures the Leyvistas had tried in 1912 and those Pablo González had executed in 1918–19, the new law was a generous mandate for the preservation of the pueblo in the state.

So ended the year 1920, in peace, with populist agrarian reform instituted as a national policy, and with the Zapatista movement established in Morelos politics. In the future through thick and thin these achievements would last. This was the claim Zapata, his chiefs, and their volunteers had forced, and Magaña had won and secured.

[3] *Periódico Oficial del Estado de Morelos,* 4th Ser., No. 1, pp. 3–4; No. 3, pp. 3–4; No. 4, p. 3.

[4] For the various preconstitutional and constitutional agrarian decrees, laws, and circulars of the Carranza government, see Fabila: op. cit., pp. 270–361.

New attitudes, new policies, new laws, new agencies, new authorities—and of the plain country people of 1910, about three fifths remained. They had won a victory too, simply in holding on as villagers, not in refuge in the state's cities or huddled into the haciendas but out where they felt they belonged, in the little towns and pueblos and ranchos, still reeking at least of "pacific Zapatismo."[5] In 1910 the bases of the only life they wanted to live had been breaking down. Although they wore themselves out, dutifully tilling their scattered patches of corn and beans, now and then trading a horse or a cow, for a few pesos marketing eggs, tomatoes, onions, chiles, or charcoal, tending their scrubby orchards, desperately sharecropping on the planters' worst land, they had nevertheless lost the struggle to keep their communities going. In store for them then there had been only a long torment of grief and shame, to labor for a wage in steaming cane fields and rice paddies, to take orders from a boss, eventually to move into huts the boss's boss owned, to watch from a distance while old friends and neighbors and kinfolk moved away too, never to rest, and at the end to die in debt anyway. Now a decade later, two souls having disappeared for every three that stayed, they were still in their bases and back in the struggle. After all, the endurance in the pueblos counted more than the new government, the new champions, the new reforms. Those small communities, burdened and threatened for centuries, had just survived the most vigorous, ruthless, and ingenious siege ever mounted against them, spoiling the best if not the last chance that usurpers would have to eradicate them. Although the villagers of Morelos emerged mangled and in mourning in 1920, they had proved their abiding commitment to the local traditions of their forebears. The faith they had inherited was a source not of ambitions but of obligations, an inspiration not to acquire but to repair, not a stimulant but a strength. This they would try to bequeath.

Several times during the war federal and national troops had demolished Anenecuilco. Weeds had grown up in its ruins and in its sloping, cobbled streets. But now its families drifted back. Soon there was a community at work again. On September 26, three weeks and a day after Parrés announced his decree about the Agrarian Commission, the Anenecuilcans filed yet another application to recover the local fields. They were the first villagers to try the new law. On September 28 Parrés returned them a provisional title to land on the old Hospital and Cuahuixtla plantations.[6]

[5] For comparative figures on the populations of cities, towns, pueblos, ranchos, and haciendas in 1910 and 1921, see Holt Büttner: op. cit., pp. 94–105.

[6] *Periódico Oficial*, 4th Ser., No. 11, pp. 1–2.

A People Keeps Faith

"The life of Anenecuilco is exemplary . . ."
—Jesús Sotelo Inclán

T HE LAND TITLES ZAPATA'S UNCLE passed on to him in September 1909
were documents almost sacred. It was no mere bundle of legal claims
that Zapata took charge of, but the collected testimony to the honor of all
Anenecuilco chiefs before him, the accumulated trust of all past generations
in the pueblo. This was his responsibility. And when a year and a half later
he decided to commit the village to revolution, he buried the titles in a
strongbox under the floor of its church.

Once when federal troops were ravaging Cuautla district, Zapata feared
they might accidentally unearth the strongbox. He sent José Robles, a close
aide and fellow Anenecuilcan, to dig it up and bring it to him. When
Robles could not enter the area because of the soldiers, Zapata sent another
Anenecuilcan, his secretary on the village council, Francisco Franco. Franco
did retrieve the titles, which Zapata turned over to Robles for safekeeping.
"If you lose them, compadre," he told him, "you'll dry out hanging from a
slick oak."

In early 1914 some emissaries from a Michoacán rebel came to his camp
at Pozo Colorado, to see whether he was sincere. What was he really fighting for? How could he prove it? He had Robles bring the Anenecuilco

documents, and he showed them to his visitors. *"Por esto peleo,"* he said. "This"—not these titles, but this record of constancy and uprightness—"I am fighting for."

As the struggle wore on, Zapata took extra precautions with the documents. He entrusted them to Franco, instructing him to stay out of dangerous zones, to consider it henceforth his sole duty to save them. Afterward Zapata often referred to the titles, but he seems to have felt more comfortable knowing they could not be lost with him. "I'm bound to die some day," he would say, "but my pueblo's papers stand to get guaranteed."

In January 1919 Zapata met Franco near Villa de Ayala and repeated his commission. He even authorized Franco, in case he turned up missing, to present the documents before Carranza's agrarian authorities.

Three months later Zapata was dead. Franco returned to Anenecuilco, but as Governors Tajonar and Rodríguez promoted no reforms, he kept the strongbox hidden. A year passed.

Then came the Agua Prieta revolt, and through mid-1920 a new regime in Mexico City and Cuernavaca. Franco now produced the documents Zapata had left, and the villagers elected him their new chief. And that fall he filed their request for the definitive and rightful restitution of their fields. To keep peace with their neighbors the Anenecuilcans did not press their full claim, which included part of Villa de Ayala's and Moyotepec's land.[1]

The governor's response was a fast shuffle, a favor instead of justice. Since the agronomists in the National Agrarian Commission and the Department of Agriculture had decided that reform deriving from the old, often faulty titles would only confuse the issue, the land Parrés provided the Anenecuilcans was not a restitution but a grant—over twelve hundred acres, about what they had asked him to recognize as their own. The Anenecuilcans had little choice but to accept. And on October 20 they took provisional possession of the grant, still subject to challenge and eviction.[2] The villagers' original titles were now practically worthless, but Franco kept them with the new documents.

Through the early 1920's Zapatistas remained powerful in Mexico City. In 1921 Soto y Gama's Agraristas threw the Chamber of Deputies into an extraordinary session and for months debated agrarianism, reading petitions from villages in every region of the Republic, citing treatises on land leg-

[1] Sotelo Inclán: op. cit., pp. 201–5.
[2] Gill: op. cit., p. 52.

islation, haranguing the galleries, all to prove publicly that the woes of Mexico's rural population were not mere phases of time or place but a disgrace basic and national. At least they convinced President Obregón, who came to an Agrarista Party meeting and promised to push for stronger reform. The result was the Agrarian Regulatory Law of April 10, 1922, until the mid-1930's the most drastic use of the new Constitution to provide official protection for the country poor. Elsewhere in the government the secretary general of the National Agrarian Commission was a Zapatista headquarters secretary of 1914–16, Miguel Mendoza L. Schwerdtfeger. In the army Magaña was less important but still influential, as head of a federal bureau of military colonies and then head of a National Agrarian Confederation.[3] And from these connections Anenecuilco benefited greatly. In November 1922 the President expanded its provisional grant to nearly 1,700 acres, with over 900 acres taken from Manuel Araoz's Cuahuixtla hacienda and over 750 from the Alonso heirs' Hospital. In February 1923 the Alonso attorneys requested an injunction from the Cuautla district court against the ruling; but Franco had the pueblo's papers in order, and the court refused to act. Finally on April 11, 1923, the village received its title of definitive possession: seventy-five heads of families became full-fledged ejidatarios.[4]

Other communities also benefited from the new regime. Over forty irregular camps, settlements, suburbs, and old hacienda quarters gained recognition from Parrés as civil corporations. And to nearly half of these and to most of the already established villages the governor dispensed grants of ejidos. By late 1923 he had provided land to 115 of the state's then 150 pueblos. On official encouragement many farmers organized unions, like the "Bolsheviki" at Tepoztlán, and affiliated with a national workers' confederation, the CROM.[5] Touring the state in 1923, an American journalist found men laboring in the fields "not dissatisfied." True, there was no more sugar cane. But villagers did not regret the ruin of the old industry. "What

[3] Personal interview with Soto y Gama. Díaz Soto y Gama: *La revolución*, pp. 292–3. Fuentes Díaz: *Partidos*, II, 25. Simpson: op. cit., pp. 82–5. Julio Cuadros Caldas: *México-Soviet* (Puebla, 1926), pp. 485–6, and *El Comunismo Criollo* (Puebla, 1930), pp. 52–9. Jesús Silva Herzog: *El agrarismo mexicano y la reforma agraria. Exposición y crítica* (México, 1959), pp. 304–10, 313–20. Meléndez: op. cit., II, 474.

[4] Sotelo Inclán: op. cit., pp. 205–6. Gill: op. cit., p. 53.

[5] *Periódico Oficial*, 4th Ser., Nos. 9–13, 15, 16, 19, 20, 22–31, 34–52, 55, 57–60. Diez: *Bibliografía*, p. ccxvii. Lewis: *Life*, p. 236.

was called prosperity for the state," they recalled, "was misery for us." As ejidatarios told the American, "We are [now] growing what we want to grow and for our own use."[6]

In return the local people were staunchly loyal to the federal government. When in December 1923 a revolt to make de la Huerta president broke out in several states, the country folk of Morelos kept their state quiet. The only suspicious maneuvers came from old Zapatista chiefs like Jesús Capistrán, who resented the political machine Parrés had built in Cuernavaca and who suspected him of rebel sympathies. And when the patriarch de la O removed Parrés and his aides and appointed a new loyalist governor on December 15, the disaffected chiefs resumed their support of the government. Later, rebels from Guerrero tried to drive up into Morelos, but de la O mobilized forces to hold them at Puente de Ixtla. He also distributed arms to villagers around the state. And never wavering, they guarded strategic points until the crisis passed.[7] Probably not since the War of Intervention sixty years before had the allegiance of the pueblos to the national authorities been so immediate and so firm.

By 1927 statistics indicated that Morelos had changed more from agrarian programs than any other state. Only four or five haciendas still functioned there, the others standing idle or transformed into civil communities. Toiling around them were over 120 villages established in their ejidos. While planters had lost over half their territory in the last seven years, some 16,800 ejidatarios had taken definitive possession of over 307,000 acres in grants and restitutions. Provisionally at least 80 per cent of the state's farming families now held fields of their own, which altogether amounted to around 75 per cent of the arable land.[8] In rich, wet, warm country like Morelos, where the only pause between harvests was for the crop to ripen, the emerging pattern of tenure was the outline of the old populist utopia. A kindly but shrewd American anthropologist researching in Tepoztlán saw rustic harmony, easiness, and contentment as the essence of life there.

[6] Ernest Gruening: *Mexico and Its Heritage* (New York, 1928), p. 162.

[7] S. Valverde: op. cit., pp. 246–7, 315. *Excélsior,* December 17, 23–25, and 30, 1923. Luis Monroy Durán: *El último caudillo, apuntes para la historia de México, acerca del movimiento armado de 1923, en contra del gobierno constituido* (México, 1924), pp. 329–37. Meléndez: op. cit., II, 141–3, 160–3. Figueroa Uriza: op. cit., II, 978–9.

[8] Holt Büttner: op. cit., pp. 29, 101–2. Tannenbaum: *Agrarian Revolution,* pp. 324–5, 498. Jorge L. Tamayo: *Geografía General de México,* 4 vols. (México, 1962), IV, 64–5.

The same vision transfixed a usually acerbic American reporter. "Tepoztlán! Will you be as self-sufficient, as heroically beautiful a hundred years from now?" he cried. "If I read the god-like palm of your destiny aright, you will forever cherish your traditions . . ."[9]

Nevertheless, despite the statistics and the rhetoric, new worries had set in. The most galling were political, the local repercussions of the conflict and disruption President Calles caused in the National Agrarista Party after he succeeded Obregón in 1924. In August 1924 the Senate deposed the governor whom de la O had installed and appointed instead Ismael Velasco, a jefe político in Jonacatepec and Tetecala before the revolution but later a Zapatista. In September the War Department reassigned de la O himself to Tlaxcala and named a Sonoran commander in chief in Morelos. In October Velasco left and Joaquín Rojas Hidalgo became governor. Sixteen months later, in February 1926, he conducted the first state elections since 1912. They featured seven parties backing four candidates, and they concluded in the rival claims to victory of three of the candidates and their respective legislatures, one in business in the Cortés palace, one in a private house in Cuernavaca, and one in Jojutla. Congress promptly dismissed Rojas Hidalgo and appointed Valentín del Llano, a federal deputy from Morelos in 1912–13. In March del Llano nullified the recent elections. In May he resigned. His lieutenant governor replaced him until December, when Congress made a new appointment, which it revoked the following February to make another, which it revoked a month later to make yet another.[1]

For the villagers the proliferation of politicians was about as welcome as a visitation of locusts. As the citizens of Santa María Alpuyeca wrote in a typical complaint to the Department of the Interior, ". . . our pueblo, like the rest of the state, has been suffering a long series of injustices and ailments of all kinds, due to the confusion and complete disorder which have reigned . . . since the time of Sr. Rojas Hidalgo, who came to impose authorities in the municipalities, these authorities being precisely the mortal enemies of the pueblo. . . . Sr. Rojas Hidalgo went, and we raised our hands

---

[9] Redfield: op. cit., pp. 54–68. Carleton Beals: *Mexican Maze* (New York, 1931), p. 137.

[1] Fuentes Díaz: *Partidos*, II, 25–6. S. Valverde: op. cit., pp. 243–55, 285. Gruening: op. cit., pp. 465–6. Diez: *Bibliografía*, pp. ccxviii–ccxx. For Velasco's early career, see *Semanario Oficial*, XII, 12, 13; XIII, 28, 17; XVI, 26, 15; XVII, 3, 15. For del Llano, see ibid., XXI, 28, 1.

to heaven thinking that we should now rest, but our disappointment was very painful when we learned that the contrary took place, for Sr. Valentín del Llano, who came afterward, and who, they say, has Gachupín blood, immediately let himself be deceived by the reactionaries and left things in that state. This gentleman left, and for three months we have not known who is at the head of the government. . . . All we know is that every day things go from bad to worse and who knows where we shall end . . ."[2]

Another trouble was the parvenu agrarians, some returning natives and some immigrants from states where land was harder to get. Attracted to Morelos by the generosity of policy and nature, they came in the thousands. Mostly they settled in the villages. And as they reclaimed old rights or competed for new grants, they cramped their hosts. The more that came, the more they advertised the state to others.

Less clear but even more deeply disturbing was a problem about money. As the national economy recovered through the mid-1920's, villagers had to pay higher prices for an increasing variety of goods. But entrenched in their corn patches, tending a few livestock, they had little chance to earn enough cash. Retouring the state in 1925, the American journalist found ejidatarios who wanted the fields in sugar cane again. But the mills were still in ruins; experts calculated that their reconstruction would require $25,000,000, not a likely investment. Some villagers tried growing rice for the metropolitan market, but they had to deal with brokers, who absorbed the profits before the crop was in. In one case squabbles over water for the paddies degenerated into pitched battle between two armed pueblos. Increasingly often farmers who wanted more than a modest subsistence had to rent from their neighbors or do jobs for wages.[3]

Veteran natives stayed in the state: their mood was not desperate, much less subversive. During 1926-8 three small outlaw bands operated in northern and eastern Morelos in support of the Catholic Cristero rebellion then raging in Jalisco, but they aroused no serious sympathy among the pueblos. They hid out in the hills, to avoid the armed and dutiful villagers. Even so one band fell victim to the pursuing forces of Adrián Castrejón, a Zapatista chief now a stalwart national general. When a military revolt flared in Veracruz in late 1927, President Calles felt so sure of Morelos that he did not bother to reinforce troops there or to mobilize the militia. And he crushed the eastern rebels without the slightest complication in the south.

[2] Cited in Gruening: op. cit., p. 467.

[3] Ibid., pp. 162-3. Memo on production of sugar in Morelos, November 8, 1924, NA, 59: 812.61351/6.

Two years later, during another abortive mutiny in the north, the same peace prevailed in Morelos.[4]

But however firm, local loyalty was no longer automatic but a strain. After 1928 it lasted mainly on the strength of gratitude and faith, for that year Morelos lost its best champion in Mexico City, Obregón, to a religious fanatic's bullet, and Calles, who owed the state nothing, became the nation's supreme political boss. In the National Revolutionary Party Calles then organized, Soto y Gama refused to accept a place. The Agraristas split, and Morelos lost even its advocates in the capital. After a provisional president decreed a record flurry of grants in the state in 1929, villages went begging.[5]

Anenecuilco meanwhile struggled on. The old kind of direct challenge was too obvious to hurt the village now—in June 1927 Manuel Araoz's attorneys appealed the expropriation of Cuahuixtla lands in the Cuautla district court, to no avail. But more devious tactics had evolved that required the villagers' special vigilance. The Alonso attorneys tried to sell two of the fields already expropriated from Hospital to the federal Loan Bank for Irrigation and Agriculture. Francisco Franco quickly exposed the maneuver in court, however, and Anenecuilcans were able to farm a few more seasons in peace.[6]

By 1929 the village was in yet another bind. As the young men married and formed new households, they pressed for local plots of their own rather than emigrate. But there was not enough land in the ejido to give them a decent stake. And official restrictions on enlarging the grant made the pinch worse. Legally Anenecuilco had no right even to request new holdings until ten years after the original grant, that is, until October 1930.

Instinctively Franco sought a way out by resorting to the old titles. On May 9, 1929, Anenecuilcans applied again for restitution of their lost lands. The request became urgent in July, when the National Agrarian Commission ruled that in September it would end agrarian reform in Morelos, dissolving the State Agrarian Commission and accepting no more pleas for restitution, new grants, or enlargements. When the National Commission

---

[4] Sheffield to the secretary of state, May 13, August 24, September 13, and October 18, 1927, and August 7, 1928, NA, 59: 812.00/28408, 28662, 28719, 28906, 29272. Mazari: "Bosquejo," p. 127. Meléndez: op. cit., II, 235–40.

[5] Fuentes Díaz: *Partidos,* II, 26–7. Meléndez: op. cit., II, 212. Holt Büttner: op. cit., p. 29. Marte R. Gómez: *La reforma agraria de México. Su crisis durante el período 1928–1934* (México, 1964), pp. 33–9.

[6] Sotelo Inclán: op. cit., pp. 205–6.

failed to carry out the ruling, however, Franco went on in late October to file an application for enlarging Anenecuilco's ejido.[7]

Neither action brought results. The request for restitution was dismissed as out of order. And the application for enlargement soon ran afoul of new legislation further restricting pueblos' rights. According to an executive decree of December 26, 1930, villagers could not even ask for more ejidal plots unless they proved that they had made "efficient use" of previous grants, and they had to pay for new expropriated fields before putting them under cultivation.[8]

To Anenecuilco these were formidable barriers, and they grew more imposing. As the federal government developed its own security, as it grew more conservative, more careful about investors' nerves, it raised the premium on political connections and discounted simply popular needs. Although a new state constitution took effect in Morelos in 1930 and elected governors and legislatures henceforth made the local rules, the real directions still came from Mexico City. And the options of plain people dwindled. In practice the Anenecuilcans could only go on supporting Francisco Franco's efforts. In December 1932 their request to enlarge the ejido finally reached the National Agrarian Commission, but prompted no action.

The pueblo's struggle became frantic over the winter of 1934–5. There had just been elections for a new president, and in the familiar manner the departing chief executive showered last-minute favors on his similarly departing colleagues. One favor, a mere token for him, was the concession of two fields south of Cuautla to a clique of generals organized as the José María Leyva Cooperative. It so happened that these fields were among the richest in Anenecuilco's ejido. They were fields Anenecuilco had always held title to, as one of the cooperative's leading generals, Maurilio Mejía, must have known. Besides, the village had won the fields "definitively" from Hospital hacienda in 1923, and successfully defended its possession in court in 1927. But the land was valuable, and lower court rulings often failed to inhibit a magnanimous president. Soon the generals sent out crews to fence in the land.

Francisco Franco now proved himself a worthy heir of Zapata's legacy, a true descendant in Anenecuilco's honorable line. He notified Mejía and his cronies that he would resist their maneuvers by again presenting Anenecuilco's titles in court. And on November 29, 1934, he did file again for restitution. Then when the generals accused him of rebellion against

[7] Gill: op. cit., p. 53. Simpson: op. cit., p. 117. Sotelo Inclán: op. cit., p. 206.
[8] Fabila: op. cit., pp. 536–9. Simpson: op. cit., pp. 114–16.

local officials and initiated a private hunt for him, he fled with the documents into the hills. He spent several months a jump ahead of death, writing when he could to various authorities. Once again that bundle of legal papers had inspired the total devotion of Anenecuilco's trustiest man.

Eventually Franco's pleas came to the attention of the new President, Lázaro Cárdenas, who had revived radical agrarianism as a national policy. And on June 29, 1935, astoundingly, the President arrived in Anenecuilco. In public proceedings he declared the generals expropriated, the pueblo entitled to the fields in question, as well as the cooperative's farm machinery, and Francisco Franco guaranteed against political abuse.

Anenecuilco's trials now seemed over. For although professional Zapatista politicians remained in eclipse, President Cárdenas actually proceeded to grant new ejidos and to carry out other reforms in Morelos that surely forecast the village's relief. After ten years of revolution and then fifteen years more of petition, Zapata's native pueblo was at last about to come into its own. Had Zapata lived, he would have been a grandfather.

There remained only the formalities, the application for an enlargement of the ejido. This Franco filed, and this President Cárdenas duly granted on May 13, 1936. For ninety-three ejidatarios Anenecuilco now disposed of 10,139 acres, as much as a small, prerevolutionary hacienda. Nearly twelve hundred acres were in the lush Ayala River bottoms, over six hundred of them irrigated; the rest were in the dry hills to the west of the village.[9]

But Anenecuilco's success was a new bone of contention. It encouraged Villa de Ayalans to request an enlargement too; and when they received their grant, they found it included lands already allotted to Anenecuilco, lands Cárdenas had verbally promised Anenecuilco a year before. Unfortunately for Anenecuilco, no one had kept an official record during the President's surprise visit, and the village could not defend itself against Villa de Ayala's challenge. Although old friends of Morelos were again influential in Mexico City, Magaña having gained the confidence of the President, himself a Michoacano, and Parrés having become undersecretary of agriculture, they did not waste themselves in pacifying two little villages. In 1937 Nicolás Zapata became municipal president in Cuautla, but he offered no help to his father's native pueblo. Unlike his father, he had learned the rudiments of politics—which rotted his sense of obligation.

[9] *Excélsior*, June 29, 1935. Gill: op. cit., pp. 53–5. Sotelo Inclán: op. cit., p. 207.

For almost two years the dispute dragged on between Anenecuilco and Villa de Ayala, the larger, richer, municipal seat. Then in May 1938 came an executive ruling in Villa de Ayala's favor. Stunned, the Anenecuilcans refused to recognize the decision. Nor would they accept lands elsewhere in compensation, especially when they learned they would have to pay half the market price for them. Still, the dispossessed would not leave their pueblo. Renting local plots or taking jobs as field hands for their neighbors, they held on.

Without knowing how or why, not in delight but in distress, the villagers could see that the basic terms of their life had changed—all ironically in the past few years of official interest in their welfare. Thus, because Cárdenas wanted to give the ejidatarios of Morelos a chance to produce a cash crop, he had ordered the construction of a giant cooperative sugar mill in Zacatepec, which he had opened in February 1938; and the fields were again in cane. But inevitably the value of the land soared. And entrepreneurs inside and outside the ejidos distorted local contracts and pressed for their own advantage. Besides, from Guerrero, Mexico, and Puebla newcomers swarmed into the state hunting for places in the pueblos growing cane for Zacatepec. By 1940, mainly from immigration, Anenecuilco had over twice as many people as in 1930. Some were renters, others part- or full-time field hands, for very high wages, but they all craved a plot in the ejido. In the fierce competition for the soil the average holding shrank to less than ten acres, around a third the size it had been seven years before.[1] There was little room for the ejido to expand in, even if the secretary of agriculture, now Parrés, favored it.

Finally the Anenecuilcans accepted land adjoining the grant they already held, and agreed to pay the expropriated owners one fifth the market value. (The owners were ex-governors, the patrons of Nicolás Zapata.) But when the fields came open, Nicolás appeared and tried to take over the best sections. And then the federal official in charge refused to release any land. The tax bills still went to Anenecuilco, but use of the land soon fell to a local kulak reputedly Spanish.

In 1940 the odds shifted even more heavily against the village. Because Magaña, the closest Zapatista contact with Cárdenas, had died the year

[1] Urbán Aguirre: op. cit., pp. 256, 265. Theodore Schwartz: "L'usage de la terre dans un village à Ejido du Mexique," *Études rurales*, 10 (July 1963), 37–49. *6° Censo de Población, 1940, Morelos* (México, 1943), pp. 13, 44. Nathan L. Whetten: *Rural Mexico* (Chicago, 1948), pp. 260, 584.

before, surviving Zapatista notables formed an official club, the Zapatista Front, including Parrés, de la O, Ayaquica, and Castrejón among the directors; and to encourage Nicolás Zapata to behave more responsibly, they gave him an honorary seat in the governing council and arranged his election to the Morelos legislature. Unreformed but now a deputy of the regime, Nicolás quickly acquired over a hundred acres in Anenecuilco's ejido. When Anenecuilcans resisted, he had them ordered off other plots, which he then conceded to his partners in the Villa de Ayala ejido.[2]

Yet the Anenecuilcans remained, as many lessees and laborers now as proper ejidatarios. Although they heard of the new jobs World War II had opened in the north, in the Federal District, and right in Morelos, they preferred a dim local hope to a bright distant risk. At home at least they would not have to steal to eat.

By 1943 Anenecuilco was in desperate straits. The villagers' misery shocked a young historian who, after hearing lectures on Zapata at the National University, had come to Morelos to discover for himself the truth about the southern chief. Determined still to hold their ground, but crowded, in debt, helpless, having just lost the fields they expected their next harvest from, the Anenecuilcans had lost faith in every defense but their titles. These the now sixty-year-old Francisco Franco finally showed the young visitor. These alone, he argued, because they proved the history of the pueblo, could prove its right to exist—which for him was not merely its political right to autonomy but also the social right of its natives to live out decent lives where they were born. To Franco and other Anenecuilcans, their heritage was the only conceivable source of their salvation. It was a depressing conviction. "In seeing them suffer," the young man thought, "it seems to me I am present at the anguish of all the past generations." Back in Mexico City, corresponding with his friends from the village, he began to fear they would take up arms again in "a tragic adventure." In the book he soon published he beseeched the new President, Manuel Ávila Camacho, to enforce Anenecuilco's titles. "Will it be possible," he asked, "that the first pueblo that went to fight for its lands will be the last to receive them, or never receive them at all?"[3]

Meanwhile Franco reorganized resistance to Nicolás. "If 'Miliano was alive," he reasoned, "he would settle for his 10 acres like everybody else."

[2] Gill: op. cit., pp. 56–7, 64. Sotelo Inclán: op. cit., p. 212. Personal interview with Palacios. *Excélsior*, June 25, 1940.

[3] Sotelo Inclán: op. cit., pp. 213–14.

The other villagers agreed, both the natives and the immigrants, and through the mid-1940's they at least kept control over the fields they had. And since fewer outsiders moved into the pueblo now and some exasperated young men even moved away, those who stayed were able to brake the fragmentation of plots and the general indebtment. In 1946 Nicolás became federal deputy for Cuautla district, and the local struggle grew vicious again; but still the Anenecuilcans carried on.

Four days before Christmas 1947, the Cuautla police came down to Anenecuilco and assaulted Franco's house. Breaking in, they demanded the village documents and tried to kill the old man. He and his family fought back, and the police fled. That night national troops arrived and opened fire. They killed Franco's two sons, Julián, 22, and Vírulo, 17. Wounded, the old man tried to escape, but the soldiers caught him and finished him off in a nearby ravine. They never found the documents.[4]

During the next twenty years massive changes went on in Mexico. The population almost doubled. The number of workers in factories and construction tripled. Acreage under cultivation doubled. Production in agriculture and industry more than tripled. Over twenty thousand miles of new roads opened, and the number of cars, trucks, and buses racing along them more than quintupled. The number of radios increased at least ten times. And switched on to beam, incessantly it seemed, were over a million TVs. New tricks in salesmanship became routine, like brand names, advertising, standard packaging. Through an Export-Import Agency the federal government began buying goods directly from domestic producers and selling them directly to consumers. The annual cargo shipped on trains alone tripled. Pulled into this boom and driving it faster, the population shifted around the Republic—out of the poor, densely settled rural areas of the center and south and into the most blatantly thriving states of the northwest and the Gulf Coast, or into the large cities, especially into the now huge metropolis of Mexico City. Although most country people stayed where they were, often because of the residual security of their ejidal plots, those who moved probably numbered over two million. By the mid-1960's barely half the working population was still in farming. The obvious prospect was a mainly urban society. Already over a third of Mexicans lived in cities of at least twenty thousand inhabitants. And over all, guiding, coaxing, compelling, there appeared a new generation of national leaders, trained in

[4] Gill: op. cit., p. 65.

the offices of the regime and intent both on preserving the order and accelerating the progress they now called the Institutional Revolution.[5]

Morelos was full in the middle of the rush and swell. There indeed the changes were extraordinarily drastic, the population doubling, the output of cash crops (sugar cane, rice, and peanuts) more than doubling, the number of industrial enterprises probably quadrupling, and the number of industrial workers probably quintupling. Typical of the local boom was the expanding operation at the Zacatepec sugar mill. Despite decrepit machinery, a labyrinthine organization, and obsolete plans, the managers of the cooperative raised production 37 per cent between 1953 and 1962. Connecting roads reached out from the big mill to all the fifty-odd ejidos producing for it. So did medical, technical, and educational services.[6] So did credit, which a National Ejidal Bank channeled through the cooperative to individual ejidos. And so did directions from the government's Export-Import Agency, concerning what to plant, how much, when to sow, when

[5] For the trends of the period, see Frank R. Brandenburg: *The Making of Modern Mexico* (Englewood Cliffs, 1964); François Chevalier: "«Ejido» et Stabilité au Mexique," *Revue Française de Science Politique,* XVI, 4 (August 1966), 717–52; Howard F. Cline: *Mexico. Revolution to Evolution, 1940–1960* (New York, 1962); Floyd and Lillian O. Dotson: "Urban Centralization and Decentralization in Mexico," *Rural Sociology,* XXI, 1 (March 1956), 41–9; Marco Antonio Durán: "Condiciones y perspectivas de la agricultura mexicana," *El Trimestre Económico,* XXVIII, 1 (January 1961), 52–79, and "Las funciones de la propiedad de la tierra en la reforma agraria mexicana," ibid., XXXI, 2 (April 1964), 228–42; Julio Durán Ochoa: *Población* (México, 1955); Edmundo Flores: *Tratado de Economía Agrícola* (México, 1961); Pablo González Casanova: *La democracia en México* (México, 1965); Paul Lamartine Yates: *El desarrollo regional de México* (2nd edn., México, 1962); Oscar Lewis: "Mexico Since Cárdenas," in Richard N. Adams et al., *Social Change in Latin America Today* (New York, 1960); Gilberto Loyo: *La población de México, estado actual y tendencia, 1960–1980* (México, 1960); Pierre Monbeig: "Le mouvement démographique au Mexique," *Tiers-Monde,* IV, 15 (July 1963), 387–406; Nathan Whetten and Robert G. Burnight: "Internal Migration in Mexico," *Rural Sociology,* XXI, 2 (June 1956), 140–51. For recent comments, see Kuhn, Loeb & Co.: *Prospectus, $15,000,000, Mexico* (New York, 1966).

[6] Holt Büttner: op. cit., pp. 23, 58–66, 71–85. *Anuario Estadístico de los Estados Unidos Mexicanos, 1958–1959* (México, 1960), pp. 444–6, 523, and *VIII Censo General de Población, 1960. 8 de Junio de 1960. Resumen General* (México, 1962), pp. 365, 392. *Resumen del Boletín mensual de la Dirección General de Economía Agrícola,* No. 428–33 (January–June 1962), p. 42; No. 434–9 (July–December 1962), pp. 38–9, 63; No. 464–9 (January–June 1965), pp. 11, 15, 17; No. 470–5 (July–December 1965), pp. 48, 52, 54. Urbán Aguirre: op. cit., pp. 258–9.

to reap. Although the state remained obviously agricultural, life there increasingly resembled life in a factory.

Morelos became a hive of newcomers. For restless and destitute immigrants it was both a frontier, where they could start again for free, and a transit camp, where they could prepare for the leap into Mexico City. For the widening class of successful metropolitans it was a retreat where they could pay down on weekend homes and hope to retire. For real-estate promoters it was a paradise to subdivide and mark skeleton streets through. For entrepreneurs in general it was a bustling market. Already by 1950 nearly one fourth of Morelos residents were not natives. In municipalities like Zacatepec, Jojutla, and Cuautla the proportion ranged from a third to nearly a half, and in Cuernavaca the natives were the minority. By 1960 the proportion of immigrants in the state was 36 per cent. Six or seven years later it approached 50 per cent. By then, as the planters had fondly dreamed half a century before, even the Japanese had arrived—not as peons, however, but as technicians for a new automobile factory outside Cuernavaca. Through the deluge the legal pattern of land tenure remained intact, over 32,000 ejidatarios in over 200 ejidos holding some 740,000 acres in fields, timber, and pasture, which was over 80 per cent of the useful soil, and around 10,000 private proprietors holding the rest, mainly in minute plots; but the development of local communities was bewilderingly different from what had gone before. Cuernavaca, Cuautla, and Jojutla grew of course into major centers. But so did Zacatepec, a pueblo of only 1,900 souls in 1940, a town of 7,000 in 1950, and a city of 13,500 by 1960, the state's second largest. And while some old villages like Huitzilac and Jonacatepec remained smaller than before the revolution, and others like Jantetelco and Coatlán del Río barely grew, a new colonia like Emiliano Zapata, founded only in 1940, burgeoned into a town of over 7,000 by 1960.[7]

Politically too the state reformed. Almost all the Zapatista old-timers passed on, like de la O in 1952, into tombs their kinfolk invoked the Virgin of Guadalupe to hallow. The few survivors were mostly too aged for more than a quiet sit in the morning sun. Only here and there was a veteran of the great ordeal still active, working a little through the week and then on

[7] *Séptimo Censo General de Población, 6 de Junio de 1950. Estado de Morelos* (México, 1953), pp. 46–7; *VIII Censo, Resumen General*, pp. 247, 363, 365, 392–3, 425, and *VIII Censo General de Población, 1960. 8 de Junio de 1960. Localidades de la República por entidades y municipios*, 2 vols. (México, 1963), I, 762–6. Urbán Aguirre: op. cit., pp. 260–1. Holt Büttner: op. cit., pp. 94–105. "Mexico, Land does not pay," *The Economist*, November 12, 1966.

Sunday taking buses around to see old comrades and gather signatures for a local petition. The new officials were young men, often graduates of the National University. Increasingly they were earnest, aware, energetic, anxious at once to keep the system functioning smoothly and "to carry out the mission which is entrusted to the modern state, to offer the maximum in public and social services to the governed."[8] By neat constitutional schedule the governors and legislatures assumed authority and then surrendered it. Between 1946 and 1958 only three strikes formally occurred in Morelos, involving only ninety-four workers.[9] True, corruption persisted at many levels of state and municipal government. So did the habit of official violence—which led in 1962 to the assassination of a popular ejidatario chief from Tlaquiltenango, Rubén Jaramillo, his wife, and three stepsons.[1] But the ensuing scandal seemed more significant than the murder, as evidence that even those urbanites who had frowned on Jaramillo believed brutality belonged to the past and now expected more subtlety from their rulers. At his inauguration in 1964 the new governor sharply condemned his predecessors' ways and promised "a new stage in the institutional life of the state."[2]

Still Anenecuilco languished. After Franco's death it grew more slowly than before, accumulating only fifteen or twenty new inhabitants each year, to remain in the 1960's a minor village of some 1,250. Even they were too many for the ejido to support. So pressing was the demand of the pueblo on the supply of land that the average ejidal holding shrank to around five acres, on which plot alone no family could make a living. The scourge of the village was no longer Nicolás Zapata, removed, according to rumor, to a rich hacienda in Veracruz, the gift of the government to keep him out of trouble in Morelos. The scourge was now the Ejidal Bank, the only bank most ejidatarios had access to. Ruling from Zacatepec, its officials would not advance credit to farmers to raise livestock or poultry, to tend orchards or apiaries, to grow melons or tomatoes, ventures that the nearby markets in Cuautla and Mexico City would reward lavishly. They would finance only the culture of cane and rice, the first paying an aver-

---

[8] *Informe que rindió ante el H. Cabildo el Sr. Valentín López González, Presidente municipal constitucional de Cuernavaca, Morelos, 1964–1965* (Cuernavaca, 1965), p. 1.

[9] *Anuario Estadístico, 1946–1950,* pp. 288–309; *1954,* pp. 373–409; *1958–1959,* pp. 400–29.

[1] *Presente!,* May 27, June 3, 10, 17, and 24, and July 1, 1962.

[2] *El Universal,* May 19, 1964.

age ejidatario around 450 pesos a year, the second paying at best around 525—between ten and twelve cents a day.

Even so villagers stayed. To eke out their income they managed various expedients. One ejidatario might rent his field to the Zacatepec mill or to a private mill in Cuautla and then work for a guaranteed minimum wage. Another might rent to a neighbor and work for him, or try a season as a migrant laborer, perhaps in the United States. A lucky few managed to buy private plots outside the ejido, lease several more inside, get credit independently, and diversify operations. Most could only work longer and harder, hiring themselves out to their palmier fellows, until they spent more time in others' fields than in their own.

Rather than invest the bank's credit in the soil, they lived off it as a salary. When they needed mules or tractors, they contracted them from outside. Their debts soared. By the late 1950's the pueblo owed altogether around 200,000 pesos, one ejidatario alone owing 23,000. In effect the villagers became the bank's employees, or peons. Anenecuilcans lamented, mistakenly but to the point: "We lived easy when we had no land!"[3]

It was quiet there, well off the highway. The road into the village and the main paths were where they had always been, and the low adobe houses looked the same as before. Though on a Sunday a writer might come down from Mexico City in search of a story, he found the tombstones in the cemetery as interesting as the local conversation—Fidencio Espejo, Zapata's father-in-law, 1909, María de Jesús Zapata, 1940, María de la Luz Zapata, 1944, Franco and his sons, 1947.[4] (Whoever succeeded Franco as chief went without publicity and its jinx.) In the early 1960's, to appease metropolitan intellectuals who wanted to bestow the benefits of a Zapatista museum on the pueblo, the federal government built a concrete pavilion over the ruins of Zapata's father's house; but only stray tourists on personal pilgrimages found their way to the site. On the morning of every August 8 state and national dignitaries gathered in the little amphitheater next to the pavilion to praise Zapata on his birthday; but by mid-afternoon, before the rain, they were gone, and the pueblo was again hot, melancholy, quiet. Usually, because the women were indoors and the men out in the fields, the village

---

[3] Gill: op. cit., pp. 58–62. *Resumen del Boletín mensual de la Dirección General de Economía Agrícola*, No. 428–33 (January–June 1962), pp. 76–8. Antonio Tapia: *La economía de la producción agrícola en el Distrito Económico de Cuautla, Estado de Morelos* (México, 1960). Ramón Fernández y Fernández: "Notas Bibliográficas," *El Trimestre Económico*, XXVIII, 2 (April 1961), 349–54.

[4] Gastón García Cantú: *Utopías mexicanas* (México, 1963), pp. 120–8.

seemed empty, almost deserted. Now and then young people appeared, on silent errands in the street or muttering hard in games in the dusty walled yard beside the church. A foreign visitor winced at seeing them. In this village, he thought, children still learned respect for elders, duty to kin, honor in work and play, curious lessons to carry into a world about to fly a man to the moon, deliberately capable of nuclear war, already guilty of genocide. But being Anenecuilcans, he decided, they would probably stand the strain.

APPENDIXES

BIBLIOGRAPHICAL NOTE

APPENDIX A

Major Plantations in Morelos, 1908–1909

THIS TABLE DERIVES from the figures of Diez and Magaña, which are incomplete. Although Southworth's directory of haciendas is also incomplete, it suggests that the Araoz, Escandón, and Amor holdings were almost twice as large, and the Alonso holdings almost fourteen times as large, as listed here.[1]

MILLS	OWNERS	HACIENDAS	ACREAGE
Zacatepec	Juan Pagaza	Zacatepec	8,480.5
San Nicolás	Juan Pagaza	San Nicolás	
Cuahuixtla	Manuel Araoz	Cuahuixtla	31,292.7
Treinta	Manuel Araoz	Treinta	
	Manuel Araoz	Acamilpa	
Santa Clara	Luis García Pimentel	Santa Clara	168,420.9
Tenango	Luis García Pimentel	Tenango	
	Luis García Pimentel	San Ignacio	
Hospital	Vicente Alonso's widow	Hospital	2,614.3
Calderón	Vicente Alonso's widow	Calderón	
Chinameca	Vicente Alonso's widow	Chinameca	
Tenextepango	Ignacio de la Torre y Mier	Tenextepango	38,750.2
Atlihuayán	Sons of Antonio Escandón	Atlihuayán	14,937.2
	Sons of Antonio Escandón	Xochimancas	
San Carlos	Estate of Tomás de la Torre	San Carlos	6,980.6
	Estate of Tomás de la Torre	Cocoyoc	
	Estate of Tomás de la Torre	Pantitlán	
Miacatlán	Romualdo Pasquel	Miacatlán	42,837.3
	Romualdo Pasquel	Acatzingo	

[1] Diez: *Dos conferencias,* p. 56. Magaña: op. cit., 1, 39. Southworth: op. cit., pp. 217–19.

Cocoyotla	Romualdo Pasquel	Cocoyotla	
San Vicente	Estate of Delfín Sánchez	San Vicente	20,538.9
	Estate of Delfín Sánchez	Chiconcuac	
	Estate of Delfín Sánchez	Dolores	
	Estate of Delfín Sánchez	San Gaspar	
	Estate of Delfín Sánchez	Atlacomulco	
San Gabriel	Emmanuel Amor	San Gabriel	50,037.8
Actopan	Emmanuel Amor	Actopan	
Santa Inés	Benito Arena's widow	Santa Inés	6,177.5
	Benito Arena's widow	Guadalupe	
	Benito Arena's widow	Buenavista	
Oacalco	Francisco A. Vélez	Oacalco	9,192.1
	Francisco A. Vélez	Michate	
Temilpa	Manuel Alarcón	Temilpa	12,288.3
Santa Cruz	J. Pliego de Pérez	Santa Cruz	1,608.6
Casasano	E. Vélez de Goríbar	Casasano	5,638.8
Temixco	Concepción T. G. de Fernández	Temixco	42,748.3
Cuauchichinola	Sixto Sarmina	Cuauchichinola	4,647.9

APPENDIX B

The Plan de Ayala

THE ZAPATISTAS SWORE BY THEIR PLAN DE AYALA. From late November 1911, when they first proclaimed it, until the spring of 1918, when they shelved it for the sake of "unification," the Zapatista chiefs considered the plan a veritable cathol-icon, much more than a program of action, almost a Scripture. They would brook no compromise of its provisions, no irreverence toward its projects—which were to issue in a classic Mexican millennium. In their own shrinking domains in Morelos and Puebla they remained its devotees until they pledged allegiance to the Plan de Agua Prieta in April 1920. Afterward the Ayala plan became famous as the premier banner of modern Mexico's most remarkable and contro-versial experiment, agrarian reform.

The plan was not an instant creation. As a statement of attitudes it had been evolving for at least some fifty years, through the public lessons Juárez had given in the supreme importance of "principles," "law," and "justice," through the formation of national pride in the resistance against the French, through the exasperation with personal promises and political abuses during Don Porfirio's long reign, and lately through the abortion of hopes in the virtuous Madero. As a statement of the specific Zapatista position in revolutionary politics, it had been gestating for about nine months. The matrix was Madero's San Luis plan, to which in March 1911 the Ayalans had announced their allegiance. Thus they demanded the dismissal of all incumbent officials, local and federal, elected and appointed, the free election and impartial appointment of new authorities, and judicial review of all disputed cases involving rural real estate. Zapata's position remained the same through the summer, even through the bitter crisis of August.

Not until late September, after the federals had chased them out of Morelos, did the Zapatistas define demands of their own. Their statement was a crude

"Memorial which contains the petitions of the Counterrevolutionaries to President of the Republic Francisco L. de la Barra." Although in their obvious suspicion of electoral solutions they anticipated features of the radical plan to follow, they were nevertheless generally committed to the old limits.

I.   We recognize and respect Francisco L. de la Barra, present Provisional President of the Republic.

II.   We declare that the present Provisional Governors be dismissed and that [their successors] be named either by the will of the people or of the Generals and Chiefs of the present Counterrevolution. As well as the Commander in Chief and the forces who garrison their [the state capitals'?] plazas.

III.   We ask that the federal forces evacuate the Plazas which they are presently occupying in the States of Morelos, Puebla, Guerrero, and Oaxaca.

IV.   That [the imminent presidential] elections be suspended.

V.   That to the pueblos there be given what in justice they deserve as to lands, timber, and water, which [claim] has been the origin of the present Counterrevolution.

VI.   We ask that Political Prefectures be abolished and that absolute liberty be given to all political prisoners of the Nation.

Effective Suffrage No-Reelection. Sn. Juan
del Río, [Puebla,] Sept. 26, 1911.

[SIGNED,] *Emiliano Zapata, Eufemio Zapata,*
José Trinidad Ruiz, Augustín Quiros, Jesús Jáuregui,
Emigdio L. Marmolejo, José Cruz, Jesús Navarro,
José Rodríguez, Jesús Sánchez, José Vergara,
Mariano Rodríguez, Próculo Capistrán, Amador Salazar.

If de la Barra granted their petitions, the Zapatistas promised to lay down their arms immediately.[1]

Six weeks later Zapata clarified his position in stating conditions for surrender to the new President, Madero. This statement was clearer and more to the point than September's because Gabriel Robles Domínguez had helped compose it. It was also more moderate, in applying only to Morelos, in dropping the demand for "justice" to the pueblos there and changing it to a demand for "an agrarian law," and in recognizing the President's role in the appointments of a new governor and state police chief.

1.   General Ambrosio Figueroa will be withdrawn from the Government of the State.

2.   The forces which Federico Morales commands will be withdrawn from the State.

3.   A general pardon will be conceded to all those risen in arms.

[1] Memorial . . . , September 26, 1911, AA.

4. There will be granted an agrarian law attempting to improve the condition of the laborer in the field.

5. Federal troops will be withdrawn from the towns in the State which they presently occupy. The period in which those forces must withdraw will remain [a matter for] the prudent judgment of the President of the Republic; but General Zapata, in representation of his companions in arms and for himself, respectfully asks Sr. Madero that this period not exceed 45 days.

6. While the federal forces retire, 500 men of General Zapata's forces will remain armed, the town or towns in which they must quarter being assigned by the [Chief] Executive. This force will have the character of rural police and will take orders therefore from the Minister of the Interior.

7. The chief of these forces will be designated by Sr. Madero, but General Zapata for himself and in representation of his second chiefs respectfully asks that the appointment fall on the person of Señor Don Raúl Madero or Eufemio Zapata.

8. Passports or safeconducts will be expedited to all chiefs of those risen in arms.

9. General Zapata will not intervene in the affairs of the Government of the State and will try to use his personal influence to make the constituted authorities respected.

10. The Federal Government will turn over the amount of 10,000 pesos to pay the loans which have been made in the revolution.

11. The Governor of the State will be named by the principal revolutionary Chiefs of the State, in accord with Sr. Madero.

12. Villa de Ayala will remain garrisoned with 50 men from the State's rural police.

13. General Zapata's forces will concentrate immediately in Villa de Ayala and Jonacatepec.

Villa de Ayala, November 11, 1911.

[SIGNED,] *General Emiliano Zapata.*[2]

Two weeks later the Zapatistas formally started their own revolution under the Plan de Ayala. On the question of who composed the plan, outsiders have given widely varying opinions. One believed that Francisco Vázquez Gómez wrote it and passed it on to Zapata.[3] Another asserted that Francisco's brother, Emilio, then in exile in San Antonio, had taken there a copy of a plan proposed by Otilio Montaño, toned it down, and sent it back to Morelos for proclamation.[4] Another declared that Emilio Vázquez, Montaño, Paulino Martínez, and En-

[2] Cited in Magaña: op. cit., II, 65–6.

[3] Ramón Prida: *De la dictadura a la anarquía* (2nd edn., México, 1958), p. 382.

[4] Teodoro Hernández: "La verdad sobre el zapatismo," *Mujeres y Deportes,* February 13, 1937.

rique Bonilla, then an editor of *Diario del Hogar,* all collaborated on the final version.[5] Yet another says that three obscure Guerrerans—Gonzalo Ávila, Salustio Carrasco Núñez, and Fidel Fuentes—produced the plan and sent it to Montaño in September 1911.[6] Others have reported that Palafox or Soto y Gama wrote it.[7] These accounts rest on very flimsy evidence. There is also an official Zapatista story of the composition, to the accuracy of which both the style and the content of the plan strongly testify.

According to this account, Zapata resented metropolitan reports that his October raids into Morelos and the Federal District were only for pillage. And he asked Montaño to draw up a program to prove that the Zapatistas were not mere bandits. Counseled by the leading chiefs, Montaño and his aides composed a tentative version. In early November Zapata examined it and praised it, but judged it no longer necessary because of the deal he was going to arrange with Robles Domínguez. After the negotiations collapsed, Zapata and Montaño escaped into the Puebla mountains together and hid out around the village of Miquetzingo. There they drafted the final version. The ideas were those Zapata took as the consensus of his chiefs; the phrasing was mostly Montaño's. When they finished, Zapata assembled all the chiefs in the area, and in the little neighboring town of Ayoxustla they heard the plan read and signed it. Zapata then moved into headquarters in the Morelos mountains near Huautla, where a parish priest typed several copies of the plan for him. These he sent to the embassies in Mexico City and to his main agent there, Gildardo Magaña. He instructed Magaña to suspend talks with "Maderismo" and to try to have the "important document" published. Of all the metropolitan editors, only Bonilla of the *Diario del Hogar* would ask Madero if he could publish it. "Yes," Madero said, "publish it so everyone will know how crazy that Zapata is." So he did on December 15, in a double edition that quickly sold out.[8]

Garbled and rambling, without a hint of metropolitan grace, the thing was truly a caution—literally as well as colloquially. Most striking were four radical changes in the Zapatista position. First, the operation Zapata and his chiefs

[5] Francisco Cosío Robelo: "El dragón de dos cabezas. Zapata y Pascual Orozco," ibid., March 6, 1937.

[6] Figueroa Uriza: op. cit., I, 275–6.

[7] E.g., Gates in *World's Work,* April 1919, p. 658.

[8] Magaña: op. cit., II, 80–3. For elaborations and confirmations of this account, see Palacios: *Zapata,* pp. 62–3, and *El Plan de Ayala. Sus orígenes y su promulgación* (3rd edn., México, 1953), pp. 47–8, 57–61; Serafín M. Robles: "Semblanza del Plan de Ayala" and "El Plan de Ayala. Cómo fue el juramento de este Histórico Documento," *El Campesino,* January 1950 and December 1954; and Gómez: *Las comisiones,* pp. 93–6.

carried on was no longer a local movement of protest in Morelos or regionally through the south, but a national movement to seize federal authority. Second, the revolutionaries would not only restore fields to pueblos that had lost them, but would also expropriate some land from rightful holders whom they judged "monopolists," and would expropriate completely landlords who opposed them. Third, they would treat Maderista revolutionaries whom they captured in battle not as prisoners of war but as traitors. Fourth, to discourage personal ambitions, they would not name a provisional president or governors until after they had taken power. Measures like the last three no other revolutionary group except the anarcho-syndicalists would advocate, much less adopt as policy, for another three years. At least the Ayala plan was an alert to politicians in Mexico City about how militant and canny part of the rural population had become. But preoccupied otherwise as they were, it only convinced them of how eccentric agrarian demands were.

Distinct traces of other revolutionary documents mark the Plan de Ayala. One is the Plan de Tacubaya in support of Emilio Vázquez for president, dated October 31, 1911. It stresses allegations of Madero's personal treachery and political incapacity, and frames the Vazquista operation as a continuation and fulfillment of the original movement of 1910. Appropriately reframed, these notions and some of the Tacubayan language figure tediously in the Ayala plan, and mainly in the same section—a long discursive preface, which in the Zapatista version runs on through the first article. The source of the Tacubayan influence was probably Paulino Martínez, cosigner of the Vazquista plan and friend of the Ayalans. Probably he exchanged complaints with Zapata and Montaño and passed on his disgust with Madero to reinforce theirs, as well as a vocabulary in which to articulate it. Quite possibly even a copy of the Tacubaya plan reached the southern camp to serve as a model of denunciation. The other imprint on the Ayala plan is that of several Liberal Party papers, dating from the program of 1906, a reasoned statement of intended reforms, to the manifesto of September 23, 1911, a vivid and moving anarcho-syndicalist call for Mexicans to expropriate land and factories and use them for the common welfare.[9] Many of the concepts and phrases that the Liberals harped on most intensely, and most recently in the September manifesto, flash repeatedly through the Ayala plan. Twelve times, for instance, appear images of blood, wounds, bloody conflicts, blood and fire, bloodshed, remarks which rarely or never occur in other plans but which are frequent in Liberal literature. Also, nationalization and expropriation are acts that only the Liberals had promoted before (for four or five years,

[9] For the manifesto, see Ricardo Flores Magón: *Vida y Obra. Semilla Libertaria,* 3 vols. (México, 1923), II, 36–45.

most vigorously since September) and which only they and the Zapatistas proposed out loud in 1911. Likewise the Liberals had argued loudly and explicitly for a merging of familial loyalties into a grand revolutionary solidarity, and assuming the argument, the Zapatistas followed them: whereas Madero in his plan had appealed only to "compatriots" and "fellow citizens," the Ayalans appealed to "our brothers." And pegged firmly into the Plan de Ayala are other words that were the political currency of the Mexican opposition but on which the Liberals always had a special claim—dictatorship, justice, tyrant, despot, chains, slaves, yoke, welfare, fatherland. Finally the plan's motto, "Liberty, Justice, and Law," is a close take on the slogan of the Liberal program of 1906, "Reform, Justice, and Law." Since there were no Liberals then agitating among the Zapatistas, the source of their semantic and political influence was probably their clandestine newspaper, *Regeneración,* which Zapata and Montaño knew and which couriers could deliver from the capital.

But the notation of its putative intellectual debts does not exhaust the work. Despite its Vazquista tones the Ayala plan was no piece of Vazquista propaganda, as many metropolitan politicians thought at the time. If it was in support of Emilio, why was it not so openly—especially at the very moment when the Vazquistas needed all the public revolutionary sympathy they could muster? Why did "the sons of the State of Morelos" not refer once to Emilio or Francisco? Why was their first choice for Supreme Chief the revolutionary then Emilio's worst rival, Pascual Orozco? Nor for all its blood and brimstone was the plan another Liberal tract. In passages the anarcho-syndicalists must have gagged on or laughed at, it recognized "God" as well as "the people" helping to initiate the revolution in 1910, indicated only obliquely that an industrial proletariat even existed, and admitted the right of private propery for pueblos and individuals. It was innocent of the idea of a struggle of classes, and reflected suppositions about international affairs that reduced to a hope for approval from "the civilized world," Edwardian Europe and the Taftian United States. Although from 1910 on the Liberals had broadcast a new slogan perfectly tailored for the southern movement, "Land and Liberty," the Ayalans went on with their old motto, amending it only to "Reform, Liberty, Justice, and Law."

The Plan de Ayala was an original, more so than most of the other revolutionary plans, programs, and manifestoes that have appeared in Mexican history. Its most important articles, for instance, six, seven, and eight, on agrarian reform, contain almost nothing borrowed from previous plans, although there was much to borrow. The special disposition in Article 8 on behalf of widows and orphans is also without precedent. So is Article 10, on traitors to the revolution.

The most original and interesting feature of the plan is the sense of history pervading it. Most other contemporary plans had few roots in the Mexican past, and then only in the immediate past. In the San Luis plan, for instance, there is one late mention in passing of the anti-reelectionist provisions in Don Porfirio's revolutionary Plans of La Noria (1871) and Tuxtepec (1876). But in the Ayala plan a major early charge against Madero is his "profound disrespect for . . . the immortal Code of '57, written with the revolutionary blood of Ayutla." And to expropriate the planters' property the "norm and example" are the laws "put in force by the immortal Juárez on ecclesiastical properties, which punished the despots and conservatives who in every time have tried to impose on us the ignominious yoke of oppression and backwardness." Nowhere in the plan is there a reference to "peace" or "progress" or "democracy," the goals professed in other plans and preeminently the concerns of the citified men of the day. Instead the aim is "to recover the liberties" of a republican people and, twice stated, to bring about "prosperity and well-being," which was no new dream in Mexico but a utopia first conceived there in the flushest times of the sixteenth century, revived during the eighteenth century by Bourbon reformers, endorsed and publicized by Humboldt, recurring constantly through the difficult attempts to establish independence, and then largely subsumed and repressed during the long Porfirian "evolution." Emerging from this oldest of Mexican fashions, the Ayala plan had a tremendous and poignant impact on men who could not imagine their country basically different. Others, for whom history was a drag, it touched not at all.

The paste-gem fanciness of the plan's rhetoric was no doubt Montaño's. An ill-paid village schoolteacher, having learned and now teaching from textbooks produced by Porfirio Díaz's educational system, Montaño lived a raggedly painful present and glorified what he believed a happier past. Ironically the glorification was easier because of the official ideology. This was to depict Díaz as one more hero in an honored republican succession, to legitimize his role in Mexican history. First came Hidalgo, then Morelos, then Juárez, then the most heroic republican, Juárez's mighty general and proper heir, Don Porfirio.[1] Presumably the next in this line, which seemed to progress in the manner of the later Hapsburgs, was Díaz's Vice President, the notoriously corrupt Ramón Corral. For country intellectuals like Montaño, the contrast was too cutting. The more outrageous the científicos became, the grander the traditional heroes looked, especially Juárez. On Villa de Ayala's centennial committee Montaño could sharpen his identification with the old champions and his fury with the new entrepreneurs.

[1] A favorite text was Manuel Payno's *Compendio de la historia de México* (6th edn., México, 1880).

Zapata also looked back to the leaders of the past for precedents and inspiration. His primary-school teacher in Anenecuilco had been a veteran of the War against the French Intervention, and Zapata remembered well his classes in history.[2] Two of his uncles had fought against the French with the Republican loyalists at Puebla, and he grew up listening to their tales. He himself often referred in conversation to Hidalgo, Morelos, and Juárez. Chief of his village and by necessity a student of its history in the sources, the land titles, Zapata knew in detail how and why it had struggled. For him as for Montaño the Plan de Ayala was one more declaration in defense of the pueblos and the people, which they could hardly tell apart.

The following translation I made from the version of the plan published in the *Diario del Hogar*, December 15, 1911. This was the first version widely known in Mexico City. There are others, among them the official Zapatista version published in Magaña: op. cit., II, 83–7. The differences are minor rewordings, omissions, and grammatical and other corrections. Of the last, the most noteworthy is the legal refinement of Article 12, which as it originally stood violated constitutional procedure—Congress, not the President, properly having the authority at first assigned to him.[3] To give a faithful translation I tried not to clarify what was obscure, nor unravel what was tangled, nor tighten what was loose. In some places, where Spanish syntax swings on but English breaks down, I had to insert words in brackets to keep an obvious meaning obvious. I also changed punctuation here and there for the same reason. Highfalutin words I tried to find equivalents for, rather than deflate them, because I thought they conveyed the rural writer's indignation better. After all, it is his show.

Liberating Plan of the sons of the State of Morelos, affiliated with the Insurgent Army which defends the fulfillment of the Plan of San Luis, with the reforms which it has believed proper to add in benefit of the Mexican Fatherland.

We who undersign, constituted in a revolutionary junta to sustain and carry out the promises which the revolution of November 20, 1910, just past, made to the country, declare solemnly before the face of the civilized world which judges us and before the nation to which we belong and which we call [*sic, llamamos,* misprint for *amamos,* love], propositions which we have formulated to end the tyranny which oppresses us and redeem the fatherland from the dictatorships which are imposed on us, which [propositions] are determined in the following plan:

1.   Taking into consideration that the Mexican people led by Don Francisco I. Madero went to shed their blood to reconquer liberties and recover their

---

[2] Palacios: *Zapata,* p. 18, and Páez in *El Sol de Puebla,* April 2, 1951.

[3] This and the official version are both in González Ramírez: *Planes,* pp. 73–83. A handwritten copy of the plan, dated November 28, 1911, is in AZ, 28: 14.

rights which had been trampled on, and not for a man to take possession of power, violating the sacred principles which he took an oath to defend under the slogan "Effective Suffrage and No Reelection," outraging thus the faith, the cause, the justice, and the liberties of the people: taking into consideration that that man to whom we refer is Don Francisco I. Madero, the same who initiated the above-cited revolution, who imposed his will and influence as a governing norm on the Provisional Government of the ex-President of the Republic Attorney Francisco L. de Barra [*sic*], causing with this deed repeated sheddings of blood and multiplicate misfortunes for the fatherland in a manner deceitful and ridiculous, having no intentions other than satisfying his personal ambitions, his boundless instincts as a tyrant, and his profound disrespect for the fulfillment of the preexisting laws emanating from the immortal code of '57, written with the revolutionary blood of Ayutla;

Taking into account that the so-called Chief of the Liberating Revolution of Mexico, Don Francisco I. Madero, through lack of integrity and the highest weakness, did not carry to a happy end the revolution which gloriously he initiated with the help of God and the people, since he left standing most of the governing powers and corrupted elements of oppression of the dictatorial government of Porfirio Díaz, which are not nor can in any way be the representation of National Sovereignty, and which, for being most bitter adversaries of ours and of the principles which even now we defend, are provoking the discomfort of the country and opening new wounds in the bosom of the fatherland, to give it its own blood to drink; taking also into account that the aforementioned Sr. Francisco I. Madero, present President of the Republic, tries to avoid the fulfillment of the promises which he made to the Nation in the Plan of San Luis Potosí, being [*sic, siendo,* misprint for *ciñendo,* restricting] the above-cited promises to the agreements of Ciudad Juárez, by means of false promises and numerous intrigues against the Nation nullifying, pursuing, jailing, or killing revolutionary elements who helped him to occupy the high post of President of the Republic;

Taking into consideration that the so-often-repeated Francisco I. Madero has tried with the brute force of bayonets to shut up and to drown in blood the pueblos who ask, solicit, or demand from him the fulfillment of the promises of the revolution, calling them bandits and rebels, condemning them to a war of extermination without conceding or granting a single one of the guarantees which reason, justice, and the law prescribe; taking equally into consideration that the President of the Republic Francisco I. Madero has made of Effective Suffrage a bloody trick on the people, already against the will of the same people imposing Attorney José M. Pino Suárez in the Vice-Presidency of the Republic, or [imposing as] Governors of the States [men] designated by him, like the so-called General Ambrosio Figueroa, scourge and tyrant of the people of Morelos, or entering into scandalous cooperation with the científico party, feudal landlords, and oppressive bosses, enemies of the revolution proclaimed by him, so as to forge new chains and follow the pattern of a new dictatorship more shameful and more terrible than that of Porfirio Díaz, for it has been clear and patent that he has outraged the sovereignty of the States, trampling on the laws without any respect for lives or interests, as has happened in the State of Morelos, and others, leading them to the most horrendous anarchy which contemporary history registers.

For these considerations we declare the aforementioned Francisco I. Madero inept at realizing the promises of the revolution of which he was the author, because he has betrayed the principles with which he tricked the will of the people and was able to get into power: incapable of governing, because he has no respect for the law and justice of the pueblos, and a traitor to the fatherland, because he is humiliating in blood and fire Mexicans who want liberties, so as to please the científicos, landlords, and bosses who enslave us, and from today on we begin to continue the revolution begun by him, until we achieve the overthrow of the dictatorial powers which exist.

2. Recognition is withdrawn from Sr. Francisco I. Madero as Chief of the Revolution and as President of the Republic, for the reasons which before were expressed, it being attempted to overthrow this official.

3. Recognized as Chief of the Liberating Revolution is the illustrious General Pascual Orozco, the second of the Leader Don Francisco I. Madero, and in case he does not accept this delicate post, recognition as Chief of the Revolution will go to General Don Emiliano Zapata.

4. The Revolutionary Junta of the State of Morelos manifests to the Nation under formal oath: that it makes its own the plan of San Luis Potosí, with the additions which are expressed below in benefit of the oppressed pueblos, and it will make itself the defender of the principles it defends until victory or death.

5. The Revolutionary Junta of the State of Morelos will admit no transactions or compromises until it achieves the overthrow of the dictatorial elements of Porfirio Díaz and Francisco I. Madero, for the nation is tired of false men and traitors who make promises like liberators and who on arriving in power forget them and constitute themselves as tyrants.

6. As an additional part of the plan we invoke, we give notice: that [regarding] the fields, timber, and water which the landlords, científicos, or bosses have usurped, the pueblos or citizens who have the titles corresponding to those properties will immediately enter into possession of that real estate of which they have been despoiled by the bad faith of our oppressors, maintaining at any cost with arms in hand the mentioned possession; and the usurpers who consider themselves with a right to them [those properties] will deduce it before the special tribunals which will be established on the triumph of the revolution.

7. In virtue of the fact that the immense majority of Mexican pueblos and citizens are owners of no more than the land they walk on, suffering the horrors of poverty without being able to improve their social condition in any way or to dedicate themselves to Industry or Agriculture, because lands, timber, and water are monopolized in a few hands, for this cause there will be expropriated the third part of those monopolies from the powerful proprietors of them, with prior indemnization, in order that the pueblos and citizens of Mexico may obtain ejidos, colonies, and foundations for pueblos, or

fields for sowing or laboring, and the Mexicans' lack of prosperity and well-being may improve in all and for all.

8. [Regarding] The landlords, científicos, or bosses who oppose the present plan directly or indirectly, their goods will be nationalized and the two third parts which [otherwise would] belong to them will go for indemnizations of war, pensions for widows and orphans of the victims who succumb in the struggle for the present plan.

9. In order to execute the procedures regarding the properties aforementioned, the laws of disamortization and nationalization will be applied as they fit, for serving us as norm and example can be those laws put in force by the immortal Juárez on ecclesiastical properties, which punished the despots and conservatives who in every time have tried to impose on us the ignominious yoke of oppression and backwardness.

10. The insurgent military chiefs of the Republic who rose up with arms in hand at the voice of Don Francisco I. Madero to defend the plan of San Luis Potosí, and who oppose with armed force the present plan, will be judged traitors to the cause which they defended and to the fatherland, since at present many of them, to humor the tyrants, for a fistful of coins, or for bribes or connivance, are shedding the blood of their brothers who claim the fulfillment of the promises which Don Francisco I. Madero made to the nation.

11. The expenses of war will be taken in conformity with Article 11 of the Plan of San Luis Potosí, and all procedures employed in the revolution we undertake will be in conformity with the same instructions which the said plan determines.

12. Once triumphant the revolution which we carry into the path of reality, a Junta of the principal revolutionary chiefs from the different States will name or designate an interim President of the Republic, who will convoke elections for the organization of the federal powers.

13. The principal revolutionary chiefs of each State will designate in Junta the Governor of the State to which they belong, and this appointed official will convoke elections for the due organization of the public powers, the object being to avoid compulsory appointments which work the misfortune of the pueblos, like the so-well-known appointment of Ambrosio Figueroa in the State of Morelos and others who drive us to the precipice of bloody conflicts, sustained by the caprice of the dictator Madero and the circle of científicos and landlords who have influenced him.

14. If President Madero and other dictatorial elements of the present and former regime want to avoid the immense misfortunes which afflict the fatherland, and [if they] possess true sentiments of love for it, let them make immediate renunciation of the posts they occupy and with that they will with something staunch the grave wounds which they have opened in the bosom of the fatherland, since, if they do not do so, on their heads will fall the blood and the anathema of our brothers.

15. Mexicans: consider that the cunning and bad faith of one man is shedding blood in a scandalous manner, because he is incapable of governing; consider that his system of government is choking the fatherland and tram-

pling with the brute force of bayonets on our institutions; and thus, as we
raised up our weapons to elevate him to power, we again raise them up
against him for defaulting on his promises to the Mexican people and for
having betrayed the revolution initiated by him, we are not personalists, we
are partisans of principles and not of men!

Mexican People, support this plan with arms in hand and you will make
the prosperity and well-being of the fatherland.

Ayala, November 25, 1911   Liberty, Justice, and Law
Signed, General in Chief Emiliano Zapata; Generals Eufemio Zapata, Fran-
cisco Mendoza, Jesús Morales, Jesús Navarro, Otilio E. Montaño, José Trini-
dad Ruiz, Próculo Capistrán; Colonels Felipe Vaquero, Cesáreo Burgos,
Quintín González, Pedro Salazar, Simón Rojas, Emigdio Marmolejo, José
Campos, Pioquinto Galis, Felipe Tijera, Rafael Sánchez, José Pérez, Santiago
Aguilar, Margarito Martínez, Feliciano Domínguez, Manuel Vergara, Cruz
Salazar, Lauro Sánchez, Amador Salazar, Lorenzo Vázquez, Catarino Per-
domo, Jesús Sánchez, Domingo Romero, Zacarías Torres, Bonifacio García,
Daniel Andrade, Ponciano Domínguez, Jesús Capistrán; Captains Daniel
Mantilla, José M. Carrillo, Francisco Alarcón, Severiano Gutiérrez; and more
signatures follow. [This] is a true copy taken from the original. Camp in the
Mountains of Puebla, December 11, 1911. Signed, General in Chief Emiliano
Zapata.

APPENDIX C

The Agrarian Law

THE ZAPATISTAS' BASIC LAW OF AGRARIAN REFORM was as original as their Plan de Ayala. In the specific limits on individual agricultural holdings, in the provisions for direct expropriation of all land beyond those limits and not in the hands of villagers, in the definition of village land as perpetually inalienable, in the prohibition of agricultural syndicates and companies, in the assertion of confiscatory rights over "enemy" property, in the establishment of special agrarian courts and federal agencies of irrigation, rural credit, and agricultural education and research, in the enormous power assigned to the secretary of agriculture, and in the resort not to state but to municipal authorities for local execution, the Zapatista law departed radically from precedent revolutionary projects, bills, and laws. Most clearly it owed little to Carranza's decree of January 6, 1915.[1] Of the probably several coauthors of the law, no doubt the most important was Palafox.

The translation that follows is mine.[2] Again, I have altered the syntax and inserted words in brackets only to keep plain in English what is plain in Spanish. As elsewhere, I have transposed hectares into acres, a measure more familiar to readers of English.

UNITED MEXICAN STATES
Executive Council of the Republic
AGRARIAN LAW

THE EXECUTIVE COUNCIL, in use of the faculties invested in it, makes known to the inhabitants of the Mexican Republic:

[1] For contrary claims, see Antonio Díaz Soto y Gama: "La Ley Agraria del Villismo," *Excélsior,* October 26, 1950, and Gómez: "La Reforma Agraria," p. 167.

[2] The original text is available in Reyes H.: op. cit., pp. 125–34. There is a poor copy, misdated October 28, 1915, in AZ, 28: 5: 3.

Considering that in the Plan de Ayala are condensed the longings of the people risen in arms, especially in regard to agrarian recoveries, the intimate reason and supreme goal of the Revolution, therefore it is of necessary urgency to regulate duly the principles confirmed in said Plan in such a form that they can forthwith be carried into practice as general laws of immediate application.

Considering that the people have shown in various ways their wish to destroy at the roots and forever the unjust monopoly of land in order to realize a social state which guarantees fully the natural right which every man has to an extension of land necessary for his own subsistence and that of his family, it is a duty of the Revolutionary Authorities to respect that popular wish, expediting all those laws which, like the present, satisfy fully those legitimate aspirations of the people.

Considering that not a few authorities, far from fulfilling the sacred duty of doing revolutionary work, which the exercise of any and every public responsibility imposes in the present times, giving thereby proofs of not being identified with the Revolution, refuse to second the steps taken to obtain the economic and social emancipation of the people, making common cause with the reactionaries, landlords, and other exploiters of the working classes, therefore it becomes necessary, to define attitudes, that the Government declare definitively that it will consider disaffected from the cause and will hold responsible all those authorities who, forgetting their character as organs of the Revolution, do not assist effectively in the triumph of the Revolution's ideals.

For the preceding considerations, and taking into account that the Executive Council is the supreme authority of the Revolution, since the Sovereign Revolutionary Convention is not at present in session, [the Council] decrees:

ARTICLE 1. To communities and to individuals the fields, timber, and water of which they were despoiled are [hereby] restored, it being sufficient that they possess legal titles dated before the year 1856, in order that they enter immediately into possession of their properties.

ARTICLE 2. Individuals or groups who believe themselves entitled to the recovered properties of which the previous article speaks will have to adduce [the title] before commissions designated by the Department of Agriculture, within the year following the date of recovery, and subject to respective regulation.

ARTICLE 3. The Nation recognizes the traditional and historic right which the pueblos, ranchos, and communities of the Republic have of possessing and administering their fields of communal distribution [común repartimiento] and communal use [ejidos] in the form which they judge proper.

ARTICLE 4. The Nation recognizes the unquestionable right which belongs to every Mexican of possessing and cultivating an extension of land, the products of which permit him to cover his needs and those of his family; consequently and in order to create small property, there will be expropriated, by reason of public utility and by means of the corresponding indemnization, all the lands of the country, with the sole exception of the fields belonging to pueblos, rancherías, and communities, and those farms which, because they do not exceed the maximum which this law fixes, must remain in the power of their present proprietors.

ARTICLE 5. Proprietors who are not enemies of the Revolution will keep as inexpropriable terrain portions which do not exceed the area which, as a maximum, the following table fixes:

CLIMATE	QUALITY OF LAND	WATER	ACREAGE
Hot	Prime	Irrigated	247.1
Hot	Prime	Seasonal	345.9
Hot	Secondary	Irrigated	296.5
Hot	Secondary	Seasonal	445.8
Temperate	Prime	Irrigated	296.5
Temperate	Prime	Seasonal	535.4
Temperate	Poor	Irrigated	345.9
Temperate	Poor	Seasonal	494.2
Cold	Prime	Irrigated	345.9
Cold	Prime	Seasonal	445.8
Cold	Poor	Irrigated	445.8
Cold	Poor	Seasonal	543.6
Rich fields of pasture			1,235.5
Poor fields of pasture			2,471.0
Rich fields of rubber shrub			741.3
Poor fields of rubber shrub			1,235.5
Henequen fields			741.3
Untilled fields in the North of the Republic—Coahuila, Chihuahua, Durango, the North of Zacatecas and the North of San Luis Potosí			3,706.5

ARTICLE 6. Declared as national property are the rural properties of the enemies of the Revolution. Enemies of the Revolution are, for the effects of the present Law:

a. Individuals who under the regime of Porfirio Díaz formed part of the group of politicians and financiers which public opinion designated with the name of "Científico Party."

b. Governors and other officials of the States who during the administrations of Porfirio Díaz and Victoriano Huerta acquired properties by fraudulent or immoral means, taking unfair advantage of their official position, appealing to violence or sacking the public treasury.

c. Politicians, public employees, and businessmen who, without having belonged to the "Científico Party," made fortunes, having recourse to criminal procedures or [operating] under the protection of concessions notoriously costly to the country.

d. The authors and accomplices of the coup of the Ciudadela [which overthrew Madero in February 1913].

e. Individuals who in the administration of Victoriano Huerta served in public posts of political character.

f. High members of the Clergy who helped to sustain the usurper Huerta, by financial means or by propaganda among the faithful; and

g. Those who directly or indirectly helped the dictatorial governments of Díaz, Huerta, and other governments hostile to the Revolution in their struggle against the same.

Included in this clause are all those who provided said governments funds or subsidies for war, supported or subventioned newspapers to combat the Revolution, attacked or denounced the supporters of the same, carried on divisive activity among revolutionary elements, or in any other manner entered into complicity with the governments who fought against the revolutionary cause.

ARTICLE 7. Fields which exceed the extension mentioned in Article 5 will be expropriated by reason of public utility, through due indemnization, calculated according to the fiscal census of 1914, and in the time and form which regulation designates.

ARTICLE 8. The Department of Agriculture and Colonization will name commissions which, in the various States of the Republic and on the basis of the information in the case, will judge who are the persons who, according to Article 6, must be considered as enemies of the Revolution and subject therefore to the penalty of confiscation in reference, which will be applied immediately.

ARTICLE 9. Decisions delivered by the commissions mentioned remain subject to the definitive ruling delivered by special Land Tribunals which, in conformity with the disposition of Article 6 of the Plan de Ayala, must be instituted, and whose organization will be a matter for another law.

ARTICLE 10. The total area of lands which are obtained in virtue of the confiscation decreed against the enemies of the revolutionary cause, and in virtue of the expropriation which must be made of the fractions of farms which exceed the maximum fixed in Article 5, will be divided in lots which will be distributed among Mexicans who solicit them, preference being given in every case to country people. Each lot will have an extension such that it permits the satisfaction of a family's needs.

ARTICLE 11. To those presently sharecroppers or renters of small farms, these [farms] will be adjudicated as property, with absolute preference [to the present sharecroppers and renters] over any other solicitant, so long as those properties do not exceed the extension which each lot has to have in conformity with the disposition of the previous article.

ARTICLE 12. In order to fix the area which the said lots must have, the Department of Agriculture and Colonization will name technical commissions composed of engineers, who will locate and duly survey said lots, respecting in every case the fields belonging to the pueblos and those which are exempt from expropriation according to Article 5.

ARTICLE 13. To carry out their works of survey and subdivision, the said commissions will decide on the claims which are made before them by small proprietors who consider themselves despoiled by virtue of usurious contracts, by abuses or complicity of political bosses, or by seizures, or by usurpations committed by great landlords.

The decisions which are thereby delivered will be reviewed by the special Land Tribunals, which Article 9 mentions.

ARTICLE 14. The farms which the Government cedes to communities or individuals are not alienable, nor can they be mortgaged in any form, all contracts which tend to go against this disposition being null.

ARTICLE 15. The rights of property to fields subdivided and ceded by the Government to farmers can be transmitted only by legitimate inheritance.

ARTICLE 16. In order that the execution of this law be as rapid and complete as possible, there is conceded to the Department of Agriculture and Colonization the exclusive power to inculcate the agrarian principles confirmed in the same, and to hear and resolve in all affairs of the [agrarian] branch, without this disposition involving an attack on the sovereignty of the States, since the point is only the speedy realization of the ideals of the Revolution in regard to the improvement of the disinherited farmers of the Republic.

ARTICLE 17. The foundation, administration, and inspection of agricultural colonies, whatever be the nature of these, as well as the recruitment of colonists, is of the exclusive competence of the Department of Agriculture and Colonization.

ARTICLE 18. The Department of Agriculture and Colonization will set up an [office of] technical inspection to execute works which will be called the "National Service of Irrigation and Construction," which will depend on the said Department.

ARTICLE 19. Stands of timber are declared national property, and their inspection will be made by the Department of Agriculture in the form in which [the Department] regulates it, and they will be exploited by the pueblos in whose jurisdiction they belong, employing for that the communal system.

ARTICLE 20. The Department of Agriculture and Colonization is authorized to establish a Mexican agricultural bank in accord with the special regulation which the said Department will make.

ARTICLE 21. It is of the exclusive competence of the Department of Agriculture and Colonization to administer the banking institution of which the previous article speaks, in accord with the administrative bases which the same Department establishes.

ARTICLE 22. For the purposes of Article 20, the Department of Agriculture and Colonization is authorized to confiscate or nationalize urban property, the material works of national or expropriated property, or works of whatever kind, including furniture, machinery, and all the objects [those properties] contain, so long as they belong to enemies of the Revolution.

ARTICLE 23. Declared void are all concessions furnished in contracts celebrated by the Department of Public Works and related to the branch of

Agriculture, or [those celebrated] by this [Department of Agriculture] in the time it existed up to December 31, 1914, it remaining to the judgment of the Department of Agriculture and Colonization to revalidate those [contracts] which it judges beneficial for the people and the Government, after scrupulous and conscientious review.

ARTICLE 24. The Department of Agriculture and Colonization is authorized to establish in the Republic regional agricultural [and] forestry schools and experimental stations.

ARTICLE 25. Persons to whom are adjudicated lots in virtue of the distribution of lands, to which Articles 10, 11, and 12 of the present law refer, remain subject to the obligations and prohibitions which the following article confirms.

ARTICLE 26. The proprietor of a lot is obliged to cultivate it duly, and if for two consecutive years he abandons this cultivation without justified cause, he will be deprived of his lot, which will go to he who solicits it.

ARTICLE 27. Twenty per cent of the income from the nationalized properties of which Article 22 speaks will be destined for the payment of indemnizations of expropriated properties, taking as a base the fiscal census of the year 1914.

ARTICLE 28. Proprietors of two or more lots will be able to unite to form Cooperative Societies with the object of exploiting their properties or selling the produce from these in common, but without those associations being able to take the form of joint-stock companies or be constituted among persons who are not directly or exclusively dedicated to the cultivation of the lots. Societies which are formed in violation of the disposition of this article will be totally null in law, and there will be popular action to denounce them.

ARTICLE 29. The Federal Government will expedite laws which regulate the constitution and functioning of the cooperative societies in reference.

ARTICLE 30. The Department of Agriculture and Colonization will expedite all regulations which may be necessary for the due application and execution of the present law.

ARTICLE 31. The fiscal value presently assigned to property does not prejudice at all future evaluations which the national treasury will have a right to make as a basis for taxes which in the future may weigh on the property.

ARTICLE 32. Declared national property are all waters utilizable and utilized for whatever use, even those which were considered as in the jurisdiction of the States, without there being reason for indemnization of any kind.

ARTICLE 33. In every use of waters preference will always be given to the demands of agriculture, and only when these are satisfied will the waters be used for power and other uses.

ARTICLE 34. It is of the exclusive competence of the Department of Agriculture and Colonization to expedite regulations on the use of waters.

ARTICLE 35. In conformity with the decree of October 1, 1914, all contracts relative to the alienation of goods belonging to enemies of the Revolution are declared of complete nullity.

Enabling Articles—

First: All Municipal Authorities of the Republic are obliged to carry out and have carried out, without loss of time and without any excuse or pretext, the dispositions of the present Law, it being their duty to put pueblos and individuals immediately in possession of the lands and other properties which, in conformity with the same Law, correspond to them, without prejudice to the fact that in their own time the Agrarian Commissions which the Department of Agriculture and Colonization will designate will make the rectifications which may arise, in the knowledge that said Authorities who are remiss or negligent in the fulfillment of their duty will be considered enemies of the Revolution and severely castigated.

Second: It is declared that the present Law forms part of the fundamental [laws] of the Republic, its observance therefore being general and all those constitutive or secondary laws which in any way are opposed to it being abolished.

Granted in the hall of pleadings and proceedings of the Municipal Building, on the twenty-second day of the month of October of nineteen hundred and fifteen.

Therefore, we order that it be published, circulated, and be given its due fulfillment.

REFORM, LIBERTY, JUSTICE, AND LAW

Cuernavaca, October 26, 1915

Manuel Palafox
    Secretary of Agriculture and Colonization
Otilio E. Montaño
    Secretary of Public Education and Fine Arts
Luis Zubiría y Campa
    Secretary of the Treasury and Public Credit
Jenaro [sic] *Amezcua*
    Chief Clerk in charge of the Department of War
Miguel Mendoza L. Schwertfegert [sic]
    Secretary of Labor and Justice

United Mexican States
Executive Council

BIBLIOGRAPHICAL NOTE

THIS NOTE is not a list of all the materials used to prepare the history of the revolution in Morelos from 1910 to 1920. Most are already listed in the bibliography of my dissertation, on file in the Harvard University Archives. Some of those and other new materials are also cited in the footnotes of this volume. Convenient and reliable bibliographies of studies of the general revolution in Mexico, from 1910 to 1940, are Luis González y González et al.: *Fuentes de la historia contemporánea de México: Libros y folletos*, 3 vols. (México, 1961–2), and Roberto Ramos: *Bibliografía de la Revolución Mexicana*, 3 vols. (2nd edn., México, 1958–9). An essential instrument of research on the revolution is the collection of notes on articles in newspapers and journals that Stanley R. Ross directed and organized at the Colegio de México. These he is now publishing as *Fuentes de la historia contemporánea de México: Periódicos y revistas,* already in one volume (México, 1965), shortly in a second, and hopefully in a third. This note is only a brief description of the records and writings particularly important in my work, an indication of other records probably related but not available to me, and a quick comment on Zapatista literature outside Mexico. (A directory of materials cited in footnotes follows this general discussion of sources.)

PRIMARY SOURCES

MANUSCRIPTS.

Because the Zapatistas were the main revolutionaries in Morelos, the basic source for the study of the revolution there is the Archivo de Zapata. This is a collection in thirty-one cardboard boxes, now in file cabinets in the Archives of the National University in Mexico City. It consists of three different kinds of material. Boxes 1 through 22 and Box 24 contain almost exclusively records from the interim presidency of Francisco León de la Barra—telegrams of congratulations, political and private correspondence, and military and police orders. Boxes 23 and 31 contain mostly the same kind of material, with some scattered records of the Revolutionary Convention of 1914–16 (newspapers and transcripts of debate mainly) and some Zapatista records. Box 25 contains scattered Convention records and Zapatista material. Box 26 is almost exclusively material from the Convention. Four boxes, 27 through 30, contain almost exclusively Zapatista records—handwritten and typed letters to and from headquarters, minutes of trials, originals and copies of appointments, commissions, decrees, manifestoes, proclamations, circulars, reports, and military dispositions, from mid-July 1911 through December 1920. The documentation is richest for research on the summer of 1911, more or less satisfactory from the summer of 1914 through the fall of 1919, and most frustrating from the fall of 1911 through the spring of 1914 and through 1920. The documents are in good condition. There is no obvious order to their arrangement, but there is a separate index.

The collection has had a difficult history of its own. In 1920 the two largest caches of Zapatista papers were in Mexico City, where federal and national officers had brought them after finding them on campaigns in the south, and in Tochimilco, at the Zapatista headquarters. After the Zapatistas made their deal with Obregón in 1920, Gildardo Magaña kept the Tochimilco archive as a personal possession. Later he collected other relevant records. Among these was the de la Barra archive, not purchased but simply claimed from a room of scrap. In the 1930's, intent on writing a serious history of Zapatismo and the agrarian movement, Magaña asked his *paisano,* President Cárdenas, if he could remove some pertinent papers from national archives for use in his work, and the President granted his wish. When Magaña died in 1939, the government's papers remained among his own. The collection then passed into the hands of his younger brother, Octavio. Through the 1950's, apparently to raise money for a political venture and to provide for an early retirement to his books and extensive correspondence, Octavio tried to sell the archive. When he found no buyer in Mexico or the United States, he put what he considered the most sensational documents on microfilm and tried to sell the copies. In 1962 he turned over a large part of the original collection to the National University. He has said that he still has as much at home as he gave away, but he would not show it to me. Thus the Archivo de Zapata has emerged bigger than it started, but still incomplete, like the movement whose record it is.

The Archivo de Amezuca is a valuable supplementary source. It is a collection excellently preserved and organized in the Centro de Estudios de Historia de México, a section of the Cultural Department of the Condumex Company, Mexico City. It consists of several binders holding the originals and copies, and contains pertinent material dating from February 1911 to May 1920. Of special interest are the service records of Zapatista officers and troops, which give the dates and places of their enlistments, their ages, marital status, actions in combat, promotions, and discharges. These are not exactly reliable, but they are nevertheless useful. Here too it is easiest to learn about 1911, hardest about 1912. Most welcome was the material for 1913, for which there are more letters, orders, and circulars than for subsequent years.

The National Archives in Washington contain interesting information on the Zapatistas and sometimes on Morelos. This is almost all in Record Group 59, the State Department Papers on the Internal Affairs of Mexico, and there mostly in file 812.00, on political affairs. A few tidbits are scattered through other files of Group 59, as well as in Groups 43 (Boxes 8, 9, 10, and 12 of the Rodgers dispatches), 45 (Box 654 of the W-E-5 subject file on Mexico), 84 (Embassy letters from Mexico City), and 94 (AGO files 2212599–2225544). Because the Zapatistas operated in an area where there were comparatively few Americans and dollars invested, the U.S. government normally paid them slight attention. Its agents discovered and reported details only when the Zapatistas seemed about to combine with a more powerful ally to bring down a government in Mexico City or to set up a new one, as in 1912, with the Orozquistas against Madero, or in 1914–15, with the Villistas against Carranza.

The Ramo de la Revolución Mexicana in the Archivo General de Relaciones Exteriores, Mexico City, is an immense source for studies of various movements from 1910 to 1920. It comprises 259 volumes, to which there is a superb guide, Berta Ulloa Ortiz: *Revolución Mexicana, 1910–1920* (México, 1963). But since Mexican consuls rarely worried about Zapatista agents abroad, there is almost nothing pertinent to Morelos. Only two or three interesting memos turned up in my search.

Other unpublished collections were useful for specific periods or problems. Most helpful for the years before the revolution were the private papers of Jesús Sotelo Inclán. These include scattered records and typed or photostatic copies of records of agrarian conflicts in Morelos, the career of Francisco Leyva, the Zapata family, and Anenecuilco. There is very little of relevance in the Leyva papers in the Archivo General de la Nación in Mexico City. And the pertinent material in the Archivo de Madero, available in the Secretaría de la Hacienda, is very sparse and scattered. Mainly it is about the twinges of opposition in Morelos in 1909 and 1910. Among the private papers of Porfirio Palacios is a useful collection of newspaper clippings, Zapatista anecdotes, and biographical notes on prominent Zapatistas.

For study of the revolution of 1910–11 the Archivo de Alfredo Robles Domínguez is a key source. It is well preserved in the Instituto Nacional de Estudios Históricos de la Revolución Mexicana, in Mexico City. Hundreds of telegrams, letters, memos, and reports provide the material for tracing local phases of the revolutionary movement. Morelos and the Maderistas there, mainly Zapata and his chiefs, are fully represented.

Records abound of federal police action in Morelos during Madero's presidency. They are mainly in bundles 645, 846, 876, and 889 of the Ramo de Gobernación in the Archivo General de la Nación. Useful material appears at random in at least six other bundles—548, 639, 647, 663, 854, and 925. Records of military action also abound, mainly in sections 177 and 178 of File XI/ 481.5, of the Archivo Histórico de Defensa Nacional. Seven other sections contain scattered items of interest—126, 158, 159, 179, 217, 218, 219. Although I could not obtain direct access to this collection, the Muro notes I used at the Colegio de México were careful copies of dates and places of maneuvers, operations, battles, and casualties.

The García Pimentels' private papers are few but fascinating. No business records are among them, except the receipts for protection payments and the two long letters recounting attempts at recovery in 1920. The bulk is the report on agricultural labor by Joaquín and the memoirs by Luis, Jr. The papers are of most value for understanding the planters' hopes, fears, and positions up to mid-1914. They give a distorted impression of the hacendados only insofar as the García Pimentels were the most refined and determined family in the group.

The private collection of Marte R. Gómez is an important source for the history of Mexican agricultural policies. It is especially important for Morelos during 1914–17, because it contains much information about Manuel Palafox, who practically ran the state during those years.

In the private papers of Juan Salazar Pérez there are documents purporting to prove the innocence of Otilio Montaño. They help clarify the divisions among the Zapatistas in 1917.

The private archive of Octavio Paz (the father of the poet) has material useful mainly for the period from 1917 to 1920, when Paz was a Zapatista agent in the United States and received reports and letters from the southern headquarters to make propaganda here. I saw only selected documents.

Important material may appear in six other archives I was not able to use. One is the archive of Genovevo de la O. Evidence that it once existed comes from a reporter who visited Morelos in mid-1913 and mentioned *"un magnífico archivo que de caer en manos de justicia, haría que la pasaran nada bien algunos de esos señores* [who paid de la O for protection]." (See *"¿Por qué existe y cómo se desarrolla el zapatismo en el E. de Morelos?" La Tribuna,* May 31, 1913.) Evidence that it survived at least until the 1930's comes from Porfirio Palacios, who describes it as being a bundle of papers nearly two feet thick. He says de la O loaned it to "General Izázaga from Michoacán" (Major Gustavo Izázaga Cárdenas?), who wanted to consult it for a book he was writing. Izázaga then died, Palacios says, without having finished the book or returned the papers, and now no one knows where they are. Another archive inaccessible to me is that of Francisco Mendoza. It is the private property of Valentín López González but currently in the possession of Armando de María y Campos, who denied my request to see it. Nor did I see the personal papers of the late Antonio Díaz Soto y Gama, which, if he kept them, must be a rich and interesting collection. There may also be an Ayaquica archive, containing correspondence like that which Ayaquica published in 1937, but I was not able to reach Ayaquica's sons, who presumably have it.

The documents I was not able to consult in the Archivo Histórico de Defensa Nacional include service records of military men prominent in campaigns in Morelos, many long dead now, officers of the old federal as well as the new national army.

If it still exists, the most valuable collection for further research would be that of Palafox. That it once existed seems clear from the reference of Gómez (*Las comisiones*, p. 43). Evidently it contained material on the agrarian reforms Palafox supervised in Morelos and elsewhere, and a personal memoir by Palafox of his Zapatista career. But Palafox died in 1959. Reportedly his archive burned, whether before or after his death I could not determine. Another memoir, reportedly dictated about 1936 to one Rose Lee Martin of Washington or Baltimore, as the basis for a history of the revolution, has also escaped me.

PRINTED MATERIAL.

Public Records: The published documents of the federal government of Mexico are basically irrelevant to the study of revolutionary Morelos. But those of the state of Morelos are essential for the years up to mid-1913. Most useful are the official gazettes, *El Orden* (1885–91), *Periódico Oficial del Gobierno de Morelos* (1883–5, 1891–5), and *Semanario Oficial del Gobierno de Morelos* (1895–1913). They contain prefectural reports on local production and trade, electoral returns, minutes of legislative and executive deliberations, texts of laws and decrees, legal notices, and other similar material. The few governors' reports that survive have supplementary data on the state's administration and economy. I found no published municipal records for the revolutionary decade. The pertinent published records of the United States are the State Department's annual *Foreign Relations* and the Senate and House hearings already cited in the footnotes of this volume. Though often wildly in error, the witnesses at the hearings also often gave interesting comments and new information.

Newspapers and Journals: After the Zapata archive, the most valuable records for tracing events in Morelos from 1910 to 1920 are the metropolitan newspapers of the era. They are on file in the Hemeroteca Nacional in Mexico City. Most helpful for the years up to 1914 are the *Diario del Hogar* (closed in 1912) and *El País*, because they printed the most dirt about the government. For just before the Maderista revolution *México Nuevo* is useful; for just afterward and up to 1913, *Nueva Era*. Stories with a científico slant appeared usually in *El Imparcial* and *The Mexican Herald*, until they closed in 1914. Newspapers of the Revolutionary Convention are almost useless, appearing sporadically and full of mistakes. But Constitutionalist dailies were regular, professional products. *El Demócrata* (founded in 1915), *El Universal* (1916), and *Excélsior* (1917) each have their political biases, but together they can give an alert and skeptical reader a reasonable impression of political, economic, and military drifts. Without them and the earlier newspapers, the pattern of collapses, booms, and conflicts in this history would develop in a dim and shifting light. Other journalistic aids are the series "Para la historia," in *La Prensa,* September 3, 1931, through February 24, 1934, recounting events twenty years previous, and the historical articles that have appeared in *El Legionario* since its foundation in 1951. American and British newspapers are understandably useless for learning about revolutionary Morelos. The only journal worth searching through is the American monthly, *World's Work.*

Archives: The only relevant published archive is that which Amado Chaverri Matamoros ran in *La Prensa,* from September 12 through October 11, 1935. It is useful mainly for clues to Zapatista attitudes in 1916–17 and to intrigues in the movement in 1919. From May 4 to December 16, 1950, Octavio Magaña published material from his archive in *El Universal* as "Historia documental de la revolución." But it was largely the reprint of passages from others' memoirs or the copy of the originals now in the National University. The documents Ayaquica published in 1937 are probably only a selection. Some relevant archival material appears printed in Figueroa Uriza's two volumes.

Memoirs: This is a difficult genre to define, so long as veterans or witnesses of the revolution give interviews and write down "histories" as well as remembrances. But however they cast it, survivors of the great ordeal have recounted much important information. The five volumes of Magaña, the first two by him personally, the last three posthumous, by Carlos Pérez Guerrero, are a prime source. So is Gómez's study of the southern agrarian commissions, on which he served. Many episodes would have remained even more confused than they still are without the books, articles, and testimonies of Joaquín Páez, Alfredo Robles Domínguez, Jesús Romero Flores, Soto y Gama, Mrs. King, Mrs. Tweedie, Carlos Reyes Avilés, Juan Andrew Almazán, Serafín M. Robles, de la O, Pablo González, Palafox, "Pedro Martínez," and many others cited throughout the text. The colorful tales Paz *père* printed weekly in *El Universal* from June 23 to December 29, 1929, are not historical but literary efforts, but even they are useful as legends.

SECONDARY WORKS

BIOGRAPHICAL

There is still no trustworthy dictionary of Mexican biography, revolutionary or general. The first serious attempt is the *Diccionario Porrúa de Historia, Biografía y Geografía* (México, 1964), which contains data on some prominent revolutionaries. But it has very little about Zapatistas, and that often not reliable—like the note on Palafox that has him shot by a Zapatista firing squad in "1918?" Naranjo's *Diccionario* includes more Zapatistas but less information, and is often wrong too. Peral's *Diccionario* is worse than useless. Arturo Langle's *Vocabulario, apodos, seudónimos, sobrenombres y hemerografía de la revolución* (México, 1966) is a reliable but slim volume. The "mil biografías en la historia de México," which Jesús Romero Flores published in *El Nacional* during 1946 and 1947, remain the most convenient source of general reliability.

I know of no monographic biographies of any Morelense prominent from 1910 to 1920 except those on Zapata. The first book in Spanish about him was Germán List Arzubide's *Emiliano Zapata* (Jalapa, 1927), and it was not really a biography or even a book, but, as the author admitted in the subtitle, an *Exaltación,* a pamphlet of praise. At least twenty other such pamphlets have appeared since then. They are good panegyrics but of little historical use. The first serious effort was Baltasar Dromundo's professed *Biografía* of 1934. It really was a book, but no less an exaltation. Heavily dependent on the memory of Juan Andrew Almazán and consciously out to raise Zapata to heroic heights, Dromundo vented powerful ambitions. He opened with a large, handsome portrait of himself and then romanticized the whole southern struggle. Still, new and important information seeped into the story, which remains a useful source for the cautious researcher. Then appeared Magaña's first two volumes (1934-7), the first obviously documented study of the Zapatista movement and the role of its chief. Magaña was modest and worked his material conscientiously, but he did not organize it into a coherent argument or story. Besides, he got only up to February 1913. Another documented version of Zapata's life formed part of Meléndez's first volume of revolutionary histories, published in 1936. This was Octavio Paz's final work. It too sailed away in rhetoric about early years, skimming over the period from 1915 to 1919. But it too contained new and interesting data, still useful, on the Convention and the last guerrillas. In 1943 Sotelo Inclán's study came out, but it was more the story of Anenecuilo than of Zapata.

Eight years passed before another serious effort. This was the new complete edition of Magaña's opus in five volumes (1951-2), Carlos Pérez Guerrero having finished it for publication by the Frente Zapatista. In the last two volumes Pérez Guerrero lost his bearings in the sea of his material. He strays from one topic to the next without reason, and ends confusingly in November 1914. Even so this set remains the most helpful published source on Zapata and the southern movement. In 1952 there appeared Mario Gill's "Zapata: su pueblo y sus hijos," *Historia mexicana,* II, 2 (October–December 1952), 294-312. There the most valuable material was about Zapata's children, whom Gill numbered incompletely as seven, all illegitimate. In the revised essay published in 1960 Gill scarcely changed this material.

Beginning in 1959 books on Zapata came fast. They vary in quality. Mena's (1959) was a weak attempt to prove that intellectuals, Jacobin "witch doctors" like Montaño and Soto y Gama, had misled Zapata, a naturally Catholic populist chief. Mena produced no new material, disappointingly, because more data on Zapatista relations with parish priests would have been interesting. Barba González's book (1960) told the same old heroic and happily partisan story; only a few twists on familiar anecdotes were new. The most careful and thorough biography yet also appeared in 1960. This was Palacios's. Based on the works of Magaña and Sotelo Inclán, interviews with many Zapatista veterans, and the archives of the Frente Zapatista, it contained much information then new and still helpful. Unlike earlier biographers, Palacios believed Zapata great enough not to need literary puffing, and the style is refreshingly plain and clear. This study is also the most balanced, moving fairly through each phase of Zapata's career. Soto y Gama's memoir-biography (1960) was largely a collection of articles he had published in *El Universal* in the 1950's. Except for a few personal notes, the material was already familiar; so was the unargued conviction that Zapata mystically represented "the people," all of them. Only the passion of the writing and the stress on Zapata's intransigence were new. Alberto Morales Jiménez's *Zapata* (México, 1961) was another slice of sweet puff. But Dromundo's revised *Vida* (1961) was an impressive tour de force. Independent now, prouder of his subject than of himself, Dromundo had produced a new book, a generally quiet and convincing story of "simply a man, a bit of humanity." It was partisan still and had little new material, but it conveyed a fine sense of the southern chief's struggle. The latest effort, Reyes H.'s (1963), has reproduced some new documents from the Zapata archive, but except for them it is derivative.

PICTORIAL.

The enormous Casasola collection appears more clearly and conveniently in its second edition, cited in the text. The method of identification is still annoying, since lists of names often bear no connection with rows of faces; but the portraits are treasures of increasing value. The chronological commentary is also more often correct in the new edition.

There are hundreds of photographs in the Archivo de Zapata. Although most are of Gildardo Magaña's political campaigns in the 1930's, there are some originals dating from the revolutionary decade.

In *Artes de México*, XIII, 79/80, and in Manuel Romero de Terreros: *Antiguas Haciendas de México* (México, 1956), there are photographs of plantation buildings in Morelos, but they are generally disappointing in their failure to show the monumentality of the houses and mills.

Two motion pictures are relevant. One is a distinguished achievement, Elia Kazan's *Viva Zapata!* (Twentieth Century–Fox, 1952). The screenplay is by John Steinbeck. In telescoping the whole revolution into one dramatic episode, the movie distorts certain events and characters, some grossly; but it quickly and vividly develops a portrayal of Zapata, the villagers, and the nature of their relations and movement that I find still subtle, powerful, and true. The movie is all the more remarkable in that it makes some facts, like Zapata's marriage, public for the first time. The other movie, Louis Malle's *Viva María!* (United Artists, 1966), is a flashy but sorry product, a parody ill informed, rarely funny, and finally stupid. Its only value for the historian of revolutionary Morelos is its location, which is Cuautla. At least it is possible to see how trains looked fifty-five years ago, chugging over bridges, through fields of tall green cane, and into ambushes. The interior of the mansion is also right and interesting.

POLITICAL.

Pertinent material on Morelos politics is scattered through the volumes on *La Vida Política* of *La República Restaurada* and *El Porfiriato,* two of the deeply and shrewdly researched eight volumes directed by Daniel Cosío Villegas as the *Historia Moderna de México*. Snippets about Morelenses in national politics are in Ricardo García Granados's two volumes covering the years from 1867 to 1914. José C. Valadés's *El Porfirismo, Historia de un régimen: El nacimiento* (México, 1941) and *El crecimiento,* 2 vols. (México, 1948), are useful analyses. The least hysterical and most generally reliable account of which chiefs after 1910 were in control around the nation, where and when, is that of Jesús Romero Flores in *Anales históricos de la revolución mexicana* (2nd edn., México, 1960), Volume I on the years *Del porfirismo a la revolución constitucionalista,* and Volume II on *La constitución de 1917 y los primeros gobiernos revolucionarios*. For a political history of Morelos up to the early 1930's, Diez's 223-page introduction to his *Bibliografía* is still the best.

SOCIAL AND ECONOMIC.

Again the most useful volumes for reference and interpretation are Cosío Villegas's *La Vida Social* and *La Vida Económica* of the *República Restaurada* and the *Porfiriato*. Relevant information is also in Silva Herzog's four volumes of reproduced pamphlets and his tome on agrarismo. A partisan but interesting account appears in the fifth of five volumes by Andrés Molina Enríquez: *Esbozo de la historia de los primeros diez años de la revolución agraria de México, de 1910 a 1920* (2nd edn., México, 1936).

Specifically on Morelos the often cited thesis of Holt Büttner is a valuable source for reference, though short on analysis. Mazari's vague and rambling "Bosquejo" remains an important introduction to the history of conflicts between plantations and villages and the growth of towns in Morelos. Redfield's study of Tepoztlán and Lewis's restudy are funds of helpful information; the danger in depending on them is that Tepoztlán is not typical of Morelos, and both scholars sometimes took as facts the mistakes their interviewees told them. Interesting comments on earlier plantations in Morelos are in Fernando Sandoval's excellent study. And Sotelo Inclán's little book still stands as a stroke of genius and an act of valor. It and Gregorio López y Fuentes's novel reveal more about rural life in Morelos in 1910 than all the other volumes together.

FOREIGN.

Among the published writings of non-Mexicans about the revolution I know of only seven directly about Morelos. The first was Gates's article in

World's Work (April 1919). Although Gates misconstrued much, he also perceived and reported much that others missed. Both for this and for the revelation of his interference in Zapatista policy, the article is useful. The next effort was *The Crimson Jester,* H. H. Dunn's 1934 potboiler. This is a bad joke. Here the reader may learn that Zapata impaled prisoners on maguey plants, married twenty-six different women, etc. Although Dunn claimed to have accompanied Zapata on campaigns and to have witnessed the atrocities he presents, there is no record except his own that he ever had any connection with the revolution in Morleos. He had been a correspondent in Mexico City for the International News Service and the National News Association, but was thrown out of the country in late 1912. An example of the accuracy of his reporting is his description of Jesús Flores Magón, the minister of the interior who deported him, as "a Caribbean Negro." (See his lament in the Senate's *Revolutions in Mexico,* pp. 714–16.) The *Jester* appeared in a translation by Emmanuel Rinon as *Zapata, L'Attila du Mexique* (Paris, 1934).

Crawford's 1940 thesis on "The Suriano Rebellion" is remarkable for being the first scholarly American attention specifically to the Zapatistas. Its strengths are a comprehensive sense of the topic, not merely the causes but the whole process of the southern movement, and an objective procedure in framing questions and answers. Its weaknesses are its sources, which are few and shallow.

The latest book in English is Edgcumb Pinchon's *Zapata the Unconquerable* (New York, 1941). Although Pinchon pretended to write no more than a historical novel, he spent a year researching in Mexico. And basing his work on Paz's monograph, Magaña's first two volumes, Reyes Avilés's *Cartones,* Mrs. King's memoir, and interviews with Serafín Robles and Soto y Gama, he produced a good popular biography. He too telescoped the decade, so that the first 306 of his 332 pages go only through Zapata's and Villa's meeting in Xochimilco in 1914, and he invented characters and scenes and mistook Soto y Gama's word as gospel, but he sketched out the essentials of personality, theme, and purpose very well. The screenplay for Kazan's movie seems partly derived from this book.

In 1960 Chevalier's article appeared in *Cuadernos Americanos,* to be translated as "Un facteur décisif de la révolution agraire au Mexique: le soulèvement de Zapata, 1911–1919," in *Annales. Économies-Sociétés-Civilisations,* XVI, 1 (January 1961), 66–82. This was the first article on the southern revolution by a professional historian, and precisely the historian best trained, because of his earlier excellent study of colonial estates, to see its origins and the particular pattern of its forces. The material he used was not new, mainly items from Sotelo Inclán and Magaña, but the interpretation is seminal. Without considering it no student of revolutionary Mexico really knows where he is.

Two young American historians have recently published relevant articles —McNeely, already cited, and Arthur G. Pettit: "Relaciones Zapata-Carranza, 1914," *Anuario de Historia,* V (1965), 69–81. Both articles are careful summaries of some Zapatista memoirs and secondary accounts.

I might have found more enlightening material if I had continued my search for published as well as private documents. But by the spring of 1967 the picture seemed clear. Not only had the hunt for more details become less fruitful, but the new details I found seemed to obscure the impression I decided was true. For the sake of Carlyle's "indispensablest beauty" I set about getting done.

Directory of Materials Cited in Footnotes

(*Mexican newspapers and magazines are on file in the Hemeroteca Nacional unless otherwise described.*)

Actualidades: Mexico City weekly, 1909.

Adame Medina, Eduardo: "De Villa de Ayala a Chinameca, 1909–1919," *El Campesino,* May 1958.

Aguilar, Herminia: "Doña Josefa Espejo, Vda. de Zapata," *El Campesino,* May 1950.

Almazán, Juan Andrew: *En defensa legítima.* México, n.d., 1958?

Alvarado, Rafael: "Zapata intentó asesinar al General Pablo González," *Todo,* November 5, 1942.

Amaya C., Luis Fernando: *La Soberana Convención Revolucionaria, 1914–1916.* México, 1966.

[Amezcua, Genaro:] *Méjico Revolucionario a los pueblos de Europa y América, 1910–1918.* Havana, n.d., 1918?

Ancona, Leopoldo: "El General Almazán y el Agrarismo de Zapata," *Novedades,* October 3, 1939.

Archivo de Amezcua, Genaro (abbreviated AA), 1911–20: in the Centro de Estudios de Historia de México of the Departamento Cultural at Condumex, S. A., Mexico City.

Archivo de García Pimentel, Luis, Jr. (abbreviated AGP), 1913–20: in the possession of José García Pimentel, Mexico City.

Archivo General de la Nación (abbreviated AGN): Papeles del General Francisco Leyva.

———: Ramo de Gobernación (abbreviated as G), 1909–13.

Archivo General de la Secretaría de Relaciones Exteriores (abbreviated AGRE): Ramo de la Revolución Mexicana, 1912–19.

Archivo Histórico de Defensa Nacional (abbreviated AHDN), Section XI/481.5, 1911–13: Muro notes in El Colegio de México, Mexico City.

Archivo de Madero, Francisco I. (abbreviated AM), 1910–11: in the Secretaría de la Hacienda.

Archivo de Paz, Octavio (abbreviated AP), 1916–20: in the possession of Paz's widow, Mexico City.

"El Archivo de la Reacción," *El Universal,* September 26 to October 12, 1917.

Archivo de Robles Domínguez, Alfredo (abbreviated ARD), 1911–14: in the Instituto Nacional de Estudios Históricos de la Revolución Mexicana.

Archivo de Sotelo Inclán, Jesús (abbreviated ASI), 1867–1919: in the possession of Jesús Sotelo Inclán, Mexico City.

Archivo de Zapata, Emiliano (abbreviated AZ), 1911–20: in the Archivo Histórico de la Universidad Nacional Autónoma de México.

Arvide Rendón, Manuel: "Labor desarrollada en el Sur en 1918," *El Legionario,* June 1953.

Ayaquica Fortino: "Cómo perdió la vida el general Domingo Arenas," serialized in *El Hombre Libre,* August 4 to November 15, 1937.

Barba González, Silvano: *La lucha por la tierra. Emiliano Zapata.* México, 1960.

Barragán, Juan: *Historia del Ejército y de la Revolución Constitucionalista.* 2 vols., México, 1946.

Barrera Fuentes, Florencio, ed.: *Crónicas y debates de las sesiones de la Soberana Convención Revolucionaria.* 3 vols., México, 1964–5.

Basave del Castillo Negrete, Carlos: *Notas para la historia de la Convención Revolucionaria (1914–1915).* México, 1947.

Beals, Carleton: *Mexican Maze.* New York, 1931.

Bejarano, Moisés: "Breves Apuntes Sobre la Muerte del Gral. Otilio E. Montaño." Manuscript, n.d., 1960?, in the private papers of Juan Salazar Pérez.

Benítez, Fernando: *El rey viejo.* México, 1959.

Benson, Nettie L: "The Preconstitutional Regime of Venustiano Carranza, 1913–1917." M.A. thesis, University of Texas, 1936.

Blaisdell, Lowell L.: *The Desert Revolution. Baja California, 1911.* Madison, 1962.

Blanquel, Eduardo: "La *Revista Postiva* de D. Augustín Aragón y la Historia de la Ciencia en México," *Memorias del Primer Coloquio Mexicano de Historia de la Ciencia,* I (1964).

Bonilla, Manuel, Jr.: *El régimen maderista.* 2nd edn., México, 1962.

Braderman, Eugene M.: "A Study of Political Parties and Politics in Mexico since 1890." Ph.D. dissertation, University of Illinois, 1938.

Brandenburg, Frank R.: *The Making of Modern Mexico.* Englewood Cliffs, 1964.

Bravo Ugarte, José: *Historia sucinta de Michoacán.* 3 vols., México, 1964.

Breceda, Alfredo: *Mexico Revolucionario, 1913–1917.* 2 vols., Madrid, 1920; México, 1941.

Bulnes, Francisco: *Los grandes problemas de México.* 2nd edn., México, 1956.

Bustamante, L. F.: "Dizque Don Pablo no Autorizó la muerte de Emiliano Zapata," *El Universal Gráfico,* November 10, 1937.

[Cabrera, Luis:] *Obras políticas del Lic. Blas Urrea.* México, 1921.

Calderón Serrano, Ricardo: "Un soldado de la Revolución," *El Nacional,* January 22, 1947.

Callahan, James H.: *American Foreign Policy in Mexican Relations.* New York, 1932.

El Campesino: Mexico City monthly, 1950–8.
"Carranza autorizó la muerte de Zapata, dice Pablo González," *Novedades,* October 28, 1942.
Carreño, Alberto María, ed.: *Archivo del General Porfirio Díaz. Memorias y documentos.* 24 vols., México, 1947–58.
Casasola, Gustavo, ed.: *Historia Gráfica de la Revolución Mexicana, 1900–1960.* 4 vols., México, 1964.
Castillo, Porfirio del: *Puebla y Tlaxcala en los díaz de la revolución.* México, 1953.
Cattell, J. McKeen: *Leaders in Education. A Biographical Directory.* New York, 1932.
Cervantes, Federico: *Felipe Ángeles en la Revolución. Biografía (1869–1919).* 3rd edn., México, 1964.
Cháverri Matamoros, Amado: "El Archivo de Zapata," serialized in *La Prensa,* September 27 to October 11, 1935.
Chávez Orozco, Luis: *El Sitio de Cuautla. La epopeya de la guerra de independencia.* México, 1931.
Chevalier, François: "«Ejido» et Stabilité au Mexique," *Revue Française de Science Politique,* XVI, 4 (August 1966), pp. 717–52.
———: "Un factor decisivo de la revolución agraria de México: 'El levantamiento de Zapata' (1911–1919)," *Cuadernos Americanos,* CXIII, 6 (November 1960), 165–87.
———: *La formation des grands domaines au Mexique. Terre et société aux xvi–xvii siècles.* Paris, 1952.
Clendenen, Clarence C.: *The United States and Pancho Villa. A Study in Unconventional Diplomacy.* Ithaca, 1961.
Cline, Howard F.: *Mexico. Revolution to Evolution, 1940–1960.* New York, 1962.
El Constitucional: Mexico City biweekly, 1910.
La Convención: Mexico City daily, 1915.
Cosío Robelo, Francisco: "Dígale a Zapata que acabe el circo," *Mujeres y Deportes,* February 6, 1937.
———: "El dragón de dos cabezas. Zapata y Pascual Orozco," *Mujeres y Deportes,* March 6, 1937.
———: "Rindiendo Cuentas," *El Universal,* December 27, 1930.
Cosío Villegas, Daniel: "Del Porfiriato a la Revolución," *Novedades,* November 2, 1952.
———, ed.: *Historia Moderna de México. El Porfiriato. La Vida Económica.* 2 vols., México, 1965.
———: *Historia Moderna de México. La República Restaurada. La Vida Política.* México, 1955.
Crawford, Douglas M.: "The Suriano Rebellion in Mexico, 1910–1919." M.A. thesis, University of California at Berkeley, 1940.
Creelman, James: "President Díaz. Hero of the Americas," *Pearson's Magazine,* XIX, 3 (March 1908), 231–77.
Cronista de la Revolución: "Sobre Veracruz," *Excélsior,* July 21, 1929.

Cronon, E. David, ed.: *The Cabinet Diaries of Josephus Daniels, 1913–1921.* Lincoln, 1963.

Cuadros Caldas, Julio: *El Comunismo Criollo.* Puebla, 1930.

———: *México-Soviet.* Puebla, 1926.

Cuernavaca: *Informe que rindió ante el H. Cabildo el Sr. Valentín López González, Presidente municipal constitucional de Cuernavaca, Morelos, 1964–1965.* Cuernavaca, 1965.

Cumberland, Charles C.: "The Jenkins Case and Mexican-American Relations," *Hispanic American Historical Review,* XXXI, 4 (November 1951), 586–607.

———: *Mexican Revolution. Genesis Under Madero.* Austin, 1952.

[DeBekker, Jan Leander:] *De cómo vino Huerta y cómo se fue.* México, 1914.

El Demócrata: Mexico City daily, 1916–20.

El Diario: Mexico City daily, 1909–12.

Diario del Hogar: Mexico City daily, 1909–12. Supplementary files are in the Biblioteca de la Secretaría de la Hacienda.

Díaz Soto y Gama, Antonio: "Cargos infundados contra Zapata," *El Universal,* May 4, 1955.

———: "El Caso de Montaño," *El Universal,* May 18, 1955.

———: "Francisco Villa," *El Universal,* August 24, 1938.

———: "La Ley Agraria del Villismo," *Excélsior,* October 26, 1950.

———: *La revolución agraria del Sur y EMILIANO ZAPATA, su Caudillo.* México, 1960.

———: "Un noble amigo de Zapata," *El Universal,* December 13, 1950.

Diez, Domingo: *Bibliografía del estado de Morelos.* México, 1933.

———: *Dos conferencias sobre el Estado de Morelos.* México, 1919.

Domínguez, Manuel: *Cuautla. Sucinta reseña de la heróica ciudad, cabecera de distrito en el estado de Morelos.* México, 1907.

Dotson, Floyd and Lillian O.: "Urban Centralization and Decentralization in Mexico," *Rural Sociology,* XXI, 1 (March 1956), 41–9.

Dromundo, Baltasar: *Emiliano Zapata. Biografía.* México, 1934.

———: *Vida de Emiliano Zapata.* México, 1961.

Dunn, H. H.: *The Crimson Jester, Zapata of Mexico.* New York, 1934.

Durán, Marco Antonio: "Condiciones y perspectivas de la agricultura mexicana," *El Trimestre Económico,* XXVIII, 1 (January 1961), 52–79.

———: "Las funciones de la propiedad de la tierra en la reforma agraria mexicana," *El Trimestre Económico,* XXXI, 2 (April 1964), 228–42.

Durán Ochoa, Julio: *Población.* México, 1955.

El Eco: Cuernavaca weekly, 1889.

Enríquez, I. C.: *The Religious Question in Mexico.* New York, 1915.

Estado Mayor del General Vicente Segura: *Historia del la Brigada Mixta "Hidalgo," 1915–1916.* México, 1917.

Estrada, Roque: *La revolución y Francisco I. Madero. Primera, segunda y tercera etapas.* Guadalajara, 1912.

Excélsior: Mexico City daily, 1917–40.

Fabila, Manuel, ed.: *Cinco siglos de legislación agraria en México, 1493–1940.* México, 1941.

Fernández y Fernández, Ramón: "Notas bibliográficas," *El Trimestre Económico,* XXVIII, 2 (April 1961), 349–54.

Ferrer Mendiolea, Gabriel: *Historia del Congreso Constituyente de 1916–1917.* México, 1957.

———: "Los secretarios del Presidente Carranza," *El Nacional,* June 29, 1954.

Figueroa Doménech, J.: *Guía general descriptiva de la República mexicana. Historia, geografía, estadística, etc., etc.* 2 vols., México, 1899.

Figueroa Uriza, Arturo: *Ciudadanos en armas. Antecedencia y datos para la historia de la revolución mexicana.* 2 vols., México, 1960.

Flores, Edmundo: *Tratado de Economía Agrícola.* México, 1961.

Flores Magón, Ricardo: *Vida y Obra. Semilla Libertaria.* 3 vols., México, 1923.

Flores Vilchis, Othón: "El problema agrario en el estado de Morelos." Facultad Nacional de Jurisprudencia thesis, U.N.A.M., 1950.

Fuentes Díaz, Vicente: *Los partidos políticos en México.* 2 vols., México, 1954–6.

———: *La revolución de 1910 en el estado de Guerrero.* México, 1960.

Furtado, Celso: *The Economic Growth of Brazil. A Survey from Colonial to Modern Times.* Berkeley, 1963.

García, Rubén: *El Antiporfirismo.* México, 1935.

García Cantú, Gastón: *Utopías mexicanas.* México, 1963.

García Granados, Ricardo: *Historia de México, desde la restauración de la República en 1867, hasta la caída de Huerta.* 2 vols., 2nd edn., México, 1956.

García Pimentel, Joaquín: "Condiciones de la gente de trabajo en el Estado de Morelos antes de la revolución de 1910, durante el período de la lucha de 1911 a 1914, y desde esa época hasta la fecha." Manuscript, 1916, Archivo de García Pimentel.

García Pimentel, Luis, Jr.: "Memorias." Manuscript, 1914, Archivo de García Pimentel.

———: "Recuerdos y reflexiones." Manuscript, n.d., Archivo de García Pimentel.

Gates, William: "The Four Governments of Mexico. Creole, Mestizo, or Indian?" *World's Work,* February 1919, pp. 385–92.

———: "The Four Governments of Mexico. Zapata—Protector of Morelos," *World's Work,* April 1919, pp. 654–65.

———: "Mexico To-day," *North American Review,* CCIX (January 1919), 68–83.

Gill, Mario: *Episodios mexicanos. México en la hoguera.* 3rd edn., México, 1960.

Gómez, Marte R.: *Las comisiones agrarias del sur.* México, 1961.

———: "Notes sobre el Gral. Manuel Palafox." Manuscript, 1966, in the private papers of the author.

————: *La reforma agraria de México. Su crisis durante el período 1928–1934,* México, 1964.

————: "La Reforma Agraria en las filas villistas." Manuscript, 1965, in the private papers of the author.

González Casanova, Pablo: *La democracia en México.* México, 1965.

González Ramírez, Manuel, ed.: *Manifiestos políticos (1892–1912).* México, 1957.

————, ed.: *Planes políticos y otros documentos.* México, 1954.

González Roa, Fernando: *El aspecto agrario de la Revolución Mexicana.* México, 1919.

Greenwalt, Emmett A.: *The Point Loma Community in California, 1897–1942. A Theosophical Experiment.* Berkeley, 1955.

Gruening, Ernest: *Mexico and Its Heritage.* New York, 1928.

Gutiérrez y Gutiérrez, Luis: "*Hoy* visita a la viuda de Zapata," *Hoy,* March 28, 1953.

Guzmán, Martín Luis: *El Águila y la Serpiente.* 9th edn., México, 1962.

"Hace 50 años," *Excélsior,* December 14, 1964.

El hacendado mexicano y fabricante de azúcar: Mexico City monthly, 1905–14. Supplementary files are in the New York Public Library.

El Heraldo de México: Mexico City daily, 1919–20.

Hernández, Teodoro: "La verdad sobre el zapatismo," *Mujeres y Deportes,* February 13, 1937.

Hernández Bravo, Jesús: "El General Serratos Combatió a Zapata y Hoy lo Defiende," *El Hombre Libre,* May 28, 1937.

Holt Büttner, Elizabeth: "Evolución de las localidades en el estado de Morelos según los censos de población, 1900–1950." Maestría de Geografía thesis, U.N.A.M., 1962.

La Idea Patriótica: Cuautla weekly, 1891–2.

El Imparcial: Mexico City daily, 1908–14.

El Independiente: Mexico City daily, 1913–14.

"La industria azucarera en Méjico," *Revista Azucarera* (Buenos Aires), VII, 74(June 1900), 160–2. Files are in Widener Library.

"Informe que rinde el Jefe de la Comisión Agraria en el Distrito de Cuernavaca . . . February 19, 1915," *El Nacional,* November 20, 1932.

International Bureau of the American Republics: *Commercial Directory of the American Republics, Supplement, Containing Corrections of Errors in Volume Two of the Commercial Directory.* Washington, 1899.

————: *Mexico. Geographical Sketch, Natural Resources, Laws, Economic Conditions, Actual Development, Prospects of Future Growth.* Washington, 1904.

The Johns Hopkins Alumni Magazine, 1918.

The Johns Hopkins University Register, 1885–1910.

King, Rosa E.: *Tempest over Mexico.* Boston, 1935.

Knapp, Frank A., Jr.: *The Life of Sebastián Lerdo de Tejada, 1823–1889. A Study of Influence and Obscurity.* Austin, 1951.

Kuhn, Loeb & Co.: *Prospectus, $15,000,000, Mexico.* New York, 1966.

Lamartine Yates, Paul: *El desarrollo regional de México.* 2nd edn., México, 1962.

Leduc, Alberto, Luis Lara y Pardo, and Carlos Roumagnac: *Diccionario de geografía, historia y biografía mexicanas.* Paris, 1910.

Lewis, Oscar: *Life in a Mexican Village: Tepoztlán Restudied.* Urbana, 1963.

———: "Mexico Since Cárdenas," in Richard N. Adams *et al., Social Change in Latin America Today.* New York, 1960.

———: *Pedro Martínez. A Mexican Peasant and His Family.* New York, 1964.

El Liberal: Mexico City daily, 1914.

El Liberal: Mexico City daily, 1920.

Liceaga, Luis: *Félix Díaz.* México, 1958.

Logan, Walter S.: *The Siege of Cuautla, The Bunker Hill of Mexico.* New York, 1893.

López, Hector F.: "¿Cuándo fue consignado Emiliano Zapata?" *El Hombre Libre,* April 5, 1937.

———: "Datos para la historia de la Revolución," *El Hombre Libre,* September 10, 1937.

———: "El maderismo en Guerrero," *El Hombre Libre,* September 3, 1937.

López, Joaquín D.: "Rectificación al General Francisco Cosío Robelo," *El Universal,* December 29, 1930.

López González, Valentín: *El Ferrocarril de Cuernavaca.* Cuernavaca, 1957.

———: *La Historia del Periodismo en Morelos.* Cuernavaca, 1957.

López y Fuentes, Gregorio: *Tierra.* México, 1933.

Loyo, Gilberto: *La población de México, estado actual y tendencia, 1960–1980.* México, 1960.

Madero, Francisco I.: *La sucesión presidencial en 1910.* San Pedro, 1908.

Magaña, Gildardo: *Emiliano Zapata y el agrarismo en México.* 3 vols., México, 1934–41.

——— and Carlos Pérez Guerrero: *Emiliano Zapata y el agrarismo en México.* 5 vols., México, 1951–2.

Magaña Cerda, Octavio: "Historia documental de la revolución," serialized in *El Universal,* May 4 to December 16, 1950.

———: *Yo acuso a los responsables, El pueblo que nos juzgue.* México, 1961.

María y Campos, Armando de: *Múgica. Crónica Biográfica.* México, 1939.

———: *La Vida del General Lucio Blanco.* México, 1963.

Márquez Sterling, Manuel: *Psicología profana.* Havana, 1905.

———: *Los últimos días del Presidente Madero (Mi gestión diplomática en México).* 2nd edn., México, 1958.

Mazari, Manuel: "Bosquejo histórico del Estado de Morelos." Manuscript, 1930, in the possession of Valentín López González.

———: *Breve estudio sobre la última epidemia de influenza en la ciudad de México.* México, 1919.

———: "Correspondencia del General D. Francisco Leyva," *Boletín del Archivo General de la Nacion,* V, 3 (May 1934), 450–71.

McBride, George M.: *The Land Systems of Mexico.* New York, 1923.

McNeely, John P.: "Origins of the Zapata Revolt in Morelos," *Hispanic American Historical Review,* XLVI, 2 (May 1966), 153–69.
Meléndez, José T., ed.: *Historia de la revolución mexicana.* 2 vols., México, 1936–40.
Melgarejo, Antonio D.: *Los crímenes del zapatismo (apuntes de un guerrillero).* México, 1913.
Mena, Mario: *Zapata.* México, 1959.
Mendoza L. Schwerdtfeger, Miguel: *¡Tierra Libre!* México, 1915.
The Mexican Herald: Mexico City daily, 1908–14.
The Mexican Yearbook, 1909–1910. New York, 1910.
Mexico: *Anuario Estadístico de los Estados Unidos Mexicanos,* 1946–59.
———: *Boletín Oficial de la Secretaría de Agricultura y Fomento,* 1920.
———: *Boletín Oficial de la Secretaría de Fomento, Colonización e Industria,* 1917.
———: *Diario de los Debates del Congreso Constituyente, 1916–1917.* 2 vols., México, 1960.
———: *Diario Oficial,* 1912.
———: *Directorio Cámara de Senadores XXVIII Leg.* México, 1920.
———: *Directorio de la Cámara de Diputados del XXIX Congreso de los Estados Unidos Mexicanos.* México, 1921.
———: *Resumen del Boletín mensual de la Dirección General de Economía Agrícola,* 1962–5.
———: *6° Censo de Población, 1940, Morelos.* México, 1943.
———: *Séptimo Censo General de Población, 6 de Junio de 1950. Estado de Morelos.* México, 1953.
———: *VIII Censo General de Población, 1960. 8 de Junio de 1960. Localidades de la República por entidades y municipios.* 2 vols., México, 1963.
———: *VIII Censo General de Población, 1960. 8 Junio de 1960. Resumen General.* México, 1962.
———: *Semanario Judicial de la Federación. Tribunal Pleno. Amparos,* 1905.
"Mexico, Land does not pay," *The Economist,* November 12, 1966.
México Nuevo: Mexico City daily, 1909–10.
"Mexico To-day a Storm-Center of Misery and Danger," *Literary Digest,* LX, 8 (February 22, 1919), 50–4.
Meyer, Michael C.: *Mexican Rebel. Pascual Orozco and the Mexican Revolution, 1910–1915.* Lincoln, 1967.
Molina Enríquez, Andrés: *Los grandes problemas nacionales.* México, 1909.
Monbeig, Pierre: "Le mouvement démographique au Mexique," *Tiers-Monde,* IV, 15 (July 1963), 387–406.
Monroy Durán, Luis: *El último caudillo, apuntes para la historia de México, acerca del movimiento armado de 1923, en contra del gobierno constituido.* México, 1924.
Montaño, Otilio Edmundo: "El Zapatismo ante la Filosofía y ante la Historia." Manuscript, 1913, Archivo de Zapata.
Morales Hesse, José: *El General Pablo González. Datos para la historia, 1910–1916.* México, 1916.

Morelos: *Memoria sobre la Administración Pública de Morelos, en los períodos de 1895 a 1902. Gob. Sr. Col. Don Manuel Alarcón.* Cuernavaca, n.d., 1902?

———: *Memoria sobre el estado de la Administración pública de Morelos, presentada al Hon. X. Congreso por el Gobernador constitucional General Jesús H. Preciado, Abril 12, 1887.* Cuernavaca, n.d., 1887?

———: *Memoria sobre el estado de la Administración Pública de Morelos. Presentada al H. XI. Congreso por el Gobernador Constitucional General Jesús H. Preciado. Abril 25 de 1890.* Cuernavaca, n.d., 1890?

———: *El Orden. Periódico Oficial del Estado de Morelos,* 1894.

———: *Periódico Oficial del Estado de Morelos,* 3rd ser., 1919.

———: *Periódico Oficial del Estado de Morelos,* 4th ser., 1920–3.

———: *Periódico Oficial del Gobierno del Estado de Morelos,* 1884.

———: *Semanario Oficial del Gobierno de Morelos,* 1896–1912.

Moreno, Martín Demófilo: "Con fantásticas inexactitudes no se escribe la historia de un pubelo," *La Prensa,* July 16, 1930.

Muñoz, Encarnación: "Breves apuntes históricos." Manuscript, 1913, Archivo de Zapata.

El Nacional: Mexico City daily, 1914.

Naranjo, Francisco: *Diccionario biográfico revolucionario.* México, 1935.

National Archives (abbreviated NA): Record Groups 43, 45, 59, and 84.

The New York *Evening Post,* 1919.

The New York Times, 1919.

Nueva Era: Mexico City daily, 1911–13.

O, Genovevo de la: "Memorias," serialized in *Impacto,* December 31, 1949, to January 21, 1950.

El Obrero Espíritu: Cuautla monthly, 1910. Files are in the Latin American Collection of the University of Texas Library.

Ochoa Campos, Moisés: *La Reforma Municipal, Historia Municipal de México.* México, 1955.

Oñate, Clemente G.: "Continúo mi aportación de datos para la verdad histórica del zapatismo y demás 'ismos' que cooperaron de la ruina del estado de Morelos," *El Hombre Libre,* September 15, 1937.

La Opinión: Mexico City daily, 1914.

La Opinión Nacional: Mexico City biweekly, 1869. Files are in the Biblioteca de la Secretaría de la Hacienda.

Orozco, Wistano Luis: *Legislación y jurisprudencia sobre terrenos baldíos.* 2 vols., México, 1895.

Páez, Joaquín: "Cuatro meses de vacaciones con Zapata," serialized in *El Sol de Puebla,* March 26 to May 30, 1951.

El País: Mexico City daily, 1908–14.

Palacios, Porfirio: *Emiliano Zapata. Datos biográficos-históricos.* México, 1960.

———: Private papers.

———: *El Plan de Ayala. Sus orígenes y su promulgación.* 3rd edn., México, 1953.

———: "Todo es según el color . . . El problema del azúcar y la visión de Zapata," *La Prensa*, February 19, 1944.

———: "Zapatismo vs. Gonzalismo," *Todo*, December 24, 1942.

Palafox, Manuel: "La paz que Carranza propuso a Zapata," *El Universal*, June 28, 1934.

"Para la historia," serialized in *La Prensa*, September 3, 1931, to February 24, 1934.

Partido Reconstrucción Nacional: *Recopilación de Documentos y Algunas Publicaciones de Importancia*. Monterrey, 1923.

Payno, Manuel: *Compendio de la historia de México*. 6th edn., México, 1880.

Paz, Ireneo: *México actual. Galería de contemporáneos*. México, 1898.

Paz, Octavio: "Estalla la bomba," *El Universal*, June 30, 1929.

———: Trágico fin del General Pacheco," *El Universal*, December 3, 1933.

Peral, Miguel Ángel: *Diccionario biográfico mexicano*. México, n.d.

Pérez Guerrero, Carlos: "Cómo vivían los bandidos zapatistas," *Mujeres y Deportes*, February 6, 1937.

———: "Por qué el general Zapata no atacó Jojutla en 1911," *El Hombre Libre*, September 8, 1937.

Pérez Hernández, José María: *Cartilla de la geografía del estado de Morelos*. México, 1876.

"¿Por qué existe y cómo se desarrolla el zapatismo en el E. de Morelos?" *La Tribuna*, May 29, 1913.

Presente!: Cuernavaca weekly, 1962.

Prida, Ramón: *De la dictadura a la anarquía*. 2nd edn., México, 1958.

Pringle, Henry F.: *The Life and Times of William Howard Taft. A Biography*. 2 vols., New York, 1939.

Prinsen Geerligs, H. C.: *The World's Cane Sugar Industry, Past and Present*. Manchester, 1912.

El Progreso de Morelos: Tepoztlán weekly, 1892.

Quirk, Robert E.: *The Mexican Revolution, 1914–1915. The Convention of Aguascalientes*. Bloomington, 1960.

Ramírez Plancarte, Francisco: *La Ciudad de México durante la revolución constitucionalista*. 2nd edn., México, 1941.

Rausch, George J., Jr.: "The Early Career of Victoriano Huerta," *The Americas*, XXI, 2 (October 1964), 136–45.

Redfield, Robert: *Tepoztlán, A Mexican Village. A Study of Folk Life*. Chicago, 1930.

La República: Mexico City weekly, 1909.

Reyes Avilés, Carlos: *Cartones Zapatistas*. México, 1928.

Reyes H., Alfonso: *Emiliano Zapata. Su Vida y su Obra*. México, 1963.

Rincón Gallardo Hope, José: "Episodios de la revolución del sur," *Revista de Revistas*, January 29, 1933.

Rivera Cambas, Manuel: *Historia de la intervención y del Imperio de Maximiliano*. 5 vols., 2nd edn., México, 1961.

Robelo, Cecilio A.: *Revistas Descriptivas del Estado de Morelos*. Cuernavaca, 1885.

Robles, Manuel N.: "Lo que supe de la muerte del General Emiliano Zapata," *La Prensa,* September 19, 1955.

Robles, Serafín M.: "El Caudillo se Casa en la Villa de Ayala, Morelos," *El Campesino,* November 1954.

———: "Emboscada del Gobernador Teniente Cnel. Escandón," *El Campesino,* November 1952.

———: "Emiliano Zapata sienta plaza como soldado el año 1910," *El Campesino,* December 1951.

———: "El General Zapata. Agricultor y Arriero," *El Campesino,* October 1951.

———: "El Plan de Ayala. Cómo fue el juramento de este Histórico Documento," *El Campesino,* December 1954.

———: "Primeros brotes a causa de la Burda Imposición," *El Campesino,* May 1954.

———: "Se Incorpora J. Morales, Toma de Chietla, Puebla," *El Campesino,* June 1952.

———: "Se Levantaron al Grito de ¡Viva Madero! ¡Muera Díaz!" *El Campesino,* March and April 1952.

———: "Semblanza del Plan de Ayala," *El Campesino,* January 1950.

———: "El Zapatismo y la Industria Azucarera en Morelos," *El Campesino,* August 1950.

Robles Domínguez, Alfredo: "Mis memorias políticas," serialized in *El Hombre Libre,* September 17 to December 10, 1930.

Rojas, Basilio: *La Soberana Convención de Aguascalientes.* México, 1961.

Rojas Zúñiga, Mateo: *La gobernación de Morelos de 1912 a 1916 y la opinión pública. Dos cartas acerca de la candidatura del Ingeniero Agustín Aragón.* México, 1912.

Romero, José Guadalupe: *Noticas para formar la historia y la estadística del Obispado de Michoacán.* México, 1860.

Romero Flores, Jesús: "Evocación luctuosa de Emiliano Zapata," *El Nacional,* April 10, 1956.

———: *Historia de la Revolución en Michoacán.* México, 1964.

———: "Mil biografías en la historia de México: Amador Salazar," *El Nacional,* December 15, 1946.

———: "Mil biografías en la historia de México: Gabriel Tepepa," *El Nacional,* December 15, 1946.

———: *La revolución como nosotros la vimos.* México, 1963.

Ross, Stanley R.: *Francisco I. Madero, Apostle of Mexican Democracy.* New York, 1955.

Ruiz, Eduardo: *Historia de la guerra de intervención en Michoacán.* 2nd edn., México, 1940.

Ruiz de Velasco, Angel: *Estudios sobre el Cultivo de la Caña de Azúcar.* Cuernavaca, 1894.

Ruiz de Velasco, Felipe: *Historia y Evoluciones del Cultivo de la Caña y de la Industria Azucarera en México, Hasta el Año de 1910.* México, 1937.

Ruvalcaba, Luis N., ed.: *Campaña Política del C. Álvaro Obregón, Candidato a la Presidencia de la República, 1920–1924.* 5 vols., México, 1923.

Salazar, Rosendo: *La Casa del Obrero Mundial.* México, 1962.

Sánchez Azcona, Juan: *La etapa maderista de la revolución.* México, 1960.

Sánchez Escobar, Rafael: *Episodios de la Revolución Mexicana en el Sur.* México, 1934.

Sánchez Septién, Salvador, ed.: *José María Lozano en la Tribuna Parlamentaria, 1910–1913.* 2nd edn., México, 1956.

Sandoval, Fernando B.: *La Industria del Azúcar en Nueva España.* México, 1951.

Schwartz, Theodore: "L'usage de la terre dans un village à Ejido du Mexique," *Études rurales,* 10 (July 1963), 37–49.

Sedano, Antonio: "Andanzas militares del Coronel Republicano Antonio Sedano y Algunos Relatos Históricos del Estado de Morelos." Manuscript, 1919, Archivo de Sotelo Inclán.

Serratos, Alfredo: "Bocetos para la historia: el abrazo Villa-Zapata," *El Universal Gráfico,* November 24 and 25, 1952.

———: "El General Serratos Refuta Unas Apreciciones," *El Hombre Libre,* June 2, 1937.

Sierra Horcasitas, Luis: *Patria. Obra Histórica-Revolucionaria. Primera Parte.* México, 1916.

Silva Herzog, Jesús: *El agrarismo mexicano y la reforma agraria. Exposición y crítica.* México, 1959.

———, ed.: *La cuestión de la tierra, 1910–1917.* 4 vols., México, 1960–2.

Simmons, Merle E.: *The Mexican CORRIDO as a Source for Interpretive Study of Modern Mexico (1870–1950).* Bloomington, 1957.

Simpson, Eyler N.: *The Ejido: Mexico's Way Out.* Chapel Hill, 1937.

El Sol: Mexico City daily, 1914.

Sotelo Inclán, Jesús: *Raíz y razón de Zapata. Anenecuilco. Investigación histórica.* México, 1943.

Southworth, John R.: *The Official Directory of Mines and Estates of Mexico.* México, 1910.

Steffens, Lincoln: *Autobiography.* New York, 1931.

Stephenson, George M.: *John Lind of Minnesota.* Minneapolis, 1935.

El Sufragio Libre: Mexico City weekly, 1909–10.

Tamayo, Jorge L.: *Geografía General de México.* 4 vols., México, 1962.

Tannenbaum, Frank: *The Mexican Agrarian Revolution.* New York, 1929.

———: *Peace by Revolution. An Interpretation of Mexico.* New York, 1933.

Tapia, Antonio: *La economía de la producción agrícola en el Distrito Económico de Cuautla, Estado de Morelos.* México, 1960.

Taracena, Alfonso: *Mi vida en el vértigo de la revolución. Anales sintéticos, 1900–1930.* México, 1936.

———: *La Tragedia Zapatista. Historia de la Revolución del Sur.* México, 1931.

Terry, T. Philip: *Terry's Mexico. Handbook for Travellers.* México, 1909.

"El testamento político de Otilio E. Montaño," *Excélsior,* January 21, 1919.

Thord-Gray, I.: *Gringo Rebel (Mexico, 1913-1914).* 3rd edn., Coral Gables, 1961.

Torres, Elías L.: "No te descuides, Zapata," *Jueves de Excélsior,* April 8, 1937.

Tovar, Pantaleón: *Historia parlamentaria del cuarto congreso constitucional.* 4 vols., México, 1872-4.

La Tribuna: Mexico City daily, 1913.

Trujillo, Daniel R.: "Memorias Revolucionarias de un suriano Zapatista," *El Legionario,* March 15, 1958.

Tweedie, Mrs. Alec: *Mexico As I Saw It.* New York, 1901.

United States Congress: *Congressional Record,* 66 Cong., 2 sess., Vol. LIX, Part I.

United States Department of Commerce and Labor, Bureau of Manufactures: *Monthly Consular and Trade Reports,* 1905-1908.

United States Department of State: *Papers Relating to the Foreign Relations of the United States, 1918.* Washington, 1930.

United States House of Representatives: *Appointment of a Committee for Investigation of Mexican Situation. Hearings Before the Committee on Rules,* 66 Cong., 1 sess. 2 parts, Washington, 1919.

United States Senate: *Investigation of Mexican Affairs. Report and Hearings before a subcommittee of the Committee on Foreign Relations,* 66 Cong., 1 sess. 2 vols., Washington, 1920.

United States Senate: *Revolutions in Mexico. Hearing before a subcommittee of the Committee on Foreign Relations,* 62 Cong., 2 sess. Washington, 1913.

El Universal: Mexico City daily, 1916-64.

Urbán Aguirre, José: *Geografía e Historia del Estado de Morelos.* 2nd edn., Cuernavaca, 1963.

Valadés, José C.: *Imaginación y realidad de Francisco I. Madero.* 2 vols., México, 1960.

Valenzuela, Clodoveo, and Amado Cháverri Matamoros: *Sonora y Carranza.* 2nd edn., México, 1921.

Valverde, Custodio: *Julián Blanco y la revolución en el estado de Guerrero.* México, 1916.

Valverde, Sergio: *Apuntes para la historia de la revolución y de la política en el estado de Morelos, desde la muerte del gobernador Alarcón.* México, 1933.

Vázquez Gómez, Francisco: *Memorias Políticas (1909-1913).* México, 1933.

Velasco, Manuel de: "La revolución maderista en el estado de Puebla." Manuscript, 1914, in the possession of José Ignacio Conde.

Villarreal, Concha de: "El indio tarasco decapitado por agrarista," *Todo,* November 4, 1937.

Whetten, Nathan L.: *Rural Mexico.* Chicago, 1948.

―――― and Robert G. Burnight: "Internal Migration in Mexico," *Rural Sociology,* XXI, 2 (June 1956), 140-51.

Womack, John, Jr.: "Emiliano Zapata and the Revolution in Morelos, 1910-1920." Ph.D. dissertation, Harvard University, 1965.

Yáñez, Agustín, and Catalina Sierra, eds.: *Archivo de Don Francisco I. Madero. Epistolario (1900-1909).* México, 1963.

INDEX

Acapulco (Gro.), 180, 182, 183, 249
Acatlipa (Mor.), 46
agrarian conflict: debates, 90, 96, 98, 101, 116, 142, 149–51; commissions, 117, 231–5, 259–60, 318, 368–9, 370, 377; laws, 229, 246, 272–3, 278, 373, 377, 404
—disputes over land, timber, and water: before 1910, 4, 15, 18, 41–7, 50, 52–4, 61; after 1910, 108, 109, 233, 247, 354–5, 376, 377
—programs: Maderista, 70, 87, 150, 155; Zapatista, 122, 172–3, 178–9, 189, 194, 199, 207, 209, 216, 230, 244, 274, 342, 394, 396; Soto y Gama's, 135, 194; planters', 142; Constitutionalists', 195, 199, 207, 209, 250, 283; Vázquez Gómez's, 307; Peláez's, 355; after 1920, 366–7, 369, 373, 377–80, 382–4
—reforms: Zapatista, 125, 131, 212, 228–32, 234–5, 246, 278; Maderista, 154–5; Villista, 196; Constitutionalist, 202, 229, 259–60, 272–3, 353; after 1920, 368–70, 373, 377–80; see also Ayalans; Department of Agriculture; Palafox, Manuel; plantations; villages; Zapata, Emiliano
agrarismo: see agrarian conflict: programs
Agrarista: see National Agrarista Party
agriculture: see plantations: technology

Agua Prieta revolt, 365, 372
Aguascalientes, 155
Aguascalientes (Ags.), 214, 216–17, 218
Aguilar, Higinio, 40, 41, 167, 212–13, 222, 264, 301, 340, 344
Aguilar, José G., 317, 333, 352–3
Ahuehuepan (Mor.), 46
Ajusco (D. F.), 261
Ajusco, Mount, 269, 340
Alarcón, Francisco, 74, 314, 357
Alarcón, Juan, 152
Alarcón, Manuel, 12, 13–18, 39–40, 51–2, 73, 134
Alcázar, Álvaro, 270
Alcázar, José María, 135
Alliance of Proletarians, 314–15
Almazán, Juan Andrew, 80, 82, 121, 122, 123, 212–13, 222, 264, 301
Alonso, Vicente, 49; attorneys, 152, 377; heirs, 373
Amacuzac (Mor.), 82
Amecac (Pue.), 305
Amecameca (Mex.), 243, 263
Americans: private citizens, 48, 112, 176–7, 184, 185, 291, 298–300, 301, 307, 310, 373–4, 375; officials, see United States; mentioned, 138, 236
Amezcua, Genaro, 202, 203, 207, 209, 210,

A NOTE ABOUT THE AUTHOR

JOHN WOMACK, JR., was born in 1937 in Norman, Oklahoma, and was raised there. He attended Harvard University, where he was a Phi Beta Kappa and graduated *summa cum laude* in 1959. He was a Rhodes Scholar at Oxford from 1959 to 1961, then returned to Harvard and received his Ph.D. in history in 1965. Mr. Womack now teaches Latin American history at Harvard.

A NOTE ON THE TYPE

THIS BOOK is set in Granjon, a type named in compliment to Robert Granjon, type-cutter and printer—Antwerp, Lyons, Rome, Paris—active from 1523 to 1590. The boldest and most original designer of his time, he was one of the first to practice the trade of type-founder apart from that of printer.

This type face was designed by George W. Jones, who based his drawings on a type used by Claude Garamond (1510–61) in his beautiful French books, and more closely resembles Garamond's own than do any of the various modern types that bear his name.

Composed, printed, and bound by
The Haddon Craftsmen, Inc., Scranton, Pennsylvania
Typography and binding design by
GUY FLEMING

John Womack, Jr., was born in 1937 in Norman, Oklahoma, and was raised there. He attended Harvard University, where he was a Phi Beta Kappa and graduated *summa cum laude* in 1959. He was a Rhodes Scholar at Oxford from 1959 to 1961, then returned to Harvard and received his Ph.D. in history in 1965. Mr. Womack now teaches Latin American history at Harvard.